Administrative Law in Context

Edited by
Colleen M. Flood and Lorne Sossin
Faculty of Law, University of Toronto

2008
EMOND MONTGOMERY PUBLICATIONS LIMITED
TORONTO, CANADA

Emond Montgomery Publications Limited
60 Shaftesbury Avenue
Toronto ON M4T 1A3
http://www.emp.ca/lawschool

Printed in Canada.
Reprinted December 2011.

We acknowledge the financial support of the Government of Canada through the Canada Book Fund for our publishing activities.

Acquisitions editor: Peggy Buchan
Marketing manager: Christine Davidson
Supervising editor: Jim Lyons
Copy editor: Diane Gula
Production editors: Cindy Fujimoto and Debbie Gervais
Proofreader: David Handelsman
Indexer: Paula Pike

Library and Archives Canada Cataloguing in Publication

Administrative law in context / [edited by] Colleen Flood, Lorne Sossin.

Includes index.
ISBN 978-1-55239-269-0

1. Administrative law—Canada—Textbooks. I. Flood, Colleen M. (Colleen Marion), 1966- II. Sossin, Lorne Mitchell, 1964- III. Title.

KE5015.A845 2008 342.71'06 C2008-901590-8
KF5402.A845 2008

Table of Contents

CHAPTER TWO THE TOOLS OF THE ADMINISTRATIVE STATE AND THE REGULATORY MIX

CHAPTER THREE DOGS AND TAILS: REMEDIES IN ADMINISTRATIVE LAW

CHAPTER FIVE THE DUTY OF FAIRNESS: FROM NICHOLSON TO BAKER AND BEYOND

CHAPTER SIX INDEPENDENCE, IMPARTIALITY, AND BIAS

Table of Cases

Foreword

Having spent close to 50 years in the law, I have been a witness to the remarkable growth and development of administrative law in Canada and abroad. In my student days, the administrative law syllabus was rather thin compared with the course topics and materials found in the contemporary administrative law course. There are many reasons for this turn of events, but chief among them is the tremendous proliferation of boards, tribunals, and agencies brought about by the perceived needs and preferences of the modern regulatory state. As a lawyer in the private and public sectors, law professor, member of an administrative tribunal, judge, and now back to being a lawyer, I have been privileged to have an almost front-row seat to view the parade of administrative law developments and growth. It is that perspective which causes me to state that I enthusiastically welcome the arrival of *Administrative Law in Context*. Allow me to explain my enthusiasm.

I agree with the basic premise of this volume that for many years excessive emphasis has been placed on judicial review of administrative tribunals. Indeed, in the beginning years of the subject, and for too long, there was, in my view, far too much attention paid to legal controls of administrative action, as reflected, for example, in the views of A.V. Dicey[1] and Lord Hewart of Bury,[2] and not enough attention to what might be called a realistic approach to the subject, as reflected in the writings of John Willis.[3]

Granted, lawyers must obviously be attuned to judicial review since legal remedies and oversight are part of the tool kit for every lawyer in advising clients. Consequently (and most appropriately), the book includes chapters on remedies, the rule of law, the duty of fairness, and judicial review. But the book goes well beyond those topics to give the reader a better understanding of what tribunals do, the complexities they face, and how they reach decisions and shape policy. Also explored are a number of theoretical issues on the legitimacy of public authority; the interplay among law, regulations, and guidelines; the choice of regulatory instruments; and other topics.

The manner of presentation of the various chapters is also noteworthy. Some 17 scholars from across the country have combined to provide a highly readable text, with a range of

1 A.V. Dicey, *An Introduction to the Study of the Constitution* (London: MacMillan & Co., 1885 and subsequent editions).

2 Lord Hewart of Bury, *The New Despotism* (London: E. Benn, 1929).

3 See, for example, John Willis, *Three Approaches to Administrative Law* (1935/36) 1 U.T.L.J. 53; John Willis, 1974 Cecil Wright Memorial Lecture, University of Toronto Faculty of Law (later published as "Canadian Administrative Law in Retrospect" (1974) 24 U.T.L.J. 225); and John Willis, "Administrative Law in Canada" (1961) 39 Can. Bar Rev. 251.

diversity reflected in the transnational backgrounds of the authors, and this has resulted in a menu of innovative and instructive commentary.

In short, the collection appropriately takes a broad view of the subject and does so in an informative and well-structured manner. I have no doubt that the book will accomplish the goal of its authors to serve as a primary resource for administrative law students throughout Canada. But the book is also an important scholarly contribution to the field in a variety of topics that will be of great benefit to lawyers and judges. And for all that, I wish to commend and thank the contributors for their efforts.

Frank Iacobucci

Preface

Standing on the shoulders of giants, we were inspired to build on the teaching and scholarship of David Mullan, Hudson Janisch, Dick Risk, and John Evans, who pioneered the first edition of Emond Montgomery's *Administrative Law: Cases and Materials*, in 1981. In particular, the present volume owes much to the most recent edition of this casebook, edited by David Mullan. On behalf of all the contributors to this volume, we express our gratitude to David and to the other previous editors of *Administrative Law* for all they have done in advancing this field, and dedicate this volume in their honour. Indeed, most of the contributors have used one or another edition of this casebook as the basis for their own instruction in administrative law.

Building on this legacy, we sought to create a new kind of text for administrative law in order to explore more fully the myriad contexts of administrative decision-making. One of our goals was to create an accessible, readable text that reflects the many perspectives in administrative law. We are proud to include in this volume scholars and teachers in administrative law from across Canada, with some of the most experienced voices in the field, as well as some new ones.

Because administrative law is ever evolving, a further goal was to create a flexible, living text. To this end, the book is accompanied by a website, at <http://www.emp.ca/adminlaw>, where both students and teachers can find edited and full-text cases for each chapter, recommendations for additional readings, and important additions, clarifications, and updates to the published text. We hope this format will do justice to the dynamic nature of the field.

While the contributions to this volume reflect distinctive voices, they also speak to shared themes and concerns. These were the subject of two lively workshops, sponsored by the Faculty of Law at the University of Toronto, that included discussions on how best to cover the diverse fields of administrative law and administrative justice. Transforming the rich array of available material into relatively short, accessible chapters is a daunting task, but all of our contributors were equal to the challenge. We believe each author has skillfully managed both to survey the field and to provide more scholarly punch than is possible in a traditional casebook. This volume has been a truly collaborative project, and we thank the contributors for their efforts, which we hope will benefit the new generation of administrative law students.

In addition to the debt we owe to our contributors, we want to acknowledge the unflagging support of the Faculty of Law at the University of Toronto, as well as the various individuals at Emond Montgomery who have done so much in getting this book to press, particularly Paul Emond, Peggy Buchan, Jim Lyons, and Cindy Fujimoto. We are also grateful for the administrative and research assistance provided by Greig Hinds and Oscar

Cabrera, and wish to express special thanks to Sujith Xavier, research manager at the Faculty of Law, University of Toronto, for his tireless efforts in helping to finalize the chapters and get this book to press. Finally, we would like to thank all our students of administrative law—past and future—who stimulate and engage us, and always hold our feet to the fire.

List of Contributors

W.A. Bogart

W.A. Bogart, BA, LLB (University of Toronto), LLM (Harvard University), teaches Access to Justice and Judicial Review at the University of Windsor, Faculty of Law. Professor Bogart is the author of several books, including, most recently, *Good Government? Good Citizens?: Courts, Politics, and Markets in a Changing Canada* (Vancouver: University of British Columbia Press, 2005). Professor Bogart was a Virtual Scholar in Residence for the Law Commission of Canada (2002-3) and is a frequent consultant to government and other public bodies regarding legal policy. He is at work on his latest book, *What Are the Odds?: Regulating Excessive Consumption and Problem Gambling*.

Geneviève Cartier

Geneviève Cartier is a Professor of Law at the University of Sherbrooke and was Associate Dean, Student Affairs of the Faculty of Law and Faculty Registrar from 2005 to 2008. She holds a doctorate from the University of Toronto and a master's from Cambridge University. She was president of the Québec Association of Law Teachers in 2001-2, a member of the Board of Directors of the University of Sherbrooke from 2001 to 2004, a member of the Consultative Committee of the Law Commission of Canada from 2003 to 2006 and president of the Canadian Association of Law Teachers in 2007-8. Her recent publications focus on the conception of discretion in administrative law, following her SJD thesis titled "Reconceiving Administrative Discretion: From Discretion as Power to Discretion as Dialogue."

Peter J. Carver

Peter Carver, MA, LLB (McGill University), LLM (University of British Columbia), is an Associate Professor, Faculty of Law, at the University of Alberta, Cross-Appointment to Faculty of Rehabilitation Medicine. Professor Carver teaches and researches in the areas of Canadian constitutional, administrative, and immigration law, disability studies, and mental health law. He is a member of the Board of the Centre for Constitutional Studies. Prior to coming to the University of Alberta, Professor Carver served as a member of the Immigration and Refugee Board and practised law in British Columbia. His most recent publications include the chapter "Recurring Constitutional Themes in Canadian Public Law" in *Public Law: Cases, Materials, and Commentary* (Toronto: Emond Montgomery, 2006) and the articles "Guides' Honour: A Case Comment on *Thamotharem v. Canada* and *Benitez v. Canada*" (2006) 40 Admin. L.R. (4th) 279-94 and "The Role and Powers of Forensic Psychiatric Review Boards in Canada: Recent Developments" (2006) 41 Health L.J. 1-20 (with Cherie Langlois-Klassen).

Colleen M. Flood

Colleen M. Flood is a Canada Research Chair in Health Law and Policy and Scientific Director of the Canadian Institutes of Health Research, Institute of Health Services and Policy Research. She is also Associate Professor of Law at the University of Toronto, cross-appointed to the Department of Health Policy, Management and Evaluation and the School of Public Policy. Professor Flood obtained her BA and LLB (Hons.) from the University of Auckland, New Zealand and her LLM and SJD from the University of Toronto. She is the author and editor of five books, including *International Health Care Reform: A Legal, Economic and Political Analysis* (London: Routledge, 2000), co-editor of *Access to Care, Access to Justice: The Legal Debate Over Private Health Insurance in Canada* (Toronto: University of Toronto Press, 2005), editor of *Just Medicare: What's In, What's Out, How We Decide* (Toronto: University of Toronto Press, 2006), co-editor of *Canadian Health Law and Policy*, 3rd ed. (Markham, ON: Butterworths, 2007), and co-editor of *Exploring Social Insurance: Can a Dose of Europe Cure Canadian Health Care Finance?* (Montreal and Kingston: McGill-Queen's, 2008).

Craig Forcese

Craig Forcese is an Associate Professor, Faculty of Law (Common Law Section), at the University of Ottawa. He teaches national security law, public international law, administrative law, and public law/legislation. Much of his current research and writing relates to national security, human rights, and democratic accountability. Craig is the author of *National Security Law: Canadian Practice in International Perspective* (Toronto: Irwin Law, 2007) and co-editor of the forthcoming *Human Rights and Anti-terrorism* (Toronto: Irwin Law, Spring 2008). He is also co-editor and co-author of *International Law: Doctrine, Practice, and Theory* (Toronto: Irwin Law, 2007), co-managing editor of *Public Law: Cases, Materials, and Commentary* (Toronto: Emond Montgomery, 2006), and co-author of *The Laws of Government: The Legal Foundations of Canadian Democracy* (Toronto: Irwin Law, 2005). Prior to joining the law school faculty, Craig practised law at the Washington, DC office of Hughes Hubbard & Reed LLP, specializing in international trade and commercial law and representing, *inter alia*, the Government of Canada. He has a BA from McGill University (1992), an MA from the Norman Paterson School of International Affairs, Carleton University (1997), an LLB (*summa cum laude*) from the University of Ottawa (where he shared the gold medal for the best graduating average of his class) (1997), and an LLM from Yale University (2001). He is a member in good standing of the bars of Ontario, New York, and the District of Columbia.

Cristie L. Ford

Cristie Ford joined the University of British Columbia as an Assistant Professor in 2005. Her academic interests include regulatory theory, comparative administrative and public law, securities regulation, and corporate governance. Professor Ford is pursuing doctoral studies in law at Columbia University, from which she holds an LLM. She received numerous fellowships and awards during her graduate studies, including an SSHRC Doctoral Fellowship and the title James Kent Scholar (for highest honours). She also taught seminars, workshops, and courses at Columbia Law School in various capacities between 2000 and 2005, and she practised law for six years, in Vancouver and in New York. Recent publications include Cristie L. Ford, "New Governance, Compliance, and Principles-Based Securities Regulation" (2008) 45 American Bus. L.J. 1, available online: <http://ssrn.com/abstract=970130>; Cristie L. Ford, "How Should We Teach Securities Regulation in a Fast-Moving World?" (2008) 46:1 Canadian Bus. L. Rev.; and David Hess & Cristie L. Ford, "Corporate Corruption and Reform Undertakings: A New Approach to an Old Problem" (2008) Cornell Int. L.J.

Evan Fox-Decent

Evan Fox-Decent is an Assistant Professor at McGill University, Faculty of Law. He teaches and publishes in legal theory, administrative law, First Nations and the law, immigration law, the law of fiduciaries, and human rights. He has worked on human rights and democratic governance reform in Latin America since 1987, beginning with advocacy and relief work in El Salvador under the auspices of Nobel Peace Prize nominee Medardo Gómez. He has since served with the UN Verification Mission in Guatemala (1996-1999), and has consulted on behalf of numerous development and research agencies, as well as on behalf of legal institutions in Latin America, including the Supreme Court of Venezuela, the European Union, the World Bank, the International Development Bank, USAID, and Canada's International Development Research Centre.

Andrew Green

Andrew Green, BA (Hons.) (Queen's University) 1987, MA (University of Toronto) 1988, LLB (University of Toronto) 1992, LLM (University of Chicago) 1994, JSD (University of Chicago) 1997, called to the Bar of Ontario in 1996, is an Assistant Professor at the University of Toronto, Faculty of Law. Prior to joining the Faculty, Professor Green practised environmental law in Toronto for six years at Davies Ward Phillips & Vineberg LLP, Osler, Hoskin & Harcourt LLP, and Hicks Morley Hamilton Stewart Storie. His practice encompassed both litigation (including prosecutions, administrative appeals, and civil actions) and transactional work. From 2002 to 2004, Professor Green was Senior Research Fellow for Ontario's Panel on the Role of Government, with Professor Michael Trebilcock and Ronald Daniels, former dean of the Faculty of Law, University of Toronto. The panel identified the major challenges that the province faces in areas such as education, health, environment, economic policy, and taxes.

Professor Green's research and teaching interests focus on environmental law, international trade, and administrative law, including how international trade rules constrain countries' ability to implement domestic environmental policy; instrument choice in environmental law (including instruments for fostering renewable energy); and the role of law (including administrative law) in fostering individuals' environmental values.

Gerald Heckman

Gerald Heckman is Assistant Professor at the Faculty of Law of the University of Manitoba. His research and teaching interests focus on public law, including administrative and constitutional law, labour law, human rights law, international human rights law, and refugee law. After receiving his LLB from the University of Toronto, he clerked for the Federal Court of Canada. He obtained an LLM in administrative law from Queen's University, where he analyzed the gatekeeping powers of Canadian human rights commissions. After practising labour, employment, and human rights law for several years, he earned his PhD at Osgoode Hall Law School at York University. His dissertation focused on the gap between domestic and international institutional and procedural safeguards in Canadian, American, and Australian refugee protection decision-making.

Grant Huscroft
Professor Grant Huscroft joined the Faculty of Law at the University of Western Ontario in 2002 following a lengthy career at the University of Auckland. His research focuses on human rights and judicial review and his work has been published internationally. He is co-author of the treatise *The New Zealand Bill of Rights* (Melbourne: Oxford University Press, 2003) and has edited five collections of essays: *Expounding the Constitution: Essays in Constitutional Theory* (New York: Cambridge University Press, 2008); *Inside and Outside Canadian Administrative Law* (Toronto: University of Toronto Press, 2006) (with Michael Taggart); *Constitutionalism in the Charter Era* (Toronto: LexisNexis-Butterworths, 2004) (with Ian Brodie); *Litigating Rights: Perspectives from Domestic and International Law* (Oxford: Hart Publishing, 2002) (with Paul Rishworth); and *Rights and Freedoms* (Wellington: Brookers, 1995) (with Paul Rishworth).

Laverne Jacobs
Laverne Jacobs joined the University of Windsor's Faculty of Law in 2007. She is a recognized administrative law scholar who teaches in many areas of public law. Her current research interests include the independence and impartiality of administrative and judicial actors; access to information and privacy law; human rights law; disability rights; parliamentary officers; comparative public law; and empirical research methodology. Professor Jacobs has authored several publications and her work has been cited by courts in many Canadian jurisdictions.

Professor Jacobs's scholarship aims to bridge the gap between public law jurisprudence and public law realities through empirical inquiry. She takes an interdisciplinary approach to her research and has employed qualitative empirical research methods from the social sciences. In 2006, Professor Jacobs was a Visiting Scholar at Cornell University Law School and, in 2005, at the University of Ottawa, Faculty of Law. Laverne Jacobs completed degrees in Common Law and Civil Law at McGill University and, upon graduating, clerked for Justice Brian Malone at the Federal Court of Appeal. She has worked for the Department of Justice Canada, where she was counsel in the Public Law Policy Sector. She currently sits on the Human Rights Tribunal of Ontario as a part-time member.

Freya Kristjanson
Freya Kristjanson, BA (Hons.) (Queen's University) 1983, LLB (University of Victoria) 1987, clerked for Justice W.R. McIntyre at the Supreme Court of Canada. She was called to the Bar of Ontario in 1989. Freya is a partner in the Toronto office of Borden Ladner Gervais LLP, where she practises in the areas of public law and commercial litigation, and serves as National Chair of the Class Action Practice Group. Ms. Kristjanson has appeared as counsel before the Supreme Court of Canada, Federal Court of Appeal, all levels of court

in Ontario, and numerous administrative tribunals, acting for both public and private sector clients. Freya also has extensive public inquiry experience. She was Legal Counsel to the Commission of Inquiry into the Actions of Canadian Officials in Relation to Maher Arar, Commission Counsel to the Walkerton Inquiry, counsel to the Rt. Hon. Kim Campbell and staff at the Somalia Inquiry, and Assistant Commission Counsel to the Hryciuk Inquiry. Freya is a Past Chair of the Ontario Bar Association Constitutional and Civil Liberties Section. She teaches Administrative Law at the Faculty of Law, University of Toronto, where she has previously taught trial advocacy.

Mary Liston
Mary Liston, BA (Hons.) (University of Western Ontario), MA (York University), LLB, PhD (University of Toronto), holds the Postdoctoral Fellow in Ethics and Law at the Centre for Ethics, University of Toronto. She teaches contemporary political philosophy, Canadian public law, and Canadian politics. She also has an abiding interest in law and literature. Her doctoral dissertation, "Honest Counsel: Institutional Dialogue and the Canadian Rule of Law," constructed a theoretical model of the democratic rule of law from a close reading of Canadian jurisprudence in public law, with a particular focus on administrative and constitutional law. At the core of this model is the concept of dialogue between courts and other state institutions, between different orders of government within the Canadian constitutional system, and between citizens and the state. Her publications include "Willis, 'Theology,' and the Rule of Law" (2005) 55 U.T.L.J. and "Alert, Alive and Sensitive: *Baker*, the Duty to Give Reasons, and the Ethos of Justification in Canadian Public Law," in David Dyzenhaus, *The Unity of Public Law* (Oxford: Hart Publishing, 2004). She was awarded the Peter Russell/Ontario Graduate Scholarship in the Department of Political Science and a Social Sciences and Humanities Research Council of Canada Scholarship for her doctoral work at the University of Toronto.

Audrey Macklin
Audrey Macklin is an Associate Professor at the University of Toronto, Faculty of Law. She holds law degrees from Yale University and the University of Toronto, and a bachelor of science degree from Alberta. After graduating from Toronto, she served as law clerk to Justice Bertha Wilson at the Supreme Court of Canada. She was appointed to the faculty of Dalhousie Law School in 1991, promoted to Associate Professor in 1998, and moved to the University of Toronto in 2000. While teaching at Dalhousie, she also served as a member of the Immigration and Refugee Board.

Professor Macklin's teaching areas include criminal law, administrative law, and immigration and refugee law. Her research and writing interests include transnational migration, citizenship, forced migration, feminist and cultural analysis, and human rights. She has published on these subjects in journals such as *Refuge* and *Canadian Woman Studies*, and in collections of essays such as *The Security of Freedom: Essays on Canada's Anti-Terrorism Bill* (Ronald J. Daniels, Patrick Macklem & Kent Roach, eds.) (Toronto: University of Toronto Press, 2001) and *Engendering Forced Migration: Theory and Practice* (Doreen Indra, ed.) (Oxford: Berghahn Books, 1998).

Leslie McIntosh

Leslie McIntosh, BA (University of Toronto) 1974, LLB (University of Western Ontario) 1977, LLM in administrative law (Osgoode Hall Law School) 2003. Leslie was called to the Bar of Ontario and started her career with the Ontario Ministry of the Attorney General in 1979. Initially, she was seconded to the Ministry of Community and Social Services, where she appeared before a broad range of administrative tribunals. In 1982, she transferred to the Crown Law Office, Civil, of the Ministry of the Attorney General, where she is now General Counsel. Her practice consists mainly of appellate work in the Supreme Court of Canada, the Court of Appeal, and the Divisional Court in the areas of civil litigation and administrative law. She was counsel for the Province of Ontario at the Inquiry into the Actions of Canadian Officials in Relation to Maher Arar, and is counsel in the SARS actions. Leslie is an Adjunct Professor of Administrative Law at the University of Toronto, Faculty of Law, and is a regular speaker at other continuing legal education events.

Lorne Sossin

Lorne Sossin is a Professor at the Faculty of Law, University of Toronto and the Academic Director of the Faculty of Law's Centre for Professionalism, Ethics and Public Service. Professor Sossin holds doctorates in Law from Columbia University and in Political Science from the University of Toronto. Prior to joining the University of Toronto in 2002, he was a faculty member at Osgoode Hall Law School, York University and was an Associate-in-Law at Columbia Law School. He is also a former litigation lawyer with Borden & Elliot (now Borden Ladner Gervais LLP) and a former law clerk to the Chief Justice of the Supreme Court of Canada. Professor Sossin is the author and editor of over 50 articles and books including *Boundaries of Judicial Review: The Law of Justiciability in Canada* (Toronto: Carswell, 1999), *Public Law* (Toronto: Carswell, 2002) (with Michael J. Bryant), *Access to Care, Access to Justice: The Legal Debate over Private Health Insurance in Canada* (Colleen Flood, Kent Roach & Lorne Sossin, eds.) (Toronto: University of Toronto Press, 2005), and *Dilemmas of Solidarity: Rethinking Redistribution in the Canadian Federation* (Sujit Choudhry, Jean-François Gaudreault-Desbiens & Lorne Sossin, eds.) (Toronto: University of Toronto Press, 2006).

Sheila Wildeman

Sheila Wildeman is an Assistant Professor at Dalhousie Law School. She was a Research Associate at Dalhousie's Health Law Institute, and an articled student at Eberts Symes Street & Corbett in Toronto. She is currently in the process of completing her SJD degree at the University of Toronto, Faculty of Law. The subject of her doctoral thesis is the legal determination of capacity to make treatment decisions in the context of involuntary psychiatric hospitalization.

CHAPTER ONE

An Introduction to (the Effervescence of) Administrative Law

COLLEEN M. FLOOD*
Faculty of Law, University of Toronto

* I would like to dedicate this introduction to Hudson Janisch and David Mullan, who through their teaching and writing have inspired my interest in administrative law and thus this book. Deep thanks to Lorne Sossin for his intellectual generosity in all things to do with public law and to Diana Ginn and Audrey Macklin, both of whom generously shared their teaching notes with me when I first began to teach administrative law, and whose ideas and concepts I draw and build on in this chapter. I would also like to thank Oscar Cabrera and Sujith Xavier for their superb research support.

If you are a student you may still be unclear about what administrative law is and its relationship to other areas of law, such as constitutional law and private law. You may also have little sense of the relevance of administrative law to your future clients or to Canadian society. If you are an expert in your field but new to administrative law, you may find familiar words like fairness and reasonableness take on new and sometimes unfamiliar meanings in the administrative law context. This introduction provides a framework for approaching administrative law that will guide you through subsequent chapters.

Many students take administrative law because they have been told it is a core course. Nevertheless, you may not be approaching the course eagerly, having heard that it is dull, complex, and tedious. With respect to complexity, administrative law probably stands guilty as charged. However, administrative law is anything but dull and tedious. Part of the problem with administrative law, or "admin law" as most of you will start calling it, is its name; it does not conjure up a clear image of the subject matter of the field, as does "criminal law" or "family law." A far better name would be something like "the citizen and the state," or "law for ordinary people," or "public justice." Most people will never see the inside of a courtroom, but they will be affected in a multitude of ways by decisions of administrative bodies. This text, representing a collaboration of leading scholars and teachers across Canada, stresses the importance of administrative decision-making in the lives of Canadians, the endless variety of administrative decision-making, and its relationship to public policy.

At a minimum, a grasp of administrative law is going to immensely broaden the range of topics that you can talk about over dinner! That is because, as mentioned above, for most Canadians, administrative law will be much more relevant than civil or criminal law. Consider, for example, your grandmother. Few of you have grandmothers who will sue or be sued and few who will be convicted of a criminal offence, but many grandmothers will at some point in their lives come in contact with the administrative state or administrative decision-making, whether in the context of health-care benefits, housing, or human rights.

I. HOW DOES ADMINISTRATIVE LAW AFFECT PEOPLE?

Let's start with your own morning ritual. You wake up and your clock radio is tuned to your favourite station. The content of the show you listen to is regulated by the Canadian Radio-television and Telecommunications Commission (CRTC). The CRTC is an administrative body whose powers have been devolved to it by the federal government through legislation. Administrative law is relevant to how the CRTC conducts its business. It governs licence renewals, the processes to be gone through in applying for a licence, and the rights that various radio, television, and telephone companies and citizens like you and me have to be heard by the CRTC and to ask a court to review any decision we are unhappy with. For those who are waking up in a rented apartment in Ontario, everything from your rent increase to the rules about pets is affected by the decisions of the Ontario Landlord and Tenant Board.

Next we move to the breakfast table where you opt for eggs and bacon. The Ontario Egg Marketing Board (OEMB)—an administrative body—allots Ontario's share of the national quota of egg production by regulating hen numbers to individual egg farmers holding production quota. The OEMB also establishes prices based on a national cost of production formula for grade A eggs. As you are eating your bacon, you could contemplate the fact that the Pork Producers Marketing Board—also an administrative body—sells live hogs on a graded basis through an electronic auction system and establishes weekly pooled prices. But what do hog farmers do when the Pork Producers Marketing Board makes a decision they are unhappy with or refuses to listen to their concerns? Administrative law speaks to the ability of those affected by decisions made under delegated governmental authority (of which I say more below) to challenge both the *process* by which the decision has been made and, in certain cases, the *substance* of the decision itself.

Perhaps you have children and, before heading to class, you drop them off at school. The Ministry of Education in each province sets education standards, and various school boards make policies and decisions about staffing, resource allocation, school closures, and suspension and discipline of pupils. Your ability to be heard by these boards, to participate in decision-making, to have legal counsel, and to be able to challenge a decision to suspend or expel your child is governed by the field of administrative law.

You finally arrive at the law school. The university as a body is empowered by government, through legislation, to more or less run its own show: the faculty of law sets standards for admission; admits and rejects applicants; and grades, passes, fails, and disciplines students. Administrative law is what you turn to if you feel that you have been treated unfairly—for example, challenging the fact that the dean of the university has disciplined you for a particular act without hearing your version of events (review for procedural fairness), or arguing that a decision made against you should be overturned because it was unreasonable or based on false assumptions (review for substantive fairness).

After graduation, law societies in each of the provinces determine standards for admission to the Bar and have the power to enforce those standards through disciplinary procedures. Again, if you don't like the decision made, you turn to administrative law to find out how to challenge the procedures followed by the Law Society and, in some cases, to challenge the substance of the decision.

Apart from the administrative web within which your own personal life is immersed, administrative law also plays a role in the following situations:

- Security officers at the airport conduct a variety of personal checks on your aunt, perhaps because her physical profile or name is associated with an ethnic group that is in turn associated with terrorism.
- Your friend is denied employment insurance.
- The Immigration and Refugee Board denies refugee status to your cousin from China.
- The school board suspends your brother from school for being in the same room as some of his classmates who were using drugs.
- The College of Physicians and Surgeons revokes your sister's medical licence because she provided a large amount of morphine to help speed up the death of a terminally ill cancer patient.
- A provincial health insurance decision denies your friend's claim for hearing aid replacements because the government has decided that they are no longer "medically necessary," or your friend's application for a new cancer treatment only available in the United States is denied on the grounds that the treatment is both expensive and "experimental."

- A friend of a friend is bought up on disciplinary charges before the Senate on a charge of plagiarism in a major paper from last semester.
- The person panhandling outside your subway stop applies for social benefits.
- Your friend, who is a brilliant physicist but has a psychiatric illness, challenges a decision to compulsorily treat her with anti-psychotic medication.
- The Parole Board denies your cousin's application for early parole.

In the next chapter, Bill Bogart provides an overview and broad classifications of the workings of the administrative state, and further illustrates the endless machinery of administrative law. Moreover, he contends that there have been fundamental changes to the administrative state over the last 25 years. He asks the question, "Is there a new governance?" In providing some responses to that question, he invites us to think of the dynamic challenges posed by the shifting nature of government and of public programs. In chapter 12, Gerald Heckman pushes the boundaries of administrative law even further and expands the workings of the administrative state beyond the domestic and into the international realm. He examines how international norms, created through Canada's international obligations, have a direct influence over administrative actions. As the reader can see, the field of administrative law is a dynamic one that is being shaped by and responding to changing political and legal institutions both domestically and globally.

II. THE CHANGING NATURE OF ADMINISTRATIVE LAW

These examples merely scratch the surface of the scope of administrative law. The sheer range of administrative decision-makers makes administrative law complex yet challenging, daunting yet interesting. It requires the application of general principles to very different contexts. For example, the rule for determining the standard of review is now the same regardless of the nature of the decision-maker, but there is no cookie-cutter method for the *application* of the rule to the different contexts of administrative decision-making. This can be frustrating for students of administrative law who in reading cases may find it hard to understand the rationale for different outcomes. Certainly, their disillusionment is deepened if a court seems to be using the discretion they have in applying general principles to different contexts to drive the decision to an outcome it prefers.

In general, administrative law governs the processes and mechanisms of the welfare and regulatory states. Administrative law plays a role when someone, other than a court or a legislature, makes a decision, and this decision affects someone's rights or interests. Almost always, the decision-maker's powers spring from legislation—that is, the power has been delegated to the decision-maker by the legislature. So, administrative law is about government action, specifically *delegated* government action where decisions are made not in and by the legislature itself (where the decision can be challenged and scrutinized by the opposition and debated in the Houses of Parliament) but by the Cabinet, federal and provincial government departments (including ministers), municipalities, and boards and tribunals. These latter institutions—boards, tribunals, and other independent administrative agencies—are the core focus of administrative law and where, for these purposes, our primary focus lies. However, many of the major cases we touch on involve the exercise of ministerial discretion (what Bill Bogart describes in the next chapter as the "übertool") that often has profound impacts on individuals—for example, in *Suresh*,[1] a ministerial decision that results in deportation on the grounds of national security to a country that allows torture, or in *Baker*,[2] a ministerial decision that results in the deportation of a woman, causing separation from her Canadian-born children.

Increasingly, administrative law is moving toward uniform principles for determining review irrespective of the nature of the decision-maker (be it a minister or a government-appointed board), but there is still enormous variety in how those principles are applied to the specific contexts of decision-making. To add to the theoretical complexity, administrative law can have relevance in areas outside of delegated governmental decision-making, where private bodies have de facto assumed a governmental stance—for example, in the case of racing authorities, amateur sports associations, religious institutions, etc.

Other branches of law are subsets of administrative law. If you practise in the areas of labour and employment, environmental law, land-use planning, human rights, municipal law, immigration and refugee law, landlord and tenant law, securities law, etc., then you will practise in administrative law. Each of these areas has its own particular legislation that practitioners therein will know all too intimately; it will become clear through this text that interpreting legislation is a key part of administrative law. Statutory interpretation is critical in order to determine what processes the legislature intended to be followed, what degree of independence the legislature wished the decision-maker to enjoy, and for the purposes of determining the level of scrutiny a court should bring to bear in reviewing a particular decision.

III. A BIT MORE ON BOARDS AND TRIBUNALS

If you think about it, the role of the state—even in capitalist societies—is widespread and pervasive. Clearly the federal and provincial governments cannot (and, in some cases, should not) directly manage every public program and every government initiative. Legislatures therefore sometimes delegate decision-making powers to various boards, tribunals, regulators, and other decision-makers.

There is an enormous range of boards and tribunals in existence. We provide a small sampling of them in table 1. (If you are a student, you should try to attend the proceedings of at least one board or tribunal to get a sense of how they function.) What connects administrative boards is that they are established by legislation in order to attain a public policy goal or goals. They are frequently somewhat independent of the government that has established them. However, explicit legislation may limit the degree of independence enjoyed (a subject pursued in much greater depth by Laverne Jacobs in chapter 6). The other connection they share is that the members of the board or tribunal are appointed in order to bring a particular expertise to decision-making and, in addition, may develop expertise over time in making decisions (although in this latter regard there can be great variation because members of some boards are appointed for several years and others may only be appointed for the hearing). They may also vary with respect to what legal qualifications they have: some boards and tribunals are required to have members with legal training, others are not.

1 *Suresh v. Canada (Minister of Citizenship and Immigration)*, [2002] 1 S.C.R. 3.

2 *Baker v. Canada (Minister of Citizenship and Immigration)*, [1999] 2 S.C.R. 817 [*Baker*].

Table 1 A Small Sample of Administrative Tribunals and Boards in Canada

Jurisdiction	Name	Legislation
Federal	Canadian Artists and Producers Professional Relations Tribunal	*Status of the Artist Act* (1992) <http://www.capprt-tcrpap.gc.ca/epic/site/capprt-tcrpap.nsf/en/h_tn00040e.html>
	Canadian Forces Grievance Board	*National Defence Act* (1998) <http://www.cfgb-cgfc.gc.ca>
	National Parole Board	*Corrections and Conditional Release Act* (CCRA) (1992) Corrections and Conditional Release Regulations (CCRR) (1992) *Criminal Code* (1985) *Criminal Records Act* (1985) *Access to Information Act* (1985) *Privacy Act* (1985) *Canadian Multiculturalism Act* (1985) <http://www.npb-cnlc.gc.ca/about/legisl_e.htm>
	Patented Medicine Prices Review Board	*Patent Act* (1985) Patented Medicines Regulations (1994) <http://www.pmprb-cepmb.gc.ca/english/view.asp?x=73>
Alberta	Environmental Appeals Board	Part 4 of the *Environmental Protection and Enhancement Act* (2000), part 9 of the *Water Act* (2000), and schedule 5 of the *Government Organization Act* (2000). <http://www.eab.gov.ab.ca/legislation.htm>
	Metis Settlements Appeal Tribunal	*Métis Settlements Act* (1990) <http://www.msat.gov.ab.ca>
Atlantic provinces	The Disabled Persons Commission (Nova Scotia)	*Disabled Persons Commission Act* (1989) <http://www.gov.ns.ca/disa>
	Dairy Farmers of Nova Scotia organization (previously the Diary Commission)	*Dairy Industry Act* (2000) <http://www.dfns.ca/index.htm>
British Columbia	British Columbia Securities Commission	*Securities Act* (1996) <http://www.bcsc.bc.ca>
	Office of the Information and Privacy Commissioner	*Freedom of Information and Protection of Privacy Act* (1996) *Personal Information Protection Act* (2003) <http://www.oipcbc.org>

(The table is continued on the next page.)

Table 1 Continued

Jurisdiction	Name	Legislation
Manitoba	Automobile Injury Compensation Appeal Commission	*Manitoba Public Insurance Corporation Act* (1987) <http://www.gov.mb.ca/finance/cca/autom/index.html>
Nunavut	Nunavut Planning Commission	Nunavut Land Claims Agreement (1992) <http://npc.nunavut.ca/eng/npc/index.html>
Ontario	Board of Funeral Services	*Funeral Directors and Establishments Act* (1990) <http://www.funeralboard.com>
	Health Services Appeal and Review Board	*Ministry of Health Appeal and Review Boards Act* (1998) Note: Monitors 14 different statutes. <http://www.hsarb.on.ca/english/about/default.htm>
	Landlord and Tenant Board	*Residential Tenancies Act* (2006) <http://www.ltb.gov.on.ca/en/index.html>
Quebec	Commission des droits de la personne et des droits de la jeunesse (Human Rights Tribunal)	Quebec *Charter of Human Rights and Freedoms* (2002) <http://www.cdpdj.qc.ca/en/home.asp?noeud1=0&noeud2=0&cle=0>
Saskatchewan	Saskatchewan Real Estate Commission	*The Real Estate Act* (1997) <http://www.srec.ca/legis.asp>
Yukon	Yukon Surface Rights Board	*Yukon Surface Rights Board Act* (1994), *Placer Mining Act* (Yukon) (2003), the *Quartz Mining Act* (Yukon) (2003), and individual Yukon First Nation Final Agreements <http://www.yukonsurfacerights.com/AboutTheBoard/index.html>

What distinguishes tribunals and boards from each other is the extent to which they employ processes that are similar to courts on the one hand, and policy-making in government on the other. In practice there is a wide range, from professional disciplinary hearings (which mimic civil proceedings) to a much more informal decision-making process, such as the processing of employment insurance. At the policy end of the spectrum, bodies such as the Ontario Energy Board and the CRTC are engaged in regulating major industries and setting important policies. What also varies is the quantity of decisions that have to be taken. While the Immigration and Refugee Board decides more than 40,000 claims per year,[3] the Competition Tribunal may only hear 12 cases per year.[4] And, finally, there is great variation across boards and tribunals as to the extent to which their decisions affect individuals.

Through statutes, legislatures give these tribunals and boards power over others. Their reasons for doing so are as varied as the types of delegated decision-makers in existence. Sometimes there is a desire to employ particular expertise that is not available within a government department; sometimes there is a need for an independent and impartial decision-maker so that decisions are not seen to be dictated by political processes; and sometimes, which is of greater concern, governments may try to bury or deflect attention from inadequate funding for programs or tough resource allocation decisions by devolving decision-making to administrative agencies with court-like powers. Judicialization can be appealing to governments, who "clothe what are essentially economic or social decisions with a sort of protective colouring that may bolster the tribunal's credibility, or at least make it a little less vulnerable to criticism."[5] Judicialization, however, may undermine access (in the sense of more flexible and less formal decision-making and dispute-resolving bodies), which is another key goal in establishing administrative boards and tribunals, as Lorne Sossin discusses in chapter 15.

Whatever the reason for the establishment of a board or tribunal, it is very important to realize that the legislature—almost always at the behest of the government—makes a conscious choice to devolve decision-making away from the legislature and not to the courts but to an administrative body. The principle of parliamentary sovereignty requires that this choice be respected (although the amount of respect shown has varied through the course of jurisprudential history and still today does not necessarily mean that courts will defer to the decision of an administrative board or tribunal). An important theme in administrative law is the marriage of administrative tribunals, boards, and agencies and the courts, and the balance of power between them. The former are specialized, the latter are generalized, but who should trump who and in what circumstances? Administrative boards and tribunals can sometimes have a huge impact on individual rights. For example, a parole board can keep someone in prison. A landlord and tenant tribunal can decide if a family has a roof over its head. The Immigration and Refugee Board can decide whether a person is deported. Thus,

---

3 Immigration and Refugee Board of Canada, Decisions, online: IRB Decisions <http://www.irb-cisr.gc.ca/en/decisions/index_e.htm>.

4 Competition Tribunal, Case Listing by Date Filed, online: Competition Tribunal <http://www.ct-tc.gc.ca/english/CaseListingByDateFiled.asp?x=219>.

5 Judith McCormack, "Nimble Justice: Revitalizing Administrative Tribunals in a Climate of Rapid Change" (1995) 59 Sask. L. Rev. 385 at 2.

to what extent should such a board be expected to act like a court? And to what extent should an individual, affected by a decision made by a decision-maker delegated power by the legislature, be able to challenge that decision before a court? And how is it possible to have different requirements in this regard to reflect the great variety of administrative boards and tribunals in existence?

As you progress through this text and the accompanying cases, keep in mind *why* a legislature might prefer decision-making to be made by an administrative tribunal and not by a court. One of the most important reasons is that a board or tribunal may have specialized expertise that a court arguably should not second-guess (for example, labour boards). Courts are generalists and cannot usually be assumed to have the same level of knowledge and insight into a particular industry or sector that a tribunal or board, whose membership has been chosen explicitly for that purpose, has. Moreover, administrative boards and tribunals may have multiple functions: in addition to adjudication or making decisions that affect individuals, they may also be required to engage in policy-making and in policy analysis, a role that the courts usually eschew. Indeed, Justice Abella has written that an administrative board is "part law, part policy, a push-me-pull-you two-headed creature designed to alleviate the burdens of judges and bureaucrats."[6] Tribunals and boards may also be required to fulfill other duties such as issuing licences and investigating or prosecuting infractions in, for example, the human rights, securities, and environmental law sectors. Furthermore, the elaborate procedural processes employed by courts may make them too slow and expensive for the resolution of disputes where many decisions need to be taken quickly (immigration, social insurance, workers' compensation, etc.) or the stakes are very small.

IV. ADMINISTRATIVE LAW AND CONSTITUTIONAL LAW

Most students' understanding of public law is grounded in constitutional law; they will be curious about how constitutional and administrative law fit together. In chapter 7, Evan Fox-Decent discusses in depth the interaction between constitutional and administrative law, both in terms of procedural and substantive review. Administrative law and constitutional law are subsets of public law and both deal with the legal framework within which government works. To different extents, both constitutional law and administrative law deal with the legality of governmental powers.

What are the major differences between a constitutional challenge and an administrative law challenge? Unlike a Charter[7] challenge, an administrative law case cannot provide an applicant with the opportunity to overturn a piece of legislation. Rather, in resorting to administrative law, the applicant is trying to ensure that governmental power is used in an accountable way vis-à-vis the ordinary citizen. Charter and constitutional challenges are about overturning and reviewing parliamentary decision-making and the compliance by the executive with very fundamental legal norms (such as the freedom from inappropriate

6 R. Abella, "Canadian Administrative Tribunals: Towards Judicialization or Dejudicialization" (1988) 2 Can. J. Admin. L. & Prac. 1 at 2.

7 *Canadian Charter of Rights and Freedoms*, Part I of the *Constitution Act, 1982*, being Schedule B to the *Canada Act, 1982* (UK), 1982, c. 110.

search and seizure), whereas administrative law is about reviewing and ensuring a more generic fairness in devolved governmental decision-making. Nor, as both Evan Fox-Decent and Cristie Ford discuss in chapters 7 and 3, can administrative law provide the wide range of remedies that a court can provide in response to a Charter challenge. Often the remedy provided for a successful administrative law challenge is a redirection to the government board or tribunal to reconsider the matter in accordance with the law. Although this may prima facie not look as powerful, in truth it often amounts to the matter being decided in a different way.

Although administrative law provides more limited remedies than those available through a Charter challenge, administrative law has a much wider reach than the Charter, which only applies to government decision-making. For example, while the Charter does not normally apply to decision-making by universities, hospitals,[8] or Crown corporations, administrative law sometimes will. Whereas it may be necessary to show a deprivation of specifically enumerated rights (such as life, liberty, or security of person) to invoke Charter remedies, administrative law extends to a broader array of rights, interests, and privileges.

V. SO WHERE DO WE START?

The context of administrative decision-making is extremely important to the resolution of issues in this field, and a variety of sectors and kinds of decisions will be examined. However, the particular valleys and mountains of immigration law, labour law, securities law, etc., have to be left for other texts; we will concentrate on the general principles of administrative law. This analysis centres on how the courts review decision-making on the part of those delegated power by the legislature.

Historically, the stance of courts toward administrative agencies has been negative: to limit, to reign in, to supervise, to oversee, and to constrain. As Mary Liston describes in chapter 4, this historical orientation of the courts toward administrative agencies and tribunals, best captured in the writings of A.V. Dicey on the rule of law, was one that was largely antithetical to the administrative state. As we will see, perspectives on the rule of law and the appropriate relationships between courts, Parliament, Cabinet, and delegated decision-makers like boards and tribunals have changed over time. The emphasis has shifted so that courts will (at least in theory, if not in practice) be deferential to administrative boards and tribunals where it seems that this was what Parliament intended. However, battles and differences in opinion over the appropriate balance between parliamentary sovereignty and the rule of law continue to play out in the jurisprudence, as do battles between progressive and more libertarian stances toward claims for social services, etc. There is still no satisfactory resolution of all the various theoretical complexities and, in the absence of an agreed upon and coherent framework, there is room for courts to obtain the results they prefer politically. Understanding the history of how Canadian courts have approached these issues over time and a theoretical overview of different conceptions of the rule of law, which Mary Liston provides in chapter 4, will help students better understand how different judges approach the cases before them.

8 Although see *Eldridge* where the Charter was found to apply to a hospital making resource allocation decisions: *Eldridge v. British Columbia (Attorney General)*, [1997] 3 S.C.R. 624.

As with most administrative law texts, this book will look carefully and critically at how courts review, view, and exchange with administrative agencies. In addition, we also try to convey a much greater sense of how administrative boards and tribunals work in practice. In chapter 15, for example, Lorne Sossin looks at how people access administrative tribunals and how decisions on budgets, staffing, websites, and translation can make the difference between justice and injustice. In chapter 14, Peter Carver takes up the challenge of looking at how administrative law works differently in the politically charged context of public inquiries. In chapter 16, Freya Kristjanson and Leslie McIntosh look at administrative law from a hands-on practitioner's perspective, providing useful checklists, tips, and an overview for those starting to practise administrative law. Administrative law scholars and teachers from across Canada have joined together to work on this text to provide multiple voices, perspectives, and approaches to administrative law and to attempt to convey a greater sense of the real world of administrative decision-making. I will leave it to those authors and the chapters that follow to illuminate this world. In the remainder of this introduction I will provide a basic overview of the core features of administrative law to help guide the student/reader through subsequent chapters.

The core function of judicial review of administrative action is to examine how and why the courts decide to intervene in the administrative process. Administrative law can be roughly divided into three parts:

1. *Procedural fairness*: First, is this an issue courts should review and, if so, did the tribunal use the proper procedures in reaching a decision?
2. *Substantive fairness*: Regarding the decision itself—did the tribunal make an error of the kind or magnitude that the court is willing to get involved in?
3. *Remedies and the legitimacy of judicial review.*

VI. REVIEW FOR PROCEDURAL FAIRNESS

Chapters 5, 6, and 7 by Grant Huscroft, Laverne Jacobs, and Evan Fox-Decent all deal with aspects of procedural fairness, both in the common law and pursuant to the Charter. When it comes to the common law of procedural fairness, the court, in reviewing the actions of the tribunal, is not interested in the actual decision that the tribunal came to in the end (the substance), but in the procedures followed by the tribunal in coming to the decision.

There are several parts to this focus on procedure: the threshold question, the content of procedural fairness, bias and independence, and institutional decision-making. What follows is a simplified and high-level summary; the hard work and necessary detail are provided in chapters 5, 6, and 7.

A. Threshold Question

First, a court should ask itself what is called the "threshold" question: Is this the kind of decision that should attract some kind of procedural right? At this stage, the court is not asking what those rights would encompass; the court is only asking itself the preliminary question of whether or not there should be any entitlement to procedural fairness at all. To put it another way, the court is asking if it should review the tribunal's procedures or if it is a situation where the court feels that it is more appropriate just to say that whatever the tribunal decides to do by way of procedure is sufficient. Generally, if, as a result of delegation by the legislature of governmental power, a decision is made that affects an individual's rights or interests there will be some minimum entitlement to procedural fairness, but there are still some exceptions. Grant Huscroft explores them in chapter 5. Exceptions include situations where the decision is a legislative or policy decision or the decision is preliminary or investigative (and then there are the exceptions to the exceptions!). Another issue to consider here is the doctrine of legitimate expectation and in what circumstances, if any, an individual should be entitled to certain procedural rights if a representation of some form has been made that such rights would be forthcoming.

Traditionally, the determination of whether this threshold had been passed was carried out at common law. In recent years, another component of this threshold discussion is the Charter. In chapter 7, Evan Fox-Decent explores the kinds of actions/decisions that fall under s. 7 of the Charter. He examines in detail how the guarantee that one is not to be deprived of life, liberty, or security of the person except in accordance with fundamental justice (s. 7) relates to the common law of procedural fairness.

As you progress through the cases you will notice that the division into two separate questions of the threshold and the content of procedures is often rather artificial. Thus, the questions whether or not the threshold has been passed and, if so, what procedures are appropriate are not easily separated from each other.

B. The Content of Procedural Fairness

If a court determines that the threshold for some form of procedural fairness has been met, the court must address what those procedures will be. The Supreme Court in *Baker*[9] identified the following five factors as relevant in determining the general level of procedural fairness: the nature of the decision and the process followed in making it, the nature of the statutory scheme, the importance of the decision to the individual affected, the legitimate expectations of the parties, and the procedure chosen by the tribunal.

Having determined the general *level* of procedural fairness, the court will then decide from a range of possibilities what *specific* procedures are required. There are many possibilities:

- *notice* that the decision is going to made,
- *disclosure* of the information on which the tribunal will base its decision,
- some opportunity to participate or make views known,
- full *hearing* similar to that which occurs in a court,
- opportunity to give *evidence* and cross examine,
- right to *counsel*, and
- oral or written *reasons* for its decision.

You may notice that many of these possibilities seem to be a way of asking, "To what extent must the administrative decision-maker act like a court?" We also need to think about who is better situated to determine what various procedures the tribunals should follow: the

9 *Baker*, *supra* note 2.

tribunals or the courts? Can courts really understand the day-to-day reality, costs, and impact of requiring different procedures from those that a tribunal would select itself?

If your client asks whether or not he or she has a right to be represented by legal counsel before an administrative board or tribunal, where should you turn to first? As I mentioned earlier, students often overlook the most important aspect of administrative law, namely the necessity for closely examining the legislation setting up the board or tribunal. Often the legislation will expressly lay out the kinds of procedures that applicants are entitled to. It is possible that the common law may expand on these, but the first port of call should be the statute itself. In addition, it is important to check whether or not the province you are in has umbrella legislation that sets out the types of procedures that must be made available for all or specific types of boards and tribunals—for example, Ontario's *Statutory Powers Procedures Act*,[10] Alberta's *Administrative Procedures and Jurisdiction Act*,[11] and Quebec's *Administrative Justice Act*.[12] In British Columbia the *Administrative Tribunals Act*[13] focuses on empowering the tribunal to enact its own rules. These acts are available on the companion website to this text. It is critical to remember that where a statute—be it umbrella or specific to the tribunal—specifies a certain kind of procedural right or specifically denies a procedural right that would otherwise have been available in the common law, the statute prevails over the common law.

In addition to the statutory regime, in practice, it is also very important to check the rules that the board or tribunal operates pursuant to (these rules go beyond the content of the enabling statutes). As Andrew Green discusses in chapter 13, these rules are critical to the day-to-day operation of boards and tribunals and, in reality, the decisions of the hundreds of boards and tribunals across the country have a far greater impact on Canadians than the relatively few decisions that are taken on judicial review to the general courts.[14] For example, the guidelines issued by the Minister of Immigration set out the basis on which immigration officers are to determine whether an individual deserves humanitarian and compassionate consideration, and these guidelines were central to the resolution of the *Baker* decision, which I discuss further below.[15]

C. Bias

Another aspect of the part of this text that focuses on procedures is the idea of bias, which is more fully explored by Laverne Jacobs in chapter 6. If a decision-maker acts in a biased manner, what then? And what do we mean by bias? Do we mean that we have actual evidence that an individual decision-maker has already made up his or her mind or has been bribed to decide in a particular way? Or is it enough that, given all the circumstances, there is an appearance of bias?

10 R.S.O. 1990, c. S.22.

11 R.S.A. 2000, c. A-3.

12 R.S.Q. c. J-3.

13 S.B.C. 2004, c. 45.

14 See Lorne Sossin, at chapter 15, and his reference to McLachlin J.'s passage from *Cooper v. Canada (Human Rights Commission)*, [1996] 3 S.C.R. 854.

15 *Baker*, *supra* note 2.

D. Independence

Laverne Jacobs also deals with the related issue of independence, which, as mentioned above, is a key feature of most boards and tribunals. Institutional independence is related to the notion of bias but is more about the systemic structure of a board or tribunal as opposed to individual decision-making. In the context of independence we ask questions such as do the members of the tribunal have financial security or do they have security of tenure? A related issue is whether they are so dependent on or connected to the government that, if appointed, they cannot be perceived as being sufficiently able to make an independent decision.

E. Institutional Decision-Making

Here we look at the thorny issue of the degree to which boards and tribunals can consult with others to whom the person affected will not have had the opportunity to present his or her case. For example, is it acceptable that, in order to deal with a high caseload, a board has set up a process whereby just one member of the board hears an application or case but the full board is involved in the final decisions? If so, in what circumstances?

VII. REVIEW FOR SUBSTANTIVE ERROR

Historically, administrative law has focused primarily on procedural review (with the implicit notion that if a sound process is followed, a fair decision will be reached). The second major focus of administrative law—substantive review—has gained in importance. Here, the courts look at the decision itself, not just at the procedures that were followed in reaching the decision. Regarding the decision itself, the courts ask themselves what the standard of review is; in other words, how big an error must the tribunal make before the court will get involved? There are three possibilities:

1. A standard of correctness, the most exacting standard of review (that is, was it a correct decision, the same decision that the court would have reached?).
2. A standard of reasonableness, the middle ground in terms of the degree of scrutiny (that is, the decision can be one that falls within a band of reasonable decisions even if it was not the exact decision that a court would itself have reached).
3. A standard of patent unreasonableness, the most forgiving standard of review (that is, if superficially the decision is not unreasonable, then the court should make no further inquiry and allow the decision to stand).[16]

In chapters 8 and 9, Audrey Macklin and Sheila Wildeman, respectively, set out in much greater detail the history of the development of the tests for the standard of review and the modern test and all its myriad twists, turns, and agonies. In chapter 10, Geneviève Cartier takes the reader through the history and modern tests for review of the exercise of discretion (which historically has been treated differently from other types of decisions), and in chapter 11, Craig Forcese provides further illustration and application of discretionary decision-making—for example, in the contexts of international security and anti-terrorism measures.

16 As this book was going to press, the Supreme Court of Canada radically overhauled the law relating to standards of review in *Dunsmuir v. New Brunswick*, 2008 SCC 9. For the case and further analysis, see the accompanying website.

ouble standard review

Having determined the standard of review—the level of intensity with which the court will review a decision—the court then applies it to the decision in question, be it a decision taken by a minister, a municipality, a board, or a tribunal. Even if a court has determined that the standard of review must be the most searching (that is, correctness), in reviewing the decision, it may nonetheless determine that the standard has been met. In other words, the decision reached by the board or tribunal is the same as that which would have been reached by the court and thus will not be overturned. Similarly, if the standard of review is patent unreasonableness—the most lenient—then it does not necessarily mean the decision will stand; it may be that the court finds that no reasonable decision-maker could have reached that conclusion. For example, in the case of *Stein v. Quebec*,[17] the court found that with respect to resource allocation decisions in health care that the Quebec Health Insurance Tribunal was owed the highest degree of deference—the standard of patent unreasonableness. However, in its decision not to refund lifesaving cancer treatment paid for by Mr. Stein in New York, the tribunal failed to meet even this most deferential of standards.

What if the statute setting up the tribunal says that the tribunal's decision is final and not open to review by the courts? This kind of provision is known as a privative or preclusive clause. The history of the court's treatment of such clauses is a twisted one, beginning with an approach that readily allowed courts to ignore such express clauses (by arguing that the error made by the board or tribunal went to the very jurisdiction it had to make the decision, and thus a decision that must be reviewable by the court) to a time where the existence of a privative or preclusive clause meant that a standard of patent unreasonableness must automatically apply. The modern approach to the standard of review is to treat the existence of a privative or preclusive clause as just one factor (albeit a significant one) among a number of factors in determining the standard of review. Yet, as Sheila Wildeman fully explores in chapter 9, it is hard to avoid this concept of jurisdiction, and the jurisprudence is frequently infiltrated by jurisdiction zombies of the past.

Just as historically a privative clause automatically attracted a standard of patent unreasonableness, the existence of a statutory right of appeal was a green light for review and attracted a standard of correctness. Now, as with the presence of a privative clause, the existence of a statutory right of appeal is just one factor among a number to be weighed in determining the standard of review. Similarly, courts historically took a different approach to review of discretion. As Geneviève Cartier explains in chapter 10, now, ostensibly at least, the court applies the same approach to review of discretion as it does to other errors.

VIII. REMEDIES AND THE LEGITIMACY OF JUDICIAL REVIEW

The third important area of administrative law is remedies, an area that is often given short shrift when taught. To emphasize the importance of this area, we have placed Cristie Ford's chapter on this topic near the beginning of the book.

Because this issue of remedies is related to the source of power that courts may have to review, I will discuss that first. Where do courts get the power to review administrative decision-making? There are three sources of review power: original jurisdiction, right of appeal, and, most important for our purposes, courts' inherent judicial review jurisdiction. These are explained in turn below.

PU + most lenient

3 source of review power.

17 *Stein v. Québec (Régie de l'Assurance-maladie)* (1999), R.J.Q. 2416 (Sup. Ct.).

A. Original Jurisdiction

The ordinary courts have jurisdiction over the decisions of administrative decision-makers when they are challenged by way of direct actions by a citizen in contract or tort on the grounds that the state has infringed an individual's private legal right. For example, in 1995 a court granted a declaration that the Liberal government had breached a contract in cancelling the agreement made by the previous Progressive Conservative government with developers for the renovation and privatization of Pearson International Airport.[18]

B. Statutory Right of Appeal

There is no general common-law right to appeal the substance of a decision. The right to appeal must be contained in a statute. However, frequently there may be a right of appeal within a statute (for example, on errors of law or for both errors of fact and law). The major exceptions occur in the regulation of labour relations and employment, where it has been general legislative policy to narrow opportunities for judicial intervention. The first thing to do is to check the statute for a right of appeal.

C. Courts' Inherent Judicial Review Jurisdiction

Third, and most important from our perspective, the superior courts in each province (the judges appointed by the federal government) may review decisions made by institutions and officials with responsibility for administering public programs through the courts' inherent judicial review jurisdiction.

The words "inherent jurisdiction" refer to the fact that the jurisdiction of the superior courts is broader than whatever may be conferred by statute. Superior courts may hear any matter unless there is a specific statute that says otherwise or grants exclusive jurisdiction to another court or tribunal. Superior courts have greater freedom to craft remedies and grant relief than courts created by statute, such as the Federal Court. This inherent jurisdiction is not jurisdiction for a general appeal, thus courts cannot directly substitute their own decision for that of the agencies. This inherent jurisdiction was inherited from the United Kingdom in the 16th and 17th centuries from the Royal Court in Westminster. The Royal Court reviewed the legality of decision-making by a whole host of what were then front-running administrative tribunals such as the Bridge Commission, the Poor House Commissions, and the Sewer Commission.[19]

At the federal level, this inherent power has been limited by the *Federal Courts Act*, which assigns almost all judicial review authority in relation to federal administrative decision-makers to the Federal Courts of Canada. The Federal Courts' jurisdiction is, therefore, a statutory one, and they are the key venue for federal administrative law adjudication.

---

18 *T1T2 Limited Partnership v. Canada*, [1995] O.J. No. 137.

19 Jerome J. Hanus, "Certiorari and Policy-Making in English History" (1968) 12 Am. J. Legal Hist. 63, n. 2; S.A. de Smith, *Judicial Review of Administrative Action*, 4th ed. by J. Evans (London: Stevens & Sons, 1980) at 584 (appendix 1) and 596 (appendix 2).

IX. REMEDIAL POWERS

Historically, courts' inherent "supervisory" power over administrative decision-makers had to be exercised through remedies available, in the main, only in respect of public duties or powers. They were known as the prerogative writs and once were tremendously important in administrative law. These prerogative writs were certiorari (to quash or set aside a decision), prohibition (to order a tribunal not to proceed), mandamus (to order the performance of a public duty), and habeas corpus (to order the release of the unlawfully imprisoned).

These writs were used by the Royal Courts in England, and subsequently by the superior provincial courts in Canada, to ensure that administrative bodies and tribunals did not exceed their legal powers and encroach on powers or matters that were the responsibility or privilege of central government. Prior to the 1970s, administrative law was all about trying to squeeze cases into one or more of the prerogative writs, and courts made very fine distinctions about, for example, whether or not a writ would lie. There were thousands of cases dealing with these fine distinctions. However, much of this old law has been done away with since the emergence of general principles of judicial review. The jurisprudence now focuses much less on the technicalities of the old prerogative writs and much more on balancing the tension between private rights and public interest.

This pattern is also present at the federal level in the *Federal Courts Act*. The Act creates remedies available on judicial review that mimics the old prerogative writs, but employs simplified terminology.

X. A BRIEF HISTORY OF THE ANGLO-CANADIAN MODEL OF JUDICIAL REVIEW

Let us pause at this point to look more closely at the relationship between the courts and administrative agencies and the ground upon which courts can review administrative decisions. When thinking about the relationship between administrative agencies/tribunals and the general courts, lessons can be learnt from comparing the continental European approach (civil-law tradition) with the Anglo-Canadian model (common-law tradition).

In the continental European approach, a clear line is drawn between traditional courts and administrative agencies and tribunals. For example, in France administrative law occupies an entirely different system and is completely separate from the civil and criminal court structure. Those who are affected by decisions made by administrative agencies and tribunals do not have recourse to the general courts; they have recourse, ultimately, to the Conseil d'État, an overseeing administrative body made up of very senior civil servants. Conseil d'État means "state council" and is the highest administrative body in France and government adviser on questions arising in connection with legislation.

The Conseil d'État is the highest administrative body, whereas the Cour de Cassation is the highest court for civil and criminal law disputes. Due to its historical development, the structure of the administrative courts does not mirror that of the criminal and civil courts, and its procedures are distinct. For example, unlike the civil courts, the administrative system does not guarantee the right of appeal on both fact and law in every case; for some matters the Conseil d'État is the judge at first and last instance.

The Anglo-Canadian approach rejects the continental European approach. A strong principle of administrative Anglo-Canadian law, modified considerably through the years

rule of law

but still having impact, is the rule of law. The rule of law stands for the proposition that any citizen should be able to access the general courts when they have a grievance with the government. This conception of the rule of law is usually associated with A.V. Dicey, a law professor at the University of Oxford in the late 1800s. Dicey's conception of the rule, the 19th-century ideal, was that

1. no one should be made to suffer except for a distinct breach of law or, in other words, that there should be a government of laws but not of men; and
2. disputes between citizens and the state were decided in the ordinary courts of the law in accordance with the ordinary law of the land.[20]

The rule of law requires, at a minimum, that governmental activity affecting an individual has to be subject to the law. But you can immediately see that there is a tension here because the courts are generalists in nature, and Dicey is asking that these generalists "supervise" often very specialized agencies. Also, of course, if courts are continually second-guessing administrative tribunals, this will undermine the very reason for establishing specialized tribunals in the first instance. However, if we have only a narrow window of appeal to the courts or narrow grounds of judicial review, then we may undermine the rule of law.

Although the rule of law is still important, we know of course that citizens cannot take all their disputes with governments or administrative agencies directly to court. We know that in practice the reach of the rule of law is much smaller than that envisaged by Dicey because we are all affected by a multitude of administrative agencies that are not courts of law. The administrative/welfare state has steadily grown, challenging Dicey's conception of the rule of law and interfering with private rights (freedom of contract, property rights, etc.) in ways never contemplated by the common law.

This is a continuing battle, a continuing tension in administrative law, that has to be resolved. As mentioned earlier, and as Mary Liston will further develop in chapter 4, historically the rule of law was usually employed to fetter, limit, and prevent administrative decision-making, and so it was viewed as inherently conservative. The courts were being called upon to essentially impede the development of the welfare state insofar as it affected private property rights. Thus the prevailing sentiment in administrative law scholarship in the 1950s, 1960s, and 1970s was to protect administrative tribunals' decision-making from overzealous courts, and this movement eventually caught on in the jurisprudence with growth in notions of deference starting, as Audrey Macklin describes in chapter 8, most famously in Canada with the *CUPE* decision.[21]

It is perhaps interesting to consider to what extent the pendulum has swung the other way from protecting what administrative agencies do to allowing for the fact that courts may be the best means to protect welfare entitlements and rights. For example, consider whether in the *Baker*[22] case (discussed further below) we see more of a sense that administrative decision-making has limitations, and we should have increased faith in the supervisory power of the courts, particularly with respect to protection of human rights.[23]

20 For a full discussion and relevant citations to Dicey see Mary Liston, chapter 4.

21 *Canadian Union of Public Employees, Local 963 v. New Brunswick Liquor Corp.*, [1979] 2 S.C.R. 227.

22 *Baker*, *supra* note 2.

23 Lorne Sossin & Colleen M. Flood, "The Contextual Turn: Iacobucci's Legacy and the Standard of Review in Administrative Law" (2007) 57 U.T.L.J. 581.

XI. THE CONSTITUTIONAL RIGHT TO REVIEW ADMINISTRATIVE DECISION-MAKERS AND SECTION 96 COURTS

I now need to digress from providing an overview to providing a bit more detail on a topic not otherwise covered in the rest of the text. As I discussed above, a privative or preclusive clause is a way in which the legislature attempts to exclude the courts from reviewing the decisions of administrative boards or tribunals. As you will see in the jurisprudence, courts historically interpreted these kinds of clauses very narrowly and did not accept even very strongly worded privative clauses as ousting their authority to review for excess of jurisdiction. Why is this? Our constitutional tradition has been such that for the most part government has only those powers conferred by legislature, so its powers are legally limited.

On some views the ultimate function of the courts is to determine the limits of governmental power, especially when such powers threaten individual rights. The court may achieve this through the discretion they have in statutory interpretation but, arguably, there are also constitutional grounds for the oversight by general courts of administrative decision-makers. The question that arises here is whether a provincial legislature or the Parliament of Canada has the constitutional capacity to exclude *all* kinds of judicial review of decisions made by an administrative agency. There is nothing *explicitly* said about this in the *Constitution Act, 1867*.[24] The argument for implying a constitutionally guaranteed right to judicial review of administrative action has centred on the judicature provisions of the *Constitution Act, 1867*, ss. 96-101.

My discussion will primarily focus on s. 96 (courts). Essentially, s. 96 of the *Constitution Act* provides that the appointment of superior court judges is the responsibility of the federal government, which means that provinces cannot de facto create a court and (conveniently) call it an administrative tribunal to get around this. The courts have developed a three-part test to determine whether or not an administrative tribunal is in fact acting like a s. 96 court:

1. Historical inquiry—whether the impugned power broadly confers to a power exclusively exercised by a superior, district, or county court at the time of Confederation (the jurisprudence suggests that this should be interpreted broadly so as to ensure the protection of s. 96 courts).
2. Is the impugned power a "judicial" power as opposed to an administrative or legislative power? A judicial power is one where there is a private dispute between parties, adjudicated through the application of a recognized body of rules, and adjudicated in a manner consistent with fairness and impartiality.
3. Has the power in its institutional setting changed its character sufficiently to negate broad conformity with superior, district, or county jurisdiction? For example, it was noted in *Tomko v. Labour Relations Board*,[25] while referring to the Nova Scotia Labour Relations Board, that the adjudicative functions of such a board were part of its broader administrative and policy-making role as administrator of the labour relations legislation. Thus, it was agreed that one could not compare a labour relations board's cease and desist order with the jurisdiction of a superior court to issue mandatory injunctions to halt illegal activities.

---

24 (U.K.) 30 & 31 Vict., c. 3, reprinted in R.S.C. 1985, App. II, No. 5.

25 [1977] 1 S.C.R. 112, as referenced in *Re Residential Tenancies Act, 1979*, [1981] 1 S.C.R. 714 at 731-32.

The leading case on administrative tribunals masquerading as s. 96 courts is *Crevier*,[26] a Supreme Court of Canada decision from 1981. In this case, Quebec legislation created a Professions Tribunal to hear appeals from discipline committees of most statutory professional bodies in Quebec. The tribunal was made up of provincially appointed judges. The act said, in effect, that the tribunal's decisions were final even if they were decisions about the reach of its own jurisdiction.

The Supreme Court asked the following: was the Quebec Professions Tribunal acting like a s. 96 court? The only function of this tribunal was to hear appeals; it was not part of a larger institutional arrangement. Justice Laskin for the Court noted that a government, in creating an administrative tribunal, could circumvent the s. 96 problem if the privative clause provides that the superior court has judicial review over questions of jurisdiction even if there is limited review of all other kinds of decisions. But, if the wording of a privative clause tries to oust review by courts over even strict jurisdictional questions, as was the case in *Crevier*, then the clause is not constitutionally valid, because a s. 96 court is created. The Court concluded that to give a provincial tribunal unlimited jurisdiction to interpret and apply law and then preclude any supervision by provincial superior courts creates a s. 96 court.

Crevier is a landmark case for its finding that provincially constituted statutory tribunals cannot constitutionally be immunized from review of decisions on matters of jurisdiction by the Superior Courts. However, because the basis of *Crevier* is not entirely clear, the dilemma left after this landmark case is whether it is about

1. preventing the provinces from usurping the federal government's power to appoint judges to the superior courts by the creation of tribunals that have an essential characteristic of superior courts, or
2. protecting the individual's right to seek relief from an independent judiciary constituted pursuant to s. 96.

The trend in the case law is that, implicit in ss. 96-100, there is a constitutionally guaranteed right to seek judicial review of administrative action on the grounds of jurisdictional error or illegality. For example, Justice Beetz said in *Bibeault* that "[t]he role of the superior courts in maintaining the rule of law is so important that it is given constitutional protection."[27] The Supreme Court seems to have finally resolved its stand on this in *MacMillan Bloedel Ltd.*[28] At stake here were provisions in *federal* legislation that attempted to clothe provincial youth courts with exclusive jurisdiction to try youths for ex facie contempt of superior courts. The Supreme Court of Canada agreed that while it was permissible to confer jurisdiction over such matters on courts staffed by provincial appointees, that jurisdiction could not be to the exclusion of the superior courts. A superior court has a constitutionally guaranteed entitlement to try youths for flouting an injunction issued by it. According to Lamer J.C., "[t]he superior courts have a core or inherent jurisdiction which is integral to their operations. The jurisdiction which forms this core cannot be removed from the superior courts by either level of government, without amending the Constitution. Without this

26 *Crevier v. Quebec*, [1981] 2 S.C.R. 220 [*Crevier*].

27 *U.E.S., Local 298 v. Bibeault*, [1988] 2 S.C.R. 1048.

28 *MacMillan Bloedel Ltd. v. Simpson*, [1996] 2 W.W.R. 1 (S.C.C.) [*MacMillan*].

core jurisdiction, s. 96 could not be said to either ensure uniformity in the judicial system throughout the country or to protect the independence of the judiciary."[29]

Despite *MacMillan Bloedel Ltd.*,[30] there remain questions about the constitutional power of courts to review administrative decisions. For example, both *Pushpanathan*[31] and *Baker*[32] involved claims where the ability of a claimant to appeal a decision of the Federal Court Trial Division is limited to the extent that the trial judge must provide leave to appeal on the grounds that the issue is certified to be of general importance. Trial judges do not have to provide reasons for refusing leave to appeal for judicial review, and their decisions in this regard are final. Could one, employing *Crevier*,[33] challenge this limitation?

Also, an issue of great importance is the need to access the evidence with respect to a jurisdictional question but at the same time to protect the integrity of the decision-maker. There has always been a strong common-law principle of deliberative secrecy limiting access to the inner workings and discussions of decision-makers. How can you assert your constitutional right to have a court review for jurisdiction when your access to materials is limited or there is an absence of fully articulated reasons?

XII. BAKER

One method of learning how to swim is to jump into the deep end. In reality, this method is rarely tried and, when tried, can result in a watery demise. Yet we recommend it (metaphorically) for admin law. To jump into the deep end and to provide an overview in the areas of procedural and substantive review, you may start by reading and analyzing the 1999 Supreme Court of Canada case, *Baker v. Canada (Minister of Citizenship and Immigration)*.[34] This is the most important Supreme Court decision on administrative law in the last 20 years. It involved a woman, about to be deported for overstaying, who requested that the Minister use his discretionary power to allow her on humanitarian and compassionate grounds to remain in Canada with her four Canadian-born children while she applied for permanent residency. Her application was denied. An immigration officer wrote up inflammatory notes about the merits of Ms. Baker's application. Despite the relatively informal nature of these notes, they were taken by the Supreme Court to be the reasons for the decision. (For a fuller summary of the facts, see Grant Huscroft, chapter 5.)

Important issues covered in *Baker* that will be the focus of attention throughout this text include what fairness required in terms of Ms. Baker's procedural rights to participate in the decision-making process (the right to make her case, have an oral hearing, etc.), the duty to give reasons and the scope of that duty, bias, and the relevance of international treaties ratified but not yet incorporated in domestic law. In terms of substantive review, the Supreme Court provided a new test for determining the standard of review for discretionary

29 *Ibid.* at para. 15.

30 *Ibid.*

31 *Pushpanathan v. Canada (Minister of Citizenship and Immigration)*, [1998] S.C.J. No. 46, [1998] 1 S.C.R. 982.

32 *Baker*, *supra* note 2.

33 *Crevier*, *supra* note 25.

34 *Baker*, *supra* note 2.

decisions such as those made by the Minister of Immigration. For administrative law redux, read *Baker* (the full decision is available on the accompanying website) and then attempt to answer the following questions.

QUESTIONS

SOURCE OF LAW

1. What sources of law did the Supreme Court consider in reaching its decision?

THE SCOPE OF THE APPEAL

2. What are the arguments for and against the Supreme Court's decision to use the certification of "a question of general importance" to be the trigger to review the whole decision? How should the courts approach statutes that preclude an administrative decision-maker being reviewed in the general courts?

PROCEDURAL FAIRNESS

3. Madam Justice L'Heureux-Dubé said that the duty of fairness required that Ms. Baker be accorded more than "minimal" procedural rights even though she was seeking a highly discretional benefit. How should the principles of procedural fairness be applied to those, like Ms. Baker, seeking a highly discretionary benefit? How does one decide what procedural rights should be available generally? What do you think of the test laid out?
4. What procedural rights was Ms. Baker found to have had? Do you think they were satisfactory? Why or why not? When do you think an oral hearing should be required?
5. Prior to *Baker* there was division of opinion over the requirement of statutory or prerogative decision-makers to provide reasons for their decisions. On what grounds was Ms. Baker found to be entitled to reasons? Why does this illustrate the absence of a bright line between procedural and substantive review? What do you think is the nature of the relationship between reviewing discretionary decision-making and the requirement to give reasons?
6. The notes of Immigration Officer Lorenz were taken to be sufficient reasons for the decisions. On what grounds did the Court decide that this was sufficient? Why is the Court's requirement for reasons such an important finding?
7. One of several factors identified by Madam Justice L'Heureux-Dubé as helpful in determining the scope of the duty of fairness is "legitimate expectation."
    a. How did she interpret the doctrine of legitimate expectation in terms of ramification for procedural and substantive rights?
    b. The Court found that the federal government signature to the *Convention on the Rights of the Child* should not be viewed as a representation. What would have been the implications if the Court had viewed this as a representation?
    c. Do you think Ms. Baker should have had to know of the existence of the *Convention on the Rights of the Child* in order to make an argument in legitimate expectation?
8. What is the test for establishing bias? At what point does a decision-maker's obvious lack of sympathy give rise to a reasonable apprehension of bias?

SUBSTANTIVE REVIEW AND ABUSE OF DISCRETION

9. *Baker* is an important decision because it is a step toward reconciling the theory on which the courts review decisions for error of law and jurisdiction and the theory on which they review for abuse of discretion. *Baker* resulted in the folding of all questions of review of discretion into the general law of review using a "pragmatic and functional" analysis. What were the factors relied upon in *Baker* to determine what the standard of review should be? What concerns arise in applying these factors to discretionary decisions?

10. With regard to review of discretionary decision-making, what three standards of review did the Supreme Court acknowledge? What standard of review did Ms. Baker seek, and what standard was found? How will you know when you should apply one standard as opposed to another?

11. As a result of *Baker*, what advice would you give clients who ask you about the impact of international agreements that Canada has ratified but not incorporated into domestic law? How does this affect discretionary decision-making?

XIII. CONCLUSION

How courts approach review of administrative decision-making depends on the type of administrative agency, the type of decisions being made by the agency, and the impact of the decisions. Some agencies appear more court-like in nature, adjudicating on particular disputes and having a huge impact on particular individuals. These kinds of agencies arguably should be required to act more like courts in terms of the type of processes that they follow in order to ensure the highest possible standard of decision-making, although this may have to be balanced against the volume of decisions that have to be adjudicated upon (for example, in the immigration area). However, many agencies and tribunals combine adjudicative-like functions with broad-based policy-making where it seems much less appropriate to restrict the agency/tribunal to a court-like process. What is fair in terms of processes in this case?

The difficulty often is that when a court reviews the actions of an administrative tribunal, the court holds the tribunal up to the standard that it expects of other courts and, unsurprisingly, frequently finds that administrative decision-makers fall short of this mark. But, at the same time, the courts have to be respectful of democratic will. This requires courts to respect the purpose for which administrative tribunals are established and the fact that these functions have explicitly *not* been delegated to courts for a reason.

Administrative decision-making and the courts' response thereto is critical to the effective implementation of public policy and the smooth operation of public programs. In what follows we hope to convey to you the complexities and challenges in administrative law and the importance of administrative decision-making and administrative law in the lives of many Canadians. We hope you find this text useful and easy to follow and that it stimulates an interest in and even a passion for administrative law. We value your feedback and thoughts on improvement for subsequent editions, and you can provide feedback on the website that accompanies this text at <http://www.emp.ca/adminlaw>.

CHAPTER TWO

The Tools of the Administrative State and the Regulatory Mix

W.A. BOGART
Faculty of Law, University of Windsor

I. INTRODUCTION

This chapter examines the various "tools" of the administrative state as part of our understanding of administrative law. The administrative state performs a host of functions: from regulating the environment to assuring minimum levels of income protection; from regulating professions to enforcing security measures in a post-9/11 world. In performing these many and varied tasks, administrative actors can be provided with a range of "tools" ("instruments," "mechanisms"). This chapter focuses on what these tools are, how they are employed, and some of the more important issues that arise regarding their use. The discussion casts lawyers primarily in the role of architects as they design and implement the many, varied aspects of regulation. The analysis is divided into four sections.

Section II contains a brief survey of legal intervention in general as the larger context in which the administrative state functions. Legal intervention with regard to a set of issues can take many forms. It can range from "soft" tools, such as legislatively authorized educational initiatives, through to the most drastic tool of law, criminal sanctions, and can use various aspects of the administrative state. This section also asks to what extent litigation should be considered a tool. It also illustrates the discussion of the many kinds of legal tools and complexities regarding their employment by reference to an issue familiar to all: the suppression of smoking.

Section III focuses on the administrative state and the tools that it employs. As part of the repertoire of legal interventions, legislatures can provide through legislation the power to some designated administrative actor to regulate the various issues that are the subject of intervention. Administrative actors themselves can also vary enormously: from independent tribunals to Cabinet ministers and government departments to, in some circumstances, other institutions such as universities and municipalities. The power that is granted usually specifies a variety of tools that the administrative actor can employ to realize legislative objectives. Moreover, the administrative actor is usually given discretion to judge the manner and circumstances in which the various tools are used. The exercise of such discretion can give rise to many issues that are briefly discussed and that will be pursued in subsequent chapters.

Section IV examines the notions of tools and "new" governance. There is a widely held view that, over the last few decades, there has been a paradigm shift in terms of how government, including the administrative state, is functioning. The "old" governance focused on "command and control," with legislatures and administrative bodies essentially imposing regulation in a myriad of areas and sanctioning any non-conforming behaviour. The new governance is about more effective and efficient government open to achieving its goals in a variety of ways by using the best mix of tools to accomplish the designated goals. This section investigates this view of two different paradigms. It suggests that differences between the two are often exaggerated and, in fact, there has been a large degree of continuity in how government and the administrative state have functioned over the last few decades. Nevertheless, there has been an important shift in emphasis. This shift is illustrated by discussing two prominent examples in the administrative state.

The final section of this chapter discusses how various tools might be evaluated. Judicial review of administrative action has long been a prime method that the legally trained have had to resort to in order to achieve accountability and transparency regarding decisions made by administrative actors. Various aspects of judicial review are discussed throughout the book.[1] Nevertheless, the role of judicial review is constrained in important ways. Thus the last section of the chapter discusses another framework for assessing the administrative state, focusing on five criteria for doing so.

1 See, for example, the chapters by Evan Fox-Decent, Audrey Macklin, and Sheila Wildeman (chapters 7, 8, and 9, respectively) in this book.

II. THE TOOLS OF LEGAL INTERVENTION: THE REGULATORY MIX

A. From Soft Intervention to the Heaviest Machinery of the State

There can, of course, be intense debate regarding any form of legal intervention with regard to any set of issues; for example, think of the arguments regarding whether and how the Internet should be regulated. However, once the decision has been made to intervene legally (that is, once the *whether* has been decided), policy-makers need to decide what kinds of legal intervention—tools—should be invoked in order to achieve the particular regulatory goals (that is, they need to decide the *how*). This section is a brief, general discussion of the tools of legal intervention. Thereafter, we will concentrate on the administrative state and the tools that it employs as a more particular but also pervasive instance of legal intervention.

Questions arise not only with regard to which tools should be used, but also the ways in which they should be employed in combination—the "mix"—in order to maximize the likelihood of realizing the ends sought to be achieved. Achieving the best mix that is possible in the circumstances raises many challenges. We will illustrate such challenges by discussing efforts to suppress smoking.

Legal intervention can involve a variety of kinds of regulation: from the most drastic (for example, prohibition by criminalizing an activity) to those that are minimally interventionist (for example, encouraging or discouraging certain behaviours through authorized programs to educate the public).[2] Most would agree that the criminal law has a role in sanctioning violent crime. All manner of other interventions might be employed to educate people regarding the harm of violence and to encourage peaceful resolution of disputes. However, when violence does occur, most would agree that the perpetrator should face criminal sanctions.

In contrast, we would be appalled at the suggestion that a person should be subject to the criminal process for being obese. At the same time, many support the idea of intervention regarding obesity, at least in terms of publicly funded programs educating people about the importance of nutritious eating and physical exercise. Others would go further and urge the invoking of other tools, such as taxation, to discourage marketing and consumption of "junk" foods and to encourage the marketing and consumption of such wholesome staples as multi-grains and fruits and vegetables.

Various forms of legal intervention—tools—such as taxation, restrictions upon advertising, self-regulation, and constraints upon how, where, and when an activity may take place can also be used to achieve policy goals.[3] Consider taxation. It has many uses as a tool of policy-making. Taxes can be employed to provide incentives for and to impose disincentives on myriad activities: investing in Canadian equities, saving for retirement, discouraging smoking, and so forth. The progressive system of taxation itself reflects our acknowledgment

---

2 See, generally, W.A. Bogart, "Achieving Compliance: Obedience and the Limits of Deterrence" (unpublished policy paper prepared for the Privy Council Office, April 2006) and Review of Regulatory Reform, *Regulatory Reform in Canada: Government Capacity to Achieve High Quality Regulation* (Paris: Organisation for Economic Co-operation and Development, 2002) [OECD, *Regulatory Reform in Canada*].

3 L. Salamon, ed., *The Tools of Government: A Guide to the New Governance* (Oxford: Oxford University Press, 2002) [Salamon, *The Tools of Government*]; P. Eliadis, *Foundation Paper: Instrument Choice in Global Democracies* (Ottawa: Policy Research Initiative, 2002) [Eliadis, *Foundation Paper*]; and R. Baldwin & M. Cave, *Understanding Regulation* (New York: Oxford University Press, 1999).

that employing notions of equity can be appropriate in achieving societal goals: those who earn more pay proportionately more tax. The overarching question that needs to be asked regarding legal intervention in any area is, What is the best mix of various forms of regulation that is likely to result in actually attaining the policy objective? That question leads to related and complex questions concerning issues such as the role of deterrence,[4] the potential of incentives,[5] the effects of litigation in achieving various policies,[6] and the relationship between law and shifting social norms in altering behaviour.[7]

In terms of the last point, the relationship between law and shifting norms, lawyers do well to remember that there are many forms of regulation in diverse settings, including the effect of social norms in guiding various aspects of human behaviour. Legal regulation is but one form, albeit a very important one, that is backed by the power of the state. Thus Hood *et al.* offer an expansive definition of regulation that includes legal forms but that goes beyond them, in the following terms: "the sustained and focused attempt to alter the behaviour of others according to defined standards or purposes with the intention of producing a broadly identified outcome or outcomes, which may involve mechanisms of standard-setting, information gathering and behaviour-modification."[8] The discussion of the suppression of smoking, below, illustrates many aspects of legal regulation and its complicated relationship to other forms of regulation, including social norms.

Let's look at this brief general discussion of the tools of legal intervention from another angle, by examining a phenomenon closely associated with lawyers and by asking, Is litigation a tool?

B. Is Litigation a Tool?

Litigation has not been much considered in the traditional literature on tools.[9] Yet, in the age of the *Canadian Charter of Rights and Freedoms* (the Charter) and related developments, the role of litigation is increasing. Lawsuits can produce a variety of effects that do have policy consequences even if those effects and consequences are not always easily ascertained.[10]

---

4 D. Nagin, "Criminal Deterrence Research at the Outset of the Twenty-First Century" (1998) 23 Crime & Justice 1; J. Braithwaite, *Restorative Justice and Responsive Regulation* (New York: Oxford University Press, 2002).

5 J. Braithwaite, "Rewards and Regulation" (2002) 29 J.L. & Soc'y 12; M. Friedland, "Rewards in the Legal System: Tenure, Airbags, and Safety Bingo" (1993) 31 Alb. L. Rev. 493.

6 D. Dewees *et al.*, *Exploring the Domain of Accident Law: Taking the Facts Seriously* (New York: Oxford University Press, 1996); W.A. Bogart, *Consequences: The Impact of Law and Its Complexity* (Toronto: University of Toronto Press, 2002) chapter 4, "Six Ideas about the Impact of Law—America the Outlier" [Bogart, *Consequences*].

7 E. Posner, *Law and Social Norms* (Cambridge, MA: Harvard University Press, 2000) [Posner, *Law and Social Norms*]; A. Etzioni, "Social Norms: Internalization, Persuasion, and History" (2000) 34 Law & Soc'y Rev. 157 [Etzioni, "Social Norms"].

8 C. Hood *et al.*, *The Government of Risk: Understanding Risk Regulation Regimes* (Oxford: Oxford University Press, 2001) 21 [Hood *et al.*, *The Government of Risk*]. See also J. Black, "Critical Reflections on Regulation" (2002) 27 Austl. J. Leg. Phil. 1 and J. Black, "Regulatory Conversations" (2002) 29 J.L. & Soc'y 163.

9 Eliadis, *Foundation Paper*, *supra* note 3.

10 See Posner, *Law and Social Norms*, *supra* note 7, and Etzioni, "Social Norms," *supra* note 7.

There are two main reasons for the hesitancy to consider litigation as a tool: first, lawsuits are usually initiated at the behest of "private" actors (not the government) and, second, government is often subjected to litigation as a defendant. The first reason simply underscores the error of the claim that only governments make policy. Courts clearly do as well, and their role needs to be taken into account in terms of tools analyses.[11] The second reason highlights the fact that, while governments are the source of policy-making and legal intervention, their actions can also be scrutinized and altered through litigation in the courts. Such questioning may occur for several reasons, including the allegation that in acting (or sometimes in failing to act), government has infringed Charter rights—for example, the right to equality. Thus, when legally intervening in a situation, governments need to assess, as accurately as they can, the kinds of issues that might give rise to litigation and, therefore, to judicial modification of such legal intervention.

There is a third point: governments themselves sometimes create rights of action in legislation, either for themselves or for private litigants, as part of the enforcement mechanism of the regulatory scheme. An example of the creation of a right of action is the anti-smoking legislation, discussed in the next section, that provides a right of recovery for governmental costs incurred in the treatment and care of diseased smokers. In these instances, lawsuits are viewed as a means to compensate those harmed by the legislatively proscribed activity and to deter such wrongful action. In such instances litigation is being invoked in ways that even traditional analyses should have taken into account: it is a tool and is part of the regulatory "mix" that is intended to achieve the goals of the specific enactments.

There are, of course, many issues regarding the employment of litigation as a tool. Questions arise regarding the actual effects of litigation, access to the courts (including the costs associated with lawsuits), institutional arrangements between courts and legislatures, and so forth. Such questions make assessments of the likely outcomes produced by litigation in any area especially complex. Nevertheless, policy-makers need to take into account, as precisely as possible, the role litigation can and should play in any area where legal intervention is contemplated. Throughout this book there will be opportunities to reflect upon the role of judicial review of administrative action and the extent to which it is a tool that shapes the boundaries of the administrative state.[12]

C. An Example of Legal Intervention and of the Regulatory Mix: The Suppression of Smoking

Legal intervention to suppress smoking is a story of such intervention interacting with shifting public attitudes and social norms regarding cigarettes. In four decades or so smoking has gone from a glamorous, sophisticated pastime to a filthy, dangerous addiction in the minds of most of the public. The shifting public attitudes and social norms have been both the cause of and the effect of legal intervention: as more people came to view smoking as unhealthy, expensive, and disgusting, support grew for regulatory intervention aimed at

11 P. Schuck, "Tort Liability" in Salamon, *The Tools of Government*, *supra* note 3 at 466.

12 See, in this book, Cristie Ford, chapter 3; Evan Fox-Decent, chapter 7; Audrey Macklin, chapter 8; and Sheila Wildeman, chapter 9.

further curtailment; as regulation intensified, more people accepted, in terms of their own views and behaviour, the obnoxiousness of cigarettes.

Legal intervention to suppress smoking is also an excellent illustration of the regulatory mix as governments resorted to a range of tools in order to achieve the policy goal of curtailing the use of tobacco. The full spectrum of tools was employed: from educating the public regarding the dangers of smoking to criminal prohibitions regarding the sale of cigarettes to children and smoking in public places. In addition, legislative restrictions were placed on the advertising of cigarettes, legislative requirements mandated ever more graphic and explicit warnings on packaging regarding the dangers of smoking, taxation on cigarettes was increased, and various attempts were made to use litigation to compensate for the harm done by tobacco and deter cigarette companies from peddling their poisons.

It is by no means the case that all legal strategies produced the effects hoped for. The tax hikes on tobacco imposed by the federal government in the late 1980s and 1990s essentially backfired. These increases resulted in the unintended consequence of promoting the smuggling of cigarettes from American states with relatively low taxes on tobacco. Estimates suggest that, at its height, black-market traffic in cigarettes constituted 20 percent of the market. After several manoeuvres, the Canadian government decided that it had no other choice and substantially lowered taxes to undercut sales on the black market.[13]

Lawsuits involving tobacco provide a good illustration of "litigation as a tool" and how complicated its use and the effects produced may be. Tort litigation in the United States against cigarette manufacturers on behalf of smokers and of governments paying the costs of care of smokers has been protracted and has, at best, produced mixed results regarding compensation.[14] In Canada, litigation was used as a defensive measure by tobacco companies. They launched successful Charter attacks on some of the restrictions on advertising.[15] However, litigation attacking subsequent legislation restricting advertising was not successful; the validity of the enactment was upheld by the Supreme Court.[16] In the early 2000s some of the provinces passed legislation conferring on their governments causes of action to sue tobacco companies to recover the costs of health and other care for smokers.[17] The Supreme Court of Canada upheld the constitutional validity of the legislation, thus permitting related actions to proceed.[18] The results of all such litigation, including in terms of actually suppressing further rates of smoking, remain to be seen.

---

13 Bogart, *Consequences*, *supra* note 6 at 195-96 and 213-14.

14 *Ibid.* at 197-203.

15 *Ibid.* at 209-12, discussing *RJR-Macdonald Inc. v. Canada (Attorney General)*, [1995] 3 S.C.R. 199.

16 *Canada (Attorney General) v. JTI-Macdonald Corp.*, 2007 SCC 30.

17 See, for example, *Tobacco Damages and Health Care Costs Recovery Act*, S.B.C. 2000, c. 30 and *Tobacco Damages and Health-Care Costs Recovery Act*, S.N.S. 2005, c. 46.

18 *British Columbia v. Imperial Tobacco Canada Ltd.*, [2005] 2 S.C.R. 473.

III. THE TOOLS OF THE ADMINISTRATIVE STATE

A. Introduction

The discussion to this point indicates that when legislatures determine to intervene in any given area, they can do so in any number of ways and can use a range of tools. Throughout the 20th century, a chief method was to confer the power to act on the Cabinet, some administrative tribunal, a government department or official, or some other institution. We will refer to all of these as "administrative actors." The core idea was that the legislature wanted to regulate some area but wished someone else, an administrative actor, to carry out the regulation for reasons of expertise, expediency, access, independence from the political process, and so forth.

This section focuses on the administrative state and emphasizes the many areas of activity that it regulates in various ways. The section serves as an introduction to many aspects of the administrative state that are analyzed in detail in subsequent chapters.[19] It describes administrative actors—that is, who they are and what they do. The section then looks at the variety of tools that administrative actors can be given and how these powers are employed. In particular, we examine the overarching importance of discretion and how it often guides the employment of various tools and how those tools are used in diverse settings.

Such discretion gives rise to many issues, including transparency and accountability. These issues will be analyzed in depth in subsequent chapters.[20] There are many other difficult legal issues confronting the administrative state in Canada that will be addressed throughout this book. Yet, at the outset, it is also important to emphasize that the administrative state in this society is capable of functioning at a high level:

> The quality of [Canada's] regulatory governance is almost certainly a key contributor to its successes in terms of both economic performance and the achievement of its social goals.[21]

Let's begin by surveying the wide scope of the administrative state in Canada.

B. The Administrative State and Its Many Areas of Regulation

In an attempt to convey the range of areas addressed by the administrative state and by various administrative actors, Mullan compiled a non-exhaustive list.[22] The following is a summary of his efforts. It is simply an indication of the vast workings of the administrative state:

---

19 For example, Lorne Sossin, chapter 15.

20 See Geneviève Cartier, chapter 10, and Craig Forcese, chapter 11.

21 OECD, *Regulatory Reform in Canada*, *supra* note 2 at 6. In referring to the Organisation for Economic Co-operation and Development (OECD), it is important to keep in mind that the OECD has a particular perspective on what constitutes effective regulation. This is not to discredit the accuracy of the above quote, which underscores the potential of the Canadian administrative state. However, one must consider the OECD's current praise for Canada within a specific and established historical context. For a further critique of the OECD's general stance, see S. Wood, "Voluntary Environmental Codes and Sustainability" in B. Richardson & S. Wood, eds., *Environmental Law for Sustainability* (Oxford: Hart Publishing, 2006) 229.

22 D. Mullan, *Administrative Law: Cases, Text, and Materials*, 5th ed. (Toronto: Emond Montgomery, 2003) 5 [Mullan, *Administrative Law*].

- *Employment*: The employment relationship can be extensively regulated by statute and through the exercise of various functions by administrative actors. For example, under legislation addressing collective bargaining, employees are given the right to be represented by unions; the relationship between the union and the employer is extensively regulated; and relevant issues are addressed by labour relation tribunals. Further examples of regulation of employment are legislative provisions dealing with minimum wage, holiday entitlement, workers' compensation for job-related injuries, vacation pay, and maximum hours of work.
- *Regulated Industries*: Certain industries are highly regulated. For example, television and radio are intensely regulated to, among other goals, foster Canadian content in the media. In a very different area, the securities industry is substantially regulated for a number of reasons, including protection of investors trading in bonds, equities, and certain other products.
- *Economic Activities*: Certain economic activities are regulated regardless of the particular industry in which they occur. For example, mergers and takeovers are scrutinized for possible adverse impact on competition. With regard to a very different activity, the development of land is regulated in the interests of community planning.
- *Professions and Trades*: The professions are granted statutory privileges to deliver services associated with the profession. In exchange, members of the professions are highly regulated by the appropriate professional body regarding the delivery of such services in terms of quality and protection of client/patient interests. Regulatory schemes operate for a wide range of trades and vocations: the selling, usually by licence, of cars, real estate, or insurance; various aspects of travel; and funeral arrangements.
- *Social Control*: A number of programs can restrict and otherwise regulate individual freedom of movement: the incarceration of the mentally ill, the detention and removal from the country of illegal immigrants, the placing of neglected children in foster care, and so forth.
- *Human Rights*: Human rights legislation specifically addresses the problem of discrimination in various areas: housing and employment, and, with regard to grounds of discrimination, sexual orientation, religion, disability, and so forth. Such legislation applies to individuals, corporations, and governments.
- *Income Support*: Various income support programs are established and regulated by the state: employment insurance, old age security, various forms of social assistance, and so forth.
- *Public Services*: Many areas of public services are regulated: health care, education, police protection, garbage collection, and so forth.

C. Agencies, Government Departments, and Other Institutions

When legislatures decide to create administrative powers they can confer them on a wide range of agencies, individuals (including specific Cabinet ministers and their government departments), and institutions such as municipalities, professional bodies, and universities. As indicated, we will refer to these agencies, departments, individuals, and institutions collectively as administrative actors. Administrative actors can exercise a wide variety of statutory powers—tools—for diverse regulatory purposes. The following is a brief sketch of these administrative actors. We will describe the tools that they can be provided with in the next subsection.

1. Agencies

The common notion of administrative actors includes the various administrative agencies (also called tribunals and commissions) that function separately from government and the public service. At the federal level such agencies include the Canadian Radio-television and Telecommunications Commission (CRTC), the Canadian Human Rights Commission, and the access to information and privacy commissions. At the provincial level, such agencies include human rights commissions, municipal boards, environmental tribunals, and securities commissions.

What the agencies do and how they do it varies widely depending on the area regulated and the powers—the tools—conferred on each agency by the legislation that creates them. By way of introduction it is useful to summarize here four characteristics that they usually possess:

- They enjoy a measure of independence from the government department with overall responsibility for the policy area in which they operate (in terms of appointment of members of the tribunal, how decisions are made, etc.).[23]
- They render decisions regarding the area that they regulate that can directly affect persons (that is, they have an adjudicatory role regarding disputes in the regulated area).
- They follow a more or less uniform decision-making process for resolving issues that directly affect persons (in terms of pre-hearing notice, admission of evidence, examination and cross-examination of witnesses, and so forth).
- They are specialized with regard to the area that they regulate (human rights, labour, immigration, etc.).[24]

2. Cabinet Ministers and Government Departments

In a variety of settings legislation may confer powers on the entire Cabinet (the governor or lieutenant governor in council) to perform certain tasks regarding the issues being regulated: for example, the Cabinet is often empowered to make subordinate legislation or regulations to address, more specifically, aspects of the regulatory scheme.[25] In certain situations there is a right of appeal, granted by the relevant statute, to the Cabinet from the decisions of agencies. For example, certain decisions of the CRTC can be appealed to the federal Cabinet.

Legislation may also authorize specific Cabinet ministers to make certain decisions. These decisions are usually made for the ministers by various government officials who are delegated such powers. For example, under applicable immigration legislation, the designated minister may allow someone to remain in Canada who is not otherwise eligible to do so; under the Ontario legislation addressing disability issues, the designated minister can enter into agreements with affected parties to provide incentives to deal with various barriers that people with disabilities encounter; environmental legislation provides powers

23 See Laverne Jacobs, chapter 6.

24 Mullan, *Administrative Law*, *supra* note 22 at 12-13.

25 See Andrew Green, chapter 13.

to designated ministers and other officials to set and enforce various standards—for example, to protect water quality.

3. Other Institutions

Almost any institution may be considered an administrative actor, at least for limited purposes. The key to being considered an administrative actor is, usually, the exercise of some statutory power that has sufficient public and regulatory dimensions. For example, the prime purpose of professional bodies (of doctors, lawyers, etc.) is to regulate members. However, such powers come from statute, usually with a specific direction that such self-regulation is to be in the public interest. Thus, such bodies are considered to be administrative actors, for example, in terms of licensing and disciplining their members. Municipalities are viewed as administrative actors in the exercise of various statutory powers conferred on them—for example, the passing of municipal bylaws. Universities (and individual professors) in the exercise of various powers, usually traced to some statute, can be considered administrative actors. Even private organizations (such as churches, sport organizations, and commercial associations), existing without any statutory authorization, can sometimes be treated as administrative actors for limited purposes if it is established that some function they perform has a sufficiently public purpose.

D. Tools and Administrative Actors: Some General Points

Administrative actors can use a wide range of tools to perform their various tasks. This range of tools and their use in different contexts is one of the main reasons why the administrative state is so varied and not easily described or given an all encompassing assessment. At the same time, a basic understanding of these tools is fundamental to coming to grips with the functioning of the administrative state.

There are a number of general points that can be made regarding the tools of administrative actors. First, the tools are almost always authorized by statute. The administrative actor must have statutory authorization to use a particular tool—for example, the creation of subordinate legislation or the power to conduct audits. Second, as with legal intervention generally, there is a vast range of tools that are potentially available to administrative actors, from those that potentially impose sanctions (the prosecution of regulatory offences) to educational programs that encourage or discourage various kinds of behaviour. A list of other tools potentially available would include investigation, mediation, adjudication, rule-making (including subordinate legislation), licensing (including the charging of fees), contracting, audits, taxation, incentives, and self-regulation.

Third, administrative actors are often given a substantial amount of discretion regarding when and how to use the various tools they have at their disposal to carry out their regulatory tasks—that is, what the appropriate regulatory mix will be. This point about discretion is an important one and will be returned to in the next section.[26] The three points mentioned before lead to a fourth one: administrative actors are very different from civil courts. Courts focus on one tool: adjudication (with negotiated settlements and other alternative dispute

26 It will also be discussed in subsequent chapters: see, for example, Geneviève Cartier, chapter 10.

resolution [ADR] techniques used in ancillary ways). Administrative actors can sometimes adjudicate in ways that closely resemble a civil court trial. However, their array of tools, of which adjudication is only one, means that administrative actors often perform their many diverse functions differently from civil courts.

E. The Mix of Tools and Administrative Actors: An Illustration—Regulating Lawyers

This variety of tools and their employment can be illustrated by an example close to home: the regulation of lawyers. In Canada, lawyers derive their authority to self-regulate "in the public interest," through their law societies, from enabling statutes in the various provinces. Law societies are charged, in the legislation, with regulating lawyers with regard to a number of issues, including stipulating conditions for admission to practice; assuring that lawyers' services are delivered at a high level of quality; assuring ethical standards through rules of professional conduct and other means; and disciplining lawyers who breach various standards of the law societies.

In carrying out their regulatory mandate, law societies can use a variety of tools with which the enabling legislation equips them. The decision to use what tools in what circumstances to achieve the best regulatory mix is largely a matter of their discretion. For example, the enabling legislation authorizes law societies to make subordinate legislation with regard to professional conduct. As a result, the law societies have promulgated rules of professional conduct.

Law societies use their licensing powers to stipulate conditions for entry to the profession (a law degree from a recognized university, passing bar admission exams, etc.) and to impose fees so that the societies are self-funding. They can use their audit powers to ensure that lawyers are handling clients' monies and other matters consistent with their professional duties. In their discretion, they can use their disciplinary powers in a variety of applicable circumstances—for example, regarding significant breaches of the rules of professional conduct. If the lawyer is found guilty there may also be discretion regarding the penalty that is imposed—for example, a reprimand, a suspension for a period of time, or, most drastically, disbarment.

More recently, many law societies have used their regulatory discretion to become more proactive regarding a number of issues. For example, to actively promote the delivery of quality services, some societies have introduced "quality assurance/practice review" programs that emphasize such strategies as continuing education, certification of specialties, and enhanced use of audit and monitoring powers. Disciplinary proceedings and lawsuits, as "after the fact" measures, to sanction substandard services are still available, but there is much more emphasis on avoiding delivery of substandard services in the first instance than on sanctioning them after they have occurred. To actively promote opportunities for women, visible minorities, and others who have historically been marginalized in the legal profession, some societies have created equity programs with a range of educational and enforcement devices.

F. Discretion: The "Übertool"?

The foregoing discussion of law societies and the authority to self-regulate illustrates the wide-ranging discretion that administrative actors may have to carry out their mandate. It is this discretion to decide when and how other tools will be utilized that leads to our description of discretion as the "übertool," the overarching power that can control the use of other tools.

Such discretion is crucial to the work of administrative actors. It equips them with the flexibility to configure the regulatory program to what can be rapidly changing circumstances. What is more, generally speaking, it is impossible for legislatures to specify with any precision the circumstances in which various tools ought to be employed in combination or how a specific tool should be used and how, if at all, it should be enforced. There are some situations in which legislatures attempt to stipulate how discretion is to be exercised in very particular instances. However, generally, such stipulation is neither possible nor desirable: "discretion is the very lifeblood of the administrative state."[27]

At the same time, such discretion does give rise to a number of very significant issues. There are continuing concerns that such power may be abused in circumstances as different as matters of national security and issues regarding the delivery of health-care services. These concerns focus on matters such as the lack of rules bounding the exercise of discretion and of transparency and accountability in its use. This is by no means to suggest that the exercise of discretion is destined to commit such errors. It is to underscore the overarching role of discretion in the administrative state and to emphasize that it needs to be employed appropriately and to be subject to scrutiny in a variety of ways.[28] Discretion is critical to the realization of regulatory goals; at the same time, discretion must be responsibly exercised within appropriate boundaries. These issues are of such importance that they will be pursued in subsequent chapters.[29]

IV. TOOLS AND THE "NEW" GOVERNANCE

A. Is There a New Governance?

Even a casual observer senses that government and the administrative state do not function in the same way as they did, say, 25 years ago. Assumptions about powerful administrative tribunals carrying out policies of big government as a realization of the public good no longer hold. Such assumptions have changed. At least some morphed into accusations that "portray[ed] government agencies as tightly structured hierarchies insulated from market forces and from effective citizen pressure and therefore free to serve the personal and institutional interests of bureaucrats instead."[30]

---

27 Mullan, *Administrative Law*, *supra* note 22 at 948.

28 *Ibid.* at chapter 12, "The Use and Misuse of Discretion," and L. Sossin, "From Neutrality to Compassion: The Place of Civil Service Values and Legal Norms in the Exercise of Administrative Discretion" (2005) 55 U.T.L.J. 427.

29 See Geneviève Cartier, chapter 10, and Craig Forcese, chapter 11.

30 Salamon, *The Tools of Government*, *supra* note 3 at 1.

New means of regulation are sometimes associated with two broad developments: the crisis and transformation of the modern welfare state and (relatedly) the emergence and growing prominence of forms of regulation "beyond" the state, both of which have potentially profound consequences for administrative law. For example, increasing delegation of rule-making and rule-enforcing authority to private industry associations or hybrid third parties (fair trade certificates, for example) increased reliance on economic instruments such as tradable pollution permits and the increased focus on new targets of regulation, including gatekeepers such as financial institutions.[31]

Traditional conceptions of government and its agencies have been questioned across the political spectrum: the right has focused on inefficiencies and government and agencies meddling in the market; the left has focused on unresponsiveness to the needs of the disadvantaged and exclusionary practices against the historically marginalized. As a result, governments and their agencies have been pushed "to be reinvented, downsized, privatized, devolved, decentralized, deregulated, delayered, subject to performance tests, and contracted out."[32]

These demands that government and the administrative state function in substantially different ways have led to analyses regarding the extent of the alterations and how such changes might be characterized. Salamon does claim that there is a "new governance": a shift in the paradigm of public programs. The "new governance" no longer has as its centrepiece agencies or programs but, rather, the tools used to realize the various goals of the "new governance." This prominence of tools and how they should be employed has altered the very character of public management and of the administrative state:

> Instead of command and control, it must emphasize negotiation and persuasion. In place of management skills, enablement skills are increasingly required instead. Far from simplifying the task of public problem solving, the proliferation of tools has importantly complicated it even while enlarging the range of options and the pool of resources potentially brought to bear.[33]

The claim here is not that Salamon's assertions regarding a paradigmatic shift are completely accurate or that the shift, whatever its exact nature, applies equally to all aspects and areas of the administrative state in all post-industrial societies. The philosophical and political premises of government and the administrative state in Canada have been challenged in ways not fully addressed by Salamon's depiction. Such forces as globalization and fundamental alterations to the social safety net are only two examples of influences that have produced effects that go beyond changes regarding the tools of legal intervention.[34] At the

---

31 Recall the definition of regulation cited earlier: Hood *et al.*, *The Government of Risk*, *supra* note 8 and accompanying text. For further readings, see S. Wood, "Three Questions About Corporate Codes: Problematizations, Authorizations and the Public/Private Divide" in Wesley Cragg, ed., *Ethics Codes, Corporations and the Challenge of Globalization* (Cheltenham, UK: Edward Elgar, 2005) 245; and S. Wood, "Green Revolution or Greenwash? Voluntary Environmental Standards, Public Law and Private Authority in Canada" in Law Commission of Canada, ed., *New Perspectives on the Public-Private Divide* (Vancouver: University of British Columbia Press, 2003) 123.

32 Salamon, *The Tools of Government*, *supra* note 3 at 1.

33 *Ibid.* at 18.

34 Regarding the globalization influence on Canadian society and government see D. Cameron & J. Gross Stein, "Street Protests and Fantasy Parks" in D. Cameron & J. Gross Stein, eds., *Street Protests and Fantasy*

same time, reacting to Salamon's contentions about a "new governance" provides an excellent opportunity for coming to grips with the various transformations that have taken place and that continue to occur in the functioning of the administrative state.[35]

Let's examine Salamon's assertions further by looking at his claim that tools have become the centrepiece of the "new governance." There is little doubt that there has been much more interest over the last decades in various tools, particularly those that promote flexibility in terms of the role of government, including allowing for a greater influence of the market in implementing policy goals. Thus certain tools, such as vouchers, privatization, self-regulation, incentives, and contracting out, have gained greater prominence and have been experimented with more extensively.

The ongoing efforts to reconfigure the generation and supply of electricity over the last 15 years represent a prominent and controversial example of the use of privatization to drastically modify the command and control model of government with regard to an essential commodity.[36] The heated debate about underwriting the cost of private/independent schools and providing more choice in education provides a very current example of the increasing interest in vouchers. In Ontario the Conservatives provided such vouchers through the Equity in Education Tax Credit; that credit/voucher was repealed by the McGuinty Liberals.[37] The Conservatives then shifted the debate in the 2007 election by promoting public funding of religious schools, but that party was unsuccessful in forming the government. The debate regarding the role for vouchers and for private/independent schools continues.

At the same time, it is important to recognize that the tools themselves are not new and that they have long been employed by the administrative state; a point also recognized by Salamon.[38] Most provinces have long used vouchers to provide access and consumer choice in the legal aid system through the certificate system: qualified individuals, based on low income, are given a legal aid certificate (voucher) to hire a lawyer of their choice from a roster of participating counsel.

It may be most helpful to think not in terms of a paradigmatic shift but of a significant change in emphasis. The tools are not new; there are many examples of continuity in use. However, there is a movement away from "command and control"—government and its agencies mandating the regulatory regime and its detailed implementation. Instead, there is an openness to a variety of ways in which overall policy objectives can be achieved, including active involvement on the part of those subject to regulation. This flexibility, when it

---

Parks (Vancouver: University of British Columbia Press, 2002) 1; regarding transformations in the models of the social safety net see K. Banting, "Dis-embedding Liberalism: The New Social Policy Paradigm in Canada" in D. Green & J. Kesselman, eds., *Dimensions of Inequality in Canada* (Vancouver: University of British Columbia Press, 2006) 417.

35 R. Macdonald, Book Review of *The Tools of Government: A Guide to the New Governance* by L. Salamon, ed. (2003) 6 Horizons 33.

36 L. Bertoldi, *The Legal Framework for New Generation Across Canada*, a paper prepared for the Conference Board of Canada, Toronto, January 2007.

37 W.A. Bogart, *Good Government? Good Citizens? Courts, Politics, and Markets in a Changing Canada* (Vancouver: University of British Columbia Press, 2005) chapter 7, "The Youngest Citizens and Education as a Public Good?" 143 at 166.

38 Salamon, *The Tools of Government*, *supra* note 3 at 9.

occurs, is largely achieved through employment of various tools in a number of ways driven by the particular context of the regulatory initiative.

B. The Changing Emphasis: Some Examples

There are many examples of this changing emphasis and the implications for how various tools are used by administrative actors. Here we will briefly discuss two overarching approaches that are illustrative: one by a very influential academic and the other by the Canadian federal government.

Braithwaite has, for some time, urged more flexible strategies in terms of enforcement of regulatory regimes. He has done this for a number of reasons, including the fact that a command and control/sanctions approach, especially with regard to corporate misbehaviour, has been demonstrated to be much less effective in achieving regulatory goals in a number of areas than advocates of that approach would claim. As a result, Braithwaite espouses the "regulatory pyramid."[39] The basis of this approach consists of educational/persuasive strategies that encourage trust and discourage defensiveness. At the same time, escalating strategies are available to promote compliance should parties demonstrate reluctance. Punitive sanctions may be imposed but are reserved for situations where these other strategies have clearly failed. Throughout, Braithwaite speaks seriously of fostering "corporate virtue" to achieve compliance and to realize regulatory goals.[40]

His approach does acknowledge that, while regulators should try to foster trust (and, therefore, achieve greater levels of compliance), they must be equipped to move to sanctions if efforts at building and maintaining trust founder.[41] Nonetheless, ideas that emphasize persuasion, trust, and attention to a range of motivations and the use of tools that reflect these ideas in order to achieve regulatory goals are at the forefront. Braithwaite's ideas enjoy wide currency, including among government policy-makers with regard to invoking various tools. How successful this shift will actually be in terms of achieving regulatory goals remains to be established in many areas.[42] Nevertheless, as Braithwaite has recently observed, "[a]pproaches to regulation that seek to identify important problems and fix them work better and more humanely than approaches oriented to imposing the right punishment."[43]

The federal government, responding to the shift in emphasis regarding the workings of the administrative state, has recently devised the Smart Regulation Program.[44] Launched in

39 I. Ayres & J. Braithwaite, *Responsive Regulation: Transcending the Deregulation Debate* (New York: Oxford University Press, 1992).

40 J. Braithwaite, "Responsive Business Regulatory Institutions" in C. Coady & C. Sampford, eds., *Business Ethics and the Law* (Sydney: The Federation Press, 1993) 83.

41 J. Braithwaite & T. Makkai, "Trust and Compliance" (1994) 4 Policing & Soc'y 1.

42 Public Management Committee (PUMA), *Reducing the Risk of Policy Failure: Challenges for Regulatory Compliance* (Paris: Organisation for Economic Co-operation and Development, 2000). Regarding a possible countertrend in the United Kingdom see R. Baldwin, "The New Punitive Regulation" (2004) 67 Mod. L. Rev. 351.

43 J. Braithwaite, *Restorative Justice and Responsive Regulation* (New York: Oxford University Press, 2002).

44 Government of Canada, *Smart Regulation: Report on Actions and Plans*, Fall 2005 update and ongoing initiatives, online: Government of Canada <http://www.regulation.gc.ca>.

2005, Smart Regulation is an ambitious program for regulatory renewal. It has survived changes in government and is more than the initiative of any one political party. Smart Regulation is based on four principles:

- *Protecting the public interest*: Smart Regulation strives to find the right blend of policy instruments [tools] …
- *Extending the values of Canadian democracy*: Decision making on regulatory matters is conducted in an open and transparent manner …
- *Leveraging the best knowledge in Canada and worldwide*: Smart Regulation recognizes that knowledge and evidence form the basis of regulation …
- *Promoting effective co-operation, partnerships, and processes*: Smart Regulation strengthens co-operation with all levels of government …

Smart Regulation has many components to it, including devising a "framework for assessing, selecting, and implementing instruments [tools] for government action." The fall 2005 report highlighted projects that have resulted in "a 33-percent increase in process efficiency concerning drug approvals, and a system that allows 233 types of businesses to access federal, provincial, and municipal permits from one Internet site." The government has committed to reporting twice a year regarding the progress of this project so as "to be transparent with respect to areas of progress, as well as areas where delay has been experienced." Whether Smart Regulation will implement its objectives and what it will achieve largely remains to be seen.[45] At the same time, the very initiation of Smart Regulation exemplifies a shift in thinking regarding the structure and functioning of the administrative state and the employment of its tools.

V. ASSESSING TOOLS AND THE ADMINISTRATIVE STATE

A. Introduction

Assessing the effects of legal intervention is critical. At the same time, assessing the effects of any legal intervention is complicated. Such evaluation is even more difficult when the effort attempts to ascertain the impact of any one tool used in combination with several others in a mix. There may be substantial difficulties assessing the effects of the mix. There can be even greater complexities establishing the outcomes produced by any one tool within that mix. Nonetheless, a primary test for law is the extent to which legal intervention actually provides solutions to the underlying societal problems that are sought to be addressed. Complexities in assessment do not justify a failure to engage in that task.

There are a number of ways in which tools can be assessed. One of them is through judicial review of administrative action. Several of the subsequent chapters devote significant sections to analyzing this curial oversight of the administrative state.[46] Judicial review has a significant role in bringing accountability and transparency to the actions of administra-

---

45 H. Benevides, *Protection and Precaution: Canadian Priorities for Federal Regulatory Policy* (Toronto: Canadian Environmental Law Association, 2005); P. Webster and J. Cuthro, "HANDS OFF—Is 'Smart Regulation' Dumb for Canada's Wilderness Areas?" Nov. 2007 *The Walrus* Special Arctic Issue 40.

46 See chapter 3, Cristie Ford; chapter 4, Mary Liston; chapter 5, Grant Huscroft; chapter 7, Evan Fox-Decent; chapter 8, Audrey Macklin; chapter 9, Sheila Wildeman; and chapter 13, Andrew Green.

tive actors. It also needs to be considered as a tool that is used by those dissatisfied with decisions of the administrative state in an attempt to challenge them and to reshape boundaries of various programs.[47]

However, as important as judicial review is, it is also limited in terms of assessing the functioning of the administrative state. Judicial review can be costly and slow. In addition, there are aspects of the administrative state that judges, rightly or not, decline to assess because, for example, they are said to involve political judgments, decisions regarding the spending power of government, or matters of expertise that courts are ill-suited to evaluate.[48]

B. Five Criteria

Another way to assess tools is by evaluating them using a generally applicable set of criteria that reflects good policy-making and implementation. Such an evaluation can be taken from within government or in the larger realm of public debate and can involve a variety of disciplines and professions. Salamon, in his analysis of the "new governance," suggests five such generally applicable criteria for assessing tools.[49]

Applying such criteria can generate controversy in many contexts. The claim here is not that the criteria produce easy assessments or even that the five are an exhaustive inventory of all relevant considerations. However, they do assist in focusing debate regarding evaluation of regulatory strategies and in making comparisons of different tools in various contexts.

In summary, the criteria are:

1. *Effectiveness*: In some respects, this is the most basic criterion. Effectiveness assesses the extent to which a tool achieves its intended objective. There are a variety of ways to evaluate effectiveness using generally accepted social science and other methodologies.[50] At the same time, gauging effectiveness can be problematic for several reasons. For example, a regulatory mix often involves several tools so that it may be difficult to establish the effectiveness of any one of them. Then, too, there can be heated debates about what "effectiveness" means in any particular context. Advocates of school vouchers are likely to argue that they are effective by the very fact that they provide choice in education. Critics of vouchers tend to look at the overall impact on quality of education as constituting effectiveness in this context.

2. *Efficiency*: This criterion takes account of both results and the costs entailed in their realization. The most efficient tool is the one that achieves the optimal balance between benefits and costs. Costs should include not only those to government but those to others as well, especially regulated parties. Thus there should be a "double balance sheet": one focused on the costs to government alone and one focused on the costs to other social actors.

47 See text above in part II.B, "Is Litigation a Tool?"

48 See Andrew Green, chapter 13.

49 Salamon, *The Tools of Government*, *supra* note 3 at 22-24.

50 Bogart, *Consequences*, *supra* note 6 at chapter 3, "The Complexities of Assessing Impact."

There can be many debates about how to assess efficiency and the weight to accord it in any context.[51] Nonetheless, discussions of this criterion can be very helpful, including differentiating between ends and means. Many in this society support gun control and its objectives; many are also concerned about the inefficiency of recent versions of the gun registry system.[52] Problems with that system may, indeed, need to be addressed; those problems should not detract from the overarching goals associated with gun control.

3. *Equity*: This criterion is critical, including for those interested in social justice. Equity can have two meanings that should be considered.

   The first focuses on basic fairness: the distribution of benefits and costs more or less evenly among those eligible. The second, and more controversial, focuses on the redistribution of benefits to those who have previously not had them or had them disproportionately less or, in other contexts, on concerns that burdens are being imposed disproportionately. Complaints that benefits, to be conferred on a per capita basis, are being distributed by some other standard would be an example where the first meaning of equity is engaged. Claims to have proactive employment equity programs to ensure that members of historically marginalized groups would be an example of the second meaning of equity in terms of benefits. Worries that deregulation of university tuition fees will create barriers for the economically disadvantaged could be an example of disproportionate imposition of burdens.

4. *Manageability*: This criterion usually focuses on issues of implementation. The more convoluted the tool and the more separate actors are involved, the more difficult it is to manage. Problems of manageability, in fact, can swamp theoretical claims regarding effectiveness, efficiency, and equity. Many would cite the electricity industry regarding issues of manageability. Whatever the theoretical claims regarding the benefits of privatization in this area, the reconfiguration of the electricity industry, at least over the short term, is giving rise to enormous manageability issues.

5. *Legitimacy and Political Feasibility*: No matter how otherwise effective, a program that cannot win political support cannot make headway. Some tools may seem to facilitate public accountability and participation—for example, self-regulation and privatization. In the political atmosphere of today, they will likely be used more in a variety of contexts. In contrast, experiments with a specific form of privatization, vouchers, particularly regarding education, remain very controversial. Whatever their merits, their political feasibility is very much in question.

---

51 J. Gross Stein, *The Cult of Efficiency* (Toronto: Anansi Press, 2001).

52 Canadian Broadcasting Corporation, "Gun registry cost soars to $2 billion," February 13, 2004, online: CBC <http://www.cbc.ca/canada/story/2004/02/13/gunregistry_rdi040213.html>.

SUGGESTED ADDITIONAL READINGS

Baldwin, R., & M. Cave. *Understanding Regulation* (New York: Oxford University Press, 1999).

Cabinet Office. *Regulatory Justice: Sanctioning in a Post-Hampton World* (London: Better Regulation Executive, 2005).

Coglianese, C. "Performance-Based Regulation: Prospects and Limitations in Health, Safety, and Environmental Protection" (2003) 55 Admin. L. Rev. 785.

Eliadis, P., *et al.*, eds. *Designing Government: From Instruments to Governance* (Montreal & Kingston: McGill-Queen's University Press, 2005).

Hood, C., *et al. The Government of Risk: Understanding Risk Regulation Regimes* (Oxford: Oxford University Press, 2001).

Katyal, N. "Deterrence's Difficulty" (1997) 95 Mich. L. Rev. 2385.

McAdams, R. "The Origins, Development, and Regulation of Norms" (1997) 96 Mich. L. Rev. 338.

CHAPTER THREE

Dogs and Tails: Remedies in Administrative Law

CRISTIE L. FORD
Faculty of Law, University of British Columbia

I. INTRODUCTION

From time to time, one hears the criticism that a particular court judgment has allowed the "tail" of the remedy to "wag the dog" of the substantive case. In traditional treatments of administrative law remedies, the metaphor may perhaps be carried even further. One has the sense that the "tail" of what is called "judicial review"—that is, court review of remedies that have been imposed by administrative law agencies and tribunals[1]—has been allowed

1 For simplicity I will use the term "tribunal" throughout to refer to the full range of administrative agencies, commissions, and other bodies. This is an oversimplification, because many administrative decision-makers do not take a tribunal form. Many administrative decisions are made by bureaucrats without a hearing or the court-style structure of a tribunal; administrative agencies also regularly make policy decisions that affect individual and social interests. However, the tribunal is perhaps the prototypical administrative structure for purposes of understanding the remedies available to a party to tribunal action.

to "wag the dog" of the discipline's entire approach to remedies. Some classic textbooks treat administrative law remedies as if they *begin* at the point at which a party to an administrative action seeks judicial review of that action through the courts.

The legal preoccupation with court action derives, to some extent, from law's discomfort with public decision-making bodies that work differently from courts. Law's role vis-à-vis administrative action is often focused on what tools courts have to police and intervene in administrative agencies' actions, to ensure that those agencies observe the rule of law and basic principles of justice. Legal scholars and practitioners (and, of course, judges) do not always trust administrative agencies to the degree they trust courts. Concerns for justice and the rule of law are legitimate. Yet, a tight focus on court action misses the hugely important first step in real life administrative action: the varied and sometimes creative remedies that the tribunal itself may impose.

If courts and legal scholars seemingly overemphasize the role of judicial review, legislators often simultaneously try to limit its practical use. One of the themes that runs through this chapter, and indeed this book, is the "dialogue" (some might say tug-of-war) that courts and legislators engage in as they try to steer the course of administrative law.[2] Administrative tribunals, although generally quite independent of the political process, are still creatures of the executive arm of government. Legislative drafters, in crafting tribunals' enabling statutes, may use various tools to limit or circumscribe the available scope of court intervention in tribunals' decision-making processes. One common mechanism is the privative clause.[3] Another technique, relevant in this chapter, is to provide for avenues of appeal of a decision that are internal to the tribunal itself. This limits recourse to judicial review, because the general (court-developed) rule is that recourse to the courts is only available after a party has exhausted all avenues of appeal, including internal appeals and any appeals to the courts provided for in the statute. By providing for appeal mechanisms, and in particular for internal appeal mechanisms with their own unique and sometimes uncourtlike structures, the executive is able to maintain a greater degree of control over the statutory scheme that it has constructed to address a particular public issue.

This chapter provides an overview of administrative law remedies as a whole, including not only judicial review but also tribunal decisions, internal and external appeals, enforcement mechanisms, and extralegal strategies. Discussing remedies near the beginning of an administrative law textbook may seem unconventional. We have chosen this approach because understanding the available remedies is an important part of understanding what one is "getting into" in administrative law, and it provides a broad structural framework on which subsequent chapters can build. The chapter is divided into three main parts, the first two of which have not traditionally been located in the "remedies" chapter of administrative law texts (if they appear at all). First, the chapter canvasses remedial options available at the initial tribunal stage. As we shall see, remedial options available to administrative agencies differ from those available to courts, and reflect the different composition of tribunals. The remedies available to them are both more limited (in terms of the tribunal's statute-derived authority to impose them) and, potentially, more expansive (as a consequence of tribunals' particular expertise and their ability to remain seized of a matter over

2 See Mary Liston, chapter 4.

3 On substantive fairness, see Sheila Wildeman, chapter 9, and Audrey Macklin, chapter 8.

time). Second, this chapter looks at the ability of a party or a tribunal to *enforce* a tribunal order against another party, either civilly or criminally. Finally, the chapter considers parties' ability to *challenge* tribunal action. This includes internal appeal options, extralegal options, appeal to the courts, and, finally, the classic administrative law remedy, judicial review. In addressing these three parts together, the goal is to provide the reader, in a systematic and chronological fashion, with a conceptual frame of reference that includes the full range of remedial options available to parties before administrative tribunals.

II. REMEDIAL OPTIONS AT THE TRIBUNAL STAGE

Administrative tribunals are as varied as the topics on which they adjudicate, and it would be unwise to generalize about the remedial powers available to them. Only two general comments about the remedies available can safely be made. First, because a tribunal does not have the general jurisdiction that a court does, the power to impose a particular remedy must be provided for in the tribunal's enabling statute. Second, most tribunals' composition, structure, and mandates are different from courts', and their approach to remedies reflects those differences. For example, certain tribunals' expertise with a more limited subject matter may help them to identify systemic problems or recurring patterns across multiple individual disputes. Their ability to stay involved in (that is, to remain "seized" of) a dispute over a longer period of time is well-established, and many tribunals are less constrained by formal rules than courts are in developing remedies. Together, on occasion, these factors allow tribunals to conceptualize and implement novel remedial strategies aimed at addressing the systemic problems they see.

A. Statutory Authority

As a creature of statute, a tribunal cannot make orders that affect individuals' rights or obligations without authority from its enabling statute.[4] Therefore, the first step in determining a tribunal's remedial options is to look at the statute itself. If a tribunal makes orders outside the scope of its enabling statute, it is exceeding its jurisdiction, and those orders will be void.

Many enabling statutes set out express lists of the remedies a tribunal may order. For example, tribunals often have the power to make declaratory orders, to order a party to repair a problem or to mitigate damage, or to order a party to comply with the tribunal's enabling statute. Licensing powers may also be given to tribunals in statutory regimes designed to protect the public (for example, through professional licensing qualifications or requirements for corporations issuing securities to public investors), or to manage natural resources (for example, fishing and forestry licences). Some tribunals can appoint conciliators and otherwise assist in settling matters before them.[5] Some enabling statutes also provide for quasi-criminal offences that impose significant fines and possible incarceration.

Other statutes accord their tribunals broad, discretionary power to fashion the remedies they see fit. For example, s. 41(1)(a) of the Ontario *Human Rights Code* gives the Ontario

---

4 *Att. Gen. of Can. v. Inuit Tapirisat et al.*, [1980] S.C.J. No. 99, [1980] 2 S.C.R. 735 [*Inuit Tapirisat*].

5 For example, *Canadian Human Rights Act*, R.S.C. 1985, c. H-6, ss. 47-48; *BC Employment Standards Act*, R.S.B.C. 1996, c. 113, s. 78.

Human Rights Tribunal the discretion to order a party who has been found to discriminate to "do anything that, in the opinion of the Tribunal, the party ought to do to achieve compliance with this Act, both in respect of the complaint and in respect of future practices."[6]

Even where a tribunal's remedial power is less certain (that is, its enabling statute does not expressly permit a particular remedy, and the tribunal has no broad discretionary power), then, subject to the exceptions that follow, one may perhaps argue that a tribunal must, as a practical necessity, have the remedial power to do the things its statute requires it to do.[7] However, orders for the payment of money, such as compensation or damages, fines, fees and levies, and costs, can generally only be ordered by tribunals that have the express statutory authority to do so. Tribunals also lack the equitable jurisdiction to order interim injunctions, although they may be given statutory authority to seek an injunction in court to enforce a statute. Finally, whether a tribunal has the power to grant remedies under the *Canadian Charter of Rights and Freedoms* must be a separate question, based on whether the tribunal is a "court of competent jurisdiction."[8]

B. Novel Administrative Remedies

Administrative tribunals and agencies vary widely in their structures and functions, but collectively they also differ from courts in important ways. The particular structures and qualities of administrative tribunals equally affect the kinds of remedies they are inclined, and empowered, to issue. This part of this chapter seeks to set out, in broad strokes, the kinds of remedies that tribunal-style administrative bodies in particular are likely to issue. The kinds of functions performed by tribunal-type administrative bodies—party-on-party dispute resolution, party-versus-agency enforcement and disciplinary proceedings, and other forms of hearings and decision-making—tend to be the most common ways in which members of the public interact with administrative bodies. These functions also square particularly well with the concept of *remedies*, defined by *Black's Law Dictionary* as "the field of law dealing with the means of enforcing rights and redressing wrongs."[9]

However, the reader should be aware that tribunal-style administrative agencies are only one facet of administrative agency operations. Parties may interact, be answerable to, and seek to influence administrative law agencies in other ways. Agencies' policy-making functions, in particular, are outside the scope of this chapter but should not be outside one's field of vision.[10] Through their statutory drafting choices, legislators regularly delegate detailed policy-making decisions to administrative tribunals. Many larger administrative agencies have formal policy-making departments, which generally operate at some remove from their tribunal departments. Administrative policy instruments can range from formal, binding interpretive releases to relatively informal, non-binding administrative guidance. Policy releases and guidelines have a direct impact on regulated entities. They are publicly avail-

6 *Human Rights Code*, R.S.O. 1990, c. H.19, s. 41(1)(a).

7 *ATCO Gas & Pipelines Ltd. v. Alberta (Energy & Utilities Board)*, [2006] 1 S.C.R. 140.

8 *Weber v. Ontario Hydro*, [1995] S.C.J. No. 59, [1995] 2 S.C.R. 929. See also Evan Fox-Decent, chapter 7.

9 *Black's Law Dictionary*, 8th ed., *s.v.* "remedies."

10 See Andrew Green, chapter 13.

able, and regulated entities are expected to know about them. Their release can be preceded by formal public consultation, providing those affected with a chance for input in advance.

Moreover, even when acting in their tribunal capacity, administrative tribunals often do, and should, take a broader perspective on a dispute than courts necessarily will. One way to understand the difference is in terms described by an American scholar, Abram Chayes, in the mid-1970s.[11] Chayes talked about courts, not administrative agencies. Nevertheless, his point illuminates the distinction between the two. Chayes described an emerging dichotomy between traditional conceptions of adjudication, and an emerging judicial role in what he described as public law litigation. In traditional adjudication, a suit involves only the private parties before the court. It is self-contained and party-initiated. A dispassionate judge identifies the private right at issue on the basis of doctrinal analysis and retrospective fact inquiry. The judge imposes relief, understood as compensation for the past violation of an identifiable existing right. (This portrayal describes party-on-party dispute resolution, but a rights-based approach also informs tribunal-on-party regulatory action.) By contrast, in public law litigation, Chayes argued that the debate is more focused on the vindication of broader statutory or constitutional policies. The lawsuit is not self-contained. The judge must manage complex trial situations involving not only the parties to the dispute, but also the many and shifting parties not before the court who nevertheless may be affected by the suit's outcome. Fact inquiry is predictive, not retrospective. Through a combination of party negotiation and continuing judicial involvement, the judge fashions relief that is ad hoc, ongoing, and prospective. On the Chayes model, judges can become change agents under whose management specific cases can have far-reaching effects.

Like Chayes's public law adjudicatory model, administrative agencies—even when acting as tribunals rather than policy-making bodies—may have a broader mandate, and the ability to leverage a broader range of tools than a traditional prosecution of rights-based claims provides. Many administrative bodies are explicitly charged with managing complex and often "polycentric" problems in a comprehensive manner. The Supreme Court of Canada has recognized this, pointing out that "while judicial procedure is premised on a bipolar opposition of parties, interests, and factual discovery, some problems [assigned to tribunals by their enabling statutes] require the consideration of numerous interests simultaneously, and the promulgation of solutions which concurrently balance benefits and costs for many different parties."[12] This has a few implications. First, it means that administrative tribunals have stronger theoretical justifications for remaining "seized" of a case over a longer period of time.[13]

11 Abram Chayes, "The Role of the Judge in Public Law Litigation" (1976) 89 Harv. L. Rev. 1281; see also D.M. Gordon, "'Administrative' Tribunals and the Courts" (1933) 49 Law Q. Rev. 94 (defining a judicial function as one that determines "pre-existing" rights and liabilities by reference to a "fixed objective standard," as contrasted with an administrative function, in which rights and liabilities are created by "policy and expediency").

12 *Pushpanathan v. Canada (Minister of Citizenship and Immigration)*, [1998] S.C.J. No. 46, [1998] 1 S.C.R. 982 at para. 36 (advising curial deference where the purpose of the enabling statute as a whole and the provision in question present the tribunal with this sort of question).

13 See, for example, *Ontario (Ministry of Correctional Services) v. Ontario (Human Rights Comm.)* (2001), 39 C.H.R.R. D/308 (Ont. Sup. Ct.), aff'd [2004] O.J. No. 5051 (C.A.) (holding that the Human Rights Tribunal of Ontario had extensive supervisory jurisdiction over its orders and could remain seized of a matter to recast its orders to deal with ongoing systemic racism at correctional facilities).

Second, it means that administrative tribunals may try to develop remedies that address underlying structural or systemic problems, in a forward-looking rather than retrospective, rights-oriented way. This is not to say that courts do not also craft systemic, forward-looking remedies; indeed, Chayes's point is that they do.[14] However, relative to courts, administrative tribunals have a degree of subject-specific expertise, field sensitivity, and the statutory mandate that make them especially well-placed to develop and implement novel remedies.

Just as importantly, administrative tribunal members are a more diverse group, especially in terms of their training and expertise, than judges are. Some tribunals' enabling statutes stipulate that a certain portion of their tribunal members should be laypersons. For example, s. 3 of the federal *Competition Tribunal Act*[15] stipulates that the tribunal shall consist of not more than six members who are Federal Court judges, and not more than eight other "lay" members (although this does not exclude lawyers). The statute goes on to stipulate that the governor in council should establish an advisory council, "to be composed of not more than ten members who are knowledgeable in economics, industry, commerce or public affairs,"[16] to advise the Minister of Industry with respect to the appointment of lay members. The result is a tribunal with substantial expertise in economics and in commerce.[17] The tribunal's expertise also makes it more likely that its members will devise remedies that reflect their training and perspective, and that may be more economic than legal.

Sometimes, the composition of tribunal membership reflects an explicit attempt to represent different interest groups, perhaps especially in subject areas where there is a perception that judges historically have been unsympathetic or not alive to some of the issues at stake. A classic example of the latter is a tripartite labour board, on which a representative of labour, a representative of management, and a third member must sit. The BC Review Board, charged under the *Criminal Code* of Canada with making dispositions with respect to individuals found unfit to stand trial, or not criminally responsible on account of mental disorder, also has a tripartite structure. The BC *Mental Health Act* requires that each panel of the Review Board consist of a doctor, a lawyer, and a person who is *neither* a doctor *nor* a lawyer.[18] The kinds of remedies that such boards devise are likely to reflect the particular priorities and assumptions of its members, and may not be limited to the universe of strictly legal remedies that spring to the legally trained mind.

Administrative law has also been affected by what is variously called "new public management" theory, neoliberalism, or administrative structures that "span the public/private divide." Effectively, these are mechanisms by which public structures, such as administra-

14 *Doucet-Boudreau v. Nova Scotia (Minister of Education)*, [2003] 3 S.C.R. 3 provides justification for structural injunction style remedies by courts.

15 R.S.C. 1985, c. 19 (2nd Supp.), s. 3(2).

16 *Ibid.*, s. 3(3).

17 *Canada (Director of Investigation and Research) v. Southam Inc.*, [1997] 1 S.C.R. 748.

18 *Mental Health Act*, R.S.B.C. 1996, c. 288, s. 24.1(3). Additional guidelines on qualifications for part-time members of the board can be found in the British Columbia Review Board, *Recruitment, Screening and Appointment Procedures* (Vancouver: British Columbia Review Board, 2004), online: <http://www.bcrb.bc.ca/BCRB%20Recruitment%20ProceduresFinal.pdf>.

tive tribunals, retain ultimate accountability for their programs but "outsource" the implementation of those programs to private or third-party actors. For example, hundreds of standards developed by private bodies are incorporated into law and used for enforcement and compliance purposes.[19] Regulators also delegate enforcement and compliance functions to private bodies.[20] These make up a deeply embedded feature of Canadian law, especially in fields where there are highly technical product or process issues to be regulated. They are also controversial, particularly as their use becomes more widespread, and it becomes clear that "technical" standards are not so easily divorced from larger social and policy considerations. Proponents of "new governance" style approaches argue that delegated implementation is the best way forward for administrative agencies that have become sclerotic and bureaucratic; that it allocates action to those bodies best equipped and with the greatest information to perform tasks effectively; that public/private partnerships are capable of accomplishing public ends more efficiently than the public sector could achieve in acting alone; and that such partnerships do not eliminate the public state, but rather "save" it from its own bureaucratic flaws.[21] Those opposed to these mechanisms argue that they are privatization by another name; that they reduce accountability and the public sector's responsibility for what should be publicly provided goods and services; that they "hollow out" the state in potentially irretrievable ways.[22] Leaving this important debate for another day, at a practical level, parties involved in administrative action should be aware that there may be a constellation of ostensibly "private" actors that may have a role to play in their interactions with public administrative tribunals.

A combination of these factors—ongoing seizin, a broad mandate, different expertise, and the trend toward crossing the public/private divide—have led some tribunals to create innovative remedies. One cluster of innovations incorporates an independent third party in trying to develop and implement remedial measures within a subject organization or corporation, where systemic problems seem to be significant. These remedies try to effectuate meaningful systemic change within the organization, based on a sustained engagement with the problem by an impartial outsider. They have become fairly common among securities regulators in particular.[23] An important function of the third party in this context is to facilitate

19 For example, since 1927, the Canadian Standards Association's Canadian Electrical Code, Canadian Standards Association Standard C22.1-06, has provided the standards for addressing shock and fire hazards of electrical products in Canada. It has been incorporated by reference into provincial regulations across the country: see, for example, *Electrical Safety Regulation*, B.C. Reg. 100/2004, s. 20.

20 For example, the Technical Standards and Safety Association (TSSA) is a delegated administrative authority for Ontario safety regulation covering elevating devices, amusement rides, boilers, and other products. The various provincial securities commissions also delegate the regulation of investment dealers and mutual fund dealers to their respective self-regulated organizations, the Investment Dealers Association (IDA) and the Mutual Fund Dealers Association (MFDA). Many professionals, including doctors and lawyers, are regulated by their self-governing professional bodies, which are not government agencies.

21 Jody Freeman, "Private Parties, Public Functions and the New Administrative Law" (2000) 52 Admin. L. Rev. 813; Richard Stewart, "Administrative Law in the Twenty-First Century" (2003) 78 N.Y.U. L. Rev. 437.

22 See, for example, Harry Arthurs, "Public Law in a Neoliberal Globalized World: The Administrative State Goes to Market (and Cries 'Wee, Wee, Wee' All the Way Home)" (2005) 55 U.T.L.J. 797.

23 See, for example, Settlement Agreement, *In the Matter of Union Securities Ltd. and John P. Thompson* (April 18, 2006), online: <http://www.ida.ca/IDAWebsite/Files/Enforcement/SettlementAgreements/

a deliberative process within the organization itself—that is, to help the troubled organization confront and work through its problems internally. Some scholars argue that transparent, accountable, and broadly participatory dialogue of this nature, potentially facilitated by such third parties, is the most legitimate and most effective mechanism for making decisions in complex organizational structures.[24]

One effort at creating such a deliberative, third-party facilitated process is ongoing within Ontario's Ministry of Correctional Services, as a response to a long-standing human rights complaint by an employee of the ministry.[25] The complainant in that case, Michael McKinnon, was a person of native Canadian ancestry and a correctional officer with the Ministry of Correctional Services. In 1998, the Human Rights Tribunal of Ontario (then the Board of Inquiry) found that Mr. McKinnon suffered discrimination and harassment at his workplace, the Toronto East Detention Centre, because of his race, ancestry, and ethnic origin. The tribunal ordered a number of systemic remedies to address what it found was a "poisoned atmosphere," including relocating certain individual respondents, publicizing the tribunal's order among Corrections employees, and establishing a human rights training program. The tribunal reconvened the hearing in 2002 because of Mr. McKinnon's allegations that the poisoned work environment had not improved. The issue for the tribunal was not whether the existing systemic remedies had been implemented in a strict sense, but whether they had been carried out in good faith.

After dealing with the question whether it could remain seized of the matter—finding that it could, as affirmed later by the Ontario Court of Appeal[26]—the tribunal ordered an additional range of systemic remedies, including training for ministry and facility management; establishing a roster of external mediators to deal with discrimination complaints; and appointing, at the ministry's expense, an independent third-party consultant nominated by the Human Rights Commission to develop and oversee the delivery of training programs ordered. The third-party consultant was to be nominated by the Ontario Human Rights Commission, paid for by the ministry, and required to report to the Human Rights Tribunal. Sadly, as of May 2005, the parties were still arguing over the scope of that consultant's responsibilities, with the consultant alleging that the ministry was attempting to gain control over the process. The process of defining the mandate of the consultant seemed itself to have become

---

SA2006041801_en.pdf>, Offer of Settlement, *In the Matter of UBS Securities Canada Inc.* (October 8, 2004), online: <http://docs.rs.ca/ArticleFile.asp?Instance=100&ID=4CDF42F183D6455D903D528E03DF0330>; Order, *In the Matter of Agnico-Eagle Mines Limited* (April 28, 2005), online: <http://www.osc.gov.on.ca/Enforcement/Proceedings/RAD/rad_20050428_agnico-eagle-mines.pdf>; Order, *In the Matter of Murray Hoult Pollitt and Pollitt & Co. Inc.* (November 17, 2004), online: <http://www.osc.gov.on.ca/Enforcement/Proceedings/RAD/rad_20041117_pollitt.pdf>.

24 See, for example, Amy Gutmann & Dennis Thompson, *Why Deliberative Democracy?* (Princeton: Princeton University Press, 2004); Michael C. Dorf, "Legal Indeterminacy and Institutional Design" (2003) 78 N.Y.U.L. Rev. 875; Lisa Blomgren Bingham, Tina Nabatchi & Rosemary O'Leary, "The New Governance: Practices and Processes for Stakeholder and Citizen Participation in the Work of Government" (2005) 65 Pub. Admin. Rev. 547.

25 *McKinnon and Ontario Human Rights Commission v. Ontario (Ministry of Correctional Services) et al.*, [2002] O.H.R.B.I.D. No. 22, November 22, 2002, online: <http://www.opseu.org/legal/MichaelMcKinnon-Decision.pdf>.

26 *Ontario v. McKinnon*, [2004] O.J. No. 5051 C41678, [2004] CarswellOnt 5191 (C.A.).

an adversarial contest that did not bode well for the consultant's ability to catalyze the hoped-for meaningful dialogue within the ministry.[27]

As a final note, both tribunal-side and policy-side administrative functions have been affected by globalization. The effects of globalization mean that domestic administrative tribunals no longer act entirely free of international and transnational agreements, organizations, standard-setting bodies, and national commitments. Some of the most notable international examples come out of the European Union, whose policy and harmonization directives and court decisions have had a direct impact on European nation states' domestic administrative law. In Canada, as well, international obligations have had an impact on federal labour policies and their subsequent administration through a variety of public bodies,[28] and international human rights norms have influenced the substantive review of administrative decisions.[29] Relevant international or transnational standards are sometimes set by governments acting together (such as the North American Free Trade Agreement [NAFTA] and its associated side agreements) and sometimes set by independent, private, and/or non-governmental bodies filling lacunae in international law (such as forest practices certification).[30] Looking at these developments, some scholars have even begun to herald the birth of a "global administrative law."[31]

The conversation about proper tribunal action spans multiple disciplines—law, public policy, organizational and political theory—and it is taking place at the levels of practice and theory, both within tribunals and with respect to them. The forces that influence tribunals, described above, produce remedies that can be more dynamic and varied than the ones we are accustomed to seeing in the courts. Court review of tribunal remedies by means of judicial review serves a valuable "sober second thought" function, based on important rule of law values, but court action is only one facet of administrative law.

III. ENFORCING TRIBUNAL ORDERS AGAINST PARTIES

After a tribunal makes a decision and imposes an order, assuming no one challenges that decision,[32] another set of administrative law remedies becomes available: the enforcement powers. These may be invoked where a tribunal needs to enforce its order against a party that is not complying with the order. This is not uncommon among self-regulatory organizations such as professional licensing bodies, where the tribunal acts against particular individuals rather than adjudicating disputes between parties. Alternatively, a party to a multiparty dis-

---

27 Human Rights Tribunal of Ontario, Interim Decisions and Rulings, *Ontario Human Rights Commission and Michael McKinnon and Ontario Ministry of Correctional Services et al.*, 2005 HRTO 15, May 19, 2005, online: <http://www.canlii.org/en/on/onhrt/doc/2005/2005hrto15/2005hrto15.html>.

28 Canada, Commission on Labour Standards Review, *Fairness at Work: Federal Labour Standards for the 21st Century* (Gatineau: Human Resources and Skills Development Canada, 2006) at 51-52, online: <http://www.hrsdc.gc.ca/en/labour/employment_standards/arthur_report/pdf/final_report.pdf>.

29 See Gerald Heckman, chapter 12.

30 Errol Meidinger, "The Administrative Law of Global Private-Public Regulation: The Case of Forestry" (2006) 17 E.J.I.L. 47.

31 Benedict Kingsbury, Nico Krisch & Richard B. Stewart, "The Emergence of Global Administrative Law" (2005) 68 *Law and Contemporary Problems* 15.

32 See part IV.

pute before a tribunal may want to enforce the tribunal's order against another party on which the order was imposed. Criminal prosecution is also a possibility. Of course, regardless of any broader social patterns or systemic factors operating, tribunal orders can only be enforced against the parties on which they are imposed.

A. The Tribunal Seeks to Enforce Its Order

Rarely, a tribunal may enforce its own orders. One tribunal that has the power to enforce its own orders—for example, an order for civil contempt—is the federal Competition Tribunal.[33] Some other tribunals are also given the authority to enforce monetary obligations, such as requiring unpaid wages or family maintenance to be paid, imposing liens, making garnishment orders, seizing assets, or even suspending driving privileges.[34] However, any enforcement powers held by a tribunal must be granted to the tribunal in its enabling statute, and that delegation of enforcement power must pass constitutional scrutiny. For example, a provincially created tribunal cannot have criminal (and therefore federal) enforcement powers.[35]

In British Columbia, certain sections of the *Administrative Tribunals Act* (ATA)[36] are intended to assist tribunals in obtaining compliance with their orders. For example, s. 18 permits certain tribunals to schedule a hearing, make a decision, or dismiss an application if a party fails to comply with an order (presumably, an order to appear). Section 31(1)(e) permits some tribunals to dismiss an application if the applicant fails to comply with a tribunal order. Section 47, which permits some tribunals to make orders for payment of costs, also allows some tribunals, under s. 47(1)(c), to require a party to pay the *tribunal's* actual costs "if the tribunal considers the conduct of a party has been improper, vexatious, frivolous or abusive." Orders for costs, on being filed in the court registry, have the same effect as a court order for the recovery of a debt (s. 47(2)).

More commonly, the tribunal must make an application in court to enforce any order it makes. Some tribunals' enabling statutes provide that, where a party has disobeyed a tribunal order, the tribunal may apply to court for an order requiring the person to comply.[37] The tribunal's order is presumed to be valid and correct if the party disobeying it failed to file an appeal, if one is available, or if the party appealed and lost.[38] Other enabling statutes al-

33 *Competition Tribunal Act*, R.S.C. 1985, c. 19, s. 8(1). See *Chrysler Canada Ltd. v. Canada (Competition Tribunal)*, [1992] S.C.J. No. 64, 92 D.L.R. (4th) 609 (holding that clear and unambiguous statutory language can override the common-law rule that only superior courts have the power to punish for contempt, and that the wording of the *Competition Tribunal Act*, s. 8(1) (as it then was), which conferred on the tribunal jurisdiction "to hear and determine all applications made under Part VIII of the *Competition Act* and any matters related thereto," constituted such clear and unambiguous statutory language).

34 For example, *Employment Standards Act*, R.S.B.C. 1996, c. 113, ss. 87-101; *Maintenance Enforcement Act*, S.N.S. 1994-95, c. 6, ss. 19, 27-30.

35 *MacMillan Bloedel Ltd. v. Simpson*, [1996] 2 W.W.R. 1 (S.C.C.); *United Nurses of Alberta v. Alberta (Attorney General)*, [1992] S.C.J. No. 37, 89 D.L.R. (4th) 609.

36 S.B.C. 2004, c. 45.

37 See, for example, *Statutory Powers Procedure Act*, R.S.O. 1990, c. S.22, s. 19.

38 *Provincial Agricultural Land Commission v. Pickell* (1980), 109 D.L.R. (3d) 465 at 473 (B.C.S.C.); *Estevan Coal Corp. v. Estevan (Rural Municipality No. 5)*, [2000] 8 W.W.R. 474, (2000), 199 Sask. R. 57 (C.A.).

low tribunal orders to be registered with the court, sometimes only with leave.[39] In Quebec, a distinct procedure known as homologation gives courts the authority to compel individuals to fulfill tribunal orders. In order to access homologation, it must be expressly provided for in the enabling statute.[40]

Once a tribunal has successfully converted its order into a court order through one of the mechanisms above, the order can be enforced in the same manner as a court judgment. Among other things, this means that contempt proceedings are available if the party continues to disregard the order.[41] Contempt proceedings may be available if a party fails to abide by a tribunal's procedural order (for example, by failing to appear as a witness or to produce documents) or a tribunal's final substantive order.[42] Contempt can be civil or, where the conduct constitutes an intentional public act of defiance of the court, criminal.[43] In a contempt proceeding, the judge does not inquire into the validity of the tribunal's underlying order. However, only violations of "clear and unambiguous" tribunal orders will form the basis of a contempt order.[44] A court can also refuse to hold a party in contempt until an appeal or judicial review application (discussed in part IV below) is completed, although parties can be required to pay monies into court in the interim.[45]

Note that legislators seem content to house tribunal order enforcement powers in the courts, even while using privative clauses to try to limit the availability of judicial review from administrative tribunals. For the executive, then, recourse to courts to *enforce* tribunal orders seems to be acceptable, while recourse to courts to *challenge* tribunal orders is less so. Does this suggest that the executive's stance has less to do with concerns for conserving scarce judicial resources than with trying to allocate those judicial resources to buttressing and reinforcing the authority of the tribunals it creates?

B. A Party Seeks to Enforce a Tribunal's Order

A party to an administrative action may also bring an action in court against another party to enforce the tribunal's order. For example, a group of teachers may seek to enforce an

39 See, for example, *Administrative Tribunals Act*, *supra* note 37, ss. 47, 54.

40 See, for example, *Regulation respecting the conciliation and arbitration procedure for the accounts of members of the Corporation professionnelle des physiothérapeutes du Québec*, R.R.Q., c. C-26, r. 141.1. For a more in-depth discussion on homologation, see René Dussault & Louis Borgeat, *Administrative Law: A Treatise*, 2d ed., vol. 2, trans. by Murray Rankin (Toronto: Carswell, 1985) at 283.

41 Tribunals themselves may have the power to make orders for "in facie" contempt (contempt "in the face of" the court during the proceedings) because this power is implicit in the designation of a tribunal as a court of record. If a tribunal is not designated as such, then the power to punish for in facie contempt, like the power to punish for "ex facie" contempt (contempt outside the proceedings), must be explicitly conferred by the enabling statute. *Chrysler Canada Ltd. v. Canada (Competition Tribunal)*, [1992] 2 S.C.R. 394.

42 See, for example, *Statutory Powers Procedure Act*, *supra* note 38, s. 13.

43 *United Nurses of Alberta v. Alberta (Attorney General)*, [1992] S.C.J. No. 37, 89 D.L.R. (4th) 609.

44 *Chrysler Canada Ltd. v. Canada (Competition Tribunal)*, [1992] S.C.J. No. 64, [1992] 2 S.C.R. 394; *United Food & Commercial Workers, Local 1252 v. Western Star*, [1995] N.J. No. 334, 130 D.L.R. (4th) 538 (S.C.(T.D)); *Toronto Transit Commission v. Ryan*, [1998] O.J. No. 51, 37 O.R. (3d) 266 (Gen. Div.).

45 *Boucher v. Logistik Unicorp Inc.*, [2001] J.Q. No. 64 (C.A.), leave to appeal to S.C.C. refused [2001] C.S.C.R. No. 115; *Sodema Inc. v. Sarafian*, [2006] J.Q. No. 5460 (C.A.).

arbitrator's order that a school board annually set aside certain funds for teachers' professional development.[46] Sara Blake has suggested that the party's success "may depend on whether the tribunal order is of a type that a court would enforce, and whether the court believes it should enforce the tribunal order in the absence of any statutory procedure for obtaining court assistance."[47] What does this mean to you? One interpretation is that courts may be more likely to grant a private application to enforce a tribunal order where the court recognizes the tribunal's order as similar to the kind of order a law court might make. However, the private applicant will first have to convince the court that it should intervene notwithstanding the potential absence of a statutory provision empowering it to do so.

C. Criminal Prosecution

Many statutes provide for quasi-criminal prosecution of persons who disobey tribunal orders. Quasi-criminal offences are prosecuted by the federal or provincial Crown, as appropriate, and they carry penalties that include fines and imprisonment. For example, a person who commits an offence under s. 155 of the BC *Securities Act*[48] is liable to a fine of not more than $3 million, or to imprisonment for not more than three years, or both. Indictable offences under the federal *Fisheries Act* may attract, at their upper end, fines of up to $500,000 or imprisonment for up two years, or both.[49]

In the absence of other provisions, it is a criminal offence to disobey a lawful order of a federal or provincial tribunal. The federal *Criminal Code* states:

> 127(1) Every one who, without lawful excuse, disobeys a lawful order made by a court of justice *or by a person or body of persons authorized by any Act to make or give the order*, other than an order for the payment of money, is, *unless a punishment or other mode of proceeding is expressly provided by law*, guilty of
>
> (a) an indictable offence and liable to imprisonment for a term not exceeding two years; or
>
> (b) an offence punishable on summary conviction.[50]

The *Criminal Code* provision is available where no other penalty is expressly provided by law. What does this mean? Superior courts' own contempt powers do not count as an "other mode of proceeding" for purposes of this section.[51] Most administrative tribunals do not have the ability to make contempt orders on their own. Therefore, the *Criminal Code* provisions should apply where no "punishment or other mode of proceeding" is explicitly

46 *Melia v. Moose Jaw Roman Catholic Separate School District No. 22*, [1979] S.J. No. 568, 108 D.L.R. (3d) 113 (C.A.); *Twentieth Century-Fox Corp. Ltd. v. Broadway Theatres Ltd.*, [1951] 3 D.L.R. 105 (Sask. C.A.).

47 Sara Blake, *Administrative Law in Canada*, 4th ed. (Markham: LexisNexis Butterworths, 2006) at 226.

48 R.S.B.C. 1996, c. 418.

49 R.S.C. 1985, c. F-14, s. 78(b).

50 R.S.C. 1985, c. C-46, s. 127(1) (emphasis added).

51 Unless the court's contempt powers are laid out comprehensively in the Rules of Court: *R. v. Clement*, [1981] 2 S.C.R. 468, [1981] S.C.J. No. 93; *R. v. Mulhall*, [2001] O.J. No. 5237 (Ct. J.). But see *Telus Communications Inc. v. Telecommunications Workers Union* (2006), 268 D.L.R. (4th) 131 (B.C.S.C.).

set out in the tribunal's enabling statute. This does not violate the constitutional separation of powers, even when dealing with provincial tribunals: the provincial tribunal makes orders that are non-criminal. Parliament, acting within its sphere, is the one that has decided that breach of those provincial provisions is a criminal offence.[52]

IV. CHALLENGING ADMINISTRATIVE ACTION

A party to an administrative action may also decide to challenge that administrative action directly. The possible bases for a party's challenge are described throughout this text: for example, a party may challenge the tribunal's jurisdiction, its procedure, its impartiality, its exercise of discretion, or the substance of its final decision. Each of these usually amounts to a direct or indirect challenge of the remedies or orders the tribunal imposes. Sometimes, these challenges are made through applications for judicial review. However, judicial review is only one method of challenging administrative action. Judicial review applications, like litigation generally, can be expensive and drawn-out affairs. Moreover, it is important to be realistic about what can be achieved through judicial review. In order to bring a successful judicial review application, a challenger must be aware of the specific remedial mechanisms available and how those mechanisms will help him or her achieve the result that he or she wants. For example, a motion to quash a tribunal decision for lack of procedural fairness, if successful, will likely lead to the court sending the matter back to the original tribunal for rehearing.[53] This result may not satisfy the challenger. Even assuming that procedural fairness is observed the second time, there is no guarantee that the party will receive the substantive outcome he or she seeks.

For these reasons, parties seeking to challenge administrative action should consider their options carefully. This part of this chapter outlines the various mechanisms available, including both non-court mechanisms and court-based mechanisms. We begin first with mechanisms that are internal to the administrative apparatus itself, then to mechanisms that exist externally to both the administrative agency and courts (for example, to an ombudsperson), finally turning to court-based mechanisms. Here we distinguish between appeals and judicial review and discuss private law remedies that may exist against tribunals.

A. Internal Tribunal Mechanisms

A party considering a challenge to tribunal action will need to understand the particular tribunal's structure and capacity, as established by its enabling statute. All tribunals can fix certain things, such as clerical errors or factual errors due to mistake or dishonesty, without express statutory authority. This is sometimes called the "slip rule."[54] Tribunals can also "change their minds" until the time a final decision is made. Therefore, what constitutes a "final decision" becomes important. For example, if a statute provides that final decisions

52 *United Nurses of Alberta v. Alberta (Attorney General)*, [1992] 1 S.C.R. 901.

53 See Grant Huscroft, chapter 5.

54 See, for example, *Chandler v. Alberta Association of Architects*, [1989] 2 S.C.R. 848 at 861; *Muscillo Transport Ltd. v. Ontario (Licence Suspension Appeal Board)* (1997), 149 D.L.R. (4th) 545 at 553 (Ont. Gen. Div.), aff'd [1998] O.J. No. 1488 (C.A).

must be in writing, then only written decisions will constitute final decisions. Preliminary rulings can also be changed until the final decision on a matter has been made.[55]

Some enabling statutes specifically provide tribunals with the ability to reconsider and rehear decisions they have made. This is most common where a particular tribunal has on-going regulatory responsibility over a particular domain, such as public utilities regulation or employer–employee relations. For example, s. 43 of the *Public Service Labour Relations Act* provides, "[s]ubject to subsection (2) [prohibiting retroactive effect of any rights acquired], the Board may review, rescind or amend any of its orders or decisions, or may rehear any application before making an order in respect of the application."[56] Absent such express statutory authority, however, for policy reasons that favour finality of proceedings, a tribunal cannot reconsider or alter a final decision made within its jurisdiction. Once it has made a final decision, the tribunal is "functus officio."[57]

Some administrative tribunals are part of multi-tiered administrative agencies. Those tribunals' enabling statutes may provide for appeals internal to the administrative agency itself. For example, parties appearing before Canada's Immigration and Refugee Board Immigration Division may appeal to its Immigration Appeal Division.[58] Similarly, provincial securities acts across the country provide that persons directly affected by decisions made by Securities Commission staff may appeal to (or, in some statutes, seek "review" from) the commission itself, to which staff reports.[59] Again, parties should be aware that internal appellate structures may not look much like courts.

These internal review proceedings do not preclude subsequent appeals to the courts. Indeed, both the *Immigration and Refugee Protection Act* and the various securities acts mentioned above provide for appeals, under certain conditions, from their appellate bodies to the courts. Where the statute does not provide for an appeal to the courts, the parties' only entrée to the courts is by means of judicial review. However, as discussed in more detail below, where a statute provides for reconsideration or appeals, a challenger should generally exhaust those avenues before making an application for judicial review.

One of the more interesting innovations in internal administrative appeals was created in 1996, with the passage of Quebec's *Act Respecting Administrative Justice*.[60] The statute creates the Tribunal administratif du Québec (TAQ), a supertribunal that hears "proceedings" brought against almost all administrative tribunals and public bodies in the province, including government departments, boards, commissions, municipalities, and health-care bodies.[61]

55 *Comeau's Sea Foods Limited v. Canada (Minister of Fisheries and Oceans)*, [1997] 1 S.C.R. 12.

56 *Public Service Labour Relations Act*, S.C. 2003, c. 22, s. 43.

57 *Chandler v. Alberta Association of Architects*, [1989] 2 S.C.R. 848. Because rights of appeal from tribunals tend to be more limited than from courts, the functus officio doctrine should be more flexible and less formulistic for such tribunals.

58 *Immigration and Refugee Protection Act*, S.C. 2001, c. 27, ss. 62-71, 174-175.

59 See, for example, Ontario *Securities Act*, R.S.O. 1990, c. S.5, s. 8(2); Alberta *Securities Act*, R.S.A. 2000, c. S-4, s. 35(1); British Columbia *Securities Act*, *supra* note 49, ss. 165(3), 167(1).

60 R.S.Q. c. J-3.

61 *Ibid.*, s. 14. The use of the word "proceedings" rather than "appeal" or "review" indicates that the tribunal can hear appeals in the traditional sense, but it can also hear various demands that look more or less like review or "révision." The scope and nature of the proceedings depend on the wording of each tribunal's enabling statute that provides for the proceeding.

As a practical matter, this means that there is now one main appellate/review body for administrative matters in the province. According to the Act, the tribunal's purpose is "to affirm the specific character of administrative justice, to ensure its quality, promptness and accessibility and to safeguard the fundamental rights of citizens."[62] It is an administrative institution, not a judicial one, but its remedial powers include judicial review-style options and, surprisingly, the ability to substitute its decision for an original tribunal's: "[i]n the case of the contestation of a decision, the Tribunal may confirm, vary or quash the contested decision and, if appropriate, make the decision which, in its opinion, should have been made initially."[63] Where the TAQ has jurisdiction to consider a proceeding, claimants should exhaust the remedies available from it rather than trying to circumvent the administrative process.[64] Avenues of appeal from the TAQ to the Superior Court of Quebec are limited.[65]

B. External Non-Court Mechanisms

A party considering a challenge to administrative action should not overlook non-legal avenues. For example, ombudspersons or similar positions exist by statute in every Canadian province. There is no overarching federal ombudsperson, but some federal departments and subject areas have their own specialized ombudspersons. Most recently, in March 2007, the federal government created a Federal Ombudsman for Victims of Crime.[66] Generally, the mandate of an ombudsperson is to provide a forum for citizens to bring their complaints regarding the way that government departments and agencies have dealt with them. There is no charge to make a complaint to an ombudsperson. Ombudspersons have discretion as to whether or not they will investigate a complaint.

An ongoing issue has been the degree to which an ombudsperson can assert jurisdiction with respect to administrative tribunal decisions and processes (as opposed to the general run of government departments—that is, "faceless bureaucracies" not possessing the statutorily created decision-making structure that tribunals have). Most legislation defines the ombudsperson's jurisdiction as being over "matters of administration," and courts have tended to define "administration" expansively as involving generic administrative processes, not simply as the antonym of "judicial" processes.[67] Among the tribunals themselves,

62 *Supra* note 61 at s. 1.

63 *Ibid.*, s. 15.

64 *Okwuobi et al. v. Lester B. Pearson School Board et al.*, [2005] 1 S.C.R. 257.

65 The tribunal is composed of four divisions (social affairs, immovable property, territory and environment, and economic affairs), but per s. 159 of the Act, an appeal to the Quebec court is only available from the immovable property division and from decisions regarding the preservation of agricultural land. This tracks the appeals that were available from those tribunals before TAQ was created; the TAQ replaced a plethora of administrative appeal bodies, but was not intended to increase the number of available appeals to the courts.

66 Canada, Press Release, "Canada's New Government Announced Federal Victims Ombudsman and New Funding for Victims of Crime," March 17, 2007, online: <http://www.justice.gc.ca/en/news/nr/2007/doc_31987.html>. The gender-neutral term "ombudsperson" seems to have become the standard term in Canada, although the word "ombudsman" is an old Scandinavian word, not a gender-specific English word. Other gender-neutral terms include "ombuds office" and simply "ombuds."

67 For example, in *British Columbia Development Corporation v. Friedmann (Ombudsman)*, [1984] 2 S.C.R. 447, the SCC ruled that policy-making activities of provincial Crown corporations were "matters of

the range of bodies subject to an ombudsperson's investigatory powers can be quite broad. In Ontario, for example, the courts have held that even largely independent bodies can be subject to ombuds review if the government pays its members' wages.[68] However, most ombuds statutes provide that an ombudsperson is not authorized to investigate a tribunal's decision until after any right of appeal or review on the merits has been exercised or until after the time limit for doing so has expired.[69]

Several other public officials similar to ombudspersons also exist, including freedom of information and privacy commissioners, the auditor general, provincial auditors, and human rights commissioners. While harder for individuals to instigate, public inquiries are another mechanism for challenging government conduct.[70]

C. Using the Courts: Statutory Appeals

The ability to challenge administrative action in the courts is a mixed, but necessary, blessing. On the downside, courts may be reluctant to embrace novel, non-courtlike, yet potentially effective remedies devised by specialized tribunals. The richness and creativity that characterize administrative law remedies could be stifled by over-judicialized, overly interventionist court scrutiny. This is one reason that the internal appeal mechanisms described above make sense. On the other hand, there are times—for example, during times of national emergency—when executive action unquestionably needs to be subject to the rule of law, as applied by independent courts.[71] As with so many things in administrative law, context matters in thinking about the legitimacy of each alternative. There may be times when it makes sense to maintain the integrity of the administrative regime through all internal appeal stages. There may also be times when what is required is faster and unapologetic recourse to the courts—for example, allowing a party to "leapfrog" the internal appeals and proceed directly to judicial review.

There are two main ways by which a party to a tribunal action can access the courts to challenge that action: appeal and judicial review. Appeal mechanisms—either to internal administrative appellate bodies or to courts—are the norm. Judicial review is the exception.[72] Significantly, it is also discretionary. The scope of a possible appeal is confined to what the statute expressly provides. This means that, even though courts struggle sometimes with knotty issues in taking appeals from administrative tribunals, relative to judicial

administration" for the purposes of the *Ombudsman Act*. The Ontario Court of Appeal has interpreted the ombudsperson's jurisdiction over "administration of a government agency" to include investigations into matters determined by administrative tribunals: *Ombudsman of Ontario v. Ontario (Labour Relations Board)* (1986), 44 D.L.R. (4th) 312 (Ont. C.A.).

68 *Ontario (Ombudsman) v. Ontario (Health Disciplines Board)* (1979), 104 D.L.R. (3d) 597 (Ont. C.A.).

69 See, for example, the Yukon *Ombudsman Act*, R.S.Y. 2002, c. 163, s. 12. The Manitoba *Ombudsman Act*, C.C.S.M. c. O45, s. 18(d) and the Saskatchewan *Ombudsman and Children's Advocate Act*, R.S.S. 1978, c. O-4, s. 15(1)(d) provide that rights of appeal or review preclude an ombudsperson's intervention "unless the Ombudsman is satisfied that in the particular case it would have been unreasonable to expect the complainant to resort to the tribunal or court," although the time limitation for appeal or review must still have run.

70 See Peter Carver, chapter 14.

71 See Mary Liston, chapter 4, and Craig Forcese, chapter 11.

72 David J. Mullan, *Administrative Law* (Toronto: Irwin Law, 2001) at 462.

review it is easier to predict the availability and likely outcome of an appeal. By contrast, judicial review doctrine is the product of decades of contentious court battles (albeit modified from time to time by statute), directly pitting "legal" values of justice and the rule of law against "bureaucratic" values such as efficiency and expertise. Even the seemingly basic questions of whether judicial review is available in a particular situation and what remedies are available through judicial review have been shaped by this debate.

1. Is an Appeal Available?

Below are the major questions a party must ask to determine whether an appeal to the courts is available to him or her.

a. Does the Tribunal's Enabling Statute Provide for a Right of Appeal?

Courts have no inherent appellate jurisdiction over administrative tribunals.[73] A right to appeal must be provided for in a tribunal's enabling statute. If a statute does not so provide, a dissatisfied party will have to access the courts by way of judicial review. Moreover, parties may not generally appeal interlocutory rulings (for example, on jurisdiction, procedural or evidentiary issues, or bias).[74] In order to be capable of appeal, the tribunal's decision must decide the merits of the matter or otherwise be a final disposition of it.[75]

Usually, a tribunal's enabling statute will also set out the court to which tribunal orders may be appealed. For federal tribunals, appeals are generally taken to the Federal Court or the Federal Court of Appeal.[76] Appeals from provincially constituted tribunals may be taken to the province's trial court of general jurisdiction,[77] to a divisional court,[78] or to the court of appeal.[79] Rarely, a statute will provide a right (seldom exercised) to appeal a tribunal decision to Cabinet itself.[80]

b. What Is the Scope of Available Appeal?

Like the provision of an appeal, the scope of an available appeal is determined entirely by the enabling statute. The scope of appeal varies enormously from tribunal to tribunal. Some statutes permit complete de novo review of a tribunal's decision, while others will be limited

73 *Medora v. Dental Society*, [1984] N.B.J. No. 236, 56 N.B.R. (2d) 145 at 147 (C.A.).

74 *Mary & David Goodine Diary Farm v. New Brunswick (Milk Marketing Board)*, [2002] N.B.J. No. 177, 217 D.L.R. (4th) 708 (C.A.); *Roosma v. Ford Motor Co. of Canada Ltd.* (1988), 66 O.R. (2d) 18 (Div. Ct.); *Newfoundland Transport Ltd. v. Newfoundland (Public Utilities Board)*, [1983] N.J. No. 92, 45 Nfld. & P.E.I.R. 76 at 78 (C.A.); *contra, Fox v. Registered Nurses' Assn.*, [2002] N.S.J. No. 376, 207 N.S.R. (2d) 330 (C.A.).

75 *Ontario (Human Rights Commission) v. Ontario Teachers' Federation*, [1994] O.J. No. 1585, 19 O.R. (3d) 371 (Gen Div.); *Prince Albert (City) v. Riocan Holding Inc.*, [2004] S.J. No. 337, 241 D.L.R. (4th) 308 (C.A.).

76 Respectively, see, for example, *Trade-marks Act*, R.S.C. 1985, c. T-13, s. 56; *Competition Tribunal Act*, R.S.C. 1985 (2nd Supp.), c. 19, s. 13.

77 See, for example, Nunavut's *Travel and Tourism Act*, R.S.N.W.T. 1988, c. T-7, s. 8.

78 See, for example, Ontario's *Expropriations Act*, R.S.O. 1990, c. E.26, s. 31.

79 See, for example, Newfoundland and Labrador's *Law Society Act, 1999*, S.N.L. 1999, c. L-9.1, s. 55.

80 See, for example, *Broadcasting Act*, S.C. 1991, c. 11, s. 28.

to issues of law, based entirely on the original record. In other words, an appellate court's jurisdiction in reviewing tribunal decisions may be different in scope from an appellate court's jurisdiction in reviewing lower court decisions. Appellate courts generally review trial court decisions for error of law or, more rarely, for palpable and overriding error. By contrast, whichever court is designated to take appeals from a tribunal's decision must look to the tribunal's enabling statute to determine the breadth and scope of its appellate powers.

Arguably, the scope of an available appeal is determined by how closely the tribunal's subject matter, and its expertise, mirror the mandate and expertise of general courts. A right to appeal to the courts is more likely to be granted where the tribunal has the power to affect individuals' common-law rights (for example, human rights tribunals, land-use planning tribunals, professional licensing). Labour relations and employment-related matters, which have long been adjudicated by tripartite boards with specialized expertise and which involve claims by organized labour to which courts were historically perceived to be hostile, cannot generally be appealed to the courts.[81] The same considerations affect the scope of available appeal. For example, a broad power to appeal on questions of fact and law exists from certain professional disciplinary tribunals, where professionals risk losing their ability to practise their profession,[82] and from human rights boards of inquiry adjudicating on violations of human rights codes.[83] Yet even where the appeal rights are broad, courts will show some deference to a tribunal's findings of fact on the assumption that the tribunal had the evidence before it and was in a better position to make those findings.[84]

c. Is an Appeal Available as of Right, or Is Leave Required? If Leave Is Required, Who May Grant It?

Appeals can be as of right or require leave, either of the original decision-maker or, more frequently, of the appellate body. For example, British Columbia's *Forest Practices Code* provides for an appeal as of right from the Forest Appeals Commission to the BC Supreme Court on questions of law or jurisdiction. By contrast, a person affected by a decision of the BC Securities Commission may appeal to the BC Court of Appeal only with leave from a justice of that court.[85] Sometimes, additional statutory criteria must also be met before such leave will be granted.[86]

---

81 David J. Mullan *et al.*, *Administrative Law: Cases, Text, and Materials*, 5th ed. (Toronto: Emond Montgomery, 2003) at 23.

82 See, for example, *Ontario College of Teachers Act, 1996*, S.O. 1996, c. 12, s. 35(4). See also *Re Reddall and College of Nurses of Ontario* (1983), 149 D.L.R. (3d) 60 (Ont. C.A.). Ontario statutes in particular tend to provide explicitly for appeal from various tribunals "on questions of law or fact or both."

83 See, for example, Ontario *Human Rights Code*, *supra* note 7, s. 42(3); also *Zurich Insurance Co. v. Ontario (Human Rights Commission)*, [1992] 2 S.C.R. 321 at 336-38.

84 *Zurich*, *ibid.*

85 Compare *Forest Practices Code of British Columbia Act*, R.S.B.C. 1996, c. 159, s. 141 with *Securities Act*, R.S.B.C. 1996, c. 418, s. 167.

86 For example, an appeal to the Federal Court of Appeal from judicial review by the Federal Court on immigration matters may be made only if the Federal Court judge certifies that "a serious question of general importance" is involved. *Immigration and Refugee Protection Act*, *supra* note 59, s. 74.

d. Is a Stay of Proceedings Automatic, or Must One Apply for It?

The rules governing stays of proceedings vary between jurisdictions and even tribunals. The Ontario *Statutory Powers Procedure Act* establishes a default rule that an appeal operates as a stay of a tribunal's proceedings.[87] The BC *Administrative Tribunals Act*, however, provides that "the commencement of an appeal does not operate as a stay or suspend the operation of the decision being appealed unless the tribunal orders otherwise."[88] Specific statutes also expressly empower their tribunals or the appellate bodies (internal or court) to which they appeal to stay enforcement of the tribunal order pending appeal.[89] Unless a statute specifically excludes it, as British Columbia's ATA does, the superior court that is the tribunal's designated appellate court has the inherent authority to grant a stay.[90]

What are the reasons for and against automatic stays of a tribunal's order pending appeal? The decision to stay a tribunal's order automatically on filing of an appeal, or not, reflects the legislature's assessment of the proper balancing of "due process" and efficiency concerns, the balance between tribunal expertise and judicial oversight, and the legislature's comfort with granting broad autonomy to the tribunal. Assuming that the stay is not automatic, these same factors underlie the legislature's decision to allocate the power to order a stay either to the tribunal, or to the court.

D. Using the Courts: Judicial Review

Now, finally, we discuss the "tail" that sometimes wags the "dog" of administrative law remedies: judicial review. Judicial review has long been the fixation of administrative law, at the expense of tribunal-based and extralegal mechanisms and statutory appeals, in part because administrative law is created primarily by judges, lawyers, and legal scholars. The legal training that these individuals receive is, predictably, preoccupied with legal mechanisms and in particular with courts and the common law.

Having tried to place it in perspective relative to other options, however, judicial review still deserves considerable attention here. It can be conceptually and logistically complex, and it differs from a straightforward appeal. As we shall come to see throughout this volume, the basic nature of judicial review is different from statutory or internal tribunal appeals, because at its root judicial review is about the inherent jurisdiction of courts to oversee and check administrative (that is, executive) action in the interest of the rule of law. This makes it a potentially sweeping remedy. Unlike appeals, which are statutorily created, judicial review is the review of executive action *beyond* what the executive itself provided for. Thus, only on judicial review will courts investigate a tribunal's procedural fairness or the alleged bias of its members.

That said, courts today also recognize that judicial rule-of-law values need to be tempered by some degree of respect for the administrative, or bureaucratic, values of efficiency

87 *Statutory Powers Procedure Act*, *supra* note 38, s. 25.

88 *Administrative Tribunals Act*, *supra* note 37, s. 25.

89 See, for example, *Re Hampton Court Resources Inc.*, 2006 ABASC 1447 (June 13, 2006) (holding that taken together, s. 38(5) of the Alberta *Securities Act* and the provisions of the Alberta Rules of Court require that a stay of a commission decision be sought in the first instance from the commission).

90 *Kooner v. College of Physicians and Surgeons of Ontario* (2002), 213 D.L.R. (4th) 707 (Ont. Div. Ct.).

and expertise that underpin the modern administrative state. Judicial review is fundamentally discretionary in a way that appeals are not: a court may refuse to grant a remedy.[91] Perhaps the most forceful statement about the contingent nature of remedies on judicial review comes from *Domtar Inc. v. Quebec*.[92] In deciding not to intervene to resolve a conflict in legal interpretation between two tribunals construing the same statutory language, the Supreme Court of Canada stated, "[t]he advisability of judicial intervention in the event of conflicting decisions among administrative tribunals, even when serious and unquestionable, cannot, in these circumstances, be determined solely by the 'triumph' of the rule of law."[93] The Court goes on, in what amounts to a striking acknowledgement that even the most deeply cherished legal values will not always point the way to the only, or perhaps even the most appropriate, response to a problem in administrative law:

> [C]ertainty of the law and decision-making consistency are chiefly notable for their relativity. Like the rules of natural justice, these objectives cannot be absolute in nature regardless of the context. The value represented by the decision-making independence and autonomy of the members of administrative tribunals goes hand in hand here with the principle that their decisions should be effective. In light of these considerations we must conclude that, *for purposes of judicial review, the principle of the rule of law must be qualified*. This is consistent with the continuing evolution of administrative law itself.[94]

A statement such as this one gives the reader a sense of just how context-specific, controversial, and frankly difficult judicial review decisions can be.

In view of this and the often convoluted case law that courts have developed over time, legislators have also tried their hand at structuring this area of law. Several important statutes have sought to clarify procedure surrounding judicial review. As discussed below, some of these overarching provincial statutes have also sought to change the substantive shape of judicial review itself. Therefore, parties considering challenging a tribunal order must be aware of the relevant statutes' provisions, in addition to the provisions of the tribunal's own enabling statutes. Key statutes that may apply are the *Federal Courts Act*, the Ontario and British Columbia *Judicial Review Procedure Acts* (JRPAs), the British Columbia *Administrative Tribunals Act*, the Prince Edward Island *Judicial Review Act*, Quebec's *Code of Civil Procedure*, and the Rules of Court in other provinces and territories.

This chapter suggests, above, that the traditional court-centric approach has perpetuated a somewhat limited understanding of administrative law focused on judicial review at the expense of attention to tribunal-level practices. This is the first way in which the "tail" of judicial review can be seen to have wagged the administrative law "dog." But there is a second way, relevant here: the historical development of the remedies available through judicial review, and especially their limitations, has actively shaped the possibilities and potential of judicial review itself. In spite of statutory reform and evolving case law, the ancient prerogative writs that were the original forms of judicial review continue to haunt its present

91 *Immeubles Port Louis Ltée v. Lafontaine (Village)*, [1991] 1 S.C.R. 326.

92 *Domtar Inc. v. Quebec (Commission d'appel en matière de lésions professionnelles)*, [1993] 2 S.C.R. 756.

93 *Ibid.* at 795.

94 *Ibid.* at 799-800 (emphasis added).

forms. The reader should keep each of these effects in mind through the sections below that consider whether and when judicial review is available; the roots of judicial review in the prerogative writs; more recent statutory reform efforts; and discretionary grounds courts have used to refuse to grant a remedy in judicial review.

1. *Is Judicial Review Available?*

Leaving to one side what *Domtar* has said about the discretionary nature of judicial review writ large, the differences in the history, purpose, and function of judicial review also mean that whether it will be available as a remedy in any particular situation depends on a set of considerations unique to administrative law.

One of the key threshold questions is whether the tribunal whose actions are being challenged is, in fact, a public body. Judicial review is available to check executive action. Therefore, only public bodies can be subject to judicial review.[95] While this may sound straightforward, some organizations in Canadian society exercise some degree of "public" function but operate at considerable remove from government. Others seem private, but have some connection to public authority. For example, stock exchanges regulate the conduct of members and issue and revoke licences, and their operations clearly go to the protection of the public. However, their authority to act as they do derives from a compact with their members rather than from any statutory grant of authority. What about corporations incorporated under the *Canada Business Corporations Act* (CBCA)? Corporations are the prototypical "private" institution, yet CBCA companies only come into existence by virtue of government action under that statute. Similarly, one should distinguish between government action qua government, and government action qua private contracting party. As a general matter, a private party will have difficulty seeking judicial review of a government board's decision not to award it a particular contract.[96]

Various factors go into determining whether a particular tribunal is a private body or a public one. Relevant considerations include the tribunal's functions and duties and the sources of its power and funding; whether the government directly or indirectly controls the body; and whether government would have to "occupy the field" if the body were not already performing the functions it does. A body or tribunal will be subject to public law, and therefore judicial review, if it is "part of the machinery of government."[97]

In addition to determining whether a tribunal is a sufficiently "public" body, a party seeking to challenge administrative action should determine whether he or she has *standing* to challenge a tribunal decision. The answer will be straightforward for individuals that are actual parties to an administrative action, but other persons may have a collateral interest in the same matter and may want to challenge a tribunal order that does not directly affect them. The question of standing, including "public interest" standing, is discussed by Lorne Sossin in chapter 15.

---

95 Private tribunals may also owe a duty of fairness that can be enforced through the private law remedies of declaration and injunction. However, these private law remedies are outside the scope of this chapter.

96 But consider the improper purpose doctrine: *Shell Canada Products Ltd. v. Vancouver (City)*, [1994] 1 S.C.R. 231.

97 *McDonald v. Anishinabek Police Service et al.* (2006), 83 O.R. (3d) 132 (Div. Ct.).

Third, a party seeking to challenge administrative action should determine to which court he or she should apply for judicial review. Both the provincial superior courts and the Federal Courts have judicial review jurisdiction. Which court has jurisdiction to conduct judicial review, unlike appeals, is not usually set out in a tribunal's enabling statute. Typically, the choice of courts is determined by whether the source of the impugned authority's power is provincial or federal.[98] Some overarching provincial statutes, such as Ontario's *Judicial Review Procedure Act*, stipulate the particular provincial court to which judicial review applications should be brought.[99]

Fourth, a party should ensure that he or she has not missed any deadlines. Some statutes impose time limits within which a party must file an application for judicial review. For example, the *Federal Courts Act* states than a judicial review application from a federal tribunal to the Federal Court must be made within 30 days of the time the underlying decision or order is first communicated.[100] In Alberta and Nova Scotia, court rules set a six-month time limit for certain kinds of judicial review.[101] In British Columbia, the general time limit is 60 days.[102] Parties should therefore check all applicable statutes, including the tribunal's enabling statutes, global procedural and judicial review acts, and Rules of Court, for time limits. However, courts are often statutorily empowered to extend the time limit for making a judicial review application—for example, where there is a reasonable explanation for the delay, where no substantial prejudice or hardship would result from such an extension, and/or where the party can demonstrate prima facie grounds for relief.[103]

The final threshold matter that a party must establish, before gaining access to judicial review, is that he or she has exhausted all other adequate means of recourse for challenging the tribunal's actions.[104] Depending on the tribunal's enabling statute, this may include almost any of the remedies above: reconsideration by the same tribunal, appeals to appellate tribunals and other intra-agency mechanisms such as grievance arbitration, and appeals to court. However, some factors may render an alternative form of review inadequate. For example, appeal mechanisms provided for by statute will be inadequate where:

98 There are some exceptions. Provincial superior courts have concurrent or exclusive jurisdiction over some specific aspects of federal statutory regimes, due to both the *Constitution Act, 1982* and the *Federal Courts Act*, R.S.C. 1985, c. F-7. In particular, provincial superior courts have concurrent jurisdiction where Charter issues are raised in attacks on federal legislative regimes. *Reza v. Canada*, [1994] 2 S.C.R. 394.

99 Ontario *Judicial Review Procedure Act* (JRPA), R.S.O. 1990, c. J.1, s. 6, says that judicial review applications shall be made to the Divisional Court, unless "the case is one of urgency and … the delay required for an application to the Divisional Court is likely to involve a failure of justice," in which case an application may be made to the Superior Court of Justice.

100 *Federal Courts Act*, *supra* note 99, s. 18.1(2).

101 Rule 753.11(1) of the Alberta Rules of Court (Alta. Reg. 390/68) imposes this time limit where the relief sought is the setting aside of a decision or act; Rule 56.06, *Nova Scotia Civil Procedure Rules, 1971* imposes the time limit on applications for relief in the nature of certiorari. Online: http://www.courts.ns.ca/Rules/rule56_61.htm. See, for example, *Marvel Metal & Glass Products Ltd. v. Annapolis (County)* (2002), 202 N.S.R. (2d) 18 (S.C.).

102 *Administrative Tribunals Act*, *supra* note 37, s. 57(1).

103 For example, Ontario *Judicial Review Procedure Act*, *supra* note 100, s. 5; British Columbia *Administrative Tribunals Act*, *supra* note 37, s. 57(2). The *Federal Courts Act*, *supra* note 99, does not set out the conditions that must be met in order for the court to grant an extension of time: s. 18.1(2).

104 *Harelkin v. University of Regina*, [1979] 2 S.C.R 561, 96 D.L.R. (3d) 14.

Inadequate where:

1. the appellate tribunal lacks statutory authority over, or is not willing to address, the issues the appellant raises;[105]
2. the appellate tribunal does not have statutory authority to grant the remedy the appellant requests;[106]
3. the appeal must be based on the record before the original tribunal, but that record does not include evidence relevant to the applicant,[107] or includes evidentiary errors that the appellate tribunal lacks authority to correct;[108] or
4. the alternative procedure is too inefficient or costly.[109]

An alternative form of appeal will not be inadequate based only on unproven allegations that an appellate tribunal will suffer from the same errors[110] or biases[111] as the original tribunal. Nor will allegations that the original tribunal lacked jurisdiction allow challengers to circumvent available appeals in favour of judicial review.[112] Also, at least in the context of Aboriginal self-government in the taxation field, the fact that appellate tribunal members lack indicia of institutional independence—that is, they may not be paid, they lack security of tenure, and they are appointed by the people whose claims they have to adjudicate—will not make that appellate body "inadequate" without concrete evidence of a lack of independence in practice.[113]

Several provinces have also legislated in this area. For example, the *Federal Courts Act* prohibits judicial review by the Federal Court, if there is an available appeal of a tribunal's decision to the Federal Court. Quebec's *Code of Civil Procedure* also prohibits a superior court from applying Quebec's version of certiorari to a tribunal decision where an appeal is available, unless the tribunal lacked or exceeded its statutory authority. On the other hand, Ontario's *Judicial Review Procedure Act* and Prince Edward Island's *Judicial Review Act* both permit judicial review notwithstanding any right of appeal.[114] Of course, the fact

105 *Canadian Pacific Ltd. v. Matsqui Indian Band*, [1995] S.C.J. No. 1 (per La Forest and Major JJ.) [*Matsqui*]; *Violette v. Dental Society*, [2004] 267 N.B.R. (2d) 205 (C.A.); *Kingsbury v. Heighton* (2003), 230 D.L.R. (4th) 654 (C.A.).

106 *Evershed v. Ontario* (1985), 50 O.R. (2d) 198 at 200 (C.A.).

107 *V.S.R. Investments Ltd. v. Laczko* (1983), 41 O.R. (2d) 62 (Div Ct.).

108 *Cimolai v. Children's and Women's Health Centre* (2003), 228 D.L.R. (4th) 420 at 443-46 ((B.C.C.A.) [*Cimolai*].

109 *Violette v. Dental Society*, *supra* note 105.

110 *Harelkin*, *supra* note 105; but see, *contra*, *Cimolai*, *supra* note 108.

111 *Turnbull v. Canadian Institute of Actuaries* (1995), 129 D.L.R. (4th) 42 (C.A.); but see, *contra*, *Batorski v. Moody* (1983), 42 O.R. (2d) 647 (Div. Ct.).

112 *Bayne (Rural Municipality No. 371) v. Saskatchewan Water Corp.* (1990), 46 Admin. L.R. 23 (Sask. C.A.); *Delmas v. Vancouver Stock Exchange* (1994), 27 Admin. L.R. (2d) 294 (S.C.), aff'd (1995), 15 B.C.L.R. (3d) 136 (C.A.).

113 *Matsqui*, *supra* note 106. It should be emphasized that, because judicial review is basically a discretionary remedy, a court has substantial freedom to exercise its discretion and grant judicial review even where an apparently adequate alternative remedy exists. A court also has substantial freedom to exercise its discretion to refuse to entertain a judicial review application even where no adequate alternative remedy exists.

114 See, respectively, the *Federal Courts Act*, *supra* note 99, s. 185; *Code of Civil Procedure*, R.S.Q. c. C-25, art. 846; *Judicial Review Procedure Act*, *supra* note 100, s. 2(1); *Judicial Review Act* (JRA), R.S.P.E.I. 1988, c. J-3, s. 4(2).

that a court *may* grant judicial review, even where a right of appeal exists, does not mean that it *will* do so. Indeed, courts are reluctant to do so.[115]

E. Remedies on Judicial Review

The remedies available on judicial review have their roots in the ancient prerogative writs, discussed further, below. Over time, they became unwieldy. In many provinces they were modified by statute to redress problems arising from the writs' extreme technicality and unjustified narrowness. However, it is still necessary to understand the ancient writs to understand the scope and range of remedies available. For example, neither the old writs nor the reform statutes, which are based on the old writs, permit a court on judicial review to substitute its views on the substance of a matter for the tribunal's views. The old writs also continue to operate in some provinces, albeit in a more limited way.[116]

A party contemplating judicial review should also be aware that unlike an appeal, an application for judicial review usually does *not* automatically stay the enforcement of the underlying tribunal order, although the tribunal or the court or both may have the power to stay the tribunal's order on application.[117] Indeed, presumably in order to keep the Canadian banking and financial systems operating smoothly, one federal statute that establishes securities clearing houses and banking and payment systems stipulates that *no* stay shall be granted for a judicial review application related to the government's administration of those systems.[118] The legislative decision to make stays automatic for many appeals but not for judicial review applications is consistent with the "last resort" nature of judicial review. The rules regarding stays vary from jurisdiction to jurisdiction and from tribunal to tribunal, so parties seeking a stay should be sure to review the relevant enabling statute, as well as the Rules of Court and any omnibus statutes governing procedure or judicial review.

The following sections introduce the prerogative writs and subsequent statutory reform. Because judicial review remains a fundamentally discretionary power, courts can and do use their discretion to refuse to grant a remedy. The bases on which courts have refused to grant a remedy are also discussed below.

---

115 *Odufowora v. Ontario (Board of Inquiry)* (1994), 76 O.A.C. 385 (Div. Ct.); *McKenna's Furniture Store v. Prince Edward Island (Fire Marshall)*, [1997] 152 Nfld. & P.E.I.R. 212 (P.E.I.S.C.(T.D.)).

116 For example, the "direct action in nullity" is a judicial review remedy that predates the Quebec *Code of Civil Procedure*, R.S.Q. 1977, c. C-25, and is not referred to in it, yet it continues to operate: *Immeubles Port Louis Ltée v. Lafontaine (Village)*, *supra* note 91. In New Brunswick, one cannot apply specifically for the traditional prerogative writs of certiorari, mandamus, or prohibition, which are now available simply as judicial review. However, a range of "alternative" remedies echoing the old prerogative writs continues to exist. See, for example, *Sullivan v. Greater Moncton Planning District Commission* (1993), 132 N.B.R. (2d) 285 (T.D.). Manitoba's Court of Queen's Bench Rules, Man. Reg. 553/88, Rule 68.01, states only that "[a] Judge on application may grant an order of mandamus, prohibition, certiorari or quo warranto." Yukon Territory has not enacted any statutory changes to the common-law writs.

117 See, for example, Ontario *Statutory Powers Procedure Act*, *supra* note 38, s. 25 (an appeal acts as a stay but judicial review is not an appeal for that purpose); New Brunswick *Energy and Utilities Board Act*, S.N.B. 2006, c. E-9.18, s. 52(2) (judicial review does not automatically stay an order, but the board itself or the Court of Appeal may stay it).

118 *Canadian Payments Act*, R.S.C. 1985, c. C-21, s. 46.

1. Introduction to the Prerogative Writs

Certiorari is the most commonly used prerogative remedy, both historically and today. Certiorari ("cause to be certified") is a special proceeding by which a superior court requires some inferior tribunal, board, or judicial officer to provide it with the record of its proceedings, for review for excess of jurisdiction. It was the established method by which the Court of King's Bench in England, from earliest times, checked the jurisdiction of inferior courts and maintained the supremacy of the royal courts. Indeed, in the United States, the vast majority of applications to the US Supreme Court are still made by way of a petition for certiorari. A successful certiorari application results in the "quashing" (effectively, the invalidating) of a tribunal's order or decision. It is an ex post facto remedy. Note, however, that generally the court cannot substitute its decision for the decision of a tribunal that the court finds had erred, because the court has not been granted the statutory decision-making authority and does not have the expertise that the tribunal has.[119]

The related writ of *prohibition* is another special proceeding, issued by an appellate court to prevent a lower court from exceeding its jurisdiction, or to prevent a non-judicial officer or entity from exercising a power. Prohibition is a kind of common-law injunction to prevent an unlawful assumption of jurisdiction. Unlike certiorari, which provides relief after a decision is made, prohibition is used to obtain relief pre-emptively. It arrests the proceedings of any tribunal, board, or person exercising judicial functions in a manner or by means not within its jurisdiction or discretion.

Mandamus (literally, "we command") is a writ issued by a superior court to compel a lower court or a government agency to perform a duty it is mandated to perform. In practice, it is often combined with an application for certiorari. Certiorari would be used to quash a decision, for example, for a lack of procedural fairness, while mandamus would be used to force the tribunal to reconsider the matter in a procedurally fair manner. A variation on mandamus is the court's ability to send a matter back to a tribunal for reconsideration with directions. Superior courts have the inherent power to order reconsideration with directions, and several provincial statutes and rules of court, as well as the *Federal Courts Act*, also grant this power. If the court issues directions, it must clearly state what the original panel is to do or what it must refrain from doing. These directions may only protect against unfair procedures or excess of power, and cannot direct the tribunals to decide in a particular way.

A *declaration* is a judgment of a court that determines the legal position of the parties, or the law that applies to them. There are two kinds of declarations: the public law variety, used to declare some government action ultra vires, and the private law variety, used to clarify the law or declare a private party's rights under a statute. The public law variety is the main concern of administrative law. Declarations are not enforceable, and they cannot require anyone to take or refrain from taking any action. Historically, this made declarations useful in actions against the Crown itself because the traditional common-law position was that relief in the nature of mandamus was not available against the Crown. It was not

119 In exceptional circumstances, a court will nevertheless make the decision that it finds the original tribunal ought to have made. See, for example, *Renaud v. Québec (Commission des affaires sociales)*, [1999] S.C.J. No. 70, 184 D.L.R. (4th) 441; *Corp. of the Canadian Civil Liberties Assn. v. Ontario (Civilian Commission on Police Services)* (2002), 61 O.R. (3d) 649 (C.A.); *Allman v. Amacon Property Management Services Inc.*, [2007] B.C.J. No. 1144 (C.A.).

thought appropriate for a court to order enforcement against the Crown because the Crown was the source of its own authority. (These prohibitions on remedies against the Crown itself were substantially, though not completely, relaxed over the course of the 20th century.) The non-coercive nature of the remedy has not generally proven to be a problem, because court declarations against government bodies in particular tend to be respected.[120]

Less common these days are the writs of habeas corpus and quo warranto. *Habeas corpus* (literally, "produce the body") is a writ employed to bring a person before a court, most frequently to ensure that the person's imprisonment or detention is not illegal. Like certiorari, habeas corpus continues to live an active life in the United States, where it is the primary mechanism for challenging state death penalty sentences in federal court. In Canada, habeas corpus applications are rare, and are mostly made by prisoners detained in correctional institutions, and by police, immigration, child welfare, and mental health detainees. *Quo warranto* ("by what warrant?" or "by what authority?") is a writ used to inquire into what authority existed to justify acts by or powers claimed by a public office. It is rarely used today, and some provinces have abolished it by statute.[121] However, quo warranto is still used in Quebec and New Brunswick to challenge the authority of municipal councillors on the basis of a prohibited conflict of interest.[122]

2. Statutory Reform

Over time, each of the prerogative writs above came to be characterized by technical complexity and arcane rules. Potentially meritorious applications were dismissed because the applicant had petitioned for the wrong writ, or because his or her claim was barred by some technical limitation. For example, although court decisions later re-expanded the writ's scope, a number of cases in Canada in the 1960s and 1970s held that certiorari and prohibition were only available to address "judicial" or "quasi-judicial" final decisions that affected the rights of citizens. Policy reasons for maintaining the distinction between the various writs eroded.

The result, in many provinces and at the Federal Court,[123] was statutory reform. Some provinces enacted omnibus statutes governing judicial review or statutory/civil procedure,[124]

120 *Lount Corp. v. Canada (Attorney General)*, [1984] 1 F.C. 332 at 365 (T.D.) (noting that "by long tradition, the executive abides by declarations of the Court even though not formally or specifically directed to do so"), aff'd *sub nom. Canada (Attorney General) v. Lount Corp.*, [1985] 2 F.C. 185 (C.A.).

121 For example, PEI JRA, *supra* note 115, s. 11; British Columbia *Judicial Review Procedure Act* (BC JRPA), R.S.B.C. 1996, c. 241, s. 18. These statutes provide that certain remedies for what would have been an information in the nature of quo warranto are still available.

122 See, for example, *R. v. Wheeler*, [1979] 2 S.C.R. 650.

123 *Federal Courts Act*, *supra* note 99, s. 18(1), provides that the Federal Court has exclusive original jurisdiction "to issue an injunction, writ of certiorari, writ of prohibition, writ of mandamus or writ of quo warranto, or grant declaratory relief, against any federal board, commission or other tribunal."

124 Ontario JRPA, BC JRPA, PEI JRA, Quebec *Code of Civil Procedure*, R.S.Q. c. C-25. Ontario and British Columbia have enacted the most comprehensive reforms. Readers should be aware that, apart from habeas corpus, terminology in Quebec is different. For example, prohibition and certiorari are codified under "evocation" and "revision" in s. 846 of the *Civil Code*. Remedies equivalent to quo warranto and mandamus are codified under ss. 838 and 844ff respectively, and the terms "quo warranto" and "mandamus" are used in practice, but they do not appear in the Code. There also exists the "declaratory judgment in motion," codified at s. 453, which allows a party to have his or her rights "declared."

while others used their Rules of Court to enact changes.[125] Only Yukon Territory seems to have left the common law untouched. The details vary from one statutory scheme to another, but key features include the following.

1. The statutes generally provide for simplified application procedures. For example, they may state that applications for orders "in the nature of" mandamus, prohibition, or certiorari shall be deemed to be applications for judicial review, to be brought by way of an originating notice or petition. The new judicial review application combines, and in the process supersedes, the old writs of certiorari, prohibition, mandamus, public law declaration, and injunction. (Some statutes include quo warranto and habeas corpus within the ambit of the statute; some abolish quo warranto; some provinces have a dedicated *Habeas Corpus Act*.) It is sufficient for a party to set out the grounds on which relief is sought and the nature of the relief sought, without having to specify under which particular writ he or she might have proceeded at common law.
2. The statutory schemes provide for simplified remedies including, for example, the power to set aside a decision or direct the tribunal to reconsider its decision, with or without directions. Some statutes also set out the court's ability to ignore technical irregularities or defects in form if the court finds no substantial wrong or miscarriage of justice has occurred.
3. The statutes generally clarify who may be parties—for example, decision-makers whose exercise of statutory authority is being questioned may be parties to a hearing. Also, they provide that notice must be given to the attorney general, who is entitled as of right to be heard on the application.
4. The statutes generally provide for a right of appeal: judicial review applications are generally made to provincial superior courts, and the statutes provide for a subsequent right of appeal to the provincial Court of Appeal.
5. The statutes may also address the inability of judicial review mechanisms to challenge interlocutory orders and to resolve interim issues. At common law, certiorari was only available with respect to "decisions"—that is, final orders. However, the British Columbia and Ontario *Judicial Review Procedure Acts* use the words "exercise of statutory power," rather than the word "decision," thereby expanding the range of judicial review to include any exercise of statutory power.[126] Other statutes permit a tribunal itself to refer a "stated case" up to the courts for determination of a question of law, after which the whole case can go back to the original tribunal for determination of the ultimate issues.[127] For example, BC tribunals that do not have jurisdiction over constitutional questions can issue a stay and refer a constitutional question to a court of competent jurisdiction.[128] Enabling statutes must authorize stated cases.

125 Alberta, Manitoba, New Brunswick, Newfoundland, Northwest Territories, Nova Scotia, Nunavut, and Saskatchewan.

126 BC JRPA, *supra* note 122, s. 3; Ontario JRPA, *supra* note 100, s. 2.

127 For example, *Federal Courts Act*, *supra* note 99, s. 18.3; BC *Administrative Tribunals Act*, *supra* note 37, s. 43.

128 *Ibid.*, ss. 44, 45.

3. Discretionary Bases for Refusing a Remedy

As alluded to above, on judicial review courts have discretion to refuse a remedy even where one is clearly warranted by the facts of a case.[129] The common-law discretionary grounds for refusing relief have survived statutory reform of judicial review. The most important basis for refusing to grant a remedy in judicial review is discussed above: that *adequate alternative remedies are available*. Parties should exhaust all prescribed avenues of appeal before proceeding to the "last resort" of judicial review.

Judicial review applications that are brought before tribunal proceedings have been concluded are usually dismissed as being *premature*. This includes challenges to the tribunal's interim procedural and evidentiary rulings. Policy rationales that underlie dismissals for prematurity include the following: (1) administrative action is meant to be more cost-effective than court proceedings, and interim judicial review fragments and protracts those proceedings; (2) preliminary complaints may become moot as the proceedings progress; and (3) the court will be in a better position to assess the situation after a full and complete record of tribunal proceedings exists.[130] To obtain judicial review of a tribunal's preliminary or interim ruling, an applicant must show special circumstances that cannot wait until the conclusion of the proceeding. A challenge to the legality of the tribunal itself, a clear question of law about the tribunal's jurisdiction, or the absence of an appropriate remedy at the end of the proceedings could constitute special or exceptional circumstances.[131]

Even if statutory time limits for filing a judicial review application have been met, parties must be aware that *delay and acquiescence* may be bases for a reviewing court to refuse a remedy.[132] Parties should object promptly to any perceived impropriety on the part of the tribunal. Similarly, choosing not to attend a hearing waives any right to judicial review.

In addition, a remedy in judicial review will not be granted where the issues are *moot*. This may be the case where a dispute is over or has not yet arisen, where a tribunal's order has expired or no longer affects the applicant, or where the litigant no longer desires the remedy that the tribunal might have granted had it not erred.[133] The court may also refuse to provide the remedy the tribunal would have granted if present circumstances make doing so impossible, or if the court believes the tribunal's error did not affect its overall conclusion.[134]

---

129 *Immeubles Port Louis Ltée v. Lafontaine (Village)*, *supra* note 91. An interesting case that discusses the discretionary bases for refusing a remedy in the nature of mandamus, in the context of an interface between a private highway-operating company and a public statutory decision maker, is *407 ETR Concession Co. v. Ontario (Registrar of Motor Vehicles)*, [2005] O.J. No. 4830 (Div. Ct.).

130 See, for example, *Sherman v. Canada (Canada Customs and Revenue Agency)*, [2006] F.C.J. No. 912; *Zündel v. Canada (Human Rights Commission)*, [2000] 4 F.C. 255 (C.A.); *Quebec (Procureur general) v. Boulaine*, [2004] J.Q. no. 4883 (C.A.), leave to SCC refused [2004] C.S.C.R. No. 290.

131 *Secord v. Saint John (City) Board of Police Commissioners*, [2006] N.B.J. No. 84 (Q.B.); *Howe v. Institute of Chartered Accountants of Ontario* (1994), 19 O.R. (3d) 483 (C.A.).

132 *Immeubles Port Louis*, *supra* note 91.

133 *Borowski v. Canada (Attorney General)*, [1989] 1 S.C.R. 342 at 353; *Bago v. Canada (Minister of Citizenship and Immigration)*, [2004] F.C.J. No. 1565.

134 *Moose Jaw Central Bingo Assn. Inc. v. Saskatchewan (Liquor & Gaming Authority)* (1994), 123 Sask. R. 47 (C.A.); *Mobil Oil Canada Ltd. v. Canada-Nfld. Offshore Petroleum Board*, [1994] 1 S.C.R. 202.

Last, the court will use its discretion to refuse to grant a remedy on judicial review where the party making the judicial review application *does not come with clean hands*. This could include seeking a remedy to facilitate illegal conduct or obtain an unfair advantage, or flouting the law or making misrepresentations.[135]

F. Private Law Remedies

Private law remedies available to parties, as against administrative agencies, are outside the scope of administrative action and judicial review. At the same time, increasingly frequent attempts to seek private law remedies from public bodies have put pressure on judicial review doctrine. The key issue is that neither the old prerogative writs, nor the new statutory remedy of judicial review, allow a party to link a judicial review remedy with a claim for monetary relief (that is, damages or restitution). In some circumstances, unhappy parties would likely prefer monetary relief to available remedies under judicial review, such as having a tribunal reconsider its decision.

The Crown and its servants can be liable to private parties for monetary relief,[136] although some statutes limit individual administrative tribunal members' liability.[137] However, to seek monetary relief, an aggrieved party must initiate a separate civil action for restitution or damages alongside, or in lieu of, a judicial review application. Parties are doing so and, although they have had limited success so far in pushing judicial review to one side, these actions illustrate the remedy-driven nature of the law in this area.

Government agencies can be sued—for example, for the tort of negligence or the special tort of misfeasance in (or abuse of) public office. The latter requires the plaintiff to prove, in addition to the basic elements of negligence, deliberate and unlawful conduct by someone in public office, and the public officer's subjective knowledge that the conduct was unlawful and likely to harm the plaintiff. The underlying purpose of the tort is to protect each citizen's reasonable expectation that public officials will not intentionally injure members of the public through deliberate and unlawful conduct in the exercise of public functions.[138] The leading case on the tort of misfeasance in public office, *Odhavji*, involved an action for damages against police officers and the Chief of the Metropolitan Toronto Police by the estate of an individual shot by the police. The plaintiffs alleged that the police officers involved in the shooting did not promptly or fully comply with their statutory duty to cooperate with an ensuing investigation, and that the chief of police did not adequately compel

---

135 *Cosman Realty Ltd. v. Winnipeg (City)* (2001), 157 Man. R. (2d) 117 (Q.B.), aff'd (2001), 160 Man. R. (2d) 32 (C.A.); *Jaouadi v. Canada (Minister of Citizenship and Immigration)* (2003), 257 F.T.R. 161.

136 The Federal Court has concurrent original jurisdiction over all actions for damages against the federal Crown. Individual servants of the Crown, including ministers, are also liable for breaches of private law duties on the same basis as other individuals. *Federal Courts Act*, *supra* note 99, s. 17; *Peter G. White Management Ltd. v. Canada (Minister of Canadian Heritage)*, [2007] 2 F.C.R. 475 (C.A.).

137 For example, BC *Administrative Tribunals Act*, *supra* note 37, s. 56.

138 *Odhavji Estate v. Woodhouse*, [2003] 3 S.C.R. 263. Note, however, that the Crown's prerogative power to grant honours (and potentially other prerogative powers that may remain with the Crown) are not justiciable in the courts and cannot form the basis of an action for misfeasance in public office: *Black v. Canada (Prime Minister)* (2001), 199 D.L.R. (4th) 228 (Ont. C.A.).

them to cooperate. The case made its way to the Supreme Court of Canada on the defendant's motion to dismiss the plaintiff's claim, where the Court determined that the plaintiff had made out a cause of action and that the matter should be allowed to proceed. In other words, the Court held that there was such a thing as the tort of misfeasance in public office.

As this case makes clear, some torts overlap with a potential judicial review application while others do not. Judicial review was not a possibility in *Odhavji* because no tribunal decision was being challenged. By contrast, where judicial review of a tribunal decision is available, courts are less willing to entertain civil actions for monetary relief. For example, a party who wishes to attack a decision of a federal institution, like a federal penitentiary, does not have the option of proceeding either by judicial review or by way of an action even if both are theoretically available under the relevant statute. Where judicial review is available, the party must proceed by judicial review.[139] Courts will approach the tort of misfeasance in public office with caution in such circumstances, although it is not totally precluded. The caution reflects concerns about the importance of finality in administrative decisions, and about circumventing courts' normally deferential stance toward tribunals through collateral attacks on government bodies. As Madam Justice Newbury of the British Columbia Court of Appeal has stated,

> the tort [of misfeasance in public office] must be used cautiously. Otherwise, the courts risk straying into the arena of political decision-making, bypassing the normal restraints associated with judicial review, and becoming the arbiters of the personal thought processes of public officials. One recent commentator has written that the court should not, by means of the tort, take on the role of "ombudsman, a parliamentary committee, or an organ of public opinion in reviewing even egregious acts of maladministration, official incompetence, or bad judgement." To avoid dangers of this kind, a balance must be sought between curbing unlawful behaviour on the part of governmental officials on the one hand, and on the other, protecting officials who are charged with making decisions for the public good, from unmeritorious claims by persons adversely affected by such decisions.[140]

V. CONCLUSION

A goal of this chapter has been to put judicial review in context, both chronologically and conceptually. Administrative law remedies are the product of multiple forces and priorities, often acting in tension with each other. They need to be considered in light of the tug-of-war between courts and legislators as demonstrated by, for example, legislators' creation of internal appeal mechanisms and courts' periodic circumvention of those internal appeals in favour of immediate judicial review. Another recurring theme is the tug-of-war between tribunals and the courts that oversee them, in terms of courts' willingness to recognize and give effect to potentially creative and uncourtlike tribunal remedies. These tensions are emblematic of a deeper contest between deeply held values around the rule of law on the one hand, and administrative expertise, efficiency, and democratic accountability on the other.

139 *The Queen v. Grenier* (2005), 262 D.L.R. (4th) 337 (F.C.A.).

140 *Powder Mountain Resorts Ltd. v. British Columbia* (2001), 94 B.C.L.R. (3d) 14 at para. 2 (C.A.) (citations omitted).

Administrative law remedies are also path-dependent, meaning that they have been shaped by their historical origins in the prerogative writs and by subsequent, sometimes piecemeal, attempts to modify judicial review. If we were to design a set of remedies out of whole cloth today, it is not obvious that we would necessarily decide to set up two separate mechanisms for accessing the courts (that is, statutory appeals and judicial review). Rather, we might create an overarching administrative review tribunal like Quebec's. The point here is that remedies have been influenced by their historical roots, and remedies in turn have influenced the development of administrative law as a whole.

In part, as a corrective for the conventional emphasis on judicial review and its idiosyncracies, this chapter tries to situate judicial review remedies within a larger context. A panoply of other remedies is available at different stages of administrative action. A rich debate (or several rich debates) exists concerning appropriate tribunal functioning and the proper scope of tribunal action. Tribunals develop remedies that are novel, by court standards, because they are differently constituted than courts are. It is the heterogeneity and depth of this experience that underlies the modern instinct, exemplified by the *Domtar* case, that courts should practise humility in exercising judicial review of tribunal decisions. This chapter also counsels respect for that difference. A conversation about administrative law remedies illustrates the larger point that animates much of this volume: judicial review and court-centred processes, which make up the bulk of this book, are nevertheless the "tail" of administrative law and practice. That tail, fascinating though it is, should not limit our appreciation of, and approach to, the complex and varied species of "dog" that administrative action represents.

SUGGESTED ADDITIONAL READINGS

CASES

407 ETR Concession Co. v. Ontario (Registrar of Motor Vehicles), [2005] O.J. No. 4830 (Div. Ct.).

Domtar v. Quebec (Commission d'appel en matière de lésions professionnelles), [1993] 2 S.C.R. 756 at 795. "The advisability of judicial intervention in the event of conflicting decisions among administrative tribunals, even when serious and unquestionable, cannot, in these circumstances, be determined solely by the 'triumph' of the rule of law. Where decisions made within jurisdiction are not patently unreasonable, the issue instead turns on whether the principles underlying curial deference should give way to other imperatives. In my opinion, the answer is no."

Harelkin v. University of Regina, [1979] 2 S.C.R. 561, re whether judicial review can jump the queue of statutory appeals—what constitutes "adequate alternative remedy."

McDonald v. Anishinabek Police Service et al. (2006), 83 O.R. (3d) 132 (Div. Ct.), on whether a particular body is a public body for purposes of judicial review.

McKinnon v. Ontario, [2003] O.J. No. 893 (Div. Ct.).

STATUTES

Relevant judicial review procedure acts, administrative tribunals acts, and rules of court (professors should incorporate their provinces' statutes or Rules of Court, if any, governing judicial review).

CHAPTER FOUR

Governments in Miniature: The Rule of Law in the Administrative State

MARY LISTON*

Centre for Ethics, University of Toronto

---

* Postdoctoral Fellow in Ethics and Law, Centre for Ethics, University of Toronto. I would like to thank David Duff, Colleen Flood, Evan Fox-Decent, Zvi Halpern, and Audrey Macklin for their careful analysis of the arguments and thoughtful suggestions for improvement.

I. INTRODUCTION

If there is one concept that ties together the seemingly disparate strands of administrative law, it is surely the rule of law. This chapter discusses several attributes of the rule of law and explores their relevance for Canadian administrative law. Although it is unlikely that the rule of law will constitute a direct and complete basis for answering a law exam question, the puzzles and tensions that administrative law evokes cannot be understood without recourse to this foundational concept.

Part II presents several of the main features of the rule of law: the rule of law as a constitutional principle, the rule of law as a political ideal involving a matrix of institutional relations and competencies, and the rule of law as a distinctive political morality.[1] Part III of this chapter assesses the Canadian articulation of the rule of law in the jurisprudence of the Supreme Court of Canada. The fourth part focuses on judicial review of administrative action as a key component of the rule of law. The conclusion argues that at least for Canadian administrative law, the rule of law is best conceived as an open set of institutional practices entailing shared responsibility for upholding the content of the rule of law, a responsibility that is distributed within and among coordinate institutions.

II. THE RULE OF LAW IN THEORY

Certain philosophical concepts—for example, democracy, freedom, autonomy, equality, rights, and the rule of law—do not have a firmly agreed-upon core of meaning and therefore can be considered essentially contested.[2] Despite this uncertain state of philosophical affairs, this part suggests that the rule of law can be characterized by three interrelated features: a jurisprudential principle of legality; an activity or practice of law-making among and within an institutional arrangement of government; and a distinctive political morality. Together, these three features affirm the rule of law as an overarching normative relationship among legal subjects and the state, seeking to prevent the arbitrary use of power, and encouraging appropriate forms of responsiveness among government institutions and between these institutions and affected individuals. While this presentation may initially seem

---

1 By political morality, I mean principles of justice that are publicly endorsed; constitute the political relationship between the state, groups, and individuals; and inform political and legal practices. These principles justify the use of coercive state power, power that the state claims universal authority to exercise over members of a political community. Principles of justice ought to be enforced by the state in society as well as within state institutions. Political morality, because it is public, is distinguishable from various private moralities that establish relations, rights, and duties among individuals. The legal and political dimensions of a political morality come together in judicial review in, for example, how judges understand their role in upholding fidelity to the concept of the rule of law in a constitutional order. Different political moralities, for example, provide different justifications for the supervisory role of courts and the scope of judicial power.

2 For an elucidation of the nature of "essentially contested concepts" with reference to the rule of law, see Jeremy Waldron, "Is the Rule of Law an Essentially Contested Concept (in Florida)?" (2002) 21 Law & Phil. 137. Waldron discusses how disagreements about underlying normative issues—issues such as what values the rule of law is meant to promote or what is the best understanding of the rule of law—are pervasive and predictable. Despite such ever-present disagreements, rival conceptions may in fact agree on many of the particular attributes or features that make up a complex concept. They may, however, disagree about the most important features, or what features are necessary but not sufficient, or about how the features work together in a successful application of the concept.

uncontroversial, deeply embedded within any discussion of the rule of law is a debate about the legitimate scope and content of judicial power, particularly in a democratic state.

A. The Purpose of the Rule of Law: The Non-Arbitrary Rule of Men (and Women)

Since Plato and Aristotle, the rule of law has been contrasted with the rule of men. Fundamentally, the rule of law means that government action must always be sourced in law and therefore bound by law in order to be considered both valid and legitimate. In practice, the rule of law requires that legal and political institutions and their associated practices control both overt and latent forms of arbitrariness within the exercise of public authority in modern states. The concept of arbitrariness itself admits many meanings, though law students will recognize several of these meanings as the concrete subject matter of administrative law.

Arbitrariness connotes an indifference about the procedures chosen to reach an outcome. One could, for example, either toss a coin or play a game of rock-paper-scissors to make a choice; the means do not necessarily matter for the quality of the outcome. More problematically, arbitrariness can also suggest that a decision-maker possesses unconstrained discretionary powers, such that he or she alone can decide on how to use these expansive powers; hence, arbitrariness can be associated with a unilateral mode of decision-making or one that is not fully reciprocal, consultative, or participatory. Most familiarly, arbitrariness is expressed in the idea of an untrammelled exercise of will, or the uncontrolled power, of an authority. A decision, for example, may exhibit unilateralness to a degree that becomes oppressive and will therefore be considered arbitrary or illegitimate; in other words, an abuse of power. This understanding informs familiar criticisms of majority decision-making that infringes minority rights. Finally, arbitrariness seems to suggest the opposite of a rule, although a rule can be applied arbitrarily by judges or administrators.

All branches of government—executive, legislative, judicial, administrative—can manifest arbitrary behaviour in relation to individuals, groups, or other parts of government. If a branch of government steps outside its allotted constitutional role or function, the action or decision will be considered arbitrary in the sense that it is ultra vires (that is, beyond the powers of) its jurisdictional limits. Division of powers cases in Canadian federalism provide examples of this kind of legal wrong. If a branch of government attempts to monopolize governmental power, or encroaches on the powers of another branch, this action will offend the doctrine of the separation of powers, a principle that authorizes a particular distribution of political power within a state. The action or decision will be considered not to be sourced in law and will be found invalid or void for that reason. If a decision-maker in government uses statutory discretion outside the purpose of the enabling statute, the resultant decision will be found arbitrary in the sense of being incorrect in law. In all of these examples, government action will be found invalid because it offends procedural justice (otherwise known as natural justice or fairness) or because it violates the formally authorized allocation of institutional roles and responsibilities in a constitution.

In contrast to the quality or appropriateness of the means used by a public authority, the decision itself may be arbitrary in substance because it is biased, illogical, unreasonable, or capricious. In other words, it will offend what appear to be shared standards of reasonableness, rationality, or morality. Such a decision may exhibit a lack of care, concern, or reflection on the part of the decision-maker toward the affected individual or group. It can, instead of a justified response, show mere opinion, preference, stereotyping, or negative discrimination. Arbitrariness in the activity of decision-making therefore includes both procedural and substantive elements and necessarily involves a normative view of the affected person(s). The normativity of a legal subject fundamentally concerns the person as a bearer of rights and responsibilities as well as an individual who enjoys autonomy, dignity, and equality. In other words, the affected person is treated as if he or she has worth as an individual, a citizen, and a member of his or her political community.[3]

The ever-present political and legal problem of the arbitrary use of public power profoundly animates rule of law concerns. Before turning to administrative law, however, this part considers legal and political theory in order to identify several features of the rule of law.

B. Attributes of the Rule of Law

The rule of law has a kind of "dual residency" in legal and political theory. In law, it acts as a constitutional metaprinciple that organizes and connects a subsidiary and open set of associated principles.[4] For example, the principle of the rule of law informs the principle of legality, the principle of the separation of powers, the principle of judicial independence, the principle of access to justice, the principles of fundamental justice, the proper administration of justice, and so on.[5] If the rule of law has a core of meaning in legal theory, it is the principle of legality. The import of the principle of legality for the rule of law is that it conveys the basic intuition that law should always authorize the use of public power and constrain the risk of the arbitrary use of public power. The principle of legality restrains arbitrary power in three ways: first, it constrains the actions of public officials; second, it regulates the activity of law-making; and third, it seeks to minimize harms that may be created by law itself. The views of three prominent legal theorists—Albert V. Dicey, Lon Fuller, and Joseph Raz—illustrate how the principle of legality constrains the misuse of public power in each of these ways.

The first model was most famously articulated by Albert V. Dicey in his theory of British constitutionalism. In Dicey's view, the rule of law possessed three features:

- the absence of arbitrary authority in government, but especially in the executive branch and the administrative state;

---

3 The benefits of the rule of law can extend to non-citizens who are present in Canadian territory. Evan Fox-Decent, in chapter 7, discusses how cases involving non-citizens in the immigration context have posed challenges for, and often been the source of extensions to the scope of, procedural fairness in administrative law.

4 See Friedrich A. von Hayek, *The Constitution of Liberty* (Chicago: University of Chicago Press, 1978) at 205 [Hayek].

5 These norms of legality differ according to the specific area of law. The principle of legality in criminal law, for example, includes the prohibition against retroactive criminalization or *ex post facto* laws as well as the void for vagueness doctrine with respect to provisions within criminal statutes. On the relationship between the rule of law and vagueness in constitutional law, chiefly in the criminal law area, see Marc Ribeiro, *Limiting Arbitrary Power: The Vagueness Doctrine in Canadian Constitutional Law* (Vancouver: University of British Columbia Press, 2004).

- formal legal equality so that every person—including and especially public officials—in the political community is subject to the law; and
- constitutional law that forms a binding part of the ordinary law of the land.

Common-law courts, in this model, provide the institutional connection between rights and remedies and are the site for the development of the general principles of the common-law constitution. According to Dicey, judge-made law combined with an unwritten constitution represented a better mode of legal constraint than written codes and constitutions because they were less vulnerable to executive attempts to suspend or remove rights. To take away the right to individual freedom in the English constitution, Dicey wrote, would require "a thorough revolution in the institutions and manners of the nation."[6] In a common-law constitutional system like Britain's, the constitution is not the source, but the consequence, of the rights of individuals as defined and enforced by the common-law courts. Dicey argued that this particular institutional advantage of the courts meant that they were best placed not only to control the political executive in the name of the rule of law, but also to provide superior protection of fundamental values, like liberty and property, in the English polity.

In the Diceyan model, Parliament was sovereign and supreme. Parliament was the source of all ordinary law[7] and ought to be the source of all governmental power. Any power that was not authorized by Parliament, or had acted beyond the powers delegated to it, would be considered ultra vires by the courts. This meant that administrative law played a particular controlling and legitimating function. In administrative law, the ultra vires principle traditionally provided a justification for curial intervention in order to control the scope of delegated power. Such justification, however, rested on a number of grounds, including (1) the institutional role of the courts as the principal external check on executive and agency powers; (2) the specific task allocated to the courts through administrative law to constrain administrative discretion by ensuring that an administrative body did not overstep the jurisdiction that the legislature had set down in the statute; and (3) the judicial perception that a fundamental role of courts was to protect and vindicate the private autonomy of affected individuals, primarily through common-law rights derived from contract, tort, and property.[8] One key consequence of the Diceyan model was that administrative bodies were viewed with distrust as almost inherently lawless forms of governance.[9] This perception worsened when it became clear that Parliament could no longer provide proper oversight of administrative agencies in the modern state through regular legislative scrutiny or through political practices centring on ministerial responsibility.

---

6 See Albert V. Dicey, *Introduction to the Study of the Law of the Constitution*, 8th ed. (Holmes Beach, FL: Gaunt, 1996) at 197.

7 Ordinary law usually means domestic law, and only international law if it has been incorporated by Parliament. This chapter focuses on domestic law. Gerald Heckman, in chapter 12, explores the relationship between international human rights norms and administrative law.

8 For a more detailed exposition of the implications of Dicey's ultra vires model, see Paul P. Craig, "The Nature and Purpose of Administrative Law" in *Administrative Law*, 5th ed. (London: Sweet & Maxwell, 2003) at 3.

9 See, for example, Hayek's characteristic overstatement: "When the administration interferes with the private sphere of the citizen … the problem of discretion becomes relevant to us; and the principle of the rule of law, in effect, means that the administrative authorities should have no discretionary powers in this respect." Hayek, *supra* note 4 at 213.

In contrast to Dicey's common-law model, which offers institutional control on forms of executive discretion through the judiciary, Lon Fuller's "inner morality" of law represents a procedural approach to understanding the principle of legality.[10] This view concerns law-making as an activity within the political community—in other words, the laws of lawfulness. If one conceives of law as the enterprise of subjecting human conduct to the governance of rules, then the purpose of the rule of law, according to Fuller, is to create and sustain a framework for successful social interaction. Compliance occurs, in part, because citizens derive benefits from following the law.[11] Lawmakers, then, have an interest in optimizing the legal conditions necessary for, and conducive to, voluntary compliance and cooperation. Fuller's eight principles of legality aim to guide lawmakers in achieving this end:

- Laws must be general. The principle of generality ensures that laws do not take the form of ad hoc or arbitrary commands.[12]
- Laws must be promulgated and public because secret laws undermine legality and frustrate the citizen's ability to know where he or she stands in relation to a system of rights, benefit distribution, and/or enforcement and punishment.
- Laws must be prospective, not retroactive. This means that laws normally should seek to control present and future behaviour, not past. One should not be punished, for example, for past conduct that was not illegal when it was undertaken.
- Laws must be non-contradictory because people will be confused about how to comply if they are pointed in two different directions. Laws should be neither in contradiction with each other nor internally within the provisions of a particular statute.
- Laws must have constancy through time. Rapid change means that people will not be able to adjust their patterns of behaviour in order to conform to the new rules. Moreover, inconstancy suggests arbitrariness in government law-making.
- Laws must be reasonably clear.[13]
- Laws must be capable of being performed. We are not obliged to obey laws commanding the impossible.
- Congruence between the rules as announced and the rules as applied must exist in order to avoid a legal system composed of arbitrary commands. This last principle deeply informs discretionary decision-making in the administrative state.

---

10 See Lon L. Fuller, *The Morality of Law*, rev. ed. (New Haven & London: Yale University Press, 1969) at 33 [Fuller].

11 Hence the rule of law provides one basis for the duty to obey the law and invokes concerns about when it is morally appropriate to disobey the law. For a discussion of the relationship between the duty to obey the law and the rule of law, see *Sauvé v. Canada (Chief Electoral Officer)*, [2002] 3 S.C.R. 519 at paras. 6-64, 90-121.

12 Generality also ensures that the law applies to all persons in the polity: general rules treat like cases alike in the application of a law or rule, thereby securing fairness, impartiality, and the lack of bias. Generality also constrains the scope of discretion in discretionary decision-making by drawing the individualized decision back toward the general or universal.

13 This feature also points to the notion of arbitrariness because lawmakers should be constrained from creating law that is unreasonable, illogical, vague, or otherwise ill-conceived. Nevertheless, this principle should not be taken to the extremes of rigidity for "[a] specious clarity can be more damaging than an honest open-ended vagueness." Fuller, *supra* note 10 at 64.

These principles act as eight standards of legality for all lawmakers in a society wishing to be governed by, and through, law. These principles guide law-making wherever it is found in the state: legislative, judicial, administrative, customary, and so on. Unlike Dicey, then, Fuller's conception of legality does not assume that administrative bodies are inherently lawless. Rather, if they follow these principles, they may be more likely to engage in lawful activity. Fuller's "internal morality" of law represents both a role morality (for example, how judges should decide cases) and an institutional morality (for example, how legislation should be enacted) that regulate whether or not legal activities are being carried out in accordance with the principles that constitute that same activity. If these activities do not, then the integrity of the institution will be severely harmed or destroyed altogether. Fuller argued that a political order committed to these principles would generate a successful legal system. A successful legal system, in turn, is itself a necessary—but not sufficient—condition for ensuring that law merits respect from both officials and citizens.

Joseph Raz provides a third well-regarded interpretation of the rule of law.[14] Though in agreement with several of Fuller's views, he believes it is possible to reduce the rule of law to one basic idea: law must be capable of guiding the behaviour of its subjects.[15] Raz further claims that most of the requirements we associate with the rule of law can be derived from this one basic idea in which the rule of law as the principle of legality acts as a practical guide for making effective law, thereby constraining the harms created by law itself. He proposes eight alternative principles, some of which overlap with Fuller's, but he also emphasizes that his theory does not enumerate all of the possible principles associated with the rule of law. As with Fuller, his principles aim to guide both the formation and application of law:

- Laws should be prospective, open, and clear.
- Laws should be relatively stable in order to help individuals with their short- and long-term planning.
- Particular laws should be informed by open, clear, stable, and general rules. These first three principles provide standards for laws to guide behaviour effectively.
- The independence of the judiciary must be guaranteed in order to preserve the rule of law. As lawmakers, the judiciary are also subject to the first three principles in order to control the exercise of their own discretionary power.
- The principles of natural justice must be observed, such as fair hearings and the absence of bias.
- Courts should have limited review powers over the implementation of other principles in parliamentary legislation and administrative decision-making in order to ensure conformity with the rule of law.
- Courts should be easily accessible.[16]

---

14 See also Andrei Marmor, who claims to hold a position in between those articulated by Fuller and Raz, in "The Rule of Law and Its Limits" (2004) 23 Law & Phil. 1.

15 Joseph Raz, "The Rule of Law and Its Virtue," in *The Authority of Law: Essays on Law and Morality* (Oxford: Clarendon Press, 1979) at 214 [Raz, *The Authority of Law*].

16 Raz offers no views on how such access should be realized in practice, and whether or not this access to the courts is a positive duty on government. Nevertheless, he writes: "Long delays or excessive costs may effectively turn the most enlightened law into a dead letter and frustrate one's ability effectively to guide oneself by the law." *Ibid.* at 217.

- The discretion of crime-preventing agencies, such as the police, should not be allowed to pervert the law. Principles four to eight ensure that the legal machinery of enforcing the law is not distorted, is capable of supervising conformity to the rule of law, and can provide effective remedies when the legal system deviates from it.[17]

The rule of law is essentially a negative value in Raz's theory and, moreover, is primarily instrumental—that is, it is primarily a means to the achievement of other goals.[18] Because law creates the danger of arbitrary power, the rule of law acts to minimize this risk, thereby minimizing harms created by law itself. Raz's theory constrains the form, production, and application of law, but it does not provide the grounds on which to judge the content of law. On his account, overbreadth, for example, is a technical deficiency of law that makes it more likely that the law will cause harm by (1) not adequately constraining the use of power; (2) not providing guidance for individual behaviour; or (3) widening the potential to infringe a specific right, such as individual liberty. Vagueness may present similar risks. A lack of generality, on the other hand, may violate legal equality or individual dignity interests because the classification or categorization may disproportionately "single out" a particular segment of the population. A lack of generality may also indicate negative discrimination on the grounds of race or sexual preference, but Raz's concept of the rule of law does not address this kind of content violation. Nevertheless, the rule of law has great moral value because conformity to it is a moral virtue, and it is a moral requirement to enable law to perform useful social functions or serve a moral purpose. The rule of law, then, fulfills an important but subservient role because conformity to the rule of law is not the ultimate goal. The idea of the rule of law stands as only one ideal for government; there are many others, and some will take priority over the rule of law.[19]

The chief reason underpinning this perspective on the rule of law is Raz's insistence on the liberal principle of state neutrality with respect to the many comprehensive conceptions of a good life that each of us holds. Though he argues that the state cannot remain morally neutral about harmful activities or beliefs, it should guarantee as far as possible the freedom of individuals to pursue their own conceptions of the good or "to choose styles and forms of life."[20] The instrumental virtue of the rule of law, then, establishes a secure framework for leading one's life, facilitates and protects the exercise of individual freedom, and is a necessary component of a state that respects human dignity. But, warns Raz, the rule of law should not be confused with the rule of *good* law.[21] On this account, for example, the guar-

17 Cristie Ford, in chapter 3, describes the variety of administrative law remedies a tribunal might impose as well as those available through judicial review.

18 Raz, *The Authority of Law*, *supra* note 15 at 223-26, 228.

19 In contrast to Fuller, Raz does not agree that deviations from the rule of law cannot be total or radical, or that there must necessarily be some moral value in a legal system committed to the rule of law.

20 Raz, *The Authority of Law*, *supra* note 15 at 220.

21 Raz, *ibid.* at 211, asserts that the rule of law is "not to be confused with democracy, justice, equality (before the law or otherwise), human rights of any kind or respect for persons or for the dignity of man. A non-democratic legal system, based on the denial of human rights, on extensive poverty, on racial segregation, sexual inequalities, and religious persecution may, in principle, conform to the requirements of the rule of law better than any of the legal systems of the more enlightened Western democracies. This does not mean that it will be better than those Western democracies. It will be an immeasurably worse legal system, but it will excel in one respect: in its conformity to the rule of law."

antee of legal equality in the rule of law helps identify apparent violations of formal equality, but it does not demand the realization of full or substantive equality.[22] Or, to take another example, a rule of law state may, in principle, be compatible with both a laissez-faire capitalist society as well as a society whose government creates redistributive programs to mitigate the pernicious effects of social and economic inequality.

How might each of these theories inform judicial understandings of their role in a rule of law order? The rule of law, for example, seems to entail an explicit role for the judiciary, but for what function? Dicey considered the courts to be the chief rule of law check on the executive in a Westminster system of government and, later, the primary means to control delegations of discretion from the executive to the administrative state. The Diceyan model therefore conceived of administrative law as the means through which the courts could control government power in order to protect individual rights. Such a view meant that courts need not defer to, or show respect for, the decisions made by administrative bodies that implicated common-law rights and interests. Courts, however, gradually became aware of the problems of legitimacy when intervening in administrative agencies and sought to set some limits to the exercise of their own discretionary powers. Although courts were wary about too overtly substituting their views for those of the agency when they held a different opinion about the merits of the decision, they could still intervene easily through their approach to statutory interpretation. Through their approach to statutory interpretation, courts could argue that intervention was justified when the legislature intended that questions of law or mixed fact and law implicated the jurisdiction of the agency, thereby requiring judicial review. Equally missing from Dicey's model are other functions of administrative law such as ensuring accountability in government by facilitating participation in the decision-making process—what the Fullerian approach endorses. Also lacking is the function of administrative law to design principles, standards, and rules in order to ensure that government performs its tasks efficiently and fairly—a view made explicit in Raz's theory.

The principle of the rule of law also requires an institutional framework, though not a specific institutional arrangement: Dicey recommends a common-law legal system, Fuller discusses law-making in general and as a shared and ideally cooperative institutional enterprise, while Raz emphasizes judicial independence as a necessary component of the rule of law. It is also clear that the idea of the rule of law suggests a role for the courts, and that this role depends on a political choice in the arrangement of institutions, as well as a political choice concerning the distribution of power among them. In political theory, the rule of law generally functions as a political ideal and suggests the need for legal institutions, a framework of positive law, and a constitutional order (with either a written or unwritten

22 For a contrary, radical argument, see Robin West, *Re-imagining Justice: Progressive Interpretations of Formal Equality, Rights, and the Rule of Law* (Aldershot: Ashgate, 2003). West, at 151, emphasizes the potential of the rule of law to advance substantive equality in society through formal legal equality: "The point of law, then, and the point of formal equality both, is to recognize the humanity of all, and their inclusion in a community constituted by mutual regard, and to extend the reach of that community well past the point by which we would be sympathetically and naturally inclined to do so: to extend it to the outmost reach of the law itself." On this view, the broadest scope of the rule of law can help create an egalitarian and inclusive community of civic equals. This community of equals is based on sympathetic engagement and concern for the well-being of others and moves the rule of law away from its usual identification with fear of others, individual self-interest, and mistrust of government power.

constitution—or both in the Canadian case).[23] Here the concept of the rule of law organizes other institutional matters, such as the doctrine of the separation of powers, the process of appointing judges, institutional checks and balances, and the fundamental precept that no one in a rule of law regime is above the law, particularly political actors in government.

The doctrine of the separation of powers provides a rationale for an institutional arrangement that effectively functions to check arbitrary power.[24] This doctrine, for example, makes explicit the separate function of courts in securing a political community committed to political moderation, the maintenance of order, political liberty, and the prevention of the abuse of power by all branches of government. Canada's Westminster system of government, however, cannot be characterized by bright-line distinctions between the three branches. A certain fluidity is endemic to this system, particularly among the executive, Cabinet, and bureaucracy, with significant implications for the legislature.[25] Nevertheless, one implication of the separation of powers is that the judiciary should have some measure of independence—but what is the nature of this independence and how much independence do judges need? Moreover, how is judicial independence related to the independence of persons appointed to administrative bodies such as tribunals? As discussed by Laverne Jacobs in chapter 6, the Supreme Court has identified three objective conditions necessary to guarantee functional independence: security of tenure, financial security, and administrative control.[26]

These three features informing the principle of judicial independence also apply to adjudicators in the administrative state who engage in more judicial-like decision-making in tribunal settings. Though the rationale for judicial independence does not exactly map onto the requirements for independence in the administrative state—given executive control of administrative bodies—strong analogies exist. But just as courts cannot treat administrative

23 Canada, as a former British colony, not only possesses a written constitution, but has also inherited the "unwritten" British constitution. In Britain, the constitution is said to be unwritten because no single constitutional document defines its constitutional system. Instead, a collection of statutes, decrees, conventions, customs or traditions, and royal prerogatives comprise the constitution. Seen from this perspective, it would be a mistake to think that a single document, even if comprehensive, could ever capture an entire constitution. For most countries, a constitution is a mix of written and unwritten sources. In Canada, as will be considered in more detail in part III, several of the most important constitutional principles are implicit and unwritten.

24 For discussion of the separation of powers in constitutional jurisprudence, see *Newfoundland (Treasury Board) v. N.A.P.E.*, [2004] 3 S.C.R. 38; *Doucet-Boudreau v. Nova Scotia (Minister of Education)*, [2003] 3 S.C.R. 3; *Cooper v. Canada (Human Rights Commission)*, [1996] 3 S.C.R. 854 [*Cooper*]; *Wells v. Newfoundland*, [1999] 3 S.C.R. 199 [*Wells*]; and *Operation Dismantle v. The Queen*, [1985] 1 S.C.R. 441 [*Operation Dismantle*].

25 As the Supreme Court writes in *Wells*, *supra* note 24 at paras. 52, 54: "The doctrine of separation of powers is an essential feature of our constitution. It maintains a separation of powers between the judiciary and the other two branches, legislature and the executive, and to some extent between the legislature and the executive. … The separation of powers is not a rigid and absolute structure. The Court should not be blind to the reality of Canadian governance that, except in certain rare cases, the executive frequently and *de facto* controls the legislature."

26 Cases that specify these three conditions include *R. v. Valente*, [1985] 2 S.C.R. 673; *Beauregard v. Canada*, [1986] 2 S.C.R. 56; and *Provincial Court Judges Association of New Brunswick v. New Brunswick (Minister of Justice)*, [2005] 2 S.C.R. 286.

bodies as they do lower courts in the hierarchy of legal institutions, courts cannot understand administrative independence as an exact analogy. In chapter 6, Laverne Jacobs more thoroughly treats the complexities involved in tribunal independence, including the appointments and removal processes, the guarantees of impartiality and lack of bias, and whether or not explicit and implicit constitutional guarantees apply.[27] She discusses how courts traditionally distrusted administrative agencies, partly due to the blurred lines of accountability, which seemingly violated the doctrine of the separation of powers. In other words, because they are hybrid bodies, or "governments in miniature,"[28] administrative agencies and tribunals possess differing combinations of policy-making, rule-making, and adjudication, which make their purposes and functions difficult to separate.[29] Even now, the Supreme Court describes administrative tribunals as creatures of statute that "span the constitutional divide between the judiciary and the executive"[30] and that have a significant policy-making role. Moreover, and in contrast to courts, one vital function of tribunals is the greater opportunity for participation by those affected by the decision-making process. Once again, a certain flexibility and attentiveness to context inheres in the rule of law relationship between courts and administrative bodies in the doctrine of the separation of powers.

III. THE SUPREME COURT OF CANADA ON THE RULE OF LAW'S SIGNIFICANCE

Legal and political theories constitute the often unstated background assumptions that inform judicial understandings of the rule of law that appear jurisprudentially in case-by-case development. The Supreme Court of Canada has articulated various features of the rule of law, but the Court has not (and perhaps never should) set out a comprehensive statement containing a fully articulated conception of the rule of law.

A. The Heart of the Canadian Rule of Law

The marked difference between formal and substantive approaches to the rule of law can be seen in an early Supreme Court case concerning the ability of courts to control the abuse of power in the administrative state. The case of *Roncarelli v. Duplessis*[31] contains several examples of arbitrary power: the existence of unlimited discretionary powers in an agency; a decision-maker acting in bad faith; inappropriate responsiveness to an individual situation where important interests are at stake; consideration of irrelevant factors in the decision;

27 See, in particular, Jacobs's discussion of *McKenzie v. Minister of Public Safety and Solicitor General et al.*, 2006 BCSC 1372, a case concerning procedural fairness, tribunal independence, the rule of law, and the dismissal of a residential tenancy arbitrator for arbitrary reasons. Online: <http://www.canlii.org/en/bc/bcsc/doc/2006/2006bcsc1372/2006bcsc1372.pdf>.

28 I borrow this phrase from John Willis, an important early Canadian public law scholar. See "Three Approaches to Administrative Law: The Judicial, the Conceptual and the Functional" (1935) U.T.L.J. 53 at 73. See also Mary Liston, "Willis, 'Theology,' and the Rule of Law" (2005) 55 U.T.L.J. 767.

29 In chapter 2, Bill Bogart outlines the many regulatory functions and tools in the administrative state.

30 *Ocean Port Hotel Ltd. v. British Columbia (General Manager, Liquor Control and Licensing Branch)*, [2001] 2 S.C.R. 781 at para. 24.

31 [1959] S.C.R. 121 [*Roncarelli*].

disregard of the purpose of a statute; and dictation of the decision by an external and unauthorized person. *Roncarelli* illustrates one of the primary functions of the rule of law: the control of executive arbitrariness.[32]

Frank Roncarelli owned a Montreal restaurant and was a Jehovah's Witness. At that time, the Quebec government and the Catholic Church joined forces to persecute Jehovah's Witnesses, whom they viewed as dangerous to the established order, seditious, and anti-Catholic. Hundreds of Jehovah's Witnesses were jailed for distributing religious pamphlets in violation of municipal bylaws. Roncarelli posted bail for fellow Witnesses. Premier Duplessis publicly warned Roncarelli to stop posting bail, and, when Roncarelli continued, Duplessis ordered that the liquor board cancel Roncarelli's permit to sell alcohol. The cancellation of the liquor licence forced Roncarelli to shut down his restaurant.

The Supreme Court examined the actions of Maurice Duplessis, who acted as both premier and attorney general, and found them invalid. Invoking the unwritten principle of the rule of law, the Court held that no public official is above the law. Duplessis had stepped outside the authorized bounds of his power as attorney general by ordering the revocation of Roncarelli's licence. He also inappropriately exercised the power that was properly given to the chairperson of the Quebec Liquor Commission by the enabling statute, *An Act Respecting Alcoholic Liquor*. Last, regardless of who actually was the decision-maker, the decision offended the rule of law because the substance of the decision was incompatible with the purpose of the statute. Being a Jehovah's Witness was irrelevant to a decision concerning the continuation of a liquor licence for operating a restaurant. The true nature of the decision was to punish Roncarelli for exercising his civil right to post bail.

There are two ways to understand the use of the principle of the rule of law in this judgment: the formal Diceyan model, discussed in part II, above; and a more value-laden substantive constitutionalism, or what David Dyzenhaus calls the unwritten "constitution of legality."[33] On the Diceyan model, the Supreme Court held that Chairman Edouard Archambault of the Quebec Liquor Commission had not made a decision at all because Duplessis had substituted his decision for that of the proper authority, thus exercising his power arbitrarily. The case confirmed that Premier Duplessis had overstepped his jurisdiction as attorney general by, in effect, telling Chairman Archambault to cancel Roncarelli's liquor licence "forever" so that his restaurant would go out of business. Under the terms of the governing statute, however, this power had been delegated to Chairman Archambault, not to the attorney general who, at most, could only provide advice on the matter.[34] The legal wrong committed against the rule of law here was the violation of the legal principle of validity, which affirms that "every official act must be justified by law" or be found ultra vires: the decision was not valid because the power to cancel licences was not given to either the premier or the attorney general.[35] As

---

32 For a detailed exposition of the relation between the rule of law and the administrative state in administrative law, see David Mullan *et al.*, "Chapter One: The Administrative State and the Rule of Law" in *Administrative Law: Cases, Text, and Materials*, 5th ed. (Toronto: Emond Montgomery, 2003).

33 See David Dyzenhaus, "The Deep Structure of Roncarelli v. Duplessis" (2004) 53 U.N.B.L.J. 111 at 124.

34 Alternatively, and to paraphrase Don Corleone in *The Godfather*, Duplessis provided "advice," the nature of which Archambault could not refuse.

35 This is the view taken by Peter Hogg, *Constitutional Law of Canada: 2001 Student Edition* (Toronto: Carswell, 2001) at 634 [Hogg].

Dyzenhaus points out, the problem with this line of argument is that had Archambault not consulted Duplessis, his decision would have been found valid, particularly because the enabling statute granted Archambault seemingly unfettered discretion.[36] Indeed, the relevant provision of the statute, s. 34, simply and broadly stated that the Commission "may refuse to grant any permit." On this basis, only when an administrative authority acts beyond the power given to it by Parliament can the courts legitimately enforce the rule of law or reaffirm the separation of powers.

By contrast, Rand J., writing in a concurring judgment for the majority, stated that public authorities, especially those with broad discretionary powers, are always constrained by the unwritten constitutional principle of the rule of law, even when the legislation contains no explicit or written constraints:

> In public regulation of this sort there is no such thing as absolute and untrammelled "discretion," that is that action can be taken on any ground or for any reason that can be suggested to the mind of the administrator; no legislative Act can, without express language, be taken to contemplate an unlimited arbitrary power exercisable for any purpose, however capricious or irrelevant, regardless of the nature or purpose of the statute. ... "Discretion" necessarily implies good faith in discharging public duty; there is always a perspective within which a statute is intended to operate; and any clear departure from its lines or objects is just as objectionable as fraud or corruption.[37]

Even if Archambault had acted on his own in cancelling Roncarelli's licence, he would have used his discretionary powers inappropriately according to Rand J. because his decision contradicted the substantive content of the rule of law:

> That, in the presence of expanding administrative regulation of economic activities, such a step and its consequences are to be suffered by the victim without recourse or remedy, that an administration according to law is to be superseded by action dictated by and according to the arbitrary likes, dislikes and irrelevant purposes of public officers acting beyond their duty, would signalize the beginning of disintegration of the rule of law as a fundamental postulate of our constitutional structure. An administration of licences on the highest level of fair and impartial treatment to all may be forced to follow the practice of "first come, first served," which makes the strictest observance of equal responsibility to all of even greater importance.[38]

Conventionally in public law, the rule of law's constraints on government actors seeks to prevent such "[virtual] vocation outlawry" through enforcement of the purpose of the statute and good faith decision-making achieved through the use of fair procedures.[39] Rand J. added more content: the administrative tribunal violated Roncarelli's rights as a citizen—freedom of religion, freedom of expression, freedom to pursue his livelihood—thereby damaging the normative relationship between the state and the citizen.

On the formalist account, administrative law concerns the written statutes, rules, and principles that govern public decision-makers, encompassing the relationships among all

---

36 *Supra* note 33 at 125.

37 *Roncarelli*, *supra* note 31 at 140.

38 *Ibid.* at 142.

39 *Ibid.* at 141.

branches of government as well as the relationships between branches of government and the groups, constituencies, corporations, and individuals with whom they interact and over whom they exercise power. Public decision-makers must not act outside their authority, must not abuse their authority, and must be seen not to do so either. Administrative law establishes the legal parameters of power that exist by virtue of statutes (such as delegated discretionary powers given to administrators) or because of royal prerogative—prerogative that is now mostly exercised by the executive in the name of the Crown. Judicial scrutiny within administrative law focuses on the limits on the authority given to decision-makers by statute or prerogative. On the substantive account, such authority is bounded by the purpose and terms of the statute, by regulations and guidelines, by the constitution, and by both written and unwritten legal principles. Formally valid exercises of discretion can offend the rule of law and can subsequently be determined to be a legal wrong as an abuse of power. *Roncarelli* still stands as a paradigmatic example of the deeper principled and purposive approach to understanding how the rule of law animates administrative law.

B. A Foundational Principle, but an "Unwritten" One

As a constitutional principle, the rule of law is both part of the written and (so-called) unwritten constitution. A constitution is more than the positive law: it includes customary law, conventions, judge-made or common-law, a civil code, and unwritten principles in addition to legislation and written constitutional documents.[40] As an implicit constitutional principle, the rule of law appears in the preamble to the *Constitution Act, 1867*, where it states that Canada will have a "Constitution similar in principle to that of the United Kingdom."[41] The rule of law also appears as an explicit principle in the preamble to the *Constitution Act, 1982*: "Whereas Canada is founded upon principles that recognize the supremacy of God and the rule of law."[42] Whether implicit or explicit, then, the principle of the rule of law applies to the entire constitutional order and every part of government. The deepest and broadest reflection on the unwritten principle of the rule of law in the Canadian order appears in two reference cases:[43] the *Manitoba Language Rights Reference*[44] and the *Secession Reference*.[45]

---

40 For further discussion of written and unwritten constitutions, see *supra* note 23 and accompanying text.

41 Preamble to the *Constitution Act, 1867* (U.K.), 30 & 31 Vict., c. 3, reprinted in R.S.C. 1985, App. II, No. 5.

42 Preamble to the *Constitution Act, 1982*, being Schedule B to the *Canada Act 1982* (U.K.), 1982, c. 11.

43 Reference cases constitute another institutional practice that blurs the bright-line distinction between law and politics. They have allowed Canadian courts to articulate, from a legal perspective, their understanding of the constitutional architecture and its normative underpinnings—a perspective that usually remains implicit and underspecified in ordinary judgments. Because the reference function is advisory, it is also non-judicial, and thus upsets the traditional understanding of the separation of powers doctrine. Mitigating this potential doctrinal disruption is the fact that a court's answer is neither binding nor of the same precedential weight as an opinion in an actual legal judgment. Nevertheless, there are no reported examples of an opinion being disregarded by the parties, which suggests that references are treated like other opinions. The key distinction between reference opinions and other judicial opinions is the limited range of remedies that are available to the judiciary in reference cases. See Hogg, *supra* note 35 at 8.6(d).

44 *Reference re Language Rights Under s. 23 of Manitoba Act, 1870 and s. 133 of Constitutional Act, 1867*, [1985] 1 S.C.R. 721 [*Manitoba Language Rights Reference*].

45 *Reference re Secession of Quebec*, [1998] 2 S.C.R. 217 [*Secession Reference*].

In *Manitoba Language Rights Reference*, the Supreme Court described the rule of law as a "highly textured expression ... conveying ... a sense of orderliness, of subjection to known legal rules and of executive accountability to legal authority."[46] The Court also recognized the rule of law as a "fundamental postulate of our constitutional structure"[47] whose constitutional status was beyond question. In coming to this understanding, the Court considered several features of the rule of law including the principle of legality, the institutional arrangements entailed by the idea of the rule of law, and its broader connection with Canadian political culture. Throughout the judgment, the Court characterized the rule of law as the principle of legality. This principle was understood in two ways. First, it meant that the law is supreme over government officials as well as private individuals and therefore excludes the influence and operation of arbitrary power.[48] Second, it meant that law and order are indispensable elements of civilized life within a political community. The rule of law therefore required "the creation and maintenance of an actual order of positive laws which preserves and embodies the more general principle of normative order. Law and order are indispensable elements of civilized life."[49] For the Court, Canada must be thought of as a "society of legal order and normative structure"[50] in which the rule of law was embedded as both an implicit and explicit constitutional principle. As an expression of a commitment to peace, order, and good government over war, anarchy, and arbitrary power, the rule of law, to the Court's mind, represented a "philosophical view of society" that "in the Western tradition is linked with basic democratic notions."[51]

How the principle of legality is linked to basic democratic notions was not spelled out fully in the *Manitoba Language Rights Reference*. Nevertheless, the Court stated that the constitution is deeply intertwined with the principle of parliamentary sovereignty, for the constitution "is a statement of the will of the people to be governed in accordance with certain principles held as fundamental and certain prescriptions restrictive of the powers of legislature and government."[52] In Canada, the people have elected to be governed through a democracy, its institutional forms, and its political ideals. Democracy and parliamentary sovereignty, then, are related but not synonymous. Moreover, Canadians have also embraced government under the concept of the rule of law. The interconnectedness of the principles of democracy, parliamentary sovereignty, and the rule of law inform general understandings of what good or responsible government means. In the *Manitoba Language Rights Reference*, the Court invoked the rule of law to conclude that the Manitoba government's repeated failure to respect the mandatory constitutional requirements of bilingualism exhibited a failure to comply with the manner and form of the legislative enactment and therefore rendered the legislative product invalid. By failing to adhere to the terms of the province's constitutional document, Manitoba had acted without legal authority, had acted

46 *Manitoba Language Rights Reference*, *supra* note 44 at para. 62.

47 *Ibid.* at para. 63.

48 *Ibid.* at para. 59.

49 *Ibid.* at para. 60.

50 *Ibid.* at para. 64.

51 *Ibid.* at para. 61.

52 *Ibid.* at para. 48.

arbitrarily, and had allowed its officials to act outside the law. The Court concluded that these actions constituted a complete transgression of the principle of legality. The remedial force of the rule of law compelled bilingual enactment of all unilingual provincial laws.

In the *Secession Reference*, the Court more clearly articulated the constitutional principle of the rule of law in the context of questions about the legal validity of a potential unilateral act of secession from Canada by the province of Quebec. In this judgment, the Court identified four unwritten principles that animate the Canadian constitutional order: federalism, democracy, constitutionalism and the rule of law, and respect for minorities. These principles do not, said the Court, stand alone; rather, they are highly interrelated and permeate every part of the Canadian order. They act as organizing principles of the state as well as aspirational ideals that the Canadian polity has sought, and continues to pursue and make real.

In its analysis of the constitutional requirements for secession, the Supreme Court considered the written constitution, unwritten norms, and the global system of rules and principles—in sum, the "vital unstated assumptions" that govern the exercise of constitutional authority. These four underlying principles, the judges said, are the "lifeblood" of the constitution and therefore mutually support every part of the Canadian state.[53] They do not function as trumps over one another. In addition to their highly persuasive interpretive import, these principles can have "*full legal force*" in certain circumstances.[54] This means that they are binding upon courts, can give rise to substantive legal obligations (both general and specific), and may function as real constraints on government action.[55] It would be impossible, the Court averred, to understand the Canadian constitutional order without these architectonic and organic principles.

In the context of a threat of unilateral secession by the province of Quebec, the Court wrote that the four fundamental principles mandate a rejection of unilateralism and a need for principled negotiation as the default position in the Canadian legal and political order.[56] On this understanding, sovereign power in a Westminster-style democracy also cannot be understood as an unrestrained will acting unilaterally. Rather, a democratic rule of law requires that sovereign power be lawful, responsive, and moderate in its actions. Along with the principle of democracy, the other three unwritten principles will also distinctively shape and constrain the exercise of sovereign authority. This conception of sovereign power, for example, ideally constrains the federal sovereign from dominating provincial sovereigns within federalism. It also constrains majorities from oppressing or discriminating against minorities within a democratic regime. The principle of the rule of law within institutional dialogue guarantees the existence of formal conduits and processes for dialogue to occur, and obliges institutions comprising the legal and political system to engage in moderate politics in order to realize these substantive constitutional commitments. The Court underscores this point in the *Secession Reference* when it declares that democracy cannot exist without the rule of law:

---

53 *Secession Reference*, *supra* note 45 at paras. 50-51.

54 *Ibid.* at paras. 51-54 (emphasis added).

55 *Ibid.* at para. 54.

56 *Ibid.* at paras. 84, 97.

> To be accorded legitimacy, democratic institutions must rest, ultimately, on a legal foundation. That is, they must allow for the participation of, and accountability to, the people, through public institutions created under the Constitution. Equally, however, a system of government cannot survive through adherence to law alone. A political system must also possess legitimacy, and in our political culture, that requires an interaction between the rule of law and the democratic principle. … Our law's claim to legitimacy also rests on an appeal to moral values, many of which are embedded in our constitutional structure. It would be a grave mistake to equate legitimacy with the "sovereign will" or majority rule alone, to the exclusion of other constitutional values.[57]

The unwritten principle of the rule of law therefore constrains the principle of parliamentary sovereignty from its tendency to define democracy merely as a set of formal institutional arrangements. But it also constrains courts from unilaterally, arbitrarily, and anti-democratically substituting their views for Parliament's in constitutional matters.

C. The New Minimalist Rule of Law

Perhaps not surprisingly, Supreme Court judges also disagree about the scope and content of the principle of the rule of law. In a trilogy of recent cases—*Imperial Tobacco*,[58] *Charkaoui*,[59] and *Christie*[60]—the Supreme Court has considerably narrowed the scope and effect of this principle within Canadian law. In Canada's constitutional house, the current decor is sleek and spare.

The Supreme Court continues to affirm the unwritten constitutional principle of the rule of law by asserting its status as a foundational principle at the root of our system of governance, implicit in the very concept of a constitution. According to the Court, the rule of law incorporates a number of familiar themes and embraces at least four principles: (1) it is supreme over private individuals as well as over government officials, who are required to exercise their authority non-arbitrarily and according to law; (2) it requires the creation and maintenance of a positive order of laws; (3) it requires the relationship between the state and the individual to be regulated by law; and (4) it is linked to the principle of judicial independence.[61] These four subsidiary attributes clearly conform to the general discussion of the rule of law presented in part II, "The Rule of Law in Theory," above.

Although the rule of law may possess additional principles, there is, however, one key attribute that the principle of the rule of law does not possess: the ability to strike down legislation based on its content.[62] The rule of law, then, does not speak "directly" to the terms of legislation (or provisions of statutes). This does not mean that the rule of law has no normative force at all, says the Court, but simply that the government action it is able to

57 *Ibid.* at paras. 67, 68.

58 *British Columbia v. Imperial Tobacco Canada Ltd.*, [2005] 2 S.C.R. 473 [*Imperial Tobacco*].

59 *Charkaoui v. Canada (Minister of Citizenship and Immigration)*, 2007 SCC 9 [*Charkaoui*].

60 *British Columbia (Attorney General) v. Christie*, 2007 SCC 21 [*Christie*].

61 *Imperial Tobacco*, *supra* note 58 at para. 58; *Charkaoui*, *supra* note 59 at para. 134; *Christie*, *supra* note 60 at para. 20.

62 *Imperial Tobacco*, *supra* note 58 at para. 59.

constrain is usually that of the executive and administrative branches. Legislatures are constrained by "manner and form" requirements in the processes of enacting, amending, or repealing legislation.[63] This is because the principles of democracy, constitutionalism, and judicial independence favour the validity of legislation that conforms to the express terms of the constitution, or those that follow as necessary implications from the express terms.[64] Nevertheless, the normative force of the rule of law on this understanding does appear to have been significantly curtailed[65] and the Court has minimized reference to substantive rule-of-law values.

The *Charkaoui* decision declared unconstitutional the detention review hearings process set out in the *Immigration and Refugee Protection Act* (IRPA). The Court held that the statutory scheme violated s. 7 principles of fundamental justice, ss. 9 and 10 guarantees against arbitrary detention, and the protection against cruel and unusual treatment in s. 12. The Court, however, could not actually review the reasonableness of security certificates (certificates issued jointly by the Ministers of Public Security and Immigration) because they are not subject to review or appeal. The Court also addressed arguments relating to the rule of law, and s. 15 of the Charter as it applies to foreign nationals, but did not consider these arguments relevant for the decision. The Court held that the use of secret evidence and the likelihood of indefinite detention without meaningful and timely review for non-citizens clearly violated due process rights. To guarantee a fair hearing under the Charter, a different procedure should be created—one that does not so greatly infringe Charter rights. But the rule of law did not support a right to appeal from the Federal Court judge's determination of the reasonableness of the certificate, nor could it prohibit automatic detention or detention on the basis of executive or ministerial decision-making.[66] While the *Charkaoui* decision should be celebrated for upholding s. 7's requirement of a fair procedure for determining an issue of vital importance to a detainee, the Court's reliance on a formal conception of the rule of law comes at a cost: it inhibits the purchase of rule-of-law values implicit in the unwritten or common-law constitution. Consideration of substantive rule-of-law values, like those found in the *Roncarelli* decision, would provide a toehold for judicial scrutiny of the failure to provide a right of appeal from the reasonableness of a security certificate, as well as the power of detention given to executive actors under IRPA.

---

63 But see *Authorson v. Canada (Attorney General)*, [2003] 2 S.C.R. 40, both for troubling insights into how an executive-controlled government can manipulate and avoid the manner and form requirements of enacting legislation, and for a tragic example of a systemic failure of accountability.

64 *Imperial Tobacco*, *supra* note 58 at para. 66.

65 This is clear in the *Charkaoui* decision where express provisions of the Charter were used to strike down the security certificate process under the *Immigration and Refugee Protection Act* (IRPA), but the rule of law argument against the certificate provisions in the IRPA was relegated to the margins. Craig Forcese, in chapter 11, discusses the truncated reach of the *Charkaoui* decision, which will be of little assistance in administrative proceedings where s. 7 of the Charter is not triggered. As he and other commentators emphasize, in a state built on the rule of law, no public power should lie beyond the reach of law. If judicial review of cases concerning national security is too deferential, alternative institutional forms of accountability must be devised.

66 The Court noted that the Federal Court is a superior court, not an administrative tribunal—such a right could be said to flow from a decision made in the administrative context. The legality of the process, according to the Court, is nevertheless reinforced because the Federal Court of Appeal can circumvent the privative clause where the constitutionality of the legislation is challenged or where the individual alleges bias on the part of the judge. *Charkaoui*, *supra* note 59 at paras. 136, 137.

The *Christie* case involved a constitutional challenge brought by Dugald Christie, a litigation lawyer, who claimed that British Columbia's 7 percent legal service tax made it impossible for some of his low-income clients to retain him to pursue their claims. The Court affirmed that one purpose of the rule of law is to ensure access to justice—an issue that is the focus of chapter 15 by Lorne Sossin. The Court noted that, when rights and obligations are at stake, individual access to justice can often only happen through lawyers whose role is to bring citizens' complaints about unlawful or abusive private or state action to courts or administrative tribunals. As a component of the rule of law, access to justice may guarantee a right to legal services, such as a right to counsel in some circumstances (particularly in the criminal context). But the rule of law does not underwrite a general right to legal services, to legal assistance, or to counsel in relation to court and tribunal proceedings.[67] It therefore also cannot constitutionalize a particular type of access to justice, such as a specific institutional form of legal aid. Although the argument against the use of the rule of law in this case does not foreclose the possibility that a right to counsel may be found in other circumstances, a general right to counsel could not be found. Because sufficient evidence did not exist to prove that low-income persons were prevented from accessing legal services, the provincial tax paid by all users of legal services, regardless of their income status, was found constitutional. The Court, however, suggested that an adequate evidentiary record in a different case might provide grounds for judicial gap-filling by finding a constitutional entitlement to legal services in relation to proceedings in courts and tribunals dealing with rights and obligations. Once again, the Court emphasized that the principle of the rule of law could not be used to strike down otherwise valid legislation.[68]

As Lorne Sossin discusses in chapter 15, the relationship between the unwritten principles of the rule of law and "access to justice" remains underspecified in Canadian law, although his chapter concretizes several factors that inform the quality of access to justice. The tensions among the rule of law, fairness, equality, and efficiency remain particularly acute in administrative law because many tribunals were established to provide access for low-income or otherwise vulnerable individuals; however, these tribunals may fail to do so and, for reasons concerning the separation of powers, recourse to the courts may not provide a remedy. Recalling the concepts of the rule of law advanced by the three theorists in part II, above, all suggested some degree of access to the legal system.[69] Each theory

67 *Christie*, *supra* note 60 at paras. 23-27.

68 The lack of congruence between the stated purpose of the tax and its actual effect in this case is troubling, though. The stated purpose of the tax was to fund legal aid in British Columbia, but instead the money went into general revenue. The Court could not determine how much—if any—of the tax actually went to fund legal aid.

69 Access to justice appears in Dicey's conception of the rule of law by necessity in his common-law model, in Fuller's procedural understanding of the rule of law, and explicitly as one of Raz's principles. Yet none of these theories dictates a particular institutional arrangement facilitating or guaranteeing access to justice. Dicey's theory relies on a common-law constitutionalism driven by private law rights of property and contract, not one oriented toward democratic access by all, including the disadvantaged. Raz's functionalist account suggests that courts should be easily accessible—but he does not specify whether this relative openness is constrained by justiciability or fiscal limits. Because Raz relies on a formal view of legal equality within the rule of law, access to justice cannot be equated with equal access to legal services by all as a democratic right. Fuller's aspirational theory is consistent with the common-law openness of Dicey's and

therefore comports with the fundamental conviction that individuals should have access to due process when their rights and interests have been affected by government action. Each also supports some measure of access within a rule of law state, but again none explicitly argues for effective equal access for all legal subjects.[70] Indeed, of all the theorists considered in this chapter, only Ronald Dworkin explicitly considers access to be a matter of fairness that benefits the least well off and satisfies the demands of legal equality in the rule of law.

Clearly, the Court has become anxious about the risks of its own forms of arbitrariness through recourse to unwritten principles and is attempting to constrain the use of these principles by judges and litigants. Because unwritten principles do not have content fixed in advance, they appear transcendent, and their articulation and use look like an unconstrained form of judicial law-making. Fears about undemocratic judicial activism arise because it could appear that the judiciary is usurping the legislative role by engaging in subjective and arbitrary decision-making. Unwritten principles therefore challenge the idea of a bright-line conception of the separation of powers.[71] This has led the Court to move to what Peter Hogg and Cara Zwibel define as the "middle" ground that, for them, is occupied by thinkers like themselves and Raz, where unwritten principles like the rule of law have no direct legal effect, but are merely influential "constitutional values."[72]

---

the institutional openness of Raz's. But it is not clear whether or not his theory would underwrite greater access to justice because citizens play a role in the maintenance of the legal system through litigation. Given the polycentric nature of public law cases, Fuller's theory could also support more limited grounds of justiciability.

70 The procedural devices available to judges by virtue of the rule of law—procedural due process (rights to representation, cross-examine witnesses, etc.), habeas corpus, the right to appeal an adverse decision, standing to raise constitutional issues—ensure that judges play a large role in Fuller's theory. Nevertheless, litigation alone is an unsatisfactory method of ensuring access to justice because "haphazard and fluctuating principles concerning this matter [standing] can produce a broken and arbitrary pattern of correspondence between the Constitution and its realization in practice." Serious disadvantages of relying solely on the courts as a bulwark against the "lawless administration of the law" include the willingness and financial ability of the affected party to litigate, the inability of the courts to properly constrain police lawlessness, and the ability of courts to make things much worse by departing from principles, not articulating reasonably clear general rules, issuing contradictory rulings, changing direction frequently or suddenly, and aggravating the already vexed problem of interpretation. Fuller, *supra* note 10 at 81-82.

71 In an important article, David Dyzenhaus illustrates how the Supreme Court's use of unwritten principles in administrative law cases is incompatible with their prior reliance on a formal conception of the doctrine of the separation of powers. Instead of a formal understanding, which he views as inherently unstable, Dyzenhaus underscores the significance of judgments like *Baker v. Canada (Minister of Citizenship and Immigration)*, [1999] 2 S.C.R. 817 [*Baker*] and *Cooper*, supra note 24, that express a vision of democratic constitutionalism which respects the legitimacy of the administrative state. This vision of Canadian constitutionalism relies on a democratic interpretation of the separation of powers and therefore recognizes the appropriate role of administrative tribunals—particularly human rights tribunals—in determining fundamental legal values. See in particular section I, "The Separation of Powers and the Administrative State" in "Constituting the Rule of Law: Fundamental Values in Administrative Law" (2002) 27 Queen's L.J. 445 at 453-87 ["Constituting Fundamental Values"].

72 Peter W. Hogg & Cara F. Zwibel, "The Rule of Law in the Supreme Court of Canada" (2005) 53 U.T.L.J. 716 at 718. Like Raz, they suggest that the claim that the rule of law requires our laws to "respect equality, human dignity, and other good moral values is really just natural law in disguise. The rule of law is not a protection against laws that are bad." Remedies for bad laws are to be found in the written constitution and democratic

Fears of arbitrariness are also related to the contested status of the rule of law. The Court took its clearest stance concerning the power of and limits on the unwritten principle of the rule of law in *Imperial Tobacco*. *Imperial Tobacco* concerned a statute enacted by the province of British Columbia, the *Tobacco Damages and Health Care Costs Recovery Act*, which allowed the province to sue manufacturers of tobacco products for compensation of tobacco-related health care costs incurred by individuals exposed to tobacco products.[73] The provincial government argued that tobacco companies were liable for these health care costs because they breached a duty of care to persons in British Columbia by producing products that could reasonably be expected to cause harm. One effect of the Act was to permit not only the recovery of current and future costs, but also to recover costs retroactively from the past 50 years. The tobacco companies challenged the validity of the statute on three constitutional grounds: extra-territoriality, judicial independence, and the rule of law. Major J., writing for the Court in *Imperial Tobacco*, focused on the debates concerning the meaning of the rule of law and what principles it might incorporate, noting with approval Strayer J.A.'s dictum in *Singh v. Canada (Attorney General)*,[74] that: "[a]dvocates tend to read into the principle of the rule of law anything which supports their particular view of what the law should be."[75] The Court affirmed that the rule of law does not require that legislation be prospective (except in criminal law) or general. It also does not prohibit the conferral of special privileges on the government, except where necessary for effective governance.[76] Lastly, it does not ensure a fair civil trial.[77] The Court claimed that to affirm these features constitutionally, as the tobacco companies had argued, would be tantamount to endorsing one particular conception of the rule of law, thereby seriously undermining the legitimacy of judicial review. The written constitution has primacy, such that the attributes of the rule of law are simply broader versions of the rights already contained in the Charter.[78] Protection from unjust or unfair legislation "properly lies not in the amorphous underlying principles of our Constitution, but in its text and the ballot box."[79] When legislatures use their powers validly but arbitrarily, and the content of such legislation does not engage an express constitutional provision, then citizens must look to internal forms of government responsibility and the democratic process of elections for accountability and correction, not to the courts.[80]

---

institutions. *Ibid.* For a sophisticated, contrary argument, see Mark D. Walters, "'Common Public Law in the Age of Legislation': David Mullan and the Unwritten Constitution" in Grant Huscroft & Michael Taggart, eds., *Inside and Outside Canadian Administrative Law* (Toronto: University of Toronto Press, 2006) at 421.

73 *Tobacco Damages and Health Care Costs Recovery Act*, S.B.C. 2000, c. 30.

74 [2000] 3 F.C. 185 (C.A.).

75 *Imperial Tobacco*, *supra* note 58 at para. 33.

76 The statute also changed rules of civil procedure in order to counter the systemic advantages that tobacco manufacturers enjoy in private law litigation by shifting the onus of proof from the government to the tobacco manufacturers. Tobacco companies had to prove, on a balance of probabilities, that their products did not and do not cause harm to affected persons in British Columbia. The tobacco companies argued that the shift of the evidentiary burden interfered both with the guarantee of a fair trial and the ability of judges to assess and weigh the relevant evidence.

77 *Imperial Tobacco*, *supra* note 58 at para. 63.

78 *Ibid.* at para. 65.

79 *Ibid.* at para. 66.

80 See *Bacon v. Saskatchewan Crop Insurance Corp.* (1999), 180 Sask. R. 20 at paras. 30, 36 (C.A.).

D. Lower Court Unruliness?

Though the Court has not completely shut down the legal and normative force of the unwritten principle of the rule of law, it has signalled a marked unwillingness to engage in any such "gap-filling" through the use of unwritten principles.[81] Such a conclusion cuts against the grain of the earlier jurisprudence concerning unwritten constitutional principles. Those who wish to see robust use of unwritten principles must look to lower court decisions where the unwritten principle of the rule of law, in conjunction with other unwritten principles, has supplemented the written constitutional text and provided grounds for invalidating legislation based on its content.[82]

Unwritten principles have also provided the justification for judicial intervention in discretionary decision-making. In *Lalonde*, for example, the Ontario Court of Appeal[83] reviewed a discretionary decision made by the Health Services Restructuring Commission to close the sole francophone hospital in Ontario, a decision allegedly made in the public interest. The statute stipulated that a right to receive French language services could only be limited if all reasonable and necessary measures to comply with the statute had been exhausted.[84] Montfort was explicitly designated as a francophone hospital for the Ottawa-Carleton community and the decision to restructure it was a shift in policy for which no explanation was given. While the Commission could exercise discretion to change and even limit the provision of these services, "it cannot simply invoke administrative convenience and vague funding concerns as the reasons for doing so."[85] The Health Services Commission forfeited its entitlement to deference by providing no justificatory policy for impinging on fundamental constitutional values. Because the Commission failed to give serious weight to the linguistic and cultural significance of the Montfort Hospital to the Franco-Ontarian minority, it acted in a contrary manner to the normative and legal import of the unwritten constitutional principle of respect for and protection of minorities; the decision was therefore quashed.

---

81 This seems to be the conclusion despite some tension with McLachlin C.J.'s public remarks: "I will suggest that actually quite a lot is going on, and that it is important. What is going on is the idea that there exist fundamental norms of justice so basic that they form part of the legal structure of governance and must be upheld by the courts, whether or not they find expression in constitutional texts. And the idea is important, going to the core of just governance and how we define the respective roles of Parliament, the executive and the judiciary." "Remarks of the Right Honourable Beverley McLachlin, P.C.," given at the 2005 Lord Cooke Lecture in Wellington, New Zealand, December 1, 2005, online: <http://www.scc-csc.gc.ca/aboutcourt/judges/speeches/UnwrittenPrinciples_e.asp>.

82 See, for example, the discussion by the majority in the Court of Appeal of British Columbia of the principle of the rule of law in relation to the principle of access to justice. *Christie v. British Columbia*, 2005 BCCA 63. The Supreme Court rejected this line of argument in its decision discussed above.

83 *Lalonde v. Ontario (Commission de restructuration des services de santé)*, 2001 CanLII 21164 (Ont. C.A.) [*Lalonde*]. In chapter 7, Evan Fox-Decent discusses unwritten principles in the relationship of procedural fairness to legislation. He notes that judges have imposed duties to give reasons where an unwritten constitutional principle was at stake and the relevant legislation was silent on the issue. In *Lalonde*, for example, the principle of the protection of minorities led to the imposition of a duty to give reasons.

84 The normative force of unwritten constitutional principles therefore animated a large and liberal interpretation of the relevant provincial statute, the *French Language Services Act*, R.S.O. 1990, c. F.32, and motivated the Court's less deferential attitude toward the Commission's decision.

85 *Lalonde*, *supra* note 83 at para. 168.

As a public law decision, *Lalonde* coheres with the lineage of *Roncarelli*. These decisions illustrate how judges can craft a decision that is grounded in the written constitution, but also further a distinctive Canadian political morality using principles of justice drawn from administrative and constitutional law. Approaching language rights purposively, the Ontario court identified several underlying constitutional principles which it used to interpret the boundaries within which the Ontario government could act. The Ontario Court of Appeal held that a fundamental unwritten principle of the constitutional order, protection of minorities, served to protect Ontario's sole francophone hospital from both closure and a substantial reduction in services. The Commission's directions were quashed because they failed to take into account the importance of francophone institutions and the preservation of Franco-Ontarian culture. In this case, the Court of Appeal relied on the Supreme Court of Canada's decision in *Baker*[86] to conclude that "the review of discretionary decisions on the basis of fundamental Canadian constitutional and societal values"[87] is possible and, despite being accorded a large degree of deference, such discretionary decisions are not immune from judicial scrutiny.

IV. ADMINISTERING THE RULE OF LAW

A. A Complex Institutional Relationship

All of the authors in this text allude to the lengthy and complex history in relations among the administrative state, democracy, and the rule of law. As discussed earlier, at the beginning of the 20th century the emerging administrative state was often seen as a threat both to parliamentary sovereignty and to the rule of law because delegated powers from the political executive operated outside legislative scrutiny. Not only did these new administrative bodies possess substantial powers to restrict freedom, redistribute property, and make decisions on matters relating to individual rights, but they also handled many more cases than courts did. Governments—and the executive in particular—could control these new bodies through the appointments process and had significant influence over delegated policy areas. The growth of regulatory law also meant an expanded scope of discretion for government officials in interpreting standards and defining goals in various statutory schemes and executive regulations. This development was extremely worrisome for those concerned with accountability, because Parliament, the responsible minister, and the courts together could not provide full oversight, given their lack of specialized policy knowledge and the sheer quantity of cases that the administrative state generated.

As a result of the expansion of the administrative state, and well before the Charter, administrative law had to struggle to construct a relationship with the modern state that respected the expertise and policy choices of various administrative agencies and boards while simultaneously recognizing the legitimacy and effectiveness of parallel bodies of justice such as administrative tribunals. Administrative law therefore served a crucial function by establishing, over time, a relationship between courts and government departments as one requiring reciprocal legal and political recognition. Because so many of these

86 *Baker*, *supra* note 71.

87 *Ibid.* at para. 177.

administrative bodies—labour and marketing boards, for example—were created to respond to political pressures and regulatory problems, courts, through administrative law, had to rethink their posture in relation to them in the postwar era. This posture was usually characterized by the term "deference." More important, the courts' view of the state had to change as well. The older and classical liberal view of the minimal state no longer matched reality, and courts had to change their institutional practices to acknowledge the legitimacy of the welfare state. Finally, administrative law served as an important pre-Charter vehicle to challenge government policy and to secure rule of law restraints on discretionary decision-making in social and economic policy, a role that contained both positive and negative features, depending on one's political perspective and the particular issue at play.

B. The Rule of Law and Post-Charter Administrative Law: Deference as Respect

While the rule of law traditionally serves as a bulwark against the executive branch of government and supports judicial oversight of broad statutory grants of discretion, this role becomes more complicated in the modern administrative state. With legislatively delegated powers to different kinds of administrative bodies, the role of courts can be understood in two contrasting ways. On the one hand, courts provide an essential accountability function by policing the exercise of delegated discretionary powers to ensure that they are confined to terms and purposes specified by the authorizing statute. On the other hand, courts are conscious of the separation of powers and, given their lack of expertise in determining the merits of certain policy-making exercises, are themselves under rule of law constraints to respect legislative and executive branches. The history of the relations between the courts and the other branches of government in administrative law began as a bipolar relationship: courts showed greater deference to executive decision-making and prerogative powers, as well as to legislation, but were highly antagonistic toward decisions made by actual administrative bodies, bodies that were not seen as credible or competent decision-makers on questions of law. The relationship of courts to other branches now aspires to a kind of respectful deference[88] (where merited) characterized by an institutional dialogue about the appropriate use and control of discretion, rather than the older command-and-control relationship.[89] Despite this new normative underpinning, the relationship among administrative bodies and courts encounters recurring problems arising from privative clauses, unwritten

---

88 Dyzenhaus, "Constituting Fundamental Values," *supra* note 71 at 489-502. See also David Dyzenhaus, "The Politics of Deference: Judicial Review and Democracy" in Michael Taggart, ed., *The Province of Administrative Law* (Oxford: Oxford University Press, 1997) where the original phrase occurs at 286. Dyzenhaus contrasts the principle of "deference as respect" to the traditional principle of judicial deference. He labels the traditional approach a Diceyan "deference as submission" where judges must submit to the intention of the legislature because of the overriding principle of parliamentary sovereignty. Deference as respect is the opposite of deference as submission. It should also be distinguished from the Dworkinian model, which places judges at the apex of the legal order and whose role is to enforce individualistic common-law values against the state.

89 See Geneviève Cartier's conception of discretion as dialogue versus discretion as power in chapter 10. See also Bill Bogart's analysis of "new governance" in chapter 2, in which negotiation, persuasion, and enabling skills have displaced command and control as a mode of regulation and public management.

principles, ministerial discretion in the national security context, statutory interpretation, and the choice of standard of review.

C. An Example of Deference as Respect: National Corn Growers

Contrasting approaches to the intensity of judicial scrutiny of agency decisions inform the substance of the differing opinions written by Gonthier J. and Wilson J. in *National Corn Growers Assn. v. Canada (Import Tribunal).*[90] The Canadian Import Tribunal conducted an inquiry into the importation of corn grain from the United States into Canada, an inquiry authorized under s. 42 of the *Special Import Measures Act* (SIMA),[91] and determined that continued importation of grain had already caused, or in the future would likely cause, injury to Canadian producers of corn grain. This decision reaffirmed the deputy minister's prior preliminary conclusions that material injury existed and, thus, provided support for his decision to impose a provisional duty on American corn in order to protect Canadian corn growers. The *Federal Court Act*,[92] however, allowed for judicial review if a board, commission, or tribunal had, among other grounds, "based its decision or order on an erroneous finding of fact that it made in a *perverse or capricious manner* or *without regard for the material before it*."[93] Because the Tribunal's decision was based on a factual finding of harm informed by its expertise, and because the Act also contained a privative clause (s. 76(1)) stating that "every order or finding of the Tribunal is final and conclusive," this meant that the decision would be assessed on the standard of patent unreasonableness so that courts could best respect legislative intent. Review turned on whether or not it was patently unreasonable for the tribunal to refer to the *General Agreement on Tariffs and Trade* (GATT)[94] in interpreting the SIMA, whether the tribunal's interpretation of s. 42 in its constitutive legislation was unreasonable, and whether the tribunal reached its decision without any cogent evidence to support its determination of material injury.

In a concurring judgment, Wilson J. evoked the *CUPE* case[95] to caution the majority (and other like-minded judges) about the effects of engaging in a probing examination of a decision. Wilson J. believed that such a detailed examination sanctioned judicial intervention rather than the restraint represented by *CUPE*. *CUPE* was a landmark case that signalled the beginning of the end of the Diceyan model for administrative law. It concerned a labour relations tribunal, the Public Service Staff Relations Board of New Brunswick,

90 [1990] 2 S.C.R. 1324 [*National Corn Growers*], online: <http://www.canlii.org/en/ca/scc/doc/1990/1990canlii49/1990canlii49.pdf>.

91 S.C. 1984, s. 25.

92 R.S.C. 1970, c. 10.

93 *Ibid.*, s. 28.1(c). Emphasis added. Readers will recall that these are familiar expressions connoting arbitrariness in decision-making.

94 The General Agreement on Tariffs and Trade was an international agreement, originally negotiated in 1947, governing trade in goods. The GATT aimed to increase international trade by reducing tariffs and other trade barriers hindering the free flow of goods across national borders. The GATT was succeeded by the World Trade Organization in 1995.

95 *Canadian Union of Public Employees, Local 963 v. New Brunswick Liquor Corp.*, [1979] 2 S.C.R. 227 [*CUPE*]. In chapter 8, Audrey Macklin describes *CUPE*'s "blockbuster" effect on the standard of review in Canadian administrative law.

which had to interpret a poorly worded provision in its enabling statute concerning the meaning of the word "employee." The legislation stated that the employer could not replace striking employees with other employees; moreover, other parts of the statute excluded management from the definition of employee. The representative union, the Canadian Union of Public Employees, complained to the Board that the employer was replacing striking employees with management personnel, contrary to the statute. The Board examined the enabling statute, provided an interpretation of the ambiguous provision, and ordered the employer not to use management to replace striking workers. The Board's decisions were protected by a privative clause. On review, the Supreme Court held that deference was owed to the tribunal based on its expertise, the privative clause, and the reasonableness of its determination. In cases of statutory ambiguity, and where there are multiple interpretations that are reasonable, a reviewing court should defer to the interpretation of the expert tribunal.

According to Wilson J., *CUPE*'s approach to the standard of review, particularly with respect to patent unreasonableness, entailed a relationship between courts and administrative agencies where the courts should recognize that (1) administrative agencies, not courts, bear primary statutory responsibility for their legislative mandate in the area of regulation; (2) administrative agencies possess expertise, experience, and contextual knowledge about which the courts know very little; and (3) statutory provisions, such as those found in *National Corn Growers*, do not admit to one uniquely correct interpretation but, rather, can sustain a variety of reasonable interpretations. Though concurring with the result reached, Wilson J. clearly feared that such a wide-ranging and probing examination of both the agency's interpretation of its enabling statute and the reasonableness of its conclusions risked reintroducing the correctness standard under the guise of reasonableness and displacing the patently unreasonable standard.[96] In other words, this approach would likely gut the hard-won jurisprudential ground symbolized by the *CUPE* decision.

Wilson J. underscored what she believed to be the appropriate institutional attitude or posture. In the face of a privative clause, courts must not engage in a wide-ranging review concerning whether or not the tribunal's conclusions are unreasonable. The merits of a tribunal's interpretation of international obligations, such as the GATT, are for the legislature to address by amending the terms of the statute if interpretive disagreement exists between institutions. And, most important, meticulous analysis of a tribunal's reasoning concerning the evidence should not become the norm. As she tersely wrote:

> Faced with the highly charged world of international trade and a clear legislative decision to create a tribunal to dispose of disputes that arise in that context, it is highly inappropriate for courts to take it upon themselves to assess the merits of the Tribunal's conclusions about when the government may respond to another country's use of subsidies. If courts were to take it upon themselves to conduct detailed reviews of these decisions on a regular basis, the Tribunal's effectiveness and authority would soon be effectively undermined.[97]

The conclusions advanced by Wilson J. explicitly rejected the older Diceyan model in which the rule of law provided the justification for judicial control of administrative agencies and

96 This worry surfaces in the discussion of the so-called intermediate standard of review, reasonableness *simpliciter*, as discussed by Audrey Macklin in chapter 8 and Sheila Wildeman in chapter 9.

97 *National Corn Growers*, *supra* note 90 at 59.

their interpretations, to be replaced by a new model where the rule of law buttressed the "pragmatic and functional" methodological approach to determine the appropriate standard of review. Instead of an unreasonable administrative body whose straitjacket laces are ever more tightly pulled by the courts, the modern judicial approach to the administrative state ought to be informed by a more flexible, respectful, and contextualized methodology that recognizes different exercises of legitimate power by competent institutional partners.

The majority decision written by Gonthier J. also concluded that the tribunal was not unreasonable with respect to any of these three matters. To reach this result, Gonthier J. delved deeply into both how the tribunal came to the decision as well as the decision's merits. In the face of criticism from the concurring judgment written by Wilson J., Gonthier J. responded: "With respect, I do not understand how a conclusion can be reached as to the reasonableness of a tribunal's interpretation of its enabling statute without considering the reasoning underlying it, and I would be surprised if that were the effect of this Court's decision in *C.U.P.E.*"[98] Gonthier J., however, did not believe that his more probing approach repudiated *CUPE*; instead, he continued to see his method of review as more respectful and deferential than that found in the traditional Diceyan model. The effect of this more probing inquiry, however, seemed to move the standard of review away from patently unreasonable and closer to correctness.

National Corn Growers illustrates how different theoretical models can help explain how judges understand their institutional role as well as how these models shed light on the underlying rationale behind the judicial choice of the standard of review. Dicey envisions the judiciary as guardians of private-law checks—in his words, "regular law"—on the arbitrary power of the executive and its delegates. In matters of agency interpretation, his theory of the rule of law argues for the primacy of a correctness standard of review. Fuller's theory, on the other hand, clearly incorporates rule of law concerns in relation to the administrative state and judicial review of administrative decisions and envisages a collaborative, cooperative endeavour among state actors and institutions to maintain the rule of law. In the confines of the case, the fact that the tribunal had not abused its discretion and had exhibited its expertise suggest that his perspective would support the more respectful approach articulated by Wilson J. Indeed, Fuller's concern for the problems that polycentricity—defined as complex networks of relationships—poses for public law underscores the importance of this conclusion.[99] On his view, the presence of polycentricity in a case means that where a reasonable range of policy choices exists, or when multiple reasonable interpretations of an ambiguous statutory term are possible, or when a decision involves balancing multiple sets of competing interests, then these functions are best left with the expert tribunal. Raz narrows the reach of the rule of law to correction for the harms created by law itself. His theory does not provide enough details concerning a role for the rule of law as a

98 *Ibid.* at 40-41.

99 In "The Form and Limits of Adjudication," Fuller controversially claimed that polycentric disputes are inherently unsuitable for adjudication and should therefore be considered non-justiciable. According to Fuller, polycentricity is both pervasive and a matter of degree. Private law disputes, by contrast, take the familiar form of a bipolar encounter between plaintiff and defendant, and will likely have few polycentric elements. The problem Fuller identified is that of knowing when polycentric elements have become so significant that the proper limits of adjudication have been reached such that these disputes should be resolved in the legislature or by the market. (1978) 92 Harv. L. Rev. 353.

check on the arbitrary use of political power exercised in "non-legal" ways, such as decision-making power within the administrative state.[100] This omission, however, points to some support for Gonthier's approach as the best way to control harms created by the administrative state, but perhaps less so for the risks created by judicial oversight. A different case might produce a different alignment. If, for example, the third standard of review—reasonableness—had been available at the time of *National Corn Growers*, a unanimous decision on the appropriateness of this standard might have been reached. As with so many aspects of administrative law, context matters greatly, though your own tendencies concerning the appropriate ways that the rule of law constrains judges and administrative decision-makers might reflect one approach more than another.

D. Two Problems for Deference as Respect: Privative Clauses and the Choice of the Standard of Review

1. Privative Clauses

As seen in the *National Corn Growers* case discussed above, privative or ouster clauses historically posed challenges for the rule of law. Several types of privative clauses exist, but the general form is a statutory provision protecting the decisions made by public officials in boards, tribunals, and ministries either from further dispute internally (that is, a finality clause) or from judicial review (that is, an ouster clause).[101] The powers conferred on administrative agencies through privative clauses were often conferred in absolute terms and, therefore, decisions were meant to be final. The conundrum for courts was that the statute prescribed limits on delegated power but, at the same time, authorized officials to act with seemingly unfettered discretion within those broad confines. The risk to the accountability function of the rule of law was that these officials could behave as a law unto themselves because they would be the sole judges of the substantive validity of their own acts. The institutional result of privative clauses was a system of competing and irreconcilable supremacies between the legislative and judicial branches of government. Those who supported the development of the administrative state, meanwhile, worried about the growth of administrative law and the consequent judicial review of administrative decisions, seeing judicial scrutiny as an altogether too constraining legalism that would hinder the flexible regulation needed in a complex industrialized society.[102]

Courts approached privative clauses in several different ways: reading them out of the statute if a jurisdictional error was implicated in the case, or deferring completely to Parliament's intent to oust judicial oversight. Finally, and later, they developed methods of statutory interpretation grounded in the common-law presumption that Parliament always intends

100 This is not an argument that his theory cannot incorporate discretionary decision-making.

101 For a discussion of privative clauses in administrative law, see Audrey Macklin, chapter 8, and Sheila Wildeman, chapter 9. For a detailed analysis of the history, types, and constitutional effects of privative clauses, see David Dyzenhaus, "Disobeying Parliament? Privative Clauses and the Rule of Law" in Richard W. Bauman & Tsvi Kahana, eds., *The Least Examined Branch: The Role of Legislatures in the Constitutional State* (Cambridge: Cambridge University Press, 2006) at 499.

102 As Audrey Macklin points out in chapter 8, the motive behind privative clauses was not to oust judicial meddling (or not primarily), but to provide efficient resolution of disputes and allocate scarce judicial resources by restricting access to the courts.

to respect procedural fairness, even with respect to statutorily delegated powers with broad scope.[103] This last approach laid the basis for deference as respect, found in the *CUPE* decision, in which the privative clause came to be viewed as a communication from the legislature that courts should recognize the interpretive authority of the tribunal within its area of expertise, but that judges could exercise their rule of law powers of oversight on constitutional and jurisdictional matters. Nevertheless, the modern development of deference and respect for administrative tribunals is both an ongoing and vulnerable achievement.

Finally, privative clauses and unwritten principles uncannily mirror each other. As discussed in part III, above, judges seem to have an interpretive monopoly on unwritten principles, thereby "ousting" interpretations from other branches of government. Robust use of unwritten principles—and ironically the rule of law itself—risks entrenching the elitist rule of judges and opens the door to judicial arbitrariness, the obverse of legislatively sanctioned administrative arbitrariness due to the power of privative clauses. This points to a conception of the rule of law, which recognizes that all branches of government have a duty to realize a rule of law state and that all branches can fail to do so in their distinctive ways.

2. *The Choice of the Standard of Review*

We have also seen that pre-Charter administrative law was limited to the review of questions of law, jurisdiction, and procedural fairness in order to determine whether or not decision-makers acted in excess of jurisdiction, without authority, or had otherwise abused their discretion on unreasonable grounds. Reviewing courts were not to examine the full merits of the decision, save on exceptional grounds, so that they would be constrained from substituting their preferred policy outcome for that of authorized decision-makers. Judicial interpretation of the rule of law and other legal principles, such as the separation of powers, animated the level of deference shown to administrative bodies. This deference was most fully exhibited in the choice of the standard of review—correctness and patent unreasonableness (with reasonableness as a post-Charter development)—that were applied in order to analyze a particular administrative decision. The standard of review therefore functioned as a prime rule-of-law constraint on judges in administrative law.

As an ideal then, the standard of review indicates a court's understanding of independence and expertise within these administrative bodies, regulates the contours of the administrative state and its exercises of power, and controls the discretionary features within the exercise of judicial review. Whether the ideal succeeds in practice, however, is the subject of several chapters in this book.[104] And, as we have seen in *National Corn Growers*, the contemporary approach to the standard of review reflects concerns about judicial legitimacy within a democratic state—a state that has wielded a democratic mandate to create administrative and policy frameworks. The pragmatic and functional approach used to weigh the criteria involved in the choice of the standard of review illustrated courts' attempts to grapple with the sheer variety of administrative bodies, while also affirming the legitimacy of review of the multiplicity of decisions and rulings. The pragmatic

103 See Evan Fox-Decent, chapter 7, for his discussion of privative clauses and procedural fairness.

104 See in particular the two chapters on the standard of review: chapter 8 by Audrey Macklin and chapter 9 by Sheila Wildeman. On Wildeman's account, this author tends toward a romantic reading of the development of the standards of review.

and functional approach responds both to the nature of the tribunal as well as the nature of the issue that is subject to appeal. Deference will be shown when a match exists between tribunal expertise and the issue. Review on the correctness standard allows courts to show very little to no deference to agency decision-making: the decision is either right or wrong. This standard is applied when the agency has very little expertise or when the issue involves the interpretation of general law or constitutional matters. Patent unreasonableness is the most deferential or respectful standard and is considered appropriate when review involves a polycentric, complex question concerning the regulation of activities within the mandate of a highly specialized agency. The court will only intervene when it is blatantly evident that the agency has made an error of law or of fact. Reasonableness, the intermediate standard, reflects a justified degree of judicial deference or respect for the challenged decision or action.

The tensions among the rule of law, deference, the standard of review, and the administrative state were forcefully made in the *Baker* case,[105] which involved the review of an immigration officer's biased decision in the context of a humanitarian and compassionate grounds application by an illegal immigrant.[106] On some accounts, *Baker* represents an instance of judicial creativity in the crafting of a context-specific duty to give reasons, particularly in the immigration sphere. Courts normally show a large degree of deference in this policy area, given the expertise of the decision-maker in immigration cases.[107] Instead, the treatment of one individual at the hands of the administrative state precipitated the expansion of the content of the duty of fairness, a vital component of the rule of law, in an area usually demanding correctness.[108] On this point, L'Heureux-Dubé J. for the majority wrote:

> The pragmatic and functional approach can take into account the fact that the more discretion that is left to a decision-maker, the more reluctant courts should be to interfere with the manner in which decision-makers have made choices among various options. However, though discretionary decisions will generally be given considerable respect, that discretion must be exercised in accordance with the boundaries imposed in the statute, the principles of the rule of law, the principles of administrative law, the fundamental values of Canadian society, and the principles of the *Charter*.[109]

According to the Court, the administrative decision in *Baker* displayed arbitrariness: it did not exhibit a mind that was attuned to the humanitarian and compassionate requirements stipulated in the department's own guidelines; it showed a lack of regard for the per-

105 *Baker*, *supra* note 71.

106 The facts of *Baker* are described more fully by Grant Huscroft in chapter 5.

107 On the one hand, the fact-specific nature of the inquiry, the role of a humanitarian and compassionate grounds application within the statutory scheme as an exception, the fact that the decision-maker is the minister, and the considerable discretion evidenced by the statutory language suggest that a large degree of deference would be appropriate. On the other hand, the absence of a privative clause, the explicit contemplation of judicial review by the Federal Court, and the individual rather than polycentric nature of the decision, argued against patent unreasonableness as the proper standard. "Reasonableness," the intermediate standard, was therefore chosen.

108 Grant Huscroft provides a more detailed examination of the scope and content of the duty of fairness in chapter 5. Historically, the duty of fairness was a jurisdictional question and therefore required correctness. Privative clauses could not protect procedural errors.

109 *Baker*, *supra* note 71 at para. 56.

son affected; and it gave the impression that important factors, such as the best interests of the children, were outweighed by discriminatory biases. The decision therefore did not meet the threshold of reasonableness that could "command respect" from the reviewers. Mavis Baker and her counsel were lucky to gain access to the "reasons" for the negative decision in her case. In order to control for the arbitrariness of luck, the Court imposed a duty to give reasons on statutory and prerogative decision-makers in certain administrative contexts where important individual interests are at stake. Despite the fact that this is not a general duty for all decision-makers in the state, it nevertheless still stands as a substantive procedural protection. Ideally, the duty to give reasons has the potential to advance both restraint and respect, thereby facilitating rule of law concerns and administrative legitimacy. Reasons stand as an opportunity for the agency to show both its expertise and its concern for affected individuals by observing procedural fairness. Judicial recognition of reasons—that is, acknowledgment that the reasons are justified and justifiable—constrains reweighing the factors and affirms specific instances of non-arbitrary decision-making. On this account, deference does not occur simply because the statute has a privative clause ordering courts not to intervene; rather, deference is the result of institutional competence, expertise, and mutual respect for the rule of law.

As others in this casebook will discuss, no *a priori* answer exists within the pragmatic and functional approach to discerning the proper scope of deference. General tendencies based on institutional history—labour boards, for example—may exist, but a "one size fits all" approach to bodies and types of decision-making should be avoided.[110] Those who appreciate certainty as a rule of law value, however, will find the lack of predictability concerning when a court will or will not recognize agency expertise both frustrating and troubling.

Despite the continuing problem of the standard of review, *Baker* nevertheless represents an important link in the rule-of-law narrative that can be traced back to *Roncarelli*. Like *Roncarelli*, *Baker* discloses that administrative and constitutional law are attuned to underlying fundamental values such as basic concerns for human dignity, the vindication of rights, and the effects of political power on individuals. Public law, on this account, discovers its normative aim in the need to find justification for all exercises of public power. Yet this awareness does not necessarily translate into judicial supremacy. Instead, courts ought to respect institutional partners that justify their use of public power as reasonable and commit to the values that underpin the exercise of that public power. Discretion, therefore, is always structured and constrained. *Baker* confirms the shift to a value-centric approach to the rule of law in a modern constitutional democracy.[111]

---

110 Colleen Flood and Lorne Sossin, for example, argue that the myriad number of delegated powers favours the perspective that a spectrum of possibilities exists within the three standards of review. The methodology should therefore mirror the approach to procedural fairness where instead of three standards, courts would look to a wide range of factors in order to determine the degree of deference using one comprehensive standard. See Lorne Sossin & Colleen M. Flood, "The Contextual Turn: Iacobucci's Legacy and the Standard of Review in Administrative Law" (2007) 57 U.T.L.J. 581.

111 See Mary Liston, "'Alert, Alive and Sensitive': *Baker*, the Duty to Give Reasons and the Ethos of Justification in Canadian Public Law" for this understanding of *Baker* in David Dyzenhaus, ed., *The Unity of Public Law* (Oxford: Hart Publishing, 2004). This collection of essays offers a multi-perspectival examination of a public law culture of justification through the lens of *Baker*.

E. Constraining the Charter

The Charter now provides many express grounds by which courts may review the exercise of statutory or discretionary powers. A recent development in the relationship between the Charter and administrative bodies is the judicial finding that an administrative tribunal may have the jurisdiction to consider Charter challenges to its enabling legislation.[112] This determination represents a major shift in the earlier approach, which arrogated the power to determine questions of law to courts, while leaving administrative bodies the power to interpret and apply their enabling legislation. Originally, only administrative tribunals that structurally and purposively mirrored courts possessed the jurisdiction to hear Charter claims. Now, sometimes the enabling legislation will empower an administrative tribunal to interpret and apply all law, including the Charter, while at other times the statutory scheme as a whole will confer an implicit jurisdiction. These changes are grounded in concerns for access to justice and a recognition of the competence and capacity of such tribunals as legal bodies to review legislation. On this understanding, jurisdiction to apply the Charter to enabling legislation is given by the legislature in the statute and does not arise solely from the constitutional text. Certain rule of law considerations stemming from the separation of powers will flow from this more restrained mandate: the scope of the remedies that an administrative tribunal can grant will be limited; the particular decision will not be binding authority as precedent for future cases; and, in subsequent judicial review, the decision will be subject to a standard of correctness, ensuring that it receives little or no curial deference.

The Charter can significantly constrain delegations of broad discretionary powers where Charter rights and freedoms are directly or indirectly implicated, or which may not be sufficiently confined by the terms of the enabling statute in question. So, while the existence of broad discretionary powers is not suspect in itself, courts could be more demanding in cases that involve broad delegations of power by ensuring that discretion is structured or confined within the parameters of the Charter. Where Charter rights and freedoms are not at issue, courts may tolerate broad discretionary powers, but they may also attend to the effects of this power in individual cases.

The ability of administrative agencies to question unconstitutional enabling provisions not only provides an economical and efficient resolution of a rights dispute (avoiding the need to go to court), but also conforms to the emerging "institutional dialogue" or "deference as respect" institutional model. This democratically informed perspective emerged clearly in the dissent written by McLachlin J. (as she then was) and L'Heureux-Dubé J. in the case *Cooper v. Canada (Human Rights Commission)*. This case concerned the fundamental question of whether or not human rights tribunals have the authority to determine the constitutionality of provisions in their enabling statutes. In *Cooper*, they wrote a resounding affirmation:

> The *Charter* is not some holy grail which only judicial initiates of the superior courts may touch. The *Charter* belongs to the people. All law and law-makers that touch the people must conform to it. Tribunals and commissions charged with deciding legal issues are no exception.

112 See Evan Fox-Decent, chapter 7, for a discussion of the difficulties in the relationship between the Charter and administrative law, including agency jurisdiction over the Charter and the recent trilogy of cases affirming tribunal authority to consider questions of law.

> Many more citizens have their rights determined by these tribunals than by the courts. If the *Charter* is to be meaningful to ordinary people, then it must find its expression in the decisions of these tribunals.[113]

The institutional aspiration underlying this vision is to create a constitutional democracy that reconciles the formerly competing sovereignties and reinforces institutional competencies for the benefit of citizens.

F. Institutional Dialogue and the Canadian Rule of Law

Political and legal theories differ in their characterization of the relationship between democracy and the rule of law, but most allude to various tensions in that relationship. Such tensions come to a head when the rule of law is associated mainly with the courts in what comes to be seen as an antagonistic relationship of judges against the legislature and democratic will formation.

As we have seen, the Diceyan conception of the rule of law supported parliamentary democracy but employed administrative law, judicially enforced in ordinary courts, to control the policy-making branches of the state—that is, the executive and the bureaucracy. But, while institutional and policy differentiation characterizes the modern state, the Diceyan rule of law authorized judges to enforce constitutional fundamentals and institutional coherence uniformly throughout the state. Principles derived from private law controlled public bodies and Dicey rejected the notion that a separate branch of public law should develop in the British system.

A similar, but different, antagonism plays out in judicial review of legislation under a written bill of rights like the Charter in cases where individual rights and public goods directly conflict. Section II.A on the legal control of substantive arbitrariness above alluded to the normativity of the legal subject animating individual rights against the state as well as the duties with which the state must comply. This normativity potentially authorizes a greater intervention, not just in the decision-making procedures, but in the very heart or substance of a public authority's decision that affects important individual interests.

A current and prominent proponent of this approach to judicial review can be found in the philosophy of Ronald Dworkin.[114] Dworkin's legal subject is an individual bearer of rights who is entitled to demand the resolution of disputes over the content of these rights through the legal system—specifically through courts, which he calls the "independent forum of principle."[115] Dworkin's theory therefore grounds a vision of a constitutionalized

113 *Cooper*, *supra* note 24 at para. 70.

114 Two significant texts for this argument are Dworkin's *A Matter of Principle* (Cambridge, MA: Harvard University Press, 1985) and *Law's Empire* (Cambridge, MA: Harvard University Press, 1986). As a legal philosopher, Dworkin participates in a branch of philosophy called deontological liberalism, a liberalism popularized by the work of John Rawls. Deontological liberalism holds that the purpose of politics is to allow people who possess many different conceptions of value to pursue their individual ends to the greatest degree possible. This form of liberalism adheres to a theory of equality that "supposes that political decisions must be, so far as it is possible, independent of any particular conception of the good life." Ronald Dworkin, "Liberalism" in *A Matter of Principle* at 191.

115 See *A Matter of Principle*, *ibid.* at 30-32 and chapter 2, "The Forum of Principle."

public morality that he calls the "rights conception of the rule of law."[116] For Dworkin, the rule of law necessarily entails the judicial determination of rights through principled interpretation in hard cases where a legal answer must be crafted by judges rather than "given" by existing legal sources. Principled interpretation is based on rules, principles, the concomitant interpretation of how these rules and principles appropriately fit with positive law, and, importantly, how a judicial decision expresses its compatibility with selected principles from a larger political morality. Government respect for individual freedom and the autonomy of non-governmental spheres of authority, for example, would be requirements of a Dworkinian political morality.

Dworkin's theory of adjudication advances a strong political morality because it has as its central focus a concept of justice designed to further political principles of autonomy, dignity, equality, and liberty for all individuals in the political community. Politics, on his account, should be held to a higher standard than pragmatism or consequentialism would allow because the political system ought to place the pursuit of justice higher than the maintenance of political power, stability, or general welfare. Liberalism, his primary political morality, takes precedence over the political morality associated with democracy, such as majority decision-making embodied in legislation, or the focus on the common good from communitarianism. One consequence of Dworkin's theory is that judges, not legislators, are ultimately charged with guarding the moral integrity of the political order because, as the chief political actors in the form of principle, they possess the knowledge and the skills—honed through their unique access to the interpretation of the law—to be the better articulators of a constitutionalized public morality.

Nevertheless, if courts should respect pluralism as a political fact, and ideological pluralism in particular, their job is not to endorse wholeheartedly one particular substantive political morality: that, many critics of Dworkin argue, is typically seen as the role of the political sphere.[117] But, when confronted with conflicting demands, courts should seek to construct a principled balance among competing goods or reconcile conflicting rights as the appropriate remedy. The interpretive role of the courts in public law means that they must construct in their rulings a reasonable normative and narrative coherence to explain the nature of the conflict and the appropriateness of the decision in favour of one balance over another. Government justification of limitations on rights and the possibility of legislative response either through reply legislation or the notwithstanding clause represent crucial institutional restraints on this form of judicial power in the Canadian order.[118] Taken together,

---

116 *Ibid.* at 11-12.

117 Many democratic theorists have attacked Dworkin's theory of adjudication and his conception of the rule of law. See, for example, the collection of essays in Allan C. Hutchinson and Patrick Monahan, eds., *The Rule of Law: Ideal or Ideology* (Toronto: Carswell, 1987); Jeremy Waldron, *Law and Disagreement* (Oxford: Oxford University Press, 1999); Christopher Manfredi, *Judicial Power and the Charter: Canada and the Paradox of Liberal Constitutionalism*, 2d ed. (Toronto: Oxford University Press, 2001); and Ran Hirschl, *Towards Juristocracy: The Origins and Consequences of the New Constitutionalism* (Cambridge, MA: Harvard University Press, 2004).

118 See, for example, Wilson J.'s characterization of s. 1 of the *Canadian Charter of Rights and Freedoms* (the Charter) Part I of the *Constitution Act, 1982*, being Schedule B to the *Canada Act 1982* (U.K.), 1982, c. 11 in her dissent in *Operation Dismantle*, *supra* note 24 at para. 104: "Section 1, in my opinion, is the uniquely Canadian mechanism through which the courts are to determine the justiciability of particular issues that

these three aspects of the rule of law—the principle of legality, institutional practices, and a distinctive political morality—argue for an understanding of the political order as a joint effort in governance on the part of institutions and citizens. In Canada, this joint effort in upholding the rule of law is often described as an "institutional dialogue."[119]

The specific nature of this joint effort in governance is controversial. Though liberal democratic theory emphasizes that no branch of government should possess complete control of sovereignty, disputes rage about whether public power should be shared equally among the state institutions or whether one branch should retain overall supremacy.[120] In Canada's pre-Charter Westminster system of government, for example, the principle of parliamentary sovereignty traditionally meant that Parliament could pass laws on any subject, and that no institution or person could override or strike down these laws. The rule of law required that statutes meet the "manner and form" criteria of enactment: that is, the legislature must be identified as the proper source of law and the proper legislative procedure must be used. Existence of these two factors sufficed in order to recognize a statute as valid or "prescribed by law," and this recognition should be considered legitimate by all institutions and persons, including the judiciary. In the pre-Charter world of public law, the authority of legislatures was not constrained by courts, but rather by political sanctions. Political sanctions manifested themselves through regular elections as well as political conventions such as ministerial responsibility in which Cabinet ministers faced demands for accountability by way of scrutiny in question period.

The enactment of the Charter has altered the principle of parliamentary sovereignty. Constitutional rights can be limited subject to the government satisfying the justificatory requirements of s. 1 in the Charter. As well, legislatures can theoretically respond to judicial rulings by using the s. 33 notwithstanding clause to override decisions temporarily. In this way, Canada continues to endorse the principle of parliamentary sovereignty, but reconciles it with the principle of the rule of law as manifested in judicial review. However, the legitimacy of judicial decision-making in matters of political controversy and policy remains in dispute, a debate that has been exacerbated by the Charter. At times, the judicial

---

come before it. It embodies through its reference to a free and democratic society the essential features of our constitution including the separation of powers, responsible government and the rule of law. It obviates the need for a 'political questions' doctrine and permits the Court to deal with what might be termed 'prudential' considerations in a principled way without renouncing its constitutional and mandated responsibility for judicial review."

119 Noteworthy articles from the voluminous literature on institutional dialogue include T.R.S. Allan, "Constitutional Dialogue and the Justification of Judicial Review" (2003) 23 Oxford J. Legal Stud. 563; Stephen Gardbaum, "The New Commonwealth Model of Constitutionalism" (2001) 49 Am. J. Comp. L. 707; Peter W. Hogg & Allison A. Bushell, "The Charter Dialogue Between Courts and Legislatures (or Perhaps the Charter of Rights Isn't Such a Bad Thing After All)" (1997) 35 Osgoode Hall L.J. 75; Christopher P. Manfredi, "The Life of a Metaphor: Dialogue in the Supreme Court, 1998-2003" (2004) 23 Sup. Ct. L. Rev. (2d) 105; Kent Roach, *The Supreme Court on Trial: Judicial Activism or Democratic Dialogue* (Toronto: Irwin Law, 2001); and Jeremy Waldron, "Some Models of Dialogue Between Judges and Legislatures" (2004) 23 Sup. Ct. L. Rev. (2d) 7.

120 See Jürgen Habermas for an argument supporting co-equal status between the principles of democracy and the rule of law: Jürgen Habermas, "Constitutional Democracy: A Paradoxical Union of Contradictory Principles" (2001) 29 Pol. Theory 766, and "On the Internal Relation Between the Rule of Law and Democracy" in Patrick Hayden, ed., *Philosophical Perspectives on Law and Politics* (New York: Peter Lang, 1999) 327.

role goes beyond applying the rule of law understood as the principle of legality to an activity that appears more legislative or discretionary in nature—that is, the ability to make law or intervene in policy development. The litmus test for this debate is whether or not one believes that in a reasonably democratic society with functioning legislatures, where its citizens disagree about the scope and content of rights, judicial review of legislation constitutes an inappropriate mode of final decision-making.[121] In administrative law, this kind of activity is particularly controversial if it means judges can, in certain cases and with a constrained approach, "reweigh" the factors that administrative decision-makers use based on their expertise and experiential knowledge, if such decisions violate constitutional values.[122] Those who support this conclusion argue that the Charter reinforces the constitutional commitment that all persons—individuals, corporations, and state actors—must adhere to the rule of law and respect fundamental constitutional values.

G. Other Routes to Accountability in the Administrative State

Just as a "one size fits all" approach does not exist in the courts, so too in the state.[123] Judicial review represents an important, but not the sole, route to securing administrative accountability. Courts should be seen as merely one among the many means by which we hold government to account. Moreover, it will be better for the legitimacy of courts if we recognize them as one among a "family" of legitimate routes to securing accountability within a liberal democratic state: public inquiries, task forces, departmental investigations, and ombudsmen. The rule of law will also inform the various institutional alternatives to judicial review of government action.[124]

121 See Jeremy Waldron, "The Core of the Case Against Judicial Review" (2006) 115 Yale L.J. 1346. Although Waldron is discussing the role of the judiciary in the United States, his argument finds purchase in Canada with critics who bemoan the growth of judicial activism and the inability of legislatures to use the notwithstanding clause to advance a different interpretation of a constitutional matter for fear of political backlash. The abeyance of s. 33, they argue, gives judges the de facto last word and ensures that the courts remain supreme over other branches of government.

122 David Dyzenhaus argues that if one recognizes a judicial role for preserving constitutional values, then judicial review of legislative and governmental decisions is premised on this role recognition and on ensuring that decision-making takes into account the content of those values. The executive and the legislature face the onus of justifying their decisions by reference to these values either within legislation, or within the arguments they make under s. 1 of the Charter. See David Dyzenhaus, "The Legitimacy of the Rule of Law" in *2005 New York University School of Law Colloquium in Legal, Political, and Social Philosophy*, online: NYU <http://www.law.nyu.edu/clppt/program2005/readings/legallegit2.pdf>; and "Constituting Fundamental Values," *supra* note 71.

123 Similarly, the principle of federalism militates in favour of provincial experimentation with institutional design. Though higher and lower courts are compelled to work toward unified standards, there need not be concordance between federal and provincial approaches to regulation and administration.

124 See Peter Carver, chapter 14, for a discussion of administrative law in relation to public inquiries.

V. CONCLUSION: A DEMOCRATIC RULE OF LAW IN THE ADMINISTRATIVE STATE?

This chapter has explained how the concept of the rule of law and its associated legal and political principles are fundamental to understanding the relationship between courts and administrative bodies. The realization of the rule of law within a democratic culture can not only legitimate the sharing of public power among courts, the executive, legislatures, and administrative bodies, but also facilitate the creation of multiple routes for citizens (and non-citizens) to secure accountability for the use of public power. All parts of and persons in the state participate in the creation and maintenance of the rule of law. The multiplicity of institutional environments, however, means that the rule of law will require different responsibilities and restraints for different institutional actors and practices. Though this makes administrative law a difficult field of study and provides unending complications for judicial review of administrative decision-making, one positive reading of such complexity suggests that this is a necessary consequence of the interaction between the rule of law and democracy. The simple system suggested by both legal and political theory, then, is capable of infinite variations and complexity in the design of institutions and their constraints. These permutations must nevertheless continue to adhere to the substance and procedures of legality—a process in which courts play an important role through legal interpretation of abstract principles and oversight of administrative practices.[125]

How a judge understands the rule of law, and his or her role in upholding it, will necessarily shape how he or she approaches the review of decisions made by an administrative tribunal. Judicial temperament is not completely predictable: judges may conceive of themselves as the Diceyan defenders of the rule of law against the administrative state; or they may view themselves the Dworkinian legal guardians of the constitution, committed to upholding the rights conception of the rule of law; or perhaps they may see their role as the Fullerian cooperative partner who recognizes democratic initiatives, but still maintains institutional fidelity to rule-of-law principles. Institutional dialogue and deference as respect stand as distinctive forms of the commitment to judicial restraint in Canadian administrative law—a restraint that simultaneously attempts to ensure judicial accountability and larger public law accountability.

125 In a new and significant case, the Supreme Court invoked rule-of-law values and attributes to justify restructuring the standard of review. *Dunsmuir v. New Brunswick*, 2008 SCC 9 illustrates judicial efforts to introduce greater clarity, fairness, consistency, and simplicity into administrative law by reducing the standards of review from three to two—correctness and reasonableness—and by rebranding the pragmatic and functional approach as a simpler "standard of review analysis" (para. 63). These efforts were informed by a conception of the rule of law that explicitly acknowledges the tension between judicial review and democracy. According to the Court, judicial review upholds the rule of law by ensuring that all exercises of public authority are lawful, reasonable, and fair. But judicial review also respects legislative supremacy through the proper approach to the standard of review; recognizing effective limits on judicial discretion such as legislative intent, privative clauses, and agency expertise; and by rejecting a "court-centric" conception of the rule of law (paras. 27-33). On this account, administrative agencies as constitutional partners do exhibit rule-of-law attributes, have embraced rule-of-law values, and can facilitate access to justice. The Court's goal in this judgment was to provide greater guidance for reviewing courts, counsel, litigants, and decision-makers in administrative law. The postscript in chapter 8 and the accompanying website further consider these recent developments.

SUGGESTED ADDITIONAL READINGS

BOOKS AND ARTICLES

Allan, T.R.S. *Constitutional Justice: A Liberal Theory of the Rule of Law* (Oxford: Oxford University Press, 2001).

Bauman, Richard W., & Tsvi Kahana, eds. *The Least Examined Branch: The Role of Legislatures in the Constitutional State* (Cambridge: Cambridge University Press, 2006).

Bellamy, Richard, ed. *The Rule of Law and the Separation of Powers* (Aldershot, UK: Ashgate/Dartmouth, 2005).

Craig, Paul P. *Administrative Law*, 5th ed. (London: Sweet & Maxwell, 2003).

Dworkin, Ronald. *A Matter of Principle* (Cambridge, MA: Harvard University Press, 1985).

Dyzenhaus, David, ed. *Recrafting the Rule of Law: The Limits of Legal Order* (Oxford: Hart, 1999).

Huscroft, Grant, & Michael Taggart, eds. *Inside and Outside Canadian Administrative Law* (Toronto: University of Toronto Press, 2006).

McLachlin, Madam Justice Beverley M. "The Role of Administrative Tribunals and Courts in Maintaining the Rule of Law" (1999) 12 Can. J. Admin. L. & Prac. 171.

Mullan, David. *Administrative Law: Cases, Text, and Materials*, 5th ed. (Toronto: Emond Montgomery, 2003).

Saunders, Cheryl, & Katherine Le Roy, eds. *The Rule of Law* (Sydney: The Federation Press, 2003).

Shapiro, Ian, ed. *NOMOS XXXVI: The Rule of Law* (New York and London: New York University Press, 1994).

Tamanaha, Brian Z. *On the Rule of Law: History, Politics, Theory* (Cambridge, UK: Cambridge University Press, 2004).

CASES

British Columbia v. Imperial Tobacco Canada Ltd., [2005] 2 S.C.R. 473.

Cooper v. Canada (Canadian Human Rights Commission), [1996] 3 S.C.R. 85.

National Corn Growers Assn. v. Canada (Import Tribunal), [1990] 2 S.C.R. 1324.

Reference re Language Rights Under s. 23 of Manitoba Act, 1870 and s. 133 of Constitutional Act, 1867, [1985] 1 S.C.R. 721.

Roncarelli v. Duplessis, [1959] S.C.R. 121.

CHAPTER FIVE

The Duty of Fairness: From Nicholson to Baker and Beyond

GRANT HUSCROFT
Faculty of Law, University of Western Ontario

I. INTRODUCTION

Administrative law was, until the latter half of the 20th century, dominated by formalism. Judicial decisions—the decisions of courts—were required to be made in accordance with the rules of natural justice. *Audi alteram partem* required a decision-maker to "hear the other side" in a dispute, and *nemo judex in sua causa* precluded a man from being a "judge in his own cause." These ancient rules were intended to guarantee unbiased hearings, but their application was limited to the judicial and quasi-judicial spheres.[1] So-called administrative

1 The historical origin of these terms is discussed in David P. Jones & Anne S. de Villars, *Principles of Administrative Law*, 4th ed. (Toronto: Thomson Carswell, 2004) at 203-4.

decisions—decisions made by executive actors—could be made without regard to any such rules. This dichotomy between judicial and administrative decisions resulted in a preoccupation with categorization, and judicial review focused on the nature of the power exercised.

The growth of the modern regulatory state, and with it the number of decisions made by everyone from bureaucrats to tribunals and ministers of the Crown, made change inevitable. It was indefensible that important decisions could be made without any procedural protection being afforded simply because they were decisions that were classified as administrative in nature. Following the lead of the House of Lords in *Ridge v. Baldwin*,[2] the Supreme Court of Canada abandoned the all-or-nothing dichotomy between judicial and administrative decisions in *Nicholson v. Haldimand-Norfolk (Regional) Police Commissioners*.[3]

Nicholson concerned the summary dismissal of a probationary police constable some 15 months into his term of service. He was not given a reason for his dismissal nor was he given notice prior to his dismissal or allowed to make any representations before he was dismissed. Regulations made under provincial legislation governing the police provided that police officers could not be penalized without a hearing and appeal, but added that the Board of Commissioners of Police had authority "to dispense with the services of any constable within eighteen months of his becoming a constable."[4]

Under the traditional approach, that would have been the end of the matter. Nicholson was not entitled to a hearing under the regulations prior to his dismissal, nor was his dismissal a "judicial or quasi-judicial" decision to which common-law natural justice protection applied. It was an administrative matter and, as such, Nicholson was not entitled to any protection. In these circumstances, a 5–4 majority of the Supreme Court held that a general duty of "procedural fairness" applies to administrative decisions. Writing for a majority of the Court, Laskin C.J. justified the new duty as follows:

> [T]he classification of statutory functions as judicial, quasi-judicial or administrative is often very difficult, to say the least; and to endow some with procedural protection while denying others any at all would work injustice when the results of statutory decisions raise the same serious consequences for those adversely affected, regardless of the classification of the function in question.[5]

On this approach, the ability of the board to dismiss Nicholson for any reason (or none at all) was irrelevant. Plainly, Nicholson could not claim the procedural protection the regulations afforded to those with 18 months of service (that is, a full oral hearing) but, according to Laskin C.J., it did not follow that he must be denied any protection at all. Nicholson was entitled to be treated fairly, not arbitrarily; he was entitled to an opportunity to make submissions—orally or in writing at the board's discretion—before he was dismissed.

Laskin C.J. did not reject the distinction between administrative and judicial/quasi-judicial decisions in *Nicholson*. Instead, he accepted as a general principle of common law the no-

2 [1964] A.C. 40 (H.L.) [*Ridge*].

3 [1979] 1 S.C.R. 311 [*Nicholson*].

4 *Ibid.* at para. 5, citing *The Police Act*, R.S.O. 1970, c. 351, Reg. 680, s. 27(b).

5 *Ibid.* at para. 23.

tion that "in the sphere of the so-called quasi-judicial the rules of natural justice run, and that in the administrative or executive field there is a general duty of fairness."[6] However, in subsequent cases, the duty of fairness came to replace natural justice as the organizing principle in administrative law, and there is no longer any reason to differentiate between the two concepts or the spheres in which they operate. The duty of fairness applies across the spectrum of decisions that may be made and the requirements of the duty vary accordingly. "Fairness" has since become short form for procedural fairness, but it is important not to lose sight of the essentially procedural character of the duty. The duty of fairness is concerned with ensuring that public authorities use fair *procedures* in making decisions. It has nothing to say about the substantive decisions they may make, and in particular does not require that their decisions be considered "fair"—a subjective and contestable concept that Canadian administrative law eschews.[7]

The duty of fairness promotes sound public administration by ensuring that decisions are made with input from those affected by them; well-informed decisions are likely to be better decisions. The larger purpose of the duty, however, extends beyond this instrumental purpose. The duty of fairness protects dignitary interests by ensuring that people are allowed to participate meaningfully in decision-making processes that affect them; it legitimates administrative processes by requiring that people be treated with respect. It follows from this purpose that the requirements of the duty of fairness are independent of the merits of the substantive matter in issue. A particular decision may be all but inevitable, yet it must be made in accordance with the duty of fairness. This point has been stated categorically by the Court:

> [T]he denial of a right to a fair hearing must always render a decision invalid, whether or not it may appear to a reviewing court that the hearing would likely have resulted in a different decision. The right to a fair hearing must be regarded as an independent, unqualified right which finds its essential justification in the sense of procedural justice which any person affected by an administrative decision is entitled to have. It is not for a court to deny that right and sense of justice on the basis of speculation as to what the result might have been had there been a hearing.[8]

In general, the duty of fairness requires two things, both of which are modern restatements of venerable natural justice protections: (1) the right to be heard and (2) the right to an independent and impartial hearing. Because fairness is a common-law concept, these requirements may be limited or even overridden by ordinary legislation, but such is their importance that courts will require specific legislative direction before concluding that this has occurred.

6 Citing *Bates v. Lord Hailsham*, [1972] 1 W.L.R. 1373 at 1378, Megarry J (Ch. D.).

7 Judicial review of the substance of decisions, as opposed to the process by which those decisions are made, is addressed by Audrey Macklin, chapter 8 and Sheila Wildeman, chapter 9. Decisions may be reviewed for correctness, reasonableness, or patent unreasonableness, but it is important to emphasize that even in this context, judicial review is not concerned with the substantive "fairness" of a decision.

8 *Cardinal v. Director of Kent Institution*, [1985] 2 S.C.R. 643 at para. 23 [*Cardinal*]. Lord Morris makes this point about the duty of fairness in *Ridge*, *supra* note 2 at 114: "[H]ere is something which is basic to our system: the importance of upholding it far transcends the significance of any particular case."

The duty of fairness is codified in some Canadian jurisdictions. At the federal level, the *Canadian Bill of Rights* protects the "right to a fair hearing in accordance with the principles of fundamental justice for the determination of his rights and obligations."[9] Procedural protection has also been codified to varying extents in several provinces including Alberta,[10] British Columbia,[11] Ontario,[12] and Quebec.[13] In addition, it is important to note that federal and provincial legislation may establish procedural requirements short of a code that apply in particular contexts. For example, human rights legislation may establish procedural requirements governing some, but not all, procedural fairness duties. For the most part, however, the duty of fairness remains a creature of the common law. It supplements existing statutory duties and fills the vacuum where none exist. The *Canadian Charter of Rights and Freedoms* (the Charter) provides a constitutional backstop for procedural protection but, as we will see, the Charter applies in a narrower range of circumstances than the common law.

Given the wide range of decisions to which the duty of fairness applies, the protection afforded by the duty is necessarily flexible. Indeed, the term "hearing" can be misleading. It suggests that oral hearings are required by the duty, but this is not necessarily the case. The modern state could not function if oral hearings were required every time an administrative decision of some sort were made—a problem not only for the state but also for those who benefit from or are subject to the burden of administrative decisions. As a result, the requirements of the duty of fairness in particular circumstances vary greatly in accordance with a number of factors. In other words, the duty may be satisfied by different things in different decision-making contexts. Thus, to say that the duty of fairness applies to a particular decision-making process is to say little. Everything depends on what the duty is understood as requiring in the circumstances—on the procedural protection the courts think *ought* to be required before a decision is made in particular circumstances. A full and formal oral hearing will be required in some cases, involving processes similar to those used in the judicial system. In other contexts, however, the duty of fairness will be satisfied by

9 R.S.C. 1960, c. 44, s. 2(e). In *Duke v. The Queen*, [1972] S.C.R. 917 at 923, Fauteux J. discussed this provision as follows: "Without attempting to formulate any final definition of those words, I would take them to mean, generally, that the tribunal which adjudicates upon his rights must act fairly, in good faith, without bias, and in a judicial temper, and must give to him the opportunity adequately to state his case." In *Re B.C. Motor Vehicle Act*, [1985] 2 S.C.R. 486 at para. 58, Lamer J. noted that the principles of fundamental justice in the *Bill of Rights* were contextually limited to procedural matters because of their qualification of the right to a fair hearing. He gave a more expansive definition to the concept of fundamental justice in s. 7 of the *Canadian Charter of Rights and Freedoms*, Part I of the *Constitution Act, 1982*, being Schedule B to the *Canada Act, 1982* (U.K.), 1982, c. 11, among other things because it arose in the context of life, liberty, and security of the person, which he considered more fundamental rights.

10 *Administrative Procedures and Jurisdiction Act*, R.S.A. 2000, c. A-3.

11 *Administrative Tribunals Act*, S.B.C. 2004, c. 45.

12 *Statutory Powers Procedure Act*, R.S.O. 1990, c. S.22.

13 Quebec has codified procedures in several statutes. The *Civil Code of Quebec*, R.S.Q. c. C-1991; the *Charter of Human Rights and Freedoms*, R.S.Q. c. C-12; the *Administrative Justice Act*, R.S.Q. c. J-3; and the *Code of Civil Procedure*, R.S.Q. c. C-25 are discussed in Denis Lemieux, "The Codification of Administrative Law in Quebec" in Grant Huscroft & Michael Taggart, eds., *Inside and Outside Canadian Administrative Law* (Toronto: University of Toronto Press, 2006).

minimal, informal procedures. For example, the right to be "heard" may be satisfied by an exchange of correspondence before a decision is made.

Two questions arise when judicial review proceedings are brought alleging a breach of the duty of fairness. First, what is the threshold for the application of the duty? Although the duty of fairness applies to a wide range of decisions, there remain decisions to which the duty of fairness does not apply. Second, how is the content of the duty of fairness determined? As we will see, courts first determine the degree of fairness that is required before particularizing the content of the duty and deciding whether or not the duty was met.

The focus of this chapter is on the first branch of the duty of fairness—the right to be heard—and the way in which it is applied by the courts. The second branch of the duty of fairness is given separate treatment by Laverne Jacobs, in chapter 6. Courts require that decisions about what the duty of fairness requires be made correctly. Nevertheless, there is room for deference to the decision-maker's conception of the appropriate content of the duty of fairness. Given that a breach of the duty of fairness almost invariably results in an order quashing the relevant decision and requiring it to be remade in accordance with the procedure mandated by the court, the stakes are high. An order quashing a decision does not affect the substantive decision that may be made subsequently (in other words, it does not require the decision-maker to make a different decision). In practice, however, it may be difficult to reach the same substantive decision that was made earlier. Thus, success on an application for judicial review on fairness grounds may have the indirect effect of securing a preferred substantive outcome. At least, it will give a disgruntled person another chance to prevail against the state, and ensure that a decision is made on a well-informed basis. Even if the same substantive decision is reached following a rehearing, it is likely that it will be seen as having greater legitimacy.

II. THE THRESHOLD TEST: WHEN IS FAIRNESS REQUIRED?

A. Rights, Interests, and Privileges

Subject to some exceptions discussed below, the duty of fairness applies to any decision that affects an individual's *rights*, *interests*, or *privileges*. There is little real dispute about the meaning of these terms. They are sufficiently broad to cover most decisions that affect or have the potential to affect an individual in important ways. Thus, fairness has been required in contexts as diverse as prison disciplinary proceedings, dismissal from statutory office, and deportation.

B. Legitimate Expectations

The doctrine of legitimate expectation expands the application of the duty of fairness based on the conduct of public officials in particular circumstances.

What is a legitimate expectation? The concept has its origins in English law, but has developed in a different manner in Canada. In *Old St. Boniface Residents Assn. Inc. v. Winnipeg (City)*, the Supreme Court of Canada reviewed the English cases in which the concept was established, and held as follows:

> The principle developed in these cases is simply an extension of the rules of natural justice and procedural fairness. It affords a party affected by the decision of a public official an opportunity to make representations in circumstances in which there otherwise would be no such opportunity. The court supplies the omission where, based on the conduct of the public official, a party has been led to believe that his or her rights would not be affected without consultation.[14]

For example, a person might be led to understand that he or she will be afforded an oral hearing before a particular decision is made, even though an oral hearing would not otherwise be required. In these circumstances, the person may have a legitimate expectation that an oral hearing will be held, and if this is so the public authority will be required to hold such a hearing before making the relevant decision.

More controversially, a legitimate expectation may arise if a person is led to expect a particular *outcome* from a decision-making process. A public authority might have policies that suggest such an outcome, or perhaps an official may give an undertaking that a particular outcome will obtain. For example, a person might be told that he or she will be granted a licence. He or she may, as a result, have a legitimate expectation of receiving a licence. This is an expectation of a particular decision, as opposed to an expectation that a particular procedure will be followed in reaching a decision, and it raises different concerns.

Fundamentally, public authorities must be entitled to change their minds; indeed, the public interest may demand that they do so. The doctrine of legitimate expectation does not, therefore, require that expectations of particular outcomes must be protected. In the example above, there is no entitlement to the grant of the licence. However, before a decision is made to deny the licence, the person promised the licence will be entitled to procedural fairness. For example, he or she may be entitled to notice of the intention not to grant the licence and be allowed to make submissions before the decision is made, and may be entitled to written reasons for the decision to deny the licence. Thus, the doctrine of legitimate expectations operates not to require a particular outcome but, instead, to require that procedural protection be provided before an expectation of a particular outcome can be dashed.

The concept of legitimate expectation is akin to promissory estoppel, an equitable doctrine that offers relief from reliance on promises that do not give rise to enforceable contracts,[15] but there are important differences.[16] The Supreme Court of Canada has on several occasions reiterated that a legitimate expectation affords only procedural protection. In *Reference Re Canada Assistance Plan (B.C.)*, the Court put the point this way:

> There is no support in Canadian or English cases for the position that the doctrine of legitimate expectations can create substantive rights. It is a part of the rules of procedural fairness which can govern administrative bodies. Where it is applicable, it can create a right to make repre-

14 [1990] 3 S.C.R. 1170 at para. 74.

15 See generally Stephen M. Waddams, *The Law of Contracts*, 5th ed. (Aurora, ON: Canada Law Book, 2005) at paras. 193-203. Estoppel is understood as a defensive concept—a "shield" rather than a "sword"—and in general does not result in the enforcement of non-contractual promises.

16 Binnie J. discusses the differences between estoppel, which he suggests may rarely be available in public law contexts, and legitimate expectation in his concurring opinion in *Mount Sinai Hospital Center v. Quebec (Minister of Health and Social Services)*, [2001] 2 S.C.R. 281.

> sentations or to be consulted. It does not fetter the decision following the representations or consultation.[17]

It is important to note that English law has taken a different path. English courts have come to allow substantive expectations to be protected by the doctrine, rather than simply procedural expectations, and the process–substance distinction has become blurred.[18] The Supreme Court of Canada has sought to maintain this distinction, as the Court makes clear in *Baker v. Canada (Minister of Citizenship and Immigration)*:

> This doctrine, as applied in Canada, is based on the principle that the "circumstances" affecting procedural fairness take into account the promises or regular practices of administrative decision-makers, and that it will generally be unfair for them to act in contravention of representations as to procedure, or to backtrack on substantive promises without according significant procedural rights.[19]

In *C.U.P.E. v. Ontario (Minister of Labour)*, Binnie J. reiterated the procedural focus of the concept while emphasizing the narrowness of the circumstances in which a legitimate expectation may arise:

> [Legitimate expectation] looks to the conduct of a Minister or other public authority in the exercise of a discretionary power including established practices, conduct or representations that can be characterized as clear, unambiguous and unqualified, that has induced in the complainants (here the unions) a reasonable expectation that they will retain a benefit or be consulted before a contrary decision is taken. To be "legitimate," such expectations must not conflict with a statutory duty. Where the conditions for its application are satisfied, the Court may grant appropriate procedural remedies to respond to the "legitimate" expectation.[20]

As a result of these cases, there is relatively limited scope for the operation of the concept of legitimate expectation in Canada.

C. A Common-Law Presumption

Given that the duty of fairness is a common-law concept, it must yield to contrary legislative instructions. However, courts have always required clear statutory direction in order to limit or oust procedural protection. In *Kane v. Board of Governors of the University of British Columbia*, Dickson J. put the point this way: "To abrogate the rules of natural justice, express language or necessary implication must be found in the statutory instrument."[21] Courts presume that the legislature intended procedural protection to apply,[22] and for their part

17 [1991] 2 S.C.R. 525 at para. 59 [*Re Canada Assistance Plan (B.C.)*].

18 See generally David Feldman, ed., *English Public Law* (Oxford: Oxford University Press, 2004) chapter 16, part B, discussing *R. v. North and East Devon Health Authority, ex p Coughlan*, [2001] Q.B. 213 (C.A.).

19 [1999] 2 S.C.R. 817 at para. 26 [*Baker*].

20 [2003] 1 S.C.R. 539 at para. 131.

21 [1980] 1 S.C.R. 1105 at 1113.

22 In *Cooper v. Wandsworth Board of Works* (1863), 14 C.B. (N.S.) 180 at 194 (C.P.), Byles J. referred to the requirement of natural justice as "supplying the omission of the legislature."

legislators draft legislation with this in mind. On this approach, the courts acknowledge the supremacy of the legislature and at the same time confer quasi-constitutional protection upon the common-law duty of fairness.

The ability of legislatures to limit or oust fairness protection is, of course, subject to the need to legislate in a manner consistent with the Charter, as discussed below.

D. Constitutional Protection

Section 7 of the Charter provides as follows:[23]

> Everyone has the right to life, liberty and security of the person and the right not to be deprived thereof except in accordance with the principles of fundamental justice.

The Supreme Court of Canada has held that the principles of fundamental justice subsume procedural fairness protection.[24] However, s. 7 applies only in the context of deprivations of life, liberty, and security of the person. Security of the person is the broadest of these concepts, but there is no doubt that the threshold for activating Charter protection is higher than the threshold for obtaining fairness protection at common law. For example, an application to renew a taxi licence activates fairness protection at common law, but it is unlikely to give rise to constitutional protection because denial of a licence does not constitute a deprivation of life, liberty, or security of the person. Moreover, economic rights are not protected by s. 7 of the Charter on the Court's current approach.[25] Thus, ordinary legislation could limit or even oust the application of the duty of fairness to the licensing scheme without infringing the Charter. However, in cases in which s. 7 is found to have been infringed, it is unlikely that legislation limiting or ousting the duty of fairness will be considered justified under s. 1 of the Charter.[26]

III. LIMITATIONS ON THE SCOPE OF THE DUTY OF FAIRNESS

Although the duty of fairness applies to a broad range of decision-making, it is important to appreciate that there are limitations on the reach of the duty, both inherent in the concept and imposed on the concept by the courts. Some of these limitations are discussed below.

---

23 The impact of the Charter on administrative law is discussed by Evan Fox-Decent in chapter 7.

24 *Re B.C. Motor Vehicle Act*, *supra* note 9. More controversially, the Court held that the principles of fundamental justice include a substantive component, despite the apparent intention to limit the right to matters of procedure. See Peter Hogg, *Constitutional Law of Canada*, looseleaf (Scarborough, ON: Carswell, 1997) at para. 44.10(a).

25 See, for example, *Gosselin v. Quebec (Attorney General)*, [2002] 4 S.C.R. 429.

26 The Supreme Court of Canada maintains that s. 1 applies to all rights, and that breaches of s. 7 can be justified, but the Court has said that justification is unlikely except perhaps in "extraordinary circumstances where concerns are grave and the challenges complex." See *Charkaoui v. Canada (Citizenship and Immigration)*, [2007] 1 S.C.R. 350 at para. 66, citing *Re B.C. Motor Vehicle Act*, *supra* note 9 at para. 83, per Lamer J. (listing "exceptional conditions such as natural disasters, the outbreak of war, epidemics, and the like"). See also Evan Fox-Decent, chapter 7.

A. The Duty Applies to Decisions

The duty of fairness applies to *decisions*, meaning final dispositions of a matter. Rarely will it apply to investigations or advisory processes that do not have any consequences, even though they may lead to more formal decision-making processes that do.[27] For one thing, the imposition of fairness duties at a preliminary stage may well compromise the relevant procedures. To take an obvious example, it would be absurd to require officials charged with investigating breaches of the law to provide notice of their investigations before commencing them. In any case, the exclusion of fairness at the preliminary stage of a matter is mitigated by observing the duty at the second stage, in the event that a decision that affects rights, interests, or privileges must be made.

That being said, investigations and advisory processes may have a considerable impact on affected persons, especially when they are conducted in public.[28] The reputation of anyone caught up in these sorts of processes may be adversely affected, and where this is so there may be a strong argument for the application of the duty of fairness.[29] Moreover, preliminary decisions may be subject to the duty of fairness where they have de facto finality. For example, invariable acceptance by the ultimate decision-maker of the results of an investigation or advice from a preliminary decision-maker may suggest that the real decision is being made at the preliminary stage, and therefore the duty of fairness may apply.

B. The Duty Does Not Apply to Legislative Decisions

The Supreme Court of Canada has always insisted that the duty of fairness does not apply to legislative decisions or functions.[30] In *Reference Re Canada Assistance Plan (B.C.)*, the Court expressed the point categorically: "[T]he rules governing procedural fairness do not apply to a body exercising purely legislative functions."[31]

The Court has never explained what it means by "legislative" functions, but it is clear that primary legislation, whether passed by Parliament or a provincial legislature, is not subject to the duty of fairness. It is exempt not because it has no impact on rights, interests, or privileges. On the contrary, it is likely to have a profound effect on all of these things, and is likely to affect large numbers of people because it applies generally. Primary legislation

27 This limitation is reflected in the Ontario *Statutory Powers Procedure Act*, *supra* note 12, s. 2(g): procedural requirements do not apply to "one or more persons required to make an investigation and to make a report, with or without recommendations, where the report is for the information or advice of the person to whom it is made and does not in any way legally bind or limit that person in any decision he or she may have power to make."

28 Public inquiries are normally conducted by judges pursuant to statutory mandates that establish elaborate procedural protection. See generally Allan Manson & David Mullan, eds., *Commissions of Inquiry: Praise or Reappraise?* (Toronto: Irwin, 2003).

29 See, for example, *Masters v. Ontario* (1994), 18 O.R. (3d) 551 (Div. Ct.). In that case, a senior provincial bureaucrat, appointed at pleasure by the premier, was entitled to minimal procedural fairness in the context of an internal investigation into allegations of sexual harassment against him, but not the right to a formal hearing before an impartial decision-maker that he sought.

30 *Att. Gen. of Can. v. Inuit Tapirisat et al.*, [1980] 2 S.C.R. 735 at 758 [*Inuit Tapirisat*], citing *Bates v. Lord Hailsham*, [1972] 3 All E.R. 1019 (Ch. D.).

31 *Supra* note 17 at para. 60.

is exempt from the duty of fairness, however, because any meaningful conception of a separation of powers between the legislature and the courts demands it. In *Reference re Resolution to Amend the Constitution*, the Court essayed the relationship between the legislature and the courts as follows:

> How Houses of Parliament proceed, how a provincial legislative assembly proceeds is in either case a matter of self definition, subject to any overriding constitutional or self-imposed statutory or indoor prescription. It is unnecessary here to embark on any historical review of the "court" aspect of Parliament and the immunity of its procedures from judicial review. Courts come into the picture when legislation is enacted and not before (unless references are made to them for their opinion on a bill or a proposed enactment). It would be incompatible with the self regulating—"inherent" is as apt a word—authority of Houses of Parliament to deny their capacity to pass any kind of resolution. Reference may appropriately be made to art. 9 of the *Bill of Rights* of 1689, undoubtedly in force as part of the law of Canada, which provides that "Proceedings in Parliament ought not to be impeached or questioned in any Court or Place out of Parliament."[32]

This rationale for exempting legislative functions from the duty of fairness was reiterated in *Wells v. Newfoundland*. In that case, the Newfoundland Legislature passed legislation abolishing a quasi-judicial position to which Wells had been appointed. Wells's argument that he should have been accorded procedural fairness was rejected summarily by the Court, which stated as follows:

> [L]egislative decision making is not subject to any known duty of fairness. Legislatures are subject to constitutional requirements for valid law-making, but within their constitutional boundaries, they can do as they see fit. The wisdom and value of legislative decisions are subject only to review by the electorate.[33]

There is no guarantee that political accountability will be meaningful, of course, but this is no concern of the courts. No one has the right to succeed in the political process, no matter how sympathetic his or her cause may seem, as *Authorson v. Canada (Attorney General)*[34] demonstrates. In that case, Parliament passed legislation retrospectively limiting the amount of money the Crown owed to disabled war veterans—decades of interest on pension and benefit funds—to whom the Crown owed fiduciary duties. The law affected thousands of veterans, none of whom was given notice of the proposed change to the law. In class action proceedings, Authorson argued that the legislation infringed the right not to be deprived of the enjoyment of property except by due process of law under the *Canadian Bill of Rights* (s. 1(a)), as well as the right to a fair hearing in accordance with the principles of fundamental justice for the determination of one's rights and obligations (s. 2(e)).

---

32 [1981] 1 S.C.R. 753 at 785.

33 [1999] 3 S.C.R. 199 at para. 59. However, Wells succeeded in a contract suit against the Crown, the Court holding that the legislation abolishing his position had not abrogated his right to seek damages against the Crown for breach of his contract of employment.

34 [2003] 2 S.C.R. 40 [*Authorson*].

This argument succeeded at trial and in the Ontario Court of Appeal, but was given short shrift in the Supreme Court of Canada. The Court emphatically rejected the notion that the *Canadian Bill of Rights* established due process procedures in regard to the passage of legislation, and reiterated that the common law had nothing to add:

> The respondent claimed a right to notice and hearing to contest the passage of s. 5.1(4) of the *Department of Veterans Affairs Act*. However, in 1960, and today, no such right exists. Long-standing parliamentary tradition makes it clear that the only procedure due any citizen of Canada is that proposed legislation receive three readings in the Senate and House of Commons and that it receive Royal Assent. Once that process is completed, legislation within Parliament's competence is unassailable.[35]

If the rationale for the exemption of legislative functions is clear, however, the idea of exemption by categorization is problematic, and recalls the long-discredited distinction between administrative and judicial/quasi-judicial decisions. It invites argument over the meaning of the term "legislative," and makes the outcome all or nothing. If an applicant for judicial review succeeds in convincing a court that a decision is subject to the duty of fairness, the court may dictate the required procedure and quash the decision if there has been a failure to observe it. Conversely, if the public authority succeeds in convincing the court that its actions are legislative in nature, then the duty of fairness does not apply and the court has nothing to say about the procedures adopted or their adequacy.

The categorical exemption of legislative functions becomes especially problematic as the concept of legislative functions extends beyond primary legislation to include secondary legislation and policy decisions, both of which are discussed below.

1. Are Cabinet and Ministerial Decisions Covered by the Legislative Exemption?

Cabinet and ministerial decisions are not subject to the legislative exemption per se, but it will often be easy to characterize Cabinet and ministerial decisions as legislative, and as a result they will be exempted from the duty.

Inuit Tapirisat provides a good example. In that case, the federal Cabinet rejected an appeal from a decision made by the Canadian Radio-television and Telecommunications Commission (CRTC) allowing a rate increase without allowing the petitioning group to be heard. The Cabinet heard from the utility and the CRTC and took advice from ministerial officials, but the petitioning group was essentially left out of the proceedings. Estey J. considered the Cabinet's power to be legislative in nature, in part because the legislation authorized Cabinet to overturn a decision of the CRTC on its own motion. This, he said, was "legislative action in its purest form."[36] Estey J. buttressed this position by accentuating the practical difficulties inherent in extending the duty of fairness. He did not want to burden the Cabinet with hearing requirements, and expressed concern about undermining the Cabinet's public policy-making role.

35 *Ibid.* at para. 37. The Court held, at para. 61, that the protection of s. 2(e) is limited to "the application of law to individual circumstances in a proceeding before a court, tribunal or similar body."

36 *Inuit Tapirisat*, *supra* note 30 at 754.

Inuit Tapirisat has been subject to extensive criticism on the basis that it overstates the difficulties inherent in applying the duty of fairness to Cabinet decisions. After all, the duty is flexible, and the content of the duty could be tailored to address some of the concerns raised by Estey J. (it is difficult to conceive of the Cabinet being required to hold an oral hearing, to take an obvious example). Moreover, the case for exempting Cabinet decisions from the duty of fairness may be thought weaker than the case for exempting primary legislation, because Cabinet decision-making is not subject to political scrutiny in the same way. Nevertheless, it is not surprising to find the courts wary of scrutinizing the decisions of the executive branch of government even for limited procedural purposes. The potential for political conflict is great.

In other contexts, the Court has emphasized the unique role and responsibilities of the executive branch as a reason for not extending the duty of fairness to ministerial decisions. In *Idziak v. Canada (Minister of Justice)*, Cory J. discussed the Minister of Justice's exercise of discretionary authority to issue a warrant of surrender in an extradition case as follows:

> Parliament chose to give discretionary authority to the Minister of Justice. It is the Minister who must consider the good faith and honour of this country in its relations with other states. It is the Minister who has the expert knowledge of the political ramifications of an extradition decision. In administrative law terms, the Minister's review should be characterized as being at the extreme legislative end of the *continuum* of administrative decision-making.[37]

Decisions involving particular individuals are most likely to give rise to the application of the duty of fairness to Cabinet and ministerial decisions but, as *Idziak* demonstrates, even in this regard the Court will sometimes be reticent to impose procedural requirements for a variety of reasons.

2. Is Subordinate Legislation Covered by the Legislative Exemption?

Political self-interest often ensures that consultation occurs prior to the promulgation of legislation, even where there is no formal requirement for it. There will, however, be times when it is not in the political interest to consult before acting, and the argument for fairness protection in these contexts may be strong, especially in regard to subordinate legislation.[38] Arguably, there is less reason to be concerned about interference in the political process where subordinate legislation is concerned, because political approval for such legislation is subsidiary in nature: subordinate legislation may be made pursuant to general authorization in the statute, and delegated law-making authority might extend to actors outside the political process—for example, independent tribunals. Moreover, American experience with "notice and comment" requirements demonstrates that procedural requirements are not unworkable.[39] On the other hand, such requirements as do exist in Canada have been

37 [1992] 3 S.C.R. 631 at para. 54.

38 Geneviève Cartier, "Procedural Fairness in Legislative Functions: The End of Judicial Abstinence?" (2003) 53 U.T.L.J. 217.

39 Federal notice and comment regulations as established under Government Organization and Employees, 5 U.S.C. §553 are discussed in Peter L. Strauss, *Administrative Justice in the United States*, 2d ed. (Durham, N.C.: Carolina Academy Press, 2002) at 220-22.

established by legislation, and it may no longer be legitimate for the common law to develop a more general obligation as a result.

The legislative exemption is itself subject to exceptions. For example, in *Homex Realty and Development Co. v. Wyoming (Village)*,[40] the Supreme Court of Canada concluded that passage of a municipal bylaw was subject to the duty of fairness. Having been unable to resolve a dispute with the developer about the provision of services in a subdivision, the village passed a bylaw deeming the lots purchased by the developer not to be a registered plan of subdivision. As a result, the developer could not sell individual lots without the village's permission. Plainly, the motivation for the bylaw was the particular dispute between a developer and the village. In these circumstances, the Court held that the village was not allowed to couch its actions in a form designed to oust the application of the duty of fairness.[41] This makes the point that substance is more important than form where the legislative exemption is concerned.

3. Are Policy Decisions Covered by the Legislative Exemption?

The legislative exemption includes decisions that may be described as "policy" decisions, as well as decisions that are general in nature. In *Martineau v. Matsqui Institution Disciplinary Board*, Dickson J. observed that "[a] purely ministerial decision, on broad grounds of public policy, will typically afford the individual no procedural protection."[42] In *Knight v. Indian Head School Division No. 19*, L'Heureux-Dubé J. noted that many administrative bodies have been required to assume duties traditionally performed by legislatures, and distinguished "decisions of a legislative and general nature" from "acts of a more administrative and specific nature."[43]

The rationale for exempting policy decisions from the duty is similar to that of formal legislative decisions. Both are inherently political in nature and are subject to political accountability. Thus, in *Imperial Oil Ltd. v. Quebec (Minister of the Environment)*, the Supreme Court held that in exercising discretionary power to require an oil company to undertake site decontamination measures (at its own expense), Quebec's Environment Minister was performing a political role in choosing from among the policy options the Act allowed, and

40 [1980] 2 S.C.R. 1011 [*Homex Realty*].

41 The majority of the Court characterized the bylaw as quasi-judicial rather than legislative in substance, a distinction that is no longer meaningful. Dickson J.'s dissenting opinion puts the case for procedural fairness protection in more modern terms, *ibid.* at 1052-53:

> What we have here is not a by-law of wide and general application which was to apply to all citizens of the municipality equally. Rather, it was a by-law aimed deliberately at limiting the rights of one individual, the appellant Homex. In these circumstances, I would hold that Homex was entitled to some procedural safeguards. This does not mean that the municipality was under a duty to observe the procedures appropriate to a court of law. But, at a minimum, it was under a duty to give Homex notice of the proposed by-law and the opportunity to be heard.

42 [1980] 1 S.C.R. 602 at 628, cited with approval in *Re Canada Assistance Plan (B.C.)*, *supra* note 17 at para. 61. Since *Baker*, *supra* note 19, however, substantive decisions taken pursuant to discretionary authority have been subject to judicial review pursuant to the pragmatic and functional approach. See Audrey Macklin, chapter 8.

43 [1990] 1 S.C.R. 653 at para. 26 [*Indian Head School*].

was not subject to the duty of fairness.[44] Governments are elected to make policy decisions and must be allowed to do so, provided that they comply with relevant constitutional requirements.

But acceptance of the political rationale does not resolve the difficulties surrounding the exemption of policy decisions. Although legislative functions may be identified by the formalities that surround the legislative process, it can be considerably more difficult to identify a policy decision. Moreover, given different judicial perceptions about institutional roles, accountability, and legitimacy, we should expect to find inconsistent decisions. In truth, it is easy for a court to characterize a decision as a policy decision if it simply does not want to interfere in a particular matter.

C. The Duty May Be Suspended or Abridged in the Event of an Emergency

The duty of fairness establishes duties that must be observed *before* a decision may be made. There will, however, sometimes be circumstances in which procedural requirements cannot be met without causing harm of some sort or other. Public safety concerns will sometimes demand an immediate decision regardless of the duty of fairness.

In these sorts of circumstances, courts may defer compliance with the duty of fairness protections until after the relevant decision has been made. For example, in *Cardinal v. Director of Kent Institution*, the Court held that although the duty of fairness applied to the imposition of isolation/segregation in a prison context, in "apparently" urgent or emergency circumstances (inmates alleged to have been involved in a hostage taking were transferred to another institution and placed in isolation to secure prison order) "there could be no requirement of prior notice and an opportunity to be heard before the decision. … [T]he process of prison administration, because of its special nature and exigencies, should not be unduly burdened or obstructed by the imposition of unreasonable or inappropriate procedural requirements."[45] However, once a recommendation to end the segregation of prisoners had been made by the review body, the duty of fairness required that the prison director inform the inmates of his intended decision to reject the recommendation, provide reasons, and afford them the opportunity to contest his intended decision. The Court regarded this as a minimal amount of fairness that would not undermine the administration of the prison.

It is not clear whether fairness is not required in emergency situations, or instead whether the content of the duty simply becomes minimal.[46] More important is the extent to which a reviewing court will (or should) defer to the decision-maker as to the existence of an emergency. Deference to the government in regard to national security matters is to be expected, but care must be taken to ensure that public authorities are not overzealous in apprehending urgent or emergency circumstances. There should be few cases in which the

---

44 [2003] 2 S.C.R. 624 [*Imperial Oil*]. The *Environment Quality Act*, R.S.Q., c. Q-2, s. 31.42 included a requirement that notice be given to interested persons and that reasons for the decision be given. The oil company argued that the Minister was not impartial, and hence in breach of the bias rule of the duty of fairness.

45 *Cardinal*, *supra* note 8 at paras. 16, 22.

46 See the discussion in Mark Aronson, Bruce Dyer & Matthew Groves, *Judicial Review of Administrative Action*, 3d ed. (Sydney: Lawbook, 2004) at 436-38.

courts will regard a situation as one that is incompatible with the imposition of minimal fairness duties before a decision is made.

IV. THE CONTENT OF THE DUTY OF FAIRNESS

As we have seen, extension of the duty of fairness to a wide range of administrative decisions in *Nicholson* contexts was facilitated by the decision to keep the content of duty flexible and context-specific. One way of thinking of the content of fairness is that it involves compliance with some, but not all, of the requirements of natural justice. Among other things, the duty of fairness may include one or more of the following components:

- a right to notice of a potential decision,[47]
- a right to disclosure of particulars,[48]
- a right to make written submissions,[49]
- a right to a hearing within a reasonable time,[50]
- a right to an oral hearing,[51]
- a right to counsel,[52]

---

47 Brown and Evans state the general rule as follows: "[N]otice must be adequate in all circumstances in order to afford to those concerned a *reasonable* opportunity to present proofs and arguments, and to respond to those presented in opposition" (Donald J.M. Brown & John M. Evans, *Judicial Review of Administrative Action in Canada*, looseleaf (Toronto: Canvasback, July 2006) at 1200 [Brown & Evans]).

48 See, for example, *May v. Ferndale Institution*, [2005] 3 S.C.R. 809 at para. 92 (noting that the disclosure principles developed in the context of the criminal law prosecution in *R. v. Stinchcombe*, [1991] 3 S.C.R. 326 do not apply to administrative proceedings. In this context, it is enough that the decision-maker discloses "the information he or she relied upon. The requirement is that the individual must know the case he or she has to meet").

49 In *Nicholson*, *supra* note 3, the Court held that Nicholson's right to make submissions concerning his dismissal could be satisfied by oral or written submissions at the Board of Commissioners' discretion. In *Baker*, *supra* note 19, the Court held that a right to written submissions met the duty of fairness in the context of a request for relief from deportation on compassionate and humanitarian grounds, and that no oral hearing was required. *Baker* is discussed at length in the text below.

50 *Blencoe v. British Columbia (Human Rights Commission)*, [2000] 2 S.C.R. 307 at para. 102 ("the principles of natural justice and the duty of fairness include the right to a fair hearing and that undue delay in the processing of an administrative proceeding that impairs the fairness of the hearing can be remedied").

51 See, for example, *Khan v. University of Ottawa* (1997), 34 O.R. (3d) 535 (C.A.) (duty of fairness requires an oral hearing where credibility is in issue). See also *Singh v. Minister of Employment and Immigration*, [1985] 1 S.C.R. 177 (right to an oral hearing where credibility is in issue protected under s. 2(e) of the *Canadian Bill of Rights* and s. 7 of the Charter).

52 The right to counsel under the Charter (s. 10(b)) is limited to circumstances of "arrest or detention." In limited circumstances, s. 7 may require state-provided counsel (*New Brunswick (Minister of Health and Community Services) v. G.J.*, [1999] 3 S.C.R. 46). As the Court put it in *British Columbia (Attorney General) v. Christie*, 2007 S.C.C. 21 at para. 27:

> We conclude that the text of the constitution, the jurisprudence and the historical understanding of the rule of law do not foreclose the possibility that a right to counsel may be recognized in specific and varied situations. But at the same time, they do not support the conclusion that there is a general constitutional right to counsel in proceedings before courts and tribunals dealing with rights and obligations.

As a result, the right to counsel in administrative proceedings must be determined on a case-by-case basis.

- a right to call and cross-examine witnesses,[53] and
- a right to written reasons for a decision.[54]

Most of these procedural rights are well-established, though of course their parameters are open to argument in particular contexts. It is easy to assert that notice is required, for example, but it may be difficult to determine the appropriate length of notice, the way in which notice should be provided, or the particulars that must be included. There is considerable case law on these sorts of questions.

The right to written reasons for a decision is the least well-developed aspect of the duty of fairness. This may seem surprising, but while detailed reasons have almost invariably been given by tribunals charged with running oral hearings, less formal proceedings were often decided without reasons being given. In *Baker*, L'Heureux-Dubé J. stated simply:

> In my opinion, it is now appropriate to recognize that, in certain circumstances, the duty of procedural fairness will require the provision of a written explanation for a decision. The strong arguments demonstrating the advantages of written reasons suggest that, in cases such as this where the decision has important significance for the individual, when there is a statutory right of appeal, or in other circumstances, some form of reasons should be required.[55]

There is considerable wiggle room here; reasons are not always required, but may be required in "certain circumstances." Reasons may be required in light of the importance of the decision in question or to facilitate an appeal process that may exist, but they may also be required in "other circumstances." Moreover, the requirement is for "some form of reasons," suggesting that the right to reasons may be satisfied in a variety of different ways. In *Baker*, for example, the Court accepted as reasons informal notes that had been prepared by one immigration officer for the benefit of another (proffered when Baker's counsel had asked for reasons).

A detailed consideration of the duty to give reasons and the other components of the duty of fairness is beyond the scope of this chapter.[56] For present purposes, it is enough to note that judicial review is concerned with deciding what the duty of fairness requires in the circumstances of a particular decision, and that the court's decision is made *after* the administrative decision-maker has acted.

The retrospective nature of fairness determinations brings to mind Jeremy Bentham's complaint about the common law.[57] The problem is mitigated by the sort of institutional

53 The right to call and cross-examine witnesses is normally part of the right to an oral hearing, but the scope of the right is subject to control by the relevant tribunal. In *Innisfil (Township) v. Vespra (Township)*, [1981] 2 S.C.R. 145 at 171, Estey J. emphasized that the right of cross-examination is not to be withheld on the basis of a judgment by the tribunal that it is of limited utility: "The decision to exercise the right is solely that of the holder of the right. He, of course, must exercise it at his peril as is the case in any other administrative or judicial proceeding where such a right arises."

54 This was established in *Baker*, *supra* note 19, discussed in the text below.

55 *Ibid.* at para. 43.

56 See generally Brown & Evans, *supra* note 47.

57 Jeremy Bentham, *The Works of Jeremy Bentham*, ed. by John Bowring, vol. 5 (Edinburgh: W. Tait, 1843) at 235, 236: "It is the judges (as we have seen) that make the common law. Do you know how they make it? Just as a man makes laws for his dog. When your dog does anything you want to break him of, you wait till

knowledge that builds up over time. Still, there may be a tendency for risk-averse administrators to provide more than the duty of fairness might otherwise be held to require, in order to ensure that their decisions can withstand judicial review.

Duty of fairness concerns are least likely to arise in the context of tribunals that run oral hearings, because the procedure for those hearings will usually be well known by all concerned. Some tribunals operate pursuant to detailed legislation that establishes procedural requirements. Others are empowered to establish their own procedures and may commit those procedures to writing, with policy statements or more formal rules that they are allowed to promulgate. The Ontario Labour Relations Board is a good example of this latter approach. The chair of the board has rule-making authority, and the board has developed its own procedural code.[58] The Canadian Transportation Agency is another example of a tribunal that has authority to control its own processes and may make its own procedural rules.[59] Still other tribunals may operate pursuant to general statutory mandates such as that established by the Ontario *Statutory Powers Procedure Act*,[60] which establishes minimum default procedural provisions for Ontario tribunals charged with running oral hearings.

For a large range of decision-makers, however, common-law considerations govern the scope and content of the duty of fairness. *Baker*, the leading case, is discussed below.

A. Baker v. Canada (Minister of Citizenship and Immigration)

Mavis Baker was an illegal immigrant from Jamaica who worked as a domestic worker for 11 years. During that time she had four children in Canada, all of whom acquired Canadian citizenship by birth. In 1992 she was ordered to be deported. Immigration legislation required applicants for permanent residence to apply from outside Canada, meaning that Ms. Baker would have to apply from Jamaica. She applied for an exemption from this requirement pursuant to regulations that provided as follows:

> The Minister is hereby authorized to exempt any person from any regulation made under subsection 114(1) of the Act or otherwise facilitate the admission to Canada of any person where the Minister is satisfied that the person should be exempted from that regulation or that person's admission should be facilitated owing to the existence of compassionate or humanitarian considerations.[61]

Baker argued she had psychiatric problems that might worsen if she were forced to return to Jamaica. Moreover, two of her Canadian-born children depended on her for their care, and she was in regular contact with the other two. They, and she, would suffer emotional hardship if she were forced to return to Jamaica.

---

he does it, and then beat him for it. This is the way you make laws for your dog: and this is the way the judges make law for you and me." (First published in 1792 as "Truth Versus Ashurst; or, Law as It Is, Contrasted with what It Is Said to Be.")

58 *Labour Relations Act*, S.O. 1995, c. 1, Sch. A, s. 110(17).

59 *Canada Transportation Act*, S.C. 1996, c. 10, s. 17.

60 R.S.O. 1990, c. S.22.

61 Immigration Regulations, 1978, SOR/98-172, as amended by SOR/93-44, 52.1.

The discretionary power involved in assessing compassionate and humanitarian considerations was exercised in the name of the Minister by an immigration officer. That officer denied Baker's request for an exemption on the advice of another officer, Officer Lorenzo, whose memorandum is set out below:

> PC is unemployed—on Welfare. No income shown—no assets. Has four Cdn.-born children—four other children in Jamaica—HAS A TOTAL OF EIGHT CHILDREN.
>
> Says only two children are in her "direct custody." (No info on who has ghe [*sic*] other two.)
>
> There is nothing for her in Jamaica—hasn't been there in a long time—no longer close to her children there—no jobs there—she has no skills other than as a domestic—children would suffer—can't take them with her and can't leave them with anyone here. Says has suffered from a mental disorder since '81—is now an outpatient and is improving. If sent back will have a relapse.
>
> Letter from Children's Aid—they say PC has been diagnosed as a paranoid schizophrenic.—children would suffer if returned—
>
> Letter of Aug. '93 from psychiatrist from Ont. Govm't.
>
> Says PC had post-partum psychosis and had a brief episode of psychosis in Jam. when was 25 yrs. old. Is now an out-patient and is doing relatively well—deportation would be an extremely stressful experience.
>
> Lawyer says PS [*sic*] is sole caregiver and single parent of two Cdn. born children. PC's mental condition would suffer a setback if she is deported etc.
>
> This case is a catastrophy [*sic*]. It is also an indictment of our "system" that the client came as a visitor in Aug. '81, was not ordered deported until Dec. '92 and in APRIL '94 IS STILL HERE!
>
> The PC is a paranoid schizophrenic and on welfare. She has no qualifications other than as a domestic. She has FOUR CHILDREN IN JAMAICA AND ANOTHER FOUR BORN HERE. She will, of course, be a tremendous strain on our social welfare systems for (probably) the rest of her life. There are no H&C factors other than her FOUR CANADIAN-BORN CHILDREN. Do we let her stay because of that? I am of the opinion that Canada can no longer afford this type of generosity. However, because of the circumstances involved, there is a potential for adverse publicity. I recommend refusal but you may wish to clear this with someone at Region.
>
> There is also a potential for violence—see charge of "assault with a weapon." [Capitalization in original.]

Baker sought judicial review of the Minister's decision, arguing among other things that the Minister failed to observe the requirements of the duty of fairness.[62] She argued that she should have been granted an oral interview before the decision-maker; that her children and their fathers should have been given notice; that they should have been allowed to make submissions at the interview; and that the fathers of her children should have been given permission to attend the interview with counsel. She argued, in addition, that she was entitled to reasons for the Minister's decision, and that the immigration officer's notes gave

62 Baker also argued that the Minister's substantive decision made pursuant to his discretionary powers was flawed. The Court's treatment of that issue made new law by subjecting discretionary exercises of power to the pragmatic and functional approach. See the discussion by Audrey Macklin, chapter 8.

rise to a reasonable apprehension of bias. The decision to deny Baker's application was upheld in the Federal Court, and she appealed to the Supreme Court of Canada.

The Supreme Court of Canada held that Baker was entitled to more than minimal procedural fairness, but not an oral hearing. It was enough that she was allowed to submit complete written documentation and that reasons for the Minister's decision were provided. However, the Court held that the reasons provided—the immigration officer's notes—gave rise to a reasonable apprehension of bias.[63]

For present purposes, the important point is that the Court used *Baker* as the occasion to reiterate the purpose of the duty of fairness and set out a number of criteria that are relevant to determining its content. L'Heureux-Dubé J. described the purpose of the duty of fairness as follows:

> [T]he purpose of the participatory rights contained within the duty of procedural fairness is to ensure that administrative decisions are made using a fair and open procedure, appropriate to the decision being made and its statutory, institutional, and social context, with an opportunity for those affected by the decision to put forward their views and evidence fully and have them considered by the decision-maker.[64]

Baker follows on from L'Heureux-Dubé J.'s decision in *Knight v. Indian Head School Division No. 19*. In that case, she argued that the duty of fairness was "entrenched in the principles governing our legal system."[65] At the same time, however, she emphasized the importance of respecting the needs of administrative decision-makers:

> It must not be forgotten that every administrative body is the master of its own procedure and need not assume the trappings of a court. The object is not to import into administrative proceedings the rigidity of all the requirements of natural justice that must be observed by a court, but rather to allow administrative bodies to work out a system that is flexible, adapted to their needs and fair. As pointed out by de Smith, the aim is not to create "procedural perfection" but to achieve a certain balance between the need for fairness, efficiency and predictability of outcome.[66]

The criteria in *Baker* are designed to give effect to these aims. These criteria were not intended to be exhaustive, but as often happens when the Court enumerates criteria, they take on prescriptive force in subsequent cases. Fairness cases since *Baker* have been argued on the basis of these criteria.

B. The Baker Synthesis

The Court enumerated the following five criteria for consideration in determining the degree of fairness that must be provided in particular circumstances:

---

63 This was enough to quash the decision, but the Court went on to hold that the Minister's discretionary decision was subject to reasonableness and was not reasonable in the circumstances, because it paid insufficient attention to the interests and needs of the children and the hardship that a return to Jamaica might cause Ms. Baker. The decision was quashed on this basis as well and remitted for reconsideration.

64 *Baker*, *supra* note 19 at para. 22.

65 *Indian Head School*, *supra* note 43 at para. 46.

66 *Ibid.* at para. 49 (internal citation omitted).

1. The nature of the decision being made and the process followed in making it.
2. The nature of the statutory scheme and the terms of the statute pursuant to which the body operates.
3. The importance of the decision to the individual/individuals.
4. The legitimate expectations of the person challenging the relevant decision.
5. Deference to the procedural choices made by the decision-maker.

Each of these criteria is addressed below.

1. The Nature of the Decision Being Made and the Process Followed in Making It

Although the classification of decisions as judicial/quasi-judicial or administrative decisions is no longer important in determining whether or not procedural protection must be provided, decisions that are seen as judicial or quasi-judicial in nature—typically, decisions that resolve disputes between parties by finding facts and applying law—are likely to demand more extensive procedural protections than administrative decisions, which have more in common with regulation than adjudication.

2. The Nature of the Statutory Scheme and the Terms of the Statute Pursuant to Which the Body Operates

It is important to pay close attention to the legislation that authorizes a particular decision to be made. Where the decision-making process includes preliminary steps, the requirements of fairness may be minimal. For example, as noted above, investigatory procedures are not normally subject to the duty of fairness, even though they might give rise to proceedings in which fairness protection will be required. Where there is but one final decision to be made however, greater fairness protection will usually be required. But a decision need not be final in order to attract a high degree of fairness protection. In some ways, procedural protection may be enhanced where a second level of proceedings is envisaged. For example, the existence of an appeal is an important consideration in deciding whether and to what extent reasons for a decision are required.

3. The Importance of the Decision to the Individual/Individuals

The more important a particular decision is to those whom it affects, the greater the level of fairness protection that will be required. This is true whether the matter affected is considered a right, an interest, or a privilege. But the importance of a particular decision to an individual must be balanced against the needs of the relevant decision-maker and, as we will see, the decision-maker may be afforded considerable deference in selecting the appropriate procedures.

4. The Legitimate Expectations of the Person Challenging the Relevant Decision

By subsuming legitimate expectations on the list of considerations relevant to determining the content of fairness, the Court reaffirmed the limited procedural focus of the concept. As discussed above, where a legitimate expectation of a particular procedure exists it may expand the content of the duty of fairness. But a legitimate expectation of a particular substantive outcome will never result in the protection of that outcome. At most, a legitimate expectation of a substantive outcome will give rise to an entitlement to enhanced procedural protection before the expectation can be dashed.

5. Deference to the Procedural Choices Made by the Decision-Maker

The content of the duty of fairness affects more than just the person whose rights, interests, or privileges are at stake. It affects the decision-maker, who may be required to make decisions in hundreds, if not thousands, of additional cases, and hence all those whose rights, interests, or privileges will be affected by those decisions. As a result, the needs of the decision-maker must be taken into account:

> [T]he analysis of what procedures the duty of fairness requires should also take into account and respect the choices of procedure made by the agency itself, particularly when the statute leaves to the decision-maker the ability to choose its own procedures, or when the agency has an expertise in determining what procedures are appropriate in the circumstances. While this, of course, is not determinative, important weight must be given to the choice of procedures made by the agency itself and its institutional constraints.[67]

It is not clear how significant deference to decision-makers' procedural choices will turn out to be. "Important weight" must be given to the decision-maker's choice of procedure, but this provides little meaningful guidance.

As with judicial review generally, courts have to be conscious of the limits of their expertise on judicial review of fairness questions. Fairness requirements that are too onerous will undermine the institutional mission of the decision-maker and, as a result, it is important to take into account the perspective of the decision-maker. Thus, one of the important tasks for respondents on judicial review is to educate the court as to the needs of their processes, which may reflect compromises necessary to allow decisions to be made within a reasonable time frame and at a reasonable cost.

V. JUDICIAL REVIEW OF THE DUTY OF FAIRNESS

It is important to appreciate the difference between judicial review of a decision on procedural grounds on the one hand, and on substantive grounds on the other. The Supreme Court of Canada has developed an elaborate approach to judicial review of substantive decisions—decisions about the matter in issue, typically involving interpretation and application of the legislation pursuant to which the decision is made. The Court has, until recently, used three standards of review—correctness, reasonableness (*simpliciter*), and patent unreasonableness—and selected the standard of review applicable in particular circumstances by considering a number of criteria in its "pragmatic and functional" approach.[68]

---

67 *Baker*, *supra* note 19 at para. 27 (internal citations omitted).

68 See, for example, *Pushpanathan v. Canada (Minister of Citizenship and Immigration)*, [1998] 1 S.C.R. 982. The Court's "pragmatic and functional" approach to judicial review is discussed by Sheila Wildeman, chapter 9. But see *Dunsmuir v. New Brunswick*, 2008 SCC 9 [*Dunsmuir*], in which the Court eliminates the patent unreasonableness standard and attempts to simplify its approach to selecting the standard of review.

No similar approach is taken in regard to the duty of fairness. Historically, compliance with the duty of fairness has been regarded as a jurisdictional question, and jurisdictional questions must be answered correctly.[69] In other words, decision-makers do not have the "right to be wrong" where procedural questions are concerned. Jurisdiction will be lost in the course of proceedings if the duty of fairness is breached. If this occurs, the relevant decision will be quashed, and the decision-maker will be required to make a fresh decision in accordance with the correct procedure.

The application of the correctness standard does not mean that there is no room for deference when it comes to the duty of fairness. As we have seen, the Court made clear in *Baker* that the needs of the particular decision-maker are a relevant consideration in fashioning the content of the duty of fairness. There is room for deference at this stage of the inquiry, albeit that the needs of the decision-maker may be outweighed by the other *Baker* criteria. In any event, once the content of the duty has been determined, the conduct of the decision-maker will be assessed and the court will ask whether or not the duty of fairness has been met—a question that it will answer on a correctness basis.

It is important to emphasize that a violation of the duty of fairness will not result in a substantive outcome. The role of the court is to supervise the decision-making *process*—to ensure that the decision has been made properly, not that the "proper" decision has been made. Although a successful application for judicial review on fairness grounds will result in an order quashing a decision and requiring it to be made anew, nothing prevents the decision-maker from reaching the same substantive decision. Nevertheless, as *Baker* demonstrates, a new hearing may well lead to a different outcome. Mavis Baker was subsequently granted the humanitarian and compassionate exception she sought and was allowed to stay in Canada.

Whether or not a different result obtains on a rehearing, the consequences of a breach of the duty of fairness may be significant. Administrative proceedings can take months—even years—and be hugely expensive for all those involved.[70] An order quashing proceedings may cause great inconvenience not only to those involved but also to the public interest, by requiring that proceedings be repeated, with all the associated cost and delay. Strict adherence to the automatic quashing remedy may result in problems from time to time. Moreover, the automatic nature of the remedy may turn out to be counterproductive to the protection of the right. It is possible that, in close cases, courts might err on the side of finding that the duty has been met, given the far-reaching consequences an order quashing a particular decision may have. As long as quashing is the usual remedy for a breach of fairness, courts may be circumspect in expanding the scope and content of the duty of fairness.

69 Such questions cannot be immunized from judicial review: *Crevier v. Quebec*, [1981] 2 S.C.R. 220.

70 See, for example, *Canada (Attorney General) v. Canada (Commission of Inquiry on the Blood System)*, [1997] 3 S.C.R. 440 (judicial review of commission of inquiry [the Krever commission] that held hearings over a two-year period).

VI. POSTSCRIPT: DUNSMUIR v. NEW BRUNSWICK

The Supreme Court of Canada has created an exception to the general principles governing the application of the duty of fairness. Following *Dunsmuir v. New Brunswick*,[71] the law will no longer draw a distinction between public office holders and other employees in dismissal cases. If the terms of an individual's employment are governed by contract, then ordinary private law contractual remedies will apply in the event of his or her dismissal, regardless of the public nature of the employment concerned. In short, the duty of fairness will, in general, have no application to the dismissal of employees.

It is important to appreciate that the Court's purpose in *Dunsmuir* was not to limit the protection of public office holders. On the contrary, the Court assumed that modern public office holders enjoy contractual employment relationships, and that their contracts address procedural fairness concerns. As a result, the protection of the common-law duty of fairness was considered unnecessary. By abandoning the distinction between public office holders and contractual employees, the Court hoped to simplify the application of the law, obviating the need for litigation concerning the nature of an individual's employment.

Nevertheless, it is clear that *Dunsmuir* limits the protection of public employees to some extent. It will no longer be possible for public office holders to be restored to their positions, since that remedy is not available for breach of contract. The Court acknowledges as much, but argues that the duty of fairness did not include a reinstatement remedy, since public office holders could be dismissed provided only that the proper procedure were followed. There is no doubt, however, that reinstatement to a position following a breach of the duty of fairness—even on an ostensibly temporary basis—was often a considerable motivation for bringing judicial review proceedings.

Following *Dunsmuir*, the "crucial consideration" is whether or not a public employee has a contract of employment. Where such a contract exists, it will be assumed that it addresses procedural fairness issues. If it does not, the normal common- or civil-law principles will govern. In either event, protection from wrongful dismissal will be governed by private law contract principles. The Court conceives of two exceptions. First, employees not protected by employment contracts, or subject to employment at pleasure, will still be protected by the duty of fairness. Second, the duty of fairness may arise by necessary implication in some statutory contexts.

In general, *Dunsmuir* narrows significantly the circumstances in which the duty of fairness applies. Although the general principles outlined in *Knight v. Indian Head School Division No. 19*[72] concerning the duty of fairness owed by administrative decision-makers remain relevant, the Court notes that on its new approach the duty would not have applied in the circumstances of that case, given the existence of an employment contract.

71 *Supra* note 68.

72 *Supra* note 43.

SUGGESTED ADDITIONAL READINGS

BOOKS

Brown, Donald, & John M. Evans. *Judicial Review of Administrative Action in Canada*, looseleaf (Toronto: Canvasback, 1998).

Dyzenhaus, David, ed. *The Unity of Public Law* (Oxford: Hart Publishing, 2004).

Jones, David P., & Anne S. de Villars. *Principles of Administrative Law*, 4th ed. (Toronto: Thomson Carswell, 2004).

Mullan, David J. *Administrative Law* (Toronto: Irwin, 2001) chapter 8.

CASES

Att. Gen. of Can. v. Inuit Tapirisat et al., [1980] 2 S.C.R. 735.

Baker v. Canada (Minister of Citizenship and Immigration), [1999] 2 S.C.R. 817.

Blencoe v. British Columbia (Human Rights Commission), [2000] 2 S.C.R. 307.

Cardinal v. Director of Kent Institution, [1985] 2 S.C.R. 643.

Dunsmuir v. New Brunswick, 2008 SCC 9.

Homex Realty and Development Co. v. Wyoming (Village), [1980] 2 S.C.R. 1011.

Knight v. Indian Head School Division No. 19, [1990] 1 S.C.R. 653.

Mount Sinai Hospital Center v. Quebec (Minister of Health and Social Services), [2001] 2 S.C.R. 281.

Nicholson v. Haldimand-Norfolk (Regional) Police Commissioners, [1979] 1 S.C.R. 311.

Reference Re Canada Assistance Plan (B.C.), [1991] 2 S.C.R. 525.

Suresh v. Canada (Minister of Citizenship and Immigration), [2002] 1 S.C.R. 3.

CHAPTER SIX

Independence, Impartiality, and Bias

LAVERNE JACOBS
*Faculty of Law, University of Windsor**

I. INTRODUCTION

This chapter addresses the controversial issues of tribunal[1] independence, impartiality, and bias. It is useful at the outset to define the relationship between these three concepts, although this relationship will be discussed in greater detail below. Put simply, independence, impartiality, and bias all centre on the notion of fairness in the administrative decision-making process. A key characteristic of a fair proceeding before an administrative body is that the decision-maker and the decision-making process not proffer any undue preferential treatment or be driven by preconceived notions. This characteristic is vital, not only to the

* This chapter draws in part from the author's doctoral dissertation.

1 The term "tribunal" is a term contested by some decision-making bodies within the administrative justice system but is used here generically to encompass all statutory decision-making bodies (variously termed agencies, boards, commissions, etc.), not simply those that are adjudicative in a court-like sense, and not simply those that render binding decisions.

litigants before the tribunal, but also to the public's confidence in the administration of justice. Most certainly, the general public would lose faith in public decision-makers if it were perceived that their decisions were based on irrelevant considerations such as relationships with litigants before them, prejudice, and undue pressure from government. As a result, our legal tradition has gone to great lengths to protect this fundamental tenet of fairness. Consequently, regardless of what the reality may be in any given administrative decision-making process, the mere perception of partiality toward a particular outcome or *bias*, provided that the perception is reasonable, is enough to have a decision overturned.

If bias is the evil that we are trying to avoid, *impartiality* refers to the ideal state of the decision-maker or decision-making institution. An impartial decision-maker is one who is able to make judgments with an open mind—that is, one who comes to the decision-making table without his or her "mind already made up" or without connections that improperly influence the decision-making process. Finally, *independence* is said to be a means of achieving impartiality. For example, by ensuring through legislation that an administrative tribunal is not too dependent on government for the necessities of its day-to-day functioning, it is theoretically less likely that government officials can pull decision-making strings.

II. SOURCES OF THE GUARANTEE OF AN INDEPENDENT AND IMPARTIAL TRIBUNAL

The guarantee of a proceeding before an independent and impartial tribunal stems from both common-law and constitutional or quasi-constitutional principles. In this way, this chapter develops the concepts of procedural fairness discussed by Grant Huscroft in chapter 5 and is a prelude to the following chapter on administrative law and the Charter by Evan Fox-Decent (chapter 7). At common law, the principles of natural justice are encapsulated in two central ideas. The first is that a decision-maker should neither judge her own cause nor have any interest in the outcome of a case before her. This idea is generally known as the rule against bias and is often summarized in a Latin maxim: *nemo judex in sua causa debet esse* (no one is fit to be the judge in his own cause). The second requires the decision-maker to hear and listen to both sides of the case before making a decision. This requirement has been summarized by the maxim *audi alteram partem*, meaning "hear the other side." Both the *nemo judex* and the *audi alteram partem* principles inform the right to an independent and impartial proceeding. The *nemo judex* rule aims to avoid circumstances in which the decision-maker acts as both prosecutor and judge in the same matter or decides for personal gain or benefit. Similarly, by requiring the decision-maker to listen to all sides of a dispute, the *audi alteram partem* rule seeks, in part, to encourage the decision-maker to focus his or her decision on the facts of the dispute and the relevant law and not on extraneous, irrelevant considerations.[2]

In addition to these common-law principles, some have argued, with limited success, that the guarantees of an independent and impartial administrative tribunal are also assured

2 I discuss the interplay of these ideas in greater detail in Laverne A. Jacobs, "Tribunal Independence and Impartiality: Rethinking the Theory After Bell and Ocean Port Hotel—A Call for Empirical Analysis" in Laverne A. Jacobs & Anne L. Mactavish, eds., *Dialogue Between Courts and Tribunals: Essays in Administrative Law and Justice (2001-2007)* (Montreal: Éditions Thémis, 2008) (forthcoming).

by unwritten constitutional principles and the rule of law.[3] Finally, the guarantee of an independent and impartial tribunal is also put into operation through the *Canadian Charter of Rights and Freedoms*[4] and through quasi-constitutional enactments at the federal and provincial levels. The table below indicates the wording of the guarantees provided by these various enactments.

Statute	Section(s)	Guarantee provided
Canadian Charter of Rights and Freedoms	s. 7	Everyone has the right to life, liberty and security of the person and the right not to be deprived thereof except in accordance with the principles of fundamental justice.
Canadian Charter of Rights and Freedoms	s. 11(d)	Any person charged with an offence has the right … to be presumed innocent until proven guilty according to law in a fair and public hearing by an independent and impartial tribunal.
Quebec *Charter of human rights and freedoms*[5]	s. 23	Every person has a right to a full and equal, public and fair hearing by an independent and impartial tribunal, for the determination of his rights and obligations or of the merits of any charge brought against him.
Canadian Bill of Rights[6]	ss. 1(a) and 2(e)	1(a) the right of the individual to life, liberty, security of the person and enjoyment of property, and the right not to be deprived thereof except by due process of law; … 2. … no law of Canada shall be construed or applied so as to … (e) deprive a person of the right to a fair hearing in accordance with the principles of fundamental justice for the determination of his rights and obligations.
Alberta Bill of Rights[7]	s. 1(a)	[T]he right of the individual to liberty, security of the person and enjoyment of property, and the right not to be deprived thereof except by due process of law.

One of the most striking aspects of this comparative chart is the difference in wording and the seeming variation in the rights protected and the standards employed to protect them. For example, while the *Canadian Bill of Rights* and the *Alberta Bill of Rights* make "due process of law" the decisive factor for determining whether one has been legally or illegally deprived of one's rights, s. 7 of the Canadian Charter speaks of "principles of fundamental justice." To what extent are the two expressions coterminous? Is one concept

3 *Ocean Port Hotel Ltd. v. British Columbia (General Manager, Liquor Control and Licensing Branch)*, [2001] 2 S.C.R. 781 [*Ocean Port Hotel*] and *McKenzie v. Minister of Public Safety and Solicitor General et al.* (2006), 61 B.C.L.R. (4th) 57 (Sup. Ct.), (2007), 71 B.C.L.R. (4th) 1 (C.A.), [2007] S.C.C.A. No. 601 (leave to appeal to the SCC filed December 18, 2007) [*McKenzie*]. Both cases are discussed below.

4 Part I of the *Constitution Act, 1982*, being Schedule B to the *Canada Act 1982* (U.K.), 1982, c. 11 [the Charter].

5 R.S.Q. c. C-12 [Quebec Charter].

6 S.C. 1960, c. 44, reprinted in R.S.C. 1985, App. III.

7 R.S.A. 2000, c. A-14.

broader than the other? And how (if at all) do these concepts—due process of law, fundamental justice, etc.—relate to the common-law principle of natural justice? These are all questions with which the courts, lawyers, academics, and students have grappled.[8]

Moreover, it is clear from the chart that many situations trigger the right to what we might call globally "an independent and impartial proceeding" to cover the various formulations. What is not always clear is how smoothly these situations translate to the various instances of socio-economic regulation that are addressed by administrative actors in the administrative state. For example, s. 11(d) of the Canadian Charter has been held to require penal consequences before it can be applied.[9] And while s. 23 of the Quebec Charter seems all-encompassing insofar as it allows for a fair hearing by an independent and impartial tribunal for the mere determination of the individual's rights and obligations, this seemingly low threshold is elevated by a legislated definition of "tribunal." The Quebec Charter defines "tribunals" as being adjudicative bodies only.[10] The acceptable degree of independence and the way in which impartiality is understood may be quite different for hearings before a body in Quebec that is established to set prices and develop policy in the natural resources sector than for hearings before a human rights tribunal.

Generally, these variations, whether they stem from legislative enactments, the common law, or judicial interpretations of both, indicate a very context-driven and at times uneven promise of independence and impartiality. In order to predict the degree of independence that any administrative body should exhibit and the ways in which impartiality and bias should be understood within the context of that body's functioning, it is important to have a thorough understanding not only of the law but also of the nature, purpose, and practical ways of operating the administrative body in question.

Challenging administrative tribunals for lack of independence has become one of the most litigated issues in administrative law. Indeed, since the advent of the Canadian Charter, some see this new preoccupation with independent decision-making as providing "a more extensive basis for challenging adjudicators and statutory regimes than has been envisaged under traditional common law conceptions of bias."[11] Because independence has attracted such attention as a means of challenging administrative regimes, this chapter focuses primarily on arguments regarding lack of independence as a source for alleging rea-

8 See, for example, *Singh v. Minister of Employment and Immigration*, [1985] 1 S.C.R. 177 [*Singh*], an immigration case, in which the Supreme Court of Canada held that at a minimum, "fundamental justice" included the notion of procedural fairness.

9 See *Alex Couture Inc. v. Canada (Attorney General)* (1991), 83 D.L.R. (4th) 577 (Qc. C.A.) [*Alex Couture*], leave to appeal to the Supreme Court of Canada refused (1992), 91 D.L.R. (4th) vii; and *Chrysler Canada Ltd. v. Canada (Competition Tribunal)*, [1992] 2 S.C.R. 394. Section 7 of the Charter seems to offer more fertile ground and has been used with some success in deportation matters (see *Charkaoui v. Canada (Citizenship and Immigration)*, 2007 SCC 9; but see also *Suresh v. Canada (Minister of Citizenship and Immigration)*, [2002] 1 S.C.R. 3.

10 Section 56 of the Quebec Charter reads:

> 56(1) In sections 9, 23, 30, 31, 34 and 38, in Chapter III of Part II and in Part IV, the word "tribunal" includes a coroner, a fire investigation commissioner, an inquiry commission, and any person or agency exercising quasi judicial functions.

11 See David J. Mullan, *Administrative Law: Cases, Text, and Materials*, 5th ed. (Toronto: Emond Montgomery, 2003) at 574.

sonable apprehension of bias on the part of individual administrative decision-makers or of administrative decision-making institutions.

In addition to independence, other common-law challenges for bias have arisen from a variety of situations. Some situations constitute traditional concerns that stem from very easy to understand occurrences that would be fatal to any decision-making system including the judiciary (such as the decision-maker having a direct, pecuniary interest in the outcome). Others stem from the very nature of the administrative state, which itself comprises a wide range of administrative actors with very different natures and purposes—from governmental ministers to adjudicative bodies. These concerns include challenges for attitudinal bias and challenges with respect to the ways in which administrative bodies promote consistency and efficiency within their work. Two administrative practices that have prompted challenges for reasonable apprehension of bias in the jurisprudence will be discussed at the end this chapter: full board meetings and the even more recent development of producing "lead cases."

III. WHAT IS "TRIBUNAL INDEPENDENCE" AND WHY IS IT IMPORTANT?

The notion of tribunal independence raises several questions. To what extent should tribunals and other administrative bodies be independent of the branches of government that have created them? How can a tribunal (and its members) best fulfill the often competing functions for which it has been created while maintaining an appropriate distance from government, litigants, and other stakeholders? And how do we define "appropriate"? We will explore the various relationships that affect the independence of tribunals and their individual decision-makers, and the ways that independence may be, or perceived to be, compromised. These relationships are examined critically from both the perspective of jurisprudential debates and the practical realities of daily tribunal operations. Specific tensions include the appointments process, removal of members, tribunals as a function of policy-making, internal interactions among tribunal members and staff, and the vexing question of the extent to which explicit and implicit constitutional guarantees do or should apply to tribunals.

By design, administrative decision-making bodies have been created in a way that leaves them open to suspicion. Most have a link with the executive branch of government through a minister of Cabinet. Generally, under their enabling statutes, tribunals, or at least their chairs, are required to maintain some contact with this minister. At the very least, they are obliged to file annual reports to this minister.[12] They may also have additional statutory obligations that force them to interact with the minister and his or her department. For example, they may be asked to provide advice to the minister or to provide him or her with additional information on developments in the regulation of the industry or sector under their management.[13] Finally, the minister will certainly be involved in the process of appointing and removing members of the tribunal.

12 A typical provision imposing the obligation to file an annual report to the minister can be found in the *Residential Tenancies Act, 2006*, S.O. 2006, c. 17, s. 180.

13 See, for example, *Alcohol and Gaming Regulation and Public Protection Act*, S.O. 1996, c. 26, Sch., s. 3(4).

Given the political nature of the executive branch of government, and in particular its responsibility to create and promote the policies of government, one can easily see how members of the general public may be confused, if not wary, that inappropriate interference may stem from the regular interactions between government departments and tribunals. Users of the tribunal might be concerned that the minister may use these opportunities to dictate, explicitly or implicitly, how particular files should be decided. This concern can be particularly acute in situations where the government is frequently an opposing party before the tribunal, such as immigration matters or disputes relating to social benefits, like disability insurance.

These introductory paragraphs point us in the direction of an initial understanding of the concept of tribunal independence and why it is important. When we speak of "independence," we are referring to the tribunal's ability to decide matters free of inappropriate interference or influence. While the executive branch of government may be one source of interference in the administrative law context, several others such as litigants, other tribunal members, and staff may also exist. As in the case of trial decisions in the criminal law context, or judicial decisions made in civil matters, independence of the decision-maker is valued as an aspect of the rule of law. In theory, when decision-makers are in an insulated zone, the public has greater confidence that the decision being made is based only on relevant considerations such as the facts of the case and the law. In the context of the administrative state, however, the difficulty is determining what constitutes "relevant" considerations or "inappropriate" interference. Some of the most interesting tensions in administrative law arise in the clash between the day-to-day realities of the work of administrative tribunals and judicial understandings of how the administrative state should work. The law on tribunal independence is no exception. Arguably, it is one of the richest areas to explore these tensions. By focusing primarily on judicial review of administrative action, administrative law has, to date, given privilege to judicial conceptions of independence while failing to integrate adequately judicial understandings with on-the-ground tribunal realities.

The following discussion provides an overview of the historical development of the law on tribunal independence and the relationship between independence and the concepts of impartiality and bias. It then explores administrative law's understandings of independence, impartiality, and bias from both judicial and tribunal perspectives using three areas as examples:

- the appointment and removal of members;
- adjudicative independence, consistency, and policy-making;
- independence, impartiality, and multifunctionality.

A. The Development of the Law of Tribunal Independence in Canada

The jurisprudence on tribunal independence in Canada is easiest understood as having developed through a series of three waves. The first wave of jurisprudence used the independence of the judiciary as a foundation on which to mould the concept of administrative tribunal independence. The second wave, marked by the decision in *Ocean Port Hotel*, affirmed the hybrid nature of tribunals and maintained that there is no general constitutional guarantee of independence where tribunals are concerned. The third wave served as a retrenchment: litigants once again pushed to have judicial declarations that administrative tribunal independence is guaranteed by the Constitution.

1. Laying the Groundwork: The Theory of Judicial Independence

A discussion about the independence of administrative bodies is best started with an overview of the theory of judicial independence. At its core, judicial independence is a means of ensuring that judges act free from any interference or influence. In Australia, Sir Guy Green has described judicial independence as the capacity of the courts "to perform their constitutional function free from actual or apparent dependence upon any persons or institutions."[14] Dickson C.J., speaking for the majority of the Supreme Court of Canada in *Beauregard v. Canada*, offered this useful definition:

> Historically, the generally accepted core of the principle of judicial independence has been the complete liberty of individual judges to hear and decide the cases that come before them: *no outsider—be it government, pressure group, individual or even another judge—should interfere in fact, or attempt to interfere, with the way in which a judge conducts his or her case and makes his or her decision.* This core continues to be central to the principle of judicial independence.[15]

How is this "complete liberty" to be ascertained? While it is certainly impossible to monitor all the contacts and communications of every judge, when it comes to assuring independence from government (the first of the outside interferences noted by Dickson C.J. above), three objective conditions have been identified as necessary to guarantee independence. These three are security of tenure, financial security, and administrative (or institutional) control. The idea behind these three conditions is that they serve to reassure the public that the possibility of interference in judicial decision-making by the executive and legislative branches of government has been reduced, if not eliminated.

With respect to security of tenure, the type of interference targeted is the ability of the government to remove a judge for such things as rendering decisions that do not meet the government's approval. As a result, the condition that a judge's tenure be secure mandates that a judge be removed only for cause. Security of tenure is guaranteed by the constitution, which provides that judges of the superior courts shall hold office during good behaviour or until they reach the age of 75.[16] Moreover, before removal, judges must be provided with an opportunity to respond to the allegations against them.[17] Consequently, at-pleasure appointments, which allow judges to be removed at the request of Cabinet,

---

14 Sir Guy Green, "The Rationale and Some Aspects of Judicial Independence" (1985) 20 A.L.R. 135. Sir Green's formulation of the concept of judicial independence was endorsed by the Supreme Court of Canada in *R. v. Valente*, [1985] 2 S.C.R. 673 at para. 18 [*Valente*], per Le Dain J.

15 *Beauregard v. Canada*, [1986] 2 S.C.R. 56 at para. 21 (emphasis added).

16 See *Constitution Act, 1867* (U.K.), 30 & 31 Vict., c. 3, s. 99.

17 An example of this is found in the federal *Judges Act*, R.S.C. 1985, c. J-1, s. 64 [*Judges Act*]. See also the website of the Canadian Judicial Council, <http://www.cjc-ccm.gc.ca>, which outlines the complaints procedure and inquiry process for the investigation of federally appointed judges. For a recent example of the judicial inquiry process in action see *Ruffo (Re)*, [2005] Q.J. No. 17953 (C.A.).

without prespecified cause and without necessarily allowing the judge to be heard, have been rendered invalid.

"Financial security" aims to satisfy two goals. The first is a guarantee that although the government is responsible for the remuneration of judges, it will not alter their pay for arbitrary reasons such as discontent with decisions rendered. To accomplish this goal, judges are guaranteed a fixed salary under the constitution.[18] As well, more recently, compensation commissions have been set up to help facilitate negotiations in judges' pay and pay-related matters, such as pensions.[19] The second goal is a promise that the amount that judges are paid will be sufficient to keep them from seeking alternative means of supplementing their income. Security of tenure and financial security have historical roots dating back to 13th-century England.[20] These concepts evolved from experiences in which the King manipulated the judiciary in order to ensure that the bench was sympathetic toward him, and from the problem of bribery caused by the underpayment of court officials, including judges.

Administrative or institutional control is the third objective guarantee of independence. Institutional control deals with the manner in which the affairs of the court are administered—from budgetary allocations for buildings and equipment to the assignment of cases. It addresses how responsibility for such administration should be divided between the judiciary and the other branches of government. While questions such as the allocation of court cases have clearly been determined to fall properly within the ambit of the chief justice of the court,[21] other matters such as obtaining budgetary allocations for equipment are more problematic.[22] For example, while allowing judges to obtain their own funding for resources instead of asking them to go through a Cabinet minister such as the attorney general might be an approach that fosters the independence of the judiciary, this method may result in judges soliciting funds from the government or others, which is equally unseemly. For the Supreme Court, the Federal Courts, and the Tax Court, issues of institutional control that rely on government allocation of resources have been addressed through the use of a negotiating office called the Federal Commissioner of Judicial Affairs.[23] The problem of balancing judicial independence and judicial administration is particularly acute at the provincial and territorial level where, as a result of our constitutional division of powers, the administration of the court system requires some involvement by the provincial legislature and executive.[24]

As with security of tenure and financial security, administrative control is concerned with making sure that judges are not put in compromising situations where they may choose to make decisions in order to protect their own employment and interests, rather than for the

18 See *Constitution Act, 1867*, *supra* note 16, s. 100.

19 See, for example, *Provincial Court Judges Association of New Brunswick v. New Brunswick (Minister of Justice)*, [2005] 2 S.C.R 286.

20 See W. R. Lederman, "The Independence of the Judiciary" (1956) 34 Can. Bar Rev. 769, 1139.

21 See *Valente*, *supra* note 14.

22 See Martin Friedland, *A Place Apart: Judicial Independence and Accountability in Canada* (Ottawa: Canadian Judicial Council, 1995); see also Jules Deschênes & Carl Baar, *Masters in Their Own House* (Ottawa: Canadian Judicial Council, 1981).

23 Established under Part III of the *Judges Act*, *supra* note 17.

24 See *Constitution Act, 1867*, *supra* note 16, s. 92(14).

sake of rendering decisions solely on the basis of their legal judgment. However, unlike the first two guarantees of independence, administrative control primarily has an institutional as opposed to individual nature. Although there may be implications that affect an individual judge, it is not the individual judge and his or her relationship with the government that is at issue, but the relationship between the government and the court as an institution. Finally, the jurisprudence has come to recognize another type of independence. This is independence from interference by other judges, known commonly as adjudicative independence.

As alluded to in the introduction, the purpose of judicial independence is to help boost public confidence in the justice system. It is not the protection of the judges that these guarantees have in mind, but the protection of the public. The mere appearance that there may reasonably be inappropriate interference with the decision-making process is enough to engender a loss of public confidence in the decision-making mechanisms of the state. Some would argue that a reasonable perception of interference may threaten public acceptance of the law itself. In this light, independence is not a goal in and of itself. Rather, judicial independence serves as a cornerstone to protect other values that are considered important within our system of justice. Most commonly, independence is said to be maintained in order to provide an appearance of impartiality in the decision-making process. Providing guarantees of independence aims to assure the public that decision-makers are in a position to make decisions impartially. Similarly, the independence of administrative tribunals seeks to achieve the same goal.

2. *From Judicial Independence to Tribunal Independence*

Over time, the criteria guaranteeing independence of the judiciary have served as a foundation from which courts have determined whether administrative tribunals are also sufficiently independent. *R. v. Valente*[25] was the first Supreme Court of Canada case in Canada to suggest the idea that the guarantees for judicial independence could also be applied to a variety of tribunals.[26] Since that time, litigants have pushed for tribunals to be held to the same degree of independence as the courts. These litigants have argued that various constitutional safeguards (namely, ss. 7 and 11(d) of the Canadian Charter as well as the unwritten constitutional principle of judicial independence) and quasi-constitutional provisions (such as s. 23 of the Quebec Charter and the *Canadian Bill of Rights*) guarantee tribunal independence.[27]

---

25 *Valente, supra* note 14.

26 *Valente, ibid.*, was the first Supreme Court case to deal with the question of judicial independence in Canada. In *Valente*, the question at issue was whether a provincial court judge, appointed under the *Provincial Courts Act*, R.S.O. 1980, c. 398 and sitting as the Ontario Provincial Court (Criminal Division) could be considered an independent tribunal under s. 11(d) of the Charter.

27 See, for example, with respect to Charter s. 7: *Singh, supra* note 8; with respect to Charter s. 11(d): *R. v. Généreux*, [1992] 1 S.C.R. 259; *Ruffo v. Québec (Conseil de la magistrature)*, [1991] A.Q. No. 1101 (Qc. Sup. Ct.) (the argument relating to Charter s. 11(d) was abandoned at the higher levels of court); *Alex Couture, supra* note 9; in relation to the unwritten constitutional principles stemming from the preamble of the Constitution see *Ocean Port Hotel, supra* note 3, and *McKenzie, supra* note 3; as regards s. 23 of the Quebec Charter see *2747-3174 Quebec Inc. v. Quebec (Régie des permis d'alcool)*, [1996] 3 S.C.R. 919, and *Montambeault v. Brazeau*, [1996] A.Q. No. 4187 (C.A.).

The test for tribunal independence is whether a reasonable, well-informed person having thought the matter through would conclude that an administrative decision-maker is sufficiently free of factors that could interfere with his or her ability to make impartial judgments.[28]

The standard for tribunal independence is not as strict as it is for judicial independence. Administrative tribunals do not have to meet the same degree of independence as the courts do. The methodological approach taken by the courts when a challenge is brought to the independence of an administrative tribunal consists of applying the guarantees of tribunal independence in a flexible way to account for the functions performed by the tribunal under scrutiny. This method was stated concisely in *Canadian Pacific Ltd. v. Matsqui Indian Band* by Lamer C.J.:

> [w]hile administrative tribunals are subject to the *Valente* principles, the test for institutional independence must be applied in light of the functions being performed by the particular tribunal at issue. The requisite level of institutional independence (i.e., security of tenure, financial security and administrative control) will depend on the nature of the tribunal, the interests at stake, and other indices of independence such as oaths of office.[29]

Reference to the operational context of the tribunal does not only take place through an examination of the tribunal's functions as declared in its enabling legislation, but also through an appreciation of the tribunal as it functions in practice. In *Matsqui*, the need to see the tribunal in practice was a point of division between the majority and minority decisions. While all the judges who addressed the issue agreed with the theoretical approach set out by Lamer C.J., outlined above, the majority opinion on this issue maintained that the test should be deferred until the tribunals had actually been up and running in order to have the benefit of knowing how they operated in practice.[30] Similarly, in *2747-3174 Quebec Inc. v. Québec (Régie des permis d'alcool)*,[31] a case argued under s. 23 of the Quebec Charter, the principles developed in *Matsqui* were applied. In *Régie*, it was held that the directors of Quebec's liquor licensing board had sufficient security of tenure despite the fact that their terms of office were limited. The Supreme Court of Canada held that the requirements of tribunal independence do not necessitate that administrative actors, like judges, hold office for life. The Court reasoned that what must be avoided, however, is that adjudicators can simply be dismissed at the pleasure of the executive branch of government. The fixed-term appointments were acceptable because the directors' orders of appointment provided expressly that the directors could be dismissed only for specific reasons. They could also contest their dismissals in court. Sanctions were therefore available for any arbitrary interference by the executive in a director's term of office. The respondent in *Régie* also chal-

28 This test, which is generally referred to as the "reasonable apprehension of bias" test, has many purposes. The same test is used to determine whether a reasonable apprehension exists that an administrative decision-maker has acted partially or exhibited bias. Moreover, the test has been applied to evaluate administrative bodies as a whole in order to determine if the institution can be said to exhibit a lack of independence or impartiality in a substantial number of cases. The reasonable apprehension of bias test is discussed below in part IV.B.1, "Reasonable Apprehension of Bias."

29 [1995] 1 S.C.R. 3 at para. 83 [*Matsqui*].

30 See *Matsqui*, *ibid.* at paras. 116-117.

31 [1996] 3 S.C.R. 919 [*Régie*].

lenged the board's administrative control. It argued that there were so many points of contact between the liquor board and the minister responsible for the board's enabling legislation that the board's institutional independence was threatened. However, the Court held that administrative control was also sufficient. The Court reasoned that it was not unusual for a minister to have many points of contact with a tribunal under its responsibility. The Court noted further that no evidence had been provided to show that the minister could affect the decision-making process.

It is very easy to state the test for tribunal independence and to give illustrations of how the test has been applied in the jurisprudence. It is more challenging to explain why flexibility is needed when applying the criteria for judicial independence to tribunals. Standard explanations point to the wide range of tribunal structures, the various ways that tribunals are connected to government, the great divergence in the nature and work of administrative bodies, and the many functions that any one administrative body may be asked to perform in tandem. These standard explanations also emphasize that the test for independence is often a way of investigating whether a reasonable apprehension of bias exists in a particular administrative context. While such explanations take us to a certain point, they do not explain why tribunals ought not to have the same guarantees of structural independence—security of tenure, financial security, administrative control—as a court. Perhaps the best judicial attempt to explain normatively why the objective guarantees of judicial independence need not apply to administrative tribunals came in the Supreme Court of Canada's decision in *Ocean Port Hotel Ltd. v. British Columbia (General Manager, Liquor Control and Licensing Branch)*,[32] discussed in the next section.

In many cases, the objective guarantees of independence for the judiciary do not meet anything near a complete match for tribunals. With regard to administrative control, most tribunal chairs, like judges, are responsible for distributing their own caseload and for tribunal management. As well, the tribunal chair usually has the authority to allocate budgetary resources as effectively as possible. However, things differ considerably from the judiciary when it comes to financial security and security of tenure. While the pay for a tribunal member is normally set by legislation, for part-time members in particular, the pay is often disproportionate to the skill contributed. Generally, tribunal service is thought of as a type of public service done more for honour than for the glory or riches.[33] In the administrative tribunal context, security of tenure shows a similar marked difference from the judiciary. Tribunal members can be appointed for a variety of terms. Some statutes provide for fixed term appointments where the fixed term can vary anywhere from months to years. In some cases, appointments may be renewable; in others, the statute may give no mention of renewal; and in others still, appointments may not be renewable at all. One type of appointment, termed an "at-pleasure appointment" because it allows the government to appoint a member for as long as the government deems fit, has generated significant controversy in the administrative law jurisprudence. In essence, the problem with at-pleasure appointments is that they theoretically enable the government to fire a decision-maker whose decisions are not in line with its expectations. Given that tribunals are to be independent or "at

32 *Supra* note 3.

33 The website of the Public Appointments Secretariat for Ontario alludes to this idea. See <http://www.pas.gov.on.ca/scripts/en/home.asp>.

arm's length" from government, at-pleasure appointments seem to open the door to the possibility of indirect interference with tribunal decision-making. Ultimately, the issue of whether at-pleasure appointments fail to provide adequate guarantees of independence from arbitrary interference from the executive branch of government was seemingly resolved in *Ocean Port Hotel*. For more than one reason, *Ocean Port Hotel* formed a turning point in the jurisprudence on the independence of administrative tribunals. It constitutes the second wave of jurisprudence in this area and we will address it next.

3. Ocean Port Hotel and Parliamentary Supremacy

In its narrowest sense, the Supreme Court of Canada decision in *Ocean Port Hotel* is significant because it attempted to lay to rest the controversial issue of whether at-pleasure appointments provide a satisfactory degree of independence for decision-makers sitting on tribunals that impose penalties. From a broader perspective, *Ocean Port Hotel* is an important administrative law case because it offers very definitive opinions regarding the nature of courts and tribunals and the distinction between the two.

The British Columbia Liquor Appeal Board was a liquor-licensing body that could impose sanctions and remove licences upon finding that a licensee had contravened the province's *Liquor Control and Licensing Act*.[34] The Royal Canadian Mounted Police (RCMP) reported that Ocean Port Hotel had been responsible for five incidents that violated the Act, the regulations enacted under the statute, and the terms of its liquor licence. A senior inspector with the Liquor Control and Licensing Branch, a regulatory branch established under the Act, held that the allegations had been substantiated on a balance of probabilities. He imposed a two-day suspension on Ocean Port's liquor licence. The Liquor Appeal Board held a hearing *de novo* and confirmed the suspension, finding that the evidence supported four of the five alleged infractions.

On appeal to the British Columbia Court of Appeal, Ocean Port argued that the Liquor Appeal Board lacked sufficient independence to render a fair hearing. It was submitted that the board's decision was therefore invalid. The hotel took issue with the terms of appointment of the members of the Liquor Appeal Board. The Act indicated that the chair and the members of the board were to serve "at the pleasure of the Lieutenant Governor in Council."

The problem with at-pleasure tribunal appointments was not a new one. In fact, it had arisen in the administrative law jurisprudence prior to *Ocean Port Hotel*. Several cases had addressed the question tangentially. In these cases, the main issue had been whether compensation was owed to board members whose terms had been terminated early due to government restructuring of their tribunals.[35] In determining that compensation was owed, some lower courts had admonished the government for interfering with terms that they had previously set through order in council.[36] These decisions stressed that the appearance of

34 R.S.B.C. 1996, c. 267.

35 See, for example, *Hewat v. Ontario* (1997), 32 O.R. (3d) 622 (Div. Ct), var'd (1998), 37 O.R. (3d) 161 (C.A.) [*Hewat*]; *Dewar v. Ontario* (1996), 30 O.R. (3d) 334 (Div. Ct.); (1998), 37 O.R. (3d) 170 (C.A.); *Wells v. Newfoundland*, [1999] 3 S.C.R. 199; and *Preston v. British Columbia* (1994), 92 B.C.L.R. (2d) 298 (C.A.).

36 See, in particular, the Ontario Court of Appeal in *Hewat*, *ibid.*

independence would be undermined if the government could freely change terms of appointment. However, the courts had never before addressed the crucial question of whether at-pleasure appointments, which were clearly not as secure as fixed term appointments, could provide an adequate image of independence from government.

In analyzing this question, the British Columbia Court of Appeal in *Ocean Port Hotel* focused on the similarities between the British Columbia Liquor Appeal Board and its sister institution in Quebec. This comparison could be made easily given that the Supreme Court of Canada decision in *Régie* had just come down. The Court of Appeal noted that Gonthier J. in *Régie* had determined that the fixed term appointments held by the directors of the Régie dès permis d'alcool would not have been valid if they had allowed the directors be removed without cause (or, in other words, at the pleasure of the executive branch of government). Since *Régie* was a judgment dealing with a body mandated to control the same industry and that had adjudicative tasks similar to the British Columbia Liquor Appeal Board, the Court of Appeal held that the Liquor Appeal Board members must also require more security of tenure than what was offered through at-pleasure appointments. In her decision, Huddart J.A. highlighted that the decision to suspend a licence closely resembled a judicial decision and that the penalty was one of serious economic consequence. The British Columbia Court of Appeal also took into account that the same contraventions of the *Liquor Control and Licensing Act* could have been prosecuted in the Provincial Court where a greater level of independence would have been guaranteed. Moreover, the statute provided a lesser penalty for offences prosecuted in the Provincial Court.

On appeal to the Supreme Court of Canada, Ocean Port Hotel added a new argument. Ocean Port submitted that, as an administrative tribunal exercising adjudicative functions, the Liquor Appeal Board required the same degree of independence guaranteed to the courts. The independence of the superior courts of inherent jurisdiction is enshrined in the constitution. Ocean Port relied on *Reference Re Remuneration of Judges of the Provincial Court (PEI)*.[37] There, the Supreme Court of Canada held that judicial independence is an unwritten constitutional principle that applies not only to the superior courts of inherent jurisdiction but also to the Provincial Court of summary jurisdiction. In *PEI Reference*, Lamer C.J. held further that this unwritten constitutional principle is affirmed by the preamble of the constitution, which indicates that Canada's constitution is "similar in Principle to that of the United Kingdom."[38] Ocean Port argued that this unwritten constitutional principle guaranteeing judicial independence should be interpreted to extend to administrative tribunals as well.

The Supreme Court of Canada disagreed. The Court held that the enshrined constitutional protection of judicial independence could not be translated to the context of administrative decision-making bodies. In its reasons, the Court emphasized that judicial independence has historically developed to protect the judiciary from interference from the executive branch of government. By contrast, administrative tribunals are not separate from the executive. In the Court's words, administrative tribunals may be seen as "spanning the constitutional divide between the executive and judicial branches of

37 [1997] 3 S.C.R. 3 [*PEI Reference*].

38 The British *Act of Settlement* of 1701 was the historical inspiration for the judicature provisions of our constitution.

government."[39] Tribunals are created precisely for the purpose of implementing the policies of the executive branch of government. In doing so, they may be required to make quasi-judicial decisions. However, their primary function as policy-makers and their status as extensions of the executive branch of government make the degree of their independence a question most appropriately determined by Parliament or provincial legislature. It is up to Parliament or the legislature to determine the structure, responsibilities, and degree of independence required of any particular tribunal. In this way, the Supreme Court of Canada in *Ocean Port Hotel* asserted that the will of the legislature should prevail in determining how much independence any given tribunal should have. The Supreme Court also affirmed that there is no free-standing constitutional guarantee of tribunal independence.

Furthermore, the Court reminded us that tribunal independence is a common-law principle of natural justice. As with all principles of natural justice, the degree of independence required at common law could be ousted by express statutory language or necessary statutory implication, so long as the statute is constitutionally valid. As a general rule, administrative tribunals do not attract *Charter or quasi-constitutional* requirements of independence. However, by virtue of the nature of their work, some tribunals may be subject to these protections. Finally, the Court pointed out that the *PEI Reference* decision made no assertions that the unwritten constitutional guarantees of judicial independence were to apply to administrative tribunals as well. In sum, *Ocean Port Hotel* affirmed no general constitutional guarantee of independence for administrative tribunals. The only way that constitutional protections can be afforded to tribunals is if the actions of the particular tribunal triggered the protections offered by the Canadian Charter or by one of the provincial or federal quasi-constitutional statutes.[40]

On a theoretical level, it can be argued that *Ocean Port Hotel* has encouraged legislative policy-makers to consider the specificities of various tribunals in thinking about guarantees of independence that are most affected. It seems that it is up to the legislature to create enabling statutes that foster factors promoting independent decision-making and eliminate those that do not. In some circumstances, use of the judicial conditions of independence may be useful. Nevertheless, policy-makers should be open to considering factors that actually affect the independence of administrative decision-makers in various contexts. In particular, one wonders if it may be useful to examine different types of tribunals according to their statutory nature. For example, in the case of parliamentary officers, such as access-to-information and privacy commissioners and ombudsmen, these bodies have a more direct link to the legislature than to an executive government department. This can lead to the absence or presence of particular challenges with respect to independence that is specific to them. As well, the perception of what a tribunal does and to whom it owes its allegiance may also affect its independence. This may be best reflected in the culture of the institution itself.

Even as early as *Valente*, which was the first Supreme Court decision to deal with the issue of judicial independence, the Court noted that the three criteria identified to guarantee independence were not fixed or exhaustive and that they may evolve over time. *Ocean Port Hotel* seems to have opened the door to allowing us to determine more genuine criteria of

39 *Ocean Port Hotel*, *supra* note 3 at para. 24.

40 See the chart and accompanying discussion in part II of this chapter.

independence for administrative tribunals. Empirical exploration of these issues would undoubtedly prove fruitful in this regard.

Ocean Port Hotel affirmed that a variety of tribunal appointments may satisfy the requirement of security of tenure so long as there are no constitutional standards at play and the terms of the appointment derive from constitutionally valid legislation. Since *Ocean Port Hotel*, some provincial jurisdictions have reinforced their legislative enactments to ensure that tribunal members have fixed terms of appointment. An example of this is found in British Columbia. The British Columbia *Administrative Tribunals Act*[41] was created in order to provide guiding principles and uniformity to various aspects of the administrative justice system in the province. Section 3 of the *Administrative Tribunals Act* suggests that tribunal members be appointed for an initial term of two to four years, with reappointment for additional terms of up to five years. An even more profound example is found in Quebec. In 2005, the enabling statute of the Administrative Tribunal of Quebec (ATQ) was modified so that members would hold tenure during good behaviour. Essentially an appointment for life, tenure on the ATQ is at the highest level of tenure possible and comparable to that of the judges of the courts of inherent jurisdiction.[42]

4. *Reasserting the Push for Independence: Unwritten Constitutional Principles, Tribunal Independence, and the Rule of Law*

The Supreme Court of Canada in *Ocean Port Hotel* was quite clear in indicating that there is no free-standing constitutional guarantee of independence for administrative tribunals.[43] As noted above, this is because administrative tribunals form part of the executive branch of government. Because constitutional guarantees of independence serve primarily to protect the judiciary from interference by the executive, they cannot work to protect tribunals from the branch of government of which they are a part. At the same time, however, Supreme Court and other Canadian jurisprudence has shown a willingness to expand the notion of "court" to allow litigants before some lesser judicial entities the benefits of constitutional guarantees of independence. The third and most current wave of tribunal independence jurisprudence is marked by litigants reasserting a push for tribunals to have the same independence as courts and that this independence be guaranteed by the unwritten constitutional principles that protect our courts of inherent jurisdiction.

In the 2006 British Columbia Supreme Court decision of *McKenzie v. Minister of Public Safety and Solicitor General et al.*,[44] the petitioner argued that the unwritten constitutional guarantees of independence should be expanded to apply to residential tenancy arbitrators. Her arguments asserted that such arbitrators were at the high end of the adjudicative spectrum. Decided shortly after *Ocean Port Hotel*, *Bell Canada v. Canadian Telephone Employees Association*[45] had suggested a spectrum of decision-making types in which highly

41 S.B.C. 2004, c. 45.

42 See *An act respecting administrative justice*, R.S.Q. c. J-3, s. 38, as amended by S.Q. 2005, c. 17, s. 2.

43 *Ocean Port Hotel*, *supra* note 3 at paras. 20-24.

44 *Supra* note 3. The British Columbia Court of Appeal did not address the issue, holding that the repeal of the provisions under which the decision was made rendered the question moot.

45 [2003] 1 S.C.R. 884 [*Bell Canada*].

adjudicative tribunals endowed with court-like powers and procedures could require more stringent requirements of procedural fairness, including a higher degree of independence.[46] Because several other courts that seemed to be on the outer edge of the judiciary had been deemed to attract these unwritten constitutional guarantees of independence, residential tenancy arbitrators, because of the nature of their work, should also attract such guarantees. The petitioner argued that if such guarantees were not given to bodies at the high end of the adjudicative spectrum, such as residential tenancy arbitrators, there would be a clear violation of the rule of law.[47] The petitioner was a residential tenancy arbitrator who had had her appointment rescinded mid-term. The respondents contended that a provision of a provincial statute, the *Public Sector Employers Act*,[48] allowed for this rescission. The court addressed two main issues in *McKenzie*—a narrow question of interpreting the *Public Sector Employers Act* and a much broader question of determining whether the position of residential tenancy arbitrator was protected from interference by constitutional guarantees of independence, including guarantees of the security of tenure.[49]

The British Columbia Supreme Court agreed with the petitioner's argument. McEwan J. first set out the principles laid down in *PEI Reference*. *PEI Reference* held that judicial independence not only stemmed from specific provisions of the Charter (namely, ss. 7 and 11(d)), but that it derived as well from unwritten constitutional principles dating back to the U.K. *Act of Settlement, 1701*. That these principles applied in Canada was evident from the preamble of the constitution, which referred to "a Constitution similar in principle to that of the United Kingdom."[50] Second, the British Columbia Supreme Court noted that the Supreme Court of Canada in *Ell v. Alberta*[51] had determined that these unwritten constitutional principles serve to protect the judicial independence of justices of the peace, a class of decision-makers for whom the issue of independence had been debatable for some time. He also noted that in Ontario, the Ontario Court of Appeal had found that deputy judges in the small claims court also attracted such constitutional guarantees.[52] In light of the extension of the principles of independence to classes of adjudicators other than superior and provincial court judges and the highly adjudicative functions of residential tenancy arbitrators in this case, and given that the jurisdiction of residential tenancy arbitrators had been taken directly from the courts of civil jurisdiction, the British Columbia Supreme Court found that judicial independence should apply to them as well. Justice McEwan reasoned that the rule of law required this result.

46 By contrast, the court held that tribunals falling at the other end of the spectrum, that dealt primarily with developing or supervising the implementation of particular government policies, may not need to offer as high a degree procedural protection and require less independence from the executive.

47 The concept of the rule of law is discussed by Mary Liston in chapter 4.

48 R.S.B.C. 1996, c. 384.

49 Indeed, one wonders if the court needed to address this broader constitutional question at all. From the way that it framed the issues, it might have been sufficient, once it had determined that the statute did not allow for the rescission, to end its judicial analysis at that point. See *McKenzie*, *supra* note 3 at para. 5.

50 See *PEI Reference*, *supra* note 37; see also the preamble to the *Constitution Act, 1867*.

51 [2003] 1 S.C.R. 857.

52 See *Ontario Deputy Judges' Association v. Ontario (Attorney General)* (2006), 210 O.A.C. 94.

McKenzie raises several interesting questions in the debate on tribunal independence, questions that help focus the issues and see the extent of their ramifications. For example, how are we to understand the notion of a constitutional guarantee for bodies that are part of the executive? Is the court's decision one of judicial functionalism as McEwan J. asserts, or does his reasoning imply an interference by the courts with the operation of the legislature? As part of its reasoning, the court maintains that the rule of law, through the affirmation of the principles of judicial independence in this case, will serve to keep the legislature from inappropriately vesting tribunals with lesser aspects of natural justice than they should have, simply because other pressures such as budgetary considerations make it convenient to do so. The court's reasoning raises a much wider question of judicial activism that is often seen in judicial review matters. This is the question of who, as between the legislature in creating the tribunal and the judiciary in reviewing its functioning, is in the best position to dictate the normative aspects of the administrative justice system.

Although the decision is still windng its way through the courts, one also wonders about other implications that could flow from *McKenzie*. For example, the success of the case lay partly in the fact that residential tenancy arbitrators are very similar to courts in most of the work that they do. While some argue for judicial independence for "purely adjudicative" administrative decision-making bodies,[53] what about administrative bodies endowed with both adjudicative and policy-making functions? Would it ever be possible for constitutional guarantees to attach solely to the adjudicative functions of a multifunctional tribunal? Moreover, how many purely adjudicative tribunals exist? Through their decision-making, all tribunals create policy. Does this policy-making alter the nature of a purely adjudicative tribunal?

IV. DISCUSSION

A. Competing Images: Views of Independence and Impartiality from the Inside and the Outside

This section presents some of the most pressing issues of independence and impartiality currently relating to tribunals. It is particularly noteworthy that although security of tenure, financial security, and administrative control may figure within the issues discussed, they do not form the main organizing issues of challenges to independence and impartiality that arise in the everyday work of tribunals.

1. The Appointment and Removal Process: Institutions, Ideologies, and Institutional Culture

Some of the most controversial and contested issues relating to the independence of administrative decision-making bodies are those dealing with appointments, removal, and the guarantee of security of tenure. Whether as a member of the legal community or a member of the tribunal community, one hears concerns expressed about partisan political appointments, about loss of livelihood as a result of short fixed-term appointments, and about the

53 See, for example, S. Ronald Ellis, "The *Justicizing* of Quasi-Judicial Tribunals (Part I)" (2006) 19 Can. J. Admin. L. & Prac. 303.

removal of members. With respect to the appointment process, to what extent is it acceptable for a tribunal to reflect a particular ideology? And whose ideology? Although we often hear controversy over appointees possibly reflecting the ideology of a political party, what about the ideology that comes from the culture of the institutional workplace of the tribunal members? Is it acceptable for a chair to seek members who will contribute to the values of the tribunal? When, if ever, is it feasible for a government to appoint members who reflect political values? This question can also be looked at from the opposite perspective, which brings it into sharper focus: in particular, is it ever possible to make appointments that completely evade political thought or ideology?

Tribunals are distinct from courts in that they are institutions in which their members and staff work together within a broad framework of regulatory governance aimed at managing a particular sector or industry through their expertise. Institutional culture can play an important part in achieving the often multifunctional goals of an administrative tribunal.[54] For example, having a workplace culture in which all members feel comfortable to air their diverse opinions on how the law should be furthered may be more constructive than having several members who each staunchly put diverse views in their decisions. In light of this, with respect to the removal process, is it legitimate to remove members who are disruptive to the workplace culture?

B. Bias, Adjudicative Independence, and Policy-Making (and Whose Policies Are They Anyway?)

Policy-making is generally accepted as being central to tribunal existence. There are several ways in which tribunals create policy in their day-to-day work. Focusing primarily on adjudicative bodies, Houle and Sossin identify three modes of policy-making by administrative tribunals: decision-making; informal rule-making through the use of soft law such as guidelines, bulletins, and manuals; and formal rule-making through delegated legislation.[55] Generally, the policies made by administrative bodies, whether they are primarily adjudicative or otherwise, serve to further the law under the statute that the tribunal has been mandated to administer, to promote consistency in the decisions rendered by the tribunal's various members, and to render the tribunal more efficient in its decision-making process. Although it can be argued that courts also further the policy of any legislation simply by rendering decisions under a statute, the methods used to create policy and the function of policy-making itself are distinctive characteristics of administrative bodies. In the context of the administrative state, policy-making relates to the expertise (in the subject matter or in managing the subject matter) possessed by the tribunals that administer and further the law under a particular statute.

---

54 See, generally, on the importance of understanding the ground values of government administration Lorne Sossin, "From Neutrality to Compassion: The Place of Civil Service Values and Legal Norms in the Exercise of Administrative Discretion" (2005) 55 U.T.L.J. 427. On the importance of institutional culture to the development of consistency, see K. Whitaker, M. Gottheil & M. Uhlmann, "Consistency in Tribunal Decision Making: What Really Goes on Behind Closed Doors ..." in Jacobs & Mactavish, *supra* note 2.

55 See France Houle & Lorne Sossin, "Tribunals and Policy Making" in Jacobs & Mactavish, *supra* note 2. Rulemaking is also discussed by Andrew Green in chapter 13.

Tensions arise, however, when the methods used by tribunals in their policy-making activities appear to infringe on the adjudicative independence of any individual tribunal decision-maker. Adjudicative independence is one guarantee of independence that is called into question quite frequently in the administrative context. Referenced briefly in the Supreme Court's decision in *Beauregard*,[56] the concept of adjudicative independence embodies the ability of a decision-maker to decide, free of inappropriate interference by other decision-makers. Such inappropriate interference may include, for example, pressure to decide a certain way or substitution of another's decision for one's own. Of all the guarantees of independence, adjudicative independence is a value that is particularly delicate in the administrative law context. There is often tension between the need for tribunal members to collaborate in order to further the law as an institution and the need to give each decision-maker space to render his or her rightful decisions. This tension has shown up most frequently with respect to the use of full board meetings to promote consistency in tribunal decision-making. Nevertheless, policy-making practices have come up against adjudicative independence more recently in other very key ways. Two such ways that we will discuss in this section deal with assisting the executive branch of government to develop its policy and the use of "lead cases" as a practice to promote adjudicative efficiency and consistency.

Adjudicative independence is two-pronged. The independence of the adjudicator is also a means of ensuring that the decision-maker is not biased. When a decision-maker decides for improper purposes, the common law has held that his or her decision-making raises a reasonable apprehension of bias. It is useful therefore to discuss the concepts relating to bias before considering examples in which administrative policy-making has been perceived to clash with adjudicative independence.

1. Reasonable Apprehension of Bias

There is a very close relationship among the concepts of independence, impartiality, and bias. However, the three concepts are distinct. The relationship among independence, impartiality, and bias was set out succinctly by the Supreme Court of Canada in *Valente*:

> Although there is obviously a close relationship between independence and impartiality, they are nevertheless separate and distinct values or requirements. Impartiality refers to a state of mind or attitude of the tribunal in relation to the issues and the parties in a particular case. The word "impartial" … connotes absence of bias, actual or perceived.[57]

As the Court indicated, impartiality deals with the attitude of the decision-maker and decision-making institution with respect to both the issues and the parties before them. The notion of impartiality is therefore not just about avoiding the preferential treatment of one particular party,[58] it expands more globally to having an open mind to the issue being litigated. Prejudgment of issues stemming from prior involvement in the matter or from having fixed views on a particular question before hearing all the evidence are examples of

56 See *supra* note 15, and accompanying text.

57 *Valente*, *supra* note 14 at para. 15.

58 Or about providing preferential treatment to oneself as the decision-maker, as the concerns about pecuniary and other material interests demonstrate.

what may constitute a closed mind to an issue. Either aspect of this dual concept—inappropriate attitude toward the parties or toward the issue—may raise a question about whether a reasonable apprehension of bias exists vis-à-vis the decision-making process.

The test for bias relies on perception. It is not a question of whether bias actually exists in any decision-making context that matters; if a reasonable person with an informed understanding of how the tribunal functions perceives that the decision-making is biased, this is enough to have the decision quashed. The classic test was formulated in *Committee for Justice and Liberty v. National Energy Board*,[59] a case in which the chair of a panel of the National Energy Board was responsible for receiving applications and issuing certificates for a pipeline. The chair, Mr. Crowe, had been involved in a study group that had put in an application for consideration. The majority of the Supreme Court of Canada held that there was a reasonable apprehension of bias with respect to Crowe's participation as chair.

The test for determining reasonable apprehension of bias was formulated in the dissenting opinion of Justice DeGrandpré. However, it has been used consistently by the Supreme Court and lower courts since that time. He articulated the test in the following way:

> [T]he apprehension of bias must be a reasonable one held by reasonable and right minded persons, applying themselves to the question and obtaining thereon the required information. In the words of the Court of Appeal, that test is "what would an informed person, viewing the matter realistically and practically—and having thought the matter through—conclude. Would he think that it is more likely than not that Mr. Crowe, whether consciously or unconsciously, would not decide fairly?"[60]

Moreover, the grounds for the apprehension of bias must be substantial. A real likelihood or probability of bias should be demonstrated. Mere suspicion of bias is insufficient for the test to be met. The courts often talk of demonstrating the likelihood of bias on a balance of probabilities. The reasonable well-informed person is also not one who is overly sensitive.[61] The application of the test has broadened to encompass not only individual decision-makers but also decision-making institutions. The test for reasonable apprehension of bias on an institutional level is essentially the same. The institutional aspect of bias was first recognized in *Lippé*, where the test was identified as determining whether there could be "a reasonable apprehension of bias in the mind of a fully informed person in a *substantial number of cases*."[62]

The standard for bias varies, depending on context. What will give rise to a reasonable apprehension of bias in one administrative decision-making context may not raise a perception of bias in another. For example, although both cases dealt with a decision-maker's prior involvement with a particular matter, the Supreme Court of Canada held that the chair of the National Energy Board's involvement caused a reasonable apprehension of bias in

59 [1978] 1 S.C.R. 369 [*Committee for Justice and Liberty*].

60 *Ibid.* at 394.

61 See generally, on the test for reasonable apprehension of bias and the standard that must be met, *Committee for Justice and Liberty*, *supra* note 59 at 394-95; *Bell Canada, supra* note 45 at para. 50; *R. v. S. (R.D.)*, [1997] 3 S.C.R. 484, at paras. 31 and 112.

62 See *R. v. Lippé*, [1991] 2 S.C.R. 114 at para. 59 (emphasis added). See also *Matsqui*, *supra* note 29, where the Court confirmed the test for the administrative context.

Committee for Justice and Liberty, discussed above, but did not find so when the Quebec Minister of the Environment ordered a company to prepare a site characterization study and decontamination measures in *Imperial Oil Ltd. v. Quebec (Minister of the Environment)*.[63] What explains the difference is the central idea animating procedural fairness in administrative law: the nature and context of the decision-making process drives the content of procedural fairness, including what will constitute impartiality. Owing primarily to the quasi-judicial nature of the National Energy Board's functions in determining applications, the Court in *Committee for Justice and Liberty* found that Mr. Crowe's involvement in the decisions leading up to one party's application to the board was enough to suggest that he may make a biased appraisal in his adjudicative capacity. By contrast, the nature of the work done by the Minister in *Imperial Oil* did not require him to act in a truly adjudicative capacity. His work was of a political nature and in the public interest. In this way, the Minister's prior involvement in decontaminating a site over which lawsuits had been brought against him did not cause him to be in a conflict of interest when he later exercised statutory authority to order a company to remedy the contamination.[64] Determining what procedural safeguards, including the degree of independence and impartiality, are needed in any particular administrative context is a matter of balancing several factors including the nature of the decision being made, the nature of the statutory scheme, and the agency's choice of procedures.[65]

2. Consistency and Decision-Making

In the administrative law context, the methods used to promote consistency in decision-making across the tribunal as an institution have given rise to allegations of reasonable apprehension of bias. At the heart of the debate over consistency is whether adjudicative independence of any individual member has been compromised. The tools used to promote consistency often involve the input of tribunal members other than those charged with determining a specific claim. As a consequence, allegations of reasonable apprehension of bias have been made by litigants concerned that the adjudicators deciding their claims may have based their decisions on considerations that they did not come across in the course of their adjudications.

The challenge of fostering coherence has become all the more important with the proliferation of larger boards across the country. Such boards have several members, sometimes in the hundreds, in various parts of the country, who may each have very distinct views on

63 [2003] 2 S.C.R. 624 [*Imperial Oil*].

64 Many different situations have been alleged to give rise to a reasonable apprehension of bias in Canadian administrative law jurisprudence.

65 The Supreme Court of Canada presented a non-exhaustive list of factors in *Baker v. Canada (Minister of Citizenship and Immigration)*, [1999] 2 S.C.R. 817. These factors include (1) the nature of the decision being made and the process followed in making it; (2) the nature of the statutory scheme and the terms of the statute pursuant to which the body operates; (3) the importance of the decision to the individual or individuals affected; (4) the legitimate expectations of the person challenging the decision; and (5) the choices of procedure made by the agency itself. For a broader discussion of these factors see Grant Huscroft, chapter 5, and *International Woodworkers of America, Local 2-69 v. Consolidated-Bathurst Packaging Ltd.*, [1990] 1 S.C.R. 282 [*Consolidated-Bathurst*].

how the law under the statute(s) should be developed. Similar decisions in similar cases show the general public how a tribunal has chosen to apply its statutes in various factual situations. The "policy" that consistent decisions develop is a form of non-binding guideline that tribunal users can refer to in deciding how to manage their affairs in the industry or sector being regulated by the tribunal. It can help them to determine whether, for example, to bring a matter before the tribunal or to settle. If tribunals were without means of promoting consistency, the general public using the tribunal services would be unable to regulate their affairs properly. In a trilogy of cases (*Consolidated-Bathurst*,[66] *Tremblay v. Quebec (Commission des affaires sociales)*,[67] and *Ellis-Don Ltd. v. Ontario (Labour Relations Board)*[68]), the Supreme Court of Canada set out the guidelines that tribunals should follow so that members can collaborate within their institution to promote consistency of outcome without compromising the adjudicative independence of any one decision-maker (or fairness to the parties).

In *Consolidated-Bathurst*, the Ontario Labour Relations Board held a meeting of the full labour board to discuss the draft reasons of one of its three-member panels. The purposes of such meetings were to facilitate understanding and appreciation of policy developments throughout the board and to evaluate the practical consequences of proposed policy initiatives on provincial labour relations and the economy. The decision discussed in this particular meeting dealt with whether a particular legal test that the board had established through its jurisprudence should be replaced by another. At issue was whether full board meetings constitute a breach of the natural justice principle, "he who hears must decide," by placing the decision-makers in a situation where they can be influenced by others who have not heard the evidence or arguments. It was also argued that such meetings are unacceptable because they do not provide the parties with adequate opportunity to answer issues that may be voiced by board members who have not heard the case. The appellant's arguments were therefore cast as a matter of improper encroachment on the adjudicative independence of the decision-makers and of lack of opportunity to know the full case to be met.

The Supreme Court acknowledged the need for full board meetings. In the majority's opinion, such meetings allowed the members of a large board[69] with a heavy case load[70] to benefit from the acquired expertise of the collective. As well, consultation was useful in achieving the Labour Board's mandate. The structure of the Labour Board was conducive to exchanges of opinions between management and union (as evidenced by its tripartite nature) in order to use its combined expertise to regulate labour relations in a prompt and final manner.[71] The majority also saw coherence as a goal to be fostered so that the outcome of disputes did not depend on the identity of the decision-maker. And lastly, in the majority's view, the fact that a privative clause protects the board's decisions made it even more incumbent on the board to take measures to avoid conflicting results.

---

66 *Ibid.*

67 [1992] 1 S.C.R. 952 [*Tremblay*].

68 [2001] 1 S.C.R. 221 [*Ellis-Don*].

69 There were 48 members in 1982-83.

70 At the time, there were approximately 266 cases per year.

71 *Consolidated-Bathurst*, *supra* note 65 at paras. 70-73.

At the same time, the Court recognized that fostering coherence should not compromise any panel member's capacity to decide in accordance with his or her conscience and opinions:

> It is obvious that no outside interference may be used to compel or pressure a decision maker to participate in discussions on policy issues raised by a case on which he must render a decision. It also goes without saying that a formalized consultation process could not be used to force or induce decision makers to adopt positions with which they do not agree. Nevertheless, discussions with colleagues do not constitute, in and of themselves, infringements on the panel members' capacity to decide the issues at stake independently. A discussion does not prevent a decision maker from adjudicating in accordance with his own conscience and opinions nor does it constitute an obstacle to this freedom. Whatever discussion may take place, the ultimate decision will be that of the decision maker for which he assumes full responsibility.[72]

The Court held that whether there is *pressure* on the decision-maker to decide against his or her own conscience and opinions is the relevant issue. The Court outlined conditions for holding such meetings so that natural justice would not be breached. The conditions are that the discussions be limited to law or policy and not factual issues and that the parties be given a reasonable opportunity to respond to any new ground arising from the meeting. In this regard, the Court approved of the checks and balances put in place by the Labour Board such as not keeping minutes of the meeting, not keeping attendance, and not holding a vote at the end of the discussion.

Tremblay was decided a few years after *Consolidated-Bathurst*. Here, the Court clarified that the imposition of consultation meetings by a member of the board who was not on the panel could amount to inappropriate constraint. The Court also held that even in situations where the consultation process is said to be voluntary, it is important to see if the operational practice of the tribunal shows evidence that the consultation in fact comprises systemic pressure.

In *Tremblay*, a decision was issued after a consultation process that was quite different than the one in *Consolidated-Bathurst*. While the consultations were optional in theory (in that they were to be called by the decision-making member of the commission), the practice at the Commission des affaires sociales (CAS) made consultation compulsory when a proposed decision was contrary to previous decisions.

Other factors that gave an appearance of constraint and apparent lack of decisional independence at the Commission des affaires sociales were that the president himself or herself could refer a matter before another member for plenary discussion. The Supreme Court noted that in such circumstances, a decision-maker may not feel free to refuse to submit a question to the consultation process. Because the statute expressly indicates that the individual decision-makers must decide matters, imposing group consultation on them amounts to an act of compulsion and goes against legislative intent. As well, the plenary meetings aimed at reaching a consensus. Many of the protective devices of which the Court had approved in *Consolidated-Bathurst* did not exist at the CAS. In particular, unlike the practice at the Ontario Labour Relations Board, at the CAS, attendance and votes by show of hands

72 *Ibid.* at para. 80.

were taken and minutes of the meetings were kept. These aspects created an appearance of "systemic pressure."

Finally, at issue in *Ellis-Don* was whether facts had been discussed at a full labour board meeting, contrary to the jurisprudential rules governing institutional decision-making set out in *Consolidated-Bathurst* and *Tremblay*. Although *Ellis-Don* focused only on the issue of providing the parties with a full opportunity to respond to matters discussed at a plenary meeting and did not deal with the questions of pressure and independence, it is useful because it sets out concisely the jurisprudential rules governing intra-agency consultation.

Since the time of the *Consolidated-Bathurst* trilogy, other tribunal practices for garnering consistency, developing policy, and addressing efficiency (another perennial concern in the face of the heavy workloads of tribunals) have come to the attention of the courts. One recent development is the use of "lead cases." In the decision of *Geza v. Canada (Minister of Citizenship and Immigration)*,[73] the Immigration and Refugee Board instituted a procedure through which it attempted to select one of several similar refugee claims that could be used to create a full evidential record for all. The Immigration and Refugee Board was attempting to deal with a large influx of refugee claims by the Hungarian Roma people. Although chosen before many Roma had had their claims heard, the claim chosen was to be representative of the issues that recurred when the Hungarian Roma people were seeking refugee status. The case used as the lead case was selected with the participation of the lawyer who had the largest inventory of pending Hungarian Roma claims. The Minister of Citizenship and Immigration was invited to participate in the hearings. This claim was then heard by an experienced panel of board members drawn from different regions of Canada and chosen for their familiarity with the relevant country conditions and experience with case management of the Roma cases. The purpose of the lead case initiative was to enable the board to have one case in which there were informed findings of fact and a relatively thorough analysis of the relevant legal issues.[74]

3. Adjudicative Independence and the Legislative Process

In *Communications, Energy and Paperworkers Union of Canada, Local 707 v. The Alberta Labour Relations Board*,[75] the Alberta Labour Relations Board was consulted for its knowledge of the field by the executive branch of government in order to help the government implement a new legislative policy. As a result, the board then faced both a legal battle in which it was said to lack independence and impartiality with respect to any matter it had to deal with touching on the policy, and a grave loss of confidence manifested by a loud public outcry by one of its major stakeholders affected by the policy. To many, this statement may ring contradictory in light of McLachlin C.J.'s now famous *dicta* in *Ocean Port Hotel* that

73 [2005] 3 F.C.R. 3 (Fed. Ct.), rev'd [2006] 4 F.C.R. 377 (C.A.) [*Geza*].

74 In a similar vein, see also *Thamotharem v. Canada (Minister of Citizenship and Immigration)*, [2006] 3 F.C.R. 168 (C.A.), and *Benitez v. Canada (Citizenship and Immigration)*, 2007 FCA 199, in which allegations of reasonable apprehension of bias were brought against the Immigration and Refugee Board for its creation of procedural guidelines that suggested the manner in which adjudicators should conduct their hearings.

75 [2004] A.J. No. 83 (Q.B.) [*Alberta Labour Relations Board*].

all tribunals exist precisely to further the policy of the executive branch of government.[76] The *Alberta Labour Relations Board* case raises a fresh and interesting question of independence in administrative law—namely, how should feedback on the industry be transferred to the executive department that has responsibility for the tribunal? The question turns on how a tribunal can communicate such information while preserving its appearance of distance and independence from the executive branch of government. Central to this question of feedback is the protection of adjudicative independence, particularly on an institutional level.

C. Multifunctionality

Unlike courts, tribunals have been created to manage and oversee areas that are often polycentric in nature. This means that the expertise required of the tribunal members and staff is not only the juristic legal expertise needed to interpret the statute, but may also include expertise in the particular technical subject area.[77] The appointments process often reflects this diversity through requirements that the tribunal be composed of experts drawn not only from lawyers, but also from other fields and sometimes even from the general public. For example, although classified as staff rather than members, the *Canadian International Trade Tribunal Act* has a provision for the appointment of technical experts.[78] These experts are mandated to assist the tribunal in an advisory manner.[79] The *Natural Resources Conservation Board Act* of Alberta has a similar appointment provision.[80] However, it is not just the appointment of experts to a tribunal that serves to reflect a tribunal's polycentric nature. The structure of many enabling statutes themselves reflects the polycentric nature of the tribunal through the plurality of functions that the tribunal may be asked to perform.

For example, the Canadian International Trade Tribunal (CITT) is endowed with both broad powers of policy development and adjudicative powers. The CITT conducts inquiries and provides advice on economic, trade, and tariff matters as referred to it by the Minister of Finance or the governor in council. It also hears appeals of decisions made under various statutes by the Canada Revenue Agency.[81] This type of plurality of function has been called into question by litigants on judicial review in cases where staff research was not revealed to all the parties, raising issues of procedural fairness.[82] Many tribunals make available to the public their staff reports, research, and even training manuals and adjudicator decision-

76 *Ocean Port Hotel*, *supra* note 3 at para. 24.

77 France Houle provides a thoughtful definition of what it means to be an "expert" in the administrative law sense in France Houle, "Le fonctionnement du régime de preuve libre dans un système non-expert : Le traitement symptomatique des preuves par la Section de la protection des réfugiés" (2004) 38 R.J.J. 263. See also generally L. Jacobs & T. Kuttner, "The Expert Tribunal" in Jacobs & Mactavish, *supra* note 2.

78 *Canadian International Trade Tribunal Act*, R.S.C. 1985, c. 47 (4th Supp.), s. 14(2).

79 *Ibid.*

80 See *Natural Resources Conservation Board Act*, R.S.A. 2000, c. N-3, s. 23.

81 *Canadian International Trade Tribunal Act*, *supra* note 78, ss. 16, 18, 19. See also the mandate of the Canadian International Trade Tribunal as laid out on its website, online: <http://www.citt-tcce.gc.ca/mandate/index_e.asp>.

82 See, in particular, *Toshiba Corp. v. Canada (Anti-Dumping Tribunal)* (1984) 8 Admin. L.R. 173 (F.C.A.).

making guides, most often by posting them on their websites.[83] Some tribunals try to maintain a *de facto* separation of powers within their work, seemingly to avoid allegations that one aspect of the tribunal's work has had an inappropriate interference with another aspect of its work, causing a reasonable apprehension of bias.[84] One wonders, though, if this may be an overly cautious internalization by tribunals of the judicial dictates on multifunctionality, especially if it hinders the expertise developed in one area of the tribunal's work from enriching the rest of the tribunal's work.

The most common complaint in relation to a tribunal's multiplicity of functions stems from a perception by the user that a tribunal has the potential to act as both prosecutor and judge in the same matter. Generally, it has been held that overlapping functions are not a problem so long as sanctioned by statute enacted in conformity with the constitution and so long as the multifunctionality does not give rise to a reasonable apprehension of bias under a quasi-constitutional statute.[85]

In some cases, tribunals may take their own proactive measures to reduce the appearance or reality that relations are too close between those acting in a prosecutorial fashion and those performing adjudicative functions. Should such proactive measures be taken into account in determining whether a reasonable person could find a lack of impartiality vis-à-vis the tribunal? *Lippé* had indicated that the test for impartiality in a substantial number of cases is whether the system is structured in a way that creates a reasonable apprehension of bias on an institutional level. Several factors could be considered in deciding whether such bias existed. Determining which factors to use was held to be a matter of looking at the tribunal in question, the way that it operates in practice, and any safeguards that may exist to prevent incidents of bias in practice. In the 2006 Federal Court of Canada decision of *Sam Lévy & Associés Inc. v. Mayrand*,[86] the Federal Court held that although the superintendent of bankruptcy was statutorily endowed with powers of investigation and adjudication, the fact that he used his delegation powers to hive off adjudicative responsibilities was sufficient to avoid a reasonable apprehension of institutional bias and to avoid violating the right to a fair hearing under the federal *Bill of Rights*. The Alberta Queen's Bench decision of *Currie v. Edmonton Remand Centre*[87] illustrates how operational practice may have a more negative effect on the outcome. In *Currie*, the court found institutional bias from the overlapping functions of the prison guards and the disciplinary board members. *Currie* dealt with the question of whether disciplinary hearings used in a provincial prison exhibited signs of institutional bias in a substantial number of cases. The disciplinary hearings were used to determine whether prisoners had committed breaches of acceptable standards

83 See, for example, the various publications of the Alberta Labour Relations Board, including its *Procedure Guide*, online: <http://www.alrb.gov.ab.ca>, and the publications of the Immigration and Refugee Board, which include policies, procedures, and research reports on various countries, online: <http://www.irb-cisr.gc.ca/en/index_e.htm>.

84 Such allegations have been made in the literature. See, for example, Colin J. Bennett, "The Privacy Commissioner of Canada: Multiple Roles, Diverse Expectations and Structural Dilemmas" (2003) 46 Can. Pub. Admin. 218.

85 See *Régie*, *supra* note 31.

86 [2006] 2 F.C.R. 543 (Fed. Ct.) (decided May 16, 2005, per Martineau J.) [*Sam Lévy*].

87 (2006), 276 D.L.R. (4th) 143 (Alta. Q.B.) [*Currie*].

of conduct within the prison and to determine appropriate punishment for contraventions of the rules and regulations of the correctional institution. However, the problem was that those who were responsible for maintaining order in the institution were also placed on the disciplinary panels. This caused an appearance of conflict—in particular, an appearance that the institution's primary decision would be maintained at the expense of the prisoner's having a fair opportunity to contest it.

The applicants argued that the provisions of the Alberta *Corrections Act*[88] and the Alberta *Correctional Institution Regulation*[89] which allowed for this decision-making structure to exist, were contrary to ss. 7 and 11(d) of the Charter. The Alberta Queen's Bench found that although section 11(d) did not apply in this case, there was indeed a breach of s. 7 of the Charter. In addition to finding that none of the traditional guarantees of independence existed in this case, the court's holding was also based in part on the fact that the culture of the institution and of these types of hearings within them, made it impossible for a prisoner to assert his or her side of the story.

In summary, multifunctionality is a very current concern of many administrative bodies. Often, tribunals use their own de facto methods of reducing the appearance of bias that can be raised by the enabling statute. The degree to which these practices will or should be taken into account is a matter of debate, and the effect that these practices have on the outcome can be quite significant.

V. CONCLUSION

As indicated in the introduction to this chapter, the debate over independence leads one to question whether a fundamental reconceiving of the nature and purpose of administrative tribunals is a necessary precondition to guaranteeing impartiality, or whether the concepts of independence and impartiality need a fresh look within the administrative context, or both. This chapter has provided a historical overview of the law of tribunal independence in Canada, linking it to its jurisprudential roots in judicial independence and to its stated goals of preserving impartiality and avoiding bias. This chapter has tried to illustrate that although security of tenure, financial security, and administrative control—the central tenets of judicial independence—may figure in the problems of independence, impartiality, and bias that affect administrative tribunals, they are by no means the main issues of independence, impartiality, and bias currently affecting tribunals in their everyday operational context. By calling attention to the issues of adjudicative independence that are intimately tied to the complex concept of "policy-making" in the administrative state and to the issue of multifunctionality, this chapter serves both as a call for a greater empirical understanding of the true challenges to the work of administrative tribunals and as a more genuine reflection of these challenges in legislative policy, measures of reform, and judicial review.

---

88 R.S.A. 2000, c. C-29, s. 15.

89 Alta. Reg. 205/2001, ss. 43, 44(3), 44(5), 45.

SUGGESTED ADDITIONAL READINGS

CASES

2747-3174 Québec Inc. v. Quebec (Régie des permis d'alcool), [1996] 3 S.C.R. 919.

Beauregard v. Canada, [1986] 2 S.C.R. 56.

Bell Canada v. Canadian Telephone Employees Association, [2003] 1 S.C.R. 884.

Canadian Pacific Ltd. v. Matsqui Indian Band, [1995] 1 S.C.R. 3.

Committee for Justice and Liberty v. National Energy Board, [1978] 1 S.C.R. 369.

Communications, Energy and Paperworkers Union of Canada, Local 707 v. The Alberta Labour Relations Board (2004), 351 A.R. 267 (Q.B.).

Ell v. Alberta, [2003] 1 S.C.R. 857.

Ellis-Don Ltd. v. Ontario (Labour Relations Board), [2001] 1 S.C.R. 221.

Geza v. Canada (Minister of Citizenship and Immigration), [2005] 3 F.C.R. 3 (Fed. Ct.), [2006] 4 F.C.R. 377 (C.A.).

International Woodworkers of America, Local 2-69 v. Consolidated-Bathurst Packaging Ltd., [1990] 1 S.C.R. 282.

Lippé, R. v., [1991] 2 S.C.R. 114.

McKenzie v. Minister of Public Safety and Solicitor General et al. (2006), 61 B.C.L.R. (4th) 57 (Sup. Ct.), (2007), 71 B.C.L.R. (4th) 1 (C.A.), [2007] S.C.C.A. No. 601 (leave to appeal to the SCC filed December 18, 2007).

Ocean Port Hotel Ltd. v. British Columbia (General Manager, Liquor Control and Licensing Branch), [2001] 2 S.C.R. 781.

Reference Re Remuneration of Judges of the Provincial Court (PEI), [1997] 3 S.C.R. 3.

Sam Lévy & Associés Inc. v. Mayrand, [2006] 2 F.C.R. 543 (Fed. Ct.).

Thamotharem v. Canada (Minister of Citizenship and Immigration), [2006] 3 F.C.R. 168 (C.A.)

Tremblay v. Quebec (Commission des affaires sociales), [1992] 1 S.C.R. 952.

Valente, R. v., [1985] 2 S.C.R. 673.

LEGISLATION

Alberta Bill of Rights, R.S.A. 2000, c. A-14, s. 1(a).

Canadian Bill of Rights, S.C. 1960, c. 44, ss. 2(e), (f), reprinted in R.S.C. 1985, App. III.

Canadian Charter of Rights and Freedoms, Part I of the *Constitution Act, 1982*, being Schedule B to the *Canada Act 1982* (U.K.), 1982, c. 11, ss. 7, 11(d).

Charter of Human Rights and Freedoms, R.S.Q. c. C-12, s. 23.

LITERATURE

Bryden, Philip. "Structural Independence of Administrative Tribunals in the Wake of *Ocean Port*" (2003) 16 Can. J. Admin. L. & Prac. 125.

Comtois, Suzanne. "Le contrôle de la cohérence décisionnelle au sein des tribunaux administratifs" (1990) 21 R.D.U.S. 77.

Jacobs, Laverne. "Tribunal Independence and Impartiality: Rethinking the Theory after *Bell* and *Ocean Port Hotel*—A Call for Empirical Analysis" in Laverne A. Jacobs & Anne L. Mactavish, eds., *Dialogue Between Courts and Tribunals: Essays in Administrative Law and Justice (2001-2007)* (Montreal: Éditions Thémis, 2008) (forthcoming), online: <http://www.ciaj-icaj.ca/english/administrativetribunals/IndependenceFeb2004.pdf>.

Macdonald, Roderick A. "The Accoustics of Accountability—Towards Well-Tempered Tribunals" in *Judicial Integrity*, ed. by András Sajó (Leiden: M. Nijhoff Publishers, 2004) 141.

Mullan, David J. "Bias and Lack of Independence" in *Administrative Law* (Toronto: Irwin Law, 2001) chapter 14.

———. "Common and Divergent Elements of Practices of the Various Tribunals: An Overview of Present and Possible Developments" in *Administrative Law: Principles, Practice and Pluralism*, Special Lectures of the Law Society of Upper Canada 1992 (Toronto: Carswell, 1993), 461.

Whitaker, K., M. Gottheil & M. Uhlmann, "Consistency in Tribunal Decision Making: What Really Goes on Behind Closed Doors …" in Laverne A. Jacobs & Anne L. Mactavish, eds., *Dialogue Between Courts and Tribunals: Essays in Administrative Law and Justice (2001-2007)* (Montreal: Éditions Thémis, 2008) (forthcoming).

Wyman, K.M. "The Independence of Administrative Tribunals in an Era of Ever Expansive Judicial Independence" (2001) 14 Can. J. Admin. L. & Prac. 61.

CHAPTER SEVEN

The Charter and Administrative Law: Cross-Fertilization in Public Law

EVAN FOX-DECENT
*Faculty of Law, McGill University**

I. INTRODUCTION

The relationship between administrative law and the Charter is complex and still unfolding. If a decision touches a Charter right, front-line decision-makers and reviewing courts alike determine the requirements of legality using the Charter, administrative law principles, or some combination of the two. There is an emerging consensus that the Charter does not replace the common law, but rather embodies and supplements fundamental legal principles contained within it.

This chapter sets out various ways in which judicial review at common law has influenced understandings of the Charter, as well as the manner in which the Charter has influenced

* I am indebted to Colleen Flood, Robert Leckey, and Mary Liston for valuable comments and suggestions.

review of administrative decisions when a Charter right is clearly at stake. As we shall see, the influence runs in both directions, and has significant implications for judicial review of both the procedure and substance of administrative action. In the realm of procedure, the courts rely on the common-law doctrine of procedural fairness to interpret the principles of fundamental justice set out in s. 7 of the Charter.[1] However, when courts review the substance rather than the procedural aspects of a decision that engages a Charter right, they tend to review the decision using the analytical framework developed in *R. v. Oakes*[2] for testing the validity of legislation. Taken together, these general features of the relationship between Charter jurisprudence and administrative law suggest that each is porous and open-textured to the other. Put another way, the relationship between the Charter and administrative law exhibits a cross-fertilization of principles and approaches that inform judicial review of administrative action.

This chapter has three main sections: parts II, III, and IV. Part II explores the relationship between the common-law duty of procedural fairness and the principles of fundamental justice found in s. 7 of the Charter. In part III we examine the different approaches that courts have used to review decisions when a Charter right is at issue. Part III refers to ideas and concepts developed at common law, so it is best to read Audrey Macklin, chapter 8, and Sheila Wildeman, chapter 9, on common-law substantive review prior to reading part III.

A further and separate issue raised by the advent of the Charter is whether administrative tribunals and agencies have jurisdiction to apply the Charter to their enabling statutes. The issue is controversial because administrative bodies, as creatures of statute belonging to the executive, are not normally viewed as having authority to refuse to apply the very legislation the legislature has entrusted them to implement. Nonetheless, the Supreme Court has affirmed that the Charter is "not some holy grail which only judicial initiates of the superior courts may touch,"[3] and has found that agencies may have jurisdiction to apply the Charter if they have authority to decide questions of law. Part IV discusses the legal basis and practical effects of agency jurisdiction over the Charter.

II. PROCEDURAL FAIRNESS AND THE PRINCIPLES OF FUNDAMENTAL JUSTICE

As discussed by Grant Huscroft in chapter 5, the duty of procedural fairness in administrative law requires decision-makers to provide a fair hearing to individuals subject to their authority. At a minimum, this usually means that front-line decision-makers must hear the other side and decide the matter before them impartially, independently, and without undue delay. The duty does not necessarily entail that the individual must receive an oral hearing (sometimes written submissions are enough), but the individual must receive notice of the

1 *Canadian Charter of Rights and Freedoms*, Part I of the *Constitution Act, 1982*, being Schedule B to the *Canada Act 1982* (U.K.), 1982, c. 11 [the Charter].

2 [1986] 1 S.C.R. 103 [*Oakes*].

3 *Nova Scotia (Workers' Compensation Board) v. Martin; Nova Scotia (Workers' Compensation Board) v. Laseur*, [2003] 2 S.C.R. 504 at para. 29 [*Martin*], per Gonthier J., citing with approval McLachlin J.'s (as she then was) dissenting dictum in *Cooper v. Canada (Human Rights Commission)*, [1996] 3 S.C.R. 854 at para. 70 [*Cooper*].

proceedings and have a full and fair opportunity to respond to the facts and contentions on which the decision-maker may ultimately rely. Implicit in the duty to hear the other side is a duty to disclose such facts and contentions, barring considerations such as privacy and national security, which may justify nondisclosure. In some cases the individual may have a right to legal counsel. These safeguards are frequently referred to as participatory rights, and they apply prior to the decision. If the decision affects an important interest, such as employment or continued residency in Canada, the decision-maker owes the individual reasons for the decision. The duty to give reasons applies after the decision has been made.

What does the Charter require in terms of procedural fairness or a fair hearing? Section 7 of the Charter stipulates that "[e]veryone has the right to life, liberty and security of the person and the right not to be deprived thereof *except in accordance with the principles of fundamental justice*" (emphasis added). Section 7 is the only rights-conferring provision in the Charter that refers to the principles of fundamental justice and, within the Charter's substantive rights-conferring provisions, only these principles have been found to include procedural fairness.[4] The presence of the principles of fundamental justice within s. 7 has led to that section's emergence as the primary source of procedural safeguards within the Charter.[5]

To access procedural safeguards in the context of s. 7, complainants must first cross the "threshold" of establishing that their "life, liberty or security" interests are impaired by the relevant decision. If the affected individual cannot establish that the impugned decision touches a s. 7 interest, procedural fairness may still be due, but as a matter of common law rather than as a consequence of s. 7 and the principles of fundamental justice.

A further important threshold issue in this context concerns the relationship of procedural fairness to legislation. Legislation can (and often does) determine the content of available procedures. At common law, judges would be very reluctant to impose onerous procedures in the face of clear statutory language that dictated less stringent (or even no) procedural safeguards.[6] Under s. 7, however, the procedural requirements of the principles of funda-

4 Arguably s. 1 implicitly contains procedural fairness (or something much like it) within the idea that infringements of rights must be limited to those that can be "demonstrably justified in a free and democratic society." Similarly, the preamble refers to the rule of law, and there too procedural fairness might be inferred. See Mary Liston, chapter 4, "The Rule of Law in Theory," for discussion of the sense in which procedural fairness informs the rule of law and the idea of a common-law constitution.

5 Sections 8 though 14 are sometimes regarded as elaborations of the principles of fundamental justice in the detention context. Naturally, the courts look to the common law to guide their interpretation of these procedural rights. But these rights are parasitical on invasive state action, and so in this sense they are not substantively "right-conferring" in the sense in which s. 7 guarantees to everyone the right to life, liberty, and security of the person independently of anything the state does.

6 Unwritten constitutional principles may complicate the usual story of the supremacy of clear legislation over the common law. Judges have imposed a duty to give reasons where an unwritten constitutional principle was at stake (protection of minorities) and the relevant legislation was silent on the issue: *Lalonde v. Ontario (Commission de restructuration des services de santé)* (2001), 56 O.R. (3d) 505 (C.A.). It remains to be seen whether they would do the same in similar circumstances if confronted with express legislation that barred the imposition of such a duty. In two cases in which the rule of law was alleged to operate as an unwritten constitutional principle, the Supreme Court declined to invalidate the impugned legislation: *British Columbia v. Imperial Tobacco Canada Ltd.*, 2005 SCC 49, [2005] 2 S.C.R. 473; *British Columbia (Attorney General) v. Christie*, 2007 SCC 21 [*Christie*]. However, judges might refuse to give effect to legislation that

mental justice are also constitutional requirements. In other words, if a s. 7 interest is engaged, procedural fairness comes into play by means of the principles of fundamental justice, and legislation must conform to them in order to be lawful.

The remainder of this part now examines the content of the principles of fundamental justice in various statutory contexts. As we shall see, the common law of procedural fairness informs both the specific content of the principles (for example, oral hearings, disclosure, the duty to give reasons, timely decision-making) and the reasons for interpreting them to have particular contents in some decision-making contexts but not in others.[7]

A. Oral Hearings and the Scope of Section 7

In 1985, *Singh v. Canada (Minister of Employment and Immigration)*[8] established that the principles of fundamental justice include procedural fairness. *Singh* involved seven refugee claimants who had no opportunity to present their cases in oral hearings before either the decision-maker at first instance (formally the Minister, acting on the recommendation of the precursor to today's Immigration and Refugee Board, the Refugee Status Advisory Committee) or the Immigration Appeal Board (IAB) on appeal. The statutory scheme at the time provided for the possibility of an oral hearing, but only before the IAB on appeal, and *only if* the IAB concluded on the basis of the asylum seeker's written submissions that there were reasonable grounds to believe that the claimant could make a successful claim at an oral hearing. Thus, the statutory scheme precluded the IAB from granting an oral hearing to claimants who failed to set out "reasonable grounds." And because the statutory scheme excluded the possibility of an oral hearing in these cases, the common law of procedural fairness could not "supply the omission of the legislature"; there was no omission but rather a clear exclusion.

Six judges took part in the judgment with three finding an infringement of s. 7 of the Charter and three finding an infringement of s. 2(e) of the *Canadian Bill of Rights*.[9] Wilson J. wrote the Charter portion of the judgment, finding that "everyone" in s. 7 includes "every human being who is physically present in Canada," and that the security interest "must encompass freedom from the threat of physical punishment as well as freedom from such punishment itself."[10] As a consequence, Wilson J. held that s. 7 applied to Singh (the threshold was crossed), and while he did not have a constitutional right to remain in Canada per se, he did have a constitutional right to have his claim determined in accordance with the

---

infringes unwritten principles if they interpret it through the same lens as they interpret privative clauses (clauses that seek to oust judicial review): judges refuse to give clear and express privative clauses full effect on unwritten constitutional grounds related to the separation of powers and judicial supremacy over determinations of agency jurisdiction. For discussion of the rule of law cases, see Mary Liston, chapter 4, and for privative clauses, see Audrey Macklin, chapter 8, and Sheila Wildeman, chapter 9.

7 For an earlier, but still exemplary, discussion of the relationship between the common law and the principles of fundamental justice, see J.M. Evans, "The Principles of Fundamental Justice: The Constitution and the Common Law" (1991) 29 Osgoode Hall L.J. 51.

8 [1985] 1 S.C.R. 177 [*Singh*].

9 S.C. 1960, c. 44, reprinted in R.S.C. 1985, App. III.

10 *Singh*, *supra* note 8 at para. 47.

principles of fundamental justice. She concluded that the interests protected under s. 7 are of such importance that generally an oral hearing will be required when those interests are engaged. And, where credibility is at stake, as it almost always is in refugee cases, she found it "difficult to conceive of a situation"[11] in which the claimant would not be entitled to prior discovery of the Minister's case and an oral hearing. She affirmed the conventional wisdom that resort to the Charter should be reserved for cases in which ordinary statutory interpretation cannot provide a remedy. However, she held that this was one such case because the principles of fundamental justice in the refugee claimant context require an oral hearing, and the statute itself expressly barred some refugee claimants from receiving such a hearing. *Singh* remains a vivid example of how review under the Charter can overcome clear legislation, usually an insurmountable obstacle to relief at common law.

Singh is also a foundational case in Canadian immigration law for both its recognition that s. 7 applies to non-citizens and for its impact on Canada's statutory and institutional framework regarding refugee claimants. At no small cost, the government overhauled the statutory scheme and established the Immigration and Refugee Board to ensure that all refugee claimants receive a fair hearing in accordance with the principles of fundamental justice.

Notice, however, that although the constitutional status of the Charter is required to overcome the language of the statutory scheme then in place, Wilson J. relies on the common-law idea from civil and criminal procedure that credibility is best assessed through an evaluation of oral testimony. In other words, the Charter can take a complainant across the normally insuperable threshold of a clear statutory bar to certain procedures, but once the threshold is crossed it is still the common law that determines the content that the procedure must have to pass constitutional muster.

B. Incorporation of the Common-Law Framework Under Section 7

Earlier chapters by Colleen Flood and Grant Huscroft have already described the landmark case of *Baker v. Canada (Minister of Citizenship and Immigration)*[12] in which the Supreme Court drew together a wide body of jurisprudence to establish a framework for determining the content of procedural fairness in a particular case. Recall that the framework the Court established in *Baker* for determining the content of procedural fairness ("the *Baker* framework") is composed of five non-exhaustive contextual factors, none of which is necessarily determinative. The first concerns the nature of the decision: the more the decision can be said to be judicial or quasi-judicial in nature, rather than administrative, the weightier the procedural safeguards must be. The second factor is the role and place of the decision within the statutory scheme. For example, if the decision constitutes an exception to the general principles of the scheme, fewer protections are due. On the other hand, if procedural safeguards are present elsewhere in the Act, and if the decision is final, these considerations would militate in favour of more stringent procedures. The third factor is the importance, in practical terms, of the decision to the individual affected. The fourth is legitimate expectations. Legitimate expectations can arise as a result of past practices or representations of public officials which, if present, may provide a basis for procedural safeguards that would

11 *Ibid.* at para. 59.

12 [1999] 2 S.C.R. 817 [*Baker*].

not otherwise be available. The fifth factor calls for a measure of deference to the Minister's or agency's choice of procedure.

The Court in *Baker* applied this framework to determine only the content of Ms. Baker's participatory rights; she had a right to make written submissions and to have those submissions fully considered, but she was not entitled to an oral hearing. As well, her children were denied independent standing on the grounds that their interest in the proceedings could be communicated to the Minister and defended by Baker's legal counsel. The Court considered the issues of bias and the duty to give reasons independently of the *Baker* framework. However, as we shall now see in *Suresh v. Canada (Minister of Citizenship and Immigration)*,[13] arguably the *Baker* framework has been extended under s. 7 to establish the specific requirements of the duty to give reasons, a duty considered here as a principle of fundamental justice.

Suresh involved a Convention refugee detained on a security certificate for alleged links with the Liberation Tigers of Tamil Eelam (LTTE). The Federal Court upheld the certificate and, in the subsequent deportation hearing, the adjudicator found Suresh to be inadmissible as a refugee on grounds of membership in a terrorist organization. Pursuant to s. 53(1)(b) of the *Immigration Act* in force at the time,[14] the Minister proceeded to issue an opinion that Suresh constituted a danger to the security of Canada and should be deported, notwithstanding an acknowledgement that Suresh would face a risk of torture upon his return to Sri Lanka. Suresh challenged the Minister's decision on constitutional and administrative law grounds. The Court held that "barring extraordinary circumstances, deportation to torture will generally violate the principles of fundamental justice protected by s. 7 of the *Charter*,"[15] but ultimately the case was decided in Suresh's favour on the basis that the Minister had breached the s. 7 principles of fundamental justice by failing to provide Suresh with adequate procedural safeguards and reasons for the decision.

Unlike the statutory provisions under scrutiny in *Singh*, s. 53(1)(b) of the *Immigration Act* did not require the Minister to adopt or follow any particular procedure. The Minister notified Suresh that she intended to consider issuing a "danger opinion" against him and gave him the opportunity to make submissions to her. Those submissions were considered by an immigration officer who weighed the importance of Canada's commitment to fight terrorism against the risk of torture to Suresh. The officer recommended in a memorandum to the Minister that she issue an opinion under s. 53(1)(b) that Suresh constitutes a danger to Canada. Suresh did not have an opportunity to see or respond to the officer's memorandum, which the Court described as "more like a prosecutor's brief than a statement of reasons for a decision."[16]

---

13 [2002] 1 S.C.R. 3 [*Suresh*].

14 R.S.C. 1985, C. I-2 (superseded by the *Immigration and Refugee Protection Act*, *infra* note 34).

15 *Supra* note 13 at para. 76. This is a notable instance in which the principles of fundamental justice are deemed to contain substantive as well as procedural guarantees. It is also an instance in which international law guides the Court's interpretation of the Charter. The international/domestic law nexus is explored by Gerald Heckman in chapter 12. Examination of the substantive guarantees implicit in the principles of fundamental justice is more a matter of constitutional than administrative law and, generally, beyond the scope of this book.

16 *Ibid.* at para. 126.

Without the guidance of statute, the Court turned to the *Baker* framework to assess the adequacy of the procedure afforded Suresh: "Insofar as procedural rights are concerned, the common law doctrine summarized in *Baker*, *supra*, properly recognizes the ingredients of fundamental justice."[17]

C. The Duty to Disclose and the Right to Reply

Weighing together the five factors referred to above, the Court concluded that Suresh did not have a right to an oral hearing, but he did have the right to disclosure of the materials on which the Minister would base her decision, including the memorandum from the immigration officer who initially reviewed Suresh's case under s. 53(1)(b). Suresh also had the right to reply to the claims set out in the memorandum, including claims relevant to the threat he posed to Canada and the risk of torture he would face if deported. The Minister then had an obligation to consider Suresh's submissions as well as those of her staff.

Now, let us explore further the interaction between the Charter, statutes, and the common law by considering what would have happened if the immigration officer who prepared the memorandum was a lawyer whose legal advice the Minister explicitly sought and whether his report to the Minister could be fairly characterized as a legal opinion. The Court said that Suresh was entitled to disclosure "[subject] to privilege or other valid reasons for reduced disclosure, such as safeguarding confidential public security documents."[18] In *Pritchard v. Ontario (Human Rights Commission)*[19] (a case of judicial review at common law rather than review under the Charter), the Court held that the common-law doctrine of solicitor–client privilege barred a complainant before the Ontario Human Rights Commission from obtaining disclosure of a legal opinion drafted by the commission's in-house counsel.[20]

In principle, an ordinary statute can oust privilege because privilege is a doctrine of the common law (the Court in *Pritchard* said that any such legislation would be interpreted restrictively). It seems to follow that a duty to disclose found to inhere in the principles of fundamental justice could also reduce the effect of privilege. However, the Court in *Pritchard* found that meeting the requirements of procedural fairness does not require the disclosure of a privileged legal opinion. Thus, if the reason disclosure is required in *Suresh* is that procedural fairness is a feature of the principles of fundamental justice, and procedural fairness does not require disclosure of a legal opinion, then the immigration officer's memorandum may not be discoverable if the Minister can convince a court that the memorandum is in substance a legal opinion. To pierce privilege, a complainant would have to distinguish procedural fairness at common law (the context in *Pritchard*) from procedural fairness under s. 7.

17 *Ibid.* at para. 113.

18 *Ibid.* at para. 122.

19 [2004] 1 S.C.R. 809 [*Pritchard*].

20 The issue of whether the Minister could use solicitor–client privilege to block disclosure of the immigration officer's memorandum did not arise in *Suresh* because the Minister simply did not disclose the report prior to making her decision. Although the report was drafted prior to the decision, it was provided to Suresh only after the decision was made, apparently as reasons for the decision.

D. The Duty to Give Reasons

Another area of procedural fairness influenced by *Suresh* is the duty to give reasons. *Baker* established that decision-makers have a duty to give reasons whenever important interests are at stake. However, in *Baker* the notes of a junior officer were deemed to satisfy the reasons requirement even though this officer did not make the final decision, and even though the notes were so riddled with stereotypes and prejudice that the Court found them to give rise to a reasonable apprehension of bias. After *Baker*, some courts interpreted the duty to require no more than a symbolic or even box-ticking exercise,[21] while others interpreted the obligation to require a substantive justification of the impugned decision.[22] In *Suresh*, the Court held that the Minister herself (not a delegated officer) must provide "responsive" reasons that demonstrate both that the individual is a danger to Canada and that there are no substantial grounds to believe he would be subject to torture. And unlike in *Baker*, the Court did not separate its discussion of participatory rights from its treatment of the duty to give reasons; both were informed by contextual analysis conducted under the *Baker* framework. Specifically, the Court made much of the importance of the security interest arising from torture to justify its expansive reading of the duty to give reasons. The Court's attentiveness to the sheer brutality of torture suggests that the justificatory burden to discharge under the duty to give reasons is likely to become heavier in rough proportion to the significance of the interest, even in non-Charter contexts.

However, because the duty to give reasons is part of the duty of procedural fairness, courts will usually review it on a standard of correctness.[23] A decision will be quashed on this standard if it does not prescribe the same outcome as the reviewing court would have prescribed. Moreover, the correctness standard is brought to bear on procedural questions without application of the context-sensitive "pragmatic and functional" approach the courts have developed to determine the standard of review applicable to particular decisions. Under this approach, correctness is the most demanding standard, patent unreasonableness is the most deferential, and reasonableness *simpliciter* occupies a middle ground.[24] For discussion of the three standards of review, see Audrey Macklin, chapter 8, and Sheila Wildeman, chapter 9. It seems that the line between procedure and substance vanished in *Suresh*, and it is far from clear which standard of review will be used to assess the "responsive" reasons given in a similar future case.

E. The Right to State-Funded Legal Counsel

In the administrative realm, the presence of lawyers is sometimes viewed as a hindrance to speedy, inexpensive, and conciliatory dispute resolution, and procedural fairness does not

21 *Liang v. Canada (Minister of Citizenship and Immigration)*, [1999] F.C.J. No. 1301 (T.D.) (QL).

22 See, for example, *Via Rail Canada Inc. v. National Transportation Agency*, [2001] 2 F.C. 25 (C.A.); and *Gray v. Director of the Ontario Disability Support Program*, [2002] O.J. No. 1531 (C.A.) (QL).

23 See David Mullan, *Administrative Law: Cases, Text, and Materials*, 5th ed. (Toronto: Emond Montgomery, 2003) at 276-80 for criticism of this approach to review of procedure.

24 *Canada (Director of Investigation and Research) v. Southam Inc.*, [1997] 1 S.C.R. 748.

necessarily entail a right to legal counsel even at one's own expense.[25] The Supreme Court has held that neither procedural fairness nor the rule of law in the administrative setting requires the state to fund legal representation.[26]

Where a decision impairs a s. 7 interest, however, in certain circumstances the state must provide the individual with legal counsel in order to satisfy the requirements of the principles of fundamental justice. In *New Brunswick (Minister of Health and Community Services) v. G.(J.)*,[27] the New Brunswick Minister of Health and Community Services sought to extend for six months a previous custody order over an indigent complainant's three young children. Lamer C.J. for the majority and L'Heureux-Dubé J. for the concurring minority held that a forced separation would have "a serious and profound effect" on the parent's psychological integrity and stigmatize her, thereby engaging her right to security of the person.[28] Furthermore, the custody hearing in such cases is adversarial and held in a court of law. Given the seriousness of the interest, the complexity of the proceedings, and the limited capacities of the individual, Lamer C.J. found that the principles of fundamental justice required a fair hearing and that in these circumstances a fair hearing required the Crown to provide legal aid to the parent.

G.(J.) also offers insight into why a majority of the Supreme Court has never found an infringement of s. 7 to be justified under s. 1. Lamer C.J. notes that s. 7 infringements are not easily saved under s. 1 because the rights protected under s. 7 are very significant, and because "rarely will a violation of the principles of fundamental justice, specifically the right to a fair hearing, be upheld as a reasonable limit demonstrably justified in a free and democratic society."[29] Although the Court in *Suresh* insisted that "the common law [of procedural fairness] is not constitutionalized" but rather "is used to inform the constitutional principles that apply,"[30] there is no question that enfolding procedural fairness into the s. 7 principles of fundamental justice has elevated the duty of fairness to new heights. The consistent refusal of a majority of the Supreme Court to find a s. 7 infringement justified under s. 1 signals the remarkable extent to which the right to a fair hearing has been constitutionalized.

F. Undue Delay

A further element of procedural fairness concerns the timeliness with which administrative proceedings are conducted. The constitution does not refer explicitly to unreasonable

---

25 *Re Men's Clothing Manufacturer's Association of the Ontario and Toronto Joint Board, Amalgamated Clothing and Textile Worker's Union* (1979), 22 L.A.C. (2d) 328 (H.W. Arthurs), quashed (1979), 104 D.L.R. (3d) 441 (Ont. Div. Ct.).

26 *Christie*, *supra* note 6. At a more general level, *Christie* may also be read to suggest that the Supreme Court will not use unwritten constitutional principles (in this case the rule of law) to invalidate legislation. In *Christie*, a provincial tax scheme was alleged to impair the ability of the underprivileged to obtain legal representation and access to the courts.

27 [1999] 3 S.C.R. 1303 [*G.(J.)*].

28 *Ibid.* at paras. 60-61 and 116.

29 *Ibid.* at para. 99. It is also noteworthy that Lamer C.J. finds the infringement unjustifiable solely on the basis of the legal aid policy's deleterious effects; in other cases in which the Court refers to deleterious effects, the reference comes only after the Court has already determined that the Crown failed to satisfy some other aspect of the test from *Oakes* (for example, lack of minimal impairment).

30 *Suresh*, *supra* note 13 at 114.

delays before administrative agencies, but in *Blencoe v. British Columbia (Human Rights Commission)*,[31] Bastarache J. speaking for the majority, acknowledged the possibility that an undue delay in the resolution of a human rights complaint could infringe the security interest protected under s. 7. Specifically, it is possible that an inordinate and undue delay could result in stigmatization and an impairment of the psychological integrity of the alleged wrongdoer, but, as we shall see, the threshold to cross is set very high.

Blencoe had been a minister in the government of British Columbia in March 1995 when one of his assistants accused him of sexual harassment. A month later the premier removed him from Cabinet and the New Democratic Party caucus. In July and August 1995, two women filed sexual harassment complaints against Blencoe with the BC Council of Human Rights (later the BC Human Rights Commission). Hearings were eventually scheduled before the BC Human Rights Tribunal in March 1998, after the commission had completed its preliminary investigation and some 30 months after the initial complaints were filed. Media attention was intense. The Court recognized that Blencoe's career as a politician was finished, that he suffered clinical depression, that his financial resources were depleted, and that he and his family had moved twice to flee the stigmatizing effects of the outstanding complaints. Nonetheless, Bastarache J. found that even on the assumption that the delay was a cause of Blencoe's grief, "the state has not interfered with the respondent and his family's ability to make essential life choices,"[32] and so the state did not infringe Blencoe's s. 7 security interest.

In addition to review under the Charter, the Court also considered whether the delay had caused Blencoe to suffer an abuse of process as a matter of common law. The majority held that in principle such a claim could be made out if there were prejudice to the hearing caused by the delay (for example, witnesses have died or are unavailable), or if the delay caused significant psychological harm or attached stigma to a person's reputation to an extent that brought the human rights system into disrepute. Bastarache J. found that this threshold had not been crossed on the specific facts of the case, but nonetheless he expressed concern with the commission's lack of efficiency and assessed costs against it.

LeBel J., speaking for himself and three others in dissent, thought that the case could (and therefore should) be settled on the basis of administrative law principles rather than on Charter grounds. LeBel J. also rejected the majority's view that determining the unreasonableness of a delay depends on whether the delay brings the human rights system into disrepute. He remarked sardonically that "[a]busive administrative process is wrong and it does not matter if it wrecks only your life and not your hearing."[33] He found that the facts of the case (including a five-month period in which the commission seemed to do absolutely nothing) did give rise to an undue delay. To take account of the interests of the women who complained against Blencoe, he held that the appropriate remedy was not a stay in proceedings (the usual remedy in the criminal context) but rather a cost award in favour of Blencoe and an order for an expedited hearing.

Now, because the majority did not find an infringement of a s. 7 interest, they did not have to consider whether the principles of fundamental justice had been compromised.

---

31 [2000] 2 S.C.R. 307 [*Blencoe*].

32 *Ibid.* at para. 86.

33 *Ibid.* at para. 154.

Were an infringement of the security interest made out in another case, one would expect the Court to import its common-law reasoning on undue delay into its analysis of the principles of fundamental justice, just as the *Baker* framework was imported into *Suresh*. In such a case, it remains to be seen whether the majority or the minority's common-law understanding of undue delay will inform the principles of fundamental justice.

G. Ex Parte, in Camera Hearings

In the wake of the events of September 11, 2001, many liberal democracies, including Canada, enacted legislation to give police and security services added powers to investigate and prosecute terrorism. However, Canada already had comprehensive legislation in place within its *Immigration and Refugee Protection Act* (IRPA)[34] that permitted the detention of foreign nationals and permanent residents (not citizens) suspected of terrorism or of having an association with terrorist organizations. Detainees under the IRPA are not charged criminally, and do not benefit from a presumption of innocence and other due process guarantees that permeate the criminal justice system. As we shall see, part of the statutory scheme envisions judicial review of the security certificates that authorize such detentions, but part of the review is conducted behind closed doors if evidence cannot be disclosed for reasons of national security. This scheme eventually gave rise to *Charkaoui v. Canada (Citizenship and Immigration)*.[35]

Canadian security agencies alleged that Adil Charkaoui, Hassan Almrei, and Mohamed Harkat were involved with terrorist organizations. Charkaoui is a permanent resident. The others are foreign nationals who had been recognized as Convention refugees. The Minister of Citizenship and Immigration and the Minister of Public Safety and Emergency Preparedness issued security certificates against them pursuant to s. 77 of the IRPA, leading to their detention pending deportation.

Under ss. 78-84 of the IRPA, the detention and the reasonableness of security certificates are subject to review by the Federal Court. During the review process, *ex parte* and *in camera* hearings (closed-door hearings in which neither the person named on the certificate nor his or her lawyer is present) are held at the request of the Crown if the judge believes that disclosure of some or all of the evidence on which the certificate is based could undermine national security. The judge then provides to the named person a summary of the evidence, but not its sources or any other details that might compromise national security. The judge may receive and rely on evidence withheld from the named person that would be inadmissible in a court of law, such as uncorroborated hearsay evidence provided by foreign security agencies known to use torture. If the judge determines that the certificate is reasonable, there is no appeal or opportunity for further judicial review.

McLachlin C.J., for a unanimous Supreme Court, found that these proceedings doubly engaged s. 7 because persons subject to security certificates face detention pending deportation (the liberty interest), and because the person's removal may be to a place where his or her life or freedom would be threatened (the security interest). The Court held that the review procedure violated the principles of fundamental justice because it denied the named

34 S.C. 2001, c. 27.

35 2007 SCC 9 [*Charkaoui*].

person a fair hearing. A fair hearing, the Court said, requires a judge to decide the case on the basis of all the relevant facts and law. Unlike in an inquisitorial system in which judges play an investigative role, in an adversarial system such as ours, judges do not have the power to investigate and gather evidence. As a consequence, the Court found, Federal Court judges may have to decide on the reasonableness of the Crown's case without the benefit of having the evidence adequately tested. A similar problem affects the law the reviewing judge must consider to meet the requirements of a fair hearing. The named person is precluded from raising legal objections to the evidence, or from basing legal arguments on it. In the result, the judge may have to decide the matter without a full and fair appraisal of all the facts and law at issue.

A further implication of the secrecy required by the statutory scheme is that the named person may never know the case that he or she has to meet, because it may be based in whole or in part on undisclosed material. In perhaps the sharpest language in her judgment, the chief justice said that the "principle [of knowing the case to meet when liberty is in jeopardy] has not merely been limited; it has been effectively gutted."[36]

An important aspect of the Court's ruling on the principles of fundamental justice concerns the issue of whether reviewing judges ought to balance the interests of the individual against those of society at the s. 7 stage of determining the content of the principles of fundamental justice. In *Thomson Newspapers Ltd. v. Canada (Director of Investigation and Research, Restrictive Trade Practices Commission)*,[37] La Forest J. wrote as part of the majority and found that determining their content requires a "just accommodation between the interests of the individual and those of the state."[38] In *Charkaoui*, the Court affirmed its more recent holding in *R. v. Malmo-Levine*[39] that s. 7 does not permit "a free-standing inquiry … into whether a particular legislative measure 'strikes the right balance' between individual and societal interests in general."[40] Such balancing, the Court said, should be conducted under s. 1.

To remedy the procedural shortcomings of the statutory scheme in *Charkaoui*, the Court suggested that an *amicus curiae* (an independent, security-cleared lawyer) could be appointed to represent the named person during *in camera* proceedings. Canada has used this method in other settings, and it is currently the regime in place in the United Kingdom. The Crown's failure to incorporate such a measure, or to otherwise correct the procedural defects referred to above, led the Court to conclude that the violation of s. 7 could not be saved under s. 1 because the infringement did not minimally impair the right at stake.

Refugee advocates heralded *Charkaoui* as a major victory, notwithstanding that the Court left open what has become known as the "*Suresh* exception," the finding of the Court in *Suresh* that exceptional circumstances may entitle Canada to deport a person to torture. *Charkaoui* is another in a line of cases stretching back to *Singh* in which s. 7 has provided procedural safeguards to non-citizens who historically were vulnerable to unstructured discretionary authority subject to only limited review.

---

36 *Ibid.* at para. 64.

37 [1990] 1 S.C.R. 425.

38 *Ibid.* at para. 176.

39 [2003] 3 S.C.R. 571.

40 Cited in *Charkaoui*, *supra* note 35 at para. 21.

Nonetheless, the bigger question that is easily lost in the minutiae of Charter review of specific statutory provisions, and which was never asked by the Court, is whether it is at all just to incarcerate foreign nationals and permanent residents without the protection of fundamental criminal law principles, such as the rules of evidence, the idea that the Crown must prove its case beyond a reasonable doubt, the proscription against double jeopardy, and the presumption of innocence. These principles lie at the heart of our justice system because they are constitutive of the rule of law, and because deprivations of liberty arising from detention are so serious. Sections 7 through 14 of the Charter reflect and embody these principles, and those sections are supposed to apply to "everyone," regardless of civil and political status. They remain in place for citizens, including the 17 charged with conspiracy to commit terrorist acts in Ontario in the spring of 2006. But for others who have yet to attain citizenship, the protections of the Charter seem to have slipped loose from their moorings. It is not just the denial of the presumption of innocence and other safeguards that is worrying. More troubling still is that our highest court does not seem to think that everyone—"every human being who is physically present in Canada"—is worthy of them.

III. REVIEW OF ADMINISTRATIVE DECISIONS UNDER THE CHARTER

We turn now to consider the extent to which the methodology developed by the courts to review legislation impugned on Charter grounds has crept into review of administrative decisions when a Charter right is at stake.

We have seen already in *Singh* (per Wilson J.) and *Blencoe* (per LeBel J.) that judges will sometimes say that resort to the Charter is unwarranted when administrative law can resolve procedural issues. Arguably, part of the rationale underlying this thought is that Charter review involves minimal deference to legislative intent; courts conducting review under the Charter merely determine whether statutory provisions and the decisions made under them are invalid because they run afoul of the constitution. Judicial review at common law, on the other hand, is often said to be about determining legislative intent (review of substance) or supplying the omission of the legislature (review of procedure). Furthermore, common-law judicial review permits the legislature to have the last word through ordinary democratic means. The legislature can "trump" the requirements of the common law by amending its legislation with clear and express language and, because the Charter is not in play, it can do so without resort to s. 33 of the Charter (the "override" provision). In other words, Charter review alone appears to have the potential to place judges above legislators in determining which laws and decisions apply to us (absent the legislature's deployment of s. 33), and thus places stress on the idea that law-making and public administration belong exclusively to the people's elected representatives and their delegates.

As we shall see now, however, when the focus of review is the decision itself (that is, substantive review) rather than the procedures leading to it, and a discrete Charter right is clearly at stake, the majority position of the Supreme Court is to review the decision using (almost) exclusively the analytical framework developed under the Charter to review legislation. Under this framework, judges engage in a two-step inquiry, determining first whether the impugned decision infringes a Charter right, and second, whether the infringement can be saved under s. 1 as a reasonable limit prescribed by law and demonstrably justified in a free and democratic society. Nonetheless, in some cases the Court did not resort to the Charter when it could have done so, and the majority position is far from a unanimous position.

Whenever courts review a decision that touches a Charter right, they have at their disposal both administrative law principles and the Charter. Thus, the possible approaches to review in this context involve review under administrative law, review under the Charter, or some combination of both. In practice, Supreme Court judges have used the following frameworks to review decisions alleged to impair Charter rights:

1. *The orthodox approach*: This is the majority position referred to above, according to which reviewing courts use the two-step Charter framework to determine the legality of an impugned decision. Administrative law is still relevant to review questions of jurisdiction, fact, and the application of law to facts, but whenever a Charter right is infringed and contending values are in play, the critical analysis takes place under s. 1.
2. *The mixed approach*: Under this framework, judges first review the legality of a decision using the principles of administrative law, including inquiry into whether the decision is ultra vires a grant of discretion or based on an unreasonable interpretation of a statutory provision. If, and only if, the decision is lawful under administrative law, it is then tested within the two-step Charter framework.
3. *The administrative law approach*: This approach eschews review under the Charter and limits scrutiny to exclusively that which is available as a matter of administrative law.

We consider now the orthodox and administrative law approaches in turn, and the mixed approach within the context of these two competing frameworks of review.

A. The Orthodox and Mixed Approaches

The Supreme Court first considered the application of the Charter to an administrative decision in *Slaight Communications Inc. v. Davidson*.[41] Davidson worked for Slaight Communications as a salesperson for almost four years prior to his termination. Davidson grieved his dismissal, and the labour adjudicator found that he had been dismissed unjustly. The adjudicator enjoyed broad discretionary authority under the *Canada Labour Code* to impose a remedy. Part of the remedy consisted of a "positive order," which required the employer to write an unembellished, factual letter of reference setting out Davidson's success relative to annual sales targets, as well as the fact that the adjudicator had found Davidson's dismissal to be unjust. The adjudicator also made a "negative order" requiring Slaight to provide the letter, and only the letter, to prospective employers making inquiries about Davidson's employment at Slaight. In other words, to protect the integrity of the positive order, Slaight was forbidden from making any negative comments about Davidson's work performance to possible future employers. Slaight sought judicial review, arguing that both the positive and the negative order infringed its freedom of expression guaranteed under s. 2(b) of the Charter, and that the infringement could not be justified under s. 1.

41 [1989] 1 S.C.R. 1038 [*Slaight Communications*].

Dickson C.J. wrote for the majority and held that although the positive and negative orders infringed s. 2(b), in both cases the infringement could be saved under s. 1. The chief justice found that the orders were both rationally connected to the laudable purpose of the enabling legislation as well as proportionate to its ultimate end—that is, remedying inequality of bargaining power between employers and employees, especially when employees are seeking employment and are at their most vulnerable. He also held that the orders were reasonable in the administrative law sense, though he declined to offer any analysis to substantiate this claim apart from the idea that "administrative law unreasonableness, as a preliminary standard of review, should not impose a more onerous standard upon government than would *Charter* review."[42] He said that administrative law review remained important, but for "questions untouched by the *Charter*" such as questions of fact, because "[i]n contrast to s. 1, patent unreasonableness rests to a large extent on unarticulated and undeveloped values and lacks the same degree of structure and sophistication of analysis."[43] Dickson C.J.'s judgment remains the basis of the orthodox approach today.

Lamer J. (as he then was) dissented in part, finding on administrative law grounds that the adjudicator had made a patently unreasonable decision and had thereby exceeded his jurisdiction by issuing the negative order. The negative order, he held, could lead a recipient of the prescribed letter to impute to Slaight an opinion it did not have. Lamer J. considered this result "totalitarian" and did not weigh it against the objective of promoting equality of bargaining power between employees searching for employment and their possible employers. However, Lamer J. did not think the positive order posed the same menace, and so upheld it as reasonable in light of the statute's purpose. He then turned to review the positive order under the Charter. Lamer J.'s use of administrative law *and* the Charter is an example of the mixed approach.

Lamer J. cited Professor Hogg for the idea that because Parliament cannot pass a law inconsistent with the Charter, neither can it authorize administrative action that violates the Charter. However, Parliament can pass laws that infringe Charter rights if those infringements can be justified under s. 1, and therefore Parliament can grant discretionary authority capable of infringing Charter rights just so long as those infringements can be saved under s. 1. If Parliament grants power to infringe a Charter right expressly or by necessary implication, then the legislation is subject to review under s. 1. If, on the other hand, Parliament grants an imprecise discretion that does not confer expressly or by necessary implication the power to infringe a Charter right, then the order rather than the legislation must be tested under s. 1. *Slaight Communications* was a case of this latter scenario, with Lamer J. finding that the positive order infringed s. 2(b) but could be saved under s. 1 for roughly the same reasons as those given by the majority.

The full Court concurred with Lamer J.'s framework regarding the applicability of the Charter to administrative decisions. Where the majority parted ways with Lamer J.'s method was in their insistence that administrative law should yield to Charter review whenever Charter rights were in play and contending values had to be weighed against one another. The majority saw the Charter as a resource with which to protect a vulnerable

42 *Ibid.* at 1040.

43 *Ibid.* at 1049.

job-seeker from the prejudice that would ensue from an unfair reference concerning his past employment. Charter jurisprudence from *Oakes* had already established that "a commitment to social justice and equality" was an underlying value of a free and democratic society.[44] The Charter thereby permitted the majority to give effect to a legislative purpose (promoting equality of bargaining power between employers and employees) that common-law judges had historically neglected when confronted with employer claims to freedom of expression.[45]

Lamer J.'s blueprint to Charter review of discretion is now well established as the framework of the orthodox position. However, courts have largely rejected his mixed approach and have instead followed Dickson C.J.'s lead regarding the relationship between the Charter and administrative law, using s. 1 to the exclusion of administrative law to determine the legality of decisions that clearly infringe Charter rights.[46] In such cases, review on administrative grounds is generally reserved to review of factual determinations or issues involving the application of law to facts and the agency's jurisdiction to make such determinations. These issues tend to be segmented away from inquiries into the scope of the Charter right and possible grounds to justify its infringement under s. 1.[47] As a rule, it appears that the Supreme Court, under the orthodox approach, will engage in substantive administrative law review when contending values are at stake only if the complainant fails to establish a prima facie infringement of a discrete Charter right, in which case s. 1 never enters the picture.[48]

The orthodox approach became further entrenched in *Multani v. Commission scolaire Marguerite-Bourgeoys*.[49] A school board's council of commissioners prohibited a Sikh boy from attending school with a kirpan (a small ceremonial dagger), notwithstanding a prior agreement between the boy's family and the school board that he would wear it sewn into

44 *R. v. Oakes*, *supra* note 2 at para. 64.

45 See *National Bank of Canada v. Retail Clerks' International Union*, [1984] 1 S.C.R. 269, and Lamer J.'s administrative law reasons for his partial dissent in *Slaight Communications*.

46 See, for example, *Eldridge v. British Columbia (Attorney General)*, [1997] 3 S.C.R. 624 (decision of the BC medical services commissioner not to provide sign language interpretation in hospitals struck down under s. 15); and *Ross v. New Brunswick School District No. 15*, [1996] 1 S.C.R. 825 [*Ross*] (infringement of a teacher's s. 2(d) freedom to make racist comments upheld under s. 1).

47 Regarding segmentation of questions of fact, see *Suresh*, *supra* note 13 (whether the facts show that an individual poses a danger to the public and faces a risk of torture upon deportation). For a similar approach regarding questions of fact and law and agency jurisdiction, see *Ross*, *supra* note 46 (whether certain acts fall within the meaning of discrimination, and whether the Human Rights Tribunal has jurisdiction to make such a determination). If courts were to conduct review using "jurisdiction" in an expansive sense (the sense in which it was used prior to *Canadian Union of Public Employees, Local 963 v. New Brunswick Liquor Corp.*, [1979] 2 S.C.R. 227 [*CUPE*]), then of course the orthodox approach would collapse into the mixed approach. The orthodox approach adumbrated here, like the pragmatic and functional approach, depends on the courts taking seriously Dickson J.'s (as he then was) instruction from *CUPE* that courts "should not be alert to brand as jurisdictional, and therefore subject to broader curial review, that which may be doubtfully so" (*ibid.* at para. 10).

48 See, for example, *Blencoe*, *supra* note 31. But see also (discussed below) *Trinity Western University v. British Columbia College of Teachers*, [2001] 1 S.C.R. 772 [*Trinity Western*]; *Chamberlain v. Surrey School District No. 36*, [2002] 4 S.C.R. 710 [*Chamberlain*]; and *Baker*, *supra* note 12.

49 [2006] 1 S.C.R. 256 [*Multani*].

and sealed within the interior of his clothing. Charron J., speaking for the majority, held that the council's decision infringed Multani's freedom of religion (s. 2(a) of the Charter), and that the infringement could not be saved under s. 1. She recognized that cases involving Charter rights could have an "administrative law component" in the senses described above, but held that review on administrative grounds in the present case was inappropriate because a Charter right was clearly at stake, and therefore compliance with the Charter was the central issue. We return to *Multani* below, and to the concurring judgment of Deschamps and Abella JJ., which rejects the orthodox view outright in favour of the administrative law approach.

The details of the orthodox position have met with other criticism we consider now, although none of them suggest abandoning this approach altogether. One of the criticisms focuses on Lamer J.'s criteria for determining whether Charter review goes to either the legislation or the orders made under it. Lamer J. begins with the conventional idea that the courts should, whenever possible, interpret impugned legislation so as to render it consistent with the Charter. If courts can so interpret the statute and its framework, their review must focus on orders made under the statute rather than on provisions of the statute itself. In a case like *Slaight Communications*, where a labour adjudicator is making a single decision between two parties, this approach appears innocuous enough. But what if the decision-maker is a government agency with broad statutory authority to make scores of individual decisions, and in making those decisions over many years it discriminates against a historically marginalized group and infringes the group's freedom of expression? This was what happened in *Little Sisters Book and Art Emporium v. Canada (Minister of Justice)*,[50] a case in which customs inspectors had been routinely seizing imported lesbian and gay literature on grounds of obscenity in what the trial judge characterized as "systematic targeting." The Supreme Court split 6–3 over whether the proper subject of review was the legislation itself or the individual censorship decisions made pursuant to it. Binnie J., for the majority, held that because customs officials *could* apply the *Customs Act* in a non-discriminatory manner, constitutional review must go to particular decisions rather than the Act.[51] Iacobucci J., speaking for the minority, held that extensive Charter violations showed that the legislation itself made no reasonable effort to ensure respect for constitutional rights, and that such an effort was required.

B. The Administrative Law and Mixed Approaches

In a number of important cases, the Supreme Court has declined to use the Charter where it was at least possible to do so. *Baker* was decided in the same year as *G.(J.)*, and in *G.(J.)* the Court found that a forced separation of a mother from her children would trigger s. 7. The deportation of Ms. Baker could have forced her to leave her children behind to further their best interests, arguably engaging exactly the s. 7 security interest that was impaired in

50 [2000] 2 S.C.R. 1120 [*Little Sisters*].

51 For scholarly critique of the majority's approach in *Little Sisters*, see Lorne Sossin, "Discretion Unbound: Reconciling the Charter and Soft Law" (2002) 45 Can. Public Admin. 465, and Sujit Choudhry & Kent Roach, "Racial and Ethnic Profiling: Statutory Discretion, Constitutional Remedies, and Democratic Accountability" (2003) 41 Osgoode Hall L.J. 1.

G.(J.). The Court did not address the Charter, electing instead to resolve the dispute on administrative law grounds.

Baker, however, does not necessarily support the administrative law approach, understood here as a framework for review that refuses as a matter of principle to review administrative decisions under the Charter. L'Heureux-Dubé J. merely said that application of the Charter was unnecessary because the case could be resolved on the basis of administrative law. *Baker*, therefore, is consistent with the mixed approach, but stands in some tension with the orthodox view if the s. 7 argument canvassed above is compelling.

Two subsequent cases, *Trinity Western* and *Chamberlain*, clearly involved Charter values, and arguably concrete rights as well, but the Court decided both without resort to the Charter framework. In *Trinity Western*, the BC College of Teachers refused to grant the Evangelical Trinity Western University (TWU) permission to assume full responsibility for its educational program. TWU required faculty and students to sign its "TWU Community Standards" code, which described same-sex relations as a "sexual sin."[52] The BC College of Teachers worried that TWU was promoting a culture of discrimination that could be passed from TWU teacher-graduates to children attending public school. A majority of the Supreme Court (L'Heureux-Dubé J. dissenting)[53] applied the pragmatic and functional approach from the common law and reviewed the decision on a standard of correctness. Iacobucci and Bastarache JJ., writing for the majority, found that analysis under the Charter was inappropriate because the s. 15 equality interests of school children were not affected. The decision of the BC College of Teachers, they held, punished TWU for its religious beliefs alone, and not for any wrong it had committed. The proper subject of censure, the majority said, is conduct rather than belief, such as discriminatory conduct in the classroom. Because there was no evidence that TWU graduates had engaged in discriminatory conduct, the majority concluded that TWU graduates had not, nor would, adversely affect the s. 15 interests of BC school children.

However, the majority clearly thought that the impugned decision infringed TWU's freedom of religion by declining TWU's request to assume full responsibility for its program on the basis of its beliefs. Moreover, contending values—freedom of religion versus equality—were undeniably at stake. Nonetheless, Iacobucci and Bastarache JJ. declined to follow the orthodox approach; they did not review the decision under ss. 2(a) and 1 of the Charter. This is puzzling because one of the principal rationales of the orthodox approach from *Slaight Communications* is that review under s. 1 permits a more structured and explicit discussion of contending values.

Chamberlain was another case involving an allegation of discrimination based on sexual orientation in the public school system.[54] In this case, a kindergarten–grade 1 (K–1) teacher asked the Surrey School Board to approve as supplementary learning resources three books that depicted same-sex parented families. The board refused. McLachlin C.J. spoke for the majority and, after application of the pragmatic and functional approach, she found that

52 *Trinity Western*, *supra* note 48.

53 L'Heureux-Dubé J. held that the appropriate standard of review was patent unreasonableness, that the decision of the BC College of Teachers was not patently unreasonable, and that any alleged infringement of TWU's freedom of expression, religion, or association could be justified under s. 1.

54 *Chamberlain*, *supra* note 48.

the decision should be reviewed on a standard of reasonableness *simpliciter*. She held that the board's decision was unreasonable because it failed to respect the principles of tolerance and secularism set out in its enabling legislation and regulations. In dissent, Gonthier and Bastarache JJ. agreed that the case should be reviewed on administrative law principles and that the appropriate standard of review was reasonableness *simpliciter*. But they concluded that discrimination was not made out on the facts because same-sex parenting could still be discussed at the K–1 level, and because human sexuality—including homosexuality—was addressed in later grades. Further, the dissenters understood the elected board to stand as a proxy for parents, and parents are presumed to know their children's best interests.

It is possible that issues of standing led the majorities in *Chamberlain* and *Trinity Western* to opt for review under administrative law rather than the Charter. In *Chamberlain* none of the appellants were either same-sex parents or children of such parents in the relevant jurisdiction. The Court would have had to grant the appellants public interest standing. In *Trinity Western*, at least so far as freedom of religion was concerned, the Court would have had to establish that a religiously based corporation (TWU) could initiate a challenge on the basis of s. 2(a). It is likely that these issues contributed to the respective majorities' reluctance to follow the orthodox approach and conduct a Charter review, though neither majority indicated that standing was determinative in this regard, and both treated administrative law as a fully adequate basis on which to dispose of the issues before them. Nonetheless, as in *Baker*, the courts in *Trinity Western* and *Chamberlain* may be read as supporting a mixed approach that permits review on administrative law grounds when constitutional rights are at stake, but that does not foreclose the possibility of review under the Charter if the decision survives preliminary scrutiny at common law. Neither decision survived administrative law review, so turning to the Charter was unnecessary.

The most principled defence of the administrative law approach is found in the concurring judgment of Deschamps and Abella JJ. in *Multani*. They departed from the majority mainly on the grounds that review of administrative decisions under s. 1 is impermissible because it is inconsistent with the rights-limiting portion of the French text of s. 1: "La *Charte canadienne des droits et libertés* garantit les droits et libertés qui y sont énoncés. Ils ne peuvent être restreints que par une *règle de droit*, dans des limites qui soient raisonnables et dont la justification puisse se démontrer dans le cadre d'une société libre et démocratique"[55] (emphasis added). Whereas the English text of s. 1 provides that a limit must be "prescribed by law," the French text uses a term of canonical importance in the civilian legal tradition: "règle de droit."

Legislation and regulations establish norms of wide and general application that conform to this category, but particularized administrative decisions do not; they simply do not exhibit the required form, and this formal requirement reflects the idea that legislated norms have a pedigree and privileged status that mere decisions do not. The concurring judges concluded that the legality of such decisions must be determined on the basis of

55 For a thorough and nuanced discussion of this point and the challenge it ultimately poses to the idea that Canada has a uniform public law inherited from Britain, see Robert Leckey, "Prescribed by Law/Une règle de droit" (2007) 45 Osgoode Hall L.J. 3 at 571-620. Leckey notes that both language versions of s. 1 are authoritative and fruitfully suggests that each one should be interpreted in light of the other. He argues that both the majority and the concurrency in *Multani* failed to do this.

administrative law, but that administrative law can incorporate Charter values.[56] In the result, they applied the pragmatic and functional approach and held that the commissioner's decision should be reviewed on a standard of reasonableness *simpliciter*. They found that the decision was unreasonable and therefore unlawful because the commissioners had not given due regard to fundamental values such as Multani's freedom of religion, nor had they considered the strict conditions that would have rendered wearing the kirpan virtually harmless.

The main argument of the concurrency is based on the alleged inapplicability of s. 1 to administrative decisions. However, if s. 1 is inapplicable to administrative decisions, there are two other possible frameworks for review the concurrency did not canvass.

First, courts could adopt a mixed approach that combines administrative law with the first stage of Charter analysis (inquiry into whether a Charter right has been infringed), but that refuses to scrutinize whether an infringement could be saved under s. 1. Second, courts could adopt a much leaner framework limited to just the first stage of review under the Charter framework, one in which administrative law plays only the limited role ascribed to it under the orthodox approach.

It is likely that the concurrency in *Multani* declined to pursue these options because, in addition to the règle de droit argument, they held that administrative decisions should be reviewed using exclusively administrative law principles because these principles are best suited to review decisions.

C. Reconciliation?

The tension between the concurrency and the majority judgments could be dissipated if a unifying interpretation of s. 1 were available that took seriously the texts and background legal traditions of both language versions. A unifying interpretation of s. 1 is urgently required if Canadians are to be governed by a constitution that posits in both official languages the same analytical framework for determining rights limitations. The idea of a shared constitution would be undermined if the French version of s. 1 permitted only the administrative law approach to review, while the English text supported just the orthodox approach. Both language versions of s. 1 are authoritative, and so the unity of judicial review in this context depends on the possibility of interpreting both texts in a manner that renders them consistent with each other. It is beyond the scope of this chapter to defend such an interpretation, but tentatively we might imagine it to take the following form.

Read purposefully, "règle de droit" in the French version of s. 1 could be interpreted to refer directly to the legislation that authorizes administrative decision-making. On this reading, inquiry under s. 1 would begin by considering whether the *scope* of the authorization contained in the legislation itself—the règle de droit—encompasses the power to make the decision under scrutiny. Scope in this context refers to the statutory authority to make decisions based on either a grant of discretionary authority or the interpretation and application of a legislative provision. If the decision under review falls within the scope of the authorizing legislation in either case, then arguably, in an important sense, it is the legislation it-

56 Deschamps and Abella JJ. cite *Baker* in support of this claim, though it is unclear how much help *Baker* can lend them because L'Heureux-Dubé J. cited *Slaight Communications* (*supra* note 41 at para. 53) when she initially affirmed that discretion must be exercised in a manner consistent with the Charter.

self, the règle de droit, that is limiting the Charter right, and we are within the ordinary meaning of the French text. Moreover, if the relevant legislation is interpreted to have the requisite scope to authorize the decision under scrutiny, then the limit in question will necessarily be a limit prescribed by law, and we are within the accepted meaning of the English text of s. 1. It follows that, per the orthodox approach, s. 1 can be used to review decisions. However, consistent with the norm/decision distinction relied on by the concurrency in *Multani*, the subject of inquiry at the prescribed by law/règle de droit stage is not the decision itself, but rather the scope of the decision's authorizing legislation.

Another way to address the tension between the orthodox and administrative law approaches involves a brief inquiry into the structure of review under administrative law and the Charter. There is no reason in principle to think that the proportionality test from *Oakes* (or significant parts of it) cannot be used to flesh out the structure of the reasoning process of judicial review under administrative law. Proportionality has been used in exactly this context in continental Europe for decades, and with the United Kingdom's accession to the European Convention on Human Rights, it is now explicitly part of UK public law as well. The rights enshrined in the Charter are not absolute, and so administrative decision-makers will frequently be called on to infringe them for the sake of a laudable statutory purpose. When contemplating a decision that would infringe a Charter right for the sake of a worthy purpose, it is reasonable to suppose that decision-makers should take into account such things as the importance of the legislative objective and whether their decision will minimally impair the right. In other words, even if s. 1 did not exist, decision-makers and courts on review ought to have due regard for statutory purposes and the possible means to achieve them. From a functional point of view sympathetic to the idea that the relationship between administrative law and the Charter is one of mutual support and cross-fertilization, it should not matter which analytical framework is used when Charter rights are at stake. The considerations at play in each should be the same.

IV. AGENCY JURISDICTION OVER THE CHARTER

It is a commonplace principle of statutory interpretation that administrative tribunals and courts alike should endeavour to interpret legislation in light of the Charter and the values contained therein. Sometimes, however, unambiguous statutory provisions may appear to infringe Charter rights under any reasonable interpretation, and thus a tribunal's application of the interpretive principle referred to above would be tantamount to a refusal to obey the law the legislature has entrusted it to implement. The issue we discuss in this section is whether administrative agencies, as creatures of statute, have authority to interpret and apply the Charter to their enabling legislation for the purpose of refusing to give effect to provisions found to violate the Charter.

A. The Old Trilogy and "Jurisdiction Over the Whole Matter"

The Supreme Court initially considered this issue in a trilogy of cases: *Douglas/Kwantlen Faculty Assn. v. Douglas College*,[57] *Cuddy Chicks Ltd. v. Ontario (Labour Relations*

57 [1990] 3 S.C.R. 570 [*Douglas College*].

Board),[58] and *Tétreault-Gadoury v. Canada (Employment and Immigration Commission)*.[59] La Forest J. wrote the majority reasons in each of these decisions. He held that because s. 52(1) of the *Constitution Act, 1982* declares the constitution to be the supreme law of the land and inconsistent law of no force and effect, administrative decision-makers with the power to interpret law must also interpret and respect this supreme law. Therefore, although administrative agencies cannot declare infringing statutory provisions to be invalid (a power reserved to the courts), s. 52(1) authorizes them both to apply the Charter to their enabling legislation and to refuse to give effect to provisions they determine to be inconsistent with it.[60]

The Supreme Court pointed out that it retained authority to review agency determinations of Charter issues on the least deferential standard of review available, correctness. Perhaps more significant, however, the Court deployed a restrictive understanding of what it would mean for an agency to have authority to interpret law, and thus authority to apply the Charter. In *Cooper*, the Court later characterized this authority as one that must evince a "general power to consider questions of law."[61] This power had to be conferred by the enabling legislation because agencies have no inherent authority to decide questions of law (more on this soon), but it could be granted explicitly or implicitly. In *Cuddy Chicks*, the Court described this authority as "jurisdiction over the whole of the matter before it, namely, the parties, subject matter and remedy sought."[62] Specifically, the authority to interpret law had to be more than the authority required to implement the legislation's basic policies and programs, because all public officials had to be capable of this much interpretation, and the Court was not prepared to say that all public officials had jurisdiction to apply the Charter.

Although the majority in *Douglas College* were careful to insist that their recognition of agency jurisdiction over the Charter did not offend the separation of powers, their restrictive understanding of authority to consider questions of law shares the separation-of-powers concerns raised by Lamer C.J. in his concurring judgment in *Cooper*. Lamer C.J. thought that recognizing agency jurisdiction over the Charter undermined the separation of powers according to which the legislature makes law and the executive applies it: permitting agencies to apply the Charter to their enabling legislation appeared, he said, to let the executive decide the limits of its own jurisdiction. Conventional wisdom has the legislature determining those limits at first instance through legislation, and the judiciary policing them once they are established through judicial review. Lamer C.J. held that allowing tribunals to hear Charter challenges to their enabling legislation means that "the executive can defeat the laws of the legislature,"[63] thus inverting the relationship between the legislature and the executive.

The Court's restrictive view of authority to consider questions of law led to the much-criticized *Cooper* decision. The case turned on whether the Canadian Human Rights Com-

58 [1991] 2 S.C.R. 5 [*Cuddy Chicks*].

59 [1991] 2 S.C.R. 22.

60 Because the remedy sought is pursuant to s. 52(1) of the *Constitution Act, 1982*, the courts in this context have not ruled on whether a particular agency is a "court of competent jurisdiction" within the meaning of s. 24(1) of the Charter: *Douglas College*, *supra* note 57 at 594-95 and 605.

61 *Cooper*, *supra* note 3 at para. 46.

62 *Cuddy Chicks*, *supra* note 58 at 14.

63 *Cooper*, *supra* note 3 at para. 25.

mission or a tribunal struck under it had jurisdiction to apply s. 15 of the Charter to s. 15(c) of the *Canadian Human Rights Act*.[64] Section 15(c) of the Act stipulated that it was not a discriminatory practice for an employer to terminate an individual if the individual reached the normal age of retirement for employees occupying a similar position. La Forest J., for the majority, held that the legislation did not confer on the commission an explicit power to consider questions of law, and that no such power was implicit to the statutory scheme because the commission's role within it was to screen complaints rather than adjudicate them. Thus, the commission had to apply s. 15(c) of the Act to the appellants in *Cooper*, disqualifying their case as one that could be sent to a tribunal for adjudication. As a consequence, neither the commission nor a tribunal could review the constitutional validity of the impugned provision. McLachlin J. (as she then was, and with L'Heureux-Dubé J.) dissented, insisting that "all law and law-makers that touch the people must conform" to the Charter,[65] and that the commission had the power to consider questions of law.

B. Vindication of the Dissent in Cooper?

A new series of unanimous decisions has now emerged that confirm the dissenters' generous understanding of what it means for a tribunal to have authority to consider questions of law. As we shall see, however, the vindication of the dissent in *Cooper* may not be complete. Two of the judgments were released together, *Nova Scotia (Workers' Compensation Board) v. Martin; Nova Scotia (Workers' Compensation Board) v. Laseur*;[66] the third is *Paul v. British Columbia (Forest Appeals Commission)*.[67] The leading case is *Martin*.

In *Martin*, the Nova Scotia *Workers' Compensation Act* and its regulations excluded chronic pain sufferers from receiving benefits under the regular workers' compensation system and provided, in lieu of benefits usually available to injured workers, a four-week functional restoration program beyond which no further benefits were available. As a result of the statutory exclusion, the Workers' Compensation Board denied benefits to two workers suffering chronic pain. The workers appealed the board's decision to the Workers' Compensation Appeals Tribunal. They alleged that the legislation infringed s. 15(1) of the Charter by denying them equality under the law and discriminating against them on the basis of their disabilities. The Appeals Tribunal held that it had jurisdiction to hear the Charter argument, and concluded that the statutory exclusion violated the Charter as the complainants alleged. The Appeals Tribunal then went on to adjudicate the claims without giving effect to the infringing legislation. The board challenged the Appeals Tribunal's jurisdiction to hear the Charter argument.

Gonthier J. wrote for the Court and rejected the board's challenge, finding that "[a]dministrative tribunals which have jurisdiction—whether explicit or implied—to decide questions of law arising under a legislative provision are presumed to have concomitant jurisdiction

64 R.S.C. 1985, c. H-6.

65 *Cooper*, *supra* note 3 at para. 70.

66 [2003] 2 S.C.R. 504 [*Martin*].

67 [2003] 2 S.C.R. 585 (agency jurisdiction extends to determinations of Aboriginal rights enshrined in s. 35 of the *Constitution Act, 1982*).

to decide the constitutional validity of that provision,"[68] and that the Appeals Tribunal had such jurisdiction. He relied on the old trilogy and overruled *Cooper* to the extent that it went the other way.

Martin's most important novelty is that it eschewed the prior restrictive understanding of what it means for an agency or tribunal to have authority to consider questions of law. The inquiry into legislative intent on this matter does not rely on whether the legislature intended the tribunal to apply the Charter. The question is "whether the empowering legislation implicitly or explicitly grants to the tribunal the jurisdiction to interpret or decide *any* question of law"[69] (emphasis in original). Gonthier J. rejected the distinction made in *Cooper* between "general" and "limited" questions of law. However, he restricted the inquiry to one that must focus on whether the tribunal has the power "to decide questions of law arising from the challenged provision."[70] These powers will typically be found to reside in tribunals with adjudicative functions, but Gonthier J. made it clear that the presence or absence of adjudicative authority is not necessarily determinative.

If the legislation does not expressly grant jurisdiction to consider questions of law, the jurisdiction may still be present implicitly and inferred from a series of factors: "the statutory mandate of the tribunal in issue and whether deciding questions of law is necessary to fulfilling this mandate effectively; the interaction of the tribunal in question with other elements of the administrative system; whether the tribunal is adjudicative in nature; and practical considerations, including the tribunal's capacity to consider questions of law."[71] The guiding principle that informs the application of these factors (save perhaps practical considerations) is whether the legislature intended the tribunal to have jurisdiction to decide questions of law.

The presence of such an intent, however, does not end the inquiry; it merely establishes a rebuttable presumption that the agency has jurisdiction to apply the Charter. The presumption can be rebutted, Gonthier J. said, by pointing to an explicit or implied statutory withdrawal of authority to determine constitutional questions.

Despite the Court's unequivocal recognition of agency jurisdiction to hear Charter challenges, some tension remains. Gonthier J. acknowledged that "the factual findings and record compiled by an administrative tribunal, as well as its informed and expert view of the various issues raised by a constitutional challenge, will often be invaluable to a reviewing court."[72] However, he insisted that courts would always review on a standard of correctness when called on to scrutinize a tribunal's determination that a legislative provision is inconsistent with the Charter. If some tribunals really are "informed and expert," an appreciation of such expertise might emerge through application of the pragmatic and functional test.

68 *Martin*, *supra* note 66 at para. 3.

69 *Ibid.* at para. 36.

70 *Ibid.* at para. 37.

71 *Ibid.* at para. 30. For insightful discussion of the explicit/implicit distinction in *Martin*, and possible uncertainties regarding its application, see J.M. Evans, "Principle and Pragmatism: Administrative Agencies' Jurisdiction Over Constitutional Issues" in G. Huscroft & M. Taggart, eds., *Inside and Outside Canadian Administrative Law: Essays in Honour of David Mullan* (Toronto: University of Toronto Press, 2006) at 377-420.

72 *Martin*, *supra* note 66 at para. 30.

Review in some cases on a standard of reasonableness—a standard fully capable of detecting arbitrary and capricious decisions—would demonstrate that the Court really did consider the expert views of the agency to be "invaluable."

There is an additional tension within the Court's more generous approach to agency jurisdiction over the Charter, one that strains the dissenters' claim in *Cooper* that "all law and law-makers that touch the people" must conform to the Charter. The tension arises from the requirement of legislative intent and one of its immediate consequences: legislatures can amend and enact law to withdraw tribunal jurisdiction over the Charter. Various provincial legislatures have now drafted omnibus legislation to insulate their statutes from agency scrutiny of constitutional matters. For example, in 2004 British Columbia passed the *Administrative Tribunals Act*,[73] a comprehensive justice reform measure that expressly denies most provincial administrative tribunals jurisdiction over Charter issues. The attorney general of British Columbia justified the jurisdiction-depriving sections of the Act on several grounds.[74] In his second-reading speech to the legislative assembly, he claimed that courts are more expert than most tribunals with respect to complex and far-reaching Charter questions. He also worried that permitting agencies to resolve these questions would require laypersons to hire (costly) legal counsel where they would not otherwise have to do so. He expressed concern over the drain on resources and the additional time required to settle Charter challenges at the agency level. These resource and access to justice problems, he said, would be exacerbated by the non-binding nature of tribunal decisions over Charter issues, because similar questions would have to be decided anew in subsequent proceedings.

Both proponents and critics of agency jurisdiction over the Charter claim that their policy is the one that, overall, minimizes the expense and time required to settle an administrative dispute involving a Charter challenge. No one denies that if the tribunal does not have jurisdiction to hear a Charter challenge, separate judicial review proceedings must be launched. Critics of agency jurisdiction reply that these constitutional issues are likely to come before the courts in any event, and thus addressing them in the tribunal adds considerable cost and time to the final resolution of the matter. There are as yet no comparative empirical studies that examine similar cases before similar tribunals in which one jurisdiction's tribunals have competence to consider Charter issues while the other's does not. Studies of this nature are needed to advance this aspect of the debate past the current speculation.

---

73 S.B.C. 2004, c. 45, ss. 43-45. The Labour Relations Board and the Securities Commission are exceptions to the rule and can decide Charter questions. Other BC tribunals can determine constitutional issues related to federalism, but cannot apply the Charter. Yet others cannot determine any constitutional issues. Alberta has passed similar legislation: *Administrative Procedures Amendment Act, 2005*, S.A. 2005, c. 4. In *Tranchemontagne v. Ontario (Director, Disability Support Program)*, [2006] 1 S.C.R. 513, the Supreme Court reaffirmed that legislatures can preclude tribunals from considering Charter questions through clear legislation, though the bar in that case was specific to the relevant statute. The majority held that such a statutory bar would not be read to deprive a tribunal of authority to apply the provincial *Human Rights Code* to its enabling statute.

74 British Columbia, Legislative Assembly, *Official Report of Debates*, vol. 25, no. 15, May 18, 2004 at 1193 *et seq.*, as cited in Deborah K. Lovett, "Administrative Tribunal Jurisdiction over Constitutional Issues and the New Administrative Tribunals Act" (2005) 63 Advocate 177 at 191-92. Lovett argues in favour of limiting constitutional review to the courts, on separation of powers and policy grounds similar to those articulated by the attorney general.

The unchallenged doctrinal assumption that merits further reflection is that agency jurisdiction to apply the Charter depends on legislative intent. Recall that the idea underlying this assumption is that tribunals have no inherent jurisdiction to decide questions of law (including constitutional questions), and so all such jurisdiction must issue from the legislature. However, the mere fact that tribunals rely on the legislature for jurisdiction to decide questions of law does not imply that the legislature has authority to deprive them of jurisdiction to apply the Charter to their enabling legislation.

Arguably, respect for the supremacy of the constitution requires agencies to have due regard for the Charter—independently of legislative intent—whenever they interpret ordinary legislation to decide questions of law. Otherwise, tribunals are not treating the constitution as the supreme law with which all other law must conform. Put another way, a plausible interpretation of the principle of constitutional supremacy is that the legislature cannot confer on agencies the authority to decide questions of law without necessarily conferring on them the authority to apply the Charter. This is entirely consistent with the idea that tribunals have no inherent jurisdiction and so must receive all their legal powers from statute. The issue is whether those legal powers can be exercised without regard for the Charter. At the level of decision-making where Charter rights are at stake, we have seen in part III that the orthodox approach to review directs tribunals to evaluate their prospective decisions in light of both the Charter and its analytical framework. To require tribunals to assess provisions of their enabling statutes in the same light is simply asking them to do at the general level that which they are already doing in particular cases, regardless of legislative intent.

When the dissenters in *Cooper* said that "[t]he *Charter* belongs to the people,"[75] they affirmed that the people should not be deprived of the opportunity to assert constitutional rights in tribunals and agencies, forums that are usually much more accessible to them than the courts. In the absence of compelling empirical evidence that tribunal jurisdiction over the Charter hinders rather than promotes effective access to administrative justice, the time is ripe to consider further the idea that legislatures can require their delegates to implement programs without regard for the constitution.

SUGGESTED ADDITIONAL READINGS

CASES

Charkaoui v. Canada (Citizenship and Immigration), 2007 SCC 9.

Multani v. Commission scolaire Marguerite-Bourgeoys, [2006] 1 S.C.R. 256.

Nova Scotia (Workers' Compensation Board) v. Martin; Nova Scotia (Workers' Compensation Board) v. Laseur, [2003] 2 S.C.R. 504.

Singh v. Canada (Minister of Employment and Immigration), [1985] 1 S.C.R. 177.

Slaight Communications Inc. v. Davidson, [1989] 1 S.C.R. 1038.

Suresh v. Canada (Minister of Citizenship and Immigration), [2002] 1 S.C.R. 3.

75 *Cooper*, *supra* note 3 at para. 70.

SECONDARY SOURCES

Choudhry, Sujit, & Kent Roach. "Racial and Ethnic Profiling: Statutory Discretion, Constitutional Remedies, and Democratic Accountability" (2003) 41 Osgoode Hall L.J. 1.

Evans, J.M. "Principle and Pragmatism: Administrative Agencies' Jurisdiction over Constitutional Issues" in G. Huscroft & M. Taggart, eds., *Inside and Outside Canadian Administrative Law: Essays in Honour of David Mullan* (Toronto: University of Toronto Press, 2006) 377-420.

———. "The Principles of Fundamental Justice: The Constitution and the Common Law" (1991) 29 Osgoode Hall L.J. 51.

Leckey, Robert. "Prescribed by Law/Une règle de droit" (2007) 45 Osgoode Hall L.J. 3 at 571-620.

Lovett, Deborah K. "Administrative Tribunal Jurisdiction Over Constitutional Issues and the New Administrative Tribunals Act" (2005) 63 Advocate 177.

Mullan, David. *Administrative Law: Cases, Text, and Materials*, 5th ed. (Toronto: Emond Montgomery, 2003) at 276-80.

Sossin, Lorne. "Discretion Unbound: Reconciling the Charter and Soft Law" (2002) 45 Can. Public Admin. 465.

CHAPTER EIGHT

Standard of Review: The Pragmatic and Functional Test

AUDREY MACKLIN*
Faculty of Law, University of Toronto

I. INTRODUCTION

When judges hear appeals from decisions made by other judges about the interpretation of application of a statutory provision, their task is straightforward: ask whether the lower court got the answer "right" or "wrong." If the answer is wrong, the appellate judges will substitute the correct answer. The question presupposes that there is always only a single

* Thanks to Lorne Sossin for his editorial assistance, and to the other contributors in the volume. I am also grateful to David Dyzenhaus for his constructive suggestions, and to Sheila Wildeman for her insightful and generous contribution to the organization and analysis in my chapter.

correct answer, and it consists of the one given by the judge occupying the higher rung in the judicial hierarchy. The main exception arises where a reviewing or appellate court is called upon to review the findings of fact. Here, higher courts may hesitate to intervene on the grounds that they have not had the advantage of first-hand exposure to the evidence, especially *viva voce* testimony, and that revisiting factual determinations of little precedential value constitutes a poor use of judicial resources.

Judicial review of administrative action brings up a different set of questions that do not generally arise in ordinary appellate jurisprudence: Is there always only a single correct answer?[1] Who is better situated to determine the answer, the first-level specialist decision-maker or the generalist reviewing judge? What criteria can assist in assessing relative expertise?

At present, the short answer to these questions is as follows. A court that is called upon to review the interpretation or application of a statutory provision by an administrative decision-maker will first apply a "pragmatic and functional" test to assess who, as between the court and the original decision-maker, is better placed to make the determination at issue. The result of this test tells the court how much deference to accord the original decision. In *Baker*, the Supreme Court of Canada endorsed David Dyzenhaus's articulation of deference as respect: "Deference as respect requires not submission but a respectful attention to the reasons offered or which could be offered in support of a decision."[2]

Deference is then quantified through the standard of review applied by the court to the impugned decision. Less deference means stricter review. An issue meriting little or no deference will be judged in terms of its "correctness." An issue attracting a lot of deference will only be set aside if it is "patently unreasonable." Matters falling in between will be quashed if they are simply "unreasonable." Under the contemporary doctrine of standard of review, courts never completely relinquish their entitlement to "have the last word," and therefore insist that no decision can be completely immunized from judicial scrutiny.[3]

The longer answer to these questions requires embarking on a tortuous route through the history of judicial review, the rise of the administrative state, critical approaches to textual interpretation, and an evolving conception of the rule of law. As Bette Davis famously warned in *All About Eve*, "Fasten your seatbelts. It's going to be a bumpy night."

II. THE PREQUEL

In chapter 1, Colleen Flood surveyed the diverse reasons for the creation of administrative agencies, tribunals, and commissions. Certain functions, such as licensing, distribution of goods or resources, or the resolution of polycentric disputes, are ill-suited to resolution in a bipolar judicial process. Some domains, such as engineering, securities, and telecommu-

---

1 Of course, one might plausibly contend that this question is (or ought to be) equally apposite to appeal as to judicial review. See discussion in David Dyzenhaus, "Constituting the Rule of Law: Fundamental Values in Administrative Law" (2002) 27 Queen's L.J. 445 at 469-70 (note 46). If there is not always a single correct answer on review, there is also not always a single correct answer on appeal.

2 *Baker v. Canada (Minister of Citizenship & Immigration)*, [1999] 2 S.C.R. 817 at para. 65 [*Baker*]; and for the facts of *Baker*, see Grant Huscroft, chapter 5.

3 See the discussion of *Crevier v. Attorney-General of Quebec*, [1981] 2 S.C.R. 220, in part IV.A.

nications, require a level and type of technical or experiential expertise that judges lack. Other areas, such as immigration, social assistance, or workers' compensation, generate such a high volume of cases (usually involving people of limited means) that the ordinary courts and ordinary judicial processes would be both overwhelmed and inaccessible. Concerns of efficiency and cost militate in favour of an administrative regime. In the 20th century, ideological conflict between the expanding administrative state and the courts (incisively and passionately critiqued by the legal realists) led governments in the Anglo-American legal world to withdraw certain domains from courts and allocate them to newly created, specialized agencies. The iconic case is labour law. Deployment of traditional common-law doctrines of freedom of contract, protection of private property, privity of contract, and prohibition on contracts in restraint of trade consistently thwarted legislation designed to provide a measure of protection to workers, standardize minimum terms of employment, and enable the emergence of an industrial relations regime based on union representation.

Frustrated with judicial hostility toward the objectives of labour relations legislation, the government not only established a parallel administrative regime of labour relations boards, but also enacted statutory provisions that purported to preclude entirely judicial review of the legality of administrative action. Ordinarily, judicial review is available for breaches of procedural fairness, errors of law, abuse of discretion, or factual findings made in the absence of evidence.

So-called privative clauses were originally intended to prevent courts from interfering with substantive outcomes of administrative action through the doctrines of error of law or lack of evidence. The motive behind privative clauses is not always the desire to keep a meddling court at bay; they may also be inserted to encourage prompt and final resolution of disputes, or as a means of allocating scarce judicial resources by restricting access to the courts. Moreover, while the dominant narrative of the 20th century depicts a progressive administrative state using privative clauses to defend social welfare legislation from the conservative grasp of a retrograde judiciary, one should not assume that the politics of judicial review are uniform or static. In recent years, for example, the Australian government has perfected the use of the privative clause in the service of precluding judicial review of extremely draconian legislation directed at asylum seekers.

Privative clauses vary in wording, but the usual elements include a grant of exclusive jurisdiction over the subject matter, a declaration of finality with respect to the outcome, and a prohibition on any court proceedings to set the outcome aside. The following example is typical:

> The board shall have exclusive jurisdiction to examine, hear and determine all matters and questions arising under this Act and any other matter in respect of which a power, authority or discretion is conferred upon the board. … The decision and finding of the board under this Act upon all questions of fact and law are final and conclusive and no proceedings by or before the board shall be restrained by injunction, prohibition or other proceeding or removable by *certiorari* or otherwise in any court.[4]

4 *The Workers Compensation Act, 1979*, S.S. 1979, c. W-17.1, s. 22, quoted in *Pasienchyk v. Saskatchewan (Workers' Compensation Board)*, [1997] 2 S.C.R. 890 at para. 5 [*Pasienchyk*].

The privative clause poses a conundrum for the traditional conception of the rule of law. On the one hand, a legislative grant of authority is always circumscribed by the terms of the statute. The common law presumes that citizens' retain access to the ordinary courts in order to ensure that creatures of statute do not exceed the jurisdiction granted to them. As the British jurist H.W.R. Wade wrote, the rule of law demands that "administrative agencies and tribunals must at all costs be prevented from being sole judges of the validity of their own acts."[5]

On the other hand, the doctrine of parliamentary supremacy dictates that the legislator enacts the law, and the court must interpret and apply the law in accordance with the legislator's intent. A privative clause pits the second principle against the first by stating rather clearly and unambiguously that the legislator intends to oust the courts from supervising the actions of the administrative actor.

Not surprisingly, judges resisted the privative clause's "plain meaning" and circumvented it through the following chain of reasoning, most powerfully articulated in the House of Lords' *Anisminic*[6] case: Decisions or findings that are not lawfully made are nullities; one way in which a decision may be unlawfully made is where the decision-maker lacks jurisdiction (legal authority) under the constitutive statute to make the decision; therefore, "decisions" or "findings" that are insulated by a privative clause do not include actions that exceed the jurisdiction granted to the decision-maker.

If a college of physicians and surgeons purported to suspend the licence of a dentist to practise dentistry, we might all agree that the putative suspension was beyond the jurisdiction of the college, and not protected by a privative clause. However, few real cases ever involved such starkly deviant administrative behaviour. Typically, the issue is the interpretation of a statutory provision, or inferences from evidence whose relevance depends on a particular statutory construction. Judges assigned themselves the task of determining whether the issue fell "within jurisdiction," and therefore within the ambit of the privative clause, or whether it was a "jurisdictional question" that determined the outer boundary of the decision-maker's authority. If it was the latter, then a court was entitled to review the decision. At this juncture, prior to the emergence of a variable standard of review, correctness was the implicit and exclusive standard of review. Rather like the early approach to natural justice, review in the face of a privative clause was an all-or-nothing affair.

The effectiveness of privative clauses in ousting the courts depended on the ease and frequency with which courts could designate an issue as determinative of jurisdiction, and therefore warranting strict judicial scrutiny. Two techniques deployed by the courts were the "preliminary or collateral question" doctrine, and the "asking the wrong question" doctrine.

In *Parkhill Bedding and Furniture Ltd. v. International Molders, Etc. Union*,[7] the employer (Parkhill) purchased the tangible assets of a bankrupt company that had been bound by a collective agreement with the union with the bankrupt company. The Manitoba Labour Board ruled that Parkhill was, under s. 18(1) of the *Labour Relations Act*, a "new employer to whom passes the ownership of the business of an employer who has entered into the

---

5 H.W.R. Wade & C.F. Forsyth, *Administrative Law*, 8th ed. (New York: Oxford University Press, 2000) at 707.

6 *Anisminic Ltd. v. Foreign Compensation Commission*, [1969] 2 A.C. 147 (H.L.).

7 (1961), 26 D.L.R. (2d) 589 (Man. C.A.).

[collective] agreement." The board ordered that Parkhill was bound by the collective agreement with the union. The employer sought judicial review of the board's order in the face of a provision stating that the board's decision "shall be final and conclusive for all purposes of this Act."[8]

The Manitoba Court of Appeal ruled that the board's order exceeded its jurisdiction. The court reasoned that the question of whether Parkhill was a "new employer" was preliminary or collateral to the main issue that the board had exclusive jurisdiction to address, namely whether the collective agreement bound Parkhill. As such, "the Board cannot give itself jurisdiction by a wrong decision on such a preliminary or collateral point upon which the limit to its jurisdiction depends."[9] The court considered that resolving whether Parkhill was a new employer turned less on labour relations law than on bankruptcy law, and especially on whether the title acquired by a purchaser of assets from a trustee in bankruptcy "is to be deemed encumbered by obligations under a collective agreement which had been entered into by the assignor in bankruptcy."[10] The court acknowledged that labelling an issue preliminary or collateral was contentious, but indicated that the designation might be warranted where an issue requires considering "legal principles that are outside the scope of the [Labour Relations] Act."[11] It did not explain why principles of bankruptcy law should be determinative in the context of a labour relations scheme. It then went on to employ its understanding of bankruptcy law to conclude that in the circumstances of the case, the board wrongly concluded that Parkhill was a new employer, and thereby "gave itself jurisdiction"[12] it did not possess to declare that the collective agreement bound Parkhill.

In *Metropolitan Life Insurance Company v. International Union of Operating Engineers, Local 796*,[13] the Supreme Court of Canada addressed an Ontario Labour Relations Board certification of a union as the sole bargaining agent for a group of employees engaged in janitorial and building maintenance work. The provision that the union relied upon for certification required evidence that at least 55 percent of the employees were members of the union. The union constitution only provided for membership by "operating engineers," but in practice that union had signed up workers of many occupational classifications. Almost two decades earlier, the Ontario Labour Relations Board had adopted a policy of imposing a uniform set of criteria for determining whether employees were members of a union applicant for certification. These consisted of an application for membership, followed by acceptance of membership, an assumption of the financial or other responsibilities of membership, and enjoyment of all the rights and privileges of union membership. Eligibility under the union constitution was only one factor, and even then, only an explicit constitutional exclusion from membership status (along with its rights and privileges) would be determinative. The board's reasons explained at length the rationale for its

8 *Ibid.* at paras. 1 and 9.

9 *Ibid.* at para. 12.

10 *Ibid.* at para. 27.

11 *Ibid.* at para. 28.

12 *Ibid.* at para. 31.

13 [1970] S.C.R. 425.

approach and specifically addressed why reliance on union constitutions as the determinant of union membership would produce incongruous outcomes and confer unfair advantages on some unions over others. In the particular case before it, the board considered that over 55 percent of the employees had become union members according to its criteria. The *Ontario Labour Relations Act* contained a form of privative clause. The employer sought judicial review and ultimately appealed to the Supreme Court of Canada.

The Court ruled that the determination by the board was not protected by the privative clause. Although the question whether 55 percent of the employees were members of the union was undoubtedly an issue within the exclusive jurisdiction of the board, the board lost jurisdiction because it employed a faulty reasoning process. According to the Court, "the Board has failed to deal with the question remitted to it (ie., whether the employees in question were members of the union at the relevant date) and instead had decided a question which was not remitted to it (ie., whether in regard to those employees there has been fulfillment of the conditions [for membership devised by the Board])."[14] Implicit in the Court's reasoning is the assumption that the union constitution is determinative of membership; indeed, the Court did not engage at all with the rationale of the board in employing different criteria. The upshot of "asking the wrong question" was that even matters otherwise within the jurisdiction of a decision-maker (and thus protected by a privative clause) could become jurisdictional and subject to judicial scrutiny if the decision-maker asked himself or herself the wrong question in the course of addressing the issue.

The doctrines of preliminary or collateral question and asking the wrong question were derided as formalistic, malleable, and instrumental devices manufactured by the courts to meddle in spheres where the legislature had deliberately and explicitly excluded them. Courts inclined to disagree with a decision could, with little effort, transform almost any issue into a preliminary or collateral question, or depict the tribunal as asking the wrong question, in order to impugn a decision as the product of a defective chain of reasoning.

The language of jurisdiction has been muted but still appears in contemporary jurisprudence, while the doctrines described above have been largely discarded. Nevertheless, it remains important to be familiar with this history for two reasons. First, the rule of law sources of judicial anxiety about jurisdiction remain salient. Secondly, it is arguable that elements of the preliminary or collateral question and asking the wrong question doctrines are forgotten but not gone. For example, the assertion that a statutory provision is properly understood according to the principles of another area of law survives in cases such as *Bibeault*.[15] A reasoning process that inquires into the effect of a given interpretation on advancing the broader objectives of the statute may still be rejected as a flawed and self-aggrandizing attempt to expand the jurisdiction of the regulator.[16]

14 *Ibid.* at para. 24.

15 *U.E.S., Local 298 v. Bibeault*, [1988] 2 S.C.R. 1048 [*Bibeault*].

16 *Barrie Public Utilities v. Canadian Cable Television Association*, [2003] 1 S.C.R. 476 [*Barrie Utilities*].

III. THE BLOCKBUSTER: CUPE v. NEW BRUNSWICK LIQUOR CORPORATION

Canadian Union of Public Employees, Local 963 v. New Brunswick Liquor Corp.[17] is to the standard of review what *Nicholson*[18] is to procedure and *Baker* is to discretion: a judgment that shifts the legal landscape onto new terrain. The facts are straightforward. A public sector union, Canadian Union of Public Employees (CUPE), went on strike. Under the terms of the New Brunswick *Public Service Labour Relations Act*, striking employees were prohibited from picketing and employers were prohibited from using replacement workers. Section 102(3) of the Act stated as follows:

> 102(3) … during the continuance of the strike
>
> (a) the employer shall not replace the striking employees or fill their position with any other employee, and
>
> (b) no employee shall picket, parade or in any manner demonstrate in or near any place of business of the employer.[19]

Section 101 of the Act contained a lengthy privative clause declaring, *inter alia*, that every "award, direction, decision, declaration, or ruling of the Board … is final and shall not be questioned or reviewed in any court."[20]

The employer complained to the NB Public Service Labour Relations Board that the union was picketing, contrary to s. 102(3)(b), and the union complained that the employer was filling striking employees' positions with management personnel, contrary to s. 102(3)(a). The board upheld the employer's complaint and ordered the union to cease and desist picketing. It also upheld the complaint against the employer, and ordered it to refrain from using management personnel to do work ordinarily performed by bargaining unit employees. The employer successfully sought judicial review of the board's order against it, and eventually the union appealed to the Supreme Court of Canada.

The issue in the case was the interpretation of s. 102(3)(a). The employer argued that the provision should be interpreted as prohibiting the temporary replacement of employees "with any other employee" or permanently filling their positions "with any other employee." Management personnel were not employees as defined in the Act, therefore s. 102(3)(a) was not breached by the use of management personnel to replace employees during the strike. The objective of the provision, argued the employer, was to preserve the positions of the employees once the strike was over. The union argued that "with any other employee" only applied to permanently filling positions, and not to temporarily replacing employees during the strike.[21]

Writing for the Supreme Court of Canada, Dickson J. (as he then was) paraphrased the board's approach to interpreting s. 102(3) as follows:

---

17 [1979] 2 S.C.R. 227 [*CUPE*].

18 *Nicholson v. Haldimand-Norfolk (Regional) Board of Commissioners of Police*, [1979] 1 S.C.R. 311.

19 *CUPE*, *supra* note 17 at para. 4; *Public Service Labour Relations Act*, R.S.N.B. 1979, c. P-25.

20 *Ibid.* at para. 14.

21 *Ibid.* at paras. 5-6.

> It was the opinion of the board that when the Legislature saw fit to grant the right to strike to public employees, it intended through the enactment of s. 102(3) to restrict the possibility of picket-line violence by prohibiting strikebreaking, on the one hand, and picketing, on the other. This apparent intention, the board held, would be frustrated [by the employer's interpretation]. The result of such an interpretation would be that strikers would have been deprived of their right to picket, but the employer would not have been deprived of the right to employ strike-breakers.[22]

The Supreme Court of Canada allowed the union's appeal. However, it did not follow the extant analytical framework toward the conclusion that the interpretation of s. 102(3) was a question within the jurisdiction of the board and thus immunized from judicial review by the privative clause. Instead, Dickson J. canvassed the reasons for the existence of privative clauses, emphasizing the legislative choice to confer certain tasks on administrative actors, the specialized expertise and accumulated experience of administrative bodies, and the virtues of judicial restraint. In the case at bar, the interpretation of s. 102(3) "would seem to lie logically at the heart of the specialized jurisdiction confided to the Board."[23] As such, a court should only interfere (by labelling as jurisdictional error), an interpretation of the provision that is "so patently unreasonable that its construction cannot be rationally supported by the relevant legislation."[24]

The Supreme Court of Canada's judgment in *CUPE* did not break with earlier jurisprudence that invoked jurisdictional error to circumvent privative clauses. Rather, it dramatically reconfigured the analysis of when, why, and how jurisdictional error ought to be deployed. Most importantly, it conveyed a spirit of curial deference, a recognition that administrative decision-makers are not merely "inferior tribunals," but specialized bodies that possess a legislative mandate to apply their expertise and experience to matters that they may be better suited to address than the "ordinary court." This change of heart regarding the appropriate role of judicial review eventually transcended the confines of privative clauses to encompass substantive judicial review in general, including the exercise of discretion.

A reading of *CUPE* reveals three sources of the Supreme Court of Canada's doctrinal change. First, the Court situates the case in a broader reappraisal of the respective roles assigned by the legislature to the courts and to administrative bodies in the implementation of regulatory regimes. Dickson J. eschews reference to administrative actors as mere "inferior tribunals," and instead describes the board as a specialized tribunal possessing a legislative mandate to apply its distinctive expertise and experience to elaborating and implementing the constitutive statute. He refers to the "considerable sensitivity and unique expertise" required by board members to maintain peace in the course of a lawful public sector strike.[25] According to Dickson J., courts should recognize and respect the fact that in such matters, these specialized decision-makers bear primary responsibility for implementing their statutory mandate and may be better suited to the interpretive task than the generalist judge.

---

22 *Ibid.* at para. 7.

23 *Ibid.* at para. 15.

24 *Ibid.* at para. 16.

25 *Ibid.* at para. 15.

Secondly, the judgment candidly admits that the provision in dispute "bristles with ambiguities";[26] no one interpretation could lay claim to being "right." Instead, there were several plausible interpretations, including that of the board, the majority of the New Brunswick Court of Appeal, and a minority opinion of the Court of Appeal. Dickson J. canvasses at length the basis for each possible interpretation, not in order to discern which one was correct, but rather to demonstrate why the board's interpretation "would seem at least as reasonable as the alternative interpretations suggested in the Court of Appeal" and, in any event, could not be described as patently unreasonable.[27] Although *CUPE* is concerned with a statutory provision whose ambiguity was largely attributable to poor drafting, *CUPE* has been amplified in subsequent cases, such as *Corn Growers*[28] (Wilson J.) and *Domtar*[29] (L'Heureux-Dubé J.) into a more radical critique of the conceit that there is always only one correct interpretation of a statutory provision. Ambiguity, gaps, silences, and contradictions can rarely (if ever) be eliminated from text. This recognition of interpretive choice makes it possible to ask who is better placed to make the choice—the tribunal or the court? In other words, it underwrites the plea for judicial humility that is at the heart of *CUPE*. Moreover, Dickson J.'s interpretive survey notably focused on the meaning of the provision in the context of the statute, its purpose, and the consequences of interpretative choices for the fulfillment of the legislative scheme's objectives. He did not resort to dictionary definitions of "fill" or "replace," invoke common-law presumptions about access to the courts, or employ formal devices of statutory interpretation.

Finally, Dickson J. acknowledges the failure of prior judicial efforts to construct a coherent, principled means of distinguishing reviewable questions from those insulated by a privative clause. He notes that the "preliminary or collateral question" method is not helpful because one can, with little effort, characterize anything as preliminary or collateral. He admits that identifying what is and is not jurisdictional can be difficult, but counsels that "courts, in my view, should not be alert to brand as jurisdictional, and therefore subject to broader curial review, that which may be doubtfully so."[30] Unfortunately, the judgment does not set out an alternative, except to suggest that "jurisdiction is typically to be determined at the outset of the inquiry"[31] and that in the case at bar, the board's statutory authority over the parties (in this case, the union and the employer) and the subject matter (the conduct of a lawful strike), indisputably conferred jurisdiction "in the narrow sense of authority to enter upon an inquiry."[32] The issue then became whether the board did "something which takes the exercise of its powers outside the protection of the privative or preclusive clause."[33] Short of a patently unreasonable interpretation of a statutory provision,

26 *Ibid.* at para. 4.

27 *Ibid.* at para. 29.

28 *National Corn Growers Association. v. Canada (Canadian Import Tribunal)*, [1990] 2 S.C.R. 1324 [*Corn Growers*].

29 *Domtar Inc. v. Quebec (Commission d'appel en matière de lesions professionnelles)*, [1993] 2 S.C.R. 756 [*Domtar*].

30 *CUPE, supra* note 17 at paras. 9-10.

31 *Ibid.* at para. 9.

32 *Ibid.* at para. 12.

33 *Ibid.* at para. 16.

courts should not interfere with the result reached by the administrative decision-maker. The shorthand description of the outcome is that a jurisdictional question is assessed according to a standard of correctness, while questions within jurisdiction are evaluated against a standard of "patent unreasonableness."

CUPE transformed the conceptual basis of substantive review through a reformulation of the institutional relationship between courts and the administrative state. As Dyzenhaus and Fox-Decent observed, however, there is a certain irony in the fact that *CUPE* was decided only a year after *Nicholson*. The latter heralded a new era in procedural review by vastly expanding the range of administrative action subject to judicial scrutiny on grounds of procedural fairness. Meanwhile, *CUPE* signalled a radical break from the existing modes of substantive review by advocating judicial retreat from the interventionism of the past. Interestingly, both *Nicholson* and *CUPE* have been and continue to be hailed by most commentators as progressive and forward-looking judgments.[34]

IV. THE SEQUELS

In the aftermath of *CUPE*, many provincial superior courts seemed to embrace the message of curial deference. The Supreme Court of Canada itself displayed more diffidence in subsequent cases, providing much fodder for academics and much frustration for practitioners. (Had it been otherwise, this chapter would be shorter and simpler.)

For example, in *L'Acadie*, decided a few years after *CUPE*, a unanimous Supreme Court of Canada resiled from the idea that jurisdiction ought to be determined at the outset, and ruled that a jurisdictional question attracting a correctness standard could arise anytime, and could apply not only to interpretation, but also to findings of fact, applications of law to facts, or in the fashioning of a remedy. Elsewhere in the jurisprudence, when addressing the capacity of tribunals to entertain Charter challenges to their constitutive statute, the Supreme Court of Canada described tribunal "jurisdiction over the whole of the matter" as jurisdiction over parties, subject matter, and remedy.[35]

In *Bibeault*,[36] the Supreme Court of Canada demonstrated the putative gap between following the spirit of *CUPE* and abiding by its letter. The case involved a school board that had terminated a contract for janitorial services with a company whose employees were on a lawful strike. The school board issued a tender and contracted with another company. The union representing the striking employees argued that the new employer was bound by the terms of the collective agreement between the previous contractor and its employees, and thus the original union represented the employees of the new contractor in respect of the school board's janitorial services. The Quebec labour statute contained a successor-employer provision stating that "the alienation or operation by another" of an undertaking would not invalidate a collective agreement in existence at the time.[37] The

34 David Dyzenhaus & Evan Fox-Decent, "Rethinking the Process/Substance Distinction: Baker v. Canada" (2001) 51 U.T.L.J. 193 [Dyzenhaus & Fox-Decent].

35 *Cuddy Chicks Ltd. v. Ontario (Labour Relations Board)*, [1991] 2 S.C.R. 5 at para. 12.

36 *Supra* note 15.

37 *Ibid.* at para. 162.

labour commissioner (Bibeault) ruled in favour of the original union. A rival union appealed. The issue whether the provision in question covered non-consensual successions was very contentious in Quebec labour law. By a 7–4 majority, a special panel of the Quebec Labour Court upheld the labour commissioner's order.

While the judgment by Beetz J. certainly cites *CUPE*, it is noteworthy that the word "deference" appears nowhere in the judgment. The task Beetz J. sets for himself is the elaboration of a test for determining what constitutes a jurisdictional question (subject to correctness) and which questions are within a tribunal's jurisdiction (subject to patent unreasonableness). He reiterates the concern with the formalism of the preliminary or collateral question doctrine, but reclaims the animating principle that "any grant of jurisdiction will necessarily include limits to the jurisdiction granted, and any grant of a power remains subject to conditions."[38] Beetz J.'s innovation is to propose a pragmatic and functional analysis for distinguishing between jurisdictional and non-jurisdiction-conferring provisions. The central question posed by the analysis is not whether a question is preliminary or collateral, but "did the legislator intend the question to be within the jurisdiction conferred on the tribunal?"[39]

Responding to this question involves an examination not only of "the wording of the enactment conferring jurisdiction on the administrative tribunal, but the purpose of the statute creating the tribunal, the reasons for its existence, the area of expertise of its members and the nature of the problem before the tribunal."[40] By framing the question in terms of legislative intent, Beetz J. retains the rule of law commitment to parliamentary supremacy and rejects an acontextual interpretation of an isolated provision. Similarly, he cites the expertise of the tribunal as a relevant factor in the analysis, which hearkens back to *CUPE*'s plea for judicial humility. Nevertheless, in his application of the criteria, Beetz J. concludes that "alienation or operation by another" is indeed a jurisdictional question that the commissioner failed to answer correctly.[41]

Rather than arrange the jurisprudence chronologically, we identify different jurisprudential instruments that play out the themes of *CUPE*—and not always in harmony. In the remainder of the chapter, we consider the constitutionalization of judicial review, the expansion of curial deference beyond privative clauses, the methodology of determining how much curial deference is warranted or, in other words, the applicable standard of review. The content given to each standard of review, as well as the actual application of the particular standard of review to the statutory provision at issue is the topic of chapter 9 by Sheila Wildeman.

A. Is Judicial Review Constitutionally Protected?

A central common-law precept of statutory construction is that interpretation expresses the will of the legislator. To the extent that the judiciary accepts the doctrine of parliamentary supremacy, a given interpretation is always defensible insofar as the legislator is free to

38 *Ibid.* at para. 118.

39 *Ibid.* at para. 120.

40 *Ibid.* at para. 123.

41 But compare *Ivanhoe Inc. v. UFCW, Local 500*, [2001] 2 S.C.R. 565, where the Court adopted a standard of patent unreasonableness for the interpretation of the same phrase in a slightly revised statute.

amend the statutory provision if judicial interpretation does not properly capture the intended meaning. In theory, then, a legislator could revise and refine a privative clause in order to better effectuate the ouster of the courts. However, a few years after *CUPE*, the Supreme Court of Canada obviated the possibility of completely insulating provincial administrative bodies from judicial review. In *Crevier v. Attorney-General of Quebec*,[42] the constitutionality of a privative clause in a Quebec statute was challenged on the basis that confiding final and unreviewable decision-making authority to an administrative tribunal would violate s. 96 of the *Constitution Act, 1867*, by depriving s. 96 judges of a quintessential judicial function.[43] Writing for the Court, Laskin C.J.C. upheld the privative clause, but only on the understanding that it did not preclude correctness review on challenges based on division of powers and, by implication, a patent unreasonableness review for matters within jurisdiction. In other words, *Crevier* constitutionalized judicial review for jurisdictional questions, thereby placing the matter beyond the reach of legislative amendment.[44]

In *Bibeault*, Beetz J. remarked in passing that "The role of the superior courts in maintaining the rule of law is so important that it is given constitutional protection,"[45] though one might cavil with the use of the passive voice and point out that the Supreme Court gave itself constitutional protection. In *Royal Oak*, the Supreme Court of Canada was confronted with a privative clause in s. 22 of the *Canada Labour Code* that purported to thwart judicial review "on any ground … including the ground that the … decision … is beyond the jurisdiction of the Board to make … or that, in the course of any proceeding, the Board for any reason exceeded or lost its jurisdiction."[46] The Court did not even pause to contemplate the legislator's intention in granting a tribunal exclusive jurisdiction to determine its own jurisdiction before proceeding to subject the decision to review, albeit on the more deferential standard of patent unreasonableness. As L'Heureux-Dubé J. stated in *Pasienchyk*, "[s]ince, as a matter of constitutional law, a legislature may not, *however clearly it expresses itself*, protect an administrative body from review on matters of jurisdiction, it also cannot be left to decide freely which matters are jurisdictional and which come within the Board's exclusive jurisdiction."[47] In terms of the rule-of-law tension between fidelity to parliamentary intent and the common-law presumption of access to the ordinary courts, suffice to say that the Supreme Court's expansive interpretation of s. 96 of the *Constitution Act, 1867* ensures that the latter trumps the former.

B. Beyond Privative Clauses

The Supreme Court of Canada demonstrated its most enthusiastic embrace of *CUPE* by making "should the court defer?" a question asked not only where statutes contain privative

42 *Supra* note 3.

43 (U.K.), 30 & 31 Vict., c. 3. Section 96 grants jurisdiction over the appointment of superior court judges to the federal government, but has been interpreted to protect "essential" judicial functions associated with superior court judges.

44 See chapter 4, Mary Liston.

45 *Bibeault*, *supra* note 15 at para. 127.

46 *Royal Oak Mines Inc. v. Canada (Labour Relations Board)*, [1996] 1 S.C.R. 369 at para. 30 [*Royal Oak*].

47 *Pasienchyk*, *supra* note 4 at para. 55 (emphasis added).

clauses, but also where statutes contain finality clauses,[48] preserve the option of judicial review, or even provide an appeal to the courts, whereby the courts are formally authorized to substitute their own conclusions of law or even facts.

Pezim v. British Columbia (Superintendent of Brokers)[49] is noteworthy because the issue concerned a question of law, and the enabling statute provided for a right of appeal. Writing for the Court, Iacobucci J.'s judgment offers a time-lapse photograph of the rapid shift in the jurisprudence from the language of "jurisdiction" and "privative clause" to "expertise" and "deference."[50] The issue was whether newly acquired information about asset value constituted a "material change" requiring disclosure. At the outset of his review of principles of judicial review, Iacobucci J. states:

> The central question in ascertaining the standard of review is to determine the legislative intent in conferring jurisdiction on the administrative tribunal. … Included in the analysis is an examination of the tribunal's role or function. Also crucial is whether or not the agency's decisions are protected by a privative clause. Finally, of fundamental importance, is whether or not the question goes to the jurisdiction of the tribunal involved.[51]

A few paragraphs later, Iacobucci J. declares that "even where there is no privative clause and where there is a statutory right of appeal, the concept of the specialization of duties requires that deference be shown to decisions of specialized tribunals on matters which fall squarely within the tribunal's expertise."[52] The presence of a privative clause is apparently not so crucial after all, and the "jurisdictional question" has been supplanted by "expertise" as the key determinant of standard of review (see also *Bradco*).[53]

In the case at bar, there was no question but that the BC Securities Commission had jurisdiction over the parties (members of the board of directors of reporting issuers on the Vancouver Stock Exchange), the subject matter (disclosure of material change), and the remedy (suspension of trading). The Court identified several factors that contributed to the conclusion that the BC Securities Commission was a highly specialized tribunal and the interpretation of material change in the British Columbia *Securities Act*[54] "arguably goes to the core of its regulatory mandate and expertise."[55] The following features of the statutory framework pointed the Court toward greater deference:

- Subject area (securities regulation) is elaborate and complex.
- Commission is granted public interest mandate, plus broad discretion to determine what is in the public interest.

---

48 A finality clause typically states that the decision of the agency is final and binding on the parties, but the clause says nothing about judicial review.

49 [1994] 2 S.C.R. 557 [*Pezim*].

50 *Canada (Director of Investigation and Research) v. Southam Inc.*, [1997] 1 S.C.R. 798 at para. 31 [*Southam*]: "There is no privative clause, and so jurisdiction is not at issue."

51 *Pezim, supra* note 49 at para. 66.

52 *Ibid.* at para. 70.

53 *United Brotherhood of Carpenters and Joiners of America, Local 579 v. Bradco Construction Ltd.*, [1993] 2 S.C.R. 316.

54 S.B.C. 1985, c. 83.

55 *Pezim, supra* note 49 at para. 68.

- Commission has broad powers to administer the statute, including authority to conduct investigations, audits, and hearings and to issue orders.
- Statutory definitions (including material change) are only meaningful within factual regulatory context.
- Agency played a policy development role in addition to adjudicative functions.
- Interpretation of the statutory provision in question "goes to the heart of the regulatory expertise and mandate of the Commission, i.e, regulating the securities markets in the public's interest."[56]

Although the Court concluded that the interpretation of the statutory provision warranted curial deference, the Court conspicuously failed to describe the applicable standard of review as patently unreasonable. Instead, Iacobucci J. simply adverted to the need for considerable deference. Three years later, in *Canada (Director of Investigation and Research) v. Southam Inc.*,[57] Iacobucci J. made explicit what he had only hinted at in *Pezim*—namely, an intermediate standard of review between patent unreasonableness and correctness. He labels the standard "reasonableness *simpliciter*" and declares it (retrospectively) as the standard of review applied in *Pezim*. To understand how the perceived need for a "middle ground" emerged, one can return to the shift in emphasis from privative clauses and relative expertise identified in *Pezim*. A focus on the presence or absence of a privative clause (and the attendant jurisdictional/non-jurisdictional question) corresponds more or less easily to two standards of review embodying the presence or absence of deference. Shifting to an emphasis on relative expertise does not map as easily onto such a stark dichotomy, and this may help to explain the impetus driving the Court to insert reasonableness *simpliciter* into the spectrum.

Southam concerned a finding by the Competition Tribunal that Southam's acquisition of various newspapers within a given advertising market substantially lessened competition. By way of remedy, the tribunal gave Southam the option of divesting itself of one of two community papers. The statute provided for an appeal directly to the Federal Court of Appeal. Two aspects of the tribunal's decision were the subject of appeal: the dimensions of the relevant market within which to assess impact on competition and the remedy of divestment.

Writing for the Court, Iacobucci J. again emphasizes the complexity of the statutory scheme. He describes the objectives of the *Competition Act* as more economic than "strictly legal." Business people and economists possess greater expertise than a "typical judge," who is more "likely to encounter difficulties in understanding the economic and commercial ramifications of the Tribunal's decisions and consequently … less able to secure the fulfillment of the purpose of the *Competition Act* than is the Tribunal."[58] This judicial modesty in relation to certain regulatory domains is presaged in an earlier concurring judgment of L'Heureux-Dubé J. in *National Corn Growers Assn. v. Canada (Import Tribunal)*, where she identifies "labour relations, telecommunications, financial markets and international economic relations" as examples where courts "may simply not be as well equipped as

56 *Ibid.* at para. 86.

57 *Southam, supra* note 50.

58 *Ibid.* at para. 49.

administrative tribunals or agencies to deal with issues which Parliament has chosen to regulate through bodies exercising delegated power."[59]

Turning to the specific composition of the tribunal, Iacobucci J. observes that the statute requires at least four members to be judges of the Federal Court, Trial Division and eight lay members to be drawn from recommendations made by experts in the field of economics, commerce, industry, and public affairs. Iacobucci J. infers from the preponderance of lay members that non-legal acumen is more important than legal expertise, although he notes that the unusual requirement that the tribunal include judges, and that judicial members have exclusive jurisdiction over questions of law, indicates Parliament's opinion that "questions of competition law are not altogether beyond the ken of judges."[60]

The characterization of the issues on appeal played an important role in the court's assessment of the standard of review. The parties agreed on the economic principles governing determination of the size of the advertising market, but disagreed on whether the tribunal had ignored certain relevant evidence in making the actual determination. Upon reviewing the tribunal's reasons, Iacobucci J. concludes that the tribunal had not ignored the evidence in question, but that the dispute really concerned the weight attributed to certain evidence. In Iacobucci J.'s view, this was not a question of law, but rather a question of mixed law and fact because it involved the application of law to facts. With minimal analysis, Iacobucci J. arrived at the similar view that the remedial issue is a mixed question of fact and law.

Having identified the various factors pertinent to the standard of review, Iacobucci J. concludes that that some factors point toward deference, and some away from it:

> Several considerations counsel deference: the fact that the dispute is over a question of mixed law and fact; the fact that the purpose of the *Competition Act* is broadly economic, and so is better served by the exercise of economic judgment; and the fact that the application of principles of competition law falls squarely within the area of the Tribunal's expertise. Other considerations counsel a more exacting form of review: the existence of an unfettered statutory right of appeal from decisions of the Tribunal and the presence of judges on the Tribunal. Because there are indications both ways, the proper standard of review falls somewhere between the ends of the spectrum. Because the expertise of the Tribunal, which is the most important consideration, suggests deference, a posture more deferential than exacting is warranted.[61]

The middle ground is, of course, reasonableness *simpliciter*: "An unreasonable decision is one that, in the main, is not supported by any reasons that can stand up to a somewhat probing examination." This examination entails an inquiry into the "evidentiary foundation or the logical process by which conclusions are sought to be drawn from it."[62] Although Iacobucci J. is not entirely clear on this point, he seems to regard the most deferential standard of patent unreasonableness as appropriate only in the presence of a privative clause where intervention must be justified by resort to jurisdictional analysis.

---

59 *Corn Growers*, *supra* note 28 at para. 80.

60 *Southam*, *supra* note 50 at para. 53.

61 *Ibid.* at para. 54.

62 *Ibid.* at para. 56.

The insertion of an intermediate standard of review did little to add predictability or determinacy to this area of administrative law. Moreover, some contended that if three standards were better than two, four standards must be better than three. Others suggested that the reasonableness standard ought to be applied flexibly—sometimes closer to correctness, sometimes closer to patent unreasonableness—depending on the balance of factors for and against deference in the particular case. The Supreme Court of Canada rejected both propositions in *Law Society of New Brunswick v. Ryan*.[63]

V. THE STORY SO FAR: PUSHPANATHAN v. CANADA

Shortly after *Southam*, the Supreme Court of Canada took the opportunity to consolidate and summarize the factors to be taken into account in determining the appropriate standard of review. *Pushpanathan v. Canada (Minister of Citizenship and Immigration)*[64] concerned the interpretation of a provision in the *Immigration Act*[65] (incorporating article 1F(c) of the *UN Convention Relating to the Status of Refugees*) that excludes from refugee status those persons "guilty of acts contrary to the purposes and principles of the United Nations." Pushpanathan had made a refugee claim in Canada. Before his claim was heard, he was convicted in Canada of the offence of conspiracy to traffic in a narcotic. He was subsequently excluded from refugee protection under article 1F(c) on the basis of his conviction. The issue in the case concerned whether "acts contrary to the purposes and principles of the United Nations" included a criminal conviction for drug trafficking in the country of asylum.[66] A distinctive feature of the *Immigration Act* was the mechanism for judicial review. The statute contained no privative clause or right of appeal. Instead, judicial review could only commence with leave of a judge of the Federal Court, and no reasons were required where leave was denied. If leave was granted and the case heard, the losing party could only appeal to the Federal Court of Appeal if the trial judge certified "a serious question of general importance."

Writing for the Court, Bastarache J. organizes the factors relevant to standard of review into four categories: (1) privative clause, (2) expertise, (3) purpose of the act as a whole and of the provision in particular, and (4) nature of the problem (question of law, fact, or mixed law and fact). Jurisprudence since *Pushpanathan* has routinely relied on these four categories, and surveys of pre-*Pushpanathan* jurisprudence also reorganize the pragmatic and functional analyses to align with them.

Although the Court identifies four separate factors, arguably there are only two ingredients in the deference calculus—that is, the legislator's direct or indirect pronouncement about judicial supervision (privative clause, finality clause, common-law judicial review, statutory judicial review, appeal) and the reviewing court's assessment of the agency's relative expertise. The inquiry into statutory purpose and nature of the problem treats these factors more or less as specific indicia of expertise. In *Pushpanathan* itself, the Court ad-

63 [2003] 1 S.C.R. 247 [*Ryan*].

64 [1998] 1 S.C.R. 982 [*Pushpanathan*].

65 R.S.C. 1985, c. I-2.

66 *Pushpanathan*, *supra* note 64 at para. 22.

mits that "purpose and expertise often overlap,"[67] and that the basis for less curial deference on general questions of law than questions of fact relates to the relative expertise of courts versus agencies.[68] Ultimately, the entire test is rationalized as an exercise in discerning legislative intent: did the legislator intend that the court defer to the agency with respect to the disputed issue? The following survey summarizes the meaning ascribed to the four elements of the *Pushpanathan* test and provides examples of their application in various cases, bearing in mind the substantial overlap just described.

A. Privative Clause

Privative clauses are not all identical, though the differences between them can be overstated by courts. In any event, as La Forest J. unhelpfully stated in *Ross v. New Brunswick Human Rights Commission* "there are privative clauses and there are privative clauses."[69] Statutory language that arguably conveys a message of judicial restraint includes a provision that the action of the agency shall not be questioned, reviewed, appealed, or otherwise set aside by any court; a grant of exclusive jurisdiction over all matters, possibly even over jurisdiction or arbitrability; a declaration that the outcome of the agency is final and binding on all parties. Finality clauses typically declare only that the outcome be final and binding on all parties. A statute may otherwise provide for judicial review or for an appeal on the merits. Where the statute is silent about judicial review, the common-law bases of substantive review (error or law, finding of fact in the absence of evidence, abuse of discretion) will apply. Alternatively, the grounds of judicial review may be set out in a general statute applicable to the agency (for example, *Federal Courts Act*, British Columbia *Judicial Review Procedure Act*, Ontario *Judicial Review Procedure Act*).

Under the pragmatic and functional test, the presence of a privative clause weighs in favour of curial deference. It never plays a determinative role, however, because the designation of a matter as a jurisdictional question (correctness standard) or as a question within jurisdiction (patently unreasonable standard) must await the outcome of the court's assessment of expertise according to the remaining three factors. The court often says that a privative clause's effect can be outweighed by the assessment of expertise; the court never says that a privative clause can outweigh expertise.

A finality clause inclines toward curial deference, but not as strongly as a privative clause. The availability of judicial review is more or less neutral with respect to its message regarding deference, while the presence of an appeal provision tilts against curial deference. As with the privative clause, however, the effect of an appeal provision can be outweighed by the assessment of expertise (as it was in *Southam*).

The judicial review provisions in *Pushpanathan* are distinctive. Section 67 of the *Immigration Act* granted the Refugee Division "sole and exclusive jurisdiction to ... determine all questions of law and fact, including questions of jurisdiction."[70] Section 82.1 of the

67 *Ibid.* at para. 36.

68 *Ibid.* at para. 37.

69 [1996] 1 S.C.R. 825 at para. 26.

70 *Pushpanathan*, *supra* note 64 at para. 39.

Immigration Act grants the Federal Court gatekeeping power over judicial review. Leave is required to seek judicial review, and the Federal Court need not provide reasons for denying leave, nor can an applicant appeal from a decision to deny leave. Furthermore, an appeal from the Federal Court to the Federal Court of Appeal is only possible if the trial judge certifies a "question of general importance" (s. 83(1)). In *Pushpanathan*, the Court considered that the privative clause (s. 67), "such as it is, is superseded with respect to questions of 'general importance.'"[71] Indeed, the Court asserts that "s. 83(1) would be incoherent if the standard of review were anything other than correctness. The key to the legislative intention as to the standard of review is the use of the words 'a serious question of *general* importance.'"[72] (The analysis blends into the nature of the problem, discussed further below). In *Baker*, decided a year later, no provision resembling a privative clause protected the exercise of discretion by the Minister's delegate. Here the Court reiterated that s. 83(1) indicated less deference, but quickly added that "this is only one of the factors involved in determining the standard of review,"[73] and ultimately arrived at the intermediate standard of reasonableness *simpliciter*.

B. Expertise

The case law is clear that relative expertise is the most important factor in determining the standard of review. In *Pushpanathan*, the Court identifies three steps in evaluating expertise: "the court must characterize the expertise of the tribunal in question; it must consider its own expertise relative to that of the tribunal; and it must identify the nature of the specific issue before the administrative decision-maker relative to this expertise."[74] Where the tribunal possesses "broad relative expertise" that it brings to bear "in some degree" on the interpretation of highly general questions, the Court may show considerable deference, despite the generality of the issue.[75] Such was the case in *Southam* ("material change") and *Corn Growers* (interpretation of a treaty provision), where the Court applied the standard of patent unreasonableness in view of the tribunal's specialized expertise. Unfortunately, it is difficult to anticipate when the Court will valorize the agency's expertise as relevant to the interpretation of a question of law, and when it will discount it.

When describing the broad expertise of an agency, the Court attends to the agency's composition and specialized knowledge in comparison to a court. Evidence of distinctive expertise may come from statutory criteria for appointment (for example, qualifications, length of term, and security of tenure), a policy-making function, or a "non-judicial means of implementing the Act."[76] The following extract from the majority judgment in *Pasiechyk v. Saskatchewan (Workers' Compensation Board)* addresses several of these factors in the context of the Saskatchewan Workers' Compensation Board. Note that the board exer-

71 *Ibid.* at para. 49.

72 *Ibid.* at para. 43 (emphasis added by the Court).

73 *Baker*, *supra* note 2 at para. 58.

74 *Pushpanathan*, *supra* note 64 at para. 32.

75 *Ibid.* at para. 34.

76 *Ibid.* at para. 32.

cises no policy-making function and many of its members are "at-pleasure" appointments. Nevertheless, the Court acknowledges the extensive expertise of the board:

> At the time that the application under s. 168 was heard, the board was composed of at least three members appointed by the Lieutenant Governor in Council (s. 13(1)). The chairman was appointed from among the members by the Lieutenant Governor in Council (s. 14(1)). The members held office at pleasure, except for the chairman, who was appointed for five years and was eligible for reappointment (s. 15). As it stands today, the board has a maximum of five full-time members, including a chairperson and an even number of members, half of whom represent employers and half of whom represent workers (s. 13(1)). The employer representatives are chosen from a list of names submitted by employer associations, and the worker representatives are chosen from a list of names submitted by labour organizations (s. 13(1.1)). The chairperson holds office for five years and may be reappointed; the other members hold office for four years and may be reappointed (s. 15). In addition to the specific powers described above, the Act imposes on the board the general duty of treating workers and their dependants in a fair and reasonable manner (s. 21.1(1)). The board is assisted in its work by a large professional staff headed by an executive director who is the chief administrative officer of the board. The board also establishes and publishes policy directives (s. 21.1(2)).
>
> The composition, tenure, and powers of the board demonstrate that it has very considerable expertise in dealing with all aspects of the workers' compensation system. Not only does the board have day-to-day expertise in handling claims for compensation, in setting assessment rates and promoting workplace safety; but it also has expertise in ensuring that the purposes of the Act are not defeated.[77]

In terms of broad expertise, bodies that deal with economic, financial, or technical matters seem to sit at the apex. Members of securities commissions, international trade tribunals, telecommunications bodies, etc. have all been recognized by the Court as possessing experience, expertise, and specialized knowledge that courts lack.

Labour boards, often protected by privative clauses, are in some ways the paradigmatic example of expert administrative tribunals. Indeed, the Court typically acknowledges their specialized knowledge and expertise in relation to industrial relations.[78] Yet labour boards tend not to benefit as consistently from curial deference as some other bodies. Stricter standards of review are usually justified on the grounds that their expertise does not extend to the nature of the problem under review (see below). Labour arbitrators are considered less expert than labour boards (even though the same people often engage in both activities), because arbitrators are usually appointed by the parties on an ad hoc basis, and the arbitrator's task is confined to the interpretation and application of a particular collective agreement, rather than the administration of the entire regime of industrial relations. The ad hoc nature of the appointment usually counts against the expertise of certain human rights tribunals as well. More broadly, the majority of the Supreme Court of Canada regards the

77 *Pasienchyk, supra* note 4 at paras. 37-38.

78 See, for example, *Canada (Attorney General) v. Public Service Alliance of Canada*, [1993] 1 S.C.R. 941; *Ivanhoe Inc. v. UFCW, Local 500, supra* note 41; *Royal Oak, supra* note 46; *Toronto (City) Board of Education v. O.S.S.T.F., District 15*, [1997] 1 S.C.R. 487.

expertise of human rights tribunals and commissions as relatively weak. The divergent judgments of La Forest J. (concurring) and L'Heureux-Dubé J. (dissenting) in *Canada (Attorney General) v. Mossop*[79] illustrate the point.

The issue in the case was whether "family status," a prohibited ground of discrimination under s. 3(1) of the *Canadian Human Rights Act*,[80] included a same-sex couple. The majority of the Supreme Court of Canada determined, contrary to the Canadian Human Rights Tribunal, that family status did not comprehend same-sex relationships. La Forest J. acknowledged that courts occasionally defer to tribunals on questions of law in the absence of a privative clause in recognition of relative expertise. However, a human rights tribunal was not analogous to a labour relation board. First, while a human rights commission engages in a variety of educational, policy-making, advisory, and investigatory roles, these functions do not confer any entitlement to deference on the tribunal in its adjudicative function.[81] Secondly, the tribunals are themselves ad hoc, like labour arbitrators, but even less deserving of deference than arbitrators.[82] Labour arbitrators are selected by the parties, often have jurisdiction over arbitrability, and operate within the narrow confines of a collective agreement entered into by the parties and only binding on them. In contrast, a human rights tribunal imposes decisions on the parties "and has direct influence on society at large in relation to basic social values."[83] La Forest J. then defines the ambit of human rights tribunals' superior expertise as "fact finding and adjudication in a human rights context," as distinct from "concepts of statutory interpretation and general legal reasoning."[84]

L'Heureux-Dubé J. offers a different assessment, one which does not distinguish between the commission and the tribunal:

> The Act, as may be seen, endows the Commission with a wide range of powers and duties. The Commission must: hear and determine complaints regarding discriminatory practices; develop and conduct information programs to foster public understanding of the Act; undertake research programs which relate to its duties and functions; maintain liaisons with other bodies to foster common policies and practices; carry out studies concerning human rights; review regulations and other instruments made pursuant to Acts of Parliament; and endeavour through persuasion, publicity and other means to discourage or reduce discriminatory practices. The breadth of these powers points in the direction of a more deferential approach.[85]
>
> ...
>
> As for the Commission itself, Parliament unquestionably intended to create a highly specialized administrative body, one with sufficient expertise to review Acts of Parliament and, as specifically provided for in the Act, to offer advice and make recommendations to the Minister

---

79 [1993] 1 S.C.R. 554 [*Mossop*].

80 R.S.C. 1985, c. H-6.

81 Note that human rights tribunals are required to be independent of the commission for reasons of bias, so it would be impossible for tribunals to perform these other functions anyway. See *MacBain v. Lederman* (1985), 22 D.L.R. (4th) 119 (F.C.A.).

82 The Canadian Human Rights Tribunal is now a permanent tribunal and does not rely on ad hoc appointments.

83 *Mossop*, *supra* note 79 at para. 46.

84 *Ibid.*

85 *Ibid.* at para. 88.

> of Justice. In the exercise of its powers and functions, the Commission would inevitably accumulate expertise and specialized understanding of human rights issues, as well as a body of governing jurisprudence. The work of the Commission and its tribunals involves the consideration and balancing of a variety of social needs and goals, and requires sensitivity, understanding, and expertise.[86]

L'Heureux-Dubé J. went on to determine that other factors pointed toward a deferential standard of review, and that the tribunal's interpretation of family status was not patently unreasonable. The majority determined the appropriate standard to be correctness and found the interpretation wrong. McLachlan and Cory JJ. (dissenting) agreed with La Forest J. on the correctness standard of review, but found the tribunal's interpretation to be correct.

To the extent that expertise is the overriding factor in the pragmatic and functional test, it is perhaps unsurprising that the majority Court resists deferring to human rights tribunals. Rights adjudication lies at the heart of the judicial function and institutional self-understanding. The Court appears to find it difficult to concede anything but a narrow compass of relative expertise to another body charged with tasks that so closely resemble those performed by courts.

On the other hand, in *Law Society of New Brunswick v. Ryan*, a case involving the sanction for misconduct imposed on a miscreant lawyer, the Court went to some length to defend the superior expertise of the Law Society's professional discipline committee. Unlike a securities commission or a competition tribunal, the expertise of a law society discipline committee could hardly be described as beyond the ken of most judges. Nevertheless, the majority explained that practising lawyers "may be more intimately acquainted with the ways that these [professional] standards play out in the everyday practice of law than judges who no longer take part in the solicitor-client relationship."[87] To the extent that at least one member of the committee is a layperson, the fact that the member is not a lawyer may place him or her "in a better position to understand how particular forms of conduct and choice of sanctions would affect the general public's perception of the profession and confidence in the administration of justice."[88] Ultimately, "owing to its composition and its familiarity with the particular issue of imposing a sanction for professional misconduct in a variety of settings, the Discipline Committee arguably has more expertise than courts on the sanction to apply to the misconduct."[89] The Court eventually decided on the intermediate standard of reasonableness.

Decision-making bodies staffed by elected officials have proven problematic subjects for the evaluation of expertise (and for the application of the pragmatic and functional test as a whole). In *Baker*, the Court dealt with the humanitarian and compassionate discretion that was statutorily conferred on the Minister of Citizenship and Immigration, but delegated to a civil servant. The Court found that the "fact that the formal decision-maker is the Minister is a factor militating in favour of deference. The Minister has some expertise relative to courts in immigration matters, particularly with respect to when exemptions should be

86 *Ibid.* at para. 90.

87 *Ryan*, *supra* note 63 at para. 31.

88 *Ibid.* at para. 32.

89 *Ibid.* at para. 34.

given from the requirements that normally apply."[90] The basis of deference is unclear, given the acknowledgment that the Minister is formally the decision-maker, but the actual decisions are made by a delegate. Is it because a minister is deemed expert in whatever portfolio he or she is assigned? Is it because the delegate is presumed to have expertise acquired through repeated processing of many humanitarian and compassionate applications? Is it because the minister is an elected official, and the grant of discretion to an elected official signals an entitlement to apply "political" factors, an activity in which politicians are more expert than judges?

In *Chamberlain v. Surrey School District No. 36*,[91] a local school board composed of elected trustees passed a resolution against authorizing three books depicting same-sex parented families to be used in the classroom. One challenge to the resolution was that the board acted outside its mandate under the *School Act* in passing the resolution. In other words, it exceeded its jurisdiction. The majority of the Court applied the pragmatic and functional test to arrive at a reasonableness standard of review, and found the resolution unreasonable. Writing for the majority, McLachlin C.J.C. described the board as expert in balancing "the interests of different groups, such as parents with widely differing moral outlooks, and children from many types of families," and acknowledged that as locally elected representatives, the board is better placed to understand community concerns than the court."[92] However, McLachlin C.J.C. went on to find that because the decision in question "has a human rights dimension" in which courts are more expert than administrative bodies, less deference is owed. Writing in dissent, Gonthier J. commented that although the board's decision clearly had a human rights aspect, "courts should be reluctant to assume that they possess greater expertise than administrative decision makers with respect to all questions having a human rights component,"[93] especially in the context of local democracy. LeBel J.'s dissent challenges the premise that expertise ought to be the basis of curial deference toward elected officials in their legislative (as opposed to adjudicative) capacity. He notes that in judicial review of municipal actors, "our Court has always focused on whether the action in question was authorized, not on whether it was reasonable."[94] In LeBel J.'s view, the animating principle is the separation of the judiciary and representative government and the need to protect each from illegitimate interference by the other. Application of the pragmatic and functional test, with the possible result of a reasonableness standard,

> fails to give due recognition to the board's role as a local government body accountable to the electorate. As long as it acts pursuant to its statutory powers, it is carrying out the will of the community it serves and in general is answerable to the community, not the courts. But if it purports to exercise powers it does not have, its actions are invalid.[95]

---

90 *Baker*, *supra* note 2 at para. 59.

91 [2002] 4 S.C.R. 710 [*Chamberlain*].

92 *Ibid.* at para. 10.

93 *Ibid.* at para. 143.

94 *Ibid.* at para. 197.

95 *Ibid.* at para. 201.

One way of understanding LeBel J.'s position is to posit that elected officials merit deference because they represent the will of the majority, not because of any expertise they may possess. The ultra vires/intra vires dichotomy is analogous to the inside/outside jurisdiction dichotomy, but is even more deferential to matters deemed intra vires. In certain respects, the disagreement between the majority and LeBel J. on this issue mirrors a similar debate about the application of the doctrine of reasonable apprehension of bias. Crudely put, it surfaces the question about the role of judicial review versus the ballot box in making elected officials accountable.

Although the Supreme Court clearly prioritizes expertise in formulating the standard of review, its inquiry is limited to the statutory role of the administrative actor, not to the particular individual occupying it. Courts will glean evidence of expertise from statute and surrounding context, but will not scrutinize the qualifications, competence, training, or experience of the specific decision-maker. Nor does administrative law provide a direct mechanism for imposing upon the state an obligation to adopt a merit-based appointment process for non-elected decision-makers. Consider the *Back to School Act* (Toronto and Windsor) 2001,[96] wherein the statute empowered the Minister of Labour to appoint as arbitrator a person who "has no previous experience as an arbitrator," and who is not "mutually acceptable to both trade unions and employers."[97] Even the doctrine on independence of decision-makers adopts fairly narrow and formal criteria for assessing independence from inappropriate government influence on decision-makers. In other words, independence identifies formal indicia of susceptibility to government influence, and standard of review examines formal indicia of expertise, but neither address actual competence. One might consider whether merit and competence ought to matter to the courts and, if so, how these concerns could be addressed in administrative law.[98] Is the standard of review a satisfactory proxy?

C. Purpose of the Statute as a Whole and the Provision in Particular

What aspect of statutory purpose is relevant to the standard of review? In *Pushpanathan*, the Court distilled prior jurisprudence into the following proposition: Where the statute and/or provision can be described as "polycentric," meaning that it engages a balancing of multiple interests, constituencies, and factors, contains a significant policy element, and articulates the legal standards in vague or open-textured language, more judicial restraint is warranted. Disputes that more closely resemble the bipolar model of opposition between parties and interests justify less curial deference. The rationale is that judges have less relative expertise in the former and more relative expertise in the latter.

At one point, the possibility existed that the Court would apply a correctness standard to any provision that appeared to directly delimit parties, subject matter, or remedy, the traditional indicia of jurisdiction in an adjudicative context.[99] However, the Court is no longer

---

96 S.O. 2001, c. 1, cited in *C.U.P.E. v. Ontario (Minister of Labour)*, [2003] 1 S.C.R. 539 at para. 81 [*Retired Judges*].

97 *Back to School Act*, *ibid.*, s. 11(4).

98 See *Retired Judges*, *supra* note 96.

99 See, for example, *Syndicat des Employés de Production du Québec et de l'Acadie v. Canada*, [1989] 2 S.C.R. 879.

wedded to this, and has ruled, for example, that the remedial power of labour tribunals is subject to the most deferential standard of patent unreasonableness.[100]

This development bodes well for the Court's commitment to curial deference, although it does strain the alleged convergence of the vocabularies of jurisdiction and standard of review. In *Pushpanathan*, the Court asserted that "[i]t should be understood that a question which "goes to jurisdiction" is simply descriptive of a provision for which the proper standard of review is correctness, based upon the outcome of the pragmatic and functional analysis."[101] Recognizing that provisions determining parties, subject matter, and remedy can indeed attract maximum deference suggests that perhaps "jurisdictional question" and "no deference" are not entirely synonymous.

D. The Nature of the Problem: Law or Fact?

Appellate and judicial review jurisprudence has long divided legal issues into questions of law, questions of mixed law and fact, and questions of fact. In administrative law, these conveniently map onto the spectrum of deference as less deference, neutral, and more deference, in accordance with courts' declining relative expertise: "Without an implied or express legislative intent to the contrary … , legislatures should be assumed to have left highly generalized propositions of law to courts."[102]

The characterization of a matter as a question of law or as a question of mixed law/fact is not straightforward,[103] and is complicated by the fact that characterizing an issue as a question of law does not necessarily preclude the possibility that the tribunal may possess greater expertise than a court in interpreting it, especially if the court otherwise regards the agency as highly expert and the legal question relates to interpretation of a provision in the agency's enabling statute.[104]

One clue that judges look for is the extent to which the determination will have precedential value in subsequent cases. The greater the precedential impact, the greater the assessment of expertise tilts toward the courts. The labelling of the issue as a "pure" question of law (*Barrie Utilities*), a "concept derived from the common law or Civil Code" (*Bibeault*), a general question of law (*Mossop*, family status), not scientific or technical (*Mattel*), or a human rights issue (*Pushpanathan*, *Chamberlain*) is a reliable signal that the Court has concluded that the legal issue is one in which it is more expert than the agency. In *Pushpanathan*, as well as in *Baker* and other immigration cases, the Court relied on the unique provision in the *Immigration Act* (now the *Immigration and Refugee Protection Act*) whereby a Federal Court judge must certify a "serious question of general importance"[105] (s. 83(1)) in order for the litigants to proceed to the Federal Court of Appeal. The statutory

100 See, for example, *Royal Oak*, *supra* note 46; *CUPE Local 301 v. Montreal (City)*, [1997] 1 S.C.R. 793. See also *Pasienchyk*, *supra* note 4 for the patent unreasonableness standard with respect to "employer" (parties).

101 *Pushpanathan*, *supra* note 64 at para. 28.

102 *Ibid.* at para. 38.

103 *Southam*, *supra* note 50 at paras. 34-35.

104 See *ibid.*

105 *Pushpanathan*, *supra* note 64 at para. 87.

requirement of generality and serious importance (as determined by the Federal Court judge) allowed the Court to declare that "s. 83(1) would be incoherent if the standard of review were anything other than correctness."[106]

What is less clear is how the Court arrives at the designation in a given case. Every statutory provision must be construed and applied in the specific context of the legislative scheme administered by the agency or tribunal, with a view to fulfilling the purposes of the statute. Agencies bring a unique awareness of the practical and "field" implications of one interpretive choice versus another. Sometimes, this suffices to ascribe to the agency relative expertise in the interpretation of its own statute, but sometimes it does not. In *Council of Canadians with Disabilities*,[107] the Court dealt with a determination by the Canadian Transportation Act that authorized the Canadian Transportation Agency to determine whether there is an "undue obstacle to the mobility of persons" on VIA Rail trains, and to order an appropriate remedy if such obstacles exist. The agency found that VIA Rail's newly acquired trains created undue obstacles for wheelchair-bound passengers and ordered VIA Rail to retrofit some of the new cars to make them accessible. VIA Rail sought judicial review, and the standard of review was one of the issues before the Court.

Writing for the majority, Abella J. rejected the claim that the human rights dimension of interpreting and applying the provision justified review on a standard of correctness:

> This unduly narrows the characterization of what the Agency was called upon to decide and disregards how inextricably interwoven the human rights and transportation issues are. Parliament gave the Agency a specific mandate to determine how to render transportation systems more accessible for persons with disabilities. … The *Canada Transportation Act* is highly specialized regulatory legislation with a strong policy focus. The scheme and object of the Act are the oxygen the Agency breathes. When interpreting the Act, including its human rights components, the Agency is expected to bring its transportation policy knowledge and experience to bear on its interpretations of its assigned statutory mandate.[108]

Abella J. echoed concerns once expressed about the formalism of pre-*CUPE* jurisprudence when she remarked that "by attributing a jurisdiction-limiting label, such as 'statutory interpretation' or 'human rights' to what is in reality a function assigned and properly exercised under the enabling legislation, a tribunal's expertise is made to defer to a court's generalism rather than the other way around."[109]

The four dissenting judges asserted that the issues at stake in the case were "pure questions of law," concerning jurisdiction and human rights, with important precedential value, and therefore no deference was owed on any component of the agency's decision. At present, one can safely say only that the sole unwavering rule that the Court always follows is that a direct Charter challenge merits no deference and always attracts review on a standard of correctness.

106 *Ibid.* at para. 43.

107 *Council of Canadians with Disabilities v. VIA Rail Canada Inc.*, 2007 SCC 15 [*Council of Canadians with Disabilities*].

108 *Ibid.* at paras. 97-98.

109 *Ibid.* at para. 96.

As noted earlier, the Court attaches weight to the precedential value of a decision in characterizing a matter as a general question of law. However, the Court has rejected the assertion that the precedential value of resolving inconsistency within or between tribunals constitutes an independent basis for adopting a correctness standard of review,[110] unless the divergent decisions create an operational conflict, whereby compliance with one order would necessitate violation of the other.[111] A significant concern for the Court in *Domtar* was the risk that real or apparent inconsistencies within or between tribunal decisions might become a pretext for undermining fidelity to the principles underlying curial deference. The Court also adverted to internal mechanisms available to tribunals to encourage consistency, and downplayed the virtues of consistency in relation to other important values served by deference. As Laverne Jacobs discusses in chapter 6, internal mechanisms encouraging conformity must balance consistency against the independence of decision-makers. If you were a decision-maker in a tribunal, would you rather that an inconsistent interpretation of a statutory provision among your peers be resolved by the courts or through an internal mechanism? What factors might affect your preference?

VI. COMING ATTRACTIONS

A. Disaggregation

Where a judicial review application raises several discrete issues, it seems uncomplicated to calibrate the standard of review separately for each issue. Where a statutory provision implicates a Charter right, the task of subjecting the Charter determination to correctness scrutiny and possibly applying a different standard to other elements of the decision becomes problematic.[112] The same may apply where the decision requires interpretation of an extrinsic statute. Beyond these exceptional cases, there seems to be little consensus. For example, in the *Retired Judges* case, Binnie J. states that the "court's task on judicial review is not to isolate … issues and subject each of them to differing standards of review."[113] In *Council of Canadians with Disabilities*, the dissenting judges relied on *Canada (Deputy Minister of National Revenue) v. Mattel Canada Inc.*,[114] in support of the opposite proposition—namely, that "standard of review jurisprudence recognizes that segmentation of a decision is appropriate in order to ascertain the nature of the questions before the tribunal and the degree of deference to be accorded to the tribunal's decisions on those questions."[115] In *Lévis (City) v. Fraternité des policières et policiers provinciaux du Québec*, a

110 *Domtar*, *supra* note 29.

111 *British Columbia Telephone Co. v. Shaw Cable Systems (B.C.) Ltd.*, [1995] 2 S.C.R. 739.

112 See, for example, *Suresh v. Canada (Minister of Citizenship & Immigration)*, [2002] 1 S.C.R. 3, where the Charter issue whether deportation to torture violates s. 7 was reviewable on a standard of correctness, while the determination of whether a refugee was also a threat to national security (thereby opening the door to deportation), and whether the refugee actually faced a substantial risk of torture if removed, were subject to maximum curial deference.

113 *Retired Judges*, *supra* note 96 at para. 97.

114 [2001] 2 S.C.R. 100.

115 *Council of Canadians with Disabilities*, *supra* note 107 at para. 278. See also *Lévis (City) v. Fraternité des policières et policiers provinciaux du Québec*, 2007 SCC 14 at para. 19 [*Lévis (City)*].

case where the majority endorsed differentiated standards of review, Abella J. (concurring) warned of "a danger that the routine segmentation of [an arbitrator's mandate relating to discipline and sanctioning] leads to an unduly interventionist approach more reminiscent of "the wrong question" or "preliminary [or] collateral matter" doctrines found in cases like *Anisminic* ... and *Metropolitan Life*, than of the more deferential approach applied by Dickson J. in [*CUPE*]."[116]

The Court has yet to tackle the issue by identifying the rationale for preferring one approach over the other, or developing criteria (beyond those described above) for distinguishing between decisions that warrant disaggregation from those that do not. The issue is particularly salient where the decision in question involves the exercise of discretion: on the one hand, it seems inimical to the very idea of discretion to assert a standard of correctness, because discretionary decisions *ex hypothesi* have no uniquely correct answer. On the other hand, if the exercise of discretion implicates individual human rights, it may be difficult for a court to resist (or justify) anything less. Perhaps this helps explain the apparent discrepancy in *Baker*, where the Court arrived at a reasonableness standard in principle, yet arguably applied a stricter review in practice when it came to the best interests of the child.[117]

B. Is Three a Crowd?

Ever since *Southam* ushered in the intermediate standard of review—reasonableness *simpliciter*—commentators, practitioners, and even some lower court judges have complained about the indeterminacy, impracticability, unpredictability, and sheer confusion generated by three standards of review. In his concurring judgment in *Toronto (City) v. CUPE, Local 79*,[118] LeBel J. canvassed the widespread discontent with the direction of Supreme Court jurisprudence. He provided a thorough and thoughtful analysis of the sordid history of the application of the three standards and issued an eloquent plea for the abandonment of three standards in favour of a return to "a two standard system of review, correctness and a revised unified standard of reasonableness."[119] A fuller elaboration of what led to LeBel J.'s "cri de coeur" will follow in the next chapter by Sheila Wildeman. At present, however, it is important to note that in *Council of Canadians with Disabilities* a 5–4 majority of the Court blended reasonableness *simpliciter* and patent unreasonableness into a single standard of "demonstrably unreasonable."[120] This move was accomplished in three sentences that cited LeBel J.'s prior concurring judgment, acknowledged the "conceptual challenge" of distinguishing between the two standards, and declared that both share a common focus on whether the impugned decision is "such a departure from what is rational, as to be unsustainable."[121] The dissenting judges tersely objected that "[i]n an appropriate

116 *Lévis (City)*, *supra* note 115 at para. 111.

117 See the analyses of *Baker* by Colleen Flood, Grant Huscroft, and Evan Fox-Decent in chapters 1, 5, and 7 respectively.

118 [2003] 3 S.C.R. 77.

119 *Ibid.* at para. 134.

120 *Council of Canadians with Disabilities*, *supra* note 107 at para. 102.

121 *Ibid.*

case—of which this is not one," the Court may wish to revisit the wisdom of three standards of review." Until then, "we do not see the need to add to the lexicon of standard of review terminology."[122] Stay tuned.

C. Converging Tests?

The pragmatic and functional test is not the only instance where a formalist methodology of bright lines and either/or propositions has given way to a balancing of multiple factors and a spectrum of possibilities. The Supreme Court of Canada's procedural fairness jurisprudence also reveals a similar shift. At present, the test for the content of procedural fairness lists five factors that are relevant to determining what procedures are required by the duty of fairness in the particular case. The points of intersection with the pragmatic and functional test are noteworthy. Both list the nature of the decision, the statutory scheme, and expertise as relevant.[123] While the Court has never explicitly resiled from the principle that procedural fairness is reviewable on a standard of correctness, *Baker* instructs that the duty of fairness "should also take into account and respect the choices of procedure made by the agency itself, particularly when the statute leaves to the decision-maker the ability to choose its own procedures, or when the agency has an expertise in determining what procedures are appropriate in the circumstances."[124]

One factor that figures prominently in the *Baker* test for the content of procedures that is conspicuously absent from the pragmatic and functional test is the "importance of the decision to the individual or individuals affected."[125] One might contend, of course, that the importance attached to human rights, especially Charter rights, tacitly informs the staunch refusal to defer on these issues. What do you think the consequences would be for adherence to the idea of curial deference if the impact of the decision were imported explicitly and generically into the pragmatic and functional test? Does the importance of the decision weigh against curial deference? If so, why? Is it more salient when the decision affects an identifiable individual or group? Is it because judges are relatively more expert in making important decisions? Certain types of decisions, such as refugee determination, access to scarce medical resources or welfare, or professional discipline are obviously very important to the individuals affected, and administrative actors are tasked with making these deci-

---

122 *Ibid.* at para. 279.

123 *Retired Judges*, *supra* note 96 at para. 103.

124 *Baker*, *supra* note 2 at para. 27. The Supreme Court has never fully articulated why procedures should always be subject to correctness review. Notably, in *Nicholson*, Laskin J. did not actually rule on what procedures would be required to comply with a duty of fairness, instead returning the case to the tribunal to devise appropriate procedures. One possible explanation for the correctness standard is a lurking concern about institutional self-interest: because the choice of procedures carries resource implications for the administrative body itself (time, money, and personnel), courts may be reluctant to defer to the administrative agency's balance between fairness on the one side and cost/efficiency on the other. For a more theoretical account of the divergence, see Dyzenhaus & Fox-Decent, *supra* note 34; see also Fox-Decent, chapter 7. For a recent case where the fairness of an agency's discretionary choice of procedure is subject to review on a standard of correctness, see *Canada (Minister of Citizenship and Immigration) v. Thamotharem*, 2007 FCA 198, leave to appeal to SCC denied.

125 *Baker*, *supra* note 2 at para. 25.

sions repeatedly on a daily basis. Does the fact that these decisions have a profound impact on the lives of those affected militate against deference in respect of all elements in the decision-making process, including fact-finding? To make the question concrete, should the question of whether Suresh faces a substantial risk of torture, or whether the danger to national security outweighs the risk of torture, be reviewed on the same standard as whether deportation to torture violates s. 7 of the Charter?

To push the speculation further, the formula for procedural fairness regards the virtue of deference as only one of several factors to be weighed in divining the appropriate procedures. One could imagine moving to a test for substantive review that does the same, effectively "balancing" relative expertise, the importance of the interests at stake, statutory purpose, etc. in order to determine whether a given decision is—is what? The search is no longer for the appropriate standard of review based on relative expertise, but for a decision that meets a single, unarticulated standard of acceptability.

D. The Last Word on Legislative Intent

In virtually every case that applies the pragmatic and functional test, the Court rehearses its insistence that it is discerning the legislator's intention regarding the appropriate level of deference: "[t]he central inquiry in determining the standard of review exercisable by a court of law is the legislative intent of the statute creating the tribunal whose decision is being reviewed."[126] If the privative clause was an exercise in communicating legislative intent about the role of the courts, suffice to say that the message was, if not lost, then at least reformulated in translation. The Court rationalized this through the constitutionalization of judicial review, and appeals to a negotiation between the rule of law and a view of parliamentary sovereignty as external to, or counterpoised against, the rule of law: "[t]he pragmatic and functional approach inquires into legislative intent, but does so against the backdrop of the courts' constitutional duty to protect the rule of law."[127]

In 2004, British Columbia enacted the *Administrative Tribunals Act*,[128] which purports to express the provincial legislator's intent regarding the appropriate standard of review. If a tribunal's enabling statute has a privative clause, the standard of review is patent unreasonableness for questions of law, fact, or the exercise of discretion, for all matters over which "the tribunal has exclusive jurisdiction." Common-law rules of natural justice and procedural fairness must be decided "having regard to whether, in all of the circumstances, the tribunal acted fairly," and a standard of correctness applies to "all other matters." Where the enabling statute has no privative clause, findings of fact are reviewable on the basis of no evidence or unreasonableness, questions of law are reviewable on correctness, the exercise of discretion is subject to a standard of patent unreasonableness, and procedural fairness is decided "having regard to whether, in all of the circumstances," the tribunal acted fairly.[129] (These provisions of the BC *Administrative Tribunals Act* on the applicable

126 *Pushapanathan*, *supra* note 64 at para. 26.

127 *Dr. Q. v. College of Physicians and Surgeons of British Columbia*, [2003] 1 S.C.R. 226 at para. 21.

128 S.B.C. 2004, c. 45.

129 *Ibid.*, ss. 58-59.

standards of review precede the latest, tentative retreat by the Supreme Court from three to two standards of review.)

Would you anticipate any impediments—derived from the constitution or the rule of law—on the legislator's ability to dictate to the courts how much deference judges ought to demonstrate? These provisions of the BC *Administrative Tribunals Act* on the applicable standards of review have not yet been subjected to judicial review.[130]

VII. REVIEW OF STANDARD OF REVIEW: I LAUGHED, I CRIED, I STOOD ON MY CHAIR AND ...

At this point, a skeptic might recite the following story about the jurisprudence on standard of review: The *Pushpanathan* test for the standard of review is little more than a veneer that thinly disguises judicial opinions on the substantive outcome. When judges believe the tribunal got it "wrong," they will arrive at a standard of correctness (and conclude that the tribunal erred); when they believe that the tribunal got it "right," they will reach a standard of patently unreasonable, and find that the decision was not patently unreasonable; or they will impose a standard of reasonableness and do whatever they want. Agencies that the Court believes often get it wrong attract little deference in comparison to those bodies in which the Court has more confidence. A principled application of the pragmatic and functional test is either impossible because the criteria are too indeterminate, or is circumvented because the criteria are so easily manipulated to achieve the result that conforms with the judge's opinion on the "right" result. We have not progressed as far as we think from the empty formalism of preliminary or collateral question, or asking the wrong question. In the result, the pragmatic and functional test has not yielded a predictable, stable, principled jurisprudence on the standard of review because some, many, or most of the judiciary have not actually internalized and committed to the principles underlying curial deference. To put it another way, after reading *Southam* or *Barrie Utilities* (among others), one might wonder whether the provision at stake in *CUPE* would attract the same deferential standard of review today.[131]

In defence of the pragmatic and functional test and the inquiry into deference, one might counter that at least the pragmatic and functional test orients judges toward asking themselves the right questions. As David Mullan observes, they provide the diligent judge with the tools to arrive at meaningful results, while the unreconstructed Diceyan judge can always find a way to evade the spirit of deference. This weakness is not distinctive to the pragmatic and functional test, but is rather an endemic feature of judicial decision-making.

Only through a careful reading of the cases, including those in the next chapter on the application of the three standards, can the reader arrive at her or his own judgment.

130 See Cristie Ford, chapter 3, on remedies for further discussion of the BC *Administrative Tribunals Act*.

131 See David Dyzenhaus, "David Mullan's Theory of the Rule of (Common) Law" in Grant Huscroft & Michael Taggart, eds., *Inside and Outside Canadian Administrative Law: Essays in Honour of David Mullan* (Toronto: University of Toronto Press, 2006) 448-81 at 460.

VIII. POSTSCRIPT: DUNSMUIR v. NEW BRUNSWICK

In *Dunsmuir v. New Brunswick*,[132] the Court unanimously reverted to two standards of review (correctness and reasonableness) and tried to offer clearer guidance on the appropriate standard of review. However, this call for clarity was somewhat muffled by the split in the Court on methodology.

Dunsmuir concerned the termination of employment of a non-unionized government employee and how the adjudicator approached the duties of the government as employer under the relevant legislation.

Writing for the majority, Bastarache and Lebel JJ. concede that the law currently "provides great flexibility but little on-the-ground guidance, and offers too many standards of review."[133] They insist, however, that a return to two standards is not merely a return to pre-*Southam* law. The "pragmatic and functional approach" is revised as the "standard of review analysis," with an emphasis on three bases for deference: the presence of a privative clause; a discrete and specialized regime; and a question of law that is not of central importance to the legal system or beyond the specialized expertise of the tribunal. The majority then provides a non-exhaustive list of situations where a reasonableness or correctness standard is presumptively appropriate. Most notably, the correctness standard will apply where "true" jurisdiction or constitutionality is at stake, or where the legal issue is both of central importance to the legal system as a whole and outside the adjudicators' specialized area of expertise.

Binnie J.'s concurring judgment considers the focus on what might be an issue of "central importance to the legal system as a whole" to be a distraction. He prefers a simpler rule that provisions of the home statute and closely related statutes attract a reasonableness standard. The concurring judgment of Deschamps J. (joined by Charron and Rothstein JJ.) advances the most formalist analysis. Deschamps J. proposes that questions of fact, mixed fact and law, discretion, and questions of law protected by a privative clause attract the deferential standard of reasonableness, while other questions of law warrant stricter scrutiny for correctness.

In returning to two standards of review, the Court must articulate the criteria for determining what is (or is not) reasonable. The majority rejects a negative approach that examines the immediacy and magnitude of the alleged defect. Instead, it advocates a positive inquiry centred on the ideal of rationality, and directs the assessment toward "the qualities that make a decision reasonable, referring both to the process of articulating the reasons and to outcomes."[134] Thus, indicia of reasonableness include the process-oriented factors of intelligibility, justification, and transparency of the reasoning, as well as an outcome that "falls within a range of possible, acceptable outcomes which are defensible in respect of the facts and law."[135] *Quaere* the relationship between the majority's explicit attention to the quality of reasoning as a component of substantive review and the common-law duty to give reasons established by *Baker*.

Binnie J.'s judgment endorses the move to two standards but is preoccupied with the implications of collapsing reasonableness *simpliciter* and patent unreasonableness into a single standard, and the need to parse different levels of deference within the new, unified reasonableness standard.

In many ways *Dunsmuir* signals a seismic shift in the jurisprudence on substantive judicial review. Only by monitoring the reverberations over time will it be possible to judge whether it is a shift on the scale of *Nicholson*, *CUPE*, and *Baker*.

---

132 *Dunsmuir v. New Brunswick*, 2008 SCC 9 [*Dunsmuir*].

133 *Ibid.* at para. 43.

134 *Ibid.* at para. 47.

135 *Ibid.*

SUGGESTED ADDITIONAL READINGS

CASES

Baker v. Canada (Minister of Citizenship and Immigration), [1999] 2 S.C.R. 817.

Barrie Public Utilities v. Canadian Cable Television Assn., [2003] 1 S.C.R. 476.

Canada (Attorney General) v. Mossop, [1993] 1 S.C.R. 554.

Canada (Director of Investigation and Research) v. Southam Inc., [1997] 1 S.C.R. 748.

Canadian Union of Public Employees, Local 963 v. New Brunswick Liquor Corp., [1979] 2 S.C.R. 227.

Council of Canadians with Disabilities v. VIA Rail Canada Inc., 2007 SCC 15.

C.U.P.E. v. Ontario (Minister of Labour), [2003] 1 S.C.R. 539.

Dunsmuir v. New Brunswick, 2008 SCC 9.

Law Society of New Brunswick v. Ryan, [2003] 1 S.C.R. 247.

National Corn Growers Assn. v. Canada (Import Tribunal), [1990] 2 S.C.R. 1324.

Pushpanathan v. Canada (Minister of Citizenship and Immigration), [1998] 1 S.C.R. 982.

Starson v. Swazye, [2003] 1 S.C.R. 722.

Toronto (City) v. CUPE, Local 79, [2003] 3 S.C.R. 77.

U.E.S., Local 298 v. Bibeault, [1988] 2 S.C.R. 1048.

SECONDARY SOURCES

Dyzenhaus, D. "The Politics of Deference: Judicial Review and Democracy" in M. Taggart, ed., *The Province of Administrative Law* (Oxford: Hart Publishing, 1997) at 279.

Lahey, B., & D. Ginn. "After the Revolution: Being Pragmatic and Functional in Canada's Trial Courts and Courts of Appeal" (2002) 25 Dal. L.J. 259.

MacLauchlan, H.W. "Transforming Administrative Law: The Didactic Role of the Supreme Court of Canada" (2001) 80 Can. Bar Rev. 281.

McLachlin, The Honourable Justice B. "The Roles of Administrative Tribunals and Courts in Maintaining the Rule of Law" (1999) 12 Can. J. Admin. L. & P. 171.

Mullan, D.J. *Administrative Law: Cases, Text, and Materials*, 5th ed. (Toronto: Emond Montgomery, 2003) chapters 9, 10.

Sossin, L., & C. Flood. "The Contextual Turn: Iacobucci's Legacy and the Standard of Review in Administrative Law" (2007) 57 U.T.L.J. 581.

CHAPTER NINE

A Fine Romance? The Modern Standards of Review in Theory and Practice

SHEILA WILDEMAN*
Dalhousie Law School

I. INTRODUCTION

Contemporary Canadian administrative law features three standards of review that represent, at least in theory, three distinct judicial postures toward disputed administrative decisions. The standards in question are correctness, wherein the decision under review is said to command low or no deference; reasonableness, wherein the decision commands some, but not great, deference; and patent unreasonableness, wherein the decision commands the highest deference. This much is generally agreed upon. But beyond that, the story of the emergence and ultimate significance of the modern standards of review is subject to starkly divergent accounts. As indicated by Audrey Macklin at the close of chapter 8, the jurisprudence elaborating the standards—that which addresses the review of substantive administrative decisions—readily lends itself to skeptical accounts. On such readings, both the exceeding intricacy of the "pragmatic and functional" analysis going to the choice of standard (the subject of chapter 8) and the elusive quality of judicial pronouncements on how to apply the standards (the subject of this chapter) amount to ornate doctrinal cloaks for the

* Thanks to the other contributors to this volume, especially Audrey Macklin. Thanks also to Vaughan Black, and to Colleen Flood and Lorne Sossin for their excellent editorial advice. Finally, thanks to my mother, Margaret Wildeman, for her assistance during my maternity leave so that I might complete this chapter.

continued privileging of judicial over administrative opinions on matters given to administrators to decide. That is, the modern standards of review, says the skeptic, are but distractions masking an indomitable judicial will to have the last word on the scope and limits of executive action.

The dominant story of the development and significance of the standards of review, however, proceeds in a more romantic fashion. On that account, the modern law on substantive review, beginning with the 1979 Supreme Court judgment in *Canadian Union of Public Employees, Local 963 v. New Brunswick Liquor Corp.*,[1] expresses a gradual reconciliation of the judiciary and the administrative state under the banner of a common "culture of justification."[2] That is, the romantic discerns in *CUPE* and the subsequent cases a radical shift away from traditional judicial tendencies to regard the administrative state as a lawless zone,[3] a conception accompanied by strategies of closely hedging administrative powers or jurisdiction through the deployment of abstract or formal legal categories. With this shift comes a concomitant evolution toward recognizing the context-specific reasonableness of, and institutional reasons for deference to, administrative decisions. *CUPE* thus heralds an era of substantive review in which judges and administrative decision-makers are acknowledged to bring different strengths to the common project of ensuring that the decisions of public bodies are not arbitrary but justified.

The mechanisms driving this romantic reconciliation are the standards of review elaborated in, and subsequent to, *CUPE*. As discussed in chapter 8, the judgment of Dickson J. for a unanimous Court in that case represents a fresh start for the relationship between the judiciary and the administrative state. There, the Court indicates that it will take seriously not only the formal indicia of the legislature's entrusting certain administrative actors with exclusive powers of decision (specifically where expressed through a privative clause), but also the practical or functional justifications for granting those decision-makers presumptive authority where their decisions are subject to legal challenge.[4] In this, *CUPE* prescribes a concertedly purposive reading of the institutional arrangements promulgated in administrative decision-makers' enabling statutes. The standard of patent unreasonableness is thus forged in an acknowledgment of the unique capacities and insights of administrative agencies.

Yet, the romantic account continues, the starkly dualist alternatives of deference and non-deference presented in *CUPE* are still bound up in overly rigid formalist strictures—in

1 [1979] 2 S.C.R. 227 [*CUPE*].

2 "[S]ocieties governed by the Rule of Law are marked by a certain ethos of justification. … Where a society is marked by a culture of justification, an exercise of public power is only appropriate where it can be justified to citizens in terms of rationality and fairness. … A culture of justification shifts the analysis from the institutions themselves to, more subtly, what those institutions are capable of doing for the rational advancement of civil society. The Rule of Law, in short, can speak in several voices so long as the resulting chorus echoes its underlying values of rationality and fairness." (The Honourable Justice B. McLachlin, "The Roles of Administrative Tribunals and Courts in Maintaining the Rule of Law" (1999) 12 Can. J. Admin. L. & P. 171 at 174-75.

3 See D. Dyzenhaus & E. Fox-Decent, "Rethinking the Process/Substance Distinction: Baker v. Canada" (2001) 51 U.T.L.J. 193 at 197-200, 204-5 ["Process/Substance"]; D. Dyzenhaus, "The Politics of Deference: Judicial Review and Democracy" in M. Taggart, ed., *The Province of Administrative Law* (Oxford: Hart Publishing, 1997) at 279 ["Politics of Deference"].

4 [*CUPE*], *supra* note 1 at paras. 13-14. See also "Process/Substance," *supra* note 3 at 200.

particular, the requirement that a privative clause be in place as a necessary condition of deference. As the pragmatic and functional analysis becomes increasingly oriented to decision-specific experience or expertise, conflicting statutory indicia (for example, where administrative expertise is accompanied by lack of a privative clause or by a right of appeal) place strain on the dualist model of deference or no deference. As a result, this model gives way to the tripartite model now familiar to us. With the insertion of the standard of reasonableness *simpliciter* between the standards of correctness and patent unreasonableness (in *Canada (Director of Investigation and Research) v. Southam Inc.*)[5] then, it seems we are well on the way to a happy ending to the romantic's story. For now judges are able to take fuller notice of the practical bases for deferring to administrative decisions, while retaining a responsibility to ensure that those decisions are justified. This development may be understood to deepen the insights of *CUPE*, as recognition of administrative legitimacy is implicit both in the extension of deference on a reasonableness standard (that is, even in the absence of a privative clause explicitly directing the court to refrain from review) and in the expectation of reasonableness under that standard (implying that administrative decision-makers have the authority and capacity to interpret their statutes in a reasonable—and not just "not patently unreasonable"—manner). The development of this standard may thus be regarded as a key expression of the idea that administrative bodies have independently valuable roles to play in shaping the contours of public justification.

Yet the forging of a third standard raises new questions for the jurisprudence on substantive review, namely, how does review for reasonableness relate to—and potentially alter the pre-existing relationship of—patent unreasonableness and correctness review? Should the three-standard model be conceived of as a broad spectrum allowing for subtle gradations of deference responsive to the glorious (and inglorious) diversity of administrative agents, such that reasonableness review effectively shades into correctness review on the one end and patent unreasonableness review on the other? Or does this model feature three discrete and determinate modes of judicial engagement? The latter question was resolved by the Supreme Court in *Law Society of New Brunswick v. Ryan*,[6] where the Court unanimously affirmed a commitment to just three distinct standards of review. But questions remain—indeed, questions that go to the very coherence and workability of the law on substantive review. In short, what exactly is the import of, and what are the differences between, the modern standards of review? Typically, as noted above, the standards are characterized in terms of graduated degrees of deference, inversely correlated to graduated degrees of stringency. In *Dr. Q.*, McLachlin C.J. informs us that correctness review is "exacting review," reasonableness review demands "significant searching and testing," and patent unreasonableness review means that the decision must be left "to the near exclusive determination of the decision-maker."[7] But what do such characterizations amount to on reflection and in practice? Increasingly, commentators are asking: Do the three standards actually do the

5 [1997] 1 S.C.R. 748 [*Southam*]. Also relevant here (as discussed by Geneviève Cartier in chapter 10) is the extension of the standard of review analysis to the exercise of discretion in *Baker v. Canada (Minister of Citizenship and Immigration)*, [1999] 2 S.C.R. 817 [*Baker*].

6 2003 SCC 20, [2003] 1 S.C.R. 247 [*Ryan*].

7 *Dr. Q. v. College of Physicians and Surgeons of British Columbia*, 2003 SCC 19, [2003] 1 S.C.R. 226 at para. 22 [*Dr. Q.*].

work they are said to do on the romantic account? Do they succeed in integrating or harmonizing judicial and administrative duties and competencies and, thus, in promoting a common culture of justification? Or do they amount to a lot of judicial smoke and mirrors?

In order to address these concerns, we begin where the previous chapter on selecting the standard of review left off. Our focus is the next step: that of applying the selected standard in order to determine the legality of the disputed decision. We are therefore concerned both with how the standards have been characterized and how they have been applied; that is, with what judges have said about the standards and what they have actually done in determining whether a given administrative decision is within or beyond the limits of legality. This seems to take us to the crowning moment of the law on substantive review: the point at which legal oversight is brought directly to bear on a contested decision. However, after all the attention given to the work of selecting the standard, the application stage often comes off as the weak final act of the substantive review judgment. Application of the correctness standard, for instance, may seem to amount merely to making the law (particularly the enabling statute) speak for itself in a way that demands uncritical assent to assertions of a plain or otherwise unitary legislative intent.[8] On such occasions we may wonder whether other perspectives on the significance of the statute—most notably, the perspective of the administrative decision-maker—are being suppressed. Moreover, where a deferential standard is in play (either reasonableness or patent unreasonableness), its application may at times seem no more than a sniff test[9] registering judicial intuitions that defy public articulation and so arguably fail to meet a fundamental criterion of the rule of law. That is to say, no matter how context-sensitive and careful the threshold analysis of the standard of review has (or has not) been, the ensuing application of the standard may nonetheless be vulnerable to the charge that the reasonableness or patent unreasonableness, correctness or incorrectness, of the impugned decision is asserted with insufficient justification. Such charges open onto the skeptical thesis that at the end of the day, the standards of review are of little or no relevance to the outcome of substantive review.

It is in trying to get our bearings at the application stage, then, that we encounter with a certain immediacy the question whether or not the case law on the standards of review offers sufficient conceptual and/or practical guidance. Indeed, we may be forgiven if our sense of disorientation is profound. For as Audrey Macklin notes in her analysis of *Council of Canadians with Disabilities v. VIA Rail Canada Inc.*,[10] it seems the Court is at a crossroads in this jurisprudence, from which position it may observe the three standards bearing down upon it in imminent collision. Whether that collision will occur and, if it does, what might be sifted from the wreckage—perhaps two reinforced standards, perhaps a single, flexible standard of reasonableness—are matters that any contemporary survey of the standards

8 See below, for example, *Canada (Attorney General) v. Mossop*, [1993] 1 S.C.R. 554 [*Mossop*] and *Barrie Public Utilities v. Canadian Cable Television Assn.*, 2003 SCC 28, [2003] 1 S.C.R. 476 [*Barrie Utilities*].

9 Or "puke test": see D. Dyzenhaus, "Constituting the Rule of Law: Fundamental Values in Administrative Law" (2002) 27 Queen's L.J. 445 at 493 (note 110) ["Fundamental Values"], referring to the position of Wilson J. in *National Corn Growers Assn. v. Canada (Import Tribunal)*, [1990] 2 S.C.R. 1324 [*National Corn Growers*].

10 2007 SCC 15 [*Council of Canadians with Disabilities*].

of review must raise. Thus while the primary objective of this chapter is to familiarize you with the language and conceptual models in which the standards have been authoritatively cast, a secondary objective is to expose you to an increasingly insistent chorus of dissent calling the prevailing three-standard model into question.

This chapter is divided into three parts. The first sets out some background points to help orient us to the ensuing discussion—in particular, observations on competing approaches to statutory interpretation. The second part examines each standard in turn, first considering how they have been characterized and then how they have been applied in selected Supreme Court decisions. The third part considers the possibility of imminent collapse of the three-standard model, concluding with a look at some alternative models. By the chapter's end, we should be better equipped to consider whether the three-standard model, or some other model, is indeed an effective plot device in advancing the romantic reconciliation of the judiciary and administrative decision-makers under the rule of law.

II. BACKGROUND: STATUTORY INTERPRETATION AND SUBSTANTIVE REVIEW

As we will see in what follows, the assessment of the substantive legality of an administrative decision is steeped in the work of statutory interpretation. Thus it may assist to begin by briefly surveying competing approaches to statutory interpretation that may be significant to or even determinative of the outcome of review.[11] We start with the "modern principle" of statutory interpretation articulated in the second edition of Driedger's *Construction of Statutes* and repeatedly endorsed by the Supreme Court:

> Today there is only one principle or approach [to statutory interpretation], namely, the words of an Act are to be read in their entire context and in their grammatical and ordinary sense harmoniously with the scheme of the Act, the object of the Act, and the intention of Parliament.[12]

Yet general judicial acceptance of this principle tends to obscure continuing conflicts among judges (and sometimes even among decisions of a single judge) as to the factors that bear relevance, or primary relevance, when interpreting contested statutory texts.[13] Here we may roughly distinguish what may be termed positivist approaches from pragmatic or normative approaches.[14]

---

11 "To a large extent judicial review of administrative action is a specialized branch of statutory interpretation": *U.E.S., Local 298 v. Bibeault*, [1988] 2 S.C.R. 1048 at 1087 [*Bibeault*], quoting S.A. de Smith, H. Street & R. Brazier, *Constitutional and Administrative Law*, 4th ed. (Harmondsworth, UK: Penguin, 1981) at 588. Compare J.M. Keyes, "Judicial Review and the Interpretation of Legislation: Who Gets the Last Word?" (2006) 19 Can. J. Admin. L. & Prac. 119.

12 E.A. Driedger, *Construction of Statutes*, 2d ed. (Toronto: Butterworths, 1983) at 87.

13 See R. Sullivan, "Statutory Interpretation in the Supreme Court of Canada" (1998) 30 Ottawa L. Rev. 175 ["Statutory Interpretation]; S. Beaulac & P. Côté, "Driedger's 'Modern Principle' at the Supreme Court of Canada: Interpretation, Justification, Legitimization" (2006) R.J.T. 131.

14 Sullivan, "Statutory Interpretation," *ibid*., distinguishes textualist and intentionalist (which I am loosely calling "positivist") from pragmatic (which I am calling "normative") approaches to statutory interpretation.

In rough terms, a positivist approach to statutory interpretation flows from the presumption that statutory language contains a singular and unified meaning that is stable over time.[15] Judges adhering to that presumption tend to accept further that ascertainment of the core meaning is to be sought through interpretive techniques proper to and perfected by the judiciary. Those techniques may involve a strict focus on the statutory text, or efforts to situate the text in its legislative context.[16] But on either variant of this approach, the objective is to "find" a determinate legislative intent. A general criticism raised to the positivist approach is that it smuggles into legal judgment contestable value-driven choices, where those choices should be explicitly submitted for public justification.[17] In administrative law, a positivist approach to statutory interpretation may further be argued to work against a meaningful conception of deference, in that it restricts the potential for judges to acknowledge the operation and thus the contestability of their own value-laden presumptions in the face of the potentially competing values or perspectives of administrative decision-makers. That said, in the face of a privative clause, the positivist approach suffers the traditional tension between acknowledgment that administrative decision-makers have been granted exclusive interpretive authority over their enabling statutes, and insistence that such authority is proper to the judiciary.

In contrast, it is the explicit submission of the value-laden bases of legal judgment for public justification that marks a normative approach to statutory interpretation.[18] Such an approach proceeds on the assumption that contested matters of statutory interpretation cannot be resolved by exclusive reference to the text, or even by situating the text in its social context, but also require judgments about the competing values or social priorities informing alternative statutory constructions. This suggests a conception of the rule of law in which the legitimacy of state action is contingent not on strict adherence to legislative or majority will but on consistency with the important public values inscribed in our social and legal traditions.[19] In the administrative law context, adherence to such a conception

---

15 See D. Dyzenhaus, "David Mullan's Theory of the Rule of (Common) Law" in G. Huscroft & M. Taggert, eds., *Inside and Outside Administrative Law: Essays in Honour of David Mullan* (Toronto: University of Toronto Press, 2006) 448 at 474 [*Inside and Outside*]: "[T]he point of the positivist conception of law is to insist that real law is the determinate content of valid law, where determinate means determinable in accordance with tests that do not rely on moral considerations and arguments, including arguments about the principles of an internal morality of law."

16 But compare J. Gardner, "Legal Positivism: 5½ Myths" (2001) 46 Am. J. Juris. 199 at 218-22, who argues that legal positivism is committed neither to textualism nor to originalism in statutory interpretation. Again, see Sullivan, "Statutory Interpretation," *supra* note 13.

17 Sullivan, *ibid.* at 220-25.

18 *Ibid.* at 184-87, 220-27 (on the "pragmatic" approach to interpretation).

19 As Sullivan, *ibid.* at 227, notes, this model is supported by the following statement of McLachlin C.J. for the Court in *Reference re Secession of Quebec*, [1998] 2 S.C.R. 217 at 247 [*Secession Reference*]:

> [A] system of government … must be capable of reflecting the aspirations of the people. But there is more. Our law's claim to legitimacy also rests on an appeal to moral values, many of which are embedded in our constitutional structure. It would be a grave mistake to equate legitimacy with the "sovereign will" or majority rule alone, to the exclusion of other constitutional values.

Compare Mary Liston's discussion of *Secession Reference* in chapter 4.

may (but arguably need not) entail an attitude of strict non-deference where an administrative decision is understood to place in issue important public values. That is, some judges may insist on correctness review in such cases in accordance with an understanding of their role as exclusive arbiters of the values expressed at common law and in the constitution.[20] Yet other judges (we may call them constitutional pluralists) may view the same interpretive problems as supportive of deference on review, on the understanding that administrative decision-makers may be uniquely positioned to work out how the basic commitments of the social, political, and legal order inform or interact with the sector-specific values and policy objectives of administrative regimes.[21]

There are tensions in each of these approaches to statutory interpretation in their implications for the relationship between courts and administrative decision-makers. A positivist insistence that there is one right answer in construing disputed statutory provisions seems inconsistent with the rationale for deference expressed in *CUPE*.[22] But such an approach is nonetheless apt to express deference by placing high and even determinative importance on the existence of a privative clause, and, further, by resisting importation of value-laden constraints on administrative decision-making absent a direct constitutional challenge. The constitutional pluralist expresses deference by acknowledging a role for administrative decision-makers in the project of defending and elaborating the rule of law. But he or she may thereby invest those decision-makers with a duty to consider and even to attribute determinative importance to the values the judge deems essential to the legitimate exercise of the relevant statutory powers.

A further matter of significant background importance to substantive review, apart from the general approach to statutory interpretation adopted in a given case, is what base of evidence and argument the reviewing court is able to draw upon to inform its interpretation of the legality of the disputed decision. Is there a record of the reasons for decision, or other means (for example, policies or guidelines) of informing the court of the considerations the decision-maker took into account? Was the administrative decision-maker able to participate in the proceedings to provide such information or otherwise assist the court?[23] Wade MacLauchlan has argued that the immediate challenges facing substantive review on the way to a culture of justification lie precisely in devising better ways for tribunals to apprise courts of the institutional and social policy considerations informing their decisions. This includes instilling better practices of reason-giving among administrative decision-makers. Such institutional developments—accompanied by developments in the capacity or willingness of courts to exhibit appropriate sensitivity to such information—are held out by

20 See "Fundamental Values," *supra* note 9 at 448-51, where Dyzenhaus points out that the Court's endorsement of "unwritten constitutional principles" in the *Secession Reference* is accompanied by other statements expressing a "formalist" vision of the separation of powers, whereby judges bear exclusive responsibility for working out those principles.

21 Dyzenhaus refers to this as the "democratic" vision of the constitutional order, and, further, argues that such a vision is implicit in the majority decision of L'Heureux-Dubé J. in *Baker*, *supra* note 5.

22 You will recall that the decision in *CUPE* suggests there may be many reasonable solutions to such disputes.

23 On the traditional restrictions on such involvement to issues relating to tribunal "jurisdiction," see D. Mullan, *Administrative Law: Cases, Texts, and Materials*, 5th ed. (Toronto: Emond Montgomery, 2003) at 704-5, 1230-41.

MacLauchlan as potentially supplanting the formalist and positivist touchstones of "legislative intent" and "jurisdiction" in this area of law.[24]

III. THEORY AND PRACTICE: THE MODERN STANDARDS OF REVIEW

With that we return to the modern standards of review. Can the jurisprudence on the meaning and application of the standards resolve the tensions that surface in substantive review between the imperative to respect administrative authority and the imperative to uphold the rule of law? Among the matters canvassed below are the following: First, how are we to understand review for correctness after *CUPE*, given that the decision calls into question a positivist approach to statutory interpretation and the thesis that only judges may legitimately interpret law? Second, has the notion of review for patent unreasonableness, introduced in *CUPE* and elaborated in subsequent cases, offered meaningful guidance about how best to conceive of and go about discerning the limits of legality under this (most) deferential standard? And finally, how does the latecomer to the standard of review jurisprudence, review for unreasonableness (or reasonableness *simpliciter* review), stand in relation to the other two standards? Is it meaningfully distinct from them, or does it collapse into and so erode the integrity of one or both of its predecessors?

A. A Contested Correctness

1. The Correctness Standard in Theory

Let us begin with the standard most expressive of the institutional authority of the judiciary: review for correctness. This standard may at first blush appear so plain in meaning as to be beyond comment. That is, asserting a criterion of correctness seems to amount to an insistence that the decision-maker get it right, full stop. But on reflection, the meaning of "getting it right" and the method by which this is evaluated are less than transparent; indeed, we will see that in some cases, these matters have been hotly contested.

In *Ryan*, Iacobucci J. writes that where a correctness standard is imposed, "the court may undertake its own reasoning process to arrive at the result it judges correct."[25] This is set in contrast to what we will see shortly is a key feature in the characterization of both patent unreasonableness and reasonableness review. That is, despite some initial dissension on this point, both of the latter standards are said not to be about adjudging the "right answer" to a disputed matter and then gauging the relative accuracy of the tribunal's answer in light of that. Just what these standards do imply is something we will take up in a moment.

Iacobucci J.'s description of correctness review implies that the court need not put any effort into specifically assessing the administrative decision-maker's reasons or casting those reasons in their best light. Nor must it admit that there may be dimensions to those reasons that lie beyond its traditional capacities or exceed its powers of appreciation. Rath-

24 H.W. MacLauchlan, "Transforming Administrative Law: The Didactic Role of the Supreme Court of Canada" (2001) 80 Can. Bar Rev. 281 at 293-94, 297-98. Also see B. Lahey & D. Ginn, "After the Revolution: Being Pragmatic and Functional in Canada's Trial Courts and Courts of Appeal" (2002) 25 Dal. L.J. 259 at 325 ["After the Revolution"].

25 *Supra* note 6 at para. 50.

er, given that the court has, through a pragmatic and functional analysis, deemed itself best placed to resolve the matter under review, it is apparently free to revisit the decision originally put to the administrative decision-maker as it sees fit.

One understanding of correctness review is that it describes the sort of oversight appropriate to decisions or statutory provisions that inherently admit of just one right answer. This is placed in contrast to the sort of interpretive dispute in issue in *CUPE*, where there was significant ambiguity or room for interpretive discretion. However, with the rise of a duty on decision-makers to give reasons in cases affecting important interests (reasons that courts seem bound to consider under a commitment to public justification), and, moreover, with the rise of purposive approaches to statutory interpretation acknowledging some discretion in all interpretive judgment, this view of the basis for correctness review becomes less convincing.[26]

While a case-specific pragmatic and functional analysis is always required to determine whether correctness review is warranted,[27] this standard typically applies in determining whether non-adjudicative decisions of municipal decision-makers are ultra vires,[28] and in reviewing decision-makers' conclusions on the constitutional or Charter limits of their statutory powers.[29] In addition, the correctness standard has traditionally been understood to apply in the review of procedural fairness, although as Macklin (chapter 8) suggests, this may be in doubt after *Baker*. Further, the standard is generally engaged in cases concerning the relative jurisdictional scope of different tribunals.[30] Finally, correctness review has been closely correlated with characterization of the question on review as "pure law," "general law," or law of "great precedential value"[31]—in addition to the traditional characterization of the question as one that goes to "jurisdiction."[32] All these are matters about which the decision-maker is deemed to lack expertise or institutional authority relative to the court. That said, as Macklin suggested in chapter 8, such characterizations of the question on review may be open to dispute.

2. Correctness Review in Practice

We focus in this section on two pre-*Southam* cases that are useful in provoking reflections on the nature and methods of correctness review. Then we briefly survey how some of the controversies reflected in these cases have been taken up in more recent case law. Throughout this section and the sections that follow, we must keep in mind that until the mid-1990s, only two standards were on offer in reviewing tribunal interpretations of law: correctness

26 See "Process/Substance," *supra* note 3 at 235-36; "Fundamental Values," *supra* note 9 at 469 (note 46).

27 *Dr. Q.*, *supra* note 7 at paras. 21-25.

28 See, for example, *Nanaimo v. Rascal Trucking Ltd.*, 2000 SCC 13, [2000] 1 S.C.R. 342.

29 But see Evan Fox-Decent's comments in chapter 7 interrogating the insistence on correctness review of all tribunal determinations of constitutional questions.

30 But see *British Columbia Telephone Co. v. Shaw Cable Systems (B.C.) Inc.*, [1995] 2 S.C.R. 739.

31 See, for example, *Southam*, *supra* note 5 at paras. 35-37; *Pushpanathan v. Canada (Minister of Citizenship and Immigration)*, [1998] 1 S.C.R. 982 at para. 47 [*Pushpanathan*]; *Chieu v. Canada (Minister of Citizenship and Immigration)*, 2002 SCC 3, [2002] 1 S.C.R. 84 at para. 26; *Dr. Q.*, *supra* note 7 at para. 34.

32 See "After the Revolution," *supra* note 24 at 322, 331-32.

and patent unreasonableness. Application of the latter standard was, with few exceptions, contingent on a privative clause.[33] From the vantage of the three-standard model, we may regard the dualist model counterposing utmost deference against strict non-deference as placing a certain strain upon both standards. For under that model, cases that might now warrant "some deference" or reasonableness review were necessarily classed on one side or the other of the deference divide. And absent a privative clause, correctness review remained the default option.

Two cases that bring out the tensions of correctness review are *Bibeault*[34] and *Mossop*.[35] You will recall *Bibeault* from chapter 8. The facts involved a school board's terminating janitorial service contracts with companies whose workers were on strike, and then contracting with another company for such services. The question was, did this fit the criterion of "alienation or operation by another" of an "undertaking" under the successor employer provisions of Quebec's labour law? If so, the union representing the employees of the original companies would represent those of the new company, continuity of the collective agreement would be assured, and the strike would carry on. Macklin notes a schism in the judgment of Beetz J., which on the one hand consolidates a set of "pragmatic" and "functional" queries for discerning whether deference is due, and on the other continues to frame its analysis in terms of a Diceyan concern to patrol the limits of administrative jurisdiction.

It is the latter concern that animates the disposition of the case. Beetz J. concludes that the issue is jurisdictional, meaning that no deference is due. This conclusion turns on his determination that the statutory language includes terms of art at civil law, the interpretation of which demands general legal expertise. From there, the objective is to determine the right answer: were the successor employer provisions engaged or not? Beetz J. canvasses the purpose of the key disputed provision (in light of the purpose of the statute as a whole); this is stated to be protection of "the benefits resulting from certification and the collective agreement."[36] He then situates that general purpose in light of the principle, derived from attention to the four corners of the statute, that collective bargaining requires a single union, a single employer, and a single undertaking. That principle, in addition to analysis of the terms "alienation" and "undertaking" at civil law, leads Beetz J. to conclude that a legal relationship between employers (in transferring a single undertaking) is required to trigger the disputed provision.

According to Beetz J., the alternative construction accepted by the labour commissioner and upheld by a majority of the Labour Court gave the terms of art in question "a non-legal and even uncommon meaning"[37]—one that more broadly was "inconsistent with the purposes of the *Labour Code*."[38] He suggests that the source of this inconsistency was the

33 Although the courts had extended deference to certain specialized tribunals on questions of law interpretation in the absence of a privative clause. See *Bell Canada v. Canada (Canadian Radio-Television and Telecommunications Commission)*, [1989] 1 S.C.R. 1722 at 1746.

34 *Supra* note 11.

35 *Supra* note 8.

36 *Bibeault*, *supra* note 11 at 1098.

37 *Ibid.* at 1110.

38 *Ibid.* at 1103.

commissioner's and tribunal's misguided "desire to protect the certification and collective agreement despite all the vicissitudes of the undertaking."[39]

The judgment of Beetz J. in *Bibeault* thus favours conceptual coherence as between the statute and the civil law over the context-inflected sympathies of the tribunal. Now, few of us will argue that coherence, in the law or in general, is inherently a bad thing. But on reading this case, are you convinced by the construction of the statute adopted by Beetz J.? What else might you want to know from the administrative decision-makers to form your opinion? More generally, how important is it that terms of art at civil or common law are preserved from novel interpretations in administrative sectors? Does your answer differ if the terms relate to commercial or contract law versus human rights?

Moving from the labour context to the human rights context, consider *Mossop*.[40] You will recall from chapter 8 that in this case a majority of the Supreme Court overturned a decision of the Canadian Human Rights Tribunal on the basis that the prohibited ground of "family status" (not otherwise defined in the *Canadian Human Rights Act*) could not be interpreted to extend protection to a same-sex couple. For reasons discussed in chapter 8, the majority, as well as two judges dissenting on the result, adopted a correctness standard. (Get used to the phenomenon of judges agreeing on the correctness standard and then disagreeing on what the "right answer" is upon applying that standard.) L'Heureux-Dubé J. wrote a dissenting judgment adopting a patent unreasonableness standard.

The concurring majority judgments in *Mossop* express two variants of what I have described above as a positivist approach to statutory interpretation. Lamer C.J. (Sopinka and Iacobucci JJ. concurring) grounds his analysis in legislative intent. This analysis is framed with a gesture toward the parallel universe of normative jurisprudence available solely to claimants invoking the Charter. That is, given that Mr. Mossop had opted to base his claim exclusively in arguments from statutory interpretation, Lamer C.J. suggests that the Court is bound by contextual indicia that "family status" was not intended to encompass same-sex relationships. Here he emphasizes the absence of "sexual orientation" from the statute's prohibited grounds of discrimination at the time the proceedings arose, even in the face of a recommendation by the Canadian Human Rights Commission that it be added. The failure of Parliament to act on the commission's recommendation, he reasons, amounted to its "refusal" to do so. Lamer C.J. states the principle driving his analysis as follows:

> Absent a *Charter* challenge of its constitutionality, when Parliamentary intent is clear, courts and administrative tribunals are not empowered to do anything else but to apply the law. If there is some ambiguity as to its meaning or scope, then the courts should, using the usual rules of interpretation, seek out the purpose of the legislation and if more than one reasonable interpretation consistent with that purpose is available, that which is more in conformity with the *Charter* should prevail.[41]

In this case, however, the legislative intent is clear, so no recourse to the Charter as an interpretive aid may be had.

---

39 *Ibid.*

40 *Supra* note 8.

41 *Ibid.* at 581-82.

In his concurring judgment, La Forest J. (writing for himself and Iacobucci J.) also focuses on legislative intent. However, his judgment is more insistently fixed on the statutory text and, specifically, the word "family." He describes his approach as consistent with "the ordinary rules of statutory interpretation" which demand that one give "to the words used in a statute their usual and ordinary sense having regard to their context and to the purpose of the statute."[42] In applying this principle, however, La Forest J. emphasizes not the general purpose of the *Canadian Human Rights Act*—that of eradicating discrimination—but the "usual and ordinary sense" of the word "family." His conclusion is that the "dominant" and thus ordinary sense of the word, or that which represents the consensus of the Canadian public, is the "traditional family." This is the meaning that therefore must be understood to have been Parliament's intent both when the statute was enacted and at the time the dispute arose.

L'Heureux-Dubé J. is alone in arguing that a patent unreasonableness standard should apply. However, her disposition of the matter is endorsed in the separate dissenting reasons of McLachlin and Cory JJ., who determine that a correctness standard is in order. This seems to indicate that for McLachlin and Cory JJ., the judgment of L'Heureux-Dubé J. represents the best account of the "right answer" to this interpretive dispute.[43] Thus, while our objective in this section is to consider correctness review, it is worth contrasting the approach taken by L'Heureux-Dubé J. with that of the majority.

The judgment of L'Heureux-Dubé J. is not the superficial gloss that we will see some have endorsed as the model of patent unreasonableness review. And yet it distinguishes itself from the approach of the majority in two key ways. First, it takes an emphatically normative approach to statutory interpretation. L'Heureux-Dubé J. expresses the distance between her approach and that of the majority as follows:

> Even if Parliament had in mind a specific idea of the scope of "family status," in the absence of a definition in the *Act* which embodies this scope, concepts of equality and liberty which appear in human rights documents are not bounded by the precise understanding of those who drafted them. Human rights codes are documents that embody fundamental principles, but which permit the understanding and application of those principles to change over time. These codes leave ample scope for interpretation by those charged with that task.[44]

The point here is that, at least with human rights statutes, it is essential to orient interpretive judgment with reference to human rights principles (in this case, specifically equality or non-discrimination). These are asserted in this passage not as statute-specific but as "fundamental." As such, they may be curtailed only by the most explicit expressions of legislative intent. Thus it seems that there is, if not a right answer in this case (and perhaps, for L'Heureux-Dubé J., there is), then at least a right and a wrong way of going about resolving the question. Both the reliance of La Forest J. on an "unexamined consensus" and the reliance of Lamer C.J. on the legislative context come in for criticism as insupportably invok-

---

42 *Ibid.* at 585.

43 The implications of this are the subject of careful analysis in Dyzenhaus, "Fundamental Values," *supra* note 9 at 464-68.

44 *Mossop*, *supra* note 8 at 621.

ing a singular majority will, and so understating the importance of human rights principles to the rule of law generally or to this instance of statutory interpretation in particular. In this way, L'Heureux-Dubé J.'s judgment reflects a commitment to a normative model of statutory interpretation, or a model of the rule of law and its place in statutory interpretation known as "common-law constitutionalism."[45] Under this model, statutes are understood not as closed systems but as requiring interpretation in light of the animating principles and values of the wider social and legal tradition.

The second major difference between L'Heureux-Dubé J.'s judgment and that of the majority (and here she differs also from her fellow dissenters) is, of course, her selection of a patent unreasonableness standard. Thus, while the tradition of common-law constitutionalism tends to place the burden of identifying and prioritizing fundamental values on the shoulders of judges alone, L'Heureux-Dubé J. indicates through her adoption of deference that the tribunal has a legitimate role in this enterprise. This is confirmed in her method of reasoning, which throughout draws upon and amplifies the evidence and argument accepted by the tribunal. That is, the decision of the tribunal is drawn upon not simply as a base of fact or policy separable from legal analysis, but as an exercise in statutory interpretation which is itself a model of the interdependency of facts and values in legal judgment. As such, L'Heureux-Dubé J. demonstrates both a respect for Parliament's will to assign the tribunal the role of administering this statute, and a commitment to the idea (again, cast as a principle of law) that in administering the statute, the tribunal's task is to transcend narrow constructions of parliamentary will.

In agreeing with L'Heureux-Dubé J.'s disposition of the case, the other dissenters, McLachlin and Cory JJ., indicate their support for the idea that the statutory text must be read in light of social context (and thus changing social conceptions of family), and with particular sensitivity to the ways that human rights principles inflect and are inflected by that text and context. According to L'Heureux-Dubé J., this sensitivity is best served by careful attention to the reasons of the tribunal. In light of the fact that the other dissenters select a correctness standard, a question that arises is whether they are to be understood to say that the "right answer" would have been secured absent the tribunal's reasons, or alternatively that in this case, correctness review is compatible with—even in some measure dependent upon—attentiveness to tribunal reasoning. Perhaps the convergence of these dissenting opinions despite their divergent standards may be chalked up to the fact that there was no reasonableness standard available at the time *Mossop* was decided.[46] That is, rule of law concerns to protect the very values that L'Heureux-Dubé J. cites may have rendered the patent unreasonableness standard unpalatable to the other judges, even if they might otherwise have been sympathetic to according the tribunal some deference.

Since *Mossop* and, moreover, since the introduction of review for reasonableness, the Court has indicated a willingness to accept that some deference to human rights tribunals on matters involving the interpretation and application of human rights statutes may, in

45 See the discussion of normative approaches to statutory interpretation in part II, above. For a penetrating account of historical and contemporary features of common-law constitutionalism, see M.D. Walters, "'Common Public Law in the Age of Legislation': David Mullan and the Unwritten Constitution" in *Inside and Outside*, *supra* note 15 at 421.

46 See Dyzenhaus, "Fundamental Values," *supra* note 9 at 467-68.

some cases, be warranted.[47] However, its insistence on the exclusive authority of the judiciary on matters of human rights holds strong in instances where the administrative decision-maker is not a human rights tribunal. This was the case in *Pushpanathan*[48] and also in *Trinity Western University v. British Columbia College of Teachers*.[49] Unlike *Mossop*, both these decisions feature majority judgments that place human rights at the core of the substantive review analysis, thus taking a concertedly normative approach to resolving the disputed exercise of administrative powers. However, both also hold that there is no basis for deference to the bodies whose decisions are under review. In these judgments, then, correctness review is arguably rooted less in the idea that the decisions under review lend themselves to one right answer than the idea that judges hold a unique institutional capacity to uphold the rule of law and, in particular, to adjudicate matters of fundamental human rights—even if, or perhaps because, such adjudication necessarily involves contestable and significantly discretionary value judgments.

In *Pushpanathan*, discussed in chapter 8, the majority and dissent differ on whether drug trafficking is "contrary to the purposes and principles of the United Nations," a condition for disqualifying persons from seeking refugee status.[50] The majority focuses, in considerable measure, on the intention of the drafters of the incorporated international convention. But it also may be understood to make a contestable value judgment in privileging the convention's commitment to human rights protection as a basis for narrowly construing the disputed provision, where it could have focused instead (as did the dissent and tribunal) on the multiple UN statements and instruments evincing a purpose of eradicating the drug trade. In casting your mind back to the pragmatic and functional analysis in this case, do you agree that there was little basis for expressing deference to the tribunal on the significance of the relevant domestic and international laws? If you are so convinced—and, moreover, convinced by the majority's approach to the interpretive problem at the heart of the case—how would you compare this decision with the application of correctness review in *Trinity Western*? That decision is discussed by Evan Fox-Decent in chapter 7.[51] In it, the majority employs a markedly abstract conceptual analysis in concluding that the BC College of Teachers (BCCT) failed to balance its equality concerns about Trinity Western's teacher-training program with a concern for the university's (and/or its students') freedom of religion. Might that analysis have been improved, or more adequately justified, with closer attention to the practical bases for BCCT's concerns? Would you say that the dissent of L'Heureux-Dubé J., who adopts a patent unreasonableness standard, demonstrates such

47 See, for example, *Pushpanathan*, *supra* note 31 at para. 45.

48 *Ibid.*

49 2001 SCC 31, [2001] 1 S.C.R. 772 [*Trinity Western*].

50 *Supra* note 31 at para. 1. You will recall that the decision turned upon interpretation of a provision of the federal immigration statute incorporating article 1F(c) of the *UN Convention Relating to the Status of Refugees*. Specifically at issue was whether Pushpanathan's conviction for drug trafficking rendered him "guilty of acts contrary to the purposes and principles of the United Nations" (the language of the incorporated convention), and thus ineligible to apply for refugee status.

51 The case involved the BC College of Teachers' refusal, under its broad public interest mandate to set educational standards, to grant Trinity Western accreditation for all five years of a teacher-training program. The tribunal's concern was the requirement that students at TWU sign a community standards contract, which included a pledge to refrain from "homosexual behaviour," described as a "sexual sin."

attentiveness? But what do you make of her assertion that religious freedom is not engaged by the decision, independent of a direct Charter claim? Is this an attempt to force the supremacy of one value without explicit justification in light of competing values?[52]

Beyond these examples of normative approaches to statutory interpretation, correctness review also continues to be applied in ways that suggest a more positivistic understanding of the enterprise. For example, in *Barrie Utilities*,[53] Gonthier J. for the majority characterizes the phrase "the supporting structure of a transmission line" as a matter of "pure statutory interpretation." He then proceeds to render its plain meaning. But on the other side are arguments that the contrary interpretation (favoured by the Canadian Radio-television and Telecommunications Commission [CRTC]) both was eminently reasonable and reflected legitimate policy goals. In expressing concern with the approach of the majority, Bastarache J. in dissent draws upon the reasons of L'Heureux-Dubé J. for a unanimous Court in *Domtar Inc. v. Quebec (Commission d'appel en matière de lésions professionnelles)*:[54]

> Substituting one's opinion for that of an administrative tribunal in order to develop one's own interpretation of a legislative provision eliminates its decision-making autonomy and special expertise. Since such intervention occurs in circumstances where the legislature has determined that the administrative tribunal is the one in the best position to rule on the disputed decision, it risks, at the same time, thwarting the original intention of the legislature. For the purposes of judicial review, statutory interpretation has ceased to be a necessarily "exact" science and this Court has, again recently, confirmed the rule of curial deference set forth for the first time in *Canadian Union of Public Employees, Local 963 v. New Brunswick Liquor Corp.*[55]

Consider what it means to say that statutory interpretation is no longer an "exact" science. In particular, what does this mean for a correctness standard of review? Examination of how correctness review was applied in the above cases reveals tensions between a positivist approach to statutory interpretation, which looks to the text (or sometimes text and legislative context) as a closed system indicative of a determinate legislative intent, and a normative approach, which views problems of statutory interpretation in light of background assessments not only of social facts but also of competing value-laden purposes. Arguably the latter approach, taken seriously, begins to erode the idea that courts need not give any weight or respect to the justificatory efforts of tribunals, even on matters reserved for correctness review. Such a position is further supported when one considers that it may be difficult if not impossible ever to achieve a surgical separation of fact and law, or policy and law. However, on the other side, how, if not through correctness review, can administrative law channel the traditional rule of law concerns to ensure consistency in the interpretation and application of core or system-wide legal principles, and to protect individual rights? Is the standard of correctness, or the application of that standard in certain cases, in some sense vital to the project of striking the right balance between the rule of law and deference to administrators?

52 Arguably, on a result-driven analysis, L'Heureux-Dubé J. does this to avoid the charge that the tribunal was patently unreasonable in failing to take into account a mandatory relevant factor (more of which below).

53 *Supra* note 8.

54 [1993] 2 S.C.R. 756 [*Domtar*].

55 *Barrie Utilities*, *supra* note 8 at para. 128 (per Bastarache J.), quoting *Domtar*, *supra* note 54 at 775.

B. In Search of Patent Unreasonableness

1. The Patent Unreasonableness Standard in Theory

You will recall from chapter 8 that *CUPE* inherits from the previous jurisprudence the idea of a strict divide, relevant to decisions protected by a privative clause, between "jurisdictional questions" going to the limits of administrative decision-makers' statutory mandates (in respect of which they must be correct) and "questions within jurisdiction" (in respect of which they command deference). On the old approach, decisions taken within jurisdiction were understood to escape review, short of misinterpretations so egregious they were deemed to exceed the statutory mandate. In *CUPE*, Dickson J. indicated that the matter of jurisdiction could be quickly dispatched, on finding that the tribunal had carriage over the subject matter and parties. Thus, the interpretive challenge in that case was "for [the board] alone to decide within its jurisdiction."[56] However, Dickson J. then posed the further question:

> Did the Board here so misinterpret the provisions of the Act as to embark on an inquiry or answer a question not remitted to it? Put another way, was the Board's interpretation so patently unreasonable that its construction cannot be rationally supported by the relevant legislation and demands intervention by the court upon review?[57]

As David Mullan has observed,[58] in these two sentences Dickson J. bridges two antithetical approaches to substantive review. That is, the first sentence alludes to a set of grounds, such as "asking the wrong question,"[59] historically deployed to frame administrative decisions as in excess of jurisdiction and so to yoke tribunals' interpretive efforts to the opinions of courts. In contrast, the second sentence—both its use of the term "patently unreasonable" and its fleshing out of this term with the idea of an interpretation that "cannot be rationally supported by the relevant legislation"—is poised to become the touchstone of generations of deferential review. In the context of Dickson J.'s judgment in *CUPE*, the second formulation conveys both the idea that statutory language may accommodate more than one reasonable interpretation, and that there is good reason for courts to defer to expert tribunals where their interpretations fall within the ambit of reasonableness.

Cases decided subsequent to *CUPE* have at times manifested the uneasy coexistence of these approaches, whereby courts ostensibly deploy patent unreasonableness review, yet

56 *CUPE*, *supra* note 1 at 237.

57 *Ibid.*

58 See, for example, D. Mullan, "A Blast from the Past: A Surreptitious Resurgence of Metropolitan Life?" (1992) 5 Admin. L.R. (2d) 97.

59 In a citation just prior to the above quotation from *CUPE*, Dickson J. refers to his previous articulation of the sorts of error that take a tribunal beyond its jurisdiction, in *Service Employees' International Union, Local No. 333 v. Nipawin District Staff Nurses Assn.* [1975] 1 S.C.R. 382 at 389 ("acting in bad faith, basing the decision on extraneous matters, failing to take relevant factors into account, breaching the provisions of natural justice or so misinterpreting the provisions of the Act so as to embark on an inquiry or answer a question not remitted to it"). This list is in turn drawn from the House of Lords case *Anisminic Ltd. v. Foreign Compensation Commission*, [1969] 2 A.C. 147 at 171 (H.L.), a case recognized as the nadir of deferential review in its support for the idea that all administrative decisions involving interpretation of law attract correctness review. *Anisminic*'s list was relied upon in Canada's equivalent low watermark of deference, *Metropolitan Life Insurance Co. v. I.U.O.E., Local 796*, [1970] S.C.R. 425.

engage in what appears to be a search for the "right answer." One might include in this class judgments that make the common analytical move on patent unreasonableness review of adopting a correctness-style assessment of statutory purposes in order to then assess whether the decision-maker "failed to take into account a relevant factor" or "took into account an irrelevant factor."[60] Continuing uncertainty about the meaning and practical implications of the search for patent unreasonableness has been expressed in the case law since *CUPE*. Cory J. struggled to quell concerns about the unpredictability inherent in this standard in *Canada (Attorney General) v. Public Service Alliance of Canada*:

> It is said that it is difficult to know what "patently unreasonable" means. What is patently unreasonable to one judge may be eminently reasonable to another. Yet any test can only be defined by words, the building blocks of all reasons. Obviously, the patently unreasonable test sets a high standard of review. In the Shorter Oxford English Dictionary "patently," an adverb, is defined as "openly, evidently, clearly." "Unreasonable" is defined as "[n]ot having the faculty of reason; irrational. … Not acting in accordance with reason or good sense." Thus, based on the dictionary definition of the words "patently unreasonable," it is apparent that if the decision the Board reached, acting within its jurisdiction, is not clearly irrational, that is to say evidently not in accordance with reason, then it cannot be said that there was a loss of jurisdiction. This is clearly a very strict test.[61]

Some later cases throw lifelines back to the phrase "clearly irrational" to add putative clarity to the central inquiry under this standard. Others formulate further variations on the theme. For instance, in *Voice Construction Ltd. v. Construction and General Workers' Union, Local 92*, Major J. states that "[a] definition of patently unreasonable is difficult, but it may be said that the result must almost border on the absurd."[62]

With the rise of the reasonableness *simpliciter* standard, the courts have had to strive to further refine the concept of patent unreasonableness. Two recent concurring judgments penned by LeBel J. have consolidated the debates around the import of the patent unreasonableness standard, particularly as it relates to the reasonableness standard.[63] LeBel J. points out that the case law has sought to distinguish and thus clarify the import of patent unreasonableness with reference on the one hand to "the magnitude of the defect necessary to render a decision patently unreasonable," and on the other, "the 'immediacy or obviousness' of the defect, and thus the relative invasiveness of the review necessary to find it."[64] LeBel J.'s assessment of the failure of either definitional strand to lend coherence to the concept of patent unreasonableness, as distinguished from correctness review

60 D. Mullan, "Deference from Baker to Suresh and Beyond—Interpreting the Conflicting Signals" in D. Dyzenhaus, ed., *The Unity of Public Law* (Portland, OR: Hart Publishing, 2004) 21 at 24 (note 9) ["Deference from Baker to Suresh"].

61 *Canada (Attorney General) v. Public Service Alliance of Canada*, [1993] 1 S.C.R. 941 at 963.

62 2004 SCC 23, [2004] 1 S.C.R. 609 [*Voice Construction*] at para. 18. To this LeBel J. rejoins (at para. 40): "With respect, adding yet another definition of patent unreasonableness would not make its application any easier nor its conceptual validity more obvious."

63 *Toronto (City) v. CUPE, Local 79*, 2003 SCC 63, [2003] 3 S.C.R. 77 [*Local 79*], and *Voice Construction, supra* note 62.

64 *Local 79, ibid.* at para. 78.

on the one end and reasonableness review on the other, is taken up in the final part of this chapter.

In *Voice Construction*, Major J. states that situations in which a pragmatic and functional analysis will justify patent unreasonableness review "will be rare."[65] That said, the standard continues to have a place in the jurisprudence. It may be assigned in connection with questions of law (where the contested statutory provisions are deemed to fall squarely within the mandate of the decision-maker), and less contentiously, questions of fact, or mixed law and fact—in addition to (since *Baker*) the exercise of discretion.[66] Where the matter in issue is deemed to be a pure question of fact, the inquiry into patent unreasonableness echoes the traditional concern with whether there was "no evidence" supporting the conclusion.[67] Patent unreasonableness review of discretion also hearkens back to the traditional grounds of review, specifically inquiring into whether the discretionary decision may be said to be "unreasonable on its face, unsupported by evidence, or vitiated by failure to consider the proper factors or apply the appropriate procedures."[68] In one case the Supreme Court articulated a multi-faceted test for determining whether the exercise of a broad remedial power was patently unreasonable.[69] But in the main, as LeBel J. suggests, guidance on the import of the standard has tended to be rooted in characterizations of the "magnitude" and/or "immediacy or obviousness" of the defect.[70]

As we turn to a few instances of application of this standard, keep a watch on judicial constructions of statutory purposes as these relate to the legal limits on decision-makers' interpretive discretion. Are such background assessments necessarily done on a correctness standard, even where utmost deference is otherwise indicated? Would the alternative (deferring to administrators' interpretations of the general ambit of statutory purposes and thus of their statutory powers) place an indefensible strain upon the rule of law?

2. Patent Unreasonableness Review in Practice

So far, we have seen some uncertainty in the characterization of the patent unreasonableness standard. Might a closer look at the case law addressing how the standard is to be applied in practice assist in resolving these issues?

A basic principle of patent unreasonableness review is that the reviewing judge must not measure the decision against his or her sense of the "correct" decision.[71] As we will see, however, questions arise as to how to gauge patent unreasonableness, if not against the

65 *Supra* note 63 at para. 18. But note Lahey and Ginn's observation in "After the Revolution" (*supra* note 24 at 274, 297) that lower courts continue to apply this standard even to decisions not protected by a privative clause.

66 See chapter 10 by Geneviève Cartier.

67 *Toronto (City) Board of Education v. O.S.S.T.F., District 15*, [1997] 1 S.C.R. 487 [*OSSTF*].

68 *Suresh v. Canada (Minister of Citizenship and Immigration)*, 2002 SCC 1, [2002] 1 S.C.R. 3 at para. 41 [*Suresh*].

69 *Royal Oak Mines Inc. v. Canada (Labour Relations Board)*, [1996] 1 S.C.R. 369. But consider in what respect, if any, this test is expressive of deference.

70 *Supra* note 64.

71 *Ryan, supra* note 6 at para. 50.

judge's opinion of the right answer. A second principle goes to the allowable level of engagement with the decision-maker's reasoning, and with the evidence and argument on the record. Thus Iacobucci J. in *Southam* suggests that while patent unreasonableness review may involve review of the record, it should not require "significant searching or testing" to detect the fatal defect.[72] Uncertainty arises, however, with the attempt to quantify the depth of probing in this manner.

In *CUPE*, more questions are raised than answered about the method of patent unreasonableness review. In chapter 8, Macklin takes up Dickson J.'s application of the newly forged patent unreasonableness standard in that case. Recall that the statutory provision in issue[73] was markedly ambiguous. Macklin suggests that Dickson J.'s survey of the competing interpretations of the provision taken by the Public Service Labour Relations Board and by the reviewing judges at the Court of Appeal advances his assertion that no single interpretation could be "said to be 'right.'"[74] Indeed, Dickson J. grants that each of these opinions was reasonable on its face. But viewed in light of his background assessment of the purpose of the disputed provision in promoting the unique *quid pro quo* of public sector collective bargaining,[75] it seems that the tribunal's conclusion that the provision prohibited the Liquor Corp. from replacing striking workers with management was, if not right (on a positivist account), then the best interpretation (on a pragmatic assessment of background norms and purposes). What do you think is doing the work in this judgment: purposive statutory interpretation or deference? Or a happy coincidence of the two?

Dickson J. suggests that he has made much of the statutory purpose only because "to some, the Board's interpretation may, at first glance, seem unreasonable if one draws too heavily upon private sector experience";[76] moreover, he exhibits restraint in his conclusion that "at a minimum, the Board's interpretation would seem at least as reasonable as the alternative interpretations suggested in the Court of Appeal."[77] But one may wonder how the judgment would have gone if the tribunal had drawn a conclusion as much at odds with the purpose of the statute and provision, as characterized by Dickson J., as the Court of Appeal's conclusion. Here the approach to patent unreasonableness taken by Dickson J. in *CUPE* might be both compared with and contrasted to the approach adopted by L'Heureux-Dubé J. in dissent in *Mossop*. Both ground their judgments in reflections on the statutory purpose, conveying a strong impression that the judge is independently verifying the interpretive judgment of the tribunal. However, it is important to note that, like L'Heureux-Dubé J. in *Mossop*, Dickson J. in *CUPE* does not arrive at his construction of statutory purpose whole cloth, of his own invention, but rather draws upon and amplifies the explicit reasoning of the board.[78]

72 See *Southam, supra* note 5 at para. 57.

73 The disputed provision of New Brunswick's *Public Service Labour Relations Act* stated: "the employer shall not replace the striking employees or fill their position with any other employee." R.S.N.B. 1973, c. P-25, s. 102(3).

74 *CUPE, supra* note 1 at 237.

75 *Ibid.* at 240-41.

76 *Ibid.* at 242.

77 *Ibid.*

78 See the comments near the end of the board decision, [1977] N.B.P.S.L.R.D. No. 7 (20 September 1977), putting forward the very *quid pro quo* argument that Dickson J. draws upon in his reasons.

Still, looking back to those strains of guidance in the case law that suggest the judge must not engage in too deep or probing a review, and must not base his or her conclusion on an independent assessment of the right answer, the question may be asked of the judgment in *CUPE* (as well as that of L'Heureux-Dubé J. in *Mossop*): would this be deemed a fitting model of patent unreasonableness review today?

Indeed, one of the first controversies that arose in the case law following *CUPE* was whether patent unreasonableness review should, or indeed must, begin with the court's assessing the "right answer" (if it found that the statute lent itself to such a determination). That controversy reaches back to Sopinka J., who, in a concurring opinion in *C.A.I.M.A.W. v. Paccar of Canada Ltd.*,[79] wrote:

> Any adjudication upon the reasonableness of a decision must involve an evaluation of the merits. Reasonableness is not a quality that exists in isolation. When a court says that a decision under review is "reasonable" or "patently unreasonable" it is making a statement about a logical relationship between the grounds of the decision and premises thought by the court to be true. Without the reference point of an opinion (if not a conclusion) on the merits, such a relative statement cannot be made.[80]

David Mullan articulated criticisms of this approach as follows:

> First, it assumes the existence of a single correct answer to the statutory interpretation exercise at stake and the capacity of the Court rather than the Tribunal to discern that answer. Secondly, in a very practical sense, it must be extremely difficult for any Court, having concluded that a tribunal has "got it wrong," to then say that the error was not a patently unreasonable one.[81]

The approach taken by Sopinka J. in *Paccar* was rejected in the subsequent case law, as most recently confirmed in a statement in *Ryan* that on applying a reasonableness (and it seems, by implication, also a patent unreasonableness) standard, "a court should not at any point ask itself what the correct decision would have been."[82]

A related controversy about how to adhere to the spirit of *CUPE* arose in the 1990 judgment in *National Corn Growers*.[83] That case involved a finding of the Canadian Import Tribunal that the importation of subsidized American grain corn into Canada was the cause of actual or potential "material injury" to Canadian corn producers, triggering the imposition of a countervailing duty. The majority judgment of Gonthier J. and concurring opinion of Wilson J. agreed that the appropriate standard was patent unreasonableness. But Wilson J. took pains to distinguish her opinion on the proper application of that standard from the approach taken by Gonthier J. Her argument with the majority turned upon the issue cast above as "depth of probing." Thus she wrote that "to embark upon a detailed analysis of the

79 [1989] 2 S.C.R. 983 [*Paccar*].

80 *Paccar*, *ibid.* at 1018 (Sopinka J. writing for himself and Lamer J.). This approach may be said to be adopted by McLachlin J. in her majority judgment in *W.W. Lester (1978) Ltd. v. U.A., Local 740*, [1990] 3 S.C.R. 644.

81 D. Mullan, "Of Chaff Midst the Corn: American Farm Bureau Federation v. Canada (Canadian Import Tribunal) and Patent Unreasonableness Review" (1991) 45 Admin L.R. 264 at 269-70.

82 See *Ryan*, *supra* note 6 at para. 50.

83 *National Corn Growers*, *supra* note 9.

extent to which the evidence will support the Tribunal's finding in the face of a privative clause is to engage in the very kind of meticulous analysis of the Tribunal's reasoning that *C.U.P.E.* made clear courts should not conduct."[84] Such meticulous analysis is by Wilson J. deemed synonymous with evaluation of the "correctness" or "merits of the Tribunal's conclusions." Wilson J. stated her alternative as follows:

> In my view … the only issue which this Court may consider, once it accepts that the interpretation of a given provision is a matter that falls within a tribunal's jurisdiction, is whether the Tribunal's interpretation of the provision is "so patently unreasonable that its construction cannot be rationally supported by the relevant legislation."[85]

These comments appear to restrict patent unreasonableness review to issues of statutory interpretation, leaving the evaluation of evidence, and the appliction of the law to the facts, off limits. On applying this approach, Wilson J. takes a concertedly acontextual approach to the language of the disputed provision, determining in short order that it "certainly cannot be said to preclude the 'broader' interpretation … that the Tribunal favoured."[86]

The competing approach of Gonthier J. proceeds on the following argument:

> In some cases, the unreasonableness of a decision may be apparent without detailed examination of the record. In others, it may be no less unreasonable but this can only be understood upon an in-depth analysis. Such was the case in the *C.U.P.E.* decision where it was found that the Board's interpretation of the legislation at issue was reasonable even though it was not the only reasonable one. Similarly, understanding of the issues raised by the appellants herein as to the reasonableness of the Tribunal's decision requires some analysis of the relevant legislation and the way in which the Tribunal has interpreted and applied it to the facts.[87]

In practice, Gonthier J. tracks the tribunal's reasons closely, breaking the decision down into a set of discrete judgments. These include its decision to refer to the General Agreement on Tariffs and Trade to assist in interpreting the disputed provision, its interpretation of that provision, and its subsequent finding of "material injury" in the circumstances of the case. In response to Wilson J.'s concerns, Gonthier J. writes:

> With respect, I do not understand how a conclusion can be reached as to the reasonableness of a tribunal's interpretation of its enabling statute without considering the reasoning underlying it, and I would be surprised if that were the effect of this Court's decision in *C.U.P.E.*[88]

However, he adds that such probing "must be undertaken in light of the overall question for determination, namely, whether or not the interpretation ultimately arrived at is patently unreasonable."[89]

84 *Ibid.* at 1349.

85 *Ibid.*

86 *Ibid.* at 1352.

87 *Ibid.* at 1370.

88 *Ibid.* at 1383.

89 *Ibid.*

The approach of Gonthier J. appears to have mostly won out in the case law on applying a patent unreasonableness (and for that matter, reasonableness) standard. First, in the review of questions of fact, examination of the record to determine whether the standard of "no evidence" is met is a generally acknowledged necessity.[90] Second, in *Southam*, Iacobucci J. elaborates upon the patent unreasonableness standard as follows (after noting that a patently unreasonable error, unlike mere unreasonableness, should not take "significant searching or testing" to expose):

> This is not to say, of course, that judges reviewing a decision on the standard of patent unreasonableness may not examine the record. If the decision under review is sufficiently difficult, then perhaps a great deal of reading and thinking will be required before the judge is able to grasp the dimensions of the problem.[91]

However, there remains resistance to close oversight on a patent unreasonableness standard. This is expressed through continuing efforts to distinguish patent unreasonableness from reasonableness review on the basis of the "immediacy or obviousness" of the defect and so the depth of probing required to reveal that defect.

Finally, the concluding comment of Gonthier J. noted above, on subordinating the careful examination of tribunal reasoning to a more general assessment of the decision's patent unreasonableness, is reflected in the principle in *Ryan* that in conducting review for reasonableness *simpliciter*,

> not every element of the reasoning given must independently pass a test for reasonableness. The question is rather whether the reasons, taken as a whole, are tenable as support for the decision. At all times, a court applying a standard of reasonableness must assess the basic adequacy of a reasoned decision remembering that the issue under review does not compel one specific result. Moreover, a reviewing court should not seize on one or more mistakes or elements of the decision which do not affect the decision as a whole.[92]

A further controversy in the case law on applying the patent unreasonableness standard relates to the division of labour between courts and tribunals in characterizing the purposes of the enabling statute or a contested provision thereof. Here it may be noted that while the case law has rejected the suggestion that deferential review must start by determining the right answer, it remains that the decision and/or reasoning of the decision-maker must be gauged against some expectation of legality. The question is: how is that expectation set? A typical reference point is the purpose of the statute and/or the disputed provision. That is, analysis of statutory purpose may fundamentally orient the determination of whether the standard is met, particularly where the charge is made that the tribunal took into account irrelevant factors or failed to take into account relevant factors.[93] This suggests that even on

90 See *OSSTF*, *supra* note 67, and D. Mullan, "Establishing the Standard of Review: The Struggle for Complexity?" (2004) 17 Can. J. Admin. L. & Prac. 59 at 92.

91 *Southam*, *supra* note 5 at para. 57.

92 *Ryan*, *supra* note 6 at para. 56.

93 *Parry Sound (District) Social Services Administration Board v. O.P.S.E.U., Local 324*, 2003 SCC 42, [2003] 2 S.C.R. 157 at para. 60, referring to *Suresh*, *supra* note 68 at para. 29.

the most deferential standard, there remains an outer limit of correctness style reasoning. But is it appropriate for a reviewing court to assess the values and interests at stake in a given case independent of the tribunal's reasoning? Alternatively, might a reviewing court be expected to defer to tribunals' assessments of statutory purposes, or of the factors relevant or irrelevant to their decisions?

A final case that brings into focus these questions about the analysis proper to patent unreasonableness review is *C.U.P.E. v. Ontario (Minister of Labour)*.[94] That case involved patent unreasonableness review of a ministerial exercise of discretion. As Geneviève Cartier relates in chapter 10, discretionary powers have only recently been drawn into the fold of the standard of review analysis with the *Baker* case. Yet it appears that the traditional grounds of review of discretion continue to drive the inquiry at the application stage, including the ground of failure to take into account a relevant factor.[95] At issue in this case—typically referred to as the *Retired Judges* case—was a decision under a section of Ontario's *Hospital Labour Disputes Arbitration Act* that stated that where parties fail to agree upon the third member of an interest arbitration panel, "the Minister shall appoint ... a person who is, in the opinion of the Minister, qualified to act."[96] For nearly 20 years, the Minister (or a delegate) had exercised this power by choosing from a roster of recognized labour arbitrators or others who were "skilled and experienced in interest arbitration" and recognized as such by both unions and employers.[97] The dispute concerned the Minister's decision to restrict these appointments to retired judges. The unions objected, on the apprehension that this class of appointees would be unsympathetic to their interests, and sought judicial review.

The majority decision, written by Binnie J., concluded that the Minister's decision was patently unreasonable. This conclusion was based in great measure on a close examination of the statute in its historical context. Yet notably, that careful analysis is positioned in Binnie J.'s judgment prior to his determination of the standard of review. Here we may ask: Should there have been any canvassing of the bases of deference prior to the majority's construction of statutory purposes? Binnie J. defends his approach with a statement from Lord Reid in a 1968 House of Lords case: "[T]he policy and objects of the Act must be determined by construing the Act as a whole and construction is always a matter of law for the court."[98] Binnie J. further draws out the rule of law rationale for this principle, namely: "The Court's mandate on judicial review is to keep the statutory decision maker within the boundaries the legislature intended."[99]

Adopting this methodology, then, Binnie J. concludes that the purpose of the HLDAA is to achieve "industrial peace by substituting compulsory arbitration for the right to strike or lockout."[100] As such, the legislative scheme is dependent upon securing the "trust and

94 2003 SCC 29, [2003] 1 S.C.R. 539 [*Retired Judges*].

95 *Ibid.* at 21 (per Bastarache J.), citing *Suresh*, *supra* note 68 at para. 41.

96 R.S.O. 1990, c. H.14, s. 6(5) [HLDAA].

97 *Supra* note 94 at para. 67.

98 *Ibid.* at para. 94, quoting *Padfield v. Minister of Agriculture, Fisheries and Food*, [1968] A.C. 997 (H.L.).

99 *Retired Judges*, *supra* note 94 at para. 98.

100 *Ibid.* at para. 94.

confidence of the parties."[101] Further consideration of the statute and the historical record leads Binnie J. to conclude that the factors essential to securing that trust in the context of HLDAA arbitrations are "impartiality, independence, expertise and general acceptability in the labour relations community."[102] In other words, these are mandatory relevant factors. Binnie J. then determines that the Minister's decision was patently unreasonable because of its failure to take the last of these factors into account.

But here we should pause and ask: What work is the patent unreasonableness standard doing in this decision? Binnie J. reasons that the deference due under this standard is qualified or constrained by the statutory purpose, leaving "a relatively narrow context"[103] within which the Minister's discretion may operate. Still, the language of patent unreasonableness is used, and he characterizes the defect in the decision as "both immediate and obvious."[104] Ultimately, Binnie J. relies on the principle, present in the substantive review jurisprudence prior to *CUPE*, that while a patent unreasonableness standard does not admit the reweighing of factors taken into account by a statutory decision-maker, the court is nonetheless "entitled to have regard to the importance of the factors that have been excluded altogether from consideration."[105] In this case, concludes Binnie J., there was no indication that the relevant factors in question, which went to the "heart" of the legislative scheme, were taken into account.[106]

Bastarache J. in dissent agrees that the review of discretion "requires that we [the Court] determine the relevant criteria for exercise of the discretion, or at least whether the Minister relied upon irrelevant criteria or failed to consider a relevant and important criterion."[107] Yet he plays up the fact that the statutory language here clearly refers to "the opinion of the Minister" as to whether persons are "qualified to act."[108] Moreover, he disagrees that the flaw in decision-making identified by the majority is either immediate or obvious. He states: "Given how much work it takes to identify the factors at issue in this appeal … and to imply them into s. 6(5), I am reluctant to conclude that weighing them less heavily than another factor, also unwritten (judicial experience), vitiated the appointments as patently unreasonable."[109] That is, it took "significant searching" on the part of the majority to find the factors deemed of mandatory relevance. Bastarache J. further characterizes the majority as smuggling in, under the auspices of a "failure to consider," reassessment of the weight to be accorded the considerations relevant to these appointments.

Bastarache J. takes pains to respond to the charge that his critique implies an abandonment of the judicial duty to uphold the rule of law and to keep executive power within legal

101 *Ibid.* at para. 109, quoting the factum of the intervener National Academy of Arbitrators.

102 *Ibid.* at para. 110.

103 *Ibid.* at paras. 153-56.

104 *Ibid.* at para. 184.

105 *Ibid.* at para. 176.

106 Given that there were no formal reasons for the Minister's decision, this finding relies in part on evidence of a senior adviser that neutrality was the sole criterion in play at the stage of searching for retired judges to take up this role. *Ibid.* at para. 182.

107 *Ibid.* at para. 28.

108 *Ibid.* at para. 30.

109 *Ibid.* at para. 36.

limits. His deferential approach, he claims, would serve to contain "extreme examples" of abuse of the appointment power—for instance, should the Minister decide "to appoint only members of his own political caucus, hospital CEOs, or union business agents."[110] But consider what the analysis of the limits of discretion would look like in such a case. How would such protections be afforded, taking into account Bastarache J.'s critiques?[111]

In concluding this look at patent unreasonableness review, let us recall the two imperatives we have seen are associated with this standard: (1) the prohibition on seeking the "right answer" and measuring the tribunal's decision against that rather than attending to whether there is a rational basis for the tribunal's decision and (2) the prohibition on undue probing. Both flow from the idea that substantive review threatens to illegitimately impose foreign judicial values and perspectives on localized administrative values and perspectives. Yet that perception of the threat of judicial review runs up against the countervailing perception that judicial vigilance is required to ensure that administrative decision-makers do not exceed their legal mandates. An attempt to mediate these competing concerns informs the traditional division of labour whereby judges have exclusive capacity to identify the factors relevant to a decision (the legal limits of the decision) and administrators have exclusive capacity to weigh or balance those factors (the merits of the decision). But is this a workable distinction? Aside from its potential manipulability, are you convinced that judges can, or should, refrain from engagement with the weight placed by decision-makers on competing factors under a patent unreasonableness—or reasonableness—standard? Is it better that their background assessments of weight be explicitly stated and subjected to public scrutiny, so alleviating the possibility of these assessments' covert operation? On the other side, should judges give weight to administrative decision-makers' opinions about the factors that are and are not of mandatory relevance to their decisions? In what circumstances, if any?

With that, we turn to our last standard—reasonableness *simpliciter*.

C. The Third Way: Reasonableness Simpliciter

1. The Reasonableness Standard in Theory

In introducing the reasonableness standard in *Southam*,[112] Iacobucci J. acknowledges the conflicting signals elicited by the pragmatic and functional analysis in that case: in particular, its featuring both a statutory right of appeal and an expert tribunal. In response, Iacobucci J. determines that "what is dictated is a standard more deferential than correctness but less deferential than 'not patently unreasonable.'" He thus characterizes this standard as a "middle ground," arrived at as "almost a necessary consequence of our standard-of-review

110 *Ibid.* at para. 40.

111 See L. Sossin, "Empty Ritual, Mechanical Exercise or the Discipline of Deference? Revisiting the Standard of Review in Administrative Law" (2003) 27 Advocates' Q. 478 at 504-5. For a trenchant critique of the majority approach in the *Retired Judges* case, emphasizing the importance of the legislature's having left the disputed decision to the Minister's "opinion," see G. Huscroft, "Judicial Review from CUPE to CUPE: Less Is Not Always More" in *Inside and Outside*, *supra* note 15 at 296.

112 *Supra* note 5 at para. 54.

jurisprudence." The new standard is then described (in a sentence much cited in subsequent case law) as follows:

> An unreasonable decision is one that, in the main, is not supported by any reasons that can stand up to a somewhat probing examination.[113]

From the start, then, this form of review focuses on the quality of the reasons for a given administrative action or decision. Iacobucci J. elaborates as follows:

> Accordingly, a court reviewing a conclusion on the reasonableness standard must look to see whether any reasons support it. The defect, if there is one, could presumably be in the evidentiary foundation itself or the logical process by which conclusions are sought to be drawn from it. An example of the former kind of defect would be an assumption that had no basis in the evidence. An example of the latter kind would be a contradiction in the premises or an invalid inference.[114]

Despite the characterization of this form of review as "somewhat probing," there seems to be no significant concern in Iacobucci J.'s judgment in *Southam* to limit examination of the record. Indeed, the permissible level of probing or scrutiny is apparently extended in the further suggestion of Iacobucci J. that while a patently unreasonable decision will be "apparent on the face of the tribunal's reasons," apprehension of an unreasonable defect may take "some significant searching or testing."[115]

Iacobucci J. adds to these comments reflections linking the reasonableness standard to a conception of deference that is contingent upon both expertise and reason-giving. He writes: "In the final result, the standard of reasonableness simply instructs reviewing courts to accord considerable weight to the views of tribunals about matters with respect to which they have significant expertise."[116] To this he appends an extended citation to the effect that unless experts are able to explain "to a fair-minded but less well-informed observer, the reasons for their conclusions," then "they are not very expert" and no deference is commanded.[117]

In a later case, *Ryan*, Iacobucci J. emphasizes (as Dickson J. had done in *CUPE*) that, "[u]nlike a review for correctness, there will often be no single right answer to the questions"[118] subject to review for reasonableness. Here he directly engages problems of statutory construction hinging on the prioritization of competing statutory purposes:

> For example, when a decision must be taken according to a set of objectives that exist in tension with each other, there may be no particular trade-off that is superior to all the others. Even if there could be, notionally, a single best answer, it is not the court's role to seek this out when deciding if the decision was unreasonable.[119]

---

113 *Ibid.* at para. 56.

114 *Ibid.*

115 *Ibid.* at para. 57.

116 *Ibid.* at para. 62.

117 *Ibid.*, citing R.P. Kerans, *Standards of Review Employed by Appellate Courts* (Edmonton: Juriliber, 1994) at 17.

118 *Ryan*, *supra* note 6 at para. 51.

119 *Ibid.*

While this statement affirms the general principle that deferential review must avoid second-guessing administrators with respect to the weight they assign competing statutory purposes, we will see that this issue is not entirely settled in the jurisprudence on this standard.

The positive side to the prohibition against seeking the "right answer" on reasonableness review is the imperative stated in *Ryan* to the effect that judges must "stay close to the reasons" for an administrative decision, while searching for a "line of analysis within the given reasons that could reasonably lead the tribunal from the evidence before it to the conclusion at which it arrived."[120] Here Iacobucci J. revives the principle that "a decision may satisfy the reasonableness standard if it is supported by a tenable explanation even if this explanation is not one that the reviewing court finds compelling."[121] A further principle of reasonableness review stated in *Ryan* and reminiscent of the case law on patent unreasonableness is that judges are to assess the "basic adequacy of a reasoned decision," while refraining from "seiz[ing] on one or more mistakes or elements of the decision which do not affect the decision as a whole."[122]

Finally, as noted above, in *Ryan*, Iacobucci J. puts paid to the idea that since the introduction of the reasonableness standard in *Southam*, further and finer gradations of deference are now implicit on the spectrum of the standards of review. On reflection, the suggestion made some sense. For if the reasonableness standard was forged in an attempt to better calibrate reviewing practices to the diversity of administrative contexts, then more standards may seem to mean even finer calibration. However, Iacobucci J. responds that this would afford increased manipulability of the standards in accordance with judges' opinions of the merits of decisions, while distracting judges from the central work of "explaining why the decision was not supported by any reasons that can bear a somewhat probing examination."[123] This statement is notable for its candour in acknowledging that while the factors surveyed in selecting the standard of review are important, judges must take care lest the business of calibrating the standard to match up to the institutional and statutory context becomes a merely formalistic exercise, displacing attention from a context-sensitive assessment of the decision in issue.

In these statements in *Ryan* and in *Southam*, Iacobucci J. makes efforts to resolve in the characterization of reasonableness review some of the uncertainty and contestation that has beset patent unreasonableness review: both the idea that deferential review must begin with an ascertainment of the correct decision (then allowing for a certain "margin of error"), and the idea that deference connotes a blunt prohibition on oversight of administrative reasoning. In sum, what animates Iacobucci J.'s characterizations of reasonableness review is a confidence in reason. This is expressed on the one hand in the idea that judges are capable of appreciating the reasons of administrative decision-makers (though they must work to do so, by turning their mind to the statutory and wider institutional bases of deference revealed through the pragmatic and functional analysis), and, on the other hand, in the idea that administrative decision-makers can communicate the reasonableness of their decisions

120 *Ibid.* at paras. 49, 55.

121 *Ibid.* at para. 55.

122 *Ibid.* at para. 56. See also *Canadian Broadcasting Corp. v. Canada (Labour Relations Board)*, [1995] 1 S.C.R. 157 at paras. 48-49.

123 *Ryan*, *supra* note 6 at para. 46.

to reviewing judges (though they too must work at this, by articulating their decisions in a manner that is sensitive to the demands of public justification).

2. Reasonableness Review in Practice

Iacobucci J.'s judgment for the Court in *Southam* provides a good example of what he appears to be getting at in his characterizations of reasonableness review. The standard of review analysis in this case is discussed in chapter 8. You will recall that the decision under review was the BC Competition Tribunal's finding that Southam's purchase of certain community newspapers (while it continued to control a number of "daily" papers) had caused a "substantial lessening in competition" in the real estate print advertising market in the lower mainland. At the stage of selecting the standard, the nature of the question was characterized as mixed fact and law. As such, oversight of the tribunal's application of the law to the facts would be required. Also in characterizing the question, Iacobucci J. specifically rejected Southam's claim that the tribunal failed to "accord adequate weight to certain factors." Here he cast the requisite gauging of a "substantial lessening in competition" in the case as involving a "balancing test" involving "things that are not readily quantifiable." He continued:

> The problem with [Southam's] suggestion is that it is inimical to the very notion of a balancing test. A balancing test is a legal rule whose application should be very subtle and flexible, but not mechanical. ... The most that can be said is that the Tribunal should consider each factor; but the according of weight to the factors should be left to the Tribunal.[124]

On applying the reasonableness standard, Iacobucci J. addressed findings at the Court of Appeal that the tribunal had failed to consider evidence essential to the analysis called for under the statute. These factors included, on the one hand, evidence of the identical market-related function of the daily and community papers and, on the other, evidence (from Southam's own expert) that the relevant papers had functioned as competitors. On the first point, Iacobucci J. found that the tribunal did not fail to consider but rather accorded minimal weight to the evidence in question. He concluded: "While I might not agree, as a matter of empirical 'fact' [that the tribunal's analysis on these points] is exhaustive, I think that it is not without its reasons." He added: "Fortunately for the Tribunal, its decision need only be reasonable and not necessarily correct."[125]

On the second point, Iacobucci J. again indicated that he was less than convinced by the tribunal's conclusion. But this did not justify overturning the decision on a reasonableness standard. He writes:

> It is possible that if I were deciding the case de novo, I might not dismiss so readily as the Tribunal did what is admittedly weighty evidence of inter-industry competition. In my view, it is very revealing that Southam's own expert ... identified the community newspapers as the source of Southam's difficulties in the Lower Mainland. To find, in the face of such evidence, that the daily newspapers and the community newspapers are not competitors is perhaps un-

---

124 *Southam, supra* note 5 at para. 43.

125 *Ibid.* at para. 68.

> usual. In that sense, the Tribunal's finding is difficult to accept. However, it is not unreasonable.[126]

Iacobucci J. here appears genuinely prepared to put aside his sense of whether the tribunal's conclusions constitute the best construction of the evidence and argument available on the record. Instead, he rests content with the minimal finding that there was some evidence for those conclusions, and that the inferences therefrom were not illogical. As such, the decision in *Southam* may be taken to epitomize the idea of reasonableness review as a form of oversight that (as we have seen stated also of patent unreasonableness review) refrains from revisiting the weight placed by the decision-maker upon discrete points of evidence or argument.

Dr. Q.[127] is also instructive in this regard. This judgment serves as an incisive corrective to the re-evaluation of evidence undertaken by a first-instance reviewing judge. The judge had quashed a decision of an inquiry committee of the BC College of Physicians and Surgeons finding Dr. Q. guilty of "infamous conduct" (having taken "physical and emotional advantage of one of his patients"). This ruling followed the judge's independent assessment of the evidence, including evidence going to witness credibility. McLachlin C.J. writes: "[W]hen the standard of review is reasonableness, the reviewing judge's role is not to posit alternate interpretations of the evidence; rather, it is to determine whether the Committee's interpretation is unreasonable." In response to the judge's specifically doubting the complainant's "ability to describe distinct bodily markings suggesting an intimate relationship," McLachlin C.J. states: "With respect, when applying a standard of reasonableness *simpliciter*, the reviewing judge's view of the evidence is beside the point; rather, the reviewing judge should have asked whether the Committee's conclusion on this point had some basis in the evidence."[128]

Both these decisions therefore indicate a reluctance to interfere with tribunal assessments of evidence on a reasonableness standard; more generally, Iacobucci J. in *Southam* suggests that courts should not interfere with the weight assigned to competing factors under a term of a statute requiring the decision-maker to enter into a "balancing process." Yet in *Baker*,[129] the message seems to be different on the latter point. You have already encountered this case in these pages (for example, see Grant Huscroft, chapter 5). In her judgment,[130] L'Heureux-Dubé J. set aside a ministerial decision to refrain from exercising a discretionary power to exempt Mavis Baker from deportation. The statutory discretion in issue depended on the Minister's being "satisfied" that an exemption was warranted "owing to the existence of humanitarian and compassionate considerations."[131] Baker's application was based in part on the argument that deporting her would be contrary to the interests of her children.

126 *Ibid.* at para. 79.

127 *Supra* note 7.

128 *Ibid.* at para. 41. Query whether inquiry under a reasonableness *simpliciter* standard into whether a decision had "some basis in the evidence" is different than inquiry under a patent unreasonableness standard into whether a decision is based in "no evidence." (See *OSSTF*, *supra* note 67 at para. 44.)

129 *Supra* note 5.

130 Iacobucci and Cory JJ. agreed on the disposition but dissented on other grounds.

131 *Immigration Act*, R.S.C. 1985, c. I-2, s. 114(2); *Immigration Regulations, 1978*, SOR/78-172, s. 2.1.

On applying a reasonableness standard to the Minister's (or rather, the Minister's delegate's) exercise of discretion, L'Heureux-Dubé J. determined that the notes of the junior officer eventually held out as reasons in the case were inconsistent with "the values underlying the grant of discretion."[132] The reasoning informing this determination is carefully parsed in chapter 10 by Geneviève Cartier. In general terms, L'Heureux-Dubé J. indicates that the values that underlie or set reasonable limits to discretionary powers issue not only from a decision-maker's enabling legislation and associated regulations, but also from instruments of soft law (that is, departmental policies and guidelines), the common law ("the principles of administrative law"), the constitution ("the principles of the rule of law" and "the principles of the Charter"), international law, and even what are rather tantalizingly (and perhaps worryingly) held out as the "fundamental values of Canadian society."[133] In *Baker*, consultation of the relevant sources (the statute, an international convention ratified but not incorporated into domestic legislation, and ministerial guidelines) indicated that "the rights, interests, and needs of children and special attention to childhood are important values that should be considered in reasonably interpreting the 'humanitarian' and 'compassionate' considerations that guide the exercise of the discretion."[134] Because the officer's notes serving as reasons failed to reflect that the decision-maker was "alive, alert, or sensitive to the interests of Ms. Baker's children," the decision failed to meet a reasonableness standard.[135]

Following the ruling in *Baker*, commentators and courts alike were concerned to settle the matter of whether this decision was a straightforward example of the tradition of vitiating a discretionary decision for failure to consider a relevant factor at all (the children's best interests). Or was it perhaps a departure from the traditional approach, amounting to a revisiting of the *weight* placed on a particular factor (those interests)? The comments of L'Heureux-Dubé J. leave some uncertainty. At one point she writes that the officer's notes were "completely dismissive of the interests of Ms. Baker's children," suggesting failure to give any consideration to a relevant factor. But in the next sentence, she writes, "the failure to give serious weight and consideration to the interests of the children constitutes an unreasonable exercise of the discretion."[136] Further uncertainty arose from L'Heureux-Dubé J.'s suggestion that, depending on the circumstances, a discretionary decision-maker may be accorded deference in connection with the factors he or she deems relevant to a given decision, and not merely in connection with the weight he or she gives to mandatory relevant factors.[137]

In *Suresh*, the Court responded to some of these uncertainties, at least in part. *Baker*, it stated, "does not authorize courts reviewing decisions on the discretionary end of the spec-

132 *Baker*, *supra* note 5 at para. 65.

133 *Ibid.* at paras. 56, 67.

134 *Ibid.* at para. 73.

135 *Ibid.*

136 *Ibid.* at para. 65. See the discussion of how these statements might be reconciled, in D. Mullan, "Deference from Baker to Suresh," *supra* note 60 at 31-37.

137 *Baker*, *supra* note 5 at para. 56: "In fact, deferential standards of review may give substantial leeway to the discretionary decision-maker in determining the 'proper purposes' or 'relevant considerations' involved in making a given determination."

trum to engage in a new weighing process, but draws on an established line of cases concerning the failure of ministerial delegates to consider and weigh implied limitations and/or other patently relevant factors."[138] But the possibility that certain factors will be deemed by courts to demand prioritization (or "*serious* weight and consideration") in light of statutory and other legal sources is left open. Moreover, the Court does not address the idea that some discretionary decision-makers may receive deference in relation to the factors they deem relevant to their decisions.

The different messages in *Baker*—endorsing on the one hand the idea that deference may be accorded even decision-makers' assessments of statutory purposes, and on the other the idea that those decision-makers must conform with the "values underlying the grant of discretion," even necessarily placing significant weight on one or another of these where the reviewing judge deems that to be required by the statutory text or context—express a tension that is arguably basic to reasonableness review, at least on the romantic account. This tension is inherent in the idea of "deference as respect" advanced by David Dyzenhaus and explicitly endorsed by L'Heureux-Dubé J.[139] Such respect places confidence in the capacity of decision-makers to discern the limits of their legal mandates in a nuanced, context-sensitive fashion, while at the same time insisting that this capacity be exercised reasonably. That is, deference under this standard carries with it an expectation of reasonableness—which includes an expectation that decision-makers can and will identify and evince appropriate sensitivity to the values (including, most central in *Baker*, the significant individual interests) that should inform the exercise of their statutory powers. But given that the courts retain the last word on reasonableness, is this really so different from correctness review? Is this just an old-time assertion of the courts' "jurisdiction," but with a kindly human rights-regarding demeanour? If not, how exactly is it different?

A last case to consider on the implications of reasonableness review in light of the above reflections on the ability or inability of courts to reweigh evidence or, perhaps even more controversially, to reweigh decision-makers' assessments of competing social and political values, is *Starson v. Swazye*.[140] This case involved a finding of Ontario's Consent and Capacity Board that Starson was incapable of making a decision about proposed psychiatric medications. A majority of the Supreme Court vitiated that decision. While the majority and dissent agreed on the basic principles of interpreting the relevant section of the *Health Care Consent Act*[141] and, moreover, agreed that a reasonableness standard was due, they conflicted markedly on whether the board's decision was reasonable in light of the evidence. Without going into the details, the position of the dissent was essentially that the majority insupportably revisited the board's evidentiary findings, in particular the weight assigned by the board to the evidence of the medical experts testifying in the case. On the other side, the majority determined that the board (and dissent) was insufficiently sensitive to the evidence given by Starson on the basis for his treatment refusal.

138 *Suresh*, *supra* note 68 at para. 37.

139 "Deference as respect requires not submission but a respectful attention to the reasons offered or which could be offered in support of a decision": *Baker*, *supra* note 5 at para. 65, citing "The Politics of Deference," *supra* note 3 at 286.

140 2003 SCC 32, [2003] 1 S.C.R. 722 [*Starson*].

141 S.O. 1996, c. 2, Sch. A, s. 4(1).

I have argued elsewhere that the majority's and dissent's starkly opposed assessments of the evidence and of the tribunal's inferences from the evidence in this case may be traced back to their different prioritizations of the statutory purposes, or the deep values embedded in those statutory purposes.[142] That is, the majority favours "liberty" (or "autonomy") while the dissent favours "welfare" (or "effective medical treatment").[143] In examining the reasoning of the majority and dissent, do you agree that the differences between them might stem from a fundamental divergence in their respective prioritizations of these values?[144] If so, does this mean that the majority illegitimately substituted its prioritization of liberty or individual autonomy over the board's prioritization of welfare or effective treatment? Does the majority thus commit the error of reweighing evidence or interfering in a sensitive balancing test? Or, following the sort of analysis we have seen from L'Heureux-Dubé J. in *Baker* (and also *Mossop*), is the majority justified in requiring that a certain priority be accorded the Charter-protected interest in individual autonomy? Does such a requirement take us back to the pre-*CUPE* conflicts wherein courts insisted on vindicating individual rights at common law over competing statutory purposes aimed at advancing the public interest? Or does it urge us forward toward a culture of justification, in which judges and administrative decision-makers alike must give serious consideration to individual interests along with other important public values?

In concluding this section on reasonableness *simpliciter*, we may recall the importance of this standard to the romantic account of substantive review, as the central mechanism for reconciling judges and administrative decision-makers through a common commitment to public justification. Indeed, with the rise of the reasonableness standard, positioned as if on a continuum between the extremes of correctness and patent unreasonableness, what used to be a binary opposition of irreconcilable modes of review is brought under an overarching conception of administrative legitimacy.[145] That is, while the reasonableness standard is drawn out of the deferential tradition of patent unreasonableness review, it plays up the attentiveness to tribunal reasons and emphasis on tribunal reasonableness that was otherwise suppressed or placed on the defensive in the patent unreasonableness case law. At the same time, the emergence of reasonableness review renders suspect the tendency toward strict non-engagement with tribunal reasons on a correctness standard. In short, on the romantic account, reasonableness review serves to reconcile the concern of Gonthier J. in *National Corn Growers* to ensure the justifiedness of administrative decisions, with the concern of Wilson J. in the same case that judges may exercise their powers of oversight in

142 S. Wildeman, "The Supreme Court of Canada at the Limits of Decisional Capacity" in Jocelyn Downie & Elaine Gibson, eds., *Health Law at the Supreme Court of Canada* (Toronto: Irwin, 2007) at 241.

143 The dissent terms the core values "autonomy" and "effective medical treatment" (*Starson*, *supra* note 140 per McLachlin J. at para. 6), and the majority "liberty and welfare" (per Major J. at para. 75).

144 For instance, note that Major J. informs his judgment with the following statement on unwanted psychiatric treatment: "The enforced injection of mind-altering drugs against the respondent's will is highly offensive to his dignity and autonomy, and is to be avoided unless it is demonstrated that he lacked the capacity to make his own decision" (*ibid.* at para. 91). Contrast this with the dissent's prefacing its judgment with references to the individual and social harms flowing from untreated mental illness (*ibid.* at paras. 6-11).

145 See D. Dyzenhaus, "David Mullan's Rule of (Common) Law" in *Inside and Outside*, *supra* note 15 at 474-75. Dyzenhaus argues that reasonableness *simpliciter* "shears the correctness standard off the continuum of the standards of review."

too meticulous a manner, thereby losing sight of the bases of legitimacy of the decision as a whole.

Some see in the romantic conception of reasonableness a new threat of judicial supremacy, with administrators now more than ever under the sway of judges through the mediation of judicial values and, in particular, judge-made "fundamental values." In response, as noted above, Dyzenhaus and others have argued that reasonableness review, and with it the concept of deference as respect, may be understood to express a pluralist model of the constitutional order, in which the legislature, judiciary, and executive—as well as the persons directly affected by administrative decisions—stand as interactive participants in the common project of identifying and giving expression to fundamental values.[146] Is that model—the romantic model of substantive review—convincing to you as either an aspiration or a description of the administrative state? To narrow the questions raised in this part to some last points for reflection: Is it more or less expressive of respect for administrative decision-makers (those exercising broad discretionary powers as well as those engaged in narrower acts of statutory interpretation) to expect them to identify and bring to bear on their reasoning the values, or sources of values, that L'Heureux-Dubé J. draws upon in *Baker*? Are such expectations consistent with, or perhaps even a necessary expression of, the rule of law?[147]

IV. CRITIQUES OF THE THREE-STANDARD MODEL

LeBel J. raises a sustained critique of the modern jurisprudence on the standards of review in a set of concurring reasons (written for himself and for Deschamps J.) in *Toronto (City) v. CUPE, Local 79*.[148] Widely referred to as LeBel J.'s "cri de coeur," this critique consolidates and lends new urgency to concerns raised over many years by administrative lawyers, academics, and judges alike. It persuasively suggests that now may be the time for the Court to revisit the standards of review.

The dual thesis of LeBel J.'s critique is that the modern jurisprudence on the standards of review exhibits conceptual confusion and inspires deep methodological uncertainty. This results in intolerable unpredictability as to which standard will be deemed appropriate in a given case, as well as the effect (if any) the chosen standard will have on the method of inquiry or that inquiry's result. Lebel J. makes this critique as a first step toward reconceiving the standards to better reflect the duty of the courts on substantive review: the duty (here he draws from McLachlin C.J. in *Dr. Q.*) to "inquir[e] into legislative intent … against the backdrop of the courts' constitutional duty to protect the rule of law."[149]

LeBel J. begins with a word on the correctness standard, targeting the tendency in the case law to draw a strict correlation between "general questions of law" and imposition of

146 See chapter 10 by Geneviève Cartier, and D. Dyzenhaus, "Fundamental Values," *supra* note 9 at 451: "Legislatures and administrative tribunals have a role in the determination of the values considered fundamental to the Canadian social, political and legal order, as do the parties who challenge the state to show that its exercises of public power are accountable to those underlying values."

147 Consider here the different conceptions of the rule of law discussed by Mary Liston in chapter 4.

148 *Supra* note 63. See also the concurring judgment of LeBel J. in *Voice Construction*, *supra* note 62.

149 *Dr. Q.*, *supra* note 7 at para. 21, quoted in *Local 79*, *supra* note 63 at para. 128.

a correctness standard. This, he argues, defeats one of the central premises of the law on deference. That premise (as we have seen in *CUPE*) is that, at least in some cases, tribunals may be best placed to "develop a body of jurisprudence that is tailored to the specialized context in which they operate."[150] On this logic, the role of the courts on encountering a question of law with broad application across an administrative regime, including interpretation of a term at civil or common law as it applies to that regime, is to determine whether that question "is closely connected to the [administrative] adjudicator's core area of expertise."[151] However, LeBel J. does not argue that there is no such thing as a "general question of law" or that there is never justification for assigning a correctness standard to such questions. Rather, he suggests that correctness review is invariably engaged by constitutional questions, by ultra vires concerns in connection with non-adjudicative powers, and by cases in which "the question at issue is so clearly a question of law that is both of central importance to the legal system as a whole and outside the adjudicator's specialized area of expertise."[152] Indeed, where such questions are identified, LeBel J. would do away with the requirement of a pragmatic and functional analysis. He thus indicates that there is a place for correctness review, but that it must be appropriately confined to matters clearly outside the authority and competence of administrative decision-makers. In this he avoids the positivist claim that some questions of law are inherently supportive of only one right answer. Instead, his attention is directed at the institutional (including constitutional) reasons for correctness review, whereby judges take responsibility for elaborating system-wide legal values and for keeping non-adjudicative decision makers within the limits of their mandates.

However, the centrepiece of LeBel J.'s argument is his critique of the patent unreasonableness standard, or of the ambiguous characterizations and applications of this standard in the modern jurisprudence. He advances this critique on two fronts, first addressing problems that have plagued the distinction between patent unreasonableness and correctness, and then addressing still deeper problems plaguing the distinction between patent unreasonableness and reasonableness. On the first point, he plays up the ambiguities in *CUPE*: is the search for patent unreasonableness a search for legal error (on the model of there being just one right answer), or is it a more flexible inquiry into whether there is a "rational basis" for the decision? He also takes note of the controversies post-*CUPE* about whether the correct outcome of a disputed decision must first be ascertained in order to adjudge patent unreasonableness, and more general tendencies in the case law to marry ostensible patent unreasonableness review with what looks like correctness-style reasoning. On this analysis, it appears that the distinction between highest deference and no deference is ever on the verge of collapse.

Next, and most insistently, LeBel J. highlights the uncertainties that plague the patent unreasonableness standard following the rise of reasonableness review. Here he argues that the patent unreasonableness and reasonableness standards share a common theoretical base in the idea that there may be no single correct answer to a given problem of statutory interpretation. Both standards thus adopt as the central animating question on review: "Was the decision of the adjudicator taken in accordance with reason?" or, alternatively, "Does the

150 *Local 79*, *ibid.* at para. 73.

151 *Ibid.* at para. 74.

152 *Ibid.* at para. 62.

decision have a rational basis?" LeBel J. argues that there is no conceptual sense to seeking "fine distinctions" between these two standards.[153]

This point is confirmed as LeBel J. traces out the implications of the two "definitional strands of patent unreasonableness." As noted earlier, one of these centres on the magnitude of the defect, and the other on the immediacy or obviousness of the defect (and with this the "relative invasiveness of review").[154] Each approach, suggests LeBel J., is unsatisfactory; the idea of defects of a greater magnitude than simple irrationality is incoherent, while the idea of greater or lesser probing on review is vague and unworkable. Moreover, each of these putative translations of patent unreasonableness is fundamentally inconsistent with the role of judges in upholding the rule of law. That is, the idea of letting unreasonable or irrational decisions stand, whether because they are not irrational enough, or because they require some work to discover, is in conflict both with the principle of parliamentary supremacy (read in the light of the long-standing common-law principle that the legislature should not be understood to intend irrationality), and with "the animating principle that, in a society governed by the rule of law, power is not to be exercised arbitrarily or capriciously."[155]

LeBel J. concludes his critique with a set of open-ended questions:

> It remains to be seen, in an appropriate case, what should be the solution to these difficulties. Should courts move to a two standard system of judicial review, correctness and a revised unified standard of reasonableness? Should we attempt to more clearly define the nature and scope of each standard or rethink their relationship and application? This is perhaps some of the work which lies ahead for courts, building on the developments of recent years as well as on the legal tradition which created the framework of the present law of judicial review.[156]

There seems to be support among some of the judges at the Supreme Court for this project of rethinking—though it is not entirely clear that the project will gain momentum or what direction it might take. In *Council of Canadians with Disabilities*,[157] a 5–4 majority indicates agreement with LeBel J.'s conclusion that the patent unreasonableness standard, or its relationship with reasonableness, requires revisiting. You will recall from chapter 8 that the case involved VIA Rail's appeal from a determination of the Canadian Transportation Agency that its new fleet of rail cars presented an "undue obstacle" to persons with disabilities.[158] Yet as Audrey Macklin notes, the majority adverts to the concerns of LeBel J. in a hasty and even perfunctory manner. Indeed, beyond adopting a patent unreasonableness standard[159] that is then qualified through acknowledgment of that standard's conceptual overlap with the standard of reasonableness (both are said to "speak to whether a tribunal's decision is demonstrably unreasonable, that is, such a marked departure from what is

153 *Ibid.* at para. 108.

154 *Ibid.* at para. 78.

155 *Ibid.* at paras. 125, 128.

156 *Ibid.* at para. 134.

157 *Supra* note 10.

158 Under the *Canada Transportation Act*, S.C. 1996, c. 10, ss. 5, 172.

159 *Supra* note 10 at para. 88.

rational, as to be unsustainable"[160]), there is little indication among this bare majority of how or even whether to proceed with the project of doctrinal reform.[161]

What is clearly important to Abella J. for the majority in characterizing the standard is the imperative to resist perforating deferential review with meticulous reassessment of the tribunal's reasoning; that is, her primary concern is to distinguish reasonableness review from correctness review. Thus she draws upon the exhortation in *Ryan* to consider whether "the reasons, taken as a whole, are tenable as support for the decision,"[162] as well as the statement of Gonthier J. in *National Corn Growers* that the central question of patent unreasonableness review is whether the decision can "be sustained on a reasonable interpretation of the facts or of the law."[163] This emphasis on a holistic appraisal of reasonableness is directly related to the concerns expressed by LeBel J., as Abella J. states that "[t]he 'immediacy or obviousness' to a reviewing court of a defective strand in the analysis is not, in the face of the inevitable subjectivity involved, a reliable guide to whether a given decision is untenable or evidences an unreasonable interpretation of the facts or law."[164] Abella J. caps off these statements with an affirmation of the judgment of Wilson J. in *National Corn Growers*:

> As Wilson J. recognized in *National Corn Growers* … it is the way a tribunal understands the question its enabling legislation asks it to answer and the factors it is to consider, rather than the specific answer a tribunal arrives at, that should be the focus of a reviewing court's inquiry.[165]

Putting aside the uncertainty of the broad implications of these statements for future developments in the standard of review doctrine, on the facts of *Council of Canadians with Disabilities* they add up to a rejection of the dissent's approach (on a correctness standard) of closely parsing the agency's reasoning—in particular, its deployment of the legal test for reasonable accommodation. Viewed in light of the proper standard of (deferential) review, the majority suggests, such close scrutiny expresses an inappropriate insistence on re-evaluating the evidence and, what is more, on re-evaluating that evidence in light of a different prioritization of the competing values and interests at stake. In *Council of Canadians with Disabilities*, then, we are reminded of the difficult judicial balancing act of simultaneously resisting overly "meticulous" review and affirming administrative legitimacy through the idea that tribunal decisions can and must be reasonably justified. Whether or how a commitment to such balancing might be better expressed through reform of the standards remains an open question.

---

160 *Ibid.* at para. 102.

161 The fact that this majority is reached by one vote may indicate that its treatment of the standard of review reflects background compromises rather than considered reflection on how to respond to the challenges raised by LeBel J. I thank my colleague Dianne Pothier for this suggestion.

162 *Council of Canadians with Disabilities*, *supra* note 10 at para. 103, quoting *Ryan*, *supra* note 6 at para. 56.

163 *Council of Canadians with Disabilities*, *ibid.* at para. 103, quoting *National Corn Growers*, *supra* note 9 at 1369-70.

164 *Council of Canadians with Disabilities*, *ibid.* at para. 103.

165 *Ibid.* at para. 104.

So, given the criticisms of the three-standard model that we have seen, what alternatives might there be? And might such alternatives better support the romantic ideal of harmonizing judicial and administrative practices of justification? One possibility, as LeBel J. suggests, would be to revert to a dualist model, so that judges on review again choose between the stark alternatives of deference and non-deference. On such a model, the work of clearly distinguishing these standards might be revitalized. But some argue that this would be to return to the bad old days of rigid formalism, and so to negate the advances in the context-sensitive calibration of the standards of review that have been won over the last three decades. Sossin and Flood, for instance, suggest that what is required is instead "a more deeply contextualized standard of review framework, one much more akin to the spectrum of procedural fairness which has been successful in providing flexibility and consistency in the setting of procedural review."[166] They therefore prescribe a shift away from fixed, abstract standards of review and from the prevailing four-factor analysis, toward a broader requirement that the reviewing court "justify why it should intervene in an administrative decision."[167] Such a development would advance not "more deference or less deference, but rather a more transparent and principled basis for review."[168] The sort of justification they have in mind would take account of the factors currently canvassed under the pragmatic and functional approach, along with at least the additional factor of the effect of the decision on individual interests. Through this and other contextual considerations going to substantive legality, Sossin and Flood suggest, "[j]udges would be able to justify decisions on the same grounds that actually lead to the decision, rather than decide a case on one set of grounds and have to justify it on another."[169]

David Dyzenhaus is another commentator who, even before LeBel J.'s cri de coeur, has argued that the current regime of standards demands rethinking. Dyzenhaus suggests that the modern jurisprudence on substantive review is best understood to express a deep commitment to public justification among both judges and administrative decision-makers.[170] As such, he calls into question the continued relevance not only of the patent unreasonableness standard but of the correctness standard as well, at least as those standards are traditionally understood.[171] That is, his account of deference as respect is at odds both with the idea that some administrative decisions may be hived off from meaningful legal oversight (an idea arguably latent in patent unreasonableness review), and the idea that some legal questions, in particular constitutional questions, attract a mode of review that negates altogether the relevance of attention to tribunal reasons. Rather, Dyzenhaus suggests, all

166 L. Sossin & C. Flood, "The Contextual Turn: Iacobucci's Legacy and the Standard of Review in Administrative Law" (2007) 57 U.T.L.J. 581 at 583.

167 *Ibid.* at 604.

168 *Ibid.* at 583.

169 *Ibid.* at 605.

170 See, for example, "Process/Substance," *supra* note 3; "Fundamental Values," *supra* note 9; and *Inside and Outside*, *supra* note 15.

171 *Ibid.* These suggestions are forcefully supported by Lahey & Ginn, "After the Revolution," *supra* note 24 at 264, 317. Lahey and Ginn's careful empirical study of the application of the Supreme Court's standard of review jurisprudence by lower courts is essential reading for the student wishing to gain a broader appreciation of this area of law.

instances of substantive review—as well as procedural review[172]—must be conducted with sensitivity to the complex factual, institutional, and normative considerations that have bearing on administrative decisions. He thus endorses the idea, registered in L'Heureux-Dubé J.'s judgment in *Baker*, that administrators and judges are co-participants in justifying state action under the rule of law. Underlying this approach is a model of law and of the legal order in which "the content of law is viewed in terms of a relationship of reciprocity between legislature and subject, so that interpretive authority is shared between the institutions of the legal order, including the subject who as citizen contests the law within the domain of its application to him."[173] Ultimately, the commitment to processes of public justification that grounds this model is most supportive of a unified, context-sensitive standard of reasonableness;[174] for arguably, only under such a model are practices of justification expected and respected across all sectors of administrative action.[175]

That said, a further possible response to the critiques consolidated by Lebel J. is that the standards of review remain in their current tripartite form, to be refined or clarified over time. Bastarache J.[176] has made public comments that favour this approach. Better that the existing standards be submitted to the slow gears of the common law, he advises, than to attempt wholesale imposition of a model that may fail to achieve even the rough compromise between predictability and flexibility that the three-standard model has done. Indeed, here we should consider further what might be lost in forgoing the standard of patent unreasonableness. That is, apart from the matter of reconciling such a move with the continued place of the privative clause in some administrative statutes, it may be noted that this standard, with all its crude insistence on an irrationality that outpaces mere unreasonableness, nonetheless boldly registers the claim that judicial and administrative perspectives are different—even radically so. Perhaps the romantic is too quick to assume that judges are capable of apprehending the reasonableness of administrative decisions that advance statu-

172 See "Process/Substance," *supra* note 3.

173 "Fundamental Values," *supra* note 9 at 501.

174 Compare Lahey & Ginn, "After the Revolution," *supra* note 24 at 329: "[A] more generalized reliance on review for simple unreasonableness might allow and encourage judges to spend more time thinking about what is actually reasonable in particular contexts, and why, rather than grappling with attempts to explain why they have chosen one of the deferential standards over the other, or what the difference between the two actually is. … [I]t may even be worthwhile to consider whether it is possible to move to a single standard of review—contextualized reasonableness—or at least to ask what the draw-backs of such an approach might be. We have just begun to ask ourselves the questions that such a development might raise, particularly relative to such issues as the implications for and from section 96 of the *Constitution Act, 1867*, for the interpretation and application of privative clauses, the judicial review of the decisions of human rights adjudicators, and so on."

175 Of course, expectations of reasonableness under the law on substantive review are now closely bound up with the duty to give reasons under the law on procedural fairness, as articulated in *Baker*. Compare "Process/Substance," *supra* note 3.

176 The Hon. Justice M. Bastarache, "Recent Developments and Future Changes in Judicial Review" (Address to Administrative Law Conference, Montreal, December 2, 2004), cited in D.P. Jones, "Recent Developments in Administrative Law," Demystifying Administrative Law: What You Need to Know in Order to Survive (Canadian Bar Association Nova Scotia Administrative Law Conference, April 7, 2006) at 41-43. Bastarache J. suggests that the meaning of the standards may be "solidified as each application of the standard acts as an example for judges to draw on in a particular case" (at 10, cited in Jones at 41). Also see the comments of Mullan, "The Struggle for Complexity," *supra* note 90 at 90-93, 96.

tory mandates markedly remote from judicial preoccupations with such constructs as individual rights. A patent unreasonableness standard may be an important means of reminding judges of their lack of expertise in such settings.[177] Yet the romantic, drawing upon Iacobucci J.'s discussion of reasonableness review in *Southam*, might respond that decision-makers must be able to justify their decisions publicly to warrant deference or, indeed, to warrant the privilege of wielding public power. If a patent unreasonableness standard functions to exempt decision-makers from that expectation, then the standard is inconsistent with the rule of law and thus with a fundamental component of constitutional democracy. As a final riposte, however, the skeptic may observe that, given that it is the judges who decide whether the requisite reasonableness is evinced, such appeals to "public" justification and so to democratic legitimacy come off as disingenuous.

Ultimately, the question whether it is better to have one, two, or three standards opens onto more concrete questions about how the assessment of substantive legality is appropriately conducted in any given case. That is, as we have seen, substantive review necessarily requires negotiation of such issues as which of the competing approaches to statutory interpretation is best adopted in a specific case or in general; whether or how deferential review might avoid assessing substantive legality against some form of correctness-style limit; whether there need be any restrictions on the objects or methods of scrutiny where deference is called for; whether reassessment of the weight placed by the decision-maker on relevant factors is to be permitted; and whether deference is ever to be accorded to decision-makers' assessments of which factors are and are not relevant. Here we might note the suggestion of Evan Fox-Decent that the evaluation of substantive legality on a reasonableness standard, at least where important interests are in play, may require a more structured analysis than has yet emerged, perhaps on the model of the proportionality test under s. 1 of the Charter.[178]

Perhaps, then, the romantic account of the standards of review finds its happiest ending in those standards' dissolution into a single, context-sensitive standard of reasonableness. That story continues to be written. Yet it is clear that the challenges raised to substantive review by the idea of a rule of law that "speaks in many voices" are only beginning to be felt.

V. POSTSCRIPT: DUNSMUIR v. NEW BRUNSWICK

In *Dunsmuir v. New Brunswick*,[179] the standards of review are reduced to two: reasonableness and correctness. (See the postscript to chapter 8 as well as the text website.) This results in renewed inquiry into the nature and assessment of administrative reasonableness. But consider: does *Dunsmuir* thereby resolve—or deepen—the controversies discussed herein?

see case + applic

177 However, Lahey and Ginn's empirical analysis of the uptake of this jurisprudence by lower courts concludes: "Canadian judges have, in significant degree, internalized the respect for the distinctive expertise of administrative decision-makers that is such a fundamental part of the doctrinal change that has taken place over the past quarter century." They add: "It is therefore questionable whether their continuing commitment to curial deference depends upon the formal existence of a spectrum of standards of review that reminds them that some cases are farther beyond their realm of experience than are others" ("After the Revolution," *supra* note 24 at 330).

178 See E. Fox-Decent, "The Internal Morality of Administration: The Form and Structure of Reasonableness" in *The Unity of Public Law*, *supra* note 60 at 143.

179 2008 SCC 9 [*Dunsmiur*].

SUGGESTED ADDITIONAL READINGS

CASES

Baker v. Canada (Minister of Citizenship and Immigration), [1999] 2 S.C.R. 817.

Barrie Public Utilities v. Canadian Cable Television Assn., [2003] 1 S.C.R. 476.

Canada (Attorney General) v. Mossop, [1993] 1 S.C.R. 554.

Canada (Director of Investigation and Research) v. Southam Inc., [1997] 1 S.C.R. 748.

Canadian Union of Public Employees, Local 963 v. New Brunswick Liquor Corp., [1979] 2 S.C.R. 227.

CUPE v. Ontario (Minister of Labour), [2003] 1 S.C.R. 539.

Dunsmuir v. New Brunswick, 2008 SCC 9.

National Corn Growers Assn. v. Canada (Import Tribunal), [1990] 2 S.C.R. 1324.

Pushpanathan v. Canada (Minister of Citizenship and Immigration), [1998] 1 S.C.R. 982.

Ryan v. Law Society of New Brunswick, [2003] 1 S.C.R. 247.

Starson v. Swazye, [2003] 1 S.C.R. 722.

Toronto (City) v. CUPE, Local 79, [2003] 3 S.C.R. 77.

U.E.S., Local 298 v. Bibeault, [1988] 2 S.C.R. 1048.

SECONDARY SOURCES

Dyzenhaus, D. "The Politics of Deference: Judicial Review and Democracy" in M. Taggart, ed., *The Province of Administrative Law* (Oxford: Hart Publishing, 1997) at 279.

Lahey, B., & D. Ginn. "After the Revolution: Being Pragmatic and Functional in Canada's Trial Courts and Courts of Appeal" (2002) 25 Dal. L.J. 259.

MacLauchlan, H.W. "Transforming Administrative Law: The Didactic Role of the Supreme Court of Canada" (2001) 80 Can. Bar Rev. 281.

McLachlin, The Honourable Justice B. "The Roles of Administrative Tribunals and Courts in Maintaining the Rule of Law" (1999) 12 Can. J. Admin. L. & P. 171.

Mullan, D.J. *Administrative Law: Cases, Text, and Materials*, 5th ed. (Toronto: Emond Montgomery, 2003) chapters 9, 10.

Sossin, L., & C. Flood. "The Contextual Turn: Iacobucci's Legacy and the Standard of Review in Administrative Law" (2007) 57 U.T.L.J. 581.

CHAPTER TEN

Keeping a Check on Discretion

GENEVIÈVE CARTIER
Faculty of Law, University of Sherbrooke

I. INTRODUCTION

The Commission may cancel any permit at its discretion.

An Act Respecting Alcoholic Liquor,
R.S.Q. 1941, c. 255, s. 35

The Minister is hereby authorized to exempt any person from any regulation made under subsection 114(1) of the Act or otherwise facilitate the admission to Canada of any person where the Minister is satisfied that the person should be exempted from that regulation or that the person's admission should be facilitated owing to the existence of compassionate or humanitarian considerations.

Immigration Regulations, 1978, SOR/78-172,
as amended by SOR/93-44

These provisions were at the heart of two of the most famous decisions ever handed down by the Supreme Court of Canada on the subject of administrative law: *Roncarelli v. Duplessis*[1] and *Baker v. Minister of Citizenship and Immigration*.[2] They are but two examples of thousands of similar provisions in legislative as well as regulatory instruments[3] that confer "discretionary powers" (or, as they were sometimes called, "administrative powers") on executive decision-makers. The aim of this chapter is to present the state of the law of discretion in Canada and to highlight the challenges that discretion poses to the rule of law and to democracy.

Administrative discretion is not an easy concept to grasp. Generally speaking, it is associated with the power of an administrative authority to make a choice between various options: "the concept of discretion refers to decisions where the law does not dictate a specific outcome, or where the decision-maker is given a choice of options within a statutorily imposed set of boundaries."[4] As such, discretion questions the view of the administrative state as a mere transmission belt between the legislature and the citizens, as the traditional articulation of the separation of powers used to depict it. According to this view, the executive simply "executes" the will of the legislature by putting into operation the projects developed by democratic representatives for their citizens. In practice, the margin of manoeuvre that is involved in making choices suggests that there is a space or distance between the expression of the will of Parliament on the one hand, and acts of the executive on the other, so that running the government exceeds "mere execution." It is in that space that discretion is exercised.

Now, if discretion gives the administrative state leeway to make decisions or adopt norms, is the administrative state governed by the rule of law?[5] In other words, is discretion a legal phenomenon, exercised in a space controlled by legal principles and subjected to judicial oversight, or is it a political phenomenon, exercised in a legal void and subjected to political controls? Central issues on administrative discretion have precisely revolved around the question whether the space in which discretion is exercised is legally constrained or not. As we shall see, that question was first approached through the perspective of a dichotomy between law and discretion: "quasi-judicial" decisions were based on law and therefore legally constrained and controllable; "administrative" (or discretionary) decisions were based on policy and could not be so controlled. Over time, however, the influence of the law/discretion dichotomy was increasingly undermined, to a point where the distinction between decisions based on discretion and those based on law has come to be seen as residing in the degree, not in the nature, of the constraints within which they are made.[6]

Part II of this chapter offers an overview of the role of discretion in the administrative state. It also briefly presents the positions of a number of influential academics on the ques-

1 [1959] S.C.R. 121 [*Roncarelli*].

2 [1999] 2 S.C.R. 817 [*Baker*].

3 In 1975, Philip Anisman identified 14,885 powers of a discretionary nature in the Revised Statutes of Canada only: see Philip Anisman, *A Catalogue of Discretionary Powers in the Revised Statutes of Canada* (Ottawa: Law Reform Commission of Canada, 1975).

4 *Baker*, *supra* note 2 at para. 52.

5 For the rule of law, see Mary Liston, chapter 4.

6 D.J. Mullan, *Administrative Law: Cases, Text, and Materials*, 5th ed. (Toronto: Emond Montgomery, 2003) at 950.

tion of discretion. Part III exposes the structure of the law of discretion as it stood from *Roncarelli* to *Baker*, and part IV explores *Baker* and its implications for that part of administrative law. In the conclusion, I raise the question of the relationship between discretion and democracy. I also suggest that a conception of discretion as "dialogue" might be a promising way to take up both the rule of law and the democratic challenges, although, as we shall see from the following chapter by Craig Forcese, one might ask whether such a metaphor can still stand in the wake of 9/11.

II. THE ROLE OF DISCRETION AND HOW IT WAS VIEWED BY ACADEMICS

A. The Role of Discretion in the Administrative State

Because discretion is part of the daily routine of many administrative decision-makers, understanding the role of that kind of power is a sensible starting point to any substantial analysis of the concept of discretion.

Discretion is essential to contemporary government: bringing the various legislative schemes that are put in place by Parliament down to the individual requires some measure of flexibility on the executive's part, either because Parliament cannot foresee every individual case that is likely to arise (and therefore chooses to let the executive decide in each case according to its own appreciation of the situation) or because it does not have the necessary expertise or knowledge to craft the norms that should apply in any given area of activity (and therefore chooses to let the executive adopt the norms).

1. Discretion to Decide Individual Cases

A great many statutory and regulatory provisions confer discretionary powers on administrative decision-makers, to be exercised in individual cases. The adoption of that kind of provision is justified by the fact that the legislator or regulating authority cannot imagine all the particular situations that are likely to arise under any given scheme, so it is impossible for them to formally conceive a comprehensive set of binding rules. Delegating discretion to decide in each case gives the decision-maker presented with concrete facts the ability to make a decision that is both adapted to that set of facts and also compatible with the legislative or regulatory scheme within which the decision-maker operates.

Baker is a good example of that kind of discretionary power.[7] In that case, the *Immigration Act* required that applications for permanent residence be made outside Canada, before the arrival in Canada of the applicant. However, a regulatory provision adopted pursuant to the Act provided that the Minister could exempt someone from the application of the statutory or regulatory provision, or otherwise facilitate his or her admission to Canada, if the Minister was satisfied that compassionate and humanitarian reasons justified such an exemption or facilitation. When called upon to decide under that provision, the Minister was thus given the ability to take into account a variety of factual situations that, although not specifically mentioned in the statute, led to "exemption" or "facilitation." The *Roncarelli* case is another example: the Liquor Commission, the administrative authority responsible

7 For the facts of *Baker*, see Grant Huscroft, chapter 5.

for the application of the *Alcoholic Liquor Act*, was delegated the power to "cancel any [liquor] permit at its discretion." Here, the statute did not even provide any formal restriction on the discretionary power, an aspect that would be central to that case.[8]

2. Discretion to Adopt General Norms

An impressive number of statutory provisions expressly confer discretionary powers on administrative decision-makers to adopt binding rules of general application. These rules are often referred to as "regulations," but they may also be termed "bylaws," "orders," "tariffs," etc. The justification for delegating the discretionary power to adopt general norms is explored elsewhere in this book (see Andrew Green, chapter 13). Generally speaking, such a justification is twofold. First, it resides in the need for expertise, which members of Parliament do not always have, given the immense variety of fields that are subjected to state intervention. Specific ministries or administrative bodies are often better equipped for such a task. Second, it responds to the problem of time (which legislators do not have when it comes to articulating specific provisions in a number of contexts) and information (which is always incomplete and which results in the need for rule modification, which is most efficiently carried out through regulation rather than legislation): delegation of rule-making powers to the executive increases the efficiency and flexibility of legislative schemes.

The executive also has implicit power to adopt non-binding rules, such as "directives," "guidelines," and "manuals." Generally speaking, they are increasingly referred to as "soft law."[9] Soft law may play various roles. For instance, when discretion to decide individual cases is delegated to an administrative authority, which in practice confers its actual exercise on many front-line officers who act simultaneously,[10] directives or guidelines may establish non-binding rules intended for decision-makers, who favour coherence and fairness in administrative decision-making. In other instances, soft law is used to set policy orientations that are likely to determine the way in which a particular legislative or regulatory scheme will be applied (see Andrew Green, chapter 13).

Discretion thus plays fundamental roles in contemporary government, and to say that it is here to stay is pretty much uncontroversial. The controversy lies in the nature of the legal regime that applies to that kind of power. To understand the evolution of that legal regime, presented in parts III and IV, it is useful to refer to the perspective and vision of academic commentators because they provide an analytical tool that helps us better understand and contrast the various trends in legal thinking about discretion.

B. Discretion and Academics

Academic debates on discretion are roughly divided between authors who associate discretion with arbitrariness and those who view discretion as an instrument that allows the welfare state to reach its legitimate objectives.

8 A detailed analysis of this case will be found in part III, below.

9 See Andrew Green, chapter 13.

10 For instance, in *Baker*, the discretion delegated to the Minister was actually exercised by many Immigration officers (by virtue of a specific provision in the statute conferring powers on the Minister).

In 1885, A.V. Dicey published *An Introduction to the Study of the Law of the Constitution*,[11] in which he set out his conception of the rule of law. In what he describes as the first "meaning" of this conception, he affirms that citizens living in a state governed by the rule of law can be subjected to state punishment only if they have breached *the law*. Dicey contrasts *law* with *discretion*, which he associates with arbitrary power:

> [The rule of law means] the absolute supremacy or predominance of regular law as opposed to the influence of arbitrary power, and *excludes the existence* of arbitrariness, or prerogative, or even *of wide discretionary authority on the part of the government*. Englishmen are ruled by the law, and by the law alone; a man may with us be punished for a breach of law, but he can be punished for nothing else.[12]

In his view, "wherever there is discretion there is room for arbitrariness, and … in a republic no less than under a monarchy discretionary authority on the part of the government must mean insecurity for legal freedom on the part of its subjects."[13]

Dicey agreed that the executive might need discretionary powers in exceptional circumstances—times of trouble, war, invasion, and the like. In such cases, executive discretion was acceptable because Parliament would need to adopt a statute to authorize the delegation and also because citizens could ultimately resort to the courts, which would ensure that statutory language was construed in light of common-law principles developed over time that protected the liberty of the subject. However, Dicey fiercely condemned the kind of legislative delegations of discretion that became commonplace in the welfare state. In his opinion, those delegations were problematic for two reasons. On the one hand, statutes delegating discretion were systematically framed to deprive courts of their supervisory power.[14] On the other hand, the discretionary matters that the executive was called upon to decide were substantively extra-legal: they dealt with "public business," which, in Dicey's view, courts were unsuited to decide. In other words, although judges were trained to answer questions of law (for example, "Was the right to freedom of expression violated by the executive?"), they were unable to settle "public business" (for example, "Does the public interest require the delivery of a permit in that part of the city?").

Dicey thus sharply contrasted law with discretion. In his view, decisions of the executive based on law (that is, quasi-judicial decisions) could be properly controlled by courts, but decisions based on discretion could not, because they dealt with public business and were therefore made in a "lawless void."

In the late 1920s, in *The New Despotism*,[15] Lord Hewart followed Dicey in condemning what he perceived as the propensity of the executive to manipulate Parliament in order to be freed from judicial control. He too denounced the legislative techniques that had the effect of placing "a large and increasing field of departmental authority and activity *beyond*

---

11 A.V. Dicey, *An Introduction to the Study of the Law of the Constitution*, 10th ed. by E.C.S. Wade (London: Macmillan, 1959) (first edition published in 1885).

12 *Ibid.* at 202 (emphasis added).

13 *Ibid.* at 188.

14 A technique that was often used to attain that objective consisted in articulating parliamentary delegations of discretion in language that sought to give discretionary decisions the force of statutes.

15 Lord Hewart, *The New Despotism* (London: Ernest Benn, 1929).

the reach of the ordinary law"[16] and of making those decision-makers a law unto themselves.[17] Some time after Lord Hewart's outburst, F.A. Von Hayek added his voice to those who expressed the view that discretion was contrary to the rule of law. In his *Road to Serfdom*,[18] he described the rule of law as a set of principles whose ideal is the prevention of arbitrary government. He formed the view that discretion, with its absence of rules announced beforehand, prevented citizens from knowing how the state will use its coercive powers and was therefore contrary to the rule of law.[19]

As a reply to those who conceived and denounced discretion as arbitrariness, supporters of the welfare state perceived discretion as an instrument of welfare. W.A. Robson, in contrast to Dicey, strongly supported the increased role of the welfare state and the setting up of administrative authorities. He did not view discretion as intrinsically arbitrary. For him, the legitimacy of the administrative state depended on administrative tribunals "exhibiting a … judicial frame of mind,"[20] or a "spirit of justice":[21] when endowed with discretion, they would hear the controversies with an open mind, further only authorized purposes, and avoid being influenced by extraneous considerations.[22]

Robson agreed, however, that while the creation of administrative tribunals proved necessary in order to escape from the rigidities of the processes and methods of the law (either through the possibility to consider imponderables or through the exercise of discretion), these tribunals had to remain under appropriate legal control.[23] But in Robson's opinion, ordinary courts had failed to demonstrate their ability to appropriately control administrative tribunals and authorities. On the one hand, they had developed a dual approach to judicial control that was based on what he viewed as a disputable distinction between "law" and "discretion" (courts claimed they could control the former, not the latter). On the other hand, he thought courts were unfit to deal with the realities of administrative authorities. As a substitute, he favoured the creation of a specialized court of law that, freed from the framework of an unworkable distinction between law and discretion and attentive to the particularities of the administrative state, could exercise control over all the activities of the executive.

Following Robson, Jennings expressed the view that Dicey's constitutional theory was ill-founded, so that contending that discretion was contrary to the rule of law was pointless. Jennings did not, however, argue that discretionary powers should go uncontrolled. Like Robson, he supported the creation of an administrative court, which he thought could be a specialized division of the High Court. He thought that this would circumvent the prejudices that ordinary courts had traditionally expressed against the government of the welfare state.[24]

---

16 *Ibid.* at 11 (emphasis added).

17 *Ibid.* at 14.

18 F.A. Von Hayek, *The Road to Serfdom* (Chicago: University of Chicago Press, 1944) at 80ff.

19 *Ibid.* at 80.

20 W.A. Robson, *Justice and Administrative Law: A Study of the British Constitution*, 3d ed. (London: Stevens & Sons, 1951) at 38.

21 *Ibid.* at 418.

22 *Ibid.* at 408-9, 610.

23 *Ibid.* at 408.

24 W.I. Jennings, *The Law and the Constitution*, 5th ed. (London: University of London, 1959) at 55.

In a similar vein, J. Willis appealed to a functional approach to be applied to administrative law,[25] as opposed to being viewed from the perspective of the judiciary (which he thought expressed clear hostility toward the administrative state) or from a conceptual point of view (involving either a categorization of functions to be shared between the judiciary and the executive or the adoption of Dicey's theory of the rule of law).

Overall, however, and notwithstanding harsh critiques, Dicey's thinking exercised a profound and enduring influence on the way in which courts conceived of their supervisory role in the administrative state. Indeed, the law/discretion dichotomy structured the law of judicial review in various ways until *Baker*, and recent judicial decisions suggest that, even as of today, it has not entirely disappeared from the legal landscape. It is to the description of this complex evolution that we now turn.

III. DISCRETION FROM RONCARELLI TO BAKER

Roncarelli is usually associated with the opening chapter of the story of judicial review of discretion in Canada.[26] This decision is remarkable in many aspects, but for our purposes, it is instructive for two reasons. On the one hand, it clearly affirmed that, even at the highest levels of executive action, discretion is limited by legal principles (although, as we shall see, the nature of those principles was debated). On the other hand, the set of majority and minority opinions respectively articulate two visions of the judicial control of discretion between which courts oscillated for decades thereafter. A close analysis of *Roncarelli* is therefore inescapable.

Frank Roncarelli owned a high-class, prosperous restaurant in Montreal. He sued the premier of Quebec, Maurice Duplessis, for damage caused by the cancellation of his liquor licence. A majority of judges gave judgment for Roncarelli, in light of two fundamental factual findings. First, even though the licence had been formally cancelled by the Quebec Liquor Commission, the latter had acted on Duplessis's orders. Second, the authorities had been motivated by a desire to curb what they perceived to be seditious activities of the Jehovah's Witnesses and to punish Roncarelli. Roncarelli, a member of that sect, acted as a bailsman for close to 400 of his fellow members, who were arrested for illegally distributing pamphlets. Duplessis considered that in so using the money he earned with his liquor licence, Roncarelli was making an illegitimate use of a privilege that was granted to him by the province.

For Rand J., not only did Duplessis lack any legal basis for acting in the circumstances of the case, but so did the commission, notwithstanding the wording of the relevant statutory provision, which stipulated that the commission could "cancel any permit at its discretion."[27] In his view, even in the case of formal delegations of apparently unfettered discretion, there were always implied limits to its exercise.

Rand J. emphasized that Roncarelli had not done anything wrong and was merely acting as a private, honourable citizen: having a religion, earning his living, and exercising his

25 J. Willis, "Three Approaches to Administrative Law: The Judicial, the Conceptual, and the Functional" (1935) 1 U.T.L.J. 53.

26 See also the discussion of *Roncarelli* in Mary Liston, chapter 4.

27 *An Act Respecting Alcoholic Liquor*, R.S.Q. 1941, c. 255, s. 35, quoted in *Roncarelli*, *supra* note 1 at 139.

right to act as bailsman. In addition, the authorities had cancelled the licence in order to "halt the activities of the Witnesses, to punish the appellant … and to warn others."[28] Hence, "the *de facto* power of the Executive over its appointees at will to such a statutory public function [had been] exercised deliberately and intentionally to destroy the vital business interests of a citizen."[29] In Rand J.'s view, however, the commission was a "public service"[30] that had to "serve"[31] the purpose of the statute and that owed a "public statutory duty" toward Roncarelli.[32] This was particularly important because the occupations and businesses that were regulated (the administration and sale of alcohol) "would be free and legitimate"[33] absent restriction in legislation. This was "steadily becoming of concern to citizens generally"[34] because an increasing number of activities became subject to statutory limitations, such as requirements of permits. For Rand J., "[i]n public regulation of this sort there is no such thing as absolute and untrammelled 'discretion,'"[35] even when the formal statutory language indicates otherwise.

Rand J. also insisted that the regulatory framework and, more specifically, the requirement of a permit had important consequences for permit holders: "[a]s its exercise continues, the economic life of the holder becomes progressively more deeply implicated with the privilege while at the same time his vocation becomes correspondingly dependent on it."[36] This necessarily influenced the way in which the cancellation of a permit could be carried out. When action was "dictated by and according to the arbitrary likes, dislikes and irrelevant purposes of public officers acting beyond their duty,"[37] administration was not made "according to law,"[38] and this was susceptible to the disintegration of the rule of law.[39] The following excerpt clearly encapsulates Rand J.'s approach to discretion:

> Here, the act done was in relation to a public administration affecting the *rights of a citizen to enjoy a public privilege*, and a *duty implied by the statute toward the victim was violated.* The existing permit was an interest for which the appellant was entitled to *protection against any unauthorized interference*, and the illegal destruction of which gave rise to a remedy for the damages suffered.[40]

In sum, for Rand J., discretion could not be viewed as a pure exercise of power, as an instrument in the hands of a decision-maker enabling him or her to make any decision he or

28 *Roncarelli, ibid.* at 134.

29 *Ibid.* at 137.

30 *Ibid.* at 139.

31 *Ibid.* at 140.

32 *Ibid.* at 141.

33 *Ibid.* at 140.

34 *Ibid.*

35 *Ibid.*

36 *Ibid.*

37 *Ibid.*

38 *Ibid.* at 142.

39 *Ibid.*

40 *Ibid.* at 143 (emphasis added).

she sees fit. For discretion to be legally exercised, it had to pursue legitimate purposes and take into account the situation of the individual affected by the decision.

By contrast, in his dissenting opinion, Cartwright J. took the perspective of the decision-maker as the starting point of his analysis. He formed the view that no actionable wrong had been committed through the cancellation of Roncarelli's licence. The authorities had honestly entertained the opinion that Roncarelli did not deserve to enjoy this privilege because he supported members of a group who attempted to disrupt public order, and courts could not "inquire as to whether there was sufficient evidence to warrant its formation or as to whether it constituted a reasonable ground for cancellation of the permit."[41] The specific language of the statute did not contain any guidance as to the "circumstances under which [the commission could] cancel a permit":[42] the commission, therefore, had unfettered discretion to so determine. Cartwright J. insisted that the decision to cancel the licence was an administrative, as opposed to a quasi-judicial decision, which prevented courts from intervening in the decision of the commission:

> A tribunal that dispenses justice, i.e. every judicial tribunal, is concerned with legal rights and liabilities, which means rights and liabilities conferred or imposed by "law"; … .
>
> In contrast, non-judicial tribunals of the type called "administrative" have invariably based their decisions and orders, not on legal rights and liabilities, but on policy and expediency. …
>
> A judicial tribunal looks for some law to guide it; an "administrative" tribunal, within its province, is a law unto itself.[43]

For Cartwright J., then, the decision-maker endowed with a broadly worded delegation of discretionary power could not be the subject of control by the courts as long as he or she acted within the limits explicitly set forth in the statute. Where no formal limits were prescribed and the delegating statute conferred entire discretion on the decision-maker, the latter was "a law unto itself."

One interpretation of Rand J.'s opinion in *Roncarelli* is that the legal regime applicable to executive exercises of discretion lies in the text of the delegating statute, read in the light of a number of "underlying" principles. The latter are usually associated with interpretive presumptions aimed at identifying the intention of Parliament. Another understanding suggests that "unwritten" principles, whose identification does not depend on the written text of the delegating statute but rather lies in the fundamental values of our legal order, are a constitutive part of the legal regime of discretion.[44] The above interpretation largely dominated administrative law in the years that followed *Roncarelli*. Two reasons might explain why. First, it was more easily reconcilable with the orthodox conception of law, positivism, which postulates that only valid positive rules are binding on judges.[45] Second, the interpretation was also compatible with the ultra vires rule that generally governed the law of

---

41 *Ibid.* at 164.

42 *Ibid.* at 167.

43 *Ibid.* (emphasis added), quoting *Ashby et al.*, [1934] O.R. 421 at 428, 3 D.L.R. 565, 62 C.C.C. 132 (C.A.).

44 For a discussion of the distinction between "underlying" and "unwritten," see D. Dyzenhaus, "The Deep Structure of Roncarelli v. Duplessis" (2004) 53 U.N.B.L.J. 111.

45 *Ibid.*

judicial review of executive action, according to which excesses of jurisdiction delegated by statute would be struck down by virtue of the supervisory power of the courts.

This interpretation translated into a series of (more or less) distinct heads or grounds of review, usually grouped under the expression of "abuse of discretion."

A. Unauthorized Object or Purpose, Improper Considerations

A number of judicial pronouncements have established that decision-makers must exercise discretion in conformity with the purposes authorized by the delegating statute. Likewise, they have held that discretion cannot be exercised on the basis or in the light of "improper" considerations. The two situations often overlap. In the first case, courts must identify the object authorized by the statute and then determine whether that object or purpose has been followed or not. Similarly, in the second case, the question whether a consideration is proper or not is usually answered with reference to the object of the statute. These grounds of review are by far the most frequently invoked. A few examples illustrate that kind of case.

In *R. v. Smith & Rhuland Ltd.*,[46] the Supreme Court held that an administrative authority (in that case a labour board) entrusted with the discretionary power to certify a union as a bargaining unit could not exercise its power to refuse certification on the basis that the secretary-treasurer of the union had communist allegiance. More recently, in *Shell Products Ltd. v. Vancouver (City)*,[47] the City of Vancouver had voted a resolution expressing its intention not to do business with Shell until that company withdrew from South Africa, then under the apartheid regime. A narrow majority formed the view that the object of the resolution was to join an international movement of boycott in order to exert pressure on the company to retreat from South Africa. As such, it did not pursue "municipal purposes," which limited the powers of the city to its territory.

B. Bad Faith

As we saw above in *Roncarelli*, Duplessis was found to have used his discretion to cancel a liquor licence with a view to punishing the licence holder for supporting the cause of members of a religious movement that was overtly hostile to the Catholic church. This prompted Rand J. to say that "'[d]iscretion' necessarily implies good faith in discharging public duty; there is always a perspective within which a statute is intended to operate; and any clear departure from its lines or objects is just as objectionable as fraud or corruption."[48] Although Rand J. referred to bad faith, Duplessis's behaviour was also said to be incompatible with the object of the statute and also based on improper considerations.

In *Landreville v. Town of Boucherville*,[49] the city was found to have used its power to expropriate, not for a legitimate purpose, but with a view to prevent a resident from operating his quarry. While Beetz J. admitted that "the burden of proof is a heavy one when it involves establishing the commission of an 'abuse of power equivalent to fraud' and 'result-

46 [1953] 2 S.C.R. 95.

47 [1994] 1 S.C.R. 231.

48 *Roncarelli*, *supra* note 1 at 140.

49 [1978] 2 S.C.R. 801.

ing in a flagrant injustice,'"[50] he formed the view that both the official documents of the city and the circumstances of the case established bad faith.

C. Acting Under Dictation or Influence

Courts presume that when Parliament chooses to delegate discretion to a particular decision-maker, only the latter can actually exercise it. Therefore, any indication that one acted under the dictation or influence of another person suggests that the power was not in fact exercised by the authority that was identified by Parliament. In *Roncarelli*, the decision-maker was found to have exercised his power under the dictation of Duplessis. This was not permitted by the delegating statute that conferred the power to decide on the Liquor Commission.

D. Wrongful Delegation of Powers

The preceding reasoning is also invoked in a slightly different way. Courts assume that discretion is bestowed on executive decision-makers on the basis of their expertise or particular situation in the administrative machinery, so that an administrative authority must exercise discretion itself without delegating that responsibility to another (except when simple matters of execution are involved, in which case delegation is possible because then the exercise of the power does not require any particular ability or expertise). Hence, in *Vic Restaurant Inc. v. Montreal (City)*,[51] the city of Montreal had adopted a bylaw that made the delivery of permits conditional on the authorization of the chief of police. This was found to be an illegal subdelegation of the power to make a decision, because the bylaw did not provide precise norms on which the chief of police could rely, *de facto* conferring on him the power to make those norms.

E. Fettering of Discretion

Decision-makers who decide in advance how they will exercise their discretion, before being presented with the particulars of a situation, transform the nature of the power that was delegated to them. This kind of situation is likely to arise in contexts where directives or guidelines are used to structure the exercise of discretion, as we alluded to in part II. If directives or guidelines are applied in a way that prevents the decision-maker from making use of his or her margin of manoeuvre in each case, he or she then transforms the discretionary power into a non-discretionary one. The legality of using those directives thus requires decision-makers to actually exercise discretion and to depart from the guidelines when cases demand it.

F. Unreasonableness

On some occasions, courts invoked the notion of "unreasonableness" to reinforce an argument already made on the basis of one of the specific grounds of review just mentioned.

---

50 *Ibid.* at 809.

51 [1959] S.C.R. 58.

But as a separate ground of review, unreasonableness was rarely invoked. This is because, in contrast to the notion of reasonableness associated with the control of decisions based on law (see Audrey Macklin, chapter 8), the notion of unreasonableness expressed in the context of discretion was usually understood in the *Wednesbury*[52] sense of "something so absurd that no sensible person could ever dream that it lay within the power of the authority."[53] That definition was later reformulated by the House of Lords as "a decision which is so outrageous in its defiance of logic or of accepted moral standards that no sensible person who had applied his mind to the question to be decided could have arrived at it."[54] The conditions required to make a case of unreasonable exercise of discretion were therefore very demanding and rarely established before the courts.

The application of these various grounds of review presented important difficulties and, in many cases, the distinction between the substance of a discretionary decision and its surrounding legal limits could hardly be neatly distinguished. This challenge may explain the periodic resurfacing of the "law unto itself" approach to discretion in the years that followed *Roncarelli* and the tendency of courts to oscillate between the majority and minority approaches expressed in that decision.[55] For example, in *Thorne's Hardware Ltd. v. The Queen.*,[56] the Supreme Court expressed the view that "the possibility of striking down an Order in Council on jurisdictional or other compelling grounds remains open, [but] it would take an egregious case to warrant such action"[57] and that "[d]ecisions of the Governor in Council in matters of public convenience and necessity are final and not reviewable in legal proceedings."[58]

By and large, the approach to judicial control of discretion just described maintained the law/discretion dichotomy in that it expressed a form of control that differed from that which applied to decisions based on law. Recall that the latter were approached along the lines of the doctrines of "preliminary or collateral questions" and "asking the wrong question" (see Audrey Macklin, chapter 8) authorizing intrusive judicial control on the substance. By contrast, the various grounds of review (enumerated above) illustrate that discretionary decisions were approached from a perspective that sought to preserve the freedom of the decision-makers to decide on the substance and to limit judicial intervention to policing the surrounding legal limits within which such freedom was exercised.

The law/discretion dichotomy persisted even with the emergence of the politics of deference inaugurated in *Canadian Union of Public Employees, Local 963 v. New Brunswick Liquor Corp.*[59] As we saw from preceding chapters, the Supreme Court mandated courts to adopt an attitude of deference toward administrative determinations of law, suggesting that

52 Named after the famous dictum by Lord Greene in *Associated Provincial Picture Houses Ltd. v. Wednesbury Corporation* (1948), 1 K.B. 223.

53 *Ibid.* at 229.

54 *Council of Civil Service Unions v. Minister for the Civil Service*, [1985] A.C. 374 at 410 (H.L.).

55 See D.J. Mullan, "Judicial Deference to Executive Decision-Making: Evolving Concepts of Responsibility" (1993) 13 Queen's L.J. 137.

56 [1983] 1 S.C.R. 106 [*Thorne's*]. See Andrew Greene's discussion of *Thorne's* in chapter 13.

57 *Thorne's*, *ibid.* at 111.

58 *Ibid.*

59 [1979] 2 S.C.R. 227 [*CUPE*].

the latter had to be protected from systematic judicial control (see Audrey Macklin, chapter 8 and Sheila Wildeman, chapter 9). What came to be termed a "pragmatic and functional approach" would be used to determine the degree of deference applicable in each case. At first glance, this seemed to narrow the gap between the judicial approach to discretion and its approach to law, because courts were invited to restrain their interventions in both cases. But different reasons justified these apparently similar results.

The hands-off approach to administrative interpretations of non-jurisdictional questions was justified by the idea that law interpretation was not the monopoly of the courts and that, in many cases, expert, administrative agencies were just as qualified as courts, and sometimes better qualified, to interpret a statutory provision. By contrast, the hands-off approach to discretion was precisely dictated by the necessity to maintain the judiciary in a position that was compatible with a formal view of the separation of powers. Because discretion required choices that could be based on political or policy considerations, subjecting discretion to substantive legal scrutiny was viewed as putting courts on the slippery slope of politics. Therefore, the heads of review available limited the potential for intrusion into the substance of those decisions and maintained the judiciary in a position that was compatible with a formal view of the separation of powers.

Thus, in the field of discretion, the justification for restraint was not based on judicial "deference," the recognition of a legitimate role for the executive in law interpretation, but on judicial "abstinence,"[60] the necessity to keep the judiciary away from decisions that were viewed as being outside the realm of the law. Although both review approaches recognized that "unreasonable" decisions mandated intervention, the nature of the latter differed. In cases of discretion, unreasonableness was understood in the *Wednesbury* sense and did not seem to require any serious involvement with the merits of the decision because the defect it punished was to clearly appear on its face. By contrast, in the context of the review of executive interpretations of the law, *CUPE* defined a patently unreasonable decision as one that could not be "rationally supported by the relevant legislation."[61]

The law/discretion dichotomy therefore seemed firmly entrenched in the law of judicial review. However, another decision of the Supreme Court handed down the same year as *CUPE* paved the way for the profound restructuring of the law of judicial review that would occur 20 years later.

As explained by Grant Huscroft in chapter 5, in *Nicholson v. Haldimand-Norfolk (Regional) Board of Commissioners of Police*[62] the Supreme Court expressly stated that the distinction between law and discretion was not a reliable criterion for determining the domain of application of procedure in administrative matters. On the one hand, it was very difficult to make formal distinctions between legal (or "quasi-judicial") decisions and discretionary ones; on the other hand, the focus on formal categories masked a fundamental aspect to be considered in the discussion, that of the consequences of a decision for the individual concerned. In so saying, the Court questioned justification for using precisely this distinction for the purpose of judicial control. In other words, if the difficulty (if not the

60 The expression is from R.A. Macdonald, "Judicial Review and Procedural Fairness in Administrative Law: I" (1980) 25 McGill L.J. 520 at 534.

61 *CUPE*, *supra* note 59 at 237.

62 [1979] 1 S.C.R. 311 [*Nicholson*].

impossibility) to neatly differentiate law and discretion, together with the necessity to shift the focus of the analysis, justified changing the conditions of application of procedural rights, it became increasingly difficult to maintain that distinction as a justification for exercising different forms of control for law and discretion.

IV. THE LAW OF DISCRETION: BAKER AND BEYOND

The decision of the Supreme Court in *Baker* marked a turning point in the law of discretion in Canada.

A. Baker

The facts of *Baker* are described more fully by Grant Huscroft in chapter 5. The *Baker* case was concerned with the legality of the Minister's refusal to exempt Ms. Baker from the application of the *Immigration Act*. Such exemptions could be accorded if the Minister was satisfied that compassionate and humanitarian considerations existed. One of the arguments that were made on behalf of Ms. Baker was that the decision of the Minister was unreasonable because insufficient attention had been given to the interests of her children.

L'Heureux-Dubé J., speaking for the Court on this particular question, elucidated the proper approach for the review of administrative discretion. She recalled that traditionally, the control of that kind of decision was limited to specific grounds, as opposed to the review of decisions interpreting rules of law, which proceeded under the "pragmatic and functional approach" (see Audrey Macklin, chapter 8). In her opinion, the traditional approach to the review of discretion, with its limited grounds of review, incorporated two central ideas. One is that the decision-maker must be given an important margin of manoeuvre when exercising discretion.[63] The other idea is that the decision-maker must nonetheless act within certain limits:

> [D]iscretionary decisions, like all other administrative decisions, must be made within the bounds of the jurisdiction conferred by the statute. … [It] must be exercised in a manner that is within a reasonable interpretation of the margin of manoeuvre contemplated by the legislature, in accordance with the principles of the rule of law (*Roncarelli v. Duplessis* …), in line with general principles of administrative law governing the exercise of discretion, and consistent with the *Canadian Charter of Rights and Freedoms* (*Slaight Communications v. Davidson*).[64]

In her opinion, no strict dichotomy could be made between discretionary and non-discretionary decisions: decisions made by the executive could never be neatly associated with either category, because they were usually composed of a mixture of characteristics that prevented such a classification. Moreover, the exercise of discretion and the interpretation of rules of law could not be easily differentiated, notably because both involved making choices between two courses (either action or inaction), or between various options opening up in cases of legal silence or ambiguity.[65]

---

63 *Baker*, *supra* note 2 at para. 53.

64 *Ibid.*

65 *Ibid.* at para. 54.

The review of discretion could follow the pragmatic and functional approach, L'Heureux-Dubé J. said, because the factors it put forward to determine the applicable standard of review in any given case could accommodate the specificity of discretionary powers. This would not lead to more intervention into that kind of decision, because the pragmatic and functional approach would take into account that discretion inherently requires leeway, while recognizing that "discretion must be exercised in accordance with the boundaries imposed in the statute, the principles of the rule of law, the principles of administrative law, the fundamental values of Canadian society, and the principles of the *Charter*."[66] In the circumstances, she concluded that the Minister's decision had to be reviewed on the standard of reasonableness *simpliciter* (see Sheila Wildeman, chapter 9) and that, on the facts of the case, the decision failed to meet the required standard. The reasons that supported the decision showed that the officer failed to give "serious weight and considerations to the interests of the children."[67] As such, this demonstrated that it was "inconsistent with the *values* underlying the grant of power"[68] and therefore unreasonable.

L'Heureux-Dubé J. argued that the reasonableness of the exercise of a discretionary power conferred by Parliament depended on the words "compassionate and humanitarian considerations" and their meaning.[69] The relevant provisions showed that Parliament's intention was that decision-makers exercise discretion "in a humanitarian and compassionate manner."[70] Now, to be able to determine the meaning of those crucial words (stated differently, to determine "whether the approach taken by the immigration officer was within the boundaries set out by the words of the statute and values of administrative law"),[71] the Court had to engage in a process of statutory interpretation, through a contextual approach. Such a contextual interpretation required taking into account the objectives of the *Immigration Act*, international instruments, and ministerial guidelines. These indications revealed that "children's rights, and attention to their interests, are central humanitarian and compassionate values in Canadian society."[72] Therefore, a reasonable exercise of the power required close attention to the interests and needs of the children.

B. Baker's Promise

By applying the pragmatic and functional approach to the control of discretion, *Baker* marked the end of the law/discretion dichotomy in the domain of substantive judicial review. The Supreme Court recognized that the substance of discretionary decisions could be made subject to a control based on reasonableness. As a result, the Court moved away from Dicey's conception of discretion, because he conceived discretion as exercised on the basis of considerations that were not part of the law, and therefore impossible to control

66 *Ibid.* at para. 56.

67 *Ibid.* at para. 65.

68 *Ibid.* (emphasis added).

69 *Ibid.* at para. 66.

70 *Ibid.*

71 *Ibid.* at para. 67.

72 *Ibid.*

judicially. The approach put forward by the Court in *Baker* is much closer to the perspective endorsed by Robson, Jennings, and Willis, who had emphasized the difficulty of differentiating decisions on the basis of their discretionary or non-discretionary content and the need to confer the control of administrative decisions to institutions attentive to the distinctive features of public administration.[73] The pragmatic and functional approach aims at the same objective. In other words, if it is not possible to clearly differentiate in any given case discretion from law, the differentiation cannot be the basis for the determination of the approach to review.

In addition, the *Baker* case softened the dichotomy between procedure and substance. The Court not only required that reasons be given for decisions having important consequences for the individuals concerned, but also required that those reasons demonstrate that the decision made was sensitive and attentive to the situation of those individuals. *Baker* thus recognized that procedure may affect the substance of the decision.[74] More generally, *Baker* is in line with the decision of the Supreme Court in *Nicholson*,[75] which shifted the starting point for determining the legality of executive action, from the nature of the power to the consequences of the exercise of that power on the individual. This is clear from the rationale put forward by the Court for imposing a duty to give reasons on decision-makers endowed with extensive discretionary powers:

> The profound importance of [a humanitarian and compassionate] decision to those affected … militates in favour of a requirement that reasons be provided. It would be unfair for a person subject to a decision such as this one which is so critical to their future not to be told why the result was reached.[76]

Therefore, the duty to give reasons does not depend on the kind of power that is exercised by the executive, but rather on the consideration that the dignity of the individual requires that she be told why a decision that is critical to her future was made.

Baker thus moves closer to a conception of discretion as exercised in a "space controlled by law,"[77] as opposed to a conception of discretion as inherently political or giving the executive "free reign within legal limits."[78]

C. Baker's Aftermath

1. What Is Left of the Previous Approach?

Baker left us with the difficult question of the remaining role of the categories or heads of review that characterized the traditional approach to the review of discretion. This question emerges because *Baker* suggests that those heads of review still have a role to play: discre-

73 For further details, see text under II.B., "Discretion and Academics," above.

74 Further discussion of this argument will be found in D. Dyzenhaus & E. Fox-Decent, "Rethinking the Process/Substance Distinction: Baker v. Canada" (2001) 51 U.T.L.J. 193.

75 *Supra* note 62.

76 *Baker*, *supra* note 2 at para. 43.

77 Dyzenhaus & Fox-Decent, *supra* note 74 at 218.

78 *Ibid.* at 204.

tion "must be exercised in a manner that is within a reasonable interpretation of the margin of manoeuvre contemplated by the legislature, in accordance with the principles of the rule of law (*Roncarelli v. Duplessis* ...), *in line with general principles of administrative law governing the exercise of discretion*, and consistent with the [Charter]."[79] The "general principles of administrative law governing the exercise of discretion" very probably refer to the grounds for review described in the preceding section. How, then, can we reconcile the pragmatic and functional approach to discretion with the necessity to ensure the conformity of executive exercises of discretion with those distinct grounds?

As suggested by David Mullan,[80] one might think that the previous grounds of review, which rely in large part on questions of fact (bad faith, wrongful delegation of power, acting under dictation or fettering of discretion), are unaffected by that approach. However, the grounds more closely related to an exercise of statutory interpretation (such as unauthorized object or purpose, irrelevant considerations or reasonableness) might need to be approached in conformity with the appropriate standard of review at the close of a pragmatic and functional analysis. In more concrete terms, this could mean that reviewing courts will be called upon to intervene only if it was patently unreasonable (or unreasonable, or incorrect, depending on the standard of review identified) for a decision-maker to have taken into account, for example, an irrelevant factor, or to have omitted a relevant one, or to have considered X or Y to be the object or purpose of the statute. This is suggested by the following passage of L'Heureux-Dubé J.: "deferential standards of review may give substantial leeway to the discretionary decision-maker in determining the 'proper purpose' or 'relevant considerations' involved in making a determination."[81]

2. *The Chilling Effect of Suresh*

Recall that, in *Baker*, the Court formed the view that a number of elements (the purposes of the legislation, administrative guidelines, and the international *Convention on the Rights of the Child*[82]) pointed to the interests of Baker's children as an important element to be taken into account in the decision to deport her or not. On the facts of the case, the Court found that the decision-maker had failed to give "serious weight and considerations to the interests of the children."[83] In so concluding, the Court clearly suggested that the evaluation of the reasonableness of the decision to deport Baker included the evaluation of the "weight" that had been given to a consideration that was considered particularly relevant to the decision: the interests of Baker's children. During the months that followed *Baker*, that aspect of the decision became the focus of judicial debate and academic discussion: when called upon to review the validity of any given exercise of discretion, can the reviewing court "reweigh" the considerations that were taken into account by the decision-maker?

---

79 *Baker*, *supra* note 2 at para. 53.

80 D.J. Mullan, "Deference from Baker to Suresh—Interpreting Conflicting Signals" in D. Dyzenhaus, ed., *The Unity of Public Law* (Oxford: Hart Publishing, 2004) 21 at 24ff.

81 *Baker*, *supra* note 2 at para. 56.

82 Can. T.S. 1992 No. 3.

83 *Baker*, *supra* note 2 at para. 65.

In *Suresh v. Canada (Minister for Citizenship and Immigration)*,[84] the Supreme Court clearly said no: the authority required to "weigh" the relevant considerations in *Baker* was the Minister, not the reviewing court:

> *Baker* does not authorize courts reviewing decisions on the discretionary end of the spectrum to engage in a new weighing process, but draws on an established line of cases concerning the failure of ministerial delegates to consider and weigh implied limitations and/or patently relevant factors.[85]

Reviewing courts must therefore limit themselves to ensuring that only relevant considerations have been taken into account; weighing is for the decision-maker alone. One can of course wonder how this is any different from the pre-*Baker* era: as we saw from the various heads of review that were used to control discretion, courts were limited to just that same role. Moreover, if we accept that discretion is not intrinsically different from law, as *Baker* indicates, then discretion should be subjected to a form of control that permits an evaluation of the reasonableness of the decision. Now, since the difference between a reasonable and an unreasonable decision sometimes depends on the relative importance, or weight, given to the relevant considerations at play, it is difficult to reconcile the principles established in *Baker* with the position in *Suresh*, according to which reviewing courts must not "reweigh" the considerations at play. With the *Suresh* approach, it is difficult to see how the application of the pragmatic and functional analysis to the review of discretion will significantly alter the traditional approach to the review of discretion, as *Baker* clearly suggested.

V. CONCLUSION

No one today denies the central, indeed, the necessary role played by discretion in the day-to-day functioning of the administrative state. Discretion allows the administrative state the flexibility that is required in order either to make individual decisions adapted to particular situations, or to conceive general, regulatory norms that will structure the way in which a particular legislative scheme is to be concretized. As we saw however, the proper place of discretion within a state governed by the rule of law is not easy to find. From *Roncarelli* to *Baker*, courts oscillated between a view of discretion as governed by politics and one governed by legal principles. The latter now seems formally recognized by the judiciary, but the concrete application of such a view of discretion is likely to be affected by the turmoil associated with preoccupation for national security. We are never far away from reverting to discretion as a "law unto itself."

In addition to its complex relationship with the rule of law, discretion questions democracy. Simply put, if executive decision-makers define the norms according to which individual cases are to be decided, or simply make individual decisions in the absence of formal legislative norms, can we say that discretion is compatible with democratic values? It is my contention that a particular conception of discretion, termed "discretion as dialogue,"

84 [2002] 1 S.C.R. 3.

85 *Ibid.* at para. 37.

as opposed to a conception of "discretion as power," is likely to take up both the challenge of the rule of law and the challenge of democracy. In what follows, and by way of conclusion, I briefly advance this conception for further thought.

As I suggested in the introduction to part III, courts have been oscillating between two different conceptions of discretion at least since *Roncarelli*. I term these contrasting conceptions as "dialogue" and "power." When conceived as the former, administrative discretion must be approached from a bottom-up perspective and thought of as a dialogue[86] between the individual affected by the decision and the public authority making that decision. The exercise of discretion is here viewed as triggering a process of communication between the decision-maker and the individual concerned, in a way that prevents the former from unilaterally imposing its decision on the latter. Dialogue builds primarily upon a bottom-up approach to discretionary power and seeks to foster a reciprocal relationship between the decision-maker and the individual. The distinctive features of a conception of discretion as dialogue relate to the content of the communication that it involves and to the effect that the dialogue produces on the outcome of the decision-making process. As to the content, it first allows the individual to expose the particularities of his or her situation and requires the decision-maker to demonstrate openness and listening. Second, it requires the parties to transcend their particular position in order to deliberate on the norms and values that should govern the exercise of discretion. The effect of the dialogue is essentially to narrow the range of outcomes that a decision-maker is legally entitled to reach, because the decision must be responsive to the dialogue that preceded it.

This notion of "discretion as dialogue" is different from what I term "discretion as power"; that is, discretion exercised from a top-down perspective or as a "one-way projection of authority,"[87] where discretionary powers are seen as "direct descendants of what were once considered to be unreviewable or unjusticiable executive prerogatives."[88]

In *Roncarelli*, Rand J. set the stage for a conception of discretion as dialogue that sharply contrasted with Cartwright J.'s view of discretion as an exercise of power, unchallengeable in courts, except when the statute explicitly indicates that such a challenge is authorized. In my view, discretion should be conceived as a dialogue, for two reasons.

First, dialogue best explains the development that has occurred in administrative law over the last 30 years. More specifically, it explains why courts have been willing to impose procedural obligations on decision-makers exercising discretion (for example, *Nicholson*) and also an obligation to justify their decisions through a duty to give reasons when the decision has important effects on an individual (for example, *Baker*). Such findings can hardly be reconciled with a view of discretion as power, because such a view posits that the decision-maker is free to impose the decision as he or she sees fit from his or her point of view.

---

86 This expression has been used by J. Handler and L. Sossin. See J. Handler, "Dependent People, the State, and the Modern/Postmodern Search for the Dialogic Community" (1988) 35 U.C.L.A. L. Rev. 999; and L. Sossin, "The Politics of Discretion: Towards a Critical Theory of Public Administration" (1993) 36 Can. Pub. Adm. 364. But Handler and Sossin focus on cases involving vulnerable people, while I contend that dialogue applies to every exercise of discretion.

87 L.L. Fuller, *The Morality of Law*, rev'd ed. (New Haven, CT: Yale University Press, 1969) at 191-95, 204, 209.

88 D. Dyzenhaus, "Introduction" in D. Dyzenhaus, ed., *The Unity of Public Law*, *supra* note 80 at 2.

Second, discretion as dialogue not only explains but also justifies the evolution of the law of discretion, at least until *Baker*, because it suggests how discretion is compatible with both the rule of law and democracy. First, discretion as dialogue, through its requirement of justification, places executive action within the realm of the rule of law through participation and accountability. Second, by creating venues for communication and deliberation, discretion as dialogue allows the individual to participate in the articulation of the norms that will be applied to him or her and substantiates the democratic value of public action.

The question whether dialogue is likely to impose itself as the background metaphor in the years to come is not an easy one to answer. Indeed, as is clear from the next chapter, by Craig Forcese, when governments are overly sensitive to questions of national security and emergency, as they are now, temptations are great to fall back on a view of discretion that moves away from considerations of participation and accountability. It is my contention, however, that to have at least a clear view of the competing articulations of discretion at play in these troubled times is the best weapon to protect individual liberty, democracy, and the rule of law.

SUGGESTED ADDITIONAL READINGS

CASES

Baker v. Canada (Minister for Citizenship and Immigration), [1999] 2 S.C.R. 817.

Roncarelli v. Duplessis, [1959] S.C.R. 121.

Suresh v. Canada (Minister for Citizenship and Immigration), [2002] 1 S.C.R. 3.

SECONDARY MATERIALS

Dyzenhaus, D. "The Deep Structure of Roncarelli v. Duplessis" (2004) 53 U.N.B.L.J. 111.

Mullan, D.J. "Deference from Baker to Suresh and Beyond—Interpreting Conflicting Signals" in D. Dyzenhaus, ed., *The Unity of Public Law* (Oxford: Hart Publishing, 2004) 21.

CHAPTER ELEVEN

Administering Security: The Limits of Administrative Law in the National Security State

CRAIG FORCESE
Faculty of Law, University of Ottawa

I. INTRODUCTION

The Roman jurist Cicero once said that "during war, the laws are silent" (*silent enim legis inter arma*). Commenting in 2006 on this maxim, Aharon Barak, then-president of the Israeli Supreme Court, wrote that such "sayings are regrettable. … It is when the cannons roar that we especially need the laws. … Every struggle of the state—against terrorism or any other enemy—is conducted according to rules and law. There is always law which the state must comply with. There are no 'black holes.'"[1] Put another way, in a system built on the rule of law,[2] there should be no circumstance lying beyond the law's writ.

Nevertheless, it is also true that the content of that law may vary in times of crisis. At the international level, for example, international human rights law does allow the suspension of many rights in times of crisis threatening the existence of the state.[3] Other rights are limited on their own terms where such limitations are necessary for purposes, *inter alia*, of "national security."[4] Where a crisis crosses the boundary to an "armed conflict," international human rights law is, at least partially, displaced by the laws of war. While the latter body of rules—reflected most famously in the Geneva conventions—does seek to protect non-combatants from attack, it is nevertheless law that regards state violence as legitimate, so long as it is directed at appropriate targets. Put another way, during wars, the law is not silent, but it does speak with a different voice.

This is true at the domestic level as well. In Canadian law, the legal checks and balances that together render government accountable come in two forms: constitutional limitations and administrative law requirements. Both areas have developed rapidly in the last several decades, constraining government activity in fashions unprecedented in Canadian history. However, both constitutional and administrative law apply differently in times of national security crises than in other instances.

The constitution's emergency provisions are well understood. Most famously, the "notwithstanding" clause in s. 33 of the *Canadian Charter of Rights and Freedoms*[5] allows Parliament or the provincial legislatures to remove a statute from Charter scrutiny (in relation to most, but not all, Charter rights) by explicitly indicating that it operates "notwithstanding" the Charter. Even if s. 33 was not used and Parliament's enactment violated the Charter, the statute could be saved from a Charter challenge by s. 1. It seems likely that courts would be prepared to endorse some abridgment of rights in a good faith emergency. For instance, in *R. v. Heywood*,[6] the Supreme Court suggested that a violation of the s. 7 right to life, liberty, and security of the person, though generally difficult to justify on s. 1 grounds, could be reasonable "in times of war or national emergencies."

Of course, there has never been a use of s. 33 or an invocation of s. 1 in an emergency of the magnitude imagined in *Heywood*. More commonplace are provisions enacted without recourse to s. 33 that extend extraordinary powers to the Canadian administrative state in the interest of protecting national security. As the recent Arar inquiry noted, the national security activities undertaken pursuant to these laws

---

1 *Public Committee v. The Government of Israel*, [2006] HCJ 769/02 at para. 61.

2 For a discussion on the rule of law, see Mary Liston, chapter 4.

3 See, for example, *International Covenant on Civil and Political Rights*, G.A. res. 2200A (XXI), 21 U.N. GAOR Supp. (No. 16) at 52, U.N. Doc. A/6316 (1966), 999 U.N.T.S. 171, art. 4, (entered into force 23 March 1976) [ICCPR].

4 See ICCPR, *ibid.* art. 19 (allowing freedom of expression to be limited in the interest of national security).

5 Part I of the *Constitution Act, 1982*, being Schedule B to the *Canada Act 1982* (U.K.), 1982, c. 11 [Charter].

6 [1994] 3 S.C.R. 761 at 802. See also *Newfoundland (Treasury Board) v. N.A.P.E.*, 2004 SCC 66, [2004] 3 S.C.R. 381 for a court citing a putative fiscal crisis in upholding a discriminatory law under s. 1.

> involve the most intrusive powers of the state: electronic surveillance; search, seizure and forfeiture of property; information collection and exchange with domestic and foreign security intelligence and law enforcement agencies; and, potentially, the detention and prosecution of individuals. The use of such powers may adversely affect individual rights and freedoms.[7]

Unlike regular criminal investigations, however, national security matters are more deeply surreptitious and secret. The writ of Canada's information access laws stops short of national security matters. Those who have been investigated may be eternally oblivious to this fact and in no position to complain about misconduct. Indeed, if no criminal charge is laid and no decision is made to commence a prosecution, none of the investigation undertaken by the authorities will ever be tested before an impartial decision-maker.

In these circumstances, careful review of national security decision-making is especially important. National security law expert and government lawyer Stanley Cohen aptly captures the standard to be applied: trust, but verify.[8] Designing the mechanics of such a verification regime is, however, difficult. In theory, national security powers are subject to conventional Charter and administrative law doctrines. In practice, administrative decision-making in the national security state is particularly opaque, governed by rules on disclosure and openness that protect secrets at the possible expense of fairness. Meanwhile, courts have often scrutinized executive decisions motivated by national security using very tender standards of review. Put another way, many of the conventional administrative law doctrines discussed in this book work imperfectly to constrain the behaviour of the national security state.

This pattern poses no small problem. David Dyzenhaus warns forcefully against "grey holes"—that is, zones in which the law putatively applies, but in such a limited procedural or substantive manner as to render legal limitations on executive power meaningless. He cautions that in these circumstances, the facade of the rule of law is maintained, but in a manner that creates a simple "rule by law" and not adherence to fundamental moral values.[9]

This chapter explores these contentions in four parts. First, it briefly highlights the prevalence of national security-related powers and doctrines in Canada's federal statutes. Second, it examines the way conventional administrative law operates in relation to national security functions, focusing on fairness concepts and the issue of court deference to the executive. Third, it examines the actual practice of judicial review of national security decision-making. Last, it discusses a particularly important alternative form of review: bureaucratic review of the national security state. The overarching purpose of this chapter is to highlight the limitations of administrative law in serving as an instrument of accountability in this area of state conduct.

7 Commission of Inquiry into the Actions of Canadian Officials in Relation to Maher Arar, *A New Review Mechanism for the RCMP's National Security Activities* (Ottawa: Gilmore Print Group, 2006) at 425-26 [Arar inquiry].

8 Stanley A. Cohen, *Privacy, Crime and Terror: Legal Rights and Security in a Time of Peril* (Markham, ON: LexisNexis Butterworths, 2005) at 561.

9 David Dyzenhaus, *The Constitution of Law: Legality in a Time of Emergency* (Cambridge: Cambridge University Press, 2006).

II. NATIONAL SECURITY IN CANADIAN LAW

The expression national security, or close equivalents such as "security of Canada," appear in at least 33 Canadian federal statutes.[10] There, they act as a potent legal concept. National security is obviously the touchstone in many specialized national security statutes, laws that greatly expand the powers of the government either to regulate or penalize. It is also an important feature of more general laws, freeing the government from constraints it would otherwise face under these statutes or expanding the range of powers to which it would otherwise be normally restricted. It is worth describing briefly several of these laws, as many will feature in the discussion that follows.

A. Creating Special Government National Security Powers

Some statutes invoke national security to authorize special government action to pre-empt, or respond to, national security concerns. The *Canadian Security Intelligence Service Act*,[11] for instance, establishes an intelligence service whose exact objective is to compile, analyze, and retain information and intelligence on "threats to the security of Canada,"[12] a carefully defined term. Other laws authorizing unusual government powers on national security grounds incorporate by reference this CSIS Act definition. For instance, the *Security Offences Act* "federalizes" prosecution and police investigations of crimes stemming from conduct constituting a "threat to the security of Canada."[13]

B. Penalizing National Security Threats

Several other statutes are punitive in nature, imposing penalties or other, special disadvantages on persons on national security grounds. The concept of national security appears in several offences found in the *Criminal Code*[14] and the *Security of Information Act*.[15] These statutes bar certain predicate acts committed for a purpose prejudicial to Canadian security. Moreover, the *Criminal Code* includes numerous other offences that, while they do not invoke national security per se, are clearly intended to preserve it. Terrorism offences are key examples in point.

For its part, the *Immigration and Refugee Protection Act* (IRPA)[16] applies its own penalties in relation to national security threats. Certainly, this law is not intended as a punitive statute; instead, it fosters the conditional presence of aliens in Canada. Nevertheless, it includes provisions that, in practice, may result in the imposition of special disadvantages on aliens, up to and including prolonged incarceration where national security concerns are engaged. For

10 For a fuller treatment of this topic, see Craig Forcese, "Through a Glass Darkly: The Role and Review of 'National Security' Concepts in Canadian Law" (2006) 43 Alta. L. Rev. 963.

11 R.S.C. 1985, c. C-23 [CSIS Act].

12 *Ibid.*, s. 12.

13 R.S.C. 1985, c. S-7, s. 2.

14 R.S.C. 1985, c. C-46.

15 R.S.C. 1985, c. O-5.

16 S.C. 2001, c. 27 [IRPA].

instance, the IRPA denies entry to Canada by a permanent resident or a foreign national for "being a danger to the security of Canada."[17] A person viewed as posing such a danger may be detained and removed following inadmissibility and removal proceedings before the Immigration Division of the Immigration and Refugee Board. "Security certificates" may also be issued by the government, resulting in the detention of aliens. If considered reasonable by a Federal Court judge, the certificate constitutes a removal order.[18] Because IRPA now technically permits removal in extreme circumstances to face torture in the destination state,[19] this immigration system may culminate in the indirect administration of a penalty far in excess of what could legally be imposed in Canada. For this reason, IRPA permits consequences in excess of the criminal law, but is dressed up as an administrative procedure.

In terms of more unambiguously administrative powers, the *Citizenship Act*[20] includes a procedure for denying citizenship to individuals where the government believes that the person constitutes a threat to the security of Canada. Under the *Charities Registration (Security Information) Act*, the government may issue a "certificate stating that it is their opinion, based on information, that there are reasonable grounds to believe that an applicant for charitable status or registered charity" has financial ties to a terrorist group.[21] If the certificate is subsequently adjudged reasonable by a Federal Court judge, the applicant is denied charitable status (or an existing such status is revoked).

C. Limiting Regular Government Obligations

Finally, a number of statutes include specific national security exemptions from the constraints otherwise imposed on government action. For instance, there are various national security exemptions under the *Access to Information Act*,[22] negating the public's general right to government information. Section 38 of the *Canada Evidence Act*,[23] discussed more fully below, can be used to similar effect in the specific context of court proceedings.

The flip side to information-limiting invocations of national security are those provisions in the *Privacy Act*[24] and elsewhere allowing select, national security-motivated interception, collection, and disclosure of information that would otherwise be protected. More generally, several laws establish a national security exemption from the usual regulatory regime established by the statute.[25]

---

17 *Ibid.*, s. 35.

18 As discussed below, certain procedural aspects of this system were declared unconstitutional by the time of this writing. However, the concept of security certificates remained intact.

19 IRPA, *supra* note 16, s. 115.

20 R.S.C. 1985, c. C-29.

21 S.C. 2001, c. 41, s. 113.

22 R.S.C. 1985, c. A-1 [Access Act].

23 R.S.C. 1985, c. C-5.

24 R.S.C. 1985, c. P-21 [Privacy Act].

25 See, for example, *Canadian Environmental Assessment Act*, S.C. 1992, c. 37, s. 59(c)(i); *Mackenzie Valley Resource Management Act*, S.C. 1998, c. 25, s. 124(1)(b); *Canadian Environmental Protection Act*, 1999, c. 33, s. 24(a)(ii); *Species at Risk Act*, S.C. 2002, c. 29, s. 83(1)(a); *Canada National Marine Conservation Area Act*, S.C. 2002, c. 18, s. 17(a); *Mutual Legal Assistance in Criminal Matters Act*, R.S.C. 1985 (4th Supp.), c. 30, s. 9.4.

III. SPECIAL QUALITIES OF NATIONAL SECURITY ADMINISTRATIVE PROCEEDINGS

The statutes discussed above vary enormously in their foci and effects. Many do, however, anticipate administrative proceedings, conducted by government officials or, in several instances, by courts charged with a reviewing or confirmation function. Examples include:

- security certificate and inadmissibility proceedings under the IRPA;
- section 38 process under the *Canada Evidence Act*;
- terrorist group listing and delisting processes in the *Criminal Code* and under the relevant regulations of the *United Nations Act*; and
- terrorist-financing charity decertification processes in the *Charities Registration (Security Information) Act*.

Two key issues are raised by administrative proceedings under these and related national security statutory provisions: notice and opportunity to comment, and discretion.

A. Notice and a Right to Be Heard

As discussed elsewhere in this book, notice and an opportunity to be heard are bedrock elements of common-law procedural fairness and, where triggered, equivalent fairness protections under the *Canadian Bill of Rights* and the *Canadian Charter of Rights and Freedoms*. Yet, in national security administrative proceedings, both notice and the right to be heard may be rudimentary.

1. A Basement Floor?

As a first point, it should be noted that the court has recognized a bare minimum of fairness that must be met in national security matters, at least where Charter interests are at stake. In *Suresh*, the applicant faced the prospect of being deported by Canada to possible torture in Sri Lanka. The Supreme Court held that, in these circumstances, Suresh was protected by the Charter's s. 7 concept of fundamental justice. This meant that he "must be informed of the case to be met" and that an "opportunity be provided to respond to the case presented to the Minister," including through the presentation of evidence countering the view that he constituted a national security threat.[26]

The Supreme Court returned to this issue in *Charkaoui*, a case concerning the legitimacy of the secretive security certificate process under Canada's immigration law. In that decision, the Court concluded:

> The procedures required to conform to the principles of fundamental justice must reflect the exigencies of the security context. Yet they cannot be permitted to erode the essence of s. 7. The principles of fundamental justice cannot be reduced to the point where they cease to provide the protection of due process that lies at the heart of s. 7 of the *Charter*. The protection may not be as complete as in a case where national security constraints do not operate. But to satisfy s. 7, meaningful and substantial protection there must be.[27]

---

26 *Suresh v. Canada (Minister of Citizenship and Immigration)*, 2002 SCC 1, [2002] 1 S.C.R. 3 at paras. 122-23 [*Suresh*].

27 *Charkaoui v. Canada (Minister of Citizenship and Immigration)*, 2007 SCC 9 at para. 27 [*Charkaoui*].

Note that despite this seemingly clarion call for due process even where national security is engaged, the Court was clear that national security might temper the precise procedural guarantees offered by s. 7. This position echoes that taken in *Suresh*. Here, the court concluded that information provided by the government to inform Suresh of the case against him was legitimately "[s]ubject to privilege or similar valid reasons for reduced disclosure, such as safeguarding confidential public security documents."[28]

2. Notice and the Right to Be Heard in Practice

These allusions to special national security immigration proceedings lead naturally to a fuller account of fairness standards in several national security-related administrative law regimes.

a. Truncated Notice

First, some national security procedures anticipate no notice being given to affected individuals. For example, under s. 83.05 of the *Criminal Code*, the governor in council (in effect, the federal Cabinet) is empowered to list an entity as a terrorist group by regulation if "on the recommendation of the Minister of Public Safety and Emergency Preparedness, the Governor in Council is satisfied that there are reasonable grounds to believe that (a) the entity has knowingly carried out, attempted to carry out, participated in or facilitated a terrorist activity; or (b) the entity is knowingly acting on behalf of, at the direction of or in association with an entity referred to in paragraph (a)."

A listing may be challenged, albeit in a process in which the challenger has a limited opportunity to know the case to be met. However, an obvious omission in this administrative listing scheme is an opportunity for the entity to have notice or opportunity to comment *prior* to listing. Commenting on this absence, Kent Roach has urged that "after-the-fact judicial review … may be too late for a group that has been erroneously placed on the official list of terrorist organizations. They will have been stigmatized as a terrorist group and people will be afraid that they may be charged with terrorism offences if they participate or give money to the organization."[29] Even if successful in its delisting application, this stigma will not be easily expunged.[30]

Similarly, in 2006, the government proposed regulations under the *Aeronautics Act* putting in place "Passenger Protect," a system that includes a passenger watch list. The regulations are used to exclude persons believed to constitute a threat to civil aviation from aircraft. There is an appeal mechanism for those who have been listed. It is not anticipated, however, that persons will be given advance notice of listing decisions; instead, they will be notified of their status only when they arrive at check in counters (or try to check in at automated wickets).

---

28 *Suresh*, *supra* note 26 at para. 122.

29 Kent Roach, *September 11: Consequences for Canada* (Montreal and Kingston, ON: McGill-Queen's University Press, 2003) at 37.

30 See the discussion in Irwin Cotler, "Terrorism, Security and Rights: The Dilemma of Democracies" (2002-2003) 14 N.J.C.L. 13 at 47.

This "no-fly" program has elicited stern responses from civil liberties organizations, who warn that it will reflect ethnic profiling[31] and is likely to be riddled with errors.[32] Moreover, they fear that listed names will be supplied by Canada to foreign jurisdictions, who may then maltreat listed persons who come within their reach. Weeks after it was introduced in June 2007, Canada's federal and provincial privacy commissioners issued a joint statement deploring the system and calling for its suspension.[33]

b. Truncated Right to Be Heard

In other circumstances, when an individual is given notice—or at least an opportunity to challenge a decision—special constraints may be imposed on his or her right to be heard. At the time of this writing, special closed-door (*in camera*) administrative proceedings conducted in the absence of counsel for the non-governmental party and that party themselves (*ex parte*) were permitted in several national security-related areas, including security certificate and inadmissibility proceedings under the *Immigration and Refugee Protection Act*, s. 38 processes under the *Canada Evidence Act*, terrorist group delisting processes in the *Criminal Code* and under the relevant regulations of the *United Nations Act*, and terrorist-financing charity decertification processes in the *Charities Registration (Security Information) Act*.

In their own ways, each of these regimes allows a Federal Court judge (here, performing a statutorily mandated review or administrative role) or a government official to deny an interested party full access to relevant information—usually intelligence from the security services marshalled by the government as evidence in the proceeding. Proceedings may (and in some instances, must) be *in camera* and *ex parte* and relevant information must be redacted to preserve security interests and may simply be disclosed in a sanitized, abbreviated summary form.

The result may be a situation in which the interested party does not know the case to be met, even in circumstances where important interests may be at stake—for example, possible removal of a foreign national from Canada to face torture at the hands of a foreign government. In 2007, the Supreme Court signalled unhappiness with these procedural limitations, at least in the context of the IRPA security certificate process, declaring them a violation of s. 7. In a passage worthy of citation in full, the Court noted the deficiencies of the IRPA system:

> The [Federal Court] judge [who is charged with assessing the reasonableness of the security certificate], working under the constraints imposed by the *IRPA*, simply cannot fill the vacuum

31 See, for example, British Columbia Civil Liberties Association, News Release, "Government Shielding No-Fly Program from Parliament" (27 October 2006), online: British Columbia Civil Liberties Association <http://www.bccla.org/pressreleases/06nofly.pdf>.

32 See, for example, British Columbia Civil Liberties Association, News Release, "BCCLA Calls for Investigation on Use of the Notorious U.S. 'No-Fly List' Within Canada" (19 January 2006), online: British Columbia Civil Liberties Association <http://www.bccla.org/pressreleases/06nofly2.htm>. See also Don Butler, "Will the No-Fly List Fly?" *Ottawa Citizen* (14 January 2007), A1.

33 Canada's Privacy Commissioners and Privacy Enforcement Officials, Resolution, "Passenger Protect Program—Canada's Aviation No-Fly List" (28 June 2007), online: Office of the Privacy Commissioner of Canada <http://www.privcom.gc.ca/nfl/res_20070628_e.asp>.

> left by the removal of the traditional guarantees of a fair hearing. The judge sees only what the ministers put before him or her. The judge, knowing nothing else about the case, is not in a position to identify errors, find omissions or assess the credibility and truthfulness of the information in the way the named person would be. Although the judge may ask questions of the named person when the hearing is reopened, the judge is prevented from asking questions that might disclose the protected information. Likewise, since the named person does not know what has been put against him or her, he or she does not know what the designated judge needs to hear. If the judge cannot provide the named person with a summary of the information that is sufficient to enable the person to know the case to meet, then the judge cannot be satisfied that the information before him or her is sufficient or reliable. Despite the judge's best efforts to question the government's witnesses and scrutinize the documentary evidence, he or she is placed in the situation of asking questions and ultimately deciding the issues on the basis of incomplete and potentially unreliable information. … The judge is … not in a position to compensate for the lack of informed scrutiny, challenge and counter-evidence that a person familiar with the case could bring. Such scrutiny is the whole point of the principle that a person whose liberty is in jeopardy must know the case to meet. Here that principle has not merely been limited; it has been effectively gutted. How can one meet a case one does not know?[34]

This violation of s. 7's promise of fundamental justice was not saved by s. 1. However, some care must be taken in extrapolating too much from the *Charkaoui* holding on the question of the right to be heard. First, it is important to note that the Court did not signal that confidentiality and a truncated opportunity to be heard are per se impermissible. In *Charkaoui*, the statute's key shortcoming in the s. 1 analysis was that the government had shown no reason why it had failed to adopt an alternative to the full *ex parte* system; that is, a "special advocate" model in which a security-cleared lawyer stands in the shoes of the named person during the closed-door sessions. Systems of this sort are employed by Canada's chief allies.[35] In the United Kingdom—the jurisdiction in which this system is most developed—the special advocate role is limited: he or she may not disclose secret information to the detainee in an effort to assess its credibility. The system has, therefore, been criticized and without question falls short of conventional fair trial standards. Nevertheless, while acknowledging its shortcomings, the Court showed evident enthusiasm for such a model, strongly suggesting that a revised IRPA security certificate system will include such a feature.

Second, the *Charkaoui* ruling will be of little significance in administrative processes that do not trigger s. 7—that is, circumstances in which life, liberty, and security of the person are not in play. The latter concept could include state action potentially inflicting serious psychological injury.[36] Even so, it is difficult to see how s. 7 would apply, for instance, to

34 *Charkaoui*, *supra* note 27 at paras. 63-64.

35 See, for example, special attorney procedure available for the U.S. Alien Terrorist Removal Court, 8 U.S.C. § 1534 (2002) and the special advocate procedure under the *Special Immigration Appeals Commission Act 1997* (U.K.), 1997, c. 68, s. 6, recently extended to control order proceedings under the *Prevention of Terrorism Act 2005* (U.K.), 2005, c. 2.

36 *Chaoulli v. Quebec (Attorney General)*, 2005 SCC 35, [2005] 1 S.C.R. 791 at para. 116 *et seq.*, McLachlin C.J.C. noting that "serious psychological effects (as well as physical harm) may engage s. 7 protection for security of the person."

the decertification of terrorist-financing charities under the *Charities Registration (Security Information) Act*.

B. Discretion

A second resounding feature of national security administrative proceedings is the swath of discretion accorded by delegating statutes to government officials. Despite its seeming prevalence in Canadian law, national security and equivalent concepts are rarely defined. Indeed, in the final analysis, only 9 of 33 federal statutes (fewer than a third) that invoke national security expressions define the concept.[37] This failure of definition produces a Canadian statute book replete with a concept whose precise content is extremely amorphous. As the Federal Court of Appeal has noted, describing the proliferation of terms describing security risks in immigration law, these concepts constitute "a veritable abstract work of art in which everyone can see or discover what they wish."[38]

The conclusion echoes observations made by other authors, focusing on certain sub-aspects of national security law. Discussing Canada's anti-terrorism laws, Sujit Choudhry and Kent Roach argue that "[i]n the war on terrorism, discretionary powers take centre stage."[39] Similarly, Faisal Bhabha complains that the anti-terrorism law "confers an overly general amount of discretion on police and governmental authorities, while it also uses language that is obscure and overly broad."[40] Lorne Sossin, discussing the concept of "terrorism" and "danger to the security of Canada," found in the then current *Immigration Act* that the problem with these expressions "is not their indeterminacy *per se* … but rather that their meaning may change with the political currents of the day. … Statutory terms which authorize state action that may jeopardize the life, liberty and security of the person … must have some inherent content beyond the particular predilections of particular ministers at particular historical junctures."[41]

Ambiguity in the understanding of national security confers substantial discretion on the executive branch to define national security as it wills. Because national security exists in the eye of the beholder, there is ample room to employ national security justifications in manners that may prove impossible to contest. Take, for example, laws permitting government to hold information secret on national security grounds. Court jurisprudence relating to the *Canada Evidence Act*, access and privacy acts, and IRPA gives some indication of the secrecy doctrines that animate the government's national security confidentiality claims. Notable among these theories is the "mosaic effect," a concept that has been raised

---

37 The most notable definition is that found in the CSIS Act, *supra* note 11, s. 2, defining a "threat to the security of Canada."

38 *Charkaoui v. Canada*, 2004 FCA 421 at para. 118.

39 Sujit Choudhry & Kent Roach, "Racial and Ethnic Profiling: Statutory Discretion, Constitutional Remedies, and Democratic Accountability" (2003) 41 Osgoode Hall L.J. 1 at 7.

40 Faisal Bhabha, "Tracking 'Terrorists' or Solidifying Stereotypes? Canada's Anti-Terrorism Act in Light of the Charter's Equality Guarantee" (2003) 16 Windsor Rev. Legal Soc. Issues 95 at 126.

41 Lorne Sossin, "Developments in Administrative Law: The 2001-2002 Term" (2002) 18 Sup. Ct. L. Rev. (2d) 41 at 53 [Sossin, "Developments in Administrative Law"].

in several cases.[42] Put simply, the mosaic effect posits that the release of even innocuous information can jeopardize national security if that information can be pieced together with other data by a knowledgeable reader. The result is a mosaic of little pieces of benign information that cumulatively discloses matters of true national security significance. As urged by one Canadian Security Intelligence Service (CSIS) official in a public affidavit in Federal Court,

> assessing the damage caused by disclosure of information cannot be done in the abstract or in isolation. It must be assumed that information will reach persons with a knowledge of Service targets and the activities subject to this investigation. In the hands of an informed reader, seemingly unrelated pieces of information, which may not in themselves be particularly sensitive, can be used to develop a more comprehensive picture when compared with information already known by the recipient or available from another source.[43]

The mosaic effect has been accepted by Canadian courts, and has guided decisions on disclosure. At core, the doctrine is sensible. As noted by the Federal Court in one of the first cases to apply the doctrine,

> in security matters, there is a requirement to not only protect the identity of human sources of information but to recognize that the following types of information might require to be protected … : information pertaining to the identity of targets of the surveillance whether they be individuals or groups, the technical means and sources of surveillance, the methods of operation of the service, the identity of certain members of the service itself, the telecommunications and cypher systems and, at times, the very fact that a surveillance is being or is not being carried out. This means for instance that evidence, which of itself might not be of any particular use in actually identifying the threat, might nevertheless require to be protected if the mere divulging of the fact that CSIS is in possession of it would alert the targeted organization to the fact that it is in fact subject to electronic surveillance or to a wiretap or to a leak from some human source within the organization.[44]

The use of the mosaic effect outside the context of security investigations involving confidential informers and techniques might, however, greatly erode open government and open courts. Because the doctrine applies to innocuous information, the future use of which can never be predicted, it could be deployed to stave off disclosure of virtually *any* piece of information. In *O'Neill v. Canada*, for example, the Royal Canadian Mounted Police (RCMP) resisted disclosure on national security grounds of the location of an RCMP building "even though it has an exterior sign indicating that it is an RCMP building."[45] Moreover,

---

42 See, for example, *Canada v. Kempo*, 2004 FC 1678 [*Kempo*]; *Re Zundel*, 2005 FC 295; *Cemerlic v. Canada (Solicitor General)*, 2003 FCT 133 (F.C.); *Canada (Minister of Citizenship and Immigration) v. Singh*, [1998] F.C.J. No. 978 (F.C.T.D.); *Ternette v. Canada*, [1992] 2 F.C. 75 (F.C.T.D.); *Henrie v. Canada (Security Intelligence Review Committee)*, [1989] 2 F.C. 229 (F.C.T.D.), aff'd [1992] F.C.J. No. 100 (C.A.) [*Henrie*]; *Re Jaballah*, 2003 FCT 640, [2003] 4 F.C. 345; and *Ruby v. Canada (Solicitor General)*, [1998] 2 F.C. 351.

43 Reproduced in *Kempo*, *ibid.* at para. 62.

44 *Henrie*, *supra* note 42 at para. 29.

45 *O'Neill v. Canada (Attorney General)*, [2004] O.J. No. 4649 at para. 69 (Sup. Ct.).

the location of the building had already been disclosed in the Arar inquiry, discussed below. Not surprisingly, the Ontario Superior Court of Justice ordered the release of the information in the *O'Neill* proceedings.

IV. COURT REVIEW OF DISCRETIONARY NATIONAL SECURITY DECISIONS

The *O'Neill* holding signals the particularly important role of the courts in policing national security decision-making. Ambiguity in statutory terms is not unique. Many expressions found in the law books are undefined and, thus, open the door to discretionary interpretations. At base, these terms may not be infinitely elastic. They may be subject to review and interpretation by courts. A complicated series of statutory interpretation rules may dispel—or at least limit—ambiguity. Put succinctly, in modern statutory interpretation, "there is only one principle or approach, namely, the words of an Act are to be read in their entire context and in their grammatical and ordinary sense harmoniously with the scheme of the Act, the object of the Act, and the intention of Parliament."[46]

This precept, as well as the more specific approaches that flow from it, helps courts breathe meaning into statutory expressions that otherwise defy easy definition. Indeed, as the discussion below notes, the Supreme Court in *Suresh* assigned some meaning to national security concepts in at least one context, immigration law. Irremediably ambiguous terms, meanwhile, may be struck down by courts as unconstitutionally vague, where their use infringes on life, liberty, or security of the person.[47] Ambiguity is not threatening, in other words, so long as the ambiguous term is subject to searching judicial review. As the Supreme Court has observed, "[j]udicial decisions may properly add precision to a statute. Legislators can never foresee all the situations that may arise, and if they did, could not practically set them all out. It is thus in the nature of our legal system that areas of uncertainty exist and that judges clarify and augment the law on a case-by-case basis."[48]

At core, however, the fundamental prerequisite to this sort of limiting interpretation is meaningful access to courts willing to carefully probe government claims of national security. The rules of statutory interpretation do not prescribe mechanical outcomes. Even in applying such doctrines to assign meaning to ambiguous terms, courts could extend deference to the initial interpretations offered by government officials.[49] Under these circumstances,

---

46 *Bristol-Myers Squibb Co. v. Canada (Attorney General)*, 2005 SCC 26, [2005] 1 S.C.R. 533 at paras. 95-96, citing E.A. Driedger, *Construction of Statutes*, 2d ed. (Toronto: Butterworths, 1983) at 87 and noting that this "modern" rule prevails in the Supreme Court's jurisprudence.

47 See *Canadian Foundation for Children, Youth and the Law v. Canada (Attorney General)*, 2004 SCC 4, [2004] 1 S.C.R. 76 at para. 15: "A law is unconstitutionally vague if it 'does not provide an adequate basis for legal debate' and 'analysis'; 'does not sufficiently delineate any area of risk'; or 'is not intelligible.' The law must offer a 'grasp to the judiciary'" (citations omitted).

48 *Ibid.* at para. 17.

49 See *Barrie Public Utilities v. Canadian Cable Television Assn.*, 2003 SCC 28, [2003] 1 S.C.R. 476 at para. 16; *J.D. Irving, Ltd. v. International Longshoremen's Assn. Local 273*, 2003 FCA 266, [2003] 4 F.C. 1080 at paras. 79-80. Both cases noted that statutory interpretation is a pure question of law, a conclusion that feeds into the court's "pragmatic and functional analysis" of how much administrative law deference to extend a government official and that counsels less deference, but that does not automatically prompt a court to be non-deferential.

how assertive Canadian courts have been in evaluating the legitimacy of government national security actions is a key question.

A. Deference as the Starting Point in National Security Matters

In part to limit uncertainty in the definition of national security, courts have occasionally added their own gloss to the concept. In *Suresh*, the Supreme Court concluded that the phrase "danger to the security of Canada" in the then current *Immigration Act* would survive constitutional challenge on vagueness grounds if it were read as requiring the government to adduce evidence producing an objectively reasonable suspicion of a serious threat of substantial harm.[50]

Although a real constraint on the absolute liberty of government to define national security, definitions such as that employed in *Suresh* leave substantial freedom of action in government hands. In *Suresh* itself, the Court applied its standard administrative law "pragmatic and functional" test to determine the degree of deference to be accorded the government in reviewing its decision on the security issue—in that case, the removal under immigration law of a suspected terrorist. The Court concluded that the Minister's decision would be overturned only in egregious circumstances. In partial support of this conclusion, the Court noted that it was the Minister—with access to special information and expertise—making the determination. This fact—read together with the limited appeal mechanism in the then *Immigration Act*, the difficult balancing of the competing humanitarian purposes of the Act, and the extremely fact-intensive and contextual nature of the national security determination—prompted the Court to apply a standard of "patently unreasonable." A "patently unreasonable" decision, in the Court's mind, was one "made arbitrarily or in bad faith, [that] cannot be supported on the evidence, or [where] the Minister failed to consider the appropriate factors."[51]

Commenting on this holding, Dyzenhaus has urged that *Suresh* signals a veritable rush by the Court to a patently unreasonable standard where discretionary decisions are being reviewed.[52] Sossin echoes this view, suggesting that, at least in national security matters, "patent unreasonableness is the 'default' standard of review where the exercise of ministerial discretion is challenged."[53]

It is notable that in coming to its conclusion in *Suresh*, the Supreme Court cited with approval the U.K. House of Lords decision in *United Kingdom (Secretary of State for the Home Department) v. Rehman*.[54] There, the appellant was denied indefinite leave to remain

50 *Suresh*, *supra* note 26 at para. 90. Vagueness is a Charter s. 7 concept, discussed more fully in chapter 7 by Evan Fox-Decent.

51 *Suresh*, *ibid.* at para. 29. For a fuller discussion on the standard of review, see Sheila Wildeman, chapter 9.

52 David Dyzenhaus, "Constituting the Rule of Law: Fundamental Values in Administrative Law" (2002) 27 Queen's L.J. 445 at 506.

53 Sossin, "Developments in Administrative Law," *supra* note 41 at 59.

54 2001 UKHL 47 [*Rehman*]. U.K. courts have traditionally not employed a spectrum of review standards, or a pragmatic and functional test; instead, they have relied on a concept of "reasonableness" in reviewing discretionary administrative decision-making. As *Rehman* illustrates, deference has recently become an important consideration in select cases, involving such things as foreign affairs and immigration. See the discussion in H.W.R. Wade & C.F. Forsyth, *Administrative Law*, 9th ed. (Oxford: Oxford University Press, 2004) at 351 *et seq.* and 369.

in the United Kingdom by virtue of an affiliation with a group defined by the U.K. government as a terrorist organization. The decision was rendered pursuant to a provision in U.K. law authorizing such a determination, and a subsequent deportation, "in the interests of national security." At issue by the time the matter reached the House of Lords was the meaning of this phrase.

In their speeches, their Lordships were not prepared to grant the government carte blanche in its assessment of national security. Lord Slynn of Hadley wrote, for example, that under the relevant statute, "'the interests of national security' cannot be used to justify any reason the Secretary of State has for wishing to deport an individual from the United Kingdom. There must be some possibility of risk or danger to the security or well-being of the nation which the Secretary of State considers makes it desirable for the public good that the individual should be deported."[55]

However, at least one Law Lord was quick to point out that the question whether a threat to national security existed or not was best left in the hands of the government. Thus, Lord Hoffman, in his speech, urged that "decisions as to whether something is or is not in the interests of national security are not a matter for judicial decision. They are entrusted to the executive."[56] In a remarkable postscript, Lord Hoffman added:

> I wrote this speech some three months before the recent events in New York and Washington. They are a reminder that in matters of national security, the cost of failure can be high. This seems to me to underline the need for the judicial arm of government to respect the decisions of ministers of the Crown on the question of whether support for terrorist activities in a foreign country constitutes a threat to national security. It is not only that the executive has access to special information and expertise in these matters. It is also that such decisions, with serious potential results for the community, require a legitimacy which can be conferred only by entrusting them to persons responsible to the community through the democratic process. If the people are to accept the consequences of such decisions, they must be made by persons whom the people have elected and whom they can remove.[57]

B. The Application of Deference

Suresh and *Rehman* underscore the difficult role of reviewing courts in the national security context: generalist judges are asked to second-guess government officials privy to arcane information and expertise on matters that might shake the state to its foundation. The temptation to err of the side of caution must be practically overwhelming.

At the same time, it is important to note that statements like those of Lord Hoffman came in the immediate aftermath of 9/11. Since that time, courts in the United Kingdom have been much more demanding of government action taken in the name of anti-terrorism,[58]

55 *Rehman*, *ibid.* at para. 15.

56 *Ibid.* at para. 50.

57 *Ibid.* at para. 62.

58 For example, in December 2004, the House of Lords declared indefinite detention of foreign terrorist suspects without trial under immigration law contrary to U.K. human rights obligations: *A and Others v. Secretary of State for the Home Department*, 2004 UKHL 56. The measures introduced by the U.K. government

attracting substantial criticism from the British government.[59] In Canada, *Suresh* has been followed by *Charkaoui*, a case in which fairness imperatives prevailed against security preoccupations.

Moreover, it is also important not to overstate the preparedness of courts to simply rubber-stamp government national security decisions. Developments under IRPA suggest that a court's understandable desire to defer in national security matters does not necessarily leave government unencumbered with judicial oversight. IRPA permits a person "inadmissible on grounds of security" to be deported, even where he or she is at risk of torture, if "in the opinion of the Minister, the person should not be allowed to remain in Canada on the basis of … danger to the security of Canada."[60] In cases to date in which the government has attempted to remove people under this provision, the Federal Court followed *Suresh*'s approach to the national security assessment by pointing to the fact-intensive nature of the government's decision and holding that the appropriate standard of review was the deferential "patently unreasonable."[61] Nevertheless, in each case, the court returned the matter to the government for re-determination, urging that the government's conclusion was based on failure to consider proper factors or was not supported on the evidence before the decision-maker.[62]

Still, the pattern of court deference in national security matters is notable and has affected the manner in which courts will intervene in national security cases. Indeed, courts have been deferential even in the area of fairness. The Supreme Court has persistently refused to extend its "pragmatic and functional" approach to deference to decision-making processes that violate doctrines of common-law procedural fairness—in other words, processes that sit poorly with the court's concepts of due process.[63] Moreover, as noted above, where s. 7 is engaged there is a basement floor of procedural entitlement that must be met. Still, applying

---

in response to this decision—control orders permitting substantial constraints on liberty imposed on terrorism suspects—have also attracted close judicial scrutiny. See, for example, *Secretary of State for the Home Department v. JJ and Others*, [2006] EWHC 1623 (Admin.) (Q.B.) (holding that "six control orders [essentially confining persons to their apartments for 18 hours a day] impose obligations that are incompatible with the Respondents' right to liberty under art. 5. It follows that the Secretary of State had no power to make the orders and they must therefore all be quashed"), aff'd [2006] EWCA Civ 1141 (C.A.).

59 See, for example, Ben Russell, "Law Lords Are Undermining 'War on Terror,' Says Clarke" *Independent* [London] (18 January 2007); Ben Leapman, "Reid Says Human Rights Laws Soft on Terrorists" *Sunday Telegraph* (12 May 2007).

60 IRPA, *supra* note 16, s. 115.

61 See, for example, *Almrei v. Canada*, 2005 FC 355 at para. 32 [*Almrei*]; *Mahjoub v. Minister of Citizenship and Immigration et al.*, 2005 FC 156 at para. 31 [*Mahjoub*].

62 *Almrei*, *ibid.* at para. 95; *Mahjoub*, *ibid.* at para. 47 *et seq.*

63 *C.U.P.E. v. Ontario (Minister of Labour)*, 2003 SCC 29, [2003] 1 S.C.R. 539 at para. 100 ("It is for the courts, not the Minister, to provide the legal answer to procedural fairness questions. It is only the ultimate exercise of the Minister's discretionary … power … that is subject to the 'pragmatic and functional' analysis, intended to assess the degree of deference intended by the legislature to be paid by the courts to the statutory decision maker, which is what we call the 'standard of review'"); *Moreau-Bérubé v. New Brunswick (Judicial Council)*, 2002 SCC 11, [2002] 1 S.C.R. 249 at para. 74 (procedural fairness requires "no assessment of the appropriate standard of judicial review. Evaluating whether procedural fairness, or the duty of fairness, has been adhered to by a tribunal requires an assessment of the procedures and safeguards required in a particular situation"). For a discussion of procedural fairness, see Grant Huscroft, chapter 5.

s. 7, the Supreme Court in *Suresh* emphasized that "*the Minister must be allowed considerable discretion* in evaluating future risk and security concerns. This factor also suggests *a degree of deference to the Minister's choice of procedures* since Parliament has signaled the difficulty of the decision by leaving to the Minister the choice of how best to make it."[64]

Moreover, in some instances, courts have extended deference that seems to exceed that anticipated by statutory language. For example, s. 38 of the *Canada Evidence Act* contains special rules limiting access to "potentially injurious information" and "sensitive information" in "proceedings," including criminal trials.[65] In essence, this is information the government views as raising national security concerns. Participants in such a trial must notify the federal attorney general when they intend (or believe another participant or person intends) to disclose these classes of information. The attorney general may then authorize disclosure or, alternatively, may deny this authorization, in which case the matter is taken up by the Federal Court.

Under s. 38.06, a specially designated Federal Court judge authorizes disclosure unless he or she is persuaded that it would be injurious to international relations, national defence, or national security. Even where disclosure would be injurious, the information may still be released if the public interest in disclosure exceeds the injury.[66] In these circumstances, the judge considers "both the public interest in disclosure and the form of and conditions to disclosure that are most likely to limit any injury to international relations or national defence or national security resulting from disclosure," and authorizes the release, "subject to any conditions that the judge considers appropriate, of all of the information, a part or summary of the information, or a written admission of facts relating to the information."[67]

On the basis of this description, courts clearly have the principal role to play under this test. As the Federal Court has indicated, "Parliament has required the designated judge to balance competing interests, not simply to protect the important and legitimate interests of the state."[68] The court has also held that under s. 38 of the Act, "the designated judge has a very broad discretion to exercise."[69] Still, when it comes to weighing whether disclosure would in fact be injurious, the Federal Court of Appeal has concluded that deference is owed the Minister:

> the Attorney General's submissions regarding his assessment of the injury to national security, national defence or international relations, because of his access to special information and expertise, should be given considerable weight by the judge. … The Attorney General assumes a protective role vis-à-vis the security and safety of the public. If his assessment of the injury is reasonable, the judge should accept it.[70]

---

64 *Suresh*, *supra* note 26 at para. 120 (emphasis added).

65 *Canada Evidence Act*, *supra* note 23, s. 38. A "proceeding" "means a proceeding before a court, person or body with jurisdiction to compel the production of information."

66 *Ibid.*, s. 38.06.

67 *Ibid.*

68 *Canada (Attorney General) v. Ribic*, 2002 FCT 839 at para. 22.

69 *Jamal v. Canada (Minister of Citizenship and Immigration)*, 2002 FCT 290 at para. 2.

70 *Canada (Attorney General) v. Ribic (F.C.A.)*, 2003 FCA 246 at para. 19.

V. OTHER FORMS OF REVIEW

The discussion in this chapter suggests that judicial review of the national security state may be attenuated, curtailed by special secrecy or other rules that constrain the full expression of the adversarial system on which Canadian justice is predicated and conducted by means of highly deferential standards of review. Moreover, judicial review by its very nature is fact- and case-specific and driven by adversarial impulses and procedures. It is myopic, in other words.

If judges are uncomfortable second-guessing the secretive deliberations of executive government in narrowly focused national security cases, other avenues of accountability are necessary. Not least, the administrative state itself might impose its own, internal checks and balances through special administrative review agencies. This chapter ends with a discussion of what, for the sake of clarity, it will call "bureaucratic review"—that is, an administrative audit and complaint system able to measure agency compliance with legal or other standards and query problematic behaviour.

Forms of bureaucratic review in national security matters do exist in the administrative state. These mechanisms include both general and specialized review.

A. General Bureaucratic Review

For the purposes of this chapter, general bureaucratic review involves either standing review mechanisms with responsibilities that may occasionally touch on national security matters or ad hoc review systems created by the governor in council under general statutes permitting public inquiries. Officers of Parliament, certain administrative tribunals, and public inquiries are cases in point.

Officers of Parliament are essentially executive arms of the legislative branch. A shared and unique attribute of officers is their obligation to report directly to Parliament, rather than to a minister. The roles of the Auditor General, the information commissioner, and the privacy commissioner are tied to their statutory mandate under the *Auditor General Act*,[71] the *Access to Information Act*,[72] and the *Privacy Act*,[73] respectively. Each in their own way may scrutinize the national security functions of the state, at least as they relate to financial probity, secrecy, and the protection of privacy. Influence over the management of executive government may also, meanwhile, be exercised by independent administrative tribunals and commissions. Examples of the former include the Canadian Human Rights Commission and the Canadian Human Rights Tribunal. Persons staffing these bodies tend to enjoy a reasonably robust level of security of tenure, financial independence, and administrative independence from the regular departments of government. National security matters lying within the jurisdiction of these entities may occasionally come before them.

Occasionally, the government may also create more specialized ad hoc independent commissions to probe particular public policy issues or scandalous events, employing its

71 R.S.C. 1985, c. A-17.

72 Access Act, *supra* note 22.

73 Privacy Act, *supra* note 24.

general powers to do so under the *Inquiries Act*.[74] Recent examples in the national security area include the Arar inquiry, the 2006 Major inquiry in the "bombing of Air India Flight 182"[75] (Air India inquiry), and the 2006 Iacobucci internal inquiry concerning the actions of "Canadian officials in relation to Abdullah Almalki, Ahmad Abou-Elmaati and Muayyed Nureddin."[76] Of less recent vintage are the 1995 inquiry into "certain matters pertaining to the deployment of Canadian Forces to Somalia,"[77] the 1977 McDonald royal commission into "certain activities of the Royal Canadian Mounted Police," and the 1969 MacKenzie royal commission on security.

B. Specialized Bureaucratic Review

It is important, however, to underscore the limitations of all of these bodies. Ad hoc tribunals are by their nature periodic and constrained by their limited mandates and duration. Existing officers of Parliament and independent tribunals, while standing bodies, have very specific mandates that do not include review of the national security state per se. In the national security area, therefore, there is a need for more specialized review bodies.

At the time of this writing, only some national security agencies were subject to robust review by specialized bureaucratic bodies. CSIS, for example, is reviewed by several tiers of review agency. The best known of these entities is the Security Intelligence Review Committee (SIRC). SIRC is tasked with, among other things, reviewing the performance by CSIS of its duties and functions. SIRC also has a public complaints function. The most generic complaint concerns "any act or thing done by the Service."[78] The committee also prepares special reports where requested by the Minister of Public Safety or at any other time, and an annual report, tabled by the Minister in Parliament, which in practice contains summaries of the committee's investigations.

Yet, other organizations performing national security functions are subject to less robust bureaucratic review. The RCMP, for example, is scrutinized only by a Commission of Public Complaints, which has a limited ability, in practice, to probe RCMP national security functions. Other entities involved in national security—such as the Canada Border Services Agency and the Department of Foreign Affairs and International Trade—are subject to no special review system. The state of bureaucratic review in the national security area is best described, therefore, as very uneven. The Arar inquiry proposed a more comprehensive approach to the review of national security functions, extending SIRC-like audit and complaint powers across the spectrum of national security agencies.[79] At the time of this writing, it was not clear how the government would act in response to these recommendations.

---

74 R.S.C. 1985, c. I-11. See the discussion in chapter 14 by Peter Carver.

75 Order in Council, 2006-293 (1 May 2006).

76 Order in Council, 2006-1526 (11 December 2006).

77 Order in Council, 1995-0042 (20 May 1995).

78 CSIS Act, *supra* note 11, s. 41.

79 Arar inquiry, *supra* note 7.

VI. CONCLUSION

Courts, like government itself, struggle to find the right balance between close oversight and impunity in assessing the national security actions of the administrative state. The analysis in this chapter points to three specific problems with the concept of national security in Canadian administrative law: first, the term is too often undefined in the governing statute law; second, government resort to this undefined term is typically reviewed pursuant to a highly deferential standard of review; last, this deferential review of an undefined term takes place outside the regular, open, adversarial system. Too often, judicial review of national security decisions in Canada is a process in which deferential judges meet with government lawyers and intelligence experts in the absence of an adversarial party, to review secret information not disclosed to that adversarial party, and decide whether national security (whatever that may be) is at issue.

While reforms of Canadian national security law now seem likely, these changes will not constitute a silver bullet. It seems almost inevitable that national security will continue to be policed by deferential courts in a fashion that may leave both courts and outside observers peering through a glass, darkly.

A better (or at least additional) solution likely lies in the administrative state itself. If courts are inherently hamstrung by their lack of expertise and their piecemeal, case-by-case approach to reviewing the national security state, Canadians will be highly dependent on effective review by special agencies within the executive itself. The state of bureaucratic review in national security matters remained, however, underdeveloped by the time of this writing. For these reasons, in the area of national security, Canadians benefit from comparatively fewer checks and balances than in other areas of administrative governance.

SUGGESTED ADDITIONAL READINGS

Charkaoui v. Canada (Minister of Citizenship and Immigration), 2007 SCC 9.

Commission of Inquiry into the Actions of Canadian Officials in Relation to Maher Arar. *A New Review Mechanism for the RCMP's National Security Activities* (Ottawa: Gilmore Print Group, 2006).

Henrie v. Canada (Security Intelligence Review Committee), [1989] 2 F.C. 229, aff'd (1992), 5 Admin. L.R. (2d) 269 (F.C.A.).

Suresh v. Canada (Minister of Citizenship and Immigration), [2002] 1 S.C.R. 3.

CHAPTER TWELVE

The Role of International Human Rights Norms in Administrative Law

GERALD HECKMAN
Faculty of Law, University of Manitoba

If we define administrative law as the set of principles and rules that place limits on the exercise by administrative decision-makers of their statutory power or authority, then international human rights law is and has long been relevant to administrative lawyers. However, it has only recently garnered attention as a source of administrative law since the controversial judgment of the Supreme Court of Canada in *Baker v. Canada (Minister of Citizenship and Immigration)*.[1]

1 (1999), 174 D.L.R. (4th) 193 (S.C.C.) [*Baker*]. For the facts of *Baker*, see Grant Huscroft, chapter 5.

International human rights norms may influence the substantive review of administrative decisions in several ways. Canadian decision-makers must exercise discretionary powers and interpret their enabling statute "in accordance with the boundaries imposed in the statute, the principles of the rule of law, the principles of administrative law, the fundamental values of Canadian society, and the principles of the *Charter*."[2] This chapter will show that international human rights norms are relevant to defining several of these boundaries. First, the interpretation of a statutory provision may be influenced by a relevant international right or obligation, especially when the statute was expressly enacted to implement this right or obligation in Canada. Second, the fundamental values of Canadian society may be reflected in the international rights and obligations that bind Canada's governments through custom or convention. The meaning of rights and freedoms under the *Canadian Charter of Rights and Freedoms*[3] may also be influenced by the scope and content of Canada's international human rights obligations, many of which the Charter was intended to implement. Finally, where an official's discretionary decision could frustrate proceedings initiated by an individual before an international treaty body to clarify his or her rights under the treaty, this may be a mandatory relevant consideration to the official's exercise of the discretionary power. In sum, public officials and administrative agencies may be required, in a variety of circumstances, to exercise their statutory discretions or interpret their enabling legislation in a manner that conforms with international human rights norms or with the values underlying these norms.

The provisions of international human rights treaties may also have an impact on the review of administrative decisions for procedural defects. In *Baker*, the Supreme Court recognized that the legitimate expectations of the person challenging a decision could be a factor in determining what procedures are required by the common law duty of procedural fairness. Moreover, the Court left open the possibility that the terms of an international instrument ratified by Canada could give rise to a legitimate expectation,[4] an approach it later adopted in *Suresh*[5] to define the content of fundamental justice under s. 7 of the Charter. In that case, the Court confirmed that it would look to international law as evidence of the principles of fundamental justice. Thus, international human rights norms may be relevant to defining the content of procedural fairness and fundamental justice and, in the latter case, may factor into a challenge of the constitutional sufficiency of statutory procedures.

It is no accident that many of the materials referred to in this chapter to describe the influence of international law on administrative law in Canada—including judicial decisions, statutes, regulations, and guidelines—are from the immigration and refugee law context. This does not mean that international human rights law is not relevant in other spheres of administrative decision-making. This reflects only that it is an important source of state obligations toward non-citizens, and that immigration and refugee lawyers have

---

2 *Ibid.* at para. 56. The Supreme Court used these words to describe the boundaries applicable to the exercise of discretionary power, but in doing so, rejected any rigid dichotomy of "discretionary" or "non-discretionary" decisions.

3 Part I of the *Constitution Act, 1982*, being Schedule B to the *Canada Act 1982* (U.K.), 1982, c. 11 [Charter].

4 *Baker*, *supra* note 1 at para. 29.

5 *Suresh v. Canada (Minister of Citizenship and Immigration)*, [2002] 1 S.C.R. 3 at para. 60 [*Suresh*].

more frequently and consistently raised international human rights norms in argument before administrative decision-makers and reviewing courts.[6] As these norms continue to proliferate and more attention is paid to them by advocates, judges, and administrative decision-makers, the opportunities to apply them in other administrative contexts will only multiply.[7]

Because many readers may not be familiar with public international law and, in particular, international human rights law, the first part of this chapter sets out a brief synopsis of the sources of international law. The second part describes the rules that govern the reception of international law into Canada's domestic legal order. The third part of this chapter examines how international human rights norms affect the review by courts of the interpretation by officials and agencies of their enabling legislation, and in particular, discretionary powers. Part IV describes the role of international human rights law in administrative procedure and, in particular, the duty of decision-makers to act in accordance with the rules of procedural fairness and the principles of fundamental justice.

I. A SHORT INTRODUCTION TO INTERNATIONAL HUMAN RIGHTS LAW

International law is derived from several sources.[8] The most important of these are international custom (customary international law) and international treaties (conventional international law).

Rules of customary international law are "reflected in the practice or conduct of states" and "accepted by them, expressly or tacitly, as being binding on the international plane."[9] To establish that a legal norm is a rule of customary international law, there must be evidence that states have consistently and generally followed the rule[10] and that they have acted in this manner because they were of the view they were obliged to do so under international law rather than for reasons of political expediency.[11] Some norms expressed in international instruments of "universal" character may become customary rules of international law. Whether a rule of customary law has crystallized from a treaty norm depends on whether ratification of the treaty is widespread among interested states and whether

6 Audrey Macklin, "The State of Law's Borders and the Law of States' Borders" in David Dyzenhaus, ed., *The Unity of Public Law* (Oxford: Hart Publishing, 2004) 173 at 174.

7 See, for example, Gerald Heckman & Lorne Sossin, "How Do Canadian Administrative Law Protections Measure Up to International Human Rights Standards?" (2005) 50 McGill L.J. 193.

8 Statute of the International Court of Justice, as found in the *Charter of the United Nations*, 26 June 1945, Can. T.S. 1945 No. 7, art. 38 [UN Charter].

9 Thomas Buergenthal & Harold Maier, *Public International Law in a Nutshell*, 2d ed. (St. Paul, MN: West Publishing, 1990) at 22.

10 Ian Brownlie, *Principles of Public International Law*, 5th ed. (Oxford: Oxford University Press, 1998) at 5-6. Evidence of official state conduct could include diplomatic correspondence, state policies and legislation, executive decisions, treaties, and UN General Assembly resolutions.

11 *Opinio juris* (opinion of justice), the sense among states that they are obligated under international law to follow a certain practice, is sometimes implied on the basis of the evidence of a consistent and general practice: *Asylum Case* (1950), 17 I.L.R. 280 at 285.

these states extensively and uniformly accept that the treaty provision sets out a rule of law that is binding as custom.[12]

Customary law is not static, and groups of states may create a new customary regime by asserting a new rule backed up with consistent and general practice. Moreover, an international treaty may displace otherwise applicable customary rules as between the parties to that treaty.[13] This is not true of *jus cogens*, or peremptory norms of customary international law, which are recognized by the international community of states as norms "from which no derogation is permitted and which can be modified only by a subsequent norm of general international law having the same character."[14] States cannot contract out of peremptory norms by acquiescing to their breach or by ratifying inconsistent treaties. Accordingly, the burden of proof to establish their existence is high. The International Court of Justice has held that peremptory norms derive "from the outlawing of acts of aggression, and of genocide, as also from the principles and rules concerning the basic rights of the human person including protection from slavery and racial discrimination."[15] The prohibition against torture may also have reached the status of a peremptory norm.

Most international human rights norms find their source in conventional—not customary—international law. Following the Second World War, to further their pledge under the UN Charter to promote "universal respect for, and observance of, human rights and fundamental freedoms for all,"[16] states engaged in an intense international effort, coordinated by the UN, to codify human rights and fundamental freedoms in declarations and treaties. Regional international organizations—the Organization of American States (OAS), the Council of Europe, and the Organization of African Unity—also developed treaty-based systems for the protection of human rights. These instruments form "a vast body of legal norms, a veritable human rights code, that gives meaning to the phrase 'human rights and fundamental freedoms.'"[17] Canada is a party to many important multilateral and regional international treaties that bind Canada at international law, some of which are discussed below.[18] Canada

12 Alan Brudner, "The Domestic Enforcement of International Covenants on Human Rights: A Theoretical Framework" (1985) 35 U.T.L.J. 219 at 248. See also Brownlie, *supra* note 10 at 12.

13 Buergenthal & Maier, *supra* note 9 at 25. In this sense, conventions play a role analogous to that of statutory law in common-law domestic legal systems.

14 Vienna Convention on the Law of Treaties, 23 May 1969, Can. T.S. 1980 No. 37, UN Doc. A/Conf. 39/26, art. 53 [Vienna Convention].

15 *Barcelona Traction*, [1970] I.C.J. Rep. 33 at para. 34.

16 UN Charter, *supra* note 8, arts. 55(c), 56.

17 Thomas Buergenthal, Dinah Shelton & David Stewart, *International Human Rights*, 3d ed. (St. Paul, MN: West Publishing, 2002) at 33.

18 These include the UN Charter, *supra* note 8; the International Covenant on Civil and Political Rights, 16 December 1966, [1976] Can. T.S. No. 47 [ICCPR]; the International Covenant on Economic, Social and Cultural Rights, 16 December 1966, [1976] Can. T.S. No. 46 [ICESCR]; the Convention Against Torture and Other Cruel, Inhuman or Degrading Treatment or Punishment, 25 May 2000, [2002] Can. T.S. No. 5 [CAT]; the 1951 Convention Relating to the Status of Refugees, 28 July 1951, [1969] Can. T.S. No. 6 [1951 Convention]; the International Convention on the Elimination of All Forms of Racial Discrimination, 21 December 1965, [1970] Can. T.S. No. 28; the Convention on the Rights of the Child, 20 November 1989, [1992] Can. T.S. No. 3 [CRC]; the Convention on the Elimination of All Forms of Discrimination Against Women, 18 December 1989, [1982] Can. T. S. No. 31 [CEAFDAW]; and the Charter of the Organization of American States, 30 April 1948, [1990] Can. T.S. No. 23 [OAS Charter],

has also adopted important declarations, including the Universal Declaration of Human Rights,[19] which, while not formally binding at international law, may "have solemn effects as the formal act of a deliberative body of global importance."[20] International treaties to which Canada is not a party are also important sources of human rights norms that could eventually bind Canada if they become customary international law.[21]

Broadly speaking, international human rights treaties contain several kinds of provisions that may be relevant to Canadian administrative decision-makers, reviewing courts, and public lawyers. Some guarantee to individuals substantive rights at international law. These range from the right to freedom from torture or cruel, inhumane, or degrading treatment, conferred by the International Covenant on Civil and Political Rights and the Convention against Torture;[22] to the right to the opportunity to gain one's living by work which one freely chooses or accepts, granted by the International Covenant on Economic, Social and Cultural Rights.[23] Others impose substantive obligations on states parties at international law, like the Convention on the Rights of the Child's duty on states' social welfare institutions, courts of law, administrative authorities, or legislative bodies to take into account the best interests of the child as a primary consideration in all actions concerning children.[24]

---

19 GA Res. 217(III), UN GAOR, 3d Sess., Supp. No. 13, UN Doc. A/810 (1948) [UDHR]. The UDHR has acquired a moral and normative status unlike that of any other declaration. The repeated reliance of state governments and international organizations on the UDHR as an authoritative expression of human rights has likely given to some of its provisions the status of customary international law: Buergenthal, Shelton & Stewart, *supra* note 17 at 41-43. See also the American Declaration of the Rights and Duties of Man, 2 May 1948, 43 A.J.I.L. 133, art. 2 [ADRDM]. The ADRDM contains and defines the fundamental rights proclaimed by OAS member states in art. 3(l) of the OAS Charter: *Interpretation of the American Declaration of the Rights and Duties of Man Within the Framework of Article 64 of the American Convention on Human Rights* (1989), Advisory Opinion OC-10/89, Inter-Am. Ct. H.R. (Ser. A), No. 10 at paras. 45-46.

20 H.J. Steiner & P. Alston, *International Human Rights in Context: Law, Politics, Morals*, 2d ed. (Oxford: Oxford University Press, 2000) at 142, describing the impact of UN General Assembly declarations.

21 These include the American Convention on Human Rights, 22 November 1969, 65 A.J.I.L. 679 [American Convention]; the European Convention for the Protection of Human Rights and Fundamental Freedoms, 4 November 1950, 213 U.N.T.S. 221 [ECHR]; and the African Charter of Human and Peoples' Rights, 27 June 1981, 1520 U.N.T.S. 217 [African Charter]. In interpreting a state's human rights obligations under the ADRDM, the Inter-American Commission on Human Rights takes the American convention into account even if the state has not ratified it because the convention represents, in many cases, "an authoritative expression of the fundamental principles set forth in the American Declaration": OAS, Inter-American Commission on Human Rights, *Report on the Situation of Human Rights of Asylum Seekers Within the Canadian Refugee Determination System*, OEA/Ser.L/V/II.106/Doc. 40, rev. 28 February 2000 at para. 38 [IACHR Report]. The ECHR is a particularly important source of international norms for Canada because it is historically and conceptually related to the ICCPR, a treaty ratified by Canada. The drafting of these treaties was conducted, in part, contemporaneously and important linkages can be drawn between their respective provisions: see P. van Dijk, "'The Interpretation of Civil Rights and Obligations' by the European Court of Human Rights—One More Step to Take" in F. Matscher & H. Petzold, eds., *Protecting Human Rights: The European Dimension—Studies in Honour of Gérard Wiarda*, 2d ed. (Berlin: Carl Heymans Verlag KG, 1990) at 137.

22 CAT, *supra* note 18; ICCPR, *supra* note 18, art. 7. These provisions were considered by the Supreme Court of Canada in *Suresh*, *supra* note 5. Compare ECHR, *supra* note 21, art. 3; American Convention, *supra* note 21, art. 5.

23 ICESCR, *supra* note 18, art. 6(1). This provision was considered by the Supreme Court of Canada in *Slaight Communications*, *infra* note 101.

24 CRC, *supra* note 18, art. 3.

Many treaties require states to provide an "effective remedy" to persons whose substantive treaty rights are violated.[25] In conjunction with the right to an effective remedy, substantive rights may imply institutional or procedural safeguards without which the substantive rights cannot be effectively implemented. Other treaty provisions expressly guarantee institutional and procedural rights at international law, such as the ICCPR right to a fair and public hearing by a competent, independent, and impartial tribunal established by law in the determination of one's rights and obligations in a suit at law,[26] or the CRC right of children, in expressing their own views on matters affecting them, to be heard in any judicial and administrative proceedings affecting them, either directly, or through a representative or an appropriate body.[27] The rights and obligations set out in the international treaties to which Canada is a party are clearly binding on Canada at international law. The extent to which they are sources of domestic law that bind Canadian courts and constrain the powers of administrative decision-makers is the more difficult question addressed in the following parts of this chapter.

Although many international human rights treaties comprise enforcement mechanisms, they rely primarily on the institutions of the signatory states to enforce their guarantees in domestic law. For example, most of the major UN treaties establish treaty bodies charged with the task of supervising states parties' implementation of the rights set out in their constituent treaties. Treaty bodies carry out several supervisory functions, including reviewing periodic reports submitted by states parties regarding their implementation efforts,[28] issuing interpretive guidelines (general comments) that give meaning to specific treaty provisions, investigating systemic violations of treaty rights,[29] and reviewing petitions alleging treaty violations by a state party filed by other states[30] or by individuals.[31] However, consistent with the primacy of state laws and institutions in protecting human rights, individual petitions are admissible before UN treaty bodies only if the petitioners have exhausted all domestic remedies available to vindicate the rights in question.[32] Canadian institutions may enforce the rights and obligations expressed in international human rights treaties or in customary international law in one of several ways.[33] For example, Parliament or the provincial legislatures may draft laws to achieve compliance with international human rights norms. Canadian courts may also give effect to these norms when they are invoked in individual cases, including those that involve procedural or substantive challenges to the deci-

---

25 ICCPR, *supra* note 18, art. 2(3). Compare ECHR, *supra* note 21, art. 13; American Convention, *supra* note 21, art. 25; ADRDM, *supra* note 19, art. XVIII.

26 ICCPR, *ibid.*, art. 14.

27 CRC, *supra* note 18, art. 12.

28 ICCPR, *supra* note 18, art. 40.

29 CAT, *supra* note 18, art. 20.

30 ICCPR, *supra* note 18, art. 41.

31 Optional Protocol to the International Covenant on Civil and Political Rights, 16 December 1966, [1976] Can. T.S. No. 47, art. 1 [Optional Protocol].

32 *Ibid.*, art. 5(2)(b).

33 For a full listing, see Armand de Mestral & Evan Fox-Decent, "Implementation and Reception: The Congeniality of Canada's Legal Order to International Law" in Oonagh E. Fitzgerald, ed., *The Globalized Rule of Law* (Toronto: Irwin Law: 2006) 31 at 42-56.

sions of administrative decision-makers. The principles governing whether courts may give effect to a norm of international law—the rules of reception—are discussed in the next part of this chapter.

II. RULES OF RECEPTION OF INTERNATIONAL LAW

When can Canadian courts take international norms into account and how can these norms shape the interpretation of statutes and constitutional provisions? Despite recent efforts by Canada's Supreme Court to clarify the rules of reception of international law into domestic law,[34] these are not as clear as they should be. The Court has been criticized for, among other things, failing to rigorously analyze and apply conventional international law, including the authoritative pronouncements of treaty-based bodies, in cases where it was arguably binding, or at least persuasive, in Canada's legal system.[35] This part examines the reception of customary and conventional international human rights law in turn.

A. Reception of Customary International Human Rights Law

After a lengthy period of relative uncertainty, the Supreme Court confirmed in its 2007 decision in *R. v. Hape* that the reception of customary international law into Canadian law is governed by the doctrine of adoption, whereby customary rules of international law are incorporated automatically, as they evolve, into domestic law:

> Following the common law tradition, it appears that the doctrine of adoption operates in Canada such that prohibitive rules of customary international law should be incorporated into domestic law in the absence of conflicting legislation. The automatic incorporation of such rules is justified on the basis that international custom, as the law of nations, is also the law of Canada unless, in a valid exercise of its sovereignty, Canada declares that its law is to the contrary. Parliamentary sovereignty dictates that a legislature may violate international law, but that it must do so expressly. Absent an express derogation, the courts may look to prohibitive rules of customary international law to aid in the interpretation of Canadian law and the development of the common law.[36]

There is a sharp contrast between the Court's tentative conclusion that, absent an express derogation, courts "may" look to customary international law to "aid" in the interpretation of Canadian law and the development of the common law and its stronger restatement of the doctrine of adoption in the preceding lines of its judgment. Under that doctrine, absent an express statutory derogation, customary international law *is* Canadian law and thus directly binding on Canadian courts. This contrast may be evidence of the Court's unease with strong presumptions requiring the invocation of international law.

---

34 See, notably, *R. v. Hape*, 2007 SCC 26.

35 Stephen J. Toope, "The Uses of Metaphor: International Law and the Supreme Court of Canada" (2001) 80 Can. Bar Rev. 534 at 536-38.

36 *Hape*, *supra* note 34 at para. 39.

B. Reception of Conventional International Human Rights Law

As a matter of international law, an international treaty is binding on Canada if it is signed and ratified by Canada and has entered into force.[37] The effect of a ratified treaty on Canada's domestic law is another question entirely. Traditionally, conventional international law and Canadian domestic law have been conceived of as two separate regimes residing on entirely distinct planes. This "dualist" relationship is founded on the doctrine of separation of powers between the executive and legislature, which underpins the legal sovereignty of Parliament. Under this traditionalist account, the federal executive may exercise its prerogative power to sign and ratify international treaties that bind Canada on the international plane, but only Parliament or the provincial legislatures may enact laws affecting legal rights and obligations within Canada.[38] If treaties created legally enforceable rights and obligations without the need to enact enabling legislation, the federal executive could legislate without the consent of Parliament or the provincial legislatures.[39] Thus, international treaty provisions must be "implemented" or "transformed" into domestic law to impose obligations or confer rights legally enforceable in domestic courts. From the traditionalist perspective, an "automatic" domestic application of treaty norms by courts leads to a "democratic deficit," which must be cured by legislative or constitutional reforms to enhance legislatures' involvement in the decision to ratify international treaties.[40] A distinct but related objection to the domestic application of international treaty norms without specific legislative implementation is that federal treaty-making may have an impact on areas of provincial legislative jurisdiction and lead to violations of Canada's constitutional division of powers.[41]

The claim that a treaty obligation binding on Canada at international law is "irrelevant" unless it is implemented by a specific statute following the treaty's ratification is hotly contested for a number of reasons. First, "not all implementing legislation is obviously so."[42] For example, Parliament may enact statutes for the purpose of implementing a treaty obligation without referring to the treaty. Moreover, "legislation that was not originally intend-

---

37 By signing a treaty, the state expresses its intent to be bound by the treaty obligations in the future. The state formally expresses its final consent to be bound by a treaty by ratifying the treaty, usually by depositing a declaration to this effect with other states parties or an agreed-upon depository like the UN Secretariat. Typically, treaties provide that they come into force once a specified number of states have ratified it: see, for example, ICCPR, *supra* note 18, arts. 48 and 49. See, generally, Mark Freeman & Gibran van Ert, *International Human Rights Law* (Toronto: Irwin Law, 2004) at 57-58.

38 *Baker*, *supra* note 1 at paras. 80-83, per Iacobucci J., dissenting. See also *Baker v. Canada (Minister of Citizenship and Immigration)* (1996), 142 D.L.R. (4th) 554 at 563-64 (F.C.A.) [*Baker* (FCA)].

39 *Attorney General for Canada v. Attorney General for Ontario (Labour Conventions)*, [1937] A.C. 326 (P.C.) [*Labour Conventions*]; Hugh M. Kindred, *International Law: Chiefly as Interpreted and Applied in Canada*, 7th ed. (Toronto: Emond Montgomery, 2006) 206. The jurisdiction to enact laws to implement a treaty resides with Parliament or the provincial legislatures, depending on the particular legislative subject matter dealt with by the treaty.

40 Joanna Harrington, "Redressing the Democratic Deficit in Treaty Law Making: (Re-)Establishing a Role for Parliament" (2005) McGill L.J. 465 at 468.

41 See *Labour Conventions*, *supra* note 39.

42 van Ert & Freeman, *supra* note 37 at 166.

ed to implement a treaty may later be relied upon by the federal government as its means of doing so."[43] Canada ratifies most international human rights treaties without adopting implementing legislation, on the assumption that Canadian constitutional, statutory, and common-law regimes already conform to the treaty norms.[44] Controversially, despite this claim of conformity, the Canadian government resists attempts to enforce human rights treaty norms in Canadian courts on the ground that, absent implementing legislation, they are not binding in Canadian law.[45] Many now convincingly argue that express statutory implementation of a treaty is required only if the treaty purports to alter existing domestic law,[46] and that implementation should be inferred where Canada premises its ratification on the prior conformity of Canadian legislation, common-law, and administrative policy.[47] Others challenge the traditionalist view by questioning the very basis of the formal separation of powers doctrine—the legislature's monopoly over the production of domestic legal norms. They point out that courts have long constrained the administrative state's exercise of statutory powers by insisting that it conform with "fundamental" or "constitutional" common-law values,[48] including the duty of procedural fairness in administrative law.[49] In their view, courts' increasing reliance on norms expressed in international human rights treaties (whether implemented by statute or not) is best understood as "the judicial updating of the catalogue of values to which the common law subjects the administrative state" from "pre-democratic, property-based values, to a more modern set of democratic values, including fundamental human rights."[50]

---

43 *Ibid.* at 167. Canada's government claims that "many laws and policies, adopted by the federal, provincial and territorial governments, assist in the implementation of Canada's international human rights obligations": *ibid.*, n. 94.

44 Irit Weiser, "Effect of International Human Rights Treaties Ratified Without Implementing Legislation" in *The Impact of International Law in the Practice of Law in Canada* (The Hague: Kluwer Law, 1999) 132 at 132. Toope, *supra* note 35 at 538.

45 See *Baker* (FCA), *supra* note 38; *Ahani v. Canada (M.C.I.)* (2002), 58 O.R. (3d) 107 (C.A.), leave to appeal denied, [2002] S.C.C.A. No. 62, online: QL (S.C.C.A.) [*Ahani*]. See also K. Norman, "Taking Human Rights Lightly: The Canadian Approach" (2001) 12 N.J.C.L. 2 at 291.

46 S. Toope & J. Brunnée, "A Hesitant Embrace: The Application of International Law by Canadian Courts" (2002) 40 Can. Y.B. Int'l Law 3 at 26-27 [Toope & Brunnée, "Hesitant"]. See *Labour Conventions*, *supra* note 39 at 347 per Lord Atkin: the performance of treaty obligations requires legislative action "if they entail alterations of existing domestic law." See also *Francis v. R.*, [1956] S.C.R. 618 at 626 per Rand J.: statutory action is needed if treaties "purport to change existing law" or restrict future legislative action.

47 Toope & Brunnée, "Hesitant," *ibid.* at 26; J. Brunnée & S. Toope, "A Hesitant Embrace: Baker and the Application of International Law by Canadian Courts" in Dyzenhaus, *supra* note 6, 357 at 363 [Brunnée & Toope, "Embrace"]. See also Hugh M. Kindred, "The Use and Abuse of International Legal Sources by Canadian Courts: Searching for a Principled Approach" in Fitzgerald, *supra* note 33, 5 at 15-17; de Mestral & Fox-Decent, *supra* note 33 at 54-55.

48 David Dyzenhaus, Murray Hunt & Michael Taggart, "The Principle of Legality in Administrative Law: Internationalisation as Constitutionalisation" (2001) 1 O.U.C.L.J. 5 at 7, 34 ["Principle of Legality"]. See also John Mark Keyes & Ruth Sullivan, "A Legislative Perspective on the Interaction of International and Domestic Law" in Fitzgerald, *supra* note 33, 277 at 292 *et seq.*

49 de Mestral & Fox-Decent, *supra* note 33 at 57-58; *Knight v. Indian Head School Division No. 19*, [1990] 1 S.C.R. 653 at paras. 22 and 24.

50 "Principle of Legality," *supra* note 48 at 7, 34.

The Supreme Court appeared to endorse the traditionalist approach when it stated, in *Baker v. Canada (Minister of Citizenship and Immigration)*,[51] that "international treaties and conventions are not part of Canadian law unless they have been implemented by statute."[52] Despite this pronouncement, it is clear that "unimplemented" treaties may still influence statutory interpretation through a well-established principle of statutory interpretation that legislation will be presumed to conform to international law, including customary international law and treaty obligations:

> The presumption of conformity is based on the rule of judicial policy that, as a matter of law, courts will strive to avoid constructions of domestic law pursuant to which the state would be in violation of its international obligations, unless the wording of the statute clearly compels that result. ... [T]he presumption has two aspects. First, the legislature is presumed to act in compliance with Canada's obligations as a signatory of international treaties and as a member of the international community. In deciding between possible interpretations, courts will avoid a construction that would place Canada in breach of those obligations. The second aspect is that the legislature is presumed to comply with the values and principles of customary and conventional international law. Those values form part of the context in which statutes are enacted, and courts will therefore prefer a construction that reflects them. The presumption is rebuttable, however. Parliamentary sovereignty requires courts to give effect to a statute that demonstrates an unequivocal legislative intent to default on an international obligation.[53]

Several academics claim that courts should and do apply the presumption of conformity with international law to interpret legislation that does not implement a treaty ratified by Canada, because the underlying rationale of the presumption—to avoid an unintended breach of Canada's international obligations through judicial misconstruction of a statute—applies as much to ordinary laws as it does to implementing legislation.[54] Notwithstanding the Supreme Court's assertion in *Hape* that the presumption of conformity is a "general principle" of statutory interpretation, it is too early to conclude that the Court has embraced a general duty on courts to interpret domestic legislation in conformity with unimplemented treaties. For example, the Court followed a more restrained approach to the reception of international norms in *Baker* when it applied "a *permissive* rule *allowing* courts to have regard to Canada's treaty obligations as an *aid* to statutory interpretation."[55] We begin our review of the impact of international human rights norms on the substantive review of administrative decisions with a closer examination of the *Baker* decision.

---

51 *Supra* note 1.

52 *Ibid.* at para. 69.

53 *Hape*, *supra* note 34 at paras. 53-54.

54 van Ert & Freeman, *supra* note 37 at 156. Toope & Brunnée, "Hesitant," *supra* note 46 at 32. See also *Canadian Foundation for Children, Youth and the Law v. Canada (Attorney General)*, 2004 SCC 4, where the Supreme Court interpreted in conformity with the CRC and ICCPR a provision of the *Criminal Code* that pre-dated these treaties and was thus not enacted to implement them.

55 John Currie, *Public International Law* (Toronto: Irwin Law, 2001) at 222-23, 226 (emphasis added).

III. INTERNATIONAL HUMAN RIGHTS NORMS AND THE SUBSTANTIVE REVIEW OF ADMINISTRATIVE DECISION-MAKING

A. The Role of Unimplemented Treaties

Baker, an illegal overstayer facing removal to Jamaica by Canadian immigration authorities, asked the Minister of Citizenship and Immigration to exercise her discretion under the *Immigration Act* to allow her, on humanitarian and compassionate grounds, to remain in Canada where she could care for her Canadian-born children and continue treatment for paranoid schizophrenia. The Minister denied her application. Although the Supreme Court decided *Baker* on the procedural issue of bias, it also held that this was an unreasonable exercise of discretion because a review of the notes of the immigration officer who examined Baker's case revealed that his decision was not made in a manner that showed attentiveness and sensitivity to the best interests of Baker's children. The Court's assessment of the reasonableness of the decision was informed by the objectives of the *Immigration Act*, in particular family reunification, ministerial guidelines that emphasized preserving family connections, and the values underlying the Convention on the Rights of the Child. The Act, the guidelines and the CRC indicated that emphasis on the rights, interests and needs of children and special attention to childhood were "important values that should be considered in reasonably interpreting 'humanitarian' and 'compassionate' considerations that should guide the exercise of the discretion."[56] The Court rejected Baker's claim that in assessing her application, the Minister of Citizenship and Immigration should have given primacy to the best interests of her children as required by art. 3(1) of the CRC[57] because, in its view, the CRC was not implemented by statute and art. 3(1) was thus not part of Canadian law and could not apply directly to structure the Minister's discretion under the Act.[58] However, L'Heureux-Dubé J., for the majority, ruled that the CRC still played an important role:

> [T]he values reflected in international human rights law may help inform the contextual approach to statutory interpretation and judicial review. As stated in R. Sullivan, Driedger on the Construction of Statutes (3rd ed. 1994), at p. 330:
>
> > [T]he legislature is presumed to respect the values and principles enshrined in international law, both customary and conventional. These constitute a part of the legal context in which legislation is enacted and read. *In so far as possible, therefore, interpretations that reflect these values and principles are preferred.* [Emphasis in original.][59]

The decision that values reflected in an unimplemented international treaty may help inform the interpretation, exercise, and judicial review of statutory discretion sparked an animated debate. Iacobucci and Cory JJ. dissented on this point, arguing that allowing reference to an unincorporated treaty during the process of statutory interpretation allowed Baker to "achieve indirectly what cannot be achieved directly, namely, to give force and effect

---

56 *Baker*, *supra* note 1 at para. 73.

57 *Supra* note 18, art. 3(1) reads: "In all actions concerning children … the best interests of the child shall be a primary consideration."

58 But see de Mestral & Fox-Decent, *supra* note 33 at 54-55 for the argument that the CRC had in fact been implemented into Canadian law.

59 *Baker*, *supra* note 1 at para. 70.

within the domestic legal system to international obligations undertaken by the executive alone that have yet to be subject to the democratic will of Parliament."[60] Arguably, however, the Court did not go far enough in giving effect to the CRC, which is ratified, in force, and thus binding on Canada. Unlike other international norms, the CRC is not "potentially persuasive," but obligatory: the Court should have applied the presumption of conformity of domestic law with Canada's international obligations, requiring it to strive, as far as possible, to interpret the *Immigration Act* in conformity with Canada's obligations under art. 3 of the CRC. Instead, *Baker* prescribes only that the values underlying the CRC "may help inform" courts' "interpretive effort,"[61] a less demanding interpretive onus, appropriate in relation to international norms not binding on Canada. Curiously, when the Supreme Court reaffirmed the presumption of conformity and its application to treaty norms in *Hape*, it did not mention *Baker* or acknowledge this inconsistency.

Craig Scott argues that *Baker* changed courts' focus from the "bindingness" to the "persuasiveness" of international norms:

> [I]t is not simply a rule-of-law concern with the formal legal status of Canada's international legal commitments that determines the depth of interpretive influence of international norms on statutory interpretation but also (and more so) those commitments' resonance with Canadian law and society's fundamental constitutive values and principles. …
>
> While the [interpretive presumption of legislative conformity with international law] … is generally applicable to Canada's international commitments, the normative force of any given commitment being called in aid must vary with the subject matter of the international norms and with some appreciation of how the context in which it has been produced relates to our "free and democratic" ideals. In other words, *Baker* helps us understand how international human rights law has a special interpretive force within Canada's legal order.[62]

This characterization of *Baker* may answer the dissenting judges' challenge to the legitimacy of the majority's decision to take into account a value expressed in an unimplemented treaty in assessing the reasonableness of the Minister's decision. The value of attentiveness to the best interests of children was reflected not only in the CRC but also in the objectives of the *Immigration Act* and in the guidelines drafted by the Minister's department to structure immigration officers' exercise of humanitarian and compassionate discretion. It already resonated with values that had significance in Canadian law. Arguably, then, requiring immigration officers' attentiveness or sensitivity to the best interests of children as a precondition to their reasonable exercise of humanitarian and compassionate discretion was neither illegitimate nor revolutionary.

What is the implication of the idea that the impact on statutory interpretation of an international human rights norm from an unimplemented treaty depends on its resonance with Canadian legal values? Most of the civil and political rights in international human rights treaties, including the right to be free from arbitrary arrest or detention, the right to be heard

60 *Ibid.* at para. 80.

61 Brunnée & Toope, "Embrace," *supra* note 47 at 372.

62 Craig Scott, "Canada's International Human Rights Obligations and Disadvantaged Members of Society: Finally into the Spotlight?" (1999) 10 Const. Forum Const. 97 at 100, 101. See also "Principle of Legality," *supra* note 48 at 33.

by an impartial and independent decision-maker, and the right to be free from discrimination, have great resonance in Canada's legal system. What about social and economic rights? They have a high potential impact on administrative decision-making, which is largely concerned with individuals' entitlement to public goods and services provided or regulated by the modern state.

Under the ICESCR, individuals are entitled to "the enjoyment of the highest attainable standard of physical and mental health," and states parties must "create conditions to assure to all medical services and medical attention in the case of sickness."[63] The Committee on Economic, Social and Cultural Rights has noted that health facilities, goods, and services must be affordable for all, and that all are entitled to equal and timely access to appropriate treatment of prevalent diseases, illnesses, injuries, and disabilities, including the provision of essential drugs.[64] There is a strong presumption that retrogressive measures in relation to the right to health are not permissible, and that the state party has the burden of proving that such measures "have been introduced after the most careful consideration of all alternatives and that they are duly justified by reference to the totality of the rights provided for in the Covenant in the context of the full use of the State Party's maximum available resources."[65] The Committee also defines as a core obligation of state parties to "provide essential drugs as from time to time defined under the WHO Action Programme on Essential Drugs."[66] ICESCR norms, as developed by the committee in its general comment, could be argued to be relevant considerations for the exercise by provincial officials of the discretion to list or delist, in the public interest, certain drugs from provincial drug formularies or treatments from provincial Medicare schedules of benefits.[67] Could it be argued that the ICESCR's "right to health" resonates with Canadian legal values? Although the Supreme Court has not recognized a freestanding constitutional right to health care,[68] it has recognized that state interference with Canadians' access to health care where the government is failing to deliver care in a reasonable manner does engage constitutionally protected life and security of the person interests.[69]

Another area of administrative decision-making that could be influenced by international norms is the state regulation of residential tenancies. Article 11(1) of the ICESCR guarantees to all the right to adequate housing. The Committee has interpreted this right to include the

63 ICESCR, *supra* note 18, art. 12.

64 Committee on Economic, Social and Cultural Rights, *General Comment 14—The Right to the Highest Attainable Standard of Health (Art. 12)*, UN Doc. E/C.12/2000/4 at paras. 12(b)(iii), 17.

65 *Ibid.* at para. 32.

66 *Ibid.* at para. 44.

67 See, for example, *Ontario Drug Benefit Act*, R.S.O. 1990, c. O.10, ss. 16-20; *Ontario Drug Benefit Regulations*, O. Reg. 201/96, amended to O. Reg. 559/06, ss. 11 *et seq*. The Ontario Drug Benefit Program covers most of the cost of prescription drug products listed on the Ontario Drug Benefit Formulary for over 2 million Ontarians who are seniors or who receive social assistance or provincial disability support.

68 *Chaoulli v. Quebec (Attorney General)*, [2005] 1 S.C.R. 791 at para. 104.

69 *Ibid.* at para. 124. Additional evidence of resonance with Canadian legal values can be found in Arbour J.'s dissenting judgment in *Gosselin v. Quebec (Attorney General)*, [2002] 4 S.C.R. 429, recognizing that s. 7 protects the positive right to life and security of person. The majority of the Supreme Court in *Gosselin* did not expressly reject this interpretation of s. 7. However, when the Court has subsequently applied s. 7, albeit in cases asserting state deprivations of life, liberty, and security of the person (the negative s. 7 right), it has been silent on the existence of a positive s. 7 right.

right to security of tenure guaranteeing legal protection against forced eviction: "evictions should not result in individuals being rendered homeless or vulnerable to the violation of other human rights."[70] Before it was repealed and replaced by the Ontario legislature in 2006, the Ontario *Tenant Protection Act* allowed for expedited evictions without a hearing and did not require adjudicators with the Ontario Rental Housing Tribunal to consider the risk that evicted households could become homeless. In its review of Canada's fifth periodic report, the Committee noted that "many evictions occurred on account of minimal arrears of rent without due consideration of [Canada's] obligations under the Covenant."[71] It could be argued, on the basis of art. 11 of the ICESCR, as interpreted by the Committee, that the risk of homelessness should be a mandatory relevant consideration in the Landlord and Tenant Board's decision whether or not to grant an application for eviction.[72] It is noteworthy that both the provision of health care and the regulation of residential tenancies are largely, if not entirely, matters within provincial legislative jurisdiction. As mentioned previously, courts or administrative decision-makers who adopt a traditionalist view of the role of international norms in domestic law may be reluctant, on division of powers grounds, to give "automatic" domestic effect in areas of provincial jurisdiction to treaties ratified by the federal executive.

Following *Baker* and notwithstanding *Hape*, it remains unclear to what extent Canadian courts will apply the common law's interpretive presumption of conformity to interpret statutes in a manner consistent with international obligations that flow from treaties not implemented by statute. Parliament and provincial legislatures can clarify the role of specific international norms by expressly implementing them into Canadian law. This is what Parliament did in the immigration and refugee protection context after *Baker*. It directed courts, tribunals, and administrators to interpret and apply the provisions of the *Immigration and Refugee Protection Act* consistently with international norms.[73] It expressly implemented art. 3 of the CRC by requiring immigration officials deciding humanitarian and compassionate applications to take into account the best interests of a child directly affected by their decisions.[74] The following section examines the impact of international human rights norms that are implemented in this manner on substantive review.

B. Implemented International Human Rights Norms and the Substantive Review of Discretion

In interpreting a statute that expressly implements an international treaty, courts must rely on the provisions of that treaty.[75] In *Pushpanathan v. Canada (Minister of Citizenship and*

70 Committee on Economic, Social and Cultural Rights, *General Comment 7—The Right to Adequate Housing (Art. 11(1) of the Covenant): Forced Evictions*, UN Doc. E/1998/22, annex IV at para. 16.

71 Concluding Observations on Canada's 4th and 5th Periodic Reports, E/C.12/CAN/CO/5, 22 May 2006, 36th Sess.

72 *Residential Tenancies Act, 2006*, S.O. 2006, c. 17, s. 83.

73 S.C. 2001, c. 27, s. 3(3)(f) [IRPA].

74 *Ibid.*, s. 25.

75 Traditionally, courts would not resort to the text of an underlying treaty as an aid to interpreting the provisions of implementing legislation unless they were satisfied that the text was patently ambiguous: Kindred, *supra* note 39 at 202-3. In *National Corn Growers Assn. v. Canada (Import Tribunal)*, [1990] 2 S.C.R. 1324

Immigration),[76] the Supreme Court reviewed the Immigration and Refugee Board's (IRB's) interpretation of a provision in the *Immigration Act* that implemented a clause in the 1951 Convention Relating to the Status of Refugees excluding from refugee protection individuals "guilty of acts contrary to the purposes and principles of the UN." Since the statutory provision sought to implement the 1951 Convention, the Court was bound to "adopt an interpretation consistent with Canada's obligations under the Convention,"[77] which it determined by analyzing the convention's text and applying the rules of treaty interpretation articulated in the Vienna Convention.[78] The Court reviewed the IRB's determination on a correctness basis, largely because the interpretation of an international human rights convention was a pure question of law of precedential value over which it could claim more expertise than the IRB.[79]

Following the Supreme Court's decision in *Baker*, Parliament amended the *Immigration Act* to expressly require officials to take into account the best interests of children directly affected by their decisions.[80] It also enacted s. 3(3)(f) of the IRPA, which provides that the Act "is to be construed and applied in a manner that ... complies with international human rights instruments to which Canada is signatory." The wording of s. 3(3)(f) is not limited to specific international instruments or to treaties addressed to refugees, nor does it require that these instruments be ratified. On its face, it extends to all human rights instruments to which Canada was already, and would become, a signatory. Interpreting s. 3(3)(f) for the first time in *De Guzman v. Canada*, the Federal Court of Appeal was troubled by the provision's broad scope, which made the meaning of IRPA "subject to ... an amorphous and open-ended body of international instruments," and transferred considerable power from Parliament to the executive.[81] It decided that s. 3(3)(f) meant that international human rights instruments that were binding at international law (signed and, if necessary, ratified by Canada) were "determinative of how IRPA must be interpreted or applied, in the absence of a contrary legislative intention."[82] It suggested in *obiter* that Parliament intended

---

at 1371, the Supreme Court jettisoned this requirement and held that it was proper to refer to the treaty at the outset of the interpretive inquiry, because implementing statutes can reveal latent ambiguities. But see Stéphane Beaulac, "International Law and Statutory Interpretation: Up with Context, Down with Presumption" in Fitzgerald, *supra* note 33, 331 at 349-51.

76 [1998] 1 S.C.R. 982 [*Pushpanathan*].

77 *Ibid.* at para. 51.

78 Article 31 of the Vienna Convention, *supra* note 14 requires that a treaty be "interpreted in good faith in accordance with the ordinary meaning to be given to the terms of the treaty in their context and in light of its object and purpose." Article 32 recognizes that if this approach to interpretation leaves the meaning of a treaty provision ambiguous or obscure or leads to manifestly absurd or unreasonable results, recourse may be had to supplementary means of interpretation, including the preparatory work of the treaty and the circumstances of its conclusion. In *Pushpanathan*, on the basis of the convention's aim of protecting the human rights of refugees and on the travaux préparatoires, the Court held, at paras. 73-75, that only persons responsible for serious and sustained violations of fundamental human rights amounting to persecution should be excluded from refugee protection.

79 *Pushpanathan*, *supra* note 76 at para. 45 *et seq.*

80 IRPA, *supra* note 73, ss. 28(2)(c), 60, 67(1)(c), 68(1), 69(2).

81 2005 FCA 436 at para. 86 [*De Guzman*].

82 *Ibid.* at para. 87.

that non-binding international human rights instruments be used, as in the *Baker* approach, only as persuasive and contextual factors in the interpretation and application of IRPA.[83] In sum, in the immigration and refugee protection context, s. 3(3)(f) clarifies the role of international instruments that bind Canada at international law. Whether expressly implemented by statute or not, such instruments are determinative of the meaning of IRPA's provisions and the validity of decisions made pursuant to these provisions unless they reveal a contrary legislative intention. Instruments that do not bind Canada at international law may, under the *Baker* approach, be persuasive and considered as part of the interpretive context.[84]

Thiara v. Canada illustrates how s. 3(3)(f) has been used to challenge the substance of an immigration officer's discretionary decision.[85] The applicant, who was to be removed from Canada, applied to remain on humanitarian and compassionate grounds, arguing that she was needed to raise her Canadian-born daughters in Canada. She claimed that forcing her to return with her daughters to India would not be in their best interests because of the poverty, poor educational opportunities, and other problems faced by young girls there and would be inconsistent with the UDHR's guarantee of parental choice in childrens' education[86] and the CEAFDAW's obligation on states parties to eliminate discrimination against women in education.[87] Forcing her to leave her children in Canada would also violate the ICESCR and CRC, which required states parties to support family unity and parents' child-rearing responsibilities.[88] The immigration officer dismissed her application. Thiara sought judicial review, arguing that the officer's failure to mention any international instruments in her decision meant that she had ignored them. The court rejected her claim, finding that the officer had in fact determined that it would be in the children's best interest to remain in Canada, but that this factor was outweighed by Thiara's past misrepresentations to Citizenship and Immigration Canada. The officer's failure to specifically cite the international instruments in her decision did not indicate that her decision was unreasonable, because her analysis of the best interests of the children was "cogent, considered and thoughtful, signifying that she was sensitive to the issues raised in the CRC, UDHR and so on."[89]

---

83 *Ibid.* at para. 89.

84 De Guzman had received permanent resident status on the basis of a misrepresentation: she had not told immigration officials that she had two sons in the Philippines. Due to her misrepresentation, she was barred by s. 117(9)(d) of the *Immigration and Refugee Protection Regulations* from later sponsoring her two sons' admission to Canada. She challenged this lifetime ban on sponsorship, claiming that IRPA did not authorize the enactment of regulations that made it non-compliant with international human rights instruments to which Canada was a signatory. In her view, the regulation subjected her family to arbitrary or unlawful interference contrary to art. 17 of the ICCPR and did not treat the best interests of her children as a primary consideration, in violation of art. 3 of the CRC. The Federal Court of Appeal found that, on the whole, IRPA did comply with these international instruments, because De Guzman's sons could apply for admission on humanitarian and compassionate grounds under s. 25 of IRPA, which directed immigration officers to consider their best interests.

85 2007 FC 387 [*Thiara*].

86 UDHR, *supra* note 19, art. 26.

87 CEAFDAW, *supra* note 18, art. 10.

88 ICESCR, *supra* note 18, art. 10; CRC, *supra* note 18, art. 18.

89 *Thiara*, *supra* note 85 at para. 41.

C. Norms of Customary International Law and Substantive Review

Norms of customary international law have also influenced the substantive review of the decisions of public bodies, including municipal councils. In *114957 Canada Ltée (Spraytech, Société d'arrosage) v. Hudson (Town)*,[90] the Supreme Court sought to determine whether a bylaw enacted by the town of Hudson restricting the use of pesticides was authorized by a general power under the Quebec *Cities and Towns Act* to enact bylaws to "secure peace, order, good government, health and general welfare" in the municipality. A majority of the Court found, on the basis of ordinary principles of statutory interpretation, that the purpose of the town's bylaw fell squarely within its power to secure citizens' health. Relying on the *Baker* approach, the majority added that its interpretation of the *Cities and Towns Act* was consistent with the precautionary principle, which had arguably crystallized into a norm of customary international law. The majority's reference to the *Baker* approach in discussing the application of customary law to statutory interpretation is problematic.[91] Under the common-law rules of reception, customary norms are binding on Canada at international law and directly applicable in Canadian law. They should not be treated, following *Baker*, as only potentially relevant to statutory interpretation.[92]

Administrative decisions must also comply with Charter principles. Here again, the Supreme Court appears to have adopted the *Baker* approach, referring to international instruments as part of the context of Charter interpretation.[93] As shown below, Canadian courts' approach to the use of international human rights law in Charter interpretation suffers from the same uncertainties and inconsistencies as its approach to the interpretation of statutes.

D. The Use of International Law in Charter Interpretation

The Charter is an important locus of reception of international law norms in Canada's legal system. Fulfilling Canada's obligations under the UDHR and ICCPR was a major impetus to drafting and adopting the Charter, and the language of the general limitation clause in s. 1, the legal rights in ss. 7-14, and the right to equality in s. 15 were derived from analogous provisions in the ICCPR.[94] Moreover, Canada represents to domestic audiences and international treaty bodies that the Charter gives effect to provisions of these treaties.[95] Accordingly, it would be open to courts or administrative decision-makers to recognize the Charter

90 [2001] 2 S.C.R. 241 [*Spraytech*].

91 Brunnée & Toope, "Embrace," *supra* note 47 at 378-79.

92 Brunnée & Toope suggest that because the court did not formally determine that the precautionary principle was custom, it may have intended only to recognize that as a non-binding international norm, the principle could inform statutory interpretation and judicial review: *ibid.* at 379.

93 The role of the Charter in administrative law is discussed by Evan Fox-Decent in chapter 7.

94 Anne Bayefsky, *International Human Rights Law—Use in Canadian Charter of Rights and Freedoms Litigation* (Toronto: Butterworths, 1992) at 49. See also G.V. La Forest, "The Expanding Role of the Supreme Court of Canada in International Law Issues" (1996) 34 Can. Y.B. Int'l Law 89 at 97.

95 Presenting Canada's fourth periodic report regarding the ICCPR's implementation to the UN Committee on Human Rights, Canada's representative stated that the Charter "was the primary mechanism" for implementing the ICCPR and that the Charter's provisions "were based on the Covenant": UN Human Rights Committee, Summary Record of the 1738th Meeting: Canada (17 March 1999), UN Doc. CCPR/C/SR.1738,

as legislation intended to implement these and other important international human rights instruments. Some academics argue that the Supreme Court should treat binding international human rights laws, whether customary or conventional, as "presumptively protected" by the Charter, while non-binding international instruments and the views of UN treaty bodies should be treated as "relevant and persuasive sources for *Charter* interpretation."[96] Others object to applying the presumption of conformity to Charter interpretation because it would allow the federal executive to "unilaterally amend" Canada's constitution.[97]

In *Re Public Service Employee Relations Act (Alberta)*, Dickson C.J. recognized that, as a party to international human rights treaties with provisions similar or identical to those in the Charter, Canada had "obliged itself internationally to ensure within its borders the protection of certain fundamental rights and freedoms which are also contained in the *Charter*."[98] Consequently, "the general principles of constitutional interpretation require that these international obligations be a relevant and persuasive factor in *Charter* interpretation":

> The content of Canada's international human rights obligations is, in my view, an important indicia of the meaning of "the full benefit of the *Charter*'s protection." I believe that the *Charter* should generally be presumed to provide protection at least as great as that afforded by similar provisions in international human rights documents which Canada has ratified.
>
> In short, though I do not believe the judiciary is bound by the norms of international law in interpreting the *Charter*, these norms provide a relevant and persuasive source for interpretation of the provisions of the *Charter*, especially when they arise out of Canada's international obligations under human rights conventions.[99]

Freeman and van Ert correctly note that this passage reveals two approaches to the use of international law in Charter interpretation.[100] The first paragraph speaks of a presumption that the Charter should be interpreted in conformity with Canada's international obligations. The second holds that these obligations should be viewed by courts as relevant and persuasive, but not binding. In subsequent decisions,[101] the Supreme Court appeared to embrace the latter approach and emphasized that international norms provide a broader context within which to determine the scope and content of Charter rights, a "weaker ver-

---

online: <http://www.unhchr.ch>. Similarly, the Canadian government informed the Inter-American Commission on Human Rights that it implemented the ADHR through refugee protection laws and its general legal system and that the Charter shared many of the ADHR's principles: IACHR Report, *supra* note 21 at para. 36.

96 Freeman & van Ert, *supra* note 37 at 194-95.

97 Irit Weiser, "Undressing the Window: Treating International Human Rights Law Meaningfully in the Canadian Commonwealth System" (2004) 37 U.B.C. L. Rev. 113 at 148. But see Toope & Brunnée, "Hesitant," *supra* note 46 at 45, n. 140 and 49, n. 200.

98 [1987] 1 S.C.R. 313 at 349 [*Alberta Reference*].

99 *Ibid.* at 349-50, dissenting on another point.

100 Freeman & van Ert, *supra* note 37 at 193.

101 *Slaight Communications Inc. v. Davidson*, [1989] 1 S.C.R. 1038 at 1056-57 [*Slaight Communications*]: Canada's international human rights obligations should "inform" the interpretation of Charter rights. See also *Kindler v. Canada*, [1991] 2 S.C.R. 779; and *United States of America v. Burns*, [2001] 1 S.C.R. 283 [*Burns*].

sion" of the presumption of conformity that does not require the court to "strive for an interpretation that is consistent with international norms."[102]

In *Suresh*, the Court extended this approach to norms of customary international law. The *Immigration Act* gave the Minister of Citizenship and Immigration the discretion to decide that a refugee found to be inadmissible on the ground of membership in a terrorist organization was a danger to the security of Canada and could be removed to a country where his or her life or freedom would be threatened. The Court held that its inquiry into whether Suresh's deportation to a country where he faced a substantial risk of torture violated the principles of fundamental justice under s. 7 would be "informed not only by Canadian experience and jurisprudence, but also by international law, including jus cogens":[103]

> [T]he principles of fundamental justice expressed in s. 7 … and the limits on rights that may be justified under s. 1 … cannot be considered in isolation from the international norms which they reflect. A complete understanding of the [*Immigration Act*] and the *Charter* requires consideration of the international perspective.[104]

However, international norms were not binding or even determinative:

> International treaty norms are not, strictly speaking, binding … unless they have been incorporated into Canadian law by enactment. However, in seeking the meaning of the Canadian Constitution, courts may be informed by international law. Our concern is not with Canada's international obligations qua obligations; rather our concern is with the principles of fundamental justice. We look to international law as evidence of these principles and not as controlling in itself.[105]

Despite international law's "virtually categoric" rejection of deportation to torture, the Court concluded that under Canadian law, the Minister retained an exceptional discretion to deport to torture after balancing the probability of prejudice to national security and the importance of the security interest at stake with the serious consequences of deportation to the deportee.[106] As long as the Minister considered the correct factors in the balancing exercise, courts could not question the weight she accorded to them.[107]

Suresh sends a mixed message regarding the potential of international human rights norms to shape the interpretation of Charter rights.[108] The Court did hold that decision-makers must consider the influence of international norms in determining the procedural and substantive content of fundamental justice under s. 7, a more onerous duty than its direction in

102 Toope & Brunnée, "Hesitant," *supra* note 46 at 33.

103 *Suresh*, *supra* note 5 at para. 46.

104 *Ibid.* at para. 59. To properly review the international perspective, courts should consider "the various sources of international human rights law—declarations, covenants, conventions, judicial and quasi-judicial decisions of international tribunals, [and] customary norms": *ibid.* at para. 46.

105 *Ibid.* at para. 60.

106 *Ibid.* at paras. 76-78.

107 *Ibid.* at para. 41. The Court could intervene only if the decision was "unreasonable on its face, unsupported by evidence, or vitiated by failure to consider the proper factors or apply the appropriate procedures."

108 For a full discussion, see Gerald Heckman, "International Human Rights Law Norms and Discretionary Powers: Recent Developments" (2003) Can. J. Admin. L. & Prac. 16 [Heckman, "Recent Developments"].

Slaight Communications that Canada's international human rights obligations "should" inform Charter interpretation.[109] On the other hand, its "international norms as evidence" approach to the role of international law in Charter interpretation allowed the Court to sidestep the question whether the prohibition on torture is a peremptory norm of customary international law.[110] Peremptory norms of international customary law are more than "evidence" of fundamental justice. They are automatically incorporated and directly enforceable in Canadian law to the extent that they are not incompatible with a contrary statute or established principle of common law. Applying the presumption of conformity, the Court could have read down the Minister's statutory discretion consistently with the international customary prohibition on torture.[111] Alternatively, it could have decided that the prohibition, incorporated into Canada's common law, was a fundamental tenet of Canada's legal system, and hence a substantive principle of fundamental justice under s. 7 of the Charter. The prohibition on torture would have constitutional force; to the extent that it conflicted with the *Immigration Act*, the Act would be inoperative.[112] Instead, looking at international law merely as "evidence" of the content of fundamental justice, the Court came to a conclusion that seems extraordinary: although "international law rejects deportation to torture, even where national security interests are at stake,"[113] fundamental justice nevertheless permits the Minister to exercise an extraordinary discretion to deport refugees to torture.

In two recent decisions, the Supreme Court has re-emphasized the role in Charter interpretation of the presumption of conformity with international law. In *Hape*, a majority of the Court held that s. 8 of the Charter, which protects individuals from unreasonable search and seizure, could not be enforced in criminal investigations carried out in another state's territory without that state's consent.[114] Declaring that "in interpreting the scope of application of the Charter, the courts should seek to ensure compliance with Canada's binding obligations under international law where the express words are capable of supporting such a construction,"[115] the Court found support for its construction of s. 32 of the Charter, which delimits its application, in the jurisdictional principles of customary international law.[116] In *Health Services and Support—Facilities Subsector Bargaining Assn. v. British Columbia*,[117] released a day after *Hape*, the Court found support in Canada's international obligations under the ICESCR, ICCPR, and UN International Labor Organization (ILO) Convention

109 *Supra* note 101.

110 *Suresh*, *supra* note 5 at para. 65. There was no lack of evidence, including legal, academic, and judicial authority, to support the recognition of the absolute prohibition on torture as a peremptory norm: see Heckman, "Recent Developments," *supra* note 108 at 52.

111 Evan Fox-Decent, "Suresh and Canada's Obligations Regarding Torture" (2001) 12 N.C.L.J. 425 at 446.

112 Neither s. 7 nor s. 1 balancing was appropriate in *Suresh* because the *jus cogens* norm prohibiting torture "should have been directly controlling within Canadian law to preclude deportation": Toope & Brunnée, "Hesitant," *supra* note 46 at 49.

113 *Suresh*, *supra* note 5 at para. 75.

114 *Hape*, *supra* note 34 at para. 69.

115 *Ibid.* at para. 56.

116 *Ibid.* at paras. 57-65.

117 2007 SCC 27 [*Facilities Subsector Bargaining*].

No. 87[118] for its conclusion that access to collective bargaining fell within the Charter's guarantee of freedom of association.[119] Significantly, the Court did not articulate the presumption of conformity using the strong language it used in *Hape*. Reiterating the traditionalist view that "the incorporation of international agreements into domestic law is properly the role of the federal Parliament and the provincial legislatures," it cited *Suresh* for the proposition that "Canada's international obligations can *assist* courts charged with interpreting the *Charter*'s guarantees."[120] Relying on *Alberta Reference*, it concluded that it was "reasonable to infer" that s. 2(d) of the Charter should be interpreted "as recognizing at least the same level of protection"[121] as the international treaties that protected union members' right to collective bargaining as part of their freedom of association.

In sum, the Supreme Court's jurisprudence on the role of international human rights norms in Charter interpretation reveals that the Court has yet to decide whether international human rights obligations simply provide evidence of the meaning of the Charter's guarantees or presumptively define the minimum content of these guarantees.

E. Discretion and Rights of Access to International Human Rights Bodies

Should administrative decision-makers, in exercising discretionary powers, take into account proceedings pending before an international human rights body that may bear on the validity of their decision at international law? This question was raised before the Ontario Court of Appeal in *Ahani v. Canada (Minister of Citizenship and Immigration)*.[122] The Canadian government considered that Ahani, like Suresh, was a danger to the public and wished to deport him. Unlike Suresh, he had not made out a prima facie case that there may be a substantial risk of torture upon his removal to Iran. Having exhausted all domestic remedies in resisting deportation, Ahani petitioned the UN Human Rights Committee, claiming that his removal by Canada violated several provisions of the ICCPR, including his right not to be returned to a state where he could be tortured, his right to a fair hearing, and his right to a review of the legality of his detention without delay. The Committee made an official request to the government of Canada to stay the deportation until it could consider Ahani's petition. Ahani contended that by adhering to the ICCPR and Optional Protocol, Canada had granted individuals like him the limited right to obtain the Committee's views on whether their ICCPR rights had been breached. It was a principle of fundamental justice that Canada also provide Ahani with a fair process and effective means to ensure that he could exercise this limited right. In particular, Ahani claimed the right to an injunction prohibiting his removal to Iran until the Committee considered his communication and

118 Convention (No. 87) Concerning Freedom of Association and Protection of the Right to Organize, 68 U.N.T.S. 17, [1973] Can. T.S. no. 14, adopted 9 July 1948, ratified 23 March 1972, entered into force 23 March 1973.

119 *Facilities Subsector Bargaining*, supra note 117 at para. 79.

120 *Ibid.* at para. 78 (emphasis added). See also para. 78: "Canada's *current* international law commitments … provide a *persuasive* source for interpreting the scope of the *Charter*" (emphasis added).

121 *Ibid.* at para. 79.

122 *Supra* note 45. For a complete discussion of this question, see Heckman, "Recent Developments," supra note 108.

expressed its views thereon. While not binding on Canada, the Committee's views had moral suasion, and the petition process should be allowed to run its course.

A majority of the Ontario Court of Appeal rejected Ahani's argument because, in its view, the ICCPR and the petition procedure under the Protocol were not legislatively incorporated into Canadian law. Neither had any legal effect beyond "informing" the content of the principles of fundamental justice under s. 7.[123] Ahani could thus not "enforce" Canada's international obligations in a domestic court. Further, these obligations were limited: Canada had not committed to be bound by the final views of the Committee or that it would stay its domestic proceedings until the Committee delivered its views. Acceding to Ahani's request for a stay would "convert a non-binding request in a Protocol, which has never been a part of Canadian law, into a binding obligation enforceable in Canada by Canadian courts, and more, into a constitutional principle of fundamental justice."[124] By signing the Protocol, Canada had provided Ahani and others a right to seek the Committee's views qualified by Canada's right to reject these views and to enforce its own laws before they were delivered.[125]

Dissenting, Rosenberg J. would have recognized Ahani's right to seek an injunction preventing his removal until the Committee had presented its views on his communication. He accepted that if Parliament created a statutory right to review a decision that could affect an individual's security of the person, it was a principle of fundamental justice that the state could not unreasonably frustrate that right or render it practically illusory, a principle he was prepared to extend to the petition process under the Protocol.[126] In his view, the principle that international conventions could not bind Canada unless they were incorporated into Canadian law was intended to protect Parliament and the people of Canada from executive law-making; the executive could not rely on that principle to shield it from the consequences of its voluntary ratification of the ICCPR and the Protocol,[127] including Canada's conferral on the Committee of jurisdiction to receive and consider communications from individuals claiming to be victims of violations by Canada of their rights under the ICCPR:

> [Ahani] does not claim that the views of the Committee about our process for removing him would create legal rights that could be enforced in a domestic court. He claims only the limited procedural right to reasonable access to the Committee upon which the federal government has conferred jurisdiction. He submits that the government having held out this right of review, however limited and non-binding, should not be entitled to render it practically illusory by returning him to Iran before he has a reasonable opportunity to access it. I agree with that submission and that it is a principle of fundamental justice that individuals in Canada have fair access to the process in the Protocol. By deporting … [Ahani] to Iran, the government will deprive … [him] of this opportunity.[128]

---

123 Arguably, the ICCPR and the Protocol were implemented in Canadian law: de Mestral & Fox-Decent, *supra* note 33 at 54-55.

124 *Ahani, supra* note 45 at para. 33.

125 *Ibid.* at para. 42.

126 *Ibid.* at paras. 86-89.

127 *Ibid.* at para. 92.

128 *Ibid.* at para. 93. Ahani was owed only a right of "reasonable" access to the Committee, because fundamental justice, according to the *Suresh* decision, required that the protection of society be balanced against the individual's interest to security of the person. Such balancing could be performed by a court as part of the test for granting an interlocutory injunction: *ibid.* at para. 107.

Canada is clearly not bound to comply with the Committee's views, but on a fair reading, the Protocol contemplates that individuals be afforded an opportunity to submit communications to the Committee, and if these are deemed admissible, to have the Committee review the communications and deliver its views to the petitioners and to Canada for consideration. This interpretation is consistent with the principle of effectiveness in international law that human rights instruments like the ICCPR and the Protocol should be interpreted to make their safeguards "practical and effective."[129] A corollary to this principle is that states may not, and should not, be presumed to intend to take steps that would render the rights recognized in a treaty nugatory or ineffective. If a petitioner establishes that his or her deportation would prevent him or her from submitting a communication or prevent the Committee from considering it and delivering its views to the petitioner and Canada, deportation would not be consistent with the purpose of the Protocol. Without "reasonable" or "fair" access to the process in the Protocol, it would be nothing more than a "hollow sham ... or cruel charade."[130] In its views on Ahani's communication, the Committee determined that Canada had breached its obligations under the Protocol by deporting Ahani in the face of its request that he not be removed until it had dealt with his petition. It held that "flouting" the Committee's authority to request interim measures, especially by irreversible measures such as deportation to face torture or death in another country, "undermined" the protection of Covenant rights through the Optional Protocol.[131]

The *Immigration Act* conferred on the Minister a broad discretion to deport individuals determined to be a danger to the security of Canada, but was silent as to the timing of the deportation. Under the *Baker* approach, which recognized that discretionary powers are constrained by the values and principles contained in international law, the adverse impacts of deportation on the effectiveness of Ahani's limited right to communicate with the Committee should have been a mandatory relevant consideration in the exercise of the Minister's discretion; failure to consider this factor should have rendered her decision to deport Ahani without delay patently unreasonable. Moreover, the Minister was bound to exercise her discretion to deport Ahani consistently with the principles of fundamental justice under s. 7 of the Charter, whose content, according to *Suresh*, is informed by Canada's international obligations. Rosenberg J.'s recognition that fundamental justice does not countenance executive acts that frustrate even a limited right to review the legality of a decision that affects an individual's security of the person is entirely consistent with the principle of effectiveness in international human rights law. Here, fundamental justice arguably required that the merits of Ahani's communication (whether it raised a serious question) and the magnitude of the harm to Ahani caused by his deportation (whether the harm was irreparable) be balanced against the government's interest in deporting him before the Committee released its views on the merits of his communication.

---

129 M.N. Shaw, *International Law*, 4th ed. (Cambridge: Cambridge University Press, 1997) at 660.

130 *Ahani, supra* note 45 at para. 98, citing *Briggs v. Baptiste*, [2000] 2 A.C. 40 at para. 47 (P.C.). See also *Barbados (A.G.) v. Boyce* (2006), CCJ (8 November 2006), where the court gave effect to convicted murderers' legitimate expectation that Barbados would not execute them before considering the views of a treaty body regarding their complaint that mandatory capital punishment infringed their rights under an international treaty.

131 *Ahani v. Canada*, Communication No. 1051/2002, UN Doc. CCPR/C/80/D/1051/2002 (2004) at paras. 8.1-8.2. For a full discussion of the committee's views, see Gerald Heckman, "International Law and Procedural Safeguards in Deportation Proceedings: Ahani v. Canada" (2004) 17 R.Q.D.I. 81.

International human rights norms clearly have a role to play in the substantive review of administrative decision-making. Administrative decisions based on the interpretation of statutory powers or discretions intended to implement an international human rights treaty obligation may be reviewed on the basis that the decision-maker incorrectly or unreasonably interpreted the statute by giving it a meaning inconsistent with the international treaty norm. Canadian courts would be justified to intervene on judicial review where an administrative decision-maker fails to apply the presumption of conformity and interpret statutory powers in a manner consistent with international human rights obligations set out in a binding but unimplemented treaty. Instead, Canadian courts have followed the *Baker* approach: binding international human rights norms from unimplemented treaties may be considered as persuasive and contextual factors in interpreting and applying statutory provisions. Accordingly, administrative decisions, including discretionary decisions, may be challenged on the ground that they are inconsistent with the values behind such international human rights norms. Whether such a challenge will succeed may depend on how deeply these international norms resonate with fundamental values of the Canadian legal system. Courts have also applied the *Baker* approach to norms of customary international law, even though they are in principle directly applicable in Canadian law. Discretionary decisions may be challenged if they are inconsistent with Charter rights. International human rights norms are relevant to such challenges because they serve as evidence of the meaning of Charter protections. Finally, although it may be possible to challenge a decision-maker's exercise of discretionary power on the basis that he or she failed to consider the impact of the decision on an affected individual's access to an international human rights remedy, such challenges have so far not succeeded.

The following part shows that international human rights norms may serve to challenge administrative decision-making on procedural as well as substantive grounds.

IV. THE ROLE OF INTERNATIONAL HUMAN RIGHTS NORMS IN THE PROCEDURAL REVIEW OF ADMINISTRATIVE DECISIONS

Procedural fairness norms set out in international human rights treaties resonate deeply with Canadian legal values. Procedural fairness is a basic tenet of Canada's legal system and a principle of fundamental justice under s. 7 of the Charter. Consistent with the previous discussion of the role of international norms in substantive review, they could likely be called upon to influence the development of procedural safeguards in Canada. In *Baker*, the applicant had invited the Federal Court of Appeal and the Supreme Court to find that she had a legitimate expectation, based on the terms of the CRC, that her children would be afforded a hearing by the immigration officer considering her humanitarian and compassionate application. In particular, art. 12 of the CRC provides that children have the right "to be heard in any judicial or administrative proceedings affecting them, either directly or through a representative or appropriate body." This provision appeared to entitle Baker's children to participate directly in the humanitarian and compassionate application process. In fact, the interests of Baker's children had only been considered through the written submissions of Baker's own counsel. The Supreme Court decided that the CRC's terms did not give rise to a legitimate expectation on Baker's part that specific procedural rights above what would normally be required under the duty of fairness would be accorded.[132] The CRC was not "the equivalent of a government representation about how humanitarian and compassionate applications will be decided, nor does it suggest that any rights beyond the participatory rights [afforded by common-law procedural fairness] will be accorded."[133] The Federal Court of Appeal more clearly explained its concerns at the prospect of giving effect to the right of Baker's children to direct representation in the humanitarian and compassionate application. It warned that giving judicial force to the procedural provisions of the CRC, a treaty ratified by the federal executive, would have a significant impact on decision-making by provincial authorities involving children, notably the administration of family law and the provision of legal aid for family law and child custody proceedings—matters of provincial jurisdiction.[134]

Curiously, in rejecting Baker's legitimate expectations argument, the Supreme Court made no mention of the High Court of Australia's judgment in *Minister for Immigration and Ethnic Affairs v. Teoh*,[135] which was raised by the applicant and discussed at length by the Federal Court of Appeal. In *Teoh*, the High Court had recognized that ratified but unimplemented international treaties could influence administrative decision-making through the doctrine of legitimate expectations. The Minister's delegate had decided that there were insufficient compassionate grounds to allow Teoh's application for a permanent entry permit, despite the fact that his deportation jeopardized the livelihood of his Australian children. A majority of the High Court decided that Australia's ratification of the CRC gave rise to a legitimate expectation that the Minister's delegate would, in conformity with the CRC, treat the best interests of Teoh's children as a primary consideration in his decision. His failure to do this, or to allow Teoh to argue against a decision inconsistent with his legitimate expectation, breached procedural fairness. Australia's ratification of the CRC, the majority held, was "not to be dismissed as a merely platitudinous or ineffectual act, particularly when the CRC evidences internationally accepted standards to be applied by courts and administrative authorities in dealing with basic human rights affecting the family and children":

> Rather, [it] is a positive statement by the executive government of this country to the world and to the Australian people that the executive government and its agencies will act in accordance with the Convention. That positive statement is an adequate foundation for a legitimate expectation, absent statutory or executive indications to the contrary, that administrative decision-makers will act in conformity with the Convention and treat the best interests of the children as "a primary consideration."[136]

Dissenting, McHugh J. complained that the majority's ruling effectively allowed the executive to amend Australian law by ratifying an international convention without involving the political branches of government, a view accepted by the Federal Court of Appeal

---

132 The doctrine of legitimate expectations is discussed further by Grant Huscroft in chapter 5.

133 *Baker*, *supra* note 1 at para. 29.

134 *Baker* (FCA), *supra* note 38 at para. 30.

135 (1995), 183 C.L.R. 273 [*Teoh*].

136 *Ibid.* at 291.

in *Baker*.[137] For this reason, successive Australian governments rejected *Teoh*'s holding,[138] and publicly declared that the act of entering into a treaty did not give rise to legitimate expectations that could form the basis for challenging administrative decisions.[139] Several High Court judges have since hinted that *Teoh* should be revisited.[140]

Although the Supreme Court dismissed Baker's legitimate expectations argument, it left open the possibility that an international instrument ratified by Canada could, in other circumstances, give rise to a legitimate expectation.[141] In *Suresh*, the Court took into account the legitimate expectation raised by the terms of the CAT in determining that Suresh was owed more procedures under the principles of fundamental justice in s. 7. To determine the procedural requirements of fundamental justice, it applied the common-law approach to determining the content of the duty of procedural fairness.[142] Several factors weighed in favour of substantial procedural safeguards, including the absence of any appeal procedure, the determinative nature of the Minister's decision, and the serious personal, financial, and emotional consequences for Suresh of deportation from Canada. The Court also considered whether Suresh had a legitimate expectation of additional procedure. It noted that the CAT prohibits the deportation of persons to states where there are "substantial grounds" for believing they would be "in danger of being subjected to torture." In the Court's view, it was "only reasonable that the same executive that bound itself to the CAT intends to act in accordance with the CAT's plain meaning."[143] Given "Canada's commitment to the CAT," and the requirement of "substantial grounds" to trigger the obligation of non-refoulement, the Court found that Suresh was entitled to an opportunity to demonstrate and defend those "grounds."[144] Suresh was not owed a full hearing or complete judicial process, but was entitled to examine the material upon which the Minister based her decision to deport (subject to claims of privilege); respond to the Minister's case and challenge her information regarding the threat he posed to national security, the risk of torture, and the value of assurances from foreign governments that he would not be tortured; and obtain written reasons from the Minister justifying her final decision.[145]

Although *Suresh* indicates that it is possible to seek procedural review of administrative decisions on the grounds that the procedures provided by the decision-maker did not live

---

137 *Ibid.* at 316. See *Baker* (FCA), *supra* note 38 at para. 39.

138 H. Charlesworth et al., "Deep Anxieties: Australia and the International Legal Order" (2003) 25 Sydney L. Rev. 423 at 437 ["Anxieties"].

139 Attempts to enact legislation to counteract *Teoh* have been unsuccessful: "Anxieties," *ibid.* at 449. However, controversy over the decision led to important reforms to enhance parliamentary participation in the treaty-making process: Harrington, *supra* note 40 at 491-97.

140 *Re Minister for Immigration and Multicultural Affairs; ex parte Lam* [2003] H.C.A. 6 at para. 102, per McHugh and Gummow JJ., and para. 145 per Callinan J. Academics have also criticized *Teoh* as a disingenuous application of the legitimate expectations doctrine: Michael Taggart, "Legitimate Expectation and Treaties in the High Court of Australia" (1996) 112 L.Q.R. 50; Murray Hunt, *Using Human Rights Law in English Courts* (Oxford: Hart Publishing, 1997) at 251-59.

141 *Baker, supra* note 1 at para. 29.

142 *Suresh, supra* note 5 at para. 113-15.

143 *Ibid.* at para. 119.

144 *Ibid.*

145 *Ibid.* at paras. 121-27.

up to the legitimate expectations of the applicant on the basis of the terms of a ratified international treaty, it is unclear when such an argument will be successful given its dramatically different treatment by the Court in *Baker* and *Suresh*. More guidance is needed from the courts as to when state obligations in ratified conventions can or cannot raise legitimate expectations.

V. CONCLUSION

There is no doubt that international human rights norms from binding international treaties, customary international law, or non-binding international instruments can play an important role in the substantive and procedural review of administrative decisions. It is also obvious that much work remains to precisely delineate what that role is and, one hopes, to strengthen it. Much of the theoretical groundwork has already been laid in the burgeoning academic commentary on this subject. It is now incumbent on public lawyers to familiarize themselves with the international human rights norms that are relevant to their area of practice and, by raising them before administrative decision-makers and courts, create opportunities for the effective domestic enforcement of significant human rights and the clarification of this important area of administrative law.

SUGGESTED ADDITIONAL READINGS

CASES

Ahani v. Canada (Minister of Citizenship and Immigration) (2002), 58 O.R. (3d) 107 (C.A.).

Baker v. Canada (Minister of Citizenship and Immigration), [1999] 2 S.C.R. 817.

De Guzman v. Canada (Minister of Citizenship and Immigration), 2005 FCA 436.

Minister for Immigration and Ethnic Affairs v. Teoh (1995), 183 C.L.R. 273.

Suresh v. Canada (Minister of Citizenship and Immigration), [2002] 1 S.C.R. 3.

SECONDARY SOURCES

Brunnée, Jutta, & Stephen Toope. "A Hesitant Embrace: Baker and the Application of International Law by Canadian Courts." In David Dyzenhaus, ed., *The Unity of Public Law* (Oxford: Hart Publishing, 2004).

Fitzgerald, Oonagh E., ed. *The Globalized Rule of Law* (Toronto: Irwin Law, 2006).

Freeman, Mark, & Gibran van Ert. *International Human Rights Law* (Toronto: Irwin Law, 2004).

Heckman, Gerald. "International Human Rights Law Norms and Discretionary Powers: Recent Developments" (2003) 16 Can. J. Admin. L. & Prac. 31.

van Ert, Gibran. *Using International Law in Canadian Courts* (The Hague: Kluwer Law, 2002).

CHAPTER THIRTEEN

Regulations and Rule-Making: The Dilemma of Delegation

ANDREW GREEN
Faculty of Law and School of Public Policy and Governance, University of Toronto

I. THE SPREAD OF REGULATIONS, RULES, AND SOFT LAW

The *Environmental Protection Act* is Ontario's main statute for addressing environmental issues. One of its principal provisions concerning air pollution prohibits the discharge of a contaminant into the natural environment in excess of limits set in regulations under the Act. The Act provides that the lieutenant governor in council (the provincial Cabinet) "may make regulations" about, among other things, the emission of contaminants.[1] When the Ontario government decided that it needed to get tougher on air pollution, the Ministry of the Environment began developing new air pollution standards to be included in a regulation. The Ministry undertook a long process of consultation with the public and with industry to try to set limits on the amount of certain pollutants that could be emitted to the air. At the end of this process, the lieutenant governor in council made a regulation based on a draft prepared by the Ministry. The regulation specified how much of various pollutants could be emitted into the air over a given time period, how these pollutants were to be measured, and the manner in which contraventions were to be reported. As discussed by

1 *Environmental Protection Act*, R.S.O. 1990, c. E.19, s. 28(9).

Bill Bogart in chapter 2, regulations are a form of law developed by the executive branch of government that typically do not set general government policy as statutes do, but rather explain how statutes will actually work. Regulations are binding on all those who are subject to them. Because these environmental regulations were complicated, the Ministry also released numerous non-binding guidelines about how these regulations were to be interpreted.

This pattern of the legislature enacting broad legislation and delegating to the executive the power to fill in the details underlies much of the Canadian regulatory structure. The legislature delegates these powers to different members of the executive such as Cabinet, an individual minister, or a particular decision-making body such as the Ontario Securities Commission. These detailed rules or guidelines govern much of our daily lives at home and at work, from the safety of the food we eat and the music we can listen to on the radio to the safety of where we work.

These rules or guidelines can be broken into two broad categories: (1) regulations and rules and (2) soft law. Regulations and rules, as noted above, are legally binding requirements and, as such, the power to make them must be expressly granted under a statute.[2] The number of regulations and rules has increased dramatically in recent years. They cover such diverse issues as permissible levels of pollution, the required content of a prospectus, working conditions in mines, and record-keeping requirements for beekeepers.[3] Because they are very similar, binding regulations or rules will be called "rules" in this chapter. Soft law, on the other hand, while also developed by the executive, is not legally binding. The power to make soft law (such as guidelines about procedures) does not have to be expressly provided in a statute. However, as we will see, soft law plays a very important role in how decision-makers make decisions, both procedurally and substantively.[4]

This chapter examines the reliance by Canadian legislators on the delegation of the power to make detailed policy decisions. It focuses primarily on the power to make legally binding rules. However, the general principles also apply to soft law, and some issues relating to soft law are discussed. Part II discusses why we may want such delegation and, in particular, the desire to take advantage of the expertise and experience of different decision-makers. Part III then turns to the risk raised by delegation that the party delegating the power loses some control over the actual rules or soft law that are put in place. Part IV examines methods used in Canada and elsewhere to limit the risks that arise from delegating the power to make rules and soft law. These methods include the structuring of the grant of discretion, legislative review, judicial review, and public participation. Finally, part V briefly discusses the ongoing struggle to find a balance between the desire to rely on expertise and the need to control those who are making the rules and guidelines.

---

2 Both regulations and rules are legally binding and arise from a statutory power. The federal *Statutory Instruments Act* includes both in the term "statutory instruments" (*Statutory Instruments Act*, R.S.C. 1985, c. S-22). The term "regulation" is generally used in statutes where there is a delegation of the power to fill in detailed requirements.

3 See W.A. Bogart, chapter 2.

4 See, for example, Lorne Sossin & Charles Smith, "Hard Choices and Soft Law: Ethical Codes, Policy Guidelines and the Role of Law in Regulating Government" (2003) 40 Alta. L. Rev. 867; and France Houle & Lorne Sossin, "Tribunals and Guidelines: Exploring the Relationship Between Fairness and Legitimacy in Administrative Decision-Making" (2006) 46 Can. Pub. Admin. 283.

II. WHY DELEGATE?

When you examine the range of issues that are covered by rules or soft law, it becomes immediately apparent how important they are to our lives.[5] Yet these detailed prescriptions about our lives are not made by the legislature but by members of the executive and sometimes by what are essentially private parties. Why is it that we rely so heavily on this structure of our elected officials enacting legislation that sets out broad principles and delegates to others the power to actually fill in what is required? Why would legislators give others the power to make such important policy decisions?[6]

The primary reason for such delegation is *expertise*. Expertise is an important concept in administrative law. As Grant Huscroft discusses in chapter 5, expertise underlies the tests related to procedural fairness and, as Audrey Macklin discusses in chapter 8, it is also central to the determination of the standard of review courts use when reviewing the substance of administrative decisions. Expertise is also central to the need to delegate responsibility for detailed requirements in the form of rules and soft law. It is impossible for legislators to have sufficient expertise to understand and evaluate all the various, detailed requirements in the vast range of areas that comprise the regulatory and welfare state. Such expertise requires education and training as well as experience in dealing with a particular issue. For example, developing the appropriate procedures for an immigration hearing may require the expertise of individuals who have been involved in many such hearings. Developing air pollution standards requires an understanding of science as well as of the manner in which industries use and dispose of various pollutants. Developing rules for a securities market requires knowledge of how these markets function, the role of the consumer, and the manner in which corporations make decisions. Although individual legislators may have some information on these issues, the concern is that legislators would be unable to make optimal rules because of their lack of expertise. The argument, therefore, is that legislators should delegate the power to make these rules to individuals or groups who do have the expertise.

There is, however, a related reason for delegation of the power to make rules and soft law. Even if they had the expertise, legislators lack the *time and information* to make all the decisions necessary for the functioning of the current regulatory and welfare state. The legislature lacks the time to think through all the different ways in which specific provisions should be structured, relate to other provisions, and may apply in particular circumstances. For example, in regulating professions such as optometry, the legislators may enact a broad provision that a member of the College of Optometry may be found guilty of professional misconduct if he or she contravenes a requirement specified in regulations. Even if it were possible to do so, legislators do not have the time to consider all the potential ways in which an optometrist might act in a manner that should be considered professional misconduct.

---

5 Taggart states that "[i]t is trite to observe that delegated legislation … often has more impact on the lives of ordinary citizens than do most full-blown Acts of Parliament." Michael Taggart, "From 'Parliamentary Powers' to Privatization: The Chequered History of Delegated Legislation in the Twentieth Century" (2005) 55 U.T.L.J. 575 [Taggart, "From 'Parliamentary Powers' to Privatization"].

6 Such shifting of responsibility raised concerns about the constitutionality of delegated powers when it became increasingly common in the early part of the 20th century. See Taggart, *ibid.*, for a discussion of the history of the delegated legislation.

However, the lack of time raises the related point that, even with time and expertise, legislators never have complete information about the future. They cannot possibly know all the different ways in which optometrists may act unprofessionally, or all the different pollutants that may be released into the atmosphere, or the different types of securities that may be developed. Legislation is therefore necessarily and unavoidably incomplete. Because legislation can be difficult and time-consuming to alter, the power to make requirements may be delegated in order to increase flexibility—to allow the requirements to be changed as new information arises. This flexibility represents another rationale for legislation. It is particularly important in rapidly changing areas such as environmental and securities regulation.

The issues of expertise, time, and information arise for both rules and soft law. While not legally binding, soft law such as policies and guidelines can have significant impacts on people's lives. For example, guidelines were central to *Baker v. Canada (Minister of Citizenship and Immigration)*.[7] In that case, Ms. Baker was an over-stayer in Canada and had been ordered deported. She applied to the Immigration Minister to exercise his discretion under the *Immigration Act* to grant humanitarian and compassionate exemptions. She was seeking to stay in Canada pending determination of her application for permanent residency.[8] As a practical matter, immigration officers (not the Minister) exercised the humanitarian and compassionate power in individual cases. However, there were Minister-issued guidelines setting out the bases on which immigration officers should decide whether the individual deserved humanitarian and compassionate consideration. Although these guidelines were not legally binding, the Supreme Court of Canada took them into account in deciding that the officer had not acted reasonably in exercising the humanitarian and compassionate power in favour of Ms. Baker. These guidelines were therefore important to the Court in deciding the limits on the discretion to be exercised under the *Immigration Act*.

Soft law has some advantages over rules. Both provide a greater measure of certainty to those who come before regulatory decision-makers. Indeed, an administrative decision-maker may choose to use its power to make rules or soft law precisely because, in many cases, it is unwilling to allow the issue to be decided piecemeal through administrative hearings.[9] However, soft law is much more easily adaptable to changing circumstances because making soft law is less likely than rules to involve time-consuming and costly procedural steps. As the Federal Court of Canada stated:

> Effective decision-making by administrative agencies often involves striking a balance between general rules and the exercise of ad hoc discretion or, to put it another way, between the benefits of certainty and consistency on the one hand, and of flexibility and fact-specific solutions on the other. Legislative instruments (including such non-legally binding "soft law" documents as policy statements, guidelines, manuals and handbooks) can assist members of the public to predict how an agency is likely to exercise its statutory discretion and to arrange their affairs accordingly, and enable an agency to deal with a problem comprehensively and pro-

7 [1999] 2 S.C.R. 817.

8 For a discussion of the facts of *Baker*, see Grant Huscroft, chapter 5.

9 An administrative decision-maker may, for example, consider the five criteria discussed by Bill Bogart in chapter 2 when deciding whether to issue a guideline or rule on an issue rather than allow it to be decided through adjudication.

> actively, rather than incrementally and reactively on a case by case basis. ... Because "soft law" instruments may be put in place relatively easily and adjusted in the light of day-to-day experience, they may be preferable to formal rules requiring external approval and, possibly, drafting appropriate for legislation.[10]

The legislature therefore may want to set out broad policy decisions in legislation. These decisions are left necessarily incomplete, either because legislators lack the expertise to make the decisions or because they lack the time and information needed to make the requirements at the time of enactment. Legislators delegate the power to make rules and soft law in order to allow others to fill in the gaps left in the legislation.

III. THE RISKS OF DELEGATION

However, while there are benefits to the delegation of the power to make requirements, it is not without its risks, nor is it necessarily as benign as the above picture implies. Such delegation raises the risk that those who are making the rules or soft law are not following the wishes or expectations of those who delegated the power (and as a consequence, at least in theory, the wishes of the electorate). This risk arises because of a *principal–agent problem* inherent in such delegation.[11] This principal–agent problem has two dimensions. First, the party making the rules or soft law (who, as we will see, can be termed "the agent") is not following the wishes of the legislature (which can be described as the "the principal"). Second, there is a further, underlying principal–agent concern because the legislature or the party making the rules or soft law (either of which could be termed the agent) may not be respecting the wishes of the ultimate principal—the public.

The principal–agent problem arises when one party (the principal) gives another party (the agent) the power to undertake some task on the principal's behalf. Principal–agent relationships arise all the time in everyday life. You ask a doctor to examine and treat you because you have fallen and hurt your ankle. You contract with a real estate agent to help you sell your house. You, as the shareholder of a company, empower management to act on your behalf in running the company. In each case, you, as the principal, are seeking to have the agent (the doctor, the real estate agent, and the manager, respectively) do something to benefit you. Similarly, a lawyer is the agent for many different principals who come to her with their problems and empower her to take action on their behalf.

These relationships arise for a number of reasons. It could be that the agent has some special expertise that the principal does not have, and so the principal cannot perform the task as effectively as the agent (or at all), as in the case of the doctor or the lawyer. The agent may also have information necessary for the task that the principal does not have, such as, in the case of a real estate agent, information about the housing market and the prices received for other similar houses in the area. Further, even if the principal has the time and the expertise, the agent may have more time than the principal. For example, I

10 *Canada (Minister of Citizenship and Immigration) v. Thamotharem*, 2007 FCA 198 at paras. 55-56.

11 For a good discussion of the principal–agent problem and its relationship to administrative law, see Matthew D. McCubbins, Roger G. Noll & Barry R. Weingast, "Administrative Procedures as Instruments of Political Control" (1987) 3 J.L. Econ. & Org. 243 [McCubbins, Noll & Weingast, "Administrative Procedures as Instruments"].

may hire a plumber to fix my sink even though I could do it myself, simply because I would rather be doing other things with my time (playing with my children or working at my job). There is therefore real value in principal–agent relationships because the agent receives compensation for doing something that the principal cannot or does not want to do himself or herself.

However, there are also real risks that arise from the same features that make principals want to have agents undertake the task for them. If you have no medical expertise, it is hard (if not impossible) to know whether the doctor has taken the appropriate level of care and attention in attending to your ankle. The doctor has the relevant expertise, and you place a large degree of trust in her in having her treat you. The real estate agent has the information about the housing market and you are relying on him to use that information to get you the best price possible for your house. The plumber has the time to take apart your sink, fix it, and put it back together. If you are not watching the plumber, you are relying on him to do a good job on all aspects of the work.

The principal's lack of expertise, information, or time means that he or she has difficulty ensuring that the agent is actually acting in his or her best interests in carrying out the task. This is the principal–agent problem. The doctor may be incompetent or may want to see as many patients as possible in the day and may therefore not use as much care as warranted in the circumstances. The real estate agent may not devote much time to your house because he has other higher valued houses that he would make more money from selling. The plumber may use cheap materials or take short cuts in fixing your sink in order to save time or money on the work.

This principal–agent problem also arises where legislators delegate the power to make rules or soft law. Legislators delegate power because they lack the expertise, time, and information to make the decisions but, at the same time, they have difficulty monitoring how this power is exercised because they lack the expertise, time, and information, which means that expertise, time, and information represent both the reasons to delegate and the causes that hinder monitoring. On a more general level, the public has delegated to legislators the power to make decisions on its behalf and has difficulty monitoring what the legislators are doing and even more difficulty monitoring the parties who make the detailed rules or soft law.

There are two risks from delegating the power to make rules or soft law. First, the agent (the party making the rules or soft law) may follow its own views and values rather than the principal's views or values in making the rules or soft law. Because legislators enact legislation setting out broad directions, the ministry or agency making regulations under such legislation has considerable scope to determine the content of the detailed rules. The rule-maker may, for example, have very different views from the legislators of what constitutes the appropriate rule or guideline in particular cases.[12] The legislator often does not

12 As discussed below in the section on structural approaches to controlling delegated legislation, the impact of such a divergence in views will depend in part on the institutional structures in place. For example, in a Westminster system, the legislature and the executive are to some extent connected. Cabinet decides in large part how much detail is provided in legislation and how much is delegated to others to fill in. The Minister is then responsible to Parliament for the resulting regulation. Although this system may provide a more direct connection and different dynamic between the rule-maker and the legislatures than the stricter separation of power in the United States, the lack of time, expertise, and information affect legislators' ability to monitor and control rule-makers in both systems.

have the expertise, time, or information to monitor the content of particular rules or guidelines. The agent may be attempting to further the public interest but is doing so in the way it (as opposed to the legislature) believes is best.

Second, the agent may not even be attempting to further the public interest; it may, instead, be seeking to further its own interest. For example, if regulated parties (such as a particular industry group) offer some form of inducement to the agents (such as future job opportunities or, in the case of elected officials, funds for future election campaigns), the agents may be influenced in how they make rules or soft law. These agents may in some cases simply not want to expend the effort to regulate in a particular area.

Similarly, legislators may delegate in order to further their own interests, such as where broad legislation with delegated rule-making powers is used as a form of blame avoidance or credit attraction by legislators or Cabinet members. The legislature could, for example, enact very broad, tough-sounding pollution control legislation and then delegate the details to Cabinet to work out. Cabinet could then exempt or "grandfather" certain parties, such as particularly powerful industry groups. The legislators seek credit for enacting strong legislation but also are able to satisfy politically powerful parties.[13]

This principal–agent problem arises in any delegation of power where it is difficult for the principal to monitor the actions of the agent. The extent of the problem will vary depending on the relationship between the principal and the agent. As discussed below, the close connection between ministers and their ministries at least provides some (though at times weak) accountability to legislators for those making rules in ministries. The problem may become worse as the power to make rules is delegated to parties more independent of government. As Taggart notes, one of the trends of most concern in delegated legislation is the involvement of private parties (including regulated parties) in making rules. For example, governments in recent years have contracted out public services to private actors, giving rise to questions about the accountability of and control by legislators over these actors.[14]

IV. CONTROLLING THE RISKS

Delegated legislation therefore gives rise to a principal–agent problem. The problem occurs either between the legislature and the executive (the body making the rules or soft law) or between the public and the legislature/executive. The breadth of delegation will depend on a number of factors, such as the capacity of the legislature to make detailed statutory rules.[15] If the members of the legislatures have the time, resources, and expertise to make particular rules, they will be more likely to set out detailed requirements in legislation. The willingness of the legislature to delegate powers will also depend on its confidence that

13 See, for example, Matthew C. Stephenson, "Legislative Allocation of Delegated Power: Uncertainty, Risk, and the Choice Between Agencies and Courts" (2006) 119 Harv. L. Rev. 1035 [Stephenson, "Legislative Allocation of Delegated Power"].

14 Taggart, "From 'Parliamentary Powers' to Privatization," *supra* note 5.

15 See, for example, John D. Huber, Charles R. Shipan & Madelaine Pfahler, "Legislatures and Statutory Control of Bureaucracy" (2001) 45 Am. J. Pol. Sci. 330 [Huber, Shipan & Pfahler, "Legislature and Statutory Control of Bureaucracy"] (discussing some of the factors influencing the degree of discretion granted by legislatures including bargaining costs, legislative capacity, and the availability of non-statutory means of control).

there are controls on the exercise of discretion. We will focus on four main approaches to controlling delegated legislation:

- *Structuring the discretion*: The breadth of discretion will depend in part on how much the legislators can trust the agent to follow the legislator's policy preferences. Can legislators either choose particular agents or structure the agents in particular ways to influence the resulting rules?
- *Legislative oversight*: To what extent can the legislature exercise some form of direct control over the actual decisions made in the exercise of discretion?
- *Substantive judicial review*: What role do the courts play in supervising the substantive content of the rules? What role should they play?
- *Process requirements*: Do process requirements (such as requiring a certain degree of public involvement in the creation of rules) aid in balancing the benefits and risks of delegated legislation?[16]

We will discuss each of these approaches in turn.

A. Structural Approaches

A legislature will be more likely to delegate broad powers to make rules the more it trusts the agent making the rules to follow the legislature's policy preferences. This trust will vary according to such factors as the level of control the legislators have over those making the policy. For example, in Canada legislators may delegate rule-making powers in broad terms because Cabinet (whose members are generally part of both the legislature and the executive) may have some control over the ministry or other body making the rules. This element of trust, however, raises the second type of principal–agent problem: trust between the public and elected officials. The ability of Cabinet to both set the scope of discretion and control the exercise of that discretion provides significant ability to the party in power to steer the details of policy at the expense of other elected members of the legislature.[17] How much power the legislature delegates may therefore depend on whether there is a majority or minority government. In a minority government situation, for example, the opposition parties have greater bargaining power and, thus, are less likely to be willing to grant broad discretion to ministries controlled by the ruling party.

Legislatures may also attempt to indirectly control the exercise of discretion through, *inter alia*, the choice of body that will exercise the discretion or the resources provided to that body.[18] For example, the rules establishing environmental constraints on rights to log a particular area may be different depending on whether the decision is delegated to an en-

16 See, for example, David Mullan, *Administrative Law* (Toronto: Irwin Law, 2001) [Mullan, *Administrative Law*] (discussing three main methods of control of delegated legislation: legislative scrutiny, public consultation, and judicial review); Huber, Shipan & Pfahler, "Legislature and Statutory Control of Bureaucracy," *supra* note 15 (discussing various means of control of bureaucracy); and David B. Spence, "Managing Delegation Ex Ante: Using Law to Steer Administrative Agencies" (1999) 28 J. Legal Stud. 413 [Spence, "Managing Delegation Ex Ante"].

17 Mullan, *Administrative Law*, *supra* note 16, and Taggart, "From 'Parliamentary Powers' to Privatization," *supra* note 5.

18 Spence, "Managing Delegation Ex Ante," *supra* note 16.

vironment ministry, a natural resources ministry, or an agency composed of a majority of members of the forestry industry. Each of these bodies may have the expertise to make the rules or soft law, but their actual policy preferences may differ depending on their mission or composition. These powers may even be delegated to an arm's-length body such as the Canadian Human Rights Commission, which has the power to make binding rules regarding the interpretation of its legislation.[19] Further, for any particular agent, the legislature may constrain the use of a delegated power by limiting the resources to the body that is granted the power.

B. Legislative Review

Instead of indirectly attempting to ensure that the power it delegates conforms to its views, the legislature could directly control the discretion by reviewing the resulting rules or soft law. The legislature itself, or more likely a committee, could examine the rules or soft law and decide whether to approve, disapprove, or amend them. Such legislative committees have been used at both the federal and the provincial level in Canada to examine regulations. For example, at the federal level, there is a joint committee of the Senate and House of Commons that reviews regulations, although the intent is to review the form of the regulation and not the underlying reasons for it.[20] Further, there may be review by Cabinet or members of Cabinet. For example, the Daniels commission into the Ontario Securities Commission's (OSC's) rule-making powers recommended that an OSC rule should come into effect when made, unless Cabinet disapproves.[21] However, the legislative reforms following the committee's report instead require the OSC to deliver to the Minister of Finance a copy of the rule, any public comments on the proposed rule, and all material relied on by the OSC. The Minister then has 60 days to approve the rule, reject the rule, or return the rule to the OSC for reconsideration.[22] Although legislative committees may review rules and regulations, there is generally no legislative oversight of soft law.

However, the use of legislative committees (or Cabinet or Cabinet ministers) to review regulations only goes part of the way to solving the principal–agent problem. As a committee, it may have some time to examine regulations that are made but, absent a significant allocation of resources, still less time than the agency or ministry, particularly if there is a desire to review not only formal regulations but all rules and even soft law. Further, it exacerbates the problem of time in some ways because it creates a system where regulations go back and forth between the legislators and the agency or rule-making authority. This

19 These rules also bind the Canadian Human Rights Tribunal. The Supreme Court of Canada has upheld the legitimacy of such delegation of rule-making. See *Bell v. CTEA*, 2003 SCC 36.

20 *Statutory Instruments Act*, R.S.C. 1985, c. S-22, s. 19. See Mullan, *Administrative Law*, *supra* note 16, describing the federal and provincial committees that have been set up to review regulations. Taggart, "From 'Parliamentary Powers' to Privatization," *supra* note 5, at 624, notes that the second half of the 20th century "was dominated by the attempt to enhance parliamentary safeguards against potential and actual 'abuses' of these delegated powers."

21 See Hudson Janisch, "Further Developments with Respect to Rulemaking by Administrative Agencies" (1995) 9 Can. J. Admin. L. & Prac. 1 [Janisch, "Further Developments re Rulemaking by Administrative Agencies"] for a discussion of the background to the Daniels committee's report on OSC rule-making.

22 *Securities Act*, R.S.O. 1990, c. S.5, s. 143.3.

oversight causes delay in implementation. More important, however, legislative review does not solve the problems concerning expertise and information. Members of the legislature are unlikely to have enough information or expertise to adequately review the regulations. This lack of expertise and information is often one of the main reasons for delegation in the first place. Legislators are likely either to largely defer to the rule-making authority, in which case the purpose of review is lost, or to take a hard look and be willing to substitute their own views, in which case the potential for errors increases significantly. Finally, legislative review does little to aid in the principal–agent problem between the public and the legislature/executive.

C. Judicial Review of Substance

The courts are an obvious candidate for control of rules and soft law. In theory, they are an independent third party that can monitor or review the substance of the rules that are made. Such monitoring may keep the agent within the bounds of the power delegated to it and control the agent where it makes mistakes, substitutes its own views of the public good, or acts in its own self-interest.[23] Such review is similar to the review of other executive decisions discussed in other chapters of this book.

One of the seminal cases in Canada is *Thorne's Hardware Ltd. v. The Queen*.[24] In that case, the federal governor in council (Cabinet) made an order in council under the *National Harbours Board Act* extending the boundaries of the Port of Saint John, New Brunswick. The applicant challenged the order in council on the basis that it was made in bad faith. It argued that Cabinet extended the boundaries in order to increase the revenues of the National Harbour Board and that such a purpose was not within the scope of Cabinet's powers under the Act. The Act provided that the boundaries of the Saint John harbour were those set out in a schedule "or as may be determined from time to time by order of the Governor in Council."[25]

The Supreme Court, however, held that while it was possible to strike down an order in council on "jurisdictional or other compelling grounds," "it would take an egregious case to warrant such action. This is not such a case."[26] It refused to examine the evidence the applicant provided of bad faith stating that "the government's reasons for expanding the harbour are in the end unknown. Governments do not publish reasons for their decisions; governments may be moved by any number of political, economic, social or partisan considerations."[27] As a result, the Court found against the applicant, stating that the harbour extension was an issue of "economic policy and politics" for which Cabinet "quite obviously believed [it] had reasonable grounds" and the Court "cannot enquire into the validity of those beliefs."[28]

---

23 Courts can also review the rule-making procedures to ensure that there is adequate participation in the process. Such review is considered in the next part.

24 [1983] 1 S.C.R. 106.

25 *National Harbours Board Act*, R.S.C. 1970, c. N-8, s. 7(2).

26 *Supra* note 24 at 111.

27 *Ibid.* at 112-13.

28 *Ibid.* at 115. The Supreme Court applied the principle in *Thorne's Hardware* in refusing to allow an applicant to examine members of a city council to determine their motives in creating a board of inquiry: *Consortium Development (Clearwater) Ltd. v. Sarnia (City of)*, [1998] 3 S.C.R. 3.

The Court in *Thorne's Hardware* therefore took a strong position against examining the actions of Cabinet in making orders in council (a form of delegated rule-making). However, as discussed by Audrey Macklin, chapter 8, the courts do review the substance of rules made by other agents under judicial review powers similar to the powers used to review other decisions of the executive. For example, *Enbridge and Union Gas v. Ontario Energy Board* involved a rule made by the Ontario Energy Board.[29] Section 44 of the *Ontario Energy Board Act* gave the board the power to make rules "governing the conduct of a gas distributer as such conduct relates to any person, (i) selling or offering to sell gas to a consumer."[30] The board made a rule—the Gas Distribution Access Rule (GDAR)—permitting gas vendors (who buy and sell the actual gas for distribution to consumers) to determine who will bill consumers for the gas they buy and for the transportation of the gas to the consumer. The vendor could choose whether both the vendor and the gas distributor (such as Enbridge Gas, which transports the gas through pipes to the consumer) issue separate bills; the vendor issues a bill for the vendor and the gas distributor; or the gas distributor issues a bill for both the vendor and the gas distributor. The Act contained a statutory right of appeal, which the gas distributors used to challenge the rule. They appeared to be concerned that the rule potentially interfered with their relationships with the consumer.

As with substantive review generally, the Ontario Court of Appeal in *Enbridge* first considered the standard of review. It held that the standard of review should be correctness whether the matter was viewed in the more traditional ultra vires framework (that is, as a question whether the board had jurisdiction to make the rule) or the more recent pragmatic and functional approach.[31] The gas distributors attempted to read s. 44 narrowly as only applying where there is a "business relationship" between the gas distributor and the vendor. However, the court found that there was nothing in the Act that narrowed the interpretation in this manner and, in fact, that this interpretation was inconsistent with the broad purposes of the Act to regulate all aspects of the gas distribution business. It emphasized that the gas distribution business was regulated and that there was no common-law right to engage in it.

Courts therefore will review the substance of rules (including regulations) for whether (as in *Enbridge*) the regulation is within the grant of power. They will also review rules for other reasons, including whether the regulation violates the *Canadian Charter of Rights and Freedoms*.[32] However, they have in many cases been reluctant to do so, in part because the discretion is often granted in such broad terms that review is difficult.[33] Courts have been even more reluctant to review soft law.[34] One exception to this reluctance to review

---

29 (2005), 74 O.R. (3d) 147 (C.A.).

30 S.O. 1998, c. 15, Sch. B, s. 44(1)(b)(i).

31 Audrey Macklin, chapter 8, discusses ultra vires review and the pragmatic and functional approach.

32 Part I of the *Constitution Act, 1982*, being Schedule B to the *Canada Act 1982* (U.K.), 1982, c. 11 [Charter]. For a discussion of some of the grounds of review, see Mullan, *Administrative Law*, *supra* note 16, chapter 7 (including that the party making the rule must act in good faith, for a proper purpose, and on relevant considerations). On the Charter and regulations, see *Eldridge v. B.C. (Attorney General)*, [1997] 3 S.C.R. 624.

33 See Taggart, "From 'Parliamentary Powers' to Privatization," *supra* note 5, and Mullan, *Administrative Law*, *supra* note 16.

34 For a discussion of soft law and the Charter, see, for example, *Little Sisters Book and Art Emporium v. Canada (Minister of Justice)*, [2000] 2 S.C.R. 1120, and Lorne Sossin, "Discretion Unbound: Reconciling Soft Law and the Charter" (2002) 45 Can. Pub. Pol'y 465.

soft law is a review of "fettering." Fettering occurs where a guideline or policy, due to its language or practical effect, is in effect mandatory or binding on a decision-maker, taking away the discretion that has been granted to him or her.[35]

Yet even if courts were willing to review rules or soft law substantively, is this something we should want them to do? There are three principal reasons why we may not. First, the process of judicial review tends at best to be random and, at worst, biased in favour of certain interest groups. Judicial review can be very time-consuming and expensive. In some cases there are only a few parties who bear the costs from a new rule, while the benefits are spread across many people. For example, if the Ontario Ministry of the Environment makes a rule limiting sulphur dioxide emissions, the rule may impose significant costs on a few industries or firms but provide benefits (in terms of lower levels of air pollution or acid rain) to a large number of people (both within and potentially outside the province). In such a case, the industries or firms affected may have the incentive to challenge the rule in court (and be willing and able to expend the resources to do so), while those who benefit each individually receive too little benefit to take on the expense of becoming involved in the application. The government agency that created the rule would have to represent the interests of those who the rule benefits. Conversely, if the costs are spread over a large number of people (for example, a rule imposing a tariff on an imported consumer product), there may be no one person who is sufficiently harmed to bear the costs of challenging the government decision. As a result, this check on government rules depends in part on such factors as how many parties benefit or bear costs and the resources of those parties.

The second concern with substantive judicial review is that, even if the "appropriate" challenges come before the courts, the courts often do not have the expertise to review the rules. There is therefore a large potential error cost from substantive judicial review—that is, courts might be less likely than the administrative decision-maker to determine the "right" answer.[36] Generalist courts that are "compulsorily ignorant" may not have the knowledge, experience, or technical expertise to review the often very detailed, technical rules.[37] For example, in *Enbridge*, how can a court determine the appropriateness of a rule concerning the billing of consumers or even the appropriate interpretation of the purposes of the legislation? The expertise of the Ontario Energy Board in issues relating to gas would aid in making these determinations. A court could defer to the decisions of the rule-maker, in which case there is no real check on the principal–agent concern. Alternatively, the court could take a hard look (potentially substituting its own view of the appropriate policy), in which case there is an increased risk that the wrong rule will be chosen. As with legislative review, the check on the principal–agent concern comes at the cost of loss of expertise.

Finally, even if the courts have the expertise to review administrative rules, this discussion of the courts' role in reviewing administrative rules has implicitly assumed that courts

35 See, for example, *Canada (Minister of Citizenship and Immigration) v. Thamotharem*, 2007 FCA 198 (finding a guideline specifying reverse-order questioning for refugee protection hearings did not constitute an unlawful fetter because it expressly directed panel members to consider the particular facts of each case to determine whether there should be an exception to this order of questioning).

36 Stephenson, "Legislative Allocation of Delegated Power," *supra* note 13.

37 See Taggart, "From 'Parliamentary Powers' to Privatization," *supra* note 5, at 589 (discussing the distaste of administrative law scholar John Willis for judicial review).

are attempting to determine the best possible interpretation of legislative power and the appropriateness of the challenged rule. However, judges also have their own policy preferences.[38] Judicial review therefore gives rise to a concern that judges' discretion over policy outcomes (the content of rules) creates a further principal–agent problem as judges seek to implement their own views of appropriate policy.[39]

The issue of the extent of desirable substantive review by courts of administrative decisions has long vexed courts, legislators, and legal scholars. This issue is more fully addressed in other chapters in this book. However, there is an interesting connection between judicial review and the discussion above of structural approaches to controlling delegated decision-making. In order to increase the likelihood that rules will align with their preferences, legislators may wish a particular agency to interpret legislative provisions in making rules rather than courts.[40] For example, legislators who are favourable to unions or workers may believe that a Ministry of Labour interpretation of a rule-making power is more likely to favour unions or workers than a court's interpretation. Thus, they may, in such cases, seek to limit judicial review. In other cases, the legislators may believe that courts' interpretations are more likely to be in accordance with their preferences and seek to expand judicial review. Such limitation or expansion on judicial review could come through, for example, a privative clause or a right to appeal, or through other cues as to who the legislature wishes to set policy. However, given the lack of clarity in how the courts interpret their "expertise" relative to that of administrative decision-makers, legislators can never be sure that their choice of delegate (either administrative decision-maker or court) will prevail over time.[41]

D. Process Requirements

A final manner in which the actions of the agent could be controlled is through the process it must follow to make the rules. There is a wide range of processes that a body creating rules could follow. At one extreme, it could make the decision based on no external information and no consultation with any other group. At the other, the body could hold a full hearing on the rule, taking submissions from different groups and engaging in consultations

38 See generally Jeffrey A. Segal & Harold J. Spaeth, *The Supreme Court and the Attitudinal Model Revisited* (Cambridge: Cambridge University Press, 2002), and Thomas J. Miles & Cass R. Sunstein, "Do Judges Make Regulatory Policy? An Empirical Investigation of Chevron" (2006) 73 U. Chicago L. Rev. 823. For an application of the attitudinal model of judicial decision-making in the Canadian context, see Benjamin Alarie & Andrew Green, "The Reasonable Justice: An Empirical Analysis of Frank Iacobucci's Career on the Supreme Court of Canada" (2007) 57 U.T.L.J. 1.

39 For example, see Stephenson, "Legislative Allocation of Delegated Power," *supra* note 13 (discussing the possible differences in policy preferences between legislatures, agencies, and courts).

40 For example, see Stephenson, "Legislative Allocation of Delegated Power," *ibid.* (arguing that legislators may wish to delegate the power to interpret legislation to agencies if they wish to produce consistent interpretation across issues, or to the courts if they wish to produce consistent interpretation across time—that is, even when other legislators are in power).

41 Adrian Vermeule, "The Delegation Lottery" (2006) 119 Harv. L. Rev. F. 105 (arguing that the choice of who interprets legislation is as much of a "lottery" for legislators as is the ultimate rule or decision that a delegate makes on the basis of broad legislative provisions). See also chapters 8 and 9 in this book discussing the Supreme Court's approach to determining the standard of review.

over draft rules. Actual decision-making processes generally fall somewhere between these extremes.

One of the key features of these process requirements is the extent of public participation. Why might we want to have a process that includes public participation? The principal reason is that it may result in better decisions. First, process requirements may ensure that those making the rules have all the relevant information. This information may, for example, be about the costs and the benefits of the particular rule, such as how much it would cost regulated parties to comply with the rule (for example, the cost of putting safety equipment on all machines to protect workers) or how the regulated activity affects the general public (such as the impact of noise pollution on their daily activities). It may also provide information on how the public and the regulated party value the changes proposed under the rule. Consider a rule limiting greenhouse gas emissions. Public consultation may provide the party making the rule with a better understanding of the extent to which the public cares about and is willing to bear costs of addressing climate change. This additional information may reduce the mistakes made by the party making the regulation about either the extent of the problem or the values of the public regarding the issue.

Second, instead of merely gathering information, such processes may promote deliberation. Deliberation involves individuals debating issues and exchanging ideas. Such debate may lead not only to better understanding of the issues but also to the growth of shared values and goals. For example, deliberation on the rules about public schools in Alberta may lead to new shared values or goals for education for citizens of the province. Some jurisdictions, such as British Columbia, have experimented with "citizen juries" for developing policies. These juries are made up of a number of citizens who are given information on an issue (or set of issues) and time to debate. The hope is that the exchange of ideas will lead to a better, more considered decision on the policy.

More formal processes for making rules therefore potentially lead to better decisions through increased information for the rule-makers or more thoughtful deliberation by citizens. Better information and deliberation may reduce the probability of mistakes by rule-makers. Further, the involvement of the public increases the openness of the process to scrutiny, which may reduce the probability that those making the rules act on their own view of the public interest (as opposed to that of the legislators or the public). It may also reduce the ability of interest groups to pressure those making the rules to decide in their favour (and against the interests of the public more generally).[42]

However, more formal processes are not without their risks. First, formal process can be very costly and time-consuming. Making proposals and holding hearings or consultations to obtain public input can be expensive. Perhaps more important, public consultation can considerably lengthen the time it takes to make a rule. Formal processes have been blamed in part for the inflexibility and slow-changing nature of the US regulatory system. An example of the time that consultations can add to rule-making is the air pollution standards process in Ontario. In the 1970s, the Ontario government made standards setting out permissible levels of emissions of particular substances. The Ministry of the Environment decided to revise these standards in the late 1980s. It engaged in public consultations from

42 See, for example, Richard Stewart, "The Reformation of American Administrative Law" (1975) 88 Harv. L. Rev. 1669.

1987 to 1990 but was unable to obtain agreement and stopped the process. It began again in 2001 and went through a series of proposals and different efforts at getting public comments. This process continued over four years before new standards were in force.[43]

Second, while formal processes may provide transparency that reduces interest-group power, the processes at the same time provide another avenue through which interest groups can pressure those making the rules. It is important to consider who is using the process and the nature of that group's involvement. Is a particular group able to use its resources to dominate the process? Little work has been done on this issue in Canada. Third, and relatedly, those making the rules may not actually attend to the public participation. They may simply go through the motions in the process and not substantively change their views.

Finally, public participation may be detrimental if the public itself makes mistakes. Many of the issues that are addressed through rules are highly technical or based on complex science. Individual members of the public may make mistakes in understanding and expressing opinions about an issue. These mistakes can lead individuals to believe that a risk is greater than it actually is. For example, individuals tend to perceive the risk of a car accident to be greater if they have seen a car accident recently. Individuals may also perceive risks to be less than they actually are. For example, individuals tend to be over-optimistic about their risks of accident. Most believe they have above-average skills and are less likely than average to have a workplace accident. Further, many of these mistakes concern the types of issues that involve regulatory choices that are difficult for individuals to understand. Individuals have difficulty, for example, understanding very small probabilities of catastrophic harm, such as a catastrophic shift in climate. They tend to ignore these very small probability risks even though they should be taken into account.[44]

A related concept is that individuals often do not invest the time or cost necessary to become informed on an issue. Instead, they may base their decisions on decisions of others. If some individuals believe, for example, that the use of a hormone in the production of meat is carcinogenic (even though there is no evidence to that effect), other people may adopt the same position, purely on the basis that the first individuals believed it. More may come to the same belief on the basis of the now greater number of people who believe that hormones are harmful. These "information cascades," where people come to believe something on the basis that others believe it, can lead to dramatic shifts in public opinion on issues.[45]

So some mistakes may make the public believe that a risk is greater than it actually is and some that it is less than it actually is. Some risks may be ignored entirely, and others may attract significant public concern on the basis of very little information. Formal public participation processes are open to individuals who express concern on the basis of such mistaken beliefs. The possibility of such mistakes has led to different types of proposals for structuring decision-making. Some commentators have called for the isolation of regulatory decision-makers from the public because of these mistakes—that is, they argue that

---

43 Environmental Commissioner of Ontario, *Annual Report 2004-2005*, at 55-58, available online: <http://www.eco.on.ca/english/publicat/ar2004.pdf>.

44 Richard Posner, *Catastrophe: Risk and Response* (Oxford: Oxford University Press, 2004).

45 Cass Sunstein, *Risk and Reason* (Cambridge: Cambridge University Press, 2002).

decisions should be made largely by experts as opposed to through "deliberation," which is likely to be based on mistaken understandings.[46] Others claim that any such isolation is inherently undemocratic and that the mistakes can be reduced through an appropriately deliberative process.[47]

Given these benefits and costs to procedures for making rules, what have we done in Canada to address these issues? Just as the courts have reviewed the substance of rules, you could imagine courts reviewing how the rules were developed and creating a common-law set of procedures that must be followed when making rules under delegated powers. However, as Grant Huscroft explains in chapter 5, there is no common-law requirement of procedural fairness where a decision is of a "legislative and general" nature.[48] Because rules are typically general (that is, apply to many parties), they tend to fall under this exception to procedural fairness. "Legislative" in this context does not necessarily mean "by the legislature." In *Att. Gen. of Can. v. Inuit Tapirisat et al.*,[49] the Inuit Tapirisat challenged a rate increase for telephone services supplied by Bell Canada. The Canadian Radio-television and Telecommunications Commission (CRTC) implemented the rate increase following hearings in which the Inuit Tapirisat had participated. The CRTC approved the rate increase without the conditions that the Inuit Tapirisat had requested. The Inuit Tapirisat appealed to the federal Cabinet under provisions of the *National Transportation Act* to have the CRTC decision set aside. As part of this appeal, the CRTC made submissions to Cabinet through the Department of Communications. The Inuit Tapirisat was not allowed to review or respond to the CRTC submission. Cabinet rejected the appeal.

The Inuit Tapirisat sought judicial review, claiming it had been denied procedural fairness in its appeal because the CRTC had made submissions to which it did not have access. The Supreme Court of Canada, however, found that Cabinet did not owe the Inuit Tapirisat procedural fairness in this case. Among other things, Estey J. found that making rates was "legislative action in its purest form" because it affected many Bell subscribers.[50] He pointed to, among other things, the fact that the legislation created procedural rules for the CRTC but not for Cabinet appeals. In the end, he found that there was no obligation on Cabinet to provide procedural fairness, such as notice, a hearing, or reasons.

Inuit Tapirisat shows that for a decision to be "legislative" in nature, the body making the decision does not have to be the legislature. The decision itself must have this "legislative and general" character. Although this legislative and general category is not self-evident, it appears to exclude rules aimed at a single party. For example, *Homex Realty v. Wyoming*[51] involved a dispute between a municipality and a developer over who should pay the costs of installing services for a new subdivision. After extended and bitter negotiations, the municipality used its powers to make bylaws to designate the developer's subdivision plan not

46 Cass Sunstein, *Law of Fear* (Cambridge: Cambridge University Press, 2005).

47 See Dan Kahan *et al.*, "Fear of Democracy: A Cultural Evaluation of Sunstein on Risk" (2006) 119 Harv. L. Rev. 1071.

48 *Board of Education of Indian Head School Division No. 19 of Saskatchewan v. Knight*, [1990] 1 S.C.R. 653.

49 [1980] 2 S.C.R. 735.

50 *Ibid.* at 754.

51 [1980] 2 S.C.R. 1011.

to be a "registered plan." It did so without notice to the developer. If the bylaw was valid, the developer would have to obtain permission from the municipality to sell parts of the development and, before providing consent, the municipality would impose conditions (such as installing services). The developer challenged the bylaw on the grounds that the municipality did not act fairly in enacting the bylaw. Estey J. held that the bylaw was not general in nature, but was aimed at resolving a dispute with one party—the developer. The municipality therefore owed a duty of fairness in such situations. Dickson J., in dissent, also agreed that there was duty on the municipality to provide procedural fairness. He stated, "[w]hat we have here is not a by-law of wide and general application which was to apply to all citizens of the municipality equally. Rather, it was a by-law aimed deliberately at limiting the rights of one individual."[52]

As a result, the general approach of courts in Canada has not been to impose common-law procedural requirements on the making of rules. There are, however, a range of statutory provisions and policies that set out the required procedures. Unlike the approach in the United States, where there is a principal statute (the *Administrative Procedures Act*) that sets out a set of fundamental procedures for rule-making, the Canadian approach has tended to be more piecemeal. There are, for example, some procedures at the federal level concerning formal regulations, such as procedures under the *Statutory Instruments Act* for publication of draft regulations.[53] More recently, a federal Cabinet directive on Streamlining Regulation came into effect on April 1, 2007, replacing the former Government of Canada Regulatory Policy. The Cabinet directive emphasizes the importance of identifying interested and affected persons when making regulations and providing them with meaningful opportunities and information for participation.[54]

There are also more specific procedures in particular substantive areas of law at both the federal and the provincial levels. For example, following a court challenge to policy guidelines of the OSC, the Ontario government struck a committee to reform the rule-making process of the OSC.[55] The legislation that grew out of this committee's work requires the OSC, in making a rule, to publish a notice of the proposed rule, including the rule itself, a

52 *Ibid.* at 1052. The majority and the dissent, therefore, agreed that the developer was owed a duty of fairness because the bylaw was not "legislative" or general. They differed on whether they should, in their discretion, grant the remedy requested by the developer. The majority held that the court should not grant the remedy because of the actions of the developer during the negotiations and litigation.

53 R.S.C. 1985, c. S-22. Since the mid-1980s, the publication of proposed regulations in the *Canada Gazette* has been accompanied by a regulatory impact analysis statement. The statement sets out the rationale for the regulation and attempts to measure the costs and benefits of the regulation. There is a more general statute in Quebec. See Janisch, "Further Developments re Rulemaking by Administrative Agencies," *supra* note 21, for a general discussion of rule-making in Canada.

54 The Cabinet directive also sets out process requirements such as analysis of the costs and benefits of proposed regulations. The federal government set up an advisory committee to examine the regulation-making process. This committee also recommended consultation with citizens, businesses, and other groups, as well as analysis of the costs and benefits of proposed rules. External Advisory Committee on Smart Regulation, *Smart Regulation: A Regulatory Strategy for Canada* (September 2004), available online: <http://www.smartregulation.gc.ca>.

55 See Janisch, "Further Developments re Rulemaking by Administrative Agencies," *supra* note 21, and Mullan, *Administrative Law*, *supra* note 16, for a discussion of the history behind the procedural rules for the OSC.

statement of the purpose of the rule, a discussion of the alternatives considered and the reasons for not adopting them, a reference to any unpublished material relied on, and a description of the anticipated costs and benefits.[56] The OSC is also required to provide an opportunity to interested parties to comment on the proposed rule. If, after publication and consideration, the OSC wishes to make material changes to the draft rule, it must provide further notice of and opportunity to comment on these proposed changes. The OSC cannot make the rule until it has provided the required opportunity for comments and considered all representations made in the process.

Ontario has enacted similar rules in other areas. For example, the Ontario *Environmental Bill of Rights*[57] creates procedural rights surrounding government decisions in the environmental area, including the making of rules. The Bill provides for the creation of an electronic registry on the Internet of all proposed rules and instruments (including regulations, formal rules, policies, orders, and approvals). There are different notice and comment procedures for different types of decisions (with, for example, longer comment periods for decisions that may have a greater impact on the environment). The Minister of the Environment is to "take every reasonable step to ensure that all comments relevant to the proposal that are received as part of the public participation process … are considered when decisions about the proposal are made."[58]

The government can be taken to court for failure to fulfill statutory procedural requirements. For example, in the *Enbridge* case,[59] Enbridge and Union Gas claimed that the Ontario Energy Board did not comply with the notice and comment requirements set out in the *Ontario Energy Board Act*. The notice and comment provisions were similar to those in the *Securities Act*, with a requirement to give notice of the proposed rule, including a description of the anticipated costs and benefits. If the board then decides to make a material change to the proposed rule, it must publish the proposed change and the anticipated costs and benefits. In this case, the Ontario Energy Board proposed the new rule, took comments, and twice gave notice of a proposed change and took further comments. However, in the judicial review, Enbridge and Union Gas argued that the board only provided anticipated costs and benefits for the proposal as a whole and did not break out the costs and benefits of the different billing arrangements. They argued that this was insufficient because the purpose of the notice and comment requirements was to impose a discipline on the board and allow the parties to make full representations.

The Ontario Court of Appeal rejected this argument. It noted that a cost–benefit analysis was not required for each provision of the proposed rule. It held that the purpose of the rule was not to impose discipline on the Ontario Energy Board and that if the legislature was concerned that the board engaged in "thoughtless rulemaking, it would surely have imposed a requirement to give reasons for rulemaking, if indeed it left the Board with any rulemaking at all."[60] The court stated that the purpose of the requirement was merely to

56 *Securities Act*, *supra* note 22, s. 143.2.

57 S.O. 1993, c. 28.

58 *Ibid.*, s. 35.

59 *Supra* note 29.

60 *Ibid.* at 160.

give interested parties the opportunity to make written submissions on the change and that the parties had ample opportunity to do so. The court therefore seems to limit the usefulness of these provisions to reduce certain principal–agent risks—in particular, the risk of making mistakes in rule-making.

Much of the public participation in rule-making in Canada therefore consists of the provision of notice of the proposed rule and the opportunity for the public to comment on the proposal. How do such notice and comment requirements fit with our discussion of the benefits and risks of process? They are beneficial in that they ensure that the public has some information about the proposed rule and the regulators potentially receive information from the public on the costs and benefits of and trade-offs in making the rule. Further, the cost of these requirements is relatively low. However, notice and comment requirements have a number of drawbacks. First, they can cause delay because those making the rules need to give notice of and time to comment on any proposed material change to a rule. Second, while notice and comment rules potentially open the rule-making process up to a greater range of parties, it is not clear who can participate. It may be that the comment process is dominated by certain parties (including, potentially, the regulated parties). Certain groups may be able to make more detailed and effective comments if they have resources and are willing to invest in the process. As was noted above, if significant costs may be imposed on relatively few parties, they have greater incentive to invest resources to oppose the rule than if the benefits (or costs) are spread over a larger number of parties. Finally, notice and comment rules do not provide scope for deliberation. The comments of each individual are provided to the government, but there is no exchange of ideas between those making the comments.[61]

The process of making rules can therefore aid in controlling the actions of the "agent." It can potentially reduce mistakes in rule-making by increasing the flow of information to rule-makers. It can also provide some transparency that may reduce the rule-makers' ability to make rules following not the interests of legislators but either their own idiosyncratic view of the public good or their own self-interest (such as where they seek to favour certain parties because of the rewards those parties can provide to them). Legislators may even be able to use the process to aid in ensuring that rules have a particular substantive content by altering procedures to favour certain parties.[62] For example, procedures that favour or encourage submissions by environmental groups may lead to rules that tend to favour their interests.

However, there is no necessary connection between these processes and results, or a reduction in interest-group power. As noted above, much depends on the relative resources of the parties and the willingness of parties to become involved in the rule-making. It also depends on the willingness of the rule-maker to take the comments of interested parties into account. Interestingly, there may be a connection between these process requirements and substantive review by the courts. If a rule-maker follows expansive procedures (including public participation), courts may be more willing to defer to the resulting decisions (rules)

61 See Andrew Green, "Creating Environmentalists: Environmental Law, Identity and Commitment" (2006) 17 J. Envtl. L. & Prac. 1 for a discussion of administrative law, deliberation, and the formation of shared values or identities.

62 McCubbins, Noll & Weingast, "Administrative Procedures as Instruments," *supra* note 11.

because, for example, the use of the procedures is a signal of better-quality decisions.[63] It is difficult, however, to ensure that the quality of decisions actually is improved and that the rule-makers actually do take public comments into account. Courts have difficulty determining whether a rule-maker actually considered particular comments because there are so many potential reasons for a decision (recall the comments of the Supreme Court in *Thorne's Hardware*[64]). Part of the answer may be to require the rule-maker to provide reasons in the hope that it will be held accountable, either by the public or by legislators. However, as discussed, such accountability can be a weak constraint where time, expertise, and information costs hinder monitoring.

V. THE ONGOING STRUGGLE

Legislators therefore take a risk when they delegate the power to make rules to other parties. They gain the use of the expertise of these other parties. Further, they expand the reach of their regulatory powers because they would not otherwise have the time to make rules in all the areas that are encompassed by a modern welfare and regulatory state. However, at the same time, they are giving a significant amount of power to parties they cannot fully monitor because of the information and time costs of such monitoring. This difficulty in monitoring creates a principal–agent problem.

Governments continue to search for better ways of overcoming this principal–agent problem. Various solutions have been proposed, such as creating administrative law courts (courts specializing in the general issues related to administrative law or to substantive areas of law in particular, such as labour law or environmental law); having electronic "billboards" for comments on rules so that everyone can review comments submitted by others (thereby, it is hoped, increasing deliberation in notice and comment processes); and increasing the resources for and power of legislative committees that review regulations. There is, however, no perfect solution. The struggle is to control the principal–agent problem while retaining the significant benefits that come with delegation. This struggle will become increasingly important as governments continue to experiment with new forms of regulation, including greater use of private markets and private parties. These new forms of regulation do not mean fewer rules. Instead, they have led to "more delegated legislation, increased delegation of governmental functions to the private sector, and more quasi-legislation (rules)"[65] and, whether or not these new forms of regulation are otherwise beneficial, to increased principal–agent concerns.

63 Matthew Stephenson, "The Strategic Substitution Effect: Textual Plausibility, Procedural Formality, and Judicial Review of Agency Statutory Interpretations" (2006) 120 Harv. L. Rev. 528.

64 *Supra* note 24.

65 Taggart, "From 'Parliamentary Powers' to Privatization," *supra* note 5 at 627.

SUGGESTED ADDITIONAL READINGS

CASES

Canada (Minister of Citizenship and Immigration) v. Thamotharem, 2007 FCA 198.

Enbridge and Union Gas v. Ontario Energy Board, [2005] O.J. No. 33 (C.A.).

Thorne's Hardware Ltd. v. Canada, [1983] 1 S.C.R 106.

SECONDARY SOURCES

McCubbins, Matthew D., Roger G. Noll & Barry R. Weingast. "Administrative Procedures as Instruments of Political Control" (1987) 3 J.L. Econ. & Org. 243.

Mullan, David. *Administrative Law* (Toronto: Irwin Law, 2001), chapter 7.

Taggart, Michael. "From 'Parliamentary Powers' to Privatization: The Chequered History of Delegated Legislation in the Twentieth Century" (2005) 55 U.T.L.J. 575.

CHAPTER FOURTEEN

Getting the Story Out: Accountability and the Law of Public Inquiries

PETER J. CARVER
Faculty of Law, University of Alberta

I. ACCOUNTABILITY AND THE PUBLIC INQUIRY

In September 2002, Maher Arar, a Syrian-born Canadian citizen living in Ottawa with his wife and two children, was returning from a visit with his parents in Tunisia. His flight from Zurich to Montreal was re-routed through New York. At New York's LaGuardia Airport, U.S. customs and law enforcement officials detained Mr. Arar on suspicion of involvement with terrorist organizations. Officials questioned Mr. Arar for a period of approximately nine days. During that time, U.S. officials spoke with members of the RCMP and CSIS. American officials suggested to Mr. Arar that they were thinking of deporting him to Syria, a country of which he remained a national. Mr. Arar objected, saying that he was Canadian, that his family and his life were in Canada, and that he feared being tortured if he was placed in Syrian hands. At one point, Mr. Arar was permitted to speak with the Canadian consul in New York, who assured him that despite the suggestions made by U.S. officials, they would not deport him to Syria but rather to Canada. Nevertheless, in early October 2002, Mr. Arar was flown to Jordan and transported over land to Syria and to a military prison. For the next year, Mr. Arar lived in an underground cell six feet by six feet by three feet, and was repeatedly beaten and tortured during questioning about his alleged involvement with radical Islamic organizations. In October 2003, Syria released Mr. Arar and he returned to Canada. Soon thereafter, Mr. Arar, his family, and many other Canadians demanded that the Canadian government be made accountable for what had happened to him.

Accountability can mean many different things. One meaning of accountability is accountability in law: that persons who have harmed others by their actions or omissions be identified as responsible for those actions and made to "pay for" the harm they caused, whether through compensation or by receiving punishment. The legal system is the social institution particularly suited to achieving accountability in this sense. It provides for accountability through two principal mechanisms: (1) the assessing of *liability* for breaches of legal obligations, and (2) the imposing of *enforceable orders* on persons found liable for wrongdoing. Several features of the standard model of legal accountability are worth noting. First, legal accountability is directed at wrongdoing defined in advance by established norms of behaviour. Second, it involves a retrospective inquiry into past events. To the degree that legal accountability is concerned with the future, it is limited to remediation of the harm and wrongdoing of the individuals involved. Third, the model is adversarial in that it assumes a contest between two or more parties seeking to prove different versions of facts and law. Largely because of the coercive aspects of legal accountability, Canadian law builds in many protections for the individual. These include strict rules for ensuring that only evidence relevant to the question of liability is received, and that the onus of proving liability is placed on the party alleging liability.

This kind of accountability was not well suited to the Arar affair. It was entirely unclear whether any prescribed laws had been breached by Canadian officials. Several large government agencies had been involved in the events surrounding his fate, each charged with carrying out different public mandates. Few individuals who were active in these events were known, let alone identified as likely wrongdoers. In short, there was no one to sue and no one to prosecute.

What Mr. Arar and his supporters sought was a different kind of accountability. They wanted answers to questions about what Canadian police, intelligence, and diplomatic officials had done before and during Mr. Arar's ordeal in Syria. Had officials informed the FBI of false suspicions that Mr. Arar had terrorist connections? Did they provide information to the Americans or Syrians for use in interrogations of Mr. Arar? Did Canadian diplomats do everything in their power to prevent harm coming to Mr. Arar and to obtain his release, and, if not, why not?

This called for accountability in the sense of "getting the story out," of finding out who did what and when and why. Accountability of this kind can be fairly easily combined with accountability for improving how similar events will be handled in the future. Historically in Canada, an important mechanism for achieving accountability in this sense has been the public inquiry. Cory J. of the Supreme Court of Canada described the difference between an inquiry and liability-based proceedings in these terms:

> A commission of inquiry is neither a criminal trial nor a civil action for the determination of liability. It cannot establish either criminal culpability or civil responsibility for damages. Rather, an inquiry is an investigation into an issue, event or series of events. The findings of a commissioner relating to that investigation are simply findings of fact and statements of opin-

> ion reached by the commissioner at the end of the inquiry. They are unconnected to normal legal criteria. They are based upon and flow from a procedure which is not bound by the evidentiary or procedural rules of a courtroom. There are no legal consequences attached to the determinations of a commissioner. They are not enforceable and do not bind courts considering the same subject matter.[1]

Fact-finding is important both to liability processes and to public inquiries. However, in liability proceedings, the proof of facts is subordinated to outcome—that is, only those facts that are relevant to circumscribed issues of liability will be explored and determined. In an inquiry, determining the facts is a primary purpose in its own right.

The point here is not to argue that one kind of accountability is better than the other, nor to suggest that they are mutually exclusive.[2] The point is rather to show that public inquiries and formal legal processes serve different accountability goals, which explains the different ways in which they operate as well as the tensions that arise when they overlap.

In the case of Maher Arar, public pressure led the federal government to announce terms of reference for an inquiry into the matter and to appoint Dennis O'Connor, Associate Chief Justice of Ontario, as commissioner of the inquiry. The Arar inquiry held hearings over the next 20 months, and issued final reports covering its findings of fact and its analysis of national security oversight procedures in September and December 2006, respectively.[3] The Arar inquiry is a striking example of the inquiry phenomenon, and we will return to it from time to time in this chapter to illustrate how inquiries work.

There are two principal reasons for including a discussion of public inquiries in an introductory text on administrative law. First, both administrative law and public inquiries serve the important function of making government operations transparent and responsible to the public. Administrative law is generally told as the story of judicial review. In this familiar narrative, the superior courts act as defenders of the rights of private persons whose interests are jeopardized by government decision-makers. The courts protect individual interests by imposing standards of fair procedure and reasoned decision-making on state officials. Administrative law is an important body of established principles constraining and guiding exercises of governmental power. As a mode of accountability, however, judicial review suffers from some of the limitations of most formal legal processes. Its focus is

---

1 *Canada (Attorney General) v. Canada (Commission of Inquiry on the Blood System)*, [1997] 3 S.C.R. 440 at para. 34 [*Krever Commission*].

2 In "Canadian Public Inquiries and Accountability" in Philip C. Stenning, ed., *Accountability for Criminal Justice: Selected Essays* (Toronto: University of Toronto Press, 1995) 268-93, Kent Roach describes three kinds of accountability that may be achieved through public inquiries: literal, organizational, and social. By literal accountability he means the need for individuals to give a full account and explanation for their actions. Organizational accountability involves making organizations account for their performance by examining systems of decision-making and their flaws. Roach describes social or moral accountability as occurring at the level of the audience, or society at large, with respect to the events and issues being addressed.

3 Commission of Inquiry into the Actions of Canadian Officials in Relation to Maher Arar, *Report of the Events Relating to Maher Arar: Factual Background*, vols. I and II (Ottawa: Queen's Printer, 2006), *Report of the Events Relating to Maher Arar: Analysis and Recommendations* (Ottawa: Queen's Printer, September 2006), and *A New Review Mechanism for the RCMP's National Security Activities* (Ottawa: Queen's Printer, December 2006).

generally directed at specific acts of governmental decision-making. Remedies in judicial review are rarely systemic, and frequently go only so far as to require decision-makers to start their process over again. On the policy level, judicial review is generally silent. The judiciary confines its role to a review of process, and of rationality in decision-making measured by legislative purposes, and does not explicitly comment on the merit of those purposes. It is therefore worth considering public inquiries as an alternative recourse to judicial review for those aggrieved by alleged government misconduct. This is explored in a general way in part I of the chapter, which deals with the different kinds of public inquiries known in the Canadian tradition and the problems of balancing the public interest with individual rights in the holding of an inquiry.

Second, public inquiries operate within the context of administrative law principles. Inquiries are exercises in delegated executive power and are subject to most rules of administrative law. However, because inquiries engage largely in investigative, fact-finding, and recommending functions, and much less in adjudicative and order-making functions, they provide a different context in which to see administrative law principles at work. Part II of the chapter looks at several of the more important principles of administrative law that are applicable to public inquiries. The chapter concludes in part III by raising a few questions about the overall benefit of public inquiries.

A. Types of Public Inquiries

The terms "royal commission," "judicial inquiry," and "public inquiry" are used almost interchangeably in media descriptions. Nevertheless, these terms have different shades of meaning that are worth noting. For instance, the term "royal commission" refers to the fact that historically many inquiries were appointed by executive government pursuant to their royal prerogative powers. That has changed, as most inquiries are now appointed pursuant to the federal and provincial inquiry statutes that exist in each Canadian jurisdiction. The term "judicial inquiry" is a colloquial term that refers to the fact that governments usually name current or former judges to be "commissioners" for conducting an inquiry. This is especially true of inquiries whose main purpose is the investigation of and reporting on a series of factual events, as with the Arar inquiry. However, there is no requirement that an inquiry be headed by a judicial official, and there are many examples in Canadian experience of inquiries being led by non-judges.

This chapter uses the term "public inquiry." It does so because of the connotations of the word "public" that assist in understanding how inquiries in this country generally work. For one thing, inquiries are largely directed at the actions of public authorities and public officials. While nothing prevents lawmakers from establishing inquiries to look into the actions of private persons, it would be questionable to spend public resources where the findings had no implications for past or future government regulation. The decision to appoint an inquiry should meet a public interest test. The term "public inquiry" implies another important feature of inquiries in Canada: they are usually carried out in public view. It is through the public nature of inquiry proceedings that the inquiry achieves one of its most important purposes: to assure members of the public that the "full story" is finally coming out, that actions and decisions that were taken behind closed doors will be exposed to the light of day.

Two kinds of public inquiries are familiar in Canadian experience: the policy-oriented or policy inquiry, and the investigative inquiry. The policy inquiry is directed at the study of broad issues of social or regulatory concern, with the purpose of leading to changes in law and policy. In Canada, policy inquiries have often been termed royal commissions. Recent such inquiries include at the federal level the Royal Commission on Aboriginal Peoples ("RCAP")[4] in the early 1990s, and the Commission on the Future of Health Care in Canada (the "Romanow Commission"),[5] which reported in 2002.

An investigative inquiry is directed at uncovering and reporting on the facts of an event or series of events in which one or more persons were seriously harmed, or which comprised an instance of alleged public misconduct (that is, a political scandal). Purely investigatory inquiries, however, are relatively infrequent in Canadian experience. Much more common is the inquiry with combined investigative and policy functions. The Arar inquiry was a combined inquiry. The inquiry's terms of reference set out both functions:

> (a) to investigate and report on the actions of Canadian officials in relation to Maher Arar, including with regard to
>
> (i) the detention of Mr. Arar in the United States,
>
> (ii) the deportation of Mr. Arar to Syria via Jordan,
>
> (iii) the imprisonment and treatment of Mr. Arar in Syria,
>
> (iv) the return of Mr. Arar to Canada, and
>
> (v) any other circumstance directly related to Mr. Arar that the Commissioner considers relevant to fulfilling this mandate, in this Order referred to as the "*factual inquiry*," and
>
> (b) to make any recommendations that he [the Commissioner] considers advisable on an independent, arm's length review mechanism for the activities of the Royal Canadian Mounted Police with respect to national security based on
>
> (i) an examination of models, both domestic and international, for that review mechanism, and
>
> (ii) an assessment of how the review mechanism would interact with existing review mechanisms,
>
> in this Order referred to as the "*policy review*."[6] [Emphasis added.]

The investigative and policy review functions of combined inquiries are often termed Phase One and Phase Two processes. This reflects the increasingly common practice of commissions of inquiry with combined functions to divide their proceedings into two distinct phases, with different parties, hearing procedures, and reports. The following discussion examines how policy or Phase Two inquiries and investigative or Phase One inquiries, respectively, pursue accountability at both the individual and organizational levels.

---

4 See *Report of the Royal Commission on Aboriginal Peoples* (Ottawa: Queen's Printer, 1996), online: Indian and Northern Affairs Canada <http://www.ainc-inac.gc.ca/ch/rcap/sg/sgmm_e.html>.

5 Health Canada, *Commission on the Future of Health Care in Canada*, online: Health Canada <http://www.hc-sc.gc.ca/english/care/romanow/index1.html>.

6 The terms of reference along with all other documents prepared for website access by the Arar inquiry are now available online at Library and Archives Canada: <http://epe.lac-bac.gc.ca/100/206/301/pco-bcp/commissions/maher_arar/index.html>, Version captured September 13, 2007.

B. The Policy or Phase Two Inquiry

Policy or Phase Two inquiries raise relatively few legal issues. Governments establish policy inquiries for the purpose of developing new approaches to complex social policy issues. Not infrequently, governments are accused of establishing policy inquiries in order to forestall having to make decisions on complex or controversial social issues. The activity of policy inquiries is legislative in nature in the sense that it is prospective (not historical), broad-based or general in impact (not specific or individualized), and open to political/policy input (not restricted by stringent rules of relevance), the features that distinguish legislative from adjudicative decision-making.

The Supreme Court has ruled that legislative decision-making and "quasi-legislative" decision-making do not attract fair process protections at common law,[7] even where government officials have created legitimate expectations of fair process.[8] These principles create an unfortunate lacuna in administrative law, leaving decision-makers unbounded by anything other than statutory requirements to hear the affected public when it comes to the most important of all governmental functions: law-making. The appropriate procedural right with respect to law-making would seem likely to be a "right to consult"—that is, a right to give one's input to a legislative decision-maker. The public inquiry is one means of addressing this gap. Inquiries act in a consultative fashion with governments, and, in turn, engage the public in this consultative activity.

The nature of a true consultative process is that the advice given in consultation be received with respect and serious attention, even if the decision-maker decides not to accept it. Policy inquiries generally operate like formalized consultative processes. Most of them adopt public hearing processes similar to those adopted in the investigative inquiries. As a consequence, policy inquiries present an intriguing combination of formal hearing-like processes with a form of legislative function. Commissions of inquiry have also adopted a number of creative methods for obtaining public input, including public opinion surveys, online consultations, and the holding of public meetings at different geographic locations. An interesting question is whether a government might in certain circumstances, including by raising expectations from past practice, create a legal duty on itself to hold a policy inquiry as a form of consultation.[9]

The success of policy inquiries is often measured by whether the recommendations made by inquiry commissioners are adopted in whole or part by governments. The quality of an inquiry's hearings and final report will undoubtedly contribute to its success in this sense. In general, however, the degree to which recommendations are accepted turns on many other factors of a political nature—timing, context, and the inclinations of the gov-

---

7 *Att. Gen. of Can. v. Inuit Tapirisat et al.*, [1980] 2 S.C.R. 735.

8 See *Reference re Canada Assistance Plan (B.C.)*, [1991] 2 S.C.R. 525, and *Mount Sinai Hospital Center v. Quebec (Minister of Health and Services)*, [2001] 1 S.C.R. 281, per Binnie J., concurring.

9 In Ontario, a series of judicial review challenges were brought with respect to the hearings and findings of the Ontario Hospital Restructuring Commission in the mid-1990s, including with respect to its alleged failure to adequately consult with interested members of the community. See, for example, *Pembroke Civic Hospital v. Ontario (Health Services Restructuring Commission)* (1997), 36 O.R. (3d) 41 (Div. Ct.). However, the commission was a delegated decision-maker, having the power to order hospital restructuring, and so these cases are not directly applicable to the public inquiry situation.

ernment of the day in making the recommended changes. Reports that issue from the Phase Two process of a combined investigative and policy inquiry have an advantage in this respect. The immediacy and specificity of the issues that led to their creation can create momentum for acceptance of their recommendations. Arguably, this was the case with Phase Two of the Commission of Inquiry into the Sponsorship Program and Advertising Activities, or Gomery inquiry, dealing with management of government public relations programs.[10]

Policy inquiries can have a significant impact on public discourse even without having their recommendations implemented. One way in which they contribute in this manner is through the generation of research. Policy commissions present an occasion for gathering the best available data and thinking on the subject at hand.[11] More important, policy inquiries may serve to mobilize public participation, or more accurately, cause groups to mobilize in order to take advantage of the opportunity presented by an inquiry. The best example of this phenomenon is the Royal Commission on the Status of Women in the early 1970s, around which formed the coalition of women's groups that became the National Action Committee on the Status of Women (NAC).[12]

C. The Investigative or Phase One Inquiry

The investigative inquiry serves to uncover the truth about events that have already happened. Cory J. commented on the value of the fact-finding function of the inquiry in *Phillips v. Nova Scotia*:

> One of the primary functions of public inquiries is fact-finding. They are often convened, in the wake of public shock, horror, disillusionment, or scepticism, in order to uncover "the truth." Inquiries are, like the judiciary, independent; unlike the judiciary, they are often endowed with wide-ranging investigative powers. In following their mandates, commissions of inquiry are, ideally, free from partisan loyalties and better able than Parliament or the legislatures to take a long-term view of the problem presented. Cynics decry public inquiries as a means used by the government to postpone acting in circumstances which often call for speedy action. Yet, these inquiries can and do fulfill an important function in Canadian society. In times of public questioning, stress and concern they provide the means for Canadians to be apprised of the conditions pertaining to a worrisome community problem and to be a part of the

10 The chair of the commission was Justice John Gomery of the Quebec Superior Court. The commission produced two reports: *Who Is Responsible? Fact Finding Report* (Ottawa: Queen's Printer, 2005) [*Who Is Responsible?*] and *Restoring Accountability* (Ottawa: Queen's Printer, 2006). Documents prepared for website access by the sponsorship inquiry are now available online at Library and Archives Canada: <http://epe.lac-bac.gc.ca/100/206/301/pco-bcp/commissions/sponsorship-ef/06-03-06/www.gomery.ca/en/default.htm>.

A lively anecdotal account of the commission's activity is given by François Perreault in *Inside Gomery*, trans. from French by Carl Angers (Toronto: Douglas & McIntyre, 2006). Perreault was the commission's media spokesperson, and Justice Gomery wrote the book's foreword.

11 See, for example, the "Resources/Research" link for the Romanow commission on the Health Canada website at <http://www.hc-sc.gc.ca/english/care/romanow/hcc0407.html>.

12 See Jill Vickers, Pauline Rankin & Christine Appelle, *Politics as if Women Mattered: A Political Analysis of the National Action Committee on the Status of Women* (Toronto: University of Toronto Press, 1993).

> recommendations that are aimed at resolving the problem. Both the status and high public respect for the commissioner and the open and public nature of the hearing help to restore public confidence not only in the institution or situation investigated but also in the process of government as a whole.[13]

In this regard, public inquiries share some qualities of other formal processes that have the investigation of historical incidents as their raison d'être. Such processes include coroner's inquests, fatality inquiries,[14] and ombudsman investigations.[15] These processes serve the human need to know what happened in the past, and how to prevent it from happening again in the future.

Unlike some investigative processes, the inquiry is not solely concerned with ascertaining historical facts. It is also concerned with bringing transparency to the investigation itself, and so with carrying the investigation out in public. Justice Samuel Grange, who headed the Ontario Commission of Inquiry into the unexplained deaths of children at Toronto's Hospital for Sick Children in the 1980s, related his surprise at discovering the significance of the dual nature of the inquiry in these terms:

> I remember once thinking egotistically that all the evidence, all the antics, had only one aim: to convince the commissioner who, after all, eventually wrote the report. But I soon discovered my error. They are not just inquiries; they are public inquiries. ... I realized that there was another purpose to the inquiry just as important as one man's solution to the mystery and that was to inform the public. Merely presenting the evidence in public, evidence which had hitherto been given only in private, served that purpose. The public has a special interest, a right to know and a right to form its opinion as it goes along.[16]

A dramatic example of this phenomenon occurred with the Gomery inquiry. The inquiry's exposure of financial improprieties in the distribution and management of federal government funds in Quebec in the post-1995 referendum period dominated headlines for weeks at a time. The televised hearings of the inquiry attracted massive audiences in Quebec, and had a profound effect on public opinion in the province.

The power of the inquiry as an instrument for accountability must be balanced against what is at stake for the individuals whose decisions, actions, and lives are at the heart of any particular investigation. This includes those, loosely described as "victims," who suffered harm as a consequence of government action or inaction. People like Maher Arar and the surviving family members of individuals who lost their lives in tragedies like the Air India bombing in 1985 and the Westray coal mine explosion in 1992 are usually in the

13 *Phillips v. Nova Scotia (Commission of Inquiry into the Westray Mine Tragedy)*, [1995] 2 S.C.R. 97 at para. 62 [*Phillips*].

14 See, for example, *Fatality Inquiries Act*, R.S.A. 2000, c. F-9.

15 See, for example, *Ombudsman Act*, R.S.B.C. 1996, c. 340. See discussion of the ombudsman complaint and investigation process as an alternative to judicial review in Cristie Ford, chapter 3. Note that ombudsman investigations generally take place in confidence, which encourages candour in government responses to ombudsman queries, but arguably limits the social accountability benefits of the process.

16 S.G.M. Grange, "How Should Lawyers and the Legal Profession Adapt?" in A. Paul Pross, Innis Christie & John A. Yogis, eds., *Commissions of Inquiry* (Toronto: Carswell, 1990) 154-55, and quoted by Cory J. in *Phillips*, *supra* note 13 at para. 63.

forefront of those calling for public inquiries to be held. They do so out of a desire to know what happened to themselves or their loved ones, with hopes that those responsible for the harm they suffered are identified and held accountable to public opinion and that it will not happen again.[17] However, victims also have much to lose. They know that their own actions will be placed under scrutiny, as will their physical and emotional injuries. They expose themselves to considerable pain in reliving the events of the tragedy in question.

The second group of individuals directly affected by a public inquiry are those people whose decisions and actions are the subject of the investigation. In the mid- to late 1990s, perceived conflict between the public interest in investigative inquiries and the interests of persons investigated caused a near-crisis in the world of Canadian public inquiries. Three inquiries into high-profile tragedies—the Krever commission into the Canadian blood system's use of tainted blood products, the Somalia inquiry into mistreatment of Somali prisoners by Canadian peacekeeping forces, and the Westray inquiry into a deadly coal mine explosion in Nova Scotia—became embroiled in lengthy litigation brought by witnesses and subjects of investigation. Delays caused by the many applications for judicial review in the course of the Somalia inquiry ultimately contributed to the controversial decision made by the government of Canada to terminate the inquiry before it could complete its evidence-gathering process. It seemed to many observers that public inquiries had become too expensive, time-consuming, and litigation-prone to be effective.[18]

The principal opinions in *Krever Commission* and *Phillips*, both written by Cory J., sent the message that the public interest value of investigative inquiries outweighs concerns about their potential harm to the individual interests of witnesses and subjects of investigation. Each case addressed one of the two main interests that have been viewed as most

---

17 Maher Arar identified his objectives for wanting a public inquiry in these terms:

> Three years ago, I made a very difficult decision to tell my painful, personal story to the Canadian public. I made it clear at that time that I wanted to achieve three objectives. The most important and first objective was to clear my name. Justice Dennis O'Connor did so in his report from the Commission of Inquiry examining my case when he stated that he was "able to say categorically that there is no evidence to indicate that Mr. Arar has committed any offence or that his activities constitute a threat to the security of Canada." My second objective was to hold those people responsible to account. The Canadian government has full access to both the public and confidential reports prepared by Justice O'Connor. Since the release of the report the Canadian public has consistently asked the government to take concrete actions to hold those Canadian officials responsible to account. But nothing has been done so far, and the public's trust in the government's ability to restore faith in our institutions has clearly been shaken. It is important to highlight that the inquiry report does not point the finger at any one person or institution alone. It is also crucial to focus on demanding concrete changes rather than focusing on asking some officials to resign from their jobs. This is because accountability is not about seeking revenge; it is about making our institutions better and a model for the rest of the world. Accountability goes to the heart of our democracy. It is a fundamental pillar that distinguishes our society from police states. My third objective was to make sure that this does not happen to any other Canadian.

Online: Maher Arar <http://www.maherarar.ca>.

18 This "crisis" of the 1990s was partly responsible for the 1999 Conference on Commissions of Inquiry at Queen's University, which produced the valuable collection of essays in Allan Manson & David Mullan, eds., *Commissions of Inquiry: Praise or Reappraise* (Toronto: Irwin Law, 2003) [*Commissions of Inquiry*].

threatened by public inquiries: (1) rights of persons who may face criminal charges, and (2) reputational interests.

1. Balancing the Rights of Individuals Facing Criminal Charges

In *Starr v. Houlden*,[19] the Supreme Court of Canada quashed an Ontario public inquiry called to inquire into the actions of an individual and a private corporation involved in political fund-raising activities. The Court confirmed that public inquiries are not permitted to make findings of civil or criminal liability against individuals. In the *Starr* case, the inquiry's terms of reference prohibited the commissioner from making a finding of criminal liability but authorized him to state whether the individual had acted in ways that described a breach of an offence set out in the *Criminal Code*. The majority of the Court ruled that this effectively turned the inquiry into a substitute police investigation and prosecution without the protections of those procedures, and that this was ultra vires the provincial government.

Compelled testimony and document production are significant investigative tools of inquiries, and give them a distinct investigative advantage in this respect over criminal trials. In the criminal setting, accused persons have the right under s. 11(c) of the Charter not to testify.[20] The danger from a civil liberties perspective is that governments may use inquiries and the power to compel witnesses to testify as a means to get around the right against self-incrimination. Indeed, the power of public inquiries to compel testimony from persons suspected of being responsible for an act or acts of wrongdoing has led to pointed questions about whether inquiries pose an improper threat to the rights of individuals.

The *Phillips* litigation addressed this issue in circumstances in which two mine managers summoned to testify before the provincial inquiry into the Westray mine disaster were also facing criminal prosecution with respect to the same events. The managers applied to quash the subpoenas issued by the inquiry, and for an order quashing or at least staying the inquiry proceedings until after the criminal charges had been resolved. They argued that it would breach their Charter rights against self-incrimination to be compelled to testify at the inquiry in advance of any criminal trial, and further that the publicity attending the hearings and findings of the inquiry would deny them a fair trial pursuant to s. 11(d) of the Charter.

By the time the matter was argued before the Supreme Court, the managers had opted to be tried by judge alone, without a jury. The criminal trial was in fact under way. In these circumstances, the majority of the Court lifted a stay of the inquiry imposed by the Nova Scotia Court of Appeal, but declined to rule on the issues of compellability or publicity, finding them to be moot. However, Cory, Iacobucci, and Major JJ. gave lengthy concurring reasons addressing the compellability and fair trial questions for the sake of future cases. Cory J. concluded that witnesses should be compellable at a public inquiry, irrespective of whether they may be subject to prosecution for the same acts being investigated by the inquiry, so long as the inquiry serves a legitimate public purpose (that is, it is not intended as a substitute form of criminal investigation). Cory J. found sufficient protection for witness-

---

19 [1990] 1 S.C.R. 1366 [*Starr*].

20 Part I of the *Constitution Act, 1982*, being Schedule B to the *Canada Act 1982* (U.K.), 1982, c. 11 [Charter].

es in Charter ss. 13 and 7. Section 13 prohibits the use of a person's testimony in subsequent criminal proceedings against him. Section 7 provides "derivative use immunity" as a matter of fundamental justice, barring the Crown from introducing evidence into a criminal trial that would not have been obtained "but for" the compelled testimony.

With respect to the risk that publicity attending inquiry proceedings might make a fair trial impossible, Cory J. said that governments must be allowed to take the risk of losing the power to prosecute an accused person, rather than have the judiciary adopt a blanket rule that would prevent public inquiries from going ahead where this risk exists. In short, the important role played by public inquiries justifies maintaining the general Canadian position of making witnesses compellable in all proceedings other than their own criminal trials, so long as their right to fair process can otherwise be preserved. Although the opinion of Cory J. represented a minority position, it remains the clearest statement of the situation in Canadian law.

2. Balancing the Reputational Interests of Individuals

Wayne MacKay and Moira McQueen note that assigning blame for things that go wrong is often what members of the public mean by accountability:

> An integral part of this growing demand for accountability is the concept of blaming. When things go wrong, people want to know whom to blame for the state of affairs. ... The focus on blame is often justified by the argument that no remedial action can be effectively taken until the causes of a disaster or problem have been completely unearthed. However, this explanation is contradicted by the fact that public and media attention seems to die down fairly quickly once names have been named. ... This may suggest that what the public wants, and what public inquiries aim to achieve, is the public shaming of those found to have acted inappropriately, rather than tangible punishment.[21]

For many individuals, public shame and harm to reputation are greater fears than are financial or other penalties, including imprisonment. While public inquiries cannot directly result in penal sanctions, damage to a person's reputation may result merely from having one's name mentioned or being called to testify before a public inquiry, let alone being found in an inquiry report to be responsible for misconduct. For politicians, the damage done to reputation by a public inquiry may result in a lost election, as was the case for the Liberal government of Prime Minister Paul Martin in 2006 following the sponsorship inquiry.

In the *Krever Commission* case, Commissioner Krever served notices at the conclusion of the formal hearing process on approximately 90 individuals and organizations pursuant to s. 13 of the federal *Inquiries Act*,[22] which reads:

> No report shall be made against any person until reasonable notice has been given to the person of the charge of misconduct alleged against him and the person has been allowed full opportunity to be heard in person or by counsel.

---

21 A. Wayne MacKay & Moira G. McQueen, "Public Inquiries and the Legality of Blaming: Truth, Justice and the Canadian Way," in *Commissions of Inquiry*, *supra* note 18, 249-92, at 250-51.

22 R.S.C. 1985, c. I-11.

The notices set out the possible findings of misconduct that might be made in the final report, and invited the recipients of the notices to make a response to the commission before it reached its conclusions. Dozens of the recipients of notices sought judicial review, objecting to matters such as the timing and detail of the notices. The Supreme Court confirmed in its *Krever Commission* ruling that the potential harm to reputation justified procedural protections at common law including adequate notice. This right could enhance or "fill out" rights set out in the statute. The Court did not find, however, that Justice Krever had failed to provide reasonable notice and a right to respond. Several of the complainants went beyond this administrative law position to argue a constitutional point: basing themselves on *Starr v. Houlden*,[23] they argued that inquiries lacked the power to make findings of misconduct against individuals, and that Commissioner Krever's authority to make findings of fact about contamination of Canada's blood supply did not extend to "naming names." The Court distinguished its ruling in *Starr* by saying that it applied in the particular circumstnces of an inquiry that was established solely to investigate specific acts of individuals. The Court also distinguished between an inquiry's making findings of "misconduct," which are permissible, and making findings of civil or criminal liability, which are not. The blood system inquiry was both a policy and investigative inquiry, and could only fulfill its broader policy purpose if it was allowed to make findings about individual responsibility for past decisions and actions. This might indeed harm the reputations of certain individuals, but while this consequence justified extending procedural fairness to the affected individuals, it could not stand in the way of the inquiry's work:

> These findings of fact may well indicate those individuals and organizations which were at fault. Obviously, reputations will be affected. But damaged reputations may be the price which must be paid to ensure that if a tragedy such as that presented to the Commission in this case can be prevented, it will be.[24]

Cory J. discouraged inquiry commissioners from stating their findings in terms that would convey the incorrect impression that they had found an individual to be civilly or criminally liable, but added that a commissioner "should not be expected to perform linguistic contortions to avoid language that might conceivably be interpreted as importing a legal finding."[25]

The constitutional status of reputation in Canadian law is worth brief attention here. In a case dealing with libellous statements made against a lawyer, the Supreme Court stated that an individual's professional reputation has almost equivalent value to the constitutional interest of free expression and deserves extensive legal protection.[26] However, in *Blencoe v. British Columbia (Human Rights Commission)*,[27] the Court ruled that an individual's reputation does not constitute a "security of person" or "liberty" interest for purposes of s. 7 of the *Charter of Rights and Freedoms*. This means that state actions that interfere with

23 *Starr*, *supra* note 19.

24 *Krever Commission*, *supra* note 1 at para. 39.

25 *Ibid.* at para. 52.

26 See *Hill v. Church of Scientology*, [1995] 2 S.C.R. 1130.

27 [2000] 2 S.C.R. 307 [*Blencoe*].

reputational interests likely do not need to meet the procedural standard of "fundamental justice."[28]

II. PUBLIC INQUIRIES AND ADMINISTRATIVE LAW PRINCIPLES

Public inquiries are exercises in delegated government authority. For this reason, inquiries operate within the context of administrative law. The practice of lawyers before commissions of inquiry is an administrative law practice. The same skills that serve counsel who appear before labour boards, broadcast regulators, environmental review boards, and other tribunals also serve those who represent parties and witnesses at inquiry hearings. The same understanding of the principles governing the exercise of delegated public power will inform that practice. The major principles of administrative law concern the lawful delegation of authority, issues of procedural fairness, and the substantive review of governmental decision-making. The discussion in part II tracks these principles by looking at the following three subjects:

A. The establishing of public inquiries, including their terms of reference, constitutional limits on the scope of an inquiry, and the role and independence of commissioners of inquiry.
B. Procedural fairness issues—that is, the rules governing the conduct of the investigative and hearing process.
C. Substantive review of the findings of a commission of inquiry.

A. Establishing an Inquiry

1. Delegation of Authority

The power to call a public inquiry into a matter of governance was long understood to be a prerogative power of the Crown. In Canada, Parliament and all 10 provinces have adopted inquiry statutes that formalize certain aspects of inquiry activity.[29] Royal commissions and public inquiries are now appointed pursuant to the statutory provisions, and clothed with the powers expressly set out by statute. In addition to general inquiry statutes, most jurisdictions make provision for inquiries to be conducted in specified areas of activity.[30] It is also not uncommon for regulatory statutes to authorize ministers of the Crown to appoint someone to investigate and report on a matter or an event, and to grant them the powers of a commissioner under the general inquiry statute.[31]

---

28 See detailed discussion of s. 7 of the Charter and administrative law in chapter 7 by Evan Fox-Decent.

29 *Public Inquiries Act*, R.S.A. 2000, c. P-39; *Inquiry Act*, R.S.B.C. 1996, c. 224; *Inquiries Act*, R.S.N.B. 1973, c. I.11; *Public Inquiries Act, 2006*, S.N.L. 2006, c. P-38.1; *Public Inquiries Act*, R.S.N.S. 1989, c. 372; *Public Inquiries Act*, R.S.O. 1990, c. P.41; *Public Inquiries Act*, R.S.P.E.I. 1988, c. P-31; *An Act Respecting Public Inquiry Commissions*, R.S.Q. c. C-37; *Public Inquiries Act*, R.S.S. 1978, c. P.38.

30 See, for example, in Ontario the *Hospitals and Charitable Institutions Inquiries Act*, R.S.O. 1990, c. H.15.

31 See, for example, the federal *Railway Safety Act*, R.S.C. 1985, c. 32 (4th Supp.), s. 40(2), with respect to investigations into railway accidents.

Inquiry statutes take the following general form. First, they set out the nature of matters that may be the subject of an inquiry. The federal *Inquiries Act* authorizes two kinds of inquiries, a Part I inquiry into "any matter connected with the good government of Canada or the conduct of any part of the public business thereof," and Part II departmental inquiries into "the state and management of the business, or any part of the business, of [a] department."[32] The Nova Scotia statute provides for a broader mandate covering "any public matter in relation to which the Legislature may make laws,"[33] under which the provincial government authorized the Westray inquiry into the operations of a private company (in addition to the regulation of mining activities).

Second, the statutes grant powers of compulsion to commissioners authorizing them to summons witness, place witnesses under oath and cite for contempt, as well as to order production of documentary evidence. These are important investigatory powers that can only be granted by statute. Third, the statutes extend procedural protections to persons being investigated or persons who may be subject to adverse findings of fact in an inquiry report. These statutory procedural rights should be viewed as minimum protections that do not exclude additional protections provided by the common law of administrative law.

Governments in Canada usually initiate public inquiries by an order-in-council issued under the authority of an inquiry statute. The order will set out the terms of reference of the inquiry, and name the individual commissioner or commissioners. Governments can appoint whomever they wish to conduct public inquiries, subject to objections going to an alleged apprehension of bias (see below under the heading "Independence and Bias"). With respect to investigative and combined inquiries, it is a common practice to appoint sitting or retired justices of a superior court. For this reason, we are used to thinking of the terms "judicial inquiries" and "public inquiries" as synonymous. Nevertheless, inquiries are executive government functions. McDonald J., who chaired the commission of inquiry into RCMP activities in the late 1970s, described the status of a sitting justice acting as an inquiry commissioner in these terms:

> The Commission is not a Court. It is not a branch of the judiciary. It fulfils Executive or administrative functions. ... Very often a Judge is the sole commissioner or chairman of a group of commissioners. One reason a Judge is chosen is that his livelihood is secure in that he can be removed from office only by joint address of the Houses of Parliament. This fact, which lies at the root of the cherished independence of the judiciary, increases the likelihood that the inquiry will not be influenced by considerations to which ordinary segments of the Executive are susceptible. Putting it another way, it ensures that the inquiry will be conducted at arm's length from the Executive.[34]

Dickson C.J. pointed out in *Re Residential Tenancies Act, 1979*[35] that because Canada does not operate on a strict separation of powers basis, members of the judiciary can carry

32 *Supra* note 22, s. 2.

33 *Public Inquiries Act*, R.S.N.S. 1989, c. 372, s. 2.

34 *Re Commission of Inquiry Concerning Certain Activities of the Royal Canadian Mounted Police* (1978), 94 D.L.R. (3d) 365 at 370.

35 [1981] 1 S.C.R. 714 at 728.

out executive functions. This does not happen in the United States, for instance, where it would be unconstitutional for a federal judge to conduct an inquiry into governmental affairs.

An episode in the Arar inquiry raises an interesting question concerning the scope of a commissioner's powers to delegate his or her duties to another person. In the course of Phase One of the inquiry, Justice O'Connor retained Professor Stephen Toope as an expert "fact-finder" to inquire into and report on what happened to Maher Arar in Jordan and Syria, and specifically whether he had been tortured. Following a review of documentary material and interviews with Mr. Arar, Professor Toope concluded that Mr. Arar had been tortured. Justice O'Connor incorporated this finding in his final report.[36] Section 11(2) of the *Inquiries Act* empowers commissioners to "authorize and depute any accountants, engineers, technical advisers or other experts … to inquire into any matter within the scope of the commission." While no party objected to the expert's role in this particular instance, an argument might nevertheless be available in future cases that the statute's language falls short of permitting subdelegation of the specific fact-finding duties originally granted to a commissioner.

2. Terms of Reference

Setting the mandate or terms of reference for an inquiry is an important first step in determining what the inquiry is intended to achieve or able to achieve. As noted, inquiry statutes give authority to Cabinet to set the terms of reference. In this way, governments can exercise a significant degree of control over how far-reaching an inquiry will be. Of course, the more politically sensitive the subject matter is, the more likely opposition politicians, the media, and members of the public will take an active role in monitoring and shaping the government's decision-making in this regard. In the case of alleged improper cash payments made by German businessman Karlheinz Schreiber to former Prime Minister Brian Mulroney, the Conservative government of Stephen Harper asked an outside individual, David Johnston, former president of McGill University, to give advice on whether an inquiry should be held and what its terms of reference should be. This move followed the previous government's decision to conduct a "pre-inquiry inquiry" into the Air India disaster before establishing the full public inquiry into that matter.[37] These actions represent attempts by governments to create the impression of an independent, arm's-length process for deciding on the structuring of an inquiry. Nevertheless, the ultimate decision rests with executive government.

The terms of reference set out in an order represent the "law of the inquiry," and have binding force on the inquiry commissioner. Nevertheless, it is useful to remember that terms of reference are a form of delegated legislation, or regulatory law. In the case of the Somalia inquiry in the mid-1990s, the Federal Court of Appeal took the position that, as

36 *Report of the Events Relating to Maher Arar: Analysis and Recommendations*, *supra* note 3 at 55-58.

37 See *Lessons to Be Learned: The Report of the Honourable Bob Rae, Independent Advisor to the Minister of Public Safety and Emergency Preparedness, on Outstanding Questions with Respect to the Bombing of Air India Flight 182* (Ottawa: Queen's Printer: November 2005), online: <http://www.publicsafety.gc.ca/prg/ns/airs/rep1-en.asp>.

with other regulatory law, an inquiry's terms of reference can be modified by the executive at its discretion (see discussion of independence under the heading "Independence and Bias," below). The commissioner of an inquiry has an important role in interpreting the terms of reference. The more brief or general the wording of the terms, the more interpretive work is necessary. Depending on how broadly the commissioner understands the scope of his or her inquiry, the more evidence will be relevant, the more questions will be probed, and the more witnesses will be called. This has significant implications for the cost and time needed for an inquiry, as well as for the nature of its findings.

A commission's interpretation of its terms of reference is subject to judicial review. This is a form of "substantive review" (see discussion under that heading, below). In early 2008, the Ontario Court of Appeal rendered judgment on a judicial review application brought by the government of Ontario and several police organizations to challenge a ruling by Commissioner Norman Glaude concerning the scope of the inquiry into the handling by various public officials of complaints of child sexual abuse in Cornwall, Ontario over a number of years.[38] The government of Ontario established the inquiry in 2005 with terms of reference reading in part:

> 2. The Commission shall inquire into and report on the institutional response of the justice system and other public institutions, including the interaction of that response with other public and community sectors, in relation to:
>
> (a) allegations of historical abuse of young people in the Cornwall area, including the policies and practices then in place to respond to such allegations, and
>
> (b) the creation and development of policies and practices that were designed to improve the response to allegations of abuse in order to make recommendations directed to the further improvement of the response in similar circumstances.[39]

Justice Glaude interpreted this mandate as extending to the question of how police in Cornwall had responded to complaints of sexual assault made by minors at any time prior to 2005. The applicants for judicial review argued that the terms of reference limited the inquiry to look into how officials had responded to allegations that a child sex abuse ring existed in Cornwall at a certain period, allegations that led to a series of criminal charges that had ultimately been stayed by the Crown. A majority of the Court of Appeal agreed with the applicants and set aside Justice Glaude's ruling on the scope of the inquiry. The majority did not apply the standard of review test for substantive matters set out in *Pushpanathan v. Canada*, but instead referred to the commissioner's interpretation of the inquiry's mandate as a "jurisdictional question." On that basis, the majority declined to grant deference to Commissioner Glaude's interpretation of the terms of reference, and found it both incorrect and unreasonable. It is worth noting that the Cornwall Public Inquiry had by the time of the court's ruling been widely criticized for going well over its original budget and timeframe. Should this decision be appealed, the Supreme Court of Canada would have the opportunity to consider the question of the appropriate standard of review to apply to commissioners' rulings on terms of reference. In the *Krever Commission* case, Cory J. indicated that leeway should be given to an inquiry when engaged in interpreting its own

38 *Ontario (Provincial Police) v. Cornwall (Public Inquiry)*, 2008 O.J. No. 153 (C.A.) (QL) (January 18, 2008).

39 *Supra* note 37 at para. 13.

mandate.[40] However, that reference might be read as applying more to issues of procedure than substance. Greater deference may be accorded to an inquiry's interpretation of its own mandate when it is engaged in policy-oriented rather than an investigative function.

3. Independence and Bias

To what degree are public inquiries independent? The credibility and effectiveness of an inquiry depends very much on the degree to which it is and appears to be independent of executive government. It may be true to say, however, that the independence of public inquiries is more a matter of personal integrity, enforced at the level of politics, than a matter of law. As noted, inquiries are created by executive government, and the executive sets the terms of reference, timeframes for reporting, and budgets, and appoints commissioners for an inquiry. While the constitutional principle of judicial independence protects the judicial careers of judges serving as commissioners of inquiry, it does not likely extend to an inquiry itself. In chapter 6, Laverne Jacobs discusses the state of the law going to whether administrative tribunals of an adjudicative nature attract the constitutional principle of independence. Inquiries, of course, are not adjudicative bodies.

The clearest challenge to date to the independence of a public inquiry occurred with the Somalia inquiry. The evidence given at the public hearings of this inquiry into the abuse of Somalis in Canadian military custody caused considerable embarrassment to military and civilian officials, and led to the resignation of the Chief of Defence Forces. When the commissioners asked for a third extension of the deadline for the hearings and final report, the government of Prime Minister Chrétien refused. This decision effectively terminated the inquiry. A legal challenge alleging that the decision exceeded Cabinet's authority and violated the rule of law succeeded at first instance, but was rejected by the Federal Court of Appeal. Marceau J. stated:

> It has often been suggested, expressly or impliedly, especially in the media but also elsewhere, that commissions of inquiry were meant to operate and act as fully independent adjudicative bodies, akin to the Judiciary and completely separate and apart from the Executive by whom they were created. This is a completely misleading suggestion, in my view. The idea of an investigative body, entirely autonomous, armed with all of the powers and authority necessary to uncover the truth and answerable to no one, may well be contemplated, if one is prepared to disregard the risks to individuals and the particularities of the Canadian context. But a commission under Part I of the *Inquiries Act* is simply not such a body. ... All this, however, does not alter, in any way, the basic truth that commissions of inquiry owe their existence to the

---

40 For example, Cory J. in *Krever Commission*, *supra* note 1, stated at para. 59:

> The question then is whether the Commissioner exceeded his jurisdiction in the notices delivered to the appellants; I think not. The potential findings of misconduct cover areas that were within the Commissioner's responsibility to investigate. The mandate of the Inquiry was extremely broad, requiring the Commissioner to review and report on "the events surrounding the contamination of the blood system in Canada in the early 1980s, by examining ... the organization and effectiveness of past and current systems designed to supply blood and blood products in Canada." This must encompass a review of the conduct and practices of the institutions and persons responsible for the blood system. The content of the notices does not indicate that the Commissioner investigated or contemplated reporting on areas that were outside his mandate.

> Executive. As agencies of the Executive, I do not see how they can operate otherwise than within the parameters established by the Governor in Council.[41]

The Federal Court of Appeal's decision in *Dixon* raises important questions concerning inquiry independence. It implies that an inquiry's terms of reference, which can be changed by Cabinet at will, do not provide a firm foundation for independence. However, fears that the experience with the Somalia inquiry would make it easier for governments to interfere in the operations of public inquiries have not borne fruit. Governments know that interfering with the mandate or the proceedings of a public inquiry in mid-course may not only undermine the inquiry's credibility, but also create a political firestorm. In this way, commissioners are not powerless in their relationship with the executive that created them.

The appointment of a particular individual as a commissioner of inquiry might be challenged on grounds of bias should that person have prior involvement with interested parties or a conflict of interest. To date, claims of bias on the part of a commissioner have tended more to arise in connection with their conduct during an inquiry. For example, Justice Gomery gave an interview in the course of the sponsorship inquiry in which he described former Prime Minister Chrétien's ordering of autographed golf balls as "small town cheap." Mr. Chrétien cited this and other statements of Justice Gomery, together with his choice as commission counsel of Bernard Roy, a partner and former adviser to Prime Minister Brian Mulroney, as creating a reasonable apprehension of bias on Justice Gomery's part. An application for disqualification was brought before Justice Gomery himself. Although he expressed regret at having given the media interview, the commissioner dismissed the motion, asserting that his mind was not made up on the facts and that the circumstances did not create an apprehension of bias on his part.[42]

During the Somalia inquiry, Commissioner Mr. Justice Gilles Letourneau was reported to have made private comments about a witness before the inquiry to the effect that "Briga-

---

41 *Dixon v. Canada (Governor in Council)*, [1997] 3 F.C. 169; leave to appeal to SCC dismissed, January 8, 1998 at para. 13. See critical comment on the Federal Court of Appeal decision by Inquiry Commissioner Peter Desbarats, "The Independence of Public Inquiries: Dixon v. Canada" (1997) 36 Alta. L. Rev. 252. It might be noted that concerns in the United States over the role of independent prosecutors not subject to executive or congressional supervision became a major issue in the year following the Somalia inquiry as a result of prosecutor Kenneth Starr's investigation into the private life of President Bill Clinton. See Cass Sunstein, "Unchecked and Unbalanced: Why the Independent Counsel Act Must Go" (2002) 38 The American Prospect, online: <http://www.prospect.org/cs/articles?article=unchecked_and_unbalanced>.

42 In his ruling, Justice Gomery stated:

> I realize now, with the benefit of hindsight, that it was an error for me to agree to be interviewed by the media before Christmas. I also recognize that some of the statements made by me during those interviews were ill-advised and inappropriate. My inexperience in handling the media is obvious to everyone, and has served to detract attention from the real objective of the Inquiry, which is to get at the truth of the matters which were the subject of Chapters 3 and 4 of the Report of the Auditor General. I very much regret this distraction.

(February 1, 2005, online: <http://epe.lac-bac.gc.ca/100/206/301/pco-bcp/commissions/sponsorship-ef/06-02-10/www.gomery.ca/en/rulingonmotionforrecusal/default.htm>.)

Mr. Chrétien subsequently dropped a judicial review application to Federal Court seeking to challenge this ruling. The episode led to a memorable appearance by the former prime minister at the inquiry in which he produced a series of autographed golf balls given to him by various heads of states, asking each time whether this would indicate those leaders were "small town cheap."

dier General Beno had not given straight answers and perhaps Beno had been trying to deceive." On learning of these remarks, Beno sought to have Justice Letourneau disqualified for having created a reasonable apprehension of bias. The Federal Court of Appeal (from which bench Justice Letourneau had been appointed to the inquiry) rejected Beno's application.[43] In doing so, the court distinguished between a public inquiry and a trial process for purposes of the bias test. The fact that an inquiry is not an adjudicative process and uses more flexible rules of evidence than does a trial indicates, the court said, that a more relaxed bias standard is appropriate. At the same time, the court rejected the idea of going so far as to apply the "closed mind" test to inquiries:

> Depending on its nature, mandate and function, the Somalia Inquiry must be situated along the *Newfoundland Telephone* spectrum somewhere between its legislative and adjudicative extremes. Because of the significant differences between this Inquiry and a civil or criminal proceeding, the adjudicative extreme would be inappropriate in this case. On the other hand, in view of the serious consequences that the report of a commission may have for those who have been served with a section 13 notice, the permissive "closed mind" standard at the legislative extreme would also be inappropriate. We are of the opinion that the Commissioners of the Somalia Inquiry must perform their duties in a way which, having regard to the special nature of their functions, does not give rise to a reasonable apprehension of bias.[44]

4. Constitutional Issues

Delegated authority in Canada is subject to the constraints and obligations imposed by the constitution. A government's decision to appoint an inquiry and its drafting of the inquiry's terms of reference may thus be open to constitutional challenge. Provincially appointed inquiries have been particularly subject to challenge on federalism grounds, especially with respect to whether they invade the federal jurisdiction over criminal law.

In the 1970s, a series of cases went to the Supreme Court of Canada addressing the jurisdiction of provinces to inquire into criminal activities, and into activities of the RCMP as a federally regulated institution. In *Di Iorio v. Warden of Montreal City Jail*,[45] the Court permitted a Quebec inquiry into organized crime to proceed as falling within provincial jurisdiction over "the administration of justice" in s. 92(14) of the *Constitution Act, 1867*. A year later, in *Keable v. Canada (Attorney General)*,[46] the Court ruled that while a provincial inquiry may investigate wrongdoing by individual police officers, it may not examine the policies and management of the RCMP.

The division of powers has played a role in limiting the authority of provinces to establish public inquiries directed at establishing individual responsibility for acts of a potentially criminal nature. In *Starr v. Houlden*,[47] the Supreme Court found that the "pith and

43 *Beno v. Canada (Commissioner and Chairperson, Commission of Inquiry into the Deployment of Canadian Forces to Somalia) (C.A.)*, [1997] 2 F.C. 527 (F.C.A.).

44 *Ibid.* at para. 26.

45 [1978] 1 S.C.R. 152.

46 [1979] 1 S.C.R. 218.

47 *Starr*, *supra* note 19.

substance" of an Ontario inquiry was alleged criminal wrongdoing by individuals, and that this infringed on the federal government's criminal law power. The Court has since narrowed the holding in *Starr*. In *Consortium Developments (Clearwater Inc.) v. City of Sarnia*,[48] the Court rejected an application by a land developer to quash a judicial inquiry initiated by Sarnia City Council into certain land transactions after the police had closed a criminal investigation file on the matter. The Court found that the inquiry was properly directed at the "good government" of the municipality. Even should it turn up misconduct of a possibly criminal nature, the inquiry lacked the power to make criminal findings. Binnie J. stated that the commissioner's duty to comply with common-law requirements of the duty of fairness were sufficient to protect the interests of the developer. The facts of *Starr*—which included quoting provisions of the *Criminal Code* in that inquiry's terms of reference—were described as unusual.

Public inquiries are likely bound by the *Charter of Rights and Freedoms* with respect to all significant activities. The Charter would certainly apply to an inquiry's exercise of its coercive statutory powers, such as the powers to subpoena witnesses or documents. There may be an issue as to whether an inquiry, given its non-adjudicative nature, is subject to the Charter with respect to its fact-finding or recommendation-making functions. In *Blencoe v. British Columbia*,[49] the Supreme Court held that the Charter applies to human rights tribunals as governmental actors. It would seem likely that an inquiry would be viewed similarly, on the basis of the test set out in *Eldridge v. British Columbia*,[50] for entities implementing important government programs or policies. On the issue of the application of the Charter to administrative tribunals and executive agencies, see chapter 7 by Evan Fox-Decent.

B. Procedural Justice Issues

The status of investigative processes in administrative law is ambiguous. Investigations directed at ascertaining evidence, but not at the determination of legal rights and obligations, are not always subject to common-law rules of fair process. In *Knight v. Indian Head School Division*,[51] L'Heureux-Dubé J. stated that the question of whether a function is final or merely preliminary in nature is a threshold question with respect to the duty of fairness. The most typical example of a "preliminary" function is the investigative stage of a decision-making process. That is, the investigation may be able to be conducted free of procedural obligations, so long as any final determination of legal rights does not occur until the evidence is tested in accord with due process.

There is little doubt, however, that investigative inquiries are subject to the duty of fairness in administrative law. This follows from three things. First, inquiry statutes authorize inquiries to compel the testimony of witnesses. This extraordinary power exposes witnesses to legal consequences, as well as denying them the right to remain silent in the face of public scrutiny and possible future prosecution. The decision to subpoena a witness is itself a

48 [1998] 3 S.C.R. 3.

49 *Blencoe*, *supra* note 27.

50 *Eldridge v. British Columbia (Medical Services Commission)*, [1997] 3 S.C.R. 624.

51 [1990] 1 S.C.R. 653.

"final" decision that should give rise to extensive protections at common law. Second, the findings of fact of an inquiry carry with them significant consequences. Inquiry findings may be the closest our society comes to "received truth." Reputations can be made or broken as a result of these findings. Third, public inquiries generally operate like judicial hearings. It is neither difficult nor inappropriate for inquiries to be required to meet standards of fair process.

The particular requirements of fair process in any particular case depend on contextual factors.[52] Courts have frequently held that the investigative nature of public inquiries and the fact that they do not have decision-making power mean that they are subject to relaxed procedural standards and rules of evidence. The question each time is whether this is appropriate in light of the individual interests at stake in a particular inquiry.

The following discussion addresses several issues of fair process that arise frequently in the course of public inquiries.

1. Inquisitorial Process

Public inquiries employ an inquisitorial rather than an adversarial approach to adducing evidence. This means that the inquiry commissioners decide what evidence to call rather than any individual parties. The inquiry may receive and act on the advice of a witness or subject of investigation as to what other evidence and other witnesses to call, but is unlikely to cede its authority. A commissioner is charged with the responsibility of conducting a thorough investigation, but must do so in an impartial and non-prosecutorial fashion. Questions as to how to accomplish this task characterize many of the individual issues of fair process that arise in the course of an inquiry's proceedings. These issues will be more acute for inquiries investigating specific acts of alleged misconduct.

Public inquiries will generally produce procedural rules to govern the hearing process at the outset of the inquiry, dealing with matters of calling witnesses and examination and cross-examination, among others. Justice O'Connor established rules for the Arar inquiry that addressed these issues in the following way:

> 35. In the ordinary course Commission counsel will call and question witnesses who testify at the Inquiry. Counsel for a party may apply to the Commissioner to lead a particular witness' evidence in-chief. If counsel is granted the right to do so, examination shall be confined to the normal rules governing the examination of one's own witness in court proceedings, unless otherwise directed by the Commissioner.
>
> 36. Commission counsel have a discretion to refuse to call or present evidence.
>
> (a) Commission counsel will lead the evidence from the witness. Except as otherwise directed by the Commissioner, Commission counsel are entitled to ask both leading and non-leading questions;
>
> (b) Parties will then have an opportunity to cross-examine the witness to the extent of their interest. The order of cross-examination will be determined by the parties and, if they are unable to reach agreement, by the Commissioner;

52 See *Baker v. Canada (Minister of Citizenship and Immigration)*, [1999] 2 S.C.R. 817, and generally the discussion in chapter 5 by Grant Huscroft.

(c) After cross-examinations, counsel for a witness may then examine the witness. Except as otherwise directed by the Commissioner, counsel for the witness is entitled to ask both leading and non-leading questions;

(d) Commission counsel will have the right to re-examine last.[53]

What is the status in law of an inquiry's published rules? In the *Phillips* case, Cory J. made the general statement that "the nature and the purpose of public inquiries require courts to give a generous interpretation to a commissioner's powers to control their own proceedings."[54]

Although the rules of an inquiry provide useful guidance to all parties and witnesses about how the hearings will unfold, the binding force of an inquiry's rules is questionable. On the one hand, disobedience of the rules might give rise to an exercise by a commissioner of his or her statutory contempt power. On the other, the rules should not be viewed as the last word on procedure before the inquiry. In the absence of an explicit statutory power to make procedural regulations, the rules adopted by an inquiry should be subject to judicial review for compliance with the principles of procedural fairness, either as a general matter or in specific applications.

2. Standing

Standing is the legal concept that defines who has a sufficient interest in proceedings to justify having a participant role in the process. In ordinary legal proceedings, standing is limited to those persons who have a direct interest in the outcome. Standing tends to be an "all or nothing" proposition—a person is either a full participant with responsibility for carrying one side of the legal dispute, or not a participant at all. For more on the issue of standing, see chapter 15 by Lorne Sossin and chapter 5 by Grant Huscroft.

The issue of standing in public inquiries is more nuanced. Who are the parties to a public inquiry? Inquiries are generally called in the public interest, and with the intention that much of the population has an interest in the outcome. To the extent that an inquiry concerns wrongdoing, individuals who may be found responsible likely have interests at stake that support their right to participate in some or all of the inquiry's proceedings. The same may be true of "victims" of the wrongdoing. In addition, other organizations such as non-profit societies, who do not have a personal stake in the proceedings but have a long-standing interest and expertise in the area of public policy under scrutiny, may wish to participate in the hearings. Standing can be granted in degrees, both in terms of the scope of participation (that is, whether the person gets to call witnesses, to question and cross-examine witnesses, etc.), and in terms of duration (that is, whether the person has these rights only for some part of the inquiry's hearings, but not for others).

In the Arar inquiry, Justice O'Connor adopted the following rules on standing, including a "substantial and direct interest" test for full party standing.

12. Commission counsel, who will assist the Commissioner to ensure the orderly conduct of the Factual Inquiry, have standing throughout the Factual Inquiry. Commission counsel

53 *Supra* note 6, see "Rules of Procedure."

54 *Phillips*, *supra* note 13 at para. 175.

> have the primary responsibility for representing the public interest at the Factual Inquiry, including the responsibility to ensure that all matters that bear upon the public interest are brought to the Commissioner's attention.
>
> 13. The Commissioner will grant party standing to all persons who satisfy the Commissioner that they have a substantial and direct interest in the subject-matter of the Factual Inquiry. Persons with party standing are referred to as parties in these Rules.
>
> 14. The Commissioner may grant intervenor standing to persons who satisfy the Commissioner that they have a genuine concern about issues raised by the Factual Inquiry mandate and have a particular perspective or expertise which may assist the Commissioner. Persons with intervenor standing are referred to as intervenors in these Rules.[55]

After receiving submissions from persons wishing standing at the inquiry, Justice O'Connor granted full party standing to Maher Arar and to the Attorney General of Canada, and standing "so far as the evidence affects" their interests to the Ontario Provincial Police, the Ottawa Police Service, and individual RCMP officers. He granted intervener standing to a coalition of non-profit organizations, including the Canadian Council on American-Islamic Relations, the Canadian Arab Federation, and Amnesty International.

3. Representation by Counsel and Role of Commission Counsel

It is generally accepted that parties to public inquiries may be represented by counsel in the proceedings. Section 12 of the federal *Inquiries Act* makes this a statutory right with respect to persons who are the subject of an investigation:

> The commissioners may allow any person whose conduct is being investigated under this Act, and shall allow any person against whom any charge is made in the course of an investigation, to be represented by counsel.

A more difficult question is whether witnesses called to testify at an inquiry are entitled to be represented by counsel, and what role counsel may play. Subject to the requirements of fair process, this is a matter for commissioners to decide depending on the nature of the inquiry and of the evidence being sought. In the Arar inquiry, witnesses were permitted to have their own counsel present during pre-hearing interviews (rule 27) and at the hearing if their interests would not be adequately represented by counsel for a party (rule 32). Counsel for witnesses were permitted to ask questions of their clients following examination in chief by commission counsel and cross-examination by counsel for parties (rule 37(c)).

Representation at an inquiry can be expensive given the period of time and amount of documentary material that may be involved. This is a serious barrier to access and participation. The Supreme Court of Canada has recognized a limited right to state-funded legal counsel in matters that implicate the rights of life, liberty, or security of the person protected by s. 7 of the Charter. Given the decision in *Blencoe*, however, the subject of an inquiry likely cannot successfully argue that she has a constitutional right to funded counsel.[56] The

---

55 *Supra* note 6, see "Rules of Procedure."

56 In *British Columbia (A.G.) v. Christie*, [2007] 1 S.C.R. 873, a challenge to the imposition of a provincial tax on legal services, the Supreme Court rejected the argument that the unwritten constitutional principle of the rule of law could serve as a basis for a right to state funding of legal counsel.

question of funding for counsel is therefore a decision for government to make on an inquiry-by-inquiry basis. In some instances, governments have provided funding for counsel for parties in the budget of an inquiry and delegated authority to distribute the funds to commissioners. More commonly, inquiry commissioners are asked by government to make recommendations concerning who should receive funding for counsel. This was the case in the Arar inquiry (rules 19 to 21). Should a recommendation be refused, the inquiry commissioner would be placed in the position of deciding whether it would be fair to continue the proceedings.

Counsel for a commission of inquiry has a unique role. Although commission counsel takes the lead in adducing evidence before the inquiry and does so in the public interest, she does not assume the role of a prosecutor in the proceeding. Rather, counsel works for and is selected by the commissioner. Justice O'Connor, who conducted the Walkerton and Arar inquiries, has described commission counsel as the "alter ego" of the commissioner. Justice O'Connor in fact chose the same lawyer, Paul Cavaluzzo, to act as commission counsel in both inquiries, having clearly established a good working relationship in the Walkerton proceedings. Counsel's responsibilities include advising the commission on matters of legal procedure, preparing the evidence in advance of hearing days, leading most witnesses through their evidence in chief, and increasingly, being a spokesperson for the inquiry and its chairperson.[57] Counsel must perform these functions in an impartial fashion that does not create an impression that the proceedings are adversarial. In the *Krever Commission* case, the Canadian Red Cross sought a ruling that commission counsel could not participate in drafting the final report because counsel had viewed confidential submissions not introduced into evidence at the inquiry. The Supreme Court of Canada found this objection premature, but agreed that in some circumstances the multiple roles of counsel could lead to an order for disqualification.[58]

4. Notice and Opportunity to Respond

The federal *Inquiry Act* requires that any person about whom a finding of misconduct may be made in a final report must be notified in advance, and given an opportunity to respond. Section 13 reads:

> No report shall be made against any person until reasonable notice has been given to the person of the charge of misconduct alleged against him and the person has been allowed full opportunity to be heard in person or by counsel.

---

57 Justice O'Connor enumerates six aspects to commission counsel's role. In addition to those just listed, he mentions maintaining communication with parties to the inquiry, and participating in drafting the inquiry report. Justice Dennis O'Connor, "The Role of Commission Counsel in Public Inquiries" (2003) 22 Advocates' Soc. J. 17.

58 Cory J. wrote: "This argument too is premature, because there is no indication that the Commissioner intends to rely upon his counsel to draft the final report. … However, in the unlikely event that the submissions also included material that was not disclosed to the parties, there could well be valid cause for concern. … If the submissions did contain new, undisclosed and untested evidence, the Commissioner should not seek advice regarding the report from counsel who received the confidential submissions" (*Krever Commission*, *supra* note 1 at para. 72).

Section 13 is a statutory embodiment of the minimal fairness duty to give notice and an opportunity to be heard to persons who may be adversely affected by an inquiry's findings. However, the provision is unclear with respect to what constitutes a "charge of misconduct," when in the process such notice should be given, and whether a "full opportunity to be heard" includes the calling of further evidence or only the right to make submissions after the evidence is in. In *Krever Commission*, several parties receiving s. 13 notices argued that the delivery of notices at the conclusion of the hearing process denied them the opportunity to make full answer and defence. Cory J. disagreed. He pointed out that the statute did not specify any particular period of notice, and that while notices

> should be given as soon as it is feasible, it is unreasonable to insist that the notices of misconduct must always be given early. There will be some inquiries where the Commissioner cannot know what the findings may be until the end or very late in the process. So long as adequate time is given to the recipients of the notices to allow them to call the evidence and make the submissions they deem necessary, the late delivery of notices will not constitute unfair procedure.[59]

5. Disclosure

We earlier discussed the compellability of witnesses who face potential criminal prosecution. Closely related to this is the issue of the scope of discovery or disclosure powers of a public inquiry. The very purpose of investigative inquiries would seem to support broad powers of discovery. These powers may, however, conflict with competing interests in confidentiality and non-disclosure. Common arguments of this nature include national security, solicitor–client privilege, rights of confidentiality to counselling records, and privacy interests.

In general, public inquiries benefit from the grant of statutory power to compel disclosure. It is up to inquiry commissioners to decide, in each case, what evidence they believe is necessary and relevant to their investigation. A commissioner could always decide not to pursue evidence by means of compulsory power. Where a commissioner issues a subpoena, a recipient who objects to production would need to make one of the following arguments: (1) the demand for disclosure or its statutory authorization is unconstitutional; (2) the evidence goes to a matter not within the terms of reference of the inquiry; (3) the statutory authorization is not broad enough to include the particular demand for disclosure in the face of a competing interest. In other words, in light of the statutory power to compel testimony or disclosure, it will rarely be sufficient to argue that the demand is unfair at common law.

In considering the issue of disclosure, it is important to differentiate between disclosure to the inquiry, and disclosure by the inquiry to the public. The latter is more a question of what can or must be done in public rather than in closed sessions or *in camera*, and is discussed in the section "Conducting Hearings in Public," below. The issue of disclosure per se goes to the power of the inquiry to obtain evidence, irrespective of claims of confidentiality or privilege.

With respect to the handling of national security information, Craig Forcese discusses in chapter 11 how Canadian statutes have increasingly placed responsibility in the hands of

59 *Ibid.* at para. 69.

judges to view information that the federal government claims is subject to a national security privilege, to decide whether in fact it is, and then to decide what part of it is disclosable in legal proceedings. That has been the general approach taken in inquiries looking at national security matters. In the Air India inquiry, commissioner John Major, a former justice of the Supreme Court of Canada, went public with his concerns that the inquiry would not be able to accomplish its mandate if the government did not change its position with respect to withholding evidence from the inquiry on national security grounds.

In *McKeigan v. Hickman*,[60] the Supreme Court dealt with an issue of claimed judicial immunity from disclosure. A Nova Scotia public inquiry held into the wrongful murder conviction of Donald Marshall sought to compel testimony and notes concerning the deliberations of the Nova Scotia Court of Appeal at the time when that court had conducted a review of Marshall's conviction. The justices opposed this demand. A majority of the Supreme Court of Canada concluded that as a matter of judicial independence, a constitutional principle, judges cannot be summoned to answer questions concerning their deliberations. Several of the justices stated that the general language of the province's *Public Inquiries Act* should be read to accord with the power of superior court judges to issue subpoenas and order discovery in civil proceedings, and that the latter power has long been understood to be subject to judicial immunity.

Solicitor–client privilege seems likely to be treated similarly. In the absence of express statutory authority, inquiries would not be able to compel disclosure of communications falling within the privilege. Other privileges, such as doctor–patient and counsellor–client privileges, have generally been viewed as having lesser status. Bryan Schwartz has argued that inquiry statutes should exclude access to counselling records from the purview of inquiries' powers of disclosure.[61]

6. Conducting Hearings in Public

As noted, carrying the inquiry process out in public is one way in which the inquiry achieves its social purposes. One would expect inquiry hearings to be held in public and able to be reported in the media unless there were strong counterbalancing factors militating in favour of *in camera* proceedings.

The Arar inquiry dealt with matters of national security, and it was understood from the outset that parts of the evidence would be received in closed sessions. The terms of reference directed the commissioner to act with discretion in protecting the confidentiality of national security information disclosed to him by government agencies, but still left it to him to rule on those questions.[62] Justice O'Connor addressed the nature of his mandate in ruling on one of several motions dealing with a request for confidentiality:

---

60 [1989] 2 S.C.R. 796.

61 Bryan Schwartz, "Public Inquiries" (1997) 40 Can. Pub. Adm. 72-85.

62 The Arar inquiry's terms of reference (*supra* note 6) stated:

> (k) the Commissioner be directed, in conducting the inquiry, to take all steps necessary to prevent disclosure of information that, if it were disclosed to the public, would, in the opinion of the Commissioner, be injurious to international relations, national defence or national security and, where applicable, to conduct the proceedings in accordance with the following procedures, namely,

> The government chose to call a public inquiry, not a private investigation. Implicit in the Terms of Reference is a direction that I maximize the disclosure of information to the public, not just in my report, but during the course of the hearings. The reason for that direction is consistent with what are now broadly accepted as two of the main purposes of public inquiries: to hear the evidence relating to the events in public so that the public can be informed directly about those events, and to provide those who are affected by the events an opportunity to participate in the inquiry process.[63]

The need to receive evidence in secrecy created a serious challenge to the inquiry's credibility, particularly in its early phases when it "disappeared" from public view for weeks and months at a time. Justice O'Connor dealt with this challenge in several ways. First, he provided a public summary of evidence received in closed sessions in September 2004. He granted access to certain confidential material to Mr. Arar for the purpose of preparing his evidence. While Justice O'Connor maintained the confidentiality of evidence and findings, which he concluded were properly protected for national security reasons, he largely succeeded in convincing Mr. Arar, the media, and other observers that the most important facts concerning the events in question had been opened to public scrutiny.

Investigative inquiries may be intended to bring little-known or unknown facts into public light, but they are not adversarial proceedings, and should rarely need to rely on surprise. It is common practice now for commission counsel to interview prospective witnesses in advance of their public testimony, so that counsel for all sides and witnesses will have a good idea what will be covered and said in open session. Whether a prospective witness is entitled to be interviewed in advance or to receive notice of questions to be asked in open session would be a matter of what fairness required in the circumstances. Had an inquiry commissioner published a rule to this effect, as did Justice O'Connor in the Arar inquiry, this would likely create a legitimate expectation of such a process for each witness.

C. Substantive Review

Substantive justice issues in administrative law deal with the substance or merits of delegated decision-making. Prior to 1998, the central preoccupation of substantive review had been to determine when an issue being decided was jurisdictional or within jurisdiction of the tribunal in question. In its *Pushpanathan*[64] decision in 1998 the Supreme Court indicated that this should no longer be the starting place for substantive review. The starting place for substantive analysis, the Court said, is to determine the appropriate standard of review to be applied to any particular decision.[65]

> (i) on the request of the Attorney General of Canada, the Commissioner shall receive information in camera and in the absence of any party and their counsel if, in the opinion of the Commissioner, the disclosure of that information would be injurious to international relations, national defence or national security.

63 Ruling Concerning RCMP Testimony, May 12, 2005, online: *supra* note 6, under "Rulings."

64 *Pushpanathan v. Canada (Minister of Citizenship and Immigration)*, [1998] 1 S.C.R. 1222.

65 See *Dixon v. Canada (Commission of Inquiry into the Deployment of Canadian Forces to Somalia)* (1997), 149 D.L.R. (4th) 269 (F.C.A.).

An interesting question about substantive review is whether and how a person who is unhappy with the ultimate findings of fact of an inquiry may be able to challenge them in judicial review. This issue arose before by Reed J. of the Federal Court Trial Division in *Morneault v. Canada*,[66] another case arising from the Somalia inquiry. Lieutenant-Colonel Paul Morneault had been involved in troop training in Canada prior to the troops' deployment to Somalia. The pre-deployment phase ended up being the only one of three time periods in the Somalia mission concerning which the commission of inquiry was able to complete its investigation and report, given the termination of the inquiry by the Chrétien government. In its report on this phase, the commissioners made findings of misconduct against Morneault with respect to the inadequacy of the training program. Lieutenant-Colonel Morneault applied to Federal Court to have these findings quashed. Reed J. had first to decide whether the finding of misconduct constituted a reviewable "decision" under s. 2(1) of the *Federal Courts Act*.[67] The respondent argued that mere findings of fact without legal consequences did not constitute a decision. Reed J. disagreed, ruling that the consequences of such findings for an individual's reputation made them a "decision," and subject to judicial review. Next, the court needed to identify the appropriate standard of review for this issue of fact determination. Reed J. concluded that the standard should be patent unreasonableness.[68] Finally, the court ruled that the commissioners had misconstrued some of the evidence and drawn improper inferences from other evidence, and that their findings of misconduct against Lieutenant-Colonel Morneault were indeed patently unreasonable. With respect to remedy, Reed J. said and ordered the following:

> What then is the appropriate disposition of his application? The Report has had wide public dissemination. The Commission no longer exists. I have concluded that the appropriate remedy is a declaration by the Court that the Commission's findings of individual misconduct against the applicant set out in chapter 35 of its Report are invalid. Also, as noted, he is entitled to a declaration that the record does not support a conclusion that the two general statements of condemnation found in the Report, identified above, apply to him. Declarations of invalidity will issue accordingly.[69]

In *Stevens v. Canada*,[70] former Conservative Cabinet minister Sinclair Stevens applied to quash the report of Commissioner William Parker, who had led an inquiry into the activities of Stevens while in government. Stevens argued that the commissioner had exceeded the jurisdiction given him by the inquiry's terms of reference. The terms directed that an inquiry and report be made into

> whether the Honourable Sinclair M. Stevens was in real or apparent conflict of interest as defined by the Conflict of Interest and Post Employment Code for Public Office Holders and the letter from the Prime Minister [Brian Mulroney] … of September 5, 1985.

---

66 [1998] F.C.J. No. 501 (QL) [*Morneault*].

67 R.S.C. 1985, c. F-7.

68 *Morneault*, *supra* note 66 at para. 59.

69 *Ibid.* at para. 114.

70 [2004] F.C. No. 2116 (O'Keefe J., December 15, 2004) (QL).

O'Keefe J. of the Federal Court agreed with Stevens, and set aside the inquiry report, which had found Stevens to have placed himself in a conflict of interest situation on six occasions during his time in Cabinet. He did so on the basis that the commissioner exceeded his authority by developing his own definition and then applied it to Stevens's actions, having found that the code of ethics in question did not in fact define "conflict of interest." O'Keefe J. did not consider the commissioner's understanding of his mandate in terms of the three standards of review known to administrative law. He rejected an argument that the court should not adopt an "overly legalistic" or strict approach to reviewing the inquiry's interpretation of its terms of reference, noting the "somewhat unusual" nature of an inquiry directed at the alleged wrongdoing of a single individual.

III. PUBLIC INQUIRIES AND PUBLIC BENEFIT

In his political memoir *My Years as Prime Minister*,[71] former Prime Minister Chrétien engages in a pointed criticism of public inquiries. He defends his decision to shut down the Somalia inquiry in mid-course on the ground that it had become overly long, expensive, and of benefit only to the many lawyers involved. After noting that "I never appointed another commission of inquiry," Mr. Chrétien writes:

> For the opposition parties, calling for a public inquiry is usually an easy way to dig up dirt or keep a hot issue on the front burner after they've exhausted their own supply of facts and questions. For the government, giving in to the calls is often a mechanism to do nothing, to dodge responsibility, or to postpone a controversial decision until after the next election. Very few of these inquiries in my experience have ever been of much use, and those few were valuable only because they didn't turn into television soap operas. … But it is in the nature of public inquiries to get turned into show trials, kangaroo courts and political entertainment. The rules of evidence don't have to be respected as they are in a court. There's not the same right of due process or even the same process to protect the innocent during the investigation into a possible wrongdoing. Scores of reputations are shattered for no good cause.[72]

Of course, this comment was made in the shadow of the Sponsorship Inquiry report of Justice Gomery that found Mr. Chrétien and his chief of staff, Jean Pelletier, responsible for the mismanagement of the sponsorship program,[73] a substantive finding that Mr. Chrétien continues to challenge in judicial proceedings. Nevertheless, Mr. Chrétien's criticism is a good sharp summary of the major concerns about inquiries.

Have Canadian inquiries become over-judicialized and too expensive? Michael Trebilcock and Wendy Austin also asked this question following the Krever inquiry into Canada's blood system in the mid-1990s. The authors noted that the inquiry cost $17.5 million, when it had originally been budgeted to cost $2.5 million, took over three years to complete, and involved the services of over 50 lawyers acting for the parties granted different forms of standing. The authors asked whether the benefits of having lawyers and judges attack

---

71 Jean Chrétien, *My Years as Prime Minister* (Toronto: A.A. Knopf Canada, 2007).

72 *Ibid.* at 187-88.

73 See *Who Is Responsible?*, supra note 10, s. 16.1, "The Responsibility of Messrs. Chretien and Pelletier," 425-29.

inquiry issues through the means of fact-finding commonly used in courts outweigh the costs and delays this entailed. Why not have experts in the field in which an inquiry takes place conduct the inquiry and evaluate the information that the inquiry collects?

Canadian public inquiries have indeed become highly lawyered enterprises. This may be an inevitable consequence of having inquiries into specific events with serious consequences in the lives of individuals. The need to respect individual rights is the principal explanation for the takeover of public inquiries by lawyers and judges, and the expenditure of time and money follows from the use of trial-like procedures. If public inquiries were ever intended to provide greater public access to government, it must nevertheless be recognized that this access is now largely filtered through the language and habits of judges and lawyers. To the extent that this is a matter of concern, it should lead to thinking about how the influence of the legal profession can be reduced where it is least needed, in policy inquiries.[74] The division between Phase One and Phase Two processes might on occasion be helpfully taken one step further, by assigning a judge to the more forensic tasks of event investigation, while naming commissioners with different backgrounds to take the lead on the more consultative and prospective task of making policy proposals.

However, we have seen that public inquiries have the potential to enhance public accountability in Canada's governing structures. Important to their doing so is their ability to bring to light actions and decisions hidden from public view, and to make independent recommendations for change following extensive public consultation. In recent years, Canada has witnessed a series of public inquiries that appear to have fulfilled this potential and met the high expectations that the public had for them. These included inquiries into several wrongful murder convictions, including those involving Donald Marshall, Guy Paul Morin, and Thomas Sophonow;[75] the Ontario commissions of inquiry into the Walkerton tragedy and the confrontation between police and First Nations protesters at Ipperwash in 1995 that resulted in the death of Dudley George;[76] and the Gomery inquiry into the federal sponsorship program. Each of these inquiries proceeded with relative dispatch, were not unduly held up by applications for judicial review and appeals, and generated considerable public interest.

The Arar inquiry deserves to be placed near the top of this list. Maher Arar himself has expressed a deep sense of vindication following the inquiry's findings, and indeed vindication of the sort he received comes rarely in this life. With respect to accountability, the

74 For a critique of the suitability of a judge to disentangle complicated issues of public administration, see Ruth Hubbard & Gilles Paquet, *Gomery's Blinders and Canadian Federalism* (Ottawa: University of Ottawa Press, 2007). The authors attribute what they view as Justice Gomery's penchant for over-emphasizing individual blame for the failed oversight of the sponsorship program to his professional background (*ibid.* at 41-42):

> First, Gomery is a judge. He has been trained to adjudicate and to find guilt or innocence, and he can no more escape from this reality than a turtle can leave its shell. He is neither an organizational design specialist nor an expert in political philosophy or public administration.

75 See *Report of the Kaufman Commission on Proceedings Involving Guy Paul Morin* (1998), online: Ministry of the Attorney General of Ontario <http://www.attorneygeneral.jus.gov.on.ca/english/about/pubs/morin>; and Manitoba, *The Inquiry Regarding Thomas Sophonow* (2001), online: <http://www.gov.mb.ca/justice/publications/sophonow/toc.html>.

76 *The Ipperwash Inquiry*, online: <http://www.ipperwashinquiry.ca>.

commissioner of the RCMP was forced to resign after failing to respond satisfactorily to parliamentary questions about his knowledge of matters covered in the inquiry report. The report's findings were cited with approval by the Supreme Court of Canada,[77] and its recommendations may well contribute to important reforms in the structure of Canada's intelligence services.

Mr. Chrétien's concern about the potential of a public inquiry to become mere "political entertainment" and to damage reputations unfairly is a useful cautionary note. Truth is notoriously elusive.[78] The balancing that goes on in our legal processes is largely predicated on that realization. Every witness to an event, let alone every interested party, tends to have a different understanding of what took place. Deciding what actually did happen is a matter of probability and hesitant inference. Canadians appear to have a tremendous faith that the public inquiry is a way to get at historical truth. This is likely a tribute to how well served this country has been by those who have participated in inquiries over the years. It also speaks to the great responsibility that those engaged in public inquiries will continue to bear.

SUGGESTED ADDITIONAL READINGS

CASES

Canada (Attorney General) v. Canada (Commission of Inquiry on the Blood System), [1997] 3 S.C.R. 440 (Krever commission).

Dixon v. Canada (Commission of Inquiry into the Deployment of Canadian Forces in Somalia), [1997] F.C.J. No. 985 (C.A.) (QL).

Phillips v. Nova Scotia (Commission of Inquiry into the Westray Mine Tragedy), [1995] 2 S.C.R. 97.

SECONDARY SOURCES

Manson, Allan, & David Mullan, eds. *Commissions of Inquiry: Praise or Reappraise?* (Toronto: Irwin Law, 2003).

Perreault, François. *Inside Gomery*, trans. from the French by Carl Angers (Toronto: Douglas & McIntyre, 2006).

---

77 *Charkaoui v. Canada (Minister of Citizenship and Immigration)*, [2007] 1 S.C.R. 350 at para. 26.

78 In the May 27, 2007 issue of *The New Yorker*, in an article about a dispute over the words spoken by Secretary of War Edwin Stanton at the moment of Abraham Lincoln's death, Adam Gopnik wrote:

> Civilization is an agreement to keep people from shouting "Fire!" in a crowded theater, but the moments we call historical occur when there is a fire in a crowded theater, and then we all try to remember afterward when we heard it, and if we ever really smelled smoke, and who went first, and what they said. The indeterminacy is built into the emotion of the moment. The past is so often unknowable not because it is befogged now but because it was befogged then, too, back when it was still the present.

This seems an apt analogy for the genesis of every investigative public inquiry.

Roach, Kent. "Canadian Public Inquiries and Accountability" in P.C. Stenning, ed. *Accountability for Criminal Justice: Selected Essays* (Toronto: University of Toronto Press, 1995).

Van Harten, Gus. "Truth Before Punishment: A Defence of Public Inquiries" (2003) 29 Queens L.J. 242.

CHAPTER FIFTEEN

Access to Administrative Justice and Other Worries

LORNE SOSSIN
Faculty of Law, University of Toronto

I. INTRODUCTION

Remarkably, until recently, texts on administrative law rarely canvassed questions of access to administrative justice. Although rule of law concerns and the ideal of one's "day in court" have come to characterize "access to justice," it is less clear what this means in the diverse variety of settings where vulnerable people come before administrative decision-makers. As LeBel J. observed in *Blencoe v. British Columbia (Human Rights Commission)*,

> not all administrative bodies are the same. Indeed, this is an understatement. At first glance, labour boards, police commissions, and milk control boards may seem to have about as much in common as assembly lines, cops, and cows! Administrative bodies do, of course, have some common features, but the diversity of their powers, mandate and structure is such that to apply particular standards from one context to another might well be entirely inappropriate.[1]

1 *Blencoe v. British Columbia (Human Rights Commission)*, 2000 SCC 44 at para. 158, per LeBel J.

Rights and important interests often are at stake in administrative justice, whether before a human rights tribunal, an immigration board, or a securities commission. Access to a decision-maker may make the difference between justice and injustice being done. The rule of law is no less significant in an administrative hearing room or decision-making process than a courtroom and, arguably, as I discuss below, it may be more so.

For the community at large generally, and for vulnerable communities specifically, it is far more likely that a person's rights and important interests will be at stake in an administrative proceeding than a judicial one. As the Chief Justice of Canada has observed, "[m]any more citizens have their rights determined by these tribunals than by the courts."[2]

This chapter builds on a key theme of this volume, which is that administrative law is concerned with the everyday practice of administrative justice, not simply the judicial review of administrative decision-making. How tribunals make policy, how tribunal members are appointed, the resources available for parties before tribunals, and the fairness and quality of administrative justice provided by those tribunals all form part of the core concern of administrative law. Although these issues could arise in a myriad of administrative settings, the analysis below is concerned primarily with adjudicative tribunals.[3]

What does access to justice mean in the context of administrative tribunals? There is no one definition to this concept expressly developed by administrative law, and the analogy of administrative tribunals to courts sometimes obscures more than it reveals. In this chapter, I will canvass the issue of access to justice before administrative decision-makers from the perspective of those affected by administrative decisions. This perspective requires attention be paid not just to the statutory provisions that empower tribunals or the court decisions that interpret those provisions, but also to the everyday practice before the tribunal. While I do not suggest that this list is exhaustive, it is possible to approach the question of access to administrative justice from this perspective in at least three distinct ways:[4]

1. *Access to the tribunal*: How do parties find the tribunal? Is it accessible in person through an office open to the public? If so, is the tribunal housed in a single office

2 *Cooper v. Canada (Human Rights Commission)*, [1996] 3 S.C.R. 854 at 899-900, per McLachlin J. (as she then was) (dissenting).

3 By "adjudicative tribunal," I refer broadly to tribunals whose primary purpose is the impartial resolution of disputes, such as labour boards, human rights tribunals, and worker compensation appeal boards. I do not mean to suggest that there are no access concerns for other kinds of agencies, boards, and commissions, but I believe the issues of access are strongest where the subject matter of a tribunal is primarily adjudicative. For a discussion on classifying tribunals as adjudicative and non-adjudicative, see Ed Ratushny, *The Independence of Federal Administrative Tribunals and Agencies in Canada* (Ottawa: Canadian Bar Association, 1990) at 46-47.

4 For a helpful conceptual review of "access to justice," see Rod McDonald, "Access to Justice in 2003: Scope, Scale and Ambitions" in J. Bass, W.A. Bogart & F.H. Zemans, eds., *Access to Justice for a New Century —The Way Forward* (Toronto: Irwin, 2005). According to McDonald, "commentators identify a broad inventory of features that would characterize an accessible justice system: (1) just results, (2) fair treatment, (3) reasonable cost, (4) reasonable speed, (5) understandable to users, (6) responsive to needs, (7) certain, and (8) effective, adequately resourced and well-organized. But, as the experiences of the last four decades illustrate, these are not features of an accessible justice system; [these] are merely features of an accessible dispute-resolution system. These experiences point to two main organizing themes of a comprehensive access to justice strategy: the strategy must be multi-dimensional and it must take a pluralistic approach to the institutions of law and justice" (*ibid.* at 23-24).

or in multiple offices in a range of communities? Is video conferencing available for those unable or unwilling to travel to attend a hearing? Is the tribunal accessible through telephone and/or Internet services, and if so, are these points of contact made available in the languages spoken by users of the tribunal?

2. *Access to legal or other knowledge necessary to obtain tribunal services*: How do parties learn what they need to know to be able to contribute to the proceedings and to support their claims? Are the relevant legislative provisions and regulations setting out the powers of a tribunal publicized to parties? Have guidelines been developed to set out the standards by which decisions will be reached, and if so, have those guidelines been made available to the public? Is tribunal staff available to assist with filling out forms or to assist in preparing a party's submissions? Again, are guidelines and/or tribunal staff available in languages spoken by users of the tribunal?
3. *Access to resources needed to navigate tribunal system*: How do people present their positions before the tribunal? Is there a right to state-funded legal representation? Do fees create barriers, and if so, is there a procedure for waiving fees? Are previous decisions of the tribunal available, and if so, are they in a form that can be searched and sorted by self-represented parties? Is there access to mediation, dispute resolution, or settlement services? Are interpreters available?

In the following analysis, I explore each of these ways of addressing access to administrative justice.

II. ACCESS TO ADMINISTRATIVE JUSTICE: THE TRIBUNAL

When we think of the mandate of a tribunal, we often mean its powers, its jurisdiction, and its statutory purposes. We rarely think of this mandate in terms that matter most to those who come before the tribunal, such as, How do I find the tribunal? Where is it located? Can I initiate proceedings and, if so, how is this done? How much will it cost? Will I have a hearing? If so, what will I have to say? Who will help me if I get confused or cannot understand what is expected of me and what I can expect of others in the process?

Although the governing statute of a tribunal typically sets out the powers of a tribunal, it is often left to the tribunal itself to decide what face it will present to the public. There are two aspects to this perspective I wish to explore: first, the issue of standing before a tribunal and, second, the issue whether a tribunal will hold oral or written hearings and, if oral hearings, whether those hearings are in person or through other, technological means.

A. Standing

The first aspect of this perspective on access is standing. Who serves as the gatekeeper for administrative justice? This question may have several answers, depending on one's perspective.

For administrative law, the first sense in which standing is understood is the standing to challenge administrative action in court.[5] Under the historical regime of prerogative writs,

---

5 See, for example, D. Mullan, *Administrative Law* (Toronto: Irwin, 2001) chapter 18.

standing was limited to those directly affected by state action. To the extent that state action concerned the public interest, remedial authority lay with the attorney general. This approach is also captured in the *Federal Courts Act*, which provides standing to the attorney general or to any party "directly affected" by state action.[6]

It remains the case that not every citizen is entitled, as of right, to challenge administrative action. Judicial review of administrative action is reserved for those who are found to have a sufficient legally recognized interest in the matter to justify the judicial review application. It is said that the test for standing is whether the applicant is a "person aggrieved" by the administrative decision. It has been said that a person aggrieved is one who will suffer some "peculiar grievance of their own beyond some grievance suffered by them in common with the rest of the public."[7]

These limits on standing are said to promote the efficiency of administrative action, by keeping the administration free from artificial or academic challenges to administrative action. They also, however, serve to respect the rights of third parties. In many cases where the applicant for judicial review cannot show that he or she is directly affected or aggrieved by the challenged administrative act, there will in fact be third parties in the community who are directly affected or aggrieved. The general policy of the court is not to decide issues in the absence of the parties whose rights are most directly affected by the court's decision. In other words, if those who are most directly affected by the administrative decision are content to "live with it," the court will not permit curious busybodies to bring applications for judicial review in their stead. If, however, those most directly affected or "aggrieved" wish to challenge the administrative action, they should be able to do so free from interference.[8]

The concept of discretionary public interest standing also has been applied to challenge the decision-making of administrative bodies in court. The leading case in this area remains *Finlay v. Canada (Minister of Finance)*.[9] In granting public interest standing to a claimant challenging a decision by the federal government not to impose penalties on Manitoba for garnishing the benefits of a social welfare recipient in apparent breach of the Canada Assistance Plan provisions, the Supreme Court accepted that this form of standing would be available to challenge administrative action and not simply legislation.

Under public interest standing, the test to be applied is threefold:

1. Is the matter serious and justiciable?
2. Is the party seeking standing genuinely interested in the matter?
3. Is there any other reasonable and effective way for the matter?[10]

---

6 *Federal Courts Act*, R.S.C. 1985, c. F-7, ss. 18(1), 28(2).

7 See, for example, *Friends of the Oldman River Society v. Association of Professional Engineers, Geologists and Geophysicists of Alberta* (1997), [1998] 5 W.W.R. 179 (Alta. Q.B.), rev'd on other grounds 2001 ABCA 107. See also T.A. Cromwell, *Locus Standi: A Commentary on the Law of Standing in Canada* (Toronto: Carswell, 1986) at 106-8.

8 For discussion, see *Alberta Liquor Store Assn. v. Alberta (Gaming and Liquor Commission)*, 2006 ABQB 904 at paras. 10-11.

9 [1986] 2 S.C.R. 607.

10 *Ibid.* at 651. This test was developed in a trilogy of public interest standing cases that preceded *Finlay*: see *Thorson v. Canada (Attorney General)*, [1975] 1 S.C.R. 138; *Nova Scotia Board of Censors v. McNeil*, [1976] 2 S.C.R. 265; *Canada (Minister of Justice) v. Borowski*, [1981] 2 S.C.R. 575.

In *Finlay*, the Court applied this test to grant standing to a recipient of social benefits to challenge the conduct of the federal government toward the province of Manitoba under the then Canada Assistance Plan. The applicant raised a serious issue with respect to the legality of the government's action (or, in this case, its inaction in failing to penalize a province for breaching the conditions of the Plan) and, as a recipient of the benefit in question, was clearly genuinely interested. Because neither the federal government nor the provinces had an interest in compelling a penalty from the federal government, the Court also concluded that there was no reasonable alternative by which the challenge would reach court.

The Court has elsewhere affirmed that the purpose of granting status is to "prevent the immunization of legislation or public acts from any challenge,"[11] and that public interest standing is available in the context of challenges that arise out of administrative tribunals,[12] but there is some suggestion that the scope of such challenges may be limited to legislative provisions and public acts of a legislative character, which would exclude most tribunal decision-making.[13]

In contrast to courts, where the law of standing is governed generally by common law, in the context of tribunals, the scope of standing is set out first and foremost by the statute governing the tribunal. As Robert Macaulay and James Sprague have noted, "[t]here are a number of cases on standing before administrative agencies in Canada, but each of them relies so specifically on the mandating legislation of that agency, or at least upon the interpretation of some judicially-oriented chairperson, that are not really very helpful as a general guide."[14]

David Mullan has observed that the issue of standing before tribunals has become more important as the duty of fairness has been interpreted more expansively in cases such as *Nicholson v. Haldimand Norfolk (Regional) Police Commissioners*.[15] One might imagine even more pressure for generous approaches to standing now that the scope of fairness continues to expand[16] and tribunal jurisdiction over the *Canadian Charter of Rights and Freedoms*[17] has also been approached more generously.[18]

Historically, the kinds of tribunals where standing has been an issue were regulatory tribunals (for example, an energy board or competition tribunal), tribunals whose decisions touched many people indirectly (for example, a municipal planning board), or labour tribunals (where the rights of some employees may have an impact on a much wider group of employees). In regulatory cases, boards typically work out representative compromises,

11 *Canadian Council of Churches v. Canada (Minister of Employment and Immigration)*, [1992] 1 S.C.R. 236 at para. 252.

12 See *Vriend v. Alberta*, [1998] 1 S.C.R. 493 at 528.

13 See *Canadian Bar Assn. v. British Columbia*, 2006 BCSC 1342 at paras. 41-42.

14 R. Macaulay & J. Sprague, *Practice and Procedure Before Administrative Tribunals*, looseleaf (Toronto: Carswell, 2001) at 9.7(b).

15 [1979] 1 S.C.R. 311. See D. Mullan, *Administrative Law: Cases, Text, and Materials*, 5th ed. (Toronto: Emond Montgomery, 2005) 1247-48.

16 See, for example, *Baker v. Canada (Minister of Citizenship and Immigration)*, [1999] 2 S.C.R. 819.

17 Part I of the *Constitution Act, 1982*, being Schedule B to the *Canada Act 1982* (U.K.), 1982, c. 11 [Charter].

18 See *Nova Scotia (Workers' Compensation Board) v. Martin; Nova Scotia (Workers' Compensation Board) v. Laseur*, [2003] 2 S.C.R. 504; *Paul v. British Columbia (Forest Appeals Commission)*, [2003] 2 S.C.R. 585. See also the discussion of the Charter and administrative law by Evan Fox-Decent in chapter 7.

whereby a ratepayers' association or citizens' group is granted standing to represent the interests of those indirectly affected by board decisions (these groups will sometimes be referred to as interveners as well). This practice may raise accountability questions because the tribunal rarely inquires into the representative character of public interest groups.

In the labour board setting, standing issues often involve third-party employees who are affected by another employee's grievance—for example, where an incumbent employee potentially would be displaced following a successful grievance. Should the incumbent employee be given the opportunity to participate in the grievance to protect his or her rights? The answer appears to be "no, except in limited circumstances."[19] As one labour arbitrator observed,

> If the rights of individual employees who are directly or indirectly affected by the outcome of arbitration proceedings were granted standing in all cases where their individual rights were affected, the numbers of potentially affected employees would be quite large, arbitration hearings would become lengthy and more expensive, and employees would come to feel some obligation to be separately represented.[20]

As these examples illustrate, the tension between fairness and efficiency is an enduring theme in settings of access to administrative justice. Fairness marks the boundary of efficiency concerns in the context of standing and may expand the scope of standing. For example, by extending the scope of those in a tribunal process entitled to fairness, the courts have altered the scope of access. To give one example, in *Taylor v. Canada*, Evans J.A., writing for the Federal Court of Appeal, recognized for the first time that complainants are entitled to a degree of fairness in the disciplinary process affecting judges through the Canadian Judicial Council.[21]

B. Hearings

The second aspect of the perspective on physical access to administrative justice is how parties interact with the tribunal. Will the tribunal conduct its process entirely in writing, or will there be an opportunity for a hearing of some kind? The types of proceeding of a tribunal are usually set out in its empowering statute.[22]

Although government may not be under a legal obligation to create tribunals, once it has chosen to do so, it may well be under a legal obligation to provide adequate funding to ensure fairness, the rule of law, and access to justice before these tribunals. For example, in *Khan v. University of Ottawa*,[23] the Ontario Court of Appeal held that an oral hearing was required in the context of a university proceeding that would determine whether a student would fail a course. The court found that where a decision affecting significant interests of an individual turns on credibility, fairness requires that the individual have an opportunity

19 See *C.U.P.W. v. Canada Post Corp. (Hall Grievance)* (2006), 149 L.A.C. (4th) 306.

20 *Re Royal Victoria Hospital and O.N.A.* (1993), 30 C.L.A.S. 355 (Starkman).

21 2003 FCA 55 at paras. 81-82.

22 For further discussion on the requirement of hearings in administrative law, see Grant Huscroft, chapter 5.

23 (1997), 34 O.R. (3d) 535 (C.A.).

to put forward his or her case in person before the decision-maker. What if the body in question is not a university, however, but a province-wide licensing body located in the capital city, and the person affected lives in a remote rural community? What if an oral hearing is simply not practicable in the context of a high-volume tribunal? As discussed elsewhere in this volume, the standard of procedural fairness required in a particular case varies, but the standards recognized by administrative law justifying a lesser degree of fairness do not expressly include questions of resources.[24]

The Ontario Landlord and Tenant Board, among other province-wide bodies, has instituted video conferencing as a substitute for in-person hearings. On the one hand, this measure provides much greater access to hearings without the long travel time and dislocation previously associated with attending hearings in person. On the other hand, many report disadvantages of a hearing by video, some of which may go to the fairness of the proceeding.[25] For this reason, rule 5.2(2) of the *Statutory Powers Procedure Act* (SPPA), states that a tribunal *shall not* hold an electronic hearing if a party satisfies the tribunal that holding an electronic rather than an oral hearing is likely to cause the party significant prejudice.[26]

In addition to the location of hearings, tribunals also face other questions of how to provide access to the public. Is it important that a tribunal have a physical presence at all, or will a "virtual" tribunal that is accessible through the internet be sufficient? Is a centralized tribunal with all of its functions in one location preferable to a decentralized tribunal?

These issues arise not as an abstract question of fairness but also as a concrete trade-off involving resources. Video conferencing, for example, is far less expensive than maintaining an office in remote centres or obtaining facilities for in-person hearings. Of course, a hearing by teleconference would be even less expensive. The question is when efficiency or cost-cutting measures begin to erode the fairness of a decision-making process.

If access turns, as it must, on resources, then the question will be what, if any, legal considerations constrain the government from reducing the resources available to tribunals. Further, where the legislation, government policies, or funding practices create barriers to access, is it the role of the tribunal to raise this issue? If so, what would be the appropriate venue in which to do so? In its annual report to the legislature? In a tribunal's decisions? In a confidential or public dialogue with government? These questions are explored further below.

III. ACCESS TO ADMINISTRATIVE JUSTICE: INFORMATION AND KNOWLEDGE

Some would argue that accessing a tribunal itself is far less difficult than accessing the legal expertise necessary to succeed at a tribunal. The way in which a tribunal communicates the information and knowledge necessary to access its services or remedies varies and is rarely

24 See the discussion of *Baker* by Grant Huscroft in chapter 5: in *Baker*, the Supreme Court held that the content of procedural fairness varies depending on the nature of the decision being made, nature of the statutory scheme, importance of the decision to the people affected, legitimate expectations, and the agency's choice of procedures.

25 For discussion, see L. Sossin & Z. Yetnikoff, "I Can See Clearly Now: Videoconference Hearings and the Legal Limit on How Tribunals Allocate Resources." Unpublished paper, 2006.

26 R.S.O. 1990, c. S.22.

set out in an empowering statute. In this, as in so many areas affecting access to administrative justice, it is the policies of the tribunal itself, not the government, that are determinative.

A. Guidelines

Many tribunals develop guidelines to ensure consistency and to structure discretion.[27] Transparency with respect to the standards of decision-making represents an emerging aspect of access to administrative justice. For this reason, it is important that guidelines be developed that set out these standards, and where this occurs, it is equally important that these guidelines be made publicly available. One interesting question is whether it can be said to be a requirement of fairness that a tribunal with significant discretion structure that discretion in some fashion. To date, the farthest a court has been willing to go is to state that where guidelines are in place, ignoring those guidelines without justification may breach the decision-maker's duty of fairness.[28]

Because tribunals are bound only by statutory provisions, it is not open to a tribunal to develop binding guidelines on its own initiative.[29] This issue has arisen in the context of the Immigration and Refugee Board (IRB).

The IRB issued *Guideline No. 7* in accordance with the legislative authority conferred on the chair of the IRB by s. 159 of the *Immigration and Refugee Protection Act*.[30] *Guideline No. 7: Concerning Preparation and Conduct of a Hearing in the Refugee Protection Division* circumscribes inquiry powers of IRB members so that they can limit the scope of the inquiry and, as such, be in position to control the conduct of the hearing in order to ensure efficient and speedy determinations of claims. *Guideline No. 7* "changes the order of questioning by having the Refugee Protection Division (RPD) leading the inquiry in the hearing room. The purpose of this change is to allow the RPD to make the best use of its expertise as a specialist tribunal by focusing on the issues which it has identified as determinative."[31]

In *Thamotharem v. Canada (Minister of Citizenship and Immigration)*,[32] *Guideline No. 7* was challenged as a breach of procedural fairness and on the grounds that it fettered the discretion of board members to decide the order of questioning appropriate to a particular

---

27 See F. Houle & L. Sossin, "Tribunals and Guidelines: Exploring the Relationships Between Fairness and Legitimacy in Administrative Decision-Making" (2006) 46 Can. Pub. Admin. 282 at 294-300. See also the discussion by Andrew Green in chapter 13.

28 *Bezaire v. Windsor Roman Catholic Separate School Board* (1992), 9 O.R. (3d) 737 (Div. Ct).

29 See *Little Sisters Book and Art Emporium v. Canada (Minister of Justice)*, 2000 SCC 69 at para. 85. Because they are not considered binding as law, guidelines are not subject to Charter scrutiny. For discussion, see L. Sossin, "Discretion Unbound: Reconciling the Charter and Soft Law" (2003) 45 Can. Pub. Admin. 465.

30 S.C. 2001, c. 27, s. 159: "(1) The Chairperson is, by virtue of holding that office, a member of each Division of the board and is the chief executive officer of the Board. In that capacity, the Chairperson: … (h) may issue guidelines in writing to members of the Board and identify decisions of the Board as jurisprudential guides."

31 Immigration and Refugee Board, *Guideline 7: Concerning Preparation and Conduct of a Hearing in the Refugee Protection Division*, paras. 19-23, online: <http://www.irb-cisr.gc.ca/en/references/policy/guidelines/preparation_e.htm#2>. *Immigration and Refugee Protection Act*, S.C. 2001, c. 27.

32 2007 FCA 198; see also *Benitez et al. v. The Minister of Citizenship and Immigration*, 2007 FCA 199.

claim. It was raised in the context of a refugee application involving a Tamil student claiming persecution if returned to Sri Lanka. The Federal Court held that *Guideline No. 7* does not violate the board's duty of fairness but is an unlawful fetter on the exercise of discretion because board members often operate as if they are bound by it. The denial of Mr. Thamotharem's refugee status was quashed on this basis. The Federal Court of Appeal affirmed the court's finding with regard to *Guideline No. 7* and the duty of fairness but reversed the aspect of the decision dealing with administrative discretion. It dismissed Thamotharem's application for judicial review on the basis that *Guideline No. 7* expressly directs members to consider the facts of the particular case before them in order to determine whether there are circumstances warranting a deviation from the standard order of questioning. Also, it was not evident that board members generally disregarded this aspect of *Guideline No. 7* and unthinkingly adhered to the standard order of questioning. Thus, while transparency calls for tribunals to develop and publicize guidelines on which parties before a tribunal may rely, the principles of administrative law limit the effectiveness of that reliance by requiring that a tribunal not treat its own guidelines as binding.

While guidelines may not be binding, tribunals often do have the authority to issue rules of practice. In Ontario, the SPPA provides that "a tribunal may make rules governing the practice and procedure before it," and also stipulates that where a tribunal does make rules of practice, it must make them available to the public.[33] By these rules, tribunals exercise significant discretion with respect to access, limited only by the requirement that rules of practice be consistent with a tribunal's enabling statute and where applicable, general procedural statutes such as the SPPA. Rules of practice will, as a practical matter, determine whether the tribunal is easy or difficult to access. These rules set out the applicable time limits for filing material, the extent of material and disclosure provided, and whether hearings will be in writing, in person, or by electronic means.

B. Simplification

Another important aspect of access to information is simplification. Being provided with forms that are unduly complex or with guidelines that are inscrutable is equivalent to closing the doors to the tribunal. According to the Council of Canadian Administrative Tribunal's report, *Literacy and Access to Administrative Justice*, the following approach should be adopted by tribunals to address the question of access:

> Administrative tribunals, like other courts, have to follow the standards set in case law. We can
>
> - make sure, as much as is possible, that our clients understand all the proceedings;
> - examine how we deal with low literacy clients and how this can affect fair administration of justice;
> - follow the lead of many organizations and use "plain language" in all our communications, written, visual, and spoken.[34]

---

33 SPPA s. 25.1, as amended by S.O. 1994, c. 27, s. 56(38).

34 Council of Canadian Administrative Tribunals, *Literacy and Access to Administrative Justice: The Promotion of Plain Language* (2005), online: <http://www.ccat-ctac.org/en/publications/> at 12.

Most tribunals are committed to simple, user-friendly forms. Some are going further, investigating services that provide assistance to individuals on how to complete forms and understand the basic process requirements of the tribunal.[35]

C. Language

Just as "plain language" may facilitate access, so may the capacity of tribunals to provide services and adjudication in the language spoken by those seeking out the tribunal.

Since *R. v. Tran*,[36] the Court has adopted a contextual approach to s. 14 of the Charter, which provides:

> A party or witness in any proceedings who does not understand or speak the language in which the proceedings are conducted or who is deaf has the right to the assistance of an interpreter.

The Court noted that the Charter right is closely linked to the common-law right to a fair hearing: in other words, the right to be heard implies a right to understand the case to be met, which in some circumstances will not be possible unless interpretation and translation services are available.

As Lamer C.J. held, writing for the Court:

> Importantly, the underlying principle behind all of the interests protected by the right to interpreter assistance under s. 14 is that of linguistic understanding. The centrality of this principle is evident not only from the general jurisprudence dealing with interpreters, but also more directly from the language of s. 14 itself, which refers to "not understanding or speak[ing] the language in which the proceedings are conducted." The level of understanding protected by s. 14 will, therefore, necessarily be high. Indeed, it has been suggested that a party must have the same basic opportunity to understand and be understood as if he or she were conversant in the language of the court.[37]

Even in the criminal context, however, it is clear that the right to an interpreter is not absolute. To establish a violation of s. 14 of the Charter, the claimant of the right must prove, on a balance of probabilities, not only that he or she was in need of assistance, but also that the interpretation received fell below the basic, guaranteed standard and did so in the course of the case being advanced. Unless the Crown is able to show on a balance of probabilities that there was a valid and effective waiver of the right that accounts for the lack of or lapse in interpretation, a violation of the right to interpreter assistance guaranteed by s. 14 of the Charter will have been made out. In terms of the guaranteed standard, it is not one of "perfection," but rather one of continuity, precision, impartiality, competency, and contemporaneousness.

The Court makes clear that not every error of translation or interpretation in the context of an accused will constitute a violation of the Charter. Further, the Court holds that the error

35 Often, this role falls to the registrar or other front-line staff of tribunals, but in 2006, Pro Bono Students Canada established an Administrative Justice initiative under which law students are recruited to work with tribunals on providing such services.

36 [1994] 2 S.C.R. 951.

37 *Ibid.* at 977-78.

must be one that goes to the "vital interests" of the accused. Thus, even a serious problem with translation on a minor point (for example, a scheduling motion) will not constitute a violation.

It is clear that the standards developed in *Tran* have to be modified to the contexts of administrative proceedings and that a spectrum of interpretation/translation rights might be more appropriate to these contexts. In *Tran*, the Court specifically noted "for future consideration the possibility that different rules may have to be developed and applied to other situations which properly arise under s. 14 of the *Charter*—for instance, where the proceedings in question are civil or administrative in nature."[38]

The right to an interpreter (and, by extension, to translation of relevant material) was considered in *Filgueira v. Garfield Container Transport Inc.*[39] In that case, the Canadian Human Rights Tribunal considered its own obligation to provide an interpreter to a complainant alleging discrimination in the workplace. The tribunal noted that the complainant had a bilingual agent assisting with his case. While this mitigated the complainant's need, and while it was acknowledged that the ruling would have an impact on scarce resources, the tribunal nonetheless ordered that fairness required that the complainant be provided with an interpreter (for at least part of the hearing).

A judicial review application of the tribunal's decision in *Filgueira* was dismissed.[40] In upholding the aspect of *Filgueira* dealing with the right to an interpreter, Hughes J. concluded:

> Thus, both the complainant and Respondent/employer, while parties before the Tribunal, are players in a larger endeavour, that of seeking to the removal of discrimination. It is within the discretion of the Tribunal to determine whether such an objective can be fairly achieved in the absence of providing, in whole or during part of the process, translation services into a language other than an official language, at taxpayer's expense, to one or more of the parties.[41]

Filgueira is an example of the principles in *Tran* being applied flexibly to the realm of administrative adjudication. Although the case law answers the question, in part, as to the legal requirements of interpretation and translation services, it raises a host of others: for example, should tribunals, legal aid, the government, or some other service providers be responsible for interpreter and translation services, and into which languages for which tribunals? Should a government sponsored or administered roster of approved interpreters and translators be established? Some tribunals have undertaken initiatives to translate brochures into languages used by user groups,[42] but linguistic access remains a significant hurdle for almost all tribunals.

---

38 *Ibid.* at 961.

39 (August 17, 2005), 2005 CHRT 32, File No. T952/7204.

40 2006 FC 785.

41 *Ibid.* at para. 38.

42 The Ontario Landlord and Tenant Board, for example, translates its brochures into Arabic, Chinese, Farsi, Korean, Punjabi, Spanish, Urdu, Tamil, Russian, and Vietnamese. See Ontario Landlord and Tenant Board, online: <http://www.ltb.gov.on.ca/en/Key_Information/157371.html>.

D. Prior Decisions

One of the most controversial aspects of access is how parties may learn about previous decisions of the tribunal. While privacy concerns make it difficult for some administrative bodies to publish their decisions,[43] in most cases making the tribunal's past decisions available is seen as a key aspect of its public interest function. In this sense, it is analogous to the rule that, absent circumstances justifying confidentiality, all tribunal proceedings should be open to the public, and documents used in those proceedings should be available to the public.[44] The practice with respect to publishing decisions is uneven. Some tribunals publish all of their decisions in an easily searchable form.[45] Still others publish anonymized versions of only those previous decisions determined to be of general significance.[46] Some tribunals also charge a fee to access earlier decisions, which appears to impose a financial burden to the process of learning the standards applied by a tribunal.

Unlike a court, tribunals are not bound by their earlier decisions. Many tribunals in practice, however, aim for consistency and will treat previous decisions as strongly influential over similar disputes. For this reason, making prior decisions available could plausibly be seen as an element of fairness and as part of the requirement that parties before the tribunal should know the "case to meet."

For all of these reasons, access to administrative justice includes access to sufficient legal and institutional knowledge.

IV. ACCESS TO RESOURCES NEEDED TO NAVIGATE THE TRIBUNAL SYSTEM

Access to administrative justice is not just a matter of obtaining the necessary information, of course, but also, as noted above, a matter of resources. This attention to financial barriers is particularly important in the context of vulnerable parties. There are several ways in which an absence of resources may create barriers to access. Below, I address three potential barriers: legal representation, fees and costs, and the budgeting and staffing of tribunals.

A. Legal Representation

The first and most significant impact of resources is the availability of adequate legal representation. In the criminal justice sphere, a right to state-funded legal representation has been long recognized. In *New Brunswick (Minister of Health and Community Services) v.*

---

43 The Canadian Human Rights Commission, for example, cites privacy concerns as the reason it does not publish its past decisions. Online: <http://www.chrc-ccdp.ca/media_room/caselaw_info_jurisprudence-en.asp>.

44 See, for example, ss. 41-42 of British Columbia's *Administrative Tribunals Act*, S.B.C. 2004, c. 45 [BC, *Administrative Tribunals Act*]. See also the discussion of this legislation by Cristie Ford in chapter 3.

45 See, for example, the Alberta Labour Relations Board, online: <http://www.alrb.gov.ab.ca/decisions.html>, or the Ontario Information and Privacy Commission, online: <http://www.ipc.on.ca/index.asp?navid=62>, which allows the public to search prior decisions by both subject and name.

46 See, for example, Ontario's Social Benefits Tribunal, online: <http://www.sbt.gov.on.ca/userfiles/HTML/nts_1_7_1.html>.

G.(J.),[47] the Supreme Court of Canada affirmed that the constitutional right to legal assistance extends beyond settings where the jeopardy of an individual is concerned. In that case, the New Brunswick Minister of Health and Community Services was seeking an extension of custody of a mother's three children for a six-month period. The mother was indigent and receiving social assistance. She applied for legal aid but was turned down because, at the time, custody applications were not covered under the legal aid guidelines in New Brunswick. The Court recognized a constitutional obligation on the New Brunswick government to provide state-funded counsel in the particular circumstances of that case.

Although the principle in G.(J.) has potential application in the context of administrative tribunals, the reach of constitutionally mandated legal aid may be modest. That said, many provincial legal aid statutes fund legal representation before administrative tribunals. For example, in Ontario, those committed to psychiatric facilities who appear before the Ontario Review Board to argue for release are covered by legal aid certificates, while specialty clinics provide limited representation for eligible claimants before the Social Benefits Tribunal, the Landlord and Tenant Board, and other administrative bodies.

Access to justice, however, does not always depend on access to lawyers. The availability of paralegal assistance and the development of self-help support networks and resources may all play a role in the administrative justice sphere.

B. Fees and Costs

The second way in which resources may affect access is through user fees or other costs associated with a tribunal's process.

1. Fees

Tribunals may be funded in a variety of ways. Regulatory tribunals are sometimes self-funded, whereby the tribunal levies an assessment on regulated individuals or organizations and funds its adjudicative operations from these levies. Consider the example of energy boards. The National Energy Board receives 90 percent of its funding from industry levies with the remaining 10 percent coming from the federal government. In Alberta, the government pays for close to 50 percent of the Alberta Energy and Utilities Board's operations while industry levies pay the rest. In British Columbia and Ontario, energy boards are entirely self-funded.[48]

Although most adjudicative tribunals are free to the parties,[49] the practice of charging fees is attracting increasing attention. The British Columbia *Administrative Tribunals Act*

47 [1999] 3 S.C.R. 46.

48 See Ontario Energy Board (OEB), *Survey of Regulatory Cost Measures* (September 2006), online: <www.oeb.gov.on.ca/documents/abouttheoeb/corpinfo_reports/rcm_surveyreport-elenchus_120906.pdf>.

49 Canadian Human Rights Commission, "Filing a Complaint," online: <http://www.chrc-ccdp.ca/complaints/filing_complaint-en.asp>; Ontario Social Benefits Tribunal, "Frequently Asked Questions," online: <http://www.sbt.gov.on.ca/userfiles/HTML/nts_1_63_1.html#187>; Ontario Workplace Safety and Insurance Board, "Worker Forms," online: <http://www.wsib.on.ca/wsib/wsibsite.nsf/public/FormsWorkers>; Ontario Pay Equity Hearings Tribunal, "Forms and Rules: Form 1 – Application," online: <http://www.labour.gov.on.ca/pec/peht/peht_forms.html>.

provides the government with the power to make regulations setting out the fees associated with filing applications before tribunals.[50] These fees can range from the $25 per complaint filing fee charged by the Ontario Assessment Review Board to the $50,000 per merger notification filing fee charged by the federal Competition Bureau.

Fees of any size have the potential to pose a barrier to access to administrative justice. This is even more relevant in the field of administrative justice because low-income individuals are more likely to have interactions with administrative decision-makers than with courts. In *Polewsky v. Home Hardware Stores Ltd.*,[51] the Ontario Divisional Court recognized that the constitutional principle of access to justice required that small claims court fees be waived in the context of an individual who otherwise would not be able to bring a case to court. Similarly, in *Pearson v. Canada*,[52] the Federal Court held that the provision of the *Federal Courts Act* that, in special circumstances, allows the court to disregard its rules[53] should be interpreted so as to allow the court to exempt impecunious parties from having to pay filing fees. In so doing, Muldoon J. observed,

> The rule of law is a feature of the law, of at least the common-law parts of Canada, and has been such since long before the adoption of the Charter, as demonstrated in part by Prof. Dicey's learned writings. So, indeed, is that precept of the rule of law—the equality of civil rights among all who claim the benefit of the sovereign's peace, in truth all the inhabitants, whether citizens or not. That which is by law reserved for poor folk—taking Court proceedings "in forma pauperis"—is a civil right and therefore available to the plaintiff herein, on even the bare evidence which he has provided in order to qualify for taking his court proceedings "in forma pauperis."[54]

Although administrative tribunals do not necessarily give rise to these same common-law civil rights, the court's approach to interpreting its statutory rules so as to provide discretion to ensure that fees do not bar access would likely be applied in an analogous fashion to the rules or enabling statute of a tribunal.[55] Consider, for example, the Ontario Landlord and Tenant Board, which charges filing fees but does not offer fee waivers.[56]

The unwritten constitutional principle of "access to justice" was described by Dickson C.J. in *British Columbia Government Employees' Union v. British Columbia (Attorney General)* (a case concerning the constitutional validity of a court-issued injunction to clear the courthouse steps of picketers during a public service strike) in the following terms:

---

50 BC *Administrative Tribunals Act*, *supra* note 44 at s. 60(c).

51 (2003), 109 C.R.R. (2d) 189 (Ont. Div. Ct.).

52 [2000] 195 F.T.R. 31.

53 *Federal Courts Act*, *supra* note 6 at s. 55.

54 *Supra* note 52 at para. 14. The principle in *Pearson* recently received positive treatment in both *Spatling v. Canada (Solicitor General)*, [2003] F.C.J. No. 620, and *Pieters v. Canada (Attorney General)*, 2004 FC 1418.

55 In *McKenzie v. B.C. (Minister of Public Safety) et al.*, 2006 BCSC 1372, for example, the rule of law concept developed in the context of civil courts was applied to the setting of a reappointment to an administrative tribunal. This decision is under appeal.

56 Ontario Landlord and Tenant Board, "Landlord and Tenant Fees," online: <http://www.ltb.gov.on.ca/en/Key_Information/STEL02_111530.html>.

> Let us turn then to s. 52(1) of the Constitution Act, 1982 which states that the Constitution of Canada is the supreme law of Canada and any law that is inconsistent with the provisions of the Constitution is, to the extent of the inconsistency, of no force or effect. Earlier sections of the *Charter* assure, in clear and specific terms, certain fundamental freedoms, democratic rights, mobility rights, legal rights and equality rights of utmost importance to each and every Canadian. ... Of what value are the rights and freedoms guaranteed by the *Charter* if a person is denied or delayed access to a court of competent jurisdiction in order to vindicate them? How can the courts independently maintain the rule of law and effectively discharge the duties imposed by the *Charter* if court access is hindered, impeded or denied? The *Charter* protections would become merely illusory, the entire *Charter* undermined.
>
> There cannot be a rule of law without access, otherwise the rule of law is replaced by a rule of men and women who decide who shall and who shall not have access to justice.[57]

Access to justice is no less imperative in tribunals than in courts. Unlike judicial independence, which is an unwritten constitutional principle applying uniquely to courts,[58] access to justice likely has broader application to all adjudicative proceedings in which rights and interests are at stake, and especially to those with jurisdiction over the Charter.

In *Christie v. British Columbia*,[59] it was argued that a tax on legal services, like pickets, prevents people from accessing the courts and tribunals and thus violates the right to access justice. The trial judge held that access to justice is a fundamental constitutional right and that taxation on a fundamental right that denies service to low-income persons unjustifiably violates s. 7 of the Charter. The Court of Appeal affirmed this decision and, in fact, went further, holding that because the right to access justice is held by all, the tax should not be levied on *any* legal services that determine rights and obligations, whether before courts or tribunals, and should be struck down for *all* citizens, not just the less affluent.

The provincial attorney general successfully appealed this decision to the Supreme Court, which held that not every limit on access is unconstitutional. The constitution does not mandate a *general* right to legal representation as an aspect of, or precondition to, the rule of law. Rather, the right to counsel is limited to instances where life, liberty, and security of the person are affected as demonstrated by ss. 7 and 10(b) of the Charter.[60] The decisions of the lower courts were reversed.

2. Costs

In addition to the question of fees, there has also been growing concern over the issue of costs in the context of tribunal adjudication and the effect of costs on access to administrative justice. Where the tribunal is deciding a dispute between two or more parties, should the winning parties be able to claim costs against the losing parties as in civil courts?

57 *British Columbia Government Employees' Union v. British Columbia (Attorney General)*, [1988] 2 S.C.R. 214 at 229-30.

58 See *Ocean Port Hotel Ltd. v. British Columbia (General Manager, Liquor Control and Licensing Branch)*, [2001] 2 S.C.R. 781 at para. 24.

59 2005 BCCA 631, 262 D.L.R. (4th) 51.

60 Section 10(b) of the Charter provides that everyone has the right to retain and instruct counsel, and to be informed of that right "on arrest or detention."

Should the tribunal itself ever be in a position to recover costs? What should the consequences be when a party is unable to pay costs?

The British Columbia *Administrative Tribunals Act* expressly provides for tribunals to develop their own costs regimes:

> Power to award costs
>
> 47(1) Subject to the regulations, the tribunal may make orders for payment as follows:
>
> (a) requiring a party to pay part of the costs of another party or an intervener in connection with the application;
>
> (b) requiring an intervener to pay part of the costs of a party or another intervener in connection with the application;
>
> (c) if the tribunal considers the conduct of a party has been improper, vexatious, frivolous or abusive, requiring the party to pay part of the actual costs and expenses of the tribunal in connection with the application.
>
> (2) An order under subsection (1), after filing in the court registry, has the same effect as an order of the court for the recovery of a debt in the amount stated in the order against the person named in it, and all proceedings may be taken on it as if it were an order of the court.[61]

One of the first decisions of a tribunal considering a costs regime developed pursuant to s. 47 was *BC Vegetable Greenhouse I, L.P. v. BC Vegetable Marketing Commission*.[62] This case concerned an application to the British Columbia Farm Industry Review Board (FIRB) by the BC Vegetable Marketing Commission ("the commission") and BC Hot House Foods Inc. ("BC Hot House") for an order that BC Vegetable Greenhouse I, L.P. ("BC Vegetable") pay the costs incurred during BC Vegetable's appeal of a commission order that required BC Vegetable to remit to the commission $376,642 in outstanding levies. Some of BC Vegetable's grounds of appeal were unsuccessful or abandoned during the proceeding, and the tribunal generally found the conduct of the company to have rendered the proceeding more costly than it should have been. The FIRB panel ordered BC Vegetables to pay the costs of the other parties (but not the FIRB's, although that option would have been open to the board as well). This decision suggests that where costs are available, unless otherwise circumscribed by a tribunal's enabling legislation, the applicable principles are similar to those developed in the civil courts, with the exception of the potential for liability on the part of losing parties to pay costs directly to the tribunal. What remains undeveloped is whether the availability of costs will discourage parties from bringing disputes to tribunals or dilute the notion of the public interest jurisdiction underlying all administrative tribunal mandates.

C. Budget and Staffing

The third area where resources play a role concerns the budget and staff allocation of the tribunal. This is a controversial area for administrative law because budgetary issues are usually seen under the rubric of public administration rather than within the sphere of administrative law. Could a court ever compel the government against its will to fund or

---

61 BC *Administrative Tribunals Act*, *supra* note 44. See also s. 17.1 of the SPPA.

62 Farm Industry Review Board, May 20, 2005.

organize a tribunal differently? The notion seems paradoxical. After all, tribunals are established as a matter of government policy through empowering legislation. There is nothing preventing a government from changing the mandate of a tribunal or repealing it altogether. How, then, could it be unlawful for the government to decide its level of funding or staffing?

Although it is true that tribunals are creatures of public policy, once established, and once the rights and interests of people depend on the fairness and reasonableness of that body's decision-making, then the duty of fairness clearly imposes constraints on government, as discussed above in the context of the requirement to hold an oral hearing in *Khan*. Perhaps the best-known example of this dynamic is *Singh v. Canada*,[63] in which the duty of fairness was held to require that the federal government provide oral hearings for refugee claimants. This decision resulted in significant expenditures for the government and the reorganization of the entire refugee determination process. In *2747-3174 Quebec Inc. v. Quebec (Régie des permis d'alcool)*,[64] the Court contemplated ordering the government of Quebec to reorganize a liquor board on independence grounds. In *Suresh v. Canada*,[65] dealing with security certificates, fairness obligations were said to constrain the ability of the government to shield disclosure of national security documents. All of these constraints implicitly may impose resource obligations on government. Courts have yet to consider the corollary issue of whether fairness could be compromised by a tribunal that is provided inadequate funding to fulfill its statutory mandate and/or to provide fair proceedings.

Some years ago, during research on how administrative independence is experienced by decision-makers in the field of humanitarian and compassionate exemptions under the *Immigration and Refugee Protection Act*, I was surprised to learn that from the perspective of decision-makers, their independence was compromised by the requirement that a certain number of cases be "cleared" each week. This clearance rate was a product of the volume of applications and the limited number of staff assigned to these units within Citizenship and Immigration Canada. The requirement, these decision-makers asserted, limited their ability to conduct interviews, to research a file, and to consider and deliberate on the evidence provided.[66]

This focus on the experience of decision-makers also raises the broader issue of how decision-makers are selected (whether on a merit principle, by political appointment, or some combination of the two). Is access to a tribunal compromised where decision-makers are viewed as extensions of the government of the day? Is access enhanced where a tribunal is representative, in the sense that the demographic makeup of members and staff reflects the community and/or user groups of the tribunal?

The line between public administration and administrative law is clearly blurring. It is no longer possible (or desirable) to exclude significant government discretion over how administrative bodies are designed, funded, and governed from the purview of administrative

63 [1985] 1 S.C.R. 177.

64 [1996] 3 S.C.R. 919.

65 2002 SCC 1.

66 For a discussion of this research and its findings, see L. Sossin, "From Neutrality to Compassion: The Place of Civil Service Values and Legal Norms in the Exercise of Administrative Discretion" (2005) 55 U.T.L.J. 427.

law principles. Where these dynamics can be tied to the fairness of a decision-making process or the reasonableness of a decision, they cease to be matters of policy preference alone.

V. CONCLUSIONS

Administrative tribunals are established for a variety of purposes but most include the following rationale:

- to resolve disputes or reach decisions on the basis of specialized expertise;
- to resolve disputes or reach decisions in a more informal and expeditious fashion, thereby reducing costs to the parties; and
- to resolve disputes in a fashion both at arm's length from the government and advancing the policy mandates set out in the applicable legislation.

Accessibility is consistent with all of these purposes. Accessibility may challenge another key value, however, namely the scarce resources of government. Accessibility, whether in the form of more and better facilities, more and better information for parties, or more and better representation services, requires resources, and given the high volume of some tribunals, the resource implications may be quite substantial.

In addition to resources, access may also depend on how a tribunal accommodates the unequal power and resources between parties. For example, consider a social benefits tribunal, where often unrepresented welfare recipients face ministry representatives. How can a decision-maker remain impartial on the one hand while ensuring a sufficiently level playing field on the other? This is a challenge familiar to courts as well, particularly in areas such as family law, where power imbalances and self-represented litigants are common. An aspect of this balancing exercise that is unique to administrative tribunals is the added feature that many tribunals are established precisely so as to empower vulnerable individuals. In the case of social benefits tribunals, for example, the whole purpose of these tribunals would be undermined if those whose benefits are wrongfully taken away cannot, in practice, access the tribunal.

Access also involves the balance between fairness and efficiency. It might be optimal for a high-volume tribunal, such as a landlord and tenant tribunal, to have facilities in every major population centre. It will be more efficient, of course, to maintain fewer facilities but invest in new technologies, such as video conferencing, that allow for far greater numbers to have access to dispute resolution. At what point does the pursuit of efficiency erode the fairness of the proceeding? This is precisely the question that administrative law will increasingly have to address.

As important as access is to the parties in administrative justice, it is largely uncharted territory for administrative law. The duty of fairness, for example, typically has not included a concern for the simplicity of forms, the transparency of guidelines, or the adequacy of a tribunal's database of prior decisions. The logic of fairness, however, is that it must be viewed from the standpoint of those affected by decision-making, and from this perspective, accessibility and fairness are inextricably linked.

Finally, the analysis thus far has assumed access relates to process. Access to justice, however, not only includes being able to understand, navigate, and participate in a tribunal's decision-making, but also presupposes that the tribunal will deliver administrative justice of high quality. In this sense, access to administrative justice extends not only to standing, guidelines, fees, and representation, but also to whether decisions are well-reasoned and delivered in a timely fashion. Access may also extend to whether decision-makers are appointed under a competitive merit-based process.

The purpose of this chapter has been to introduce issues of access to administrative justice and to show how integrated such questions are with the broader principles of administrative law on the one hand, and the everyday practice of diverse tribunals on the other hand. Ultimately, this analysis leads to a challenge for administrative law, to do justice to questions of access both as part of traditional fairness determinations and as an emerging, independent aspect of the legal framework within which tribunals are established and operate. The many implications of this new focus on access to administrative justice remain to be further developed.

SUGGESTED ADDITIONAL READINGS

LEGISLATION

Administrative Tribunals Act, S.B.C. 2004, c. 45.

Statutory Powers Procedure Act, R.S.O. 1990, c. S.22.

CASES

British Columbia (Attorney General) v. Christie, 2005 BCCA 631, 262 DLR (4th) 51.

Finlay v. Canada (Minister of Finance), [1986] 2 S.C.R. 607.

Polewsky v. Home Hardware Stores Ltd. (2003), 109 C.R.R. (2d) 189 (Ont. Div. Ct.).

Thamotharem v. Canada (Minister of Citizenship and Immigration), 2007 FCA 198.

SECONDARY SOURCES

Houle, F., & L. Sossin. "Tribunals and Guidelines: Exploring the Relationships Between Fairness and Legitimacy in Administrative Decision-Making" (2006) 46 Can. Pub. Admin. 189.

Mullan, D. *Administrative Law* (Toronto: Irwin, 2001) chapter 18.

CHAPTER SIXTEEN

Advocacy Before Administrative Tribunals

FREYA KRISTJANSON
Borden Ladner Gervais LLP

LESLIE McINTOSH
Ontario Ministry of the Attorney General

I. INTRODUCTION

Advocacy is the art of persuasion. Does the art of persuasion before administrative tribunals differ from advocacy in civil and criminal courts? Does it vary from tribunal to tribunal?

This book aims to situate administrative law in context. The earlier chapters illustrate that appreciating the different contexts in which various tribunals operate is the key to understanding many administrative law concepts, such as the duty of fairness and the standard of review. Differences between administrative tribunals and courts, as well as among administrative tribunals, also dictate different techniques of advocacy.

Therefore, the cardinal rule of advocacy before administrative tribunals is: know the tribunal.

This chapter is divided into three: first, the sources of administrative law that are essential to the presentation of a case; second, pre-hearing issues; and third, advocacy at an administrative hearing.

II. APPLICABLE LAW

In any administrative law proceeding, the advocate must consider which of the following sources of law apply, and how each affects the nature of the advocacy:

- the governing statutes, regulations, and general regulatory context;
- statutory procedural codes such as the *Statutory Powers Procedure Act*[1] (SPPA) (Ontario) or the *Administrative Tribunals Act*[2] (British Columbia);
- tribunal rules, policies, and guidelines;
- common-law principles of procedural fairness;
- *Canadian Charter of Rights and Freedoms* (the Charter) and other constitutional law principles; and
- other applicable laws, particularly the rules of evidence.

A. Governing Statutes and Regulations

It is critical to start with the tribunal's governing statute or statutes. It is important to remember that the statute that establishes the administrative decision-maker may not be the same statute pursuant to which the particular proceeding arises. For example, in Ontario most administrative pension proceedings arise under the *Pension Benefits Act*.[3] However, the tribunal that hears those matters—namely, the Financial Services Tribunal—is established under a separate statute, the *Financial Services Commission of Ontario Act*.[4]

The governing statutes and accompanying regulations should be examined not only for provisions that create unique procedural requirements, but also to *characterize* the tribunal.

---

1 R.S.O. 1990, c. S.22 [SPPA]; in the discussion below, reference is made to the SPPA as an example of general legislation conferring procedural powers on tribunals.

2 S.B.C. 2004, c. 45.

3 R.S.O. 1990, c. P.8.

4 S.O. 1997, c. 28.

Is it primarily an adjudicative tribunal, deciding disputes between two parties? Is it a regulatory tribunal with a broad public policy mandate? Is it a licensing tribunal deciding whether persons can engage in particular livelihoods? Does it review government decisions with respect to various benefits? The characterization of the administrative decision-maker often dictates the type of advocacy that will be required, as well as the procedural protections that may be available at common law.

The regulatory context is a key factor in advocacy before administrative tribunals. An administrative law case is generally argued in the context of a particular statute, before a statutory decision-maker with statutory jurisdiction. In addition to legal constraints, these statutes (often supplemented by tribunal rules and guidelines) reflect normative policy choices: providing income for injured workers, investor protection and the stability of capital markets, encouraging competition, or protecting the public. The good advocate discerns these normative policy choices and uses them to support all of his or her advocacy choices in the context of a specific administrative setting.

A good advocate rereads the tribunal's constituent statute and the statute under which the particular proceeding arises each time a new file is opened. Rereading the statute or statutes and regulations in the context of a specific file can shed new light on what may seem to be familiar provisions.

It is important to be familiar with all the sections that are relevant, because the statutory decision-maker must make a decision in accordance with his or her statutory mandate. The burden is on the advocate to ensure that all statutory preconditions are met and that the appropriate evidence is called to establish what the statute requires. As part of this, the advocate should take time to think about the purpose of the statute. Perhaps one of the fundamental distinctions between criminal and civil advocacy on the one hand and administrative advocacy on the other, is the importance of the purpose of the statutory scheme. A good advocate presents a case that the decision-maker will think is just and in accordance with the purpose of the statute.

The statutory context, including the purpose of the statute, also provides a theme within which the case will be argued. For example, the *Workplace Safety and Insurance Act, 1997*,[5] an income replacement system for injured workers, has a purpose clause that reads:

> 1. The purpose of this Act is to accomplish the following in a financially responsible and accountable manner:
>
> 1. To promote health and safety in workplaces and to prevent and reduce the occurrence of workplace injuries and occupational diseases.
> 2. To facilitate the return to work and recovery of workers who sustain personal injury arising out of and in the course of employment or who suffer from an occupational disease.
> 3. To facilitate the re-entry into the labour market of workers and spouses of deceased workers.
> 4. To provide compensation and other benefits to workers and to the survivors of deceased workers.

Advocacy literature teaches that cases are built around the development of a "theme." In administrative law it is important to use the statute to develop a theme that will resonate

5 S.O. 1997, c. 16, Sch. A, s. 1.

with the administrative decision-maker. The purpose clause in the *Workplace Safety and Insurance Act, 1997*, set out above, provides the advocate with a significant set of themes that should be used to develop a case from inception to conclusion. In a dispute between the worker and the employer over whether, when, and how return to work should take place after an accident, each side could use these themes to structure their presentation. From the employer's perspective, the theme could be "financially responsible" decision-making (for example, the injured worker is asking for too much). From the injured worker's perspective, emphasis might be placed on the importance of accountability for "facilitating re-entry" into the labour market.

B. Statutory Procedural Codes

Many provinces have statutory procedural codes that set minimum standards of procedural fairness for administrative proceedings, such as the *Ontario* SPPA, the Alberta *Administrative Procedures Act,*[6] the Quebec *Administrative Justice Act,*[7] and the BC *Administrative Tribunals Act.*[8] Of note, the federal system does not have a statutory procedural code.

These procedural codes are very important in administrative law. For example, s. 32 of the SPPA provides that the SPPA prevails over conflicting provisions in other statutes, regulations, rules, or bylaws unless it is expressly provided in the other statute that "its provisions and regulations, rules or by-laws made under it apply despite anything in the [SPPA]."

The question of who may be a party to a proceeding is a good example of the interaction among the statutes governing the tribunal, statutory procedural codes such as the SPPA, and the common law. The starting point, as always, should be the statute or statutes governing the tribunal. The different functions of tribunals often dictate different provisions with respect to who may be a party. For example, in professional discipline cases, the statute may provide that in addition to the governing body and the professional, the complainant may be a party. In environmental or planning cases, the tribunals may have the statutory authority to admit interveners in the public interest.

If the statute expressly sets out who may be a party and does not provide authority to add others as parties, it appears that the tribunal has no authority to do so.[9] However, many statutes provide that persons who are "interested" or "affected" by the proceeding may be parties. The SPPA provides that any person "entitled by law," including the common law, may be a party. The common law of procedural fairness provides, depending on the nature of the decision and the statutory decision-maker, that a person seeking party status demonstrate that the subject matter of the inquiry may seriously affect him or her. Therefore, the good administrative advocate must consider whether his or her client is or should be a party; whether other parties should be added or provided with notice of a hearing; and whether he or she should oppose the addition of parties in a proceeding.

---

6 R.S.A. 1980, c. A-2.

7 R.S.Q. c. J-3.

8 S.B.C. 2004, c. 45.

9 *Ontario (Royal Commission on the Northern Environment) (Re)*, [1983] O.J. No. 994, 144 D.L.R. (3d) 416 at 419 (Div. Ct.).

C. Tribunal Rules, Policies, and Guidelines

Statutes, regulations, and statutory procedural codes are the obvious sources of a tribunal's authority. Those are "rules" that have been imposed upon administrative tribunals from the outside—that is, the common law by courts, and statutes and regulations by the legislature and the executive, respectively.

There may also be rules promulgated by tribunals themselves.[10] Although it was initially not without controversy, there is now general agreement that rule-making by tribunals is a good thing. Rule-making is advantageous for the same reason that it is appropriate to have different statutory provisions for different tribunals—that is, the diversity of administrative tribunals.

The real issue remains how to reconcile fairness with efficiency in rule-making; for example, how much consultation there should be before rules are promulgated, and how much flexibility should be left to the tribunal to depart from the rules in the interest of fairness.[11]

"Rules" is a broad term encompassing two broad categories of instruments: formal, legally binding instruments made under the authority of a statute, and informal instruments like interpretive principles and non-binding policy statements and guidelines where no statutory authority is necessary. It is important to note that the terminology is not determinative. There is no "bright line" between the two categories. Some "policy statements" can in fact be legally binding if made under the authority of a statute.[12] Some so-called rules may not be legally binding.[13] Tribunals have the power to issue non-binding instruments in the nature of policies, guidelines without any express statutory authority, so long as they do not conflict with the governing statute or regulations and do not fetter the discretion of the tribunal.[14] Rules can deal with procedural or substantive matters or both. The optimal balance between rules and discretion in each case depends on the subject matter of the issue.

Even the most informal of tribunals has likely engaged in rule-making in a number of areas. Tribunal rules typically deal with such basic topics as the circumstances in which the tribunal will grant an adjournment, service of documents, motions, and prerequisites for reconsideration of decisions. Because the tribunal is intimately familiar with its own rules, it is crucial that the advocate have the same degree of familiarity. Failure to comply with a tribunal's rules may cause delay and expense for the client and erode the patience of the tribunal.

Tribunals also have various other sources of internal law, set out in policies, directives, guidelines, precedents, procedural orders, or notices of hearing. Often, such materials may be found only at the tribunal's offices. The registrars or secretaries of tribunals and their in-house counsel are good sources of information about the tribunal's internal laws.

---

10 See also Andrew Green, chapter 13.

11 In most Canadian jurisdictions, no procedure is prescribed for rule-making by tribunals. In the United States, the *Administrative Procedure Act* requires the publication of proposed rules and an opportunity for interested parties to comment before rules are promulgated by a tribunal.

12 *Ontario Disability Support Program Act*, S.O. 1997, c. 25, Sch. B, s. 55 [ODSPA].

13 *Ainsley Financial Corporation v. Ontario Securities Commission* (1995), 21 O.R. (3d) 105 (C.A.).

14 *Capital Cities Communications Inc. et al. v. CRTC et al.*, [1978] 2 S.C.R. 141.

Externally, administrative tribunals are accountable to a ministry or department of government. Their constituent statutes are administered by a ministry or department of the government. Tribunals may be overseen by various means, such as memoranda of understanding or ministerial policy statements. The statute creating the government ministry or department may also shed some light on the context in which the tribunal operates. A good advocate will understand the policy behind the creation of the tribunal and the role it is intended to fulfil in the broader scheme.

D. Common-Law Principles of Procedural Fairness

In any administrative proceeding, the types of procedural protections to which one is entitled vary widely depending on the context. Does procedural fairness require a full oral hearing, or is the nature of the decision such that the affected party's rights are protected by the ability to make written submissions? What level of disclosure is required? Has the administrative body created "legitimate expectations"? Does "the right to state one's case" require cross-examination and representation by counsel? None of these questions can be answered in the abstract. They all require a careful examination of the type of interest at stake, the regulatory context, and the impact of the decision. One of the chief duties of an administrative advocate is to consider what level of procedural protection should be sought pursuant to common-law principles of procedural fairness.

The Supreme Court of Canada's decision in *Baker v. Canada (Minister of Citizenship and Immigration)* established the modern common-law approach to the duty of fairness.[15] This case is the subject of extensive commentary in this book.[16] One of the legacies of *Baker* is that there is no longer any bright line between administrative decision-makers who are subject to fairness duties and those who are not, nor is there any strict application of those rights once triggered. Administrative decision-making is now seen as falling somewhere on a spectrum between quasi-judicial and legislative decision-making, with procedural entitlements varying according to placement on the spectrum. Once an individual's "rights, privileges or interests" are at stake, the duty of fairness applies and the question then becomes one of degree.[17]

The five *Baker* factors attempt to balance the need to give effect to legislative intention in crafting administrative processes, which include accessibility, efficiency, informality, and cost, with the need to ensure that those processes protect individual interests and the public interest. In any administrative proceeding, the advocate must be prepared to argue about the procedural protections being sought on the basis of the five *Baker* principles, making reference to fundamental principles of administrative law.

It is important to recognize that clear legislative restrictions will oust the procedural protections that would normally be afforded at common law or by a statutory procedural code such as the SPPA. In such circumstances, only the Charter or constitutional rights can override legislative restrictions.[18] In other words, if a tribunal's enabling statute expressly

15 *Baker v. Canada (Minister of Citizenship and Immigration)*, [1999] 2 S.C.R. 817 [*Baker*].

16 See in particular Grant Huscroft, chapter 5.

17 *Baker, supra* note 15 at para. 20.

18 *Ocean Port Hotel Ltd. v. British Columbia (General Manager, Liquor Control and Licensing Branch)*, [2001] 2 S.C.R. 781.

disavows any right to a hearing, the common law does not override express statutory language, and no hearing will be required. However, courts tend to interpret rights-limiting statutory provisions quite narrowly.

E. Charter of Rights/Constitutional Law

It is important to consider whether there are any Charter or constitutional rights in issue, and if so, whether the tribunal has jurisdiction to entertain a Charter or constitutional argument or whether it must be brought before a court.[19] Many tribunals now have jurisdiction over Charter and constitutional questions, following the Supreme Court of Canada's decisions in *Nova Scotia (Workers' Compensation Board) v. Martin* and *Paul v. British Columbia (Forest Appeals Commission)*.[20] In British Columbia and Alberta, however, the *Administrative Tribunals Act* and the *Administrative Procedures Act* expressly distinguish those tribunals with jurisdiction to decide constitutional questions from those that do not. The tribunal's constituent statute may also address whether it can hear Charter issues.[21]

If both the tribunal and the court have jurisdiction, it appears from the decision of the Supreme Court of Canada in *Tranchemontange*[22] that counsel is no longer required to make a strategic decision as to which ought to be asked to decide the question. Rather, the tribunal is obliged to exercise its jurisdiction.

If the constitutional validity or applicability of an act is raised in an administrative hearing, notice generally must be provided to the appropriate attorneys general.[23]

III. PRE-HEARING ISSUES

Before the hearing, the advocate must consider all the steps that lead up to the hearing. The decisions at each step are products of judgment and the strategic assessment of the case. Each of the following steps provides opportunities for advocacy:

- notice,
- disclosure,
- oral or written hearing,
- agreed statement of facts, and
- witnesses.

A. Notice

The proceeding has presumably been commenced by the client's receipt of a notice of a hearing or of another administrative decision. The fundamental question is whether the

19 See generally Evan Fox-Decent, chapter 7.

20 *Nova Scotia (Workers' Compensation Board) v. Martin; Nova Scotia (Workers' Compensation Board) v. Laseur*, [2003] 2 S.C.R. 504; *Paul v. British Columbia (Forest Appeals Commission)*, [2003] 2 S.C.R. 585; see also *Tranchemontagne v. Ontario (Director, Disability Support Program)*, [2006] 1 S.C.R. 513 [*Tranchemontagne*].

21 ODSPA, *supra* note 12.

22 *Tranchemontagne*, *supra* note 20.

23 See, for example, *Courts of Justice Act*, R.S.O. 1990, c. C.43, s. 109.

notice is sufficient. Does it comply with statutory and common-law requirements, as well as with the tribunal's own rules? Is the scope of the hearing properly set out? Have the proper parties been identified and provided with the notice? Failure to provide the necessary notice may give rise to a pre-hearing motion, a challenge to the tribunal's jurisdiction, or a judicial review or appeal. The advocate should consider, however, what can be accomplished by an objection to the sufficiency of the notice. If the client is genuinely prejudiced, then an objection at the outset of the hearing is necessary and appropriate, and the proper remedy is a deferral of the decision or an adjournment of the hearing pending the delivery of notice adequate to permit the client to respond.

B. Disclosure

Disclosure is an increasingly complex issue in administrative hearings. It is incumbent on an administrative advocate to turn his or her mind to the myriad issues involved. The starting point, again, will be the constituent statute and the statutory procedural code. However, it is rare for statutes and procedural codes to address this issue, except to provide that the tribunal may issue orders to control its own process or that the tribunal may make rules governing disclosure.[24]

Tribunals commonly make rules governing the exchange of documents by the parties, the exchange of witness statements, the provision of expert reports, and the provision of particulars. Some tribunals have rules providing for interrogatories or establishing discovery-like pre-hearing procedures. However, rules do not generally address all of the issues regarding disclosure. For example, there may be issues about investigative files containing informant information or redactions to notes and files. If there are third-party records at issue, an *O'Connor*[25] application may be required.

In addition to the tribunal's rules, the extent of the disclosure obligation is governed by the common law. At common law, the degree of disclosure required varies depending on the nature of the tribunal and the nature of the interest affected. In the case of licensing or regulatory tribunals, a representative of the regulator acts as a "prosecutor." The Supreme Court of Canada has held that the *Stinchcombe*[26] principles do not apply in the administrative context. The general administrative law duty is to ensure that the individual knows the case to meet, so that they may address evidence prejudicial to their position and bring forward evidence to support their case.[27] Where, however, a decision may result in a "loss of livelihood and damage to professional reputation," the duty of disclosure may be similar to the duty placed on Crown prosecutors in the criminal context.[28] This standard, described by the Supreme Court of Canada in *R. v. Stinchcombe*,[29] requires disclosure of all relevant in-

24 SPPA, *supra* note 1, ss. 23(1), 5.4.

25 *R. v. O'Connor*, [1995] 4 S.C.R. 411.

26 *R. v. Stinchcombe*, [1991] 3 S.C.R. 326 [*Stinchcombe*].

27 *May v. Ferndale Institution*, 2005 SCC 82, [2005] 3 S.C.R. 809 at paras. 91-92.

28 *Sheriff v. Canada (Attorney General)*, [2006] F.C.J. No. 580 (F.C.A.) (QL), 2006 FCA 139 (CanLII) at paras. 32-34; see also *Waxman v. Ontario (Racing Commission)*, [2006] O.J. No. 4226 (Div. Ct.) (QL).

29 *Stinchcombe*, *supra* note 26 at 343.

formation, both that which the prosecution intends to introduce in evidence and that which it does not, subject to legal privileges. The evolution of disclosure obligations in the professional discipline context is in contrast to the more traditional administrative law test, which is disclosure of the case to be met. The advocate must therefore characterize the tribunal and the nature of the interest affected in order to make the case for a higher degree of disclosure.

There are other ways of obtaining information that may be helpful to the case. Increasingly, advocates are using freedom of information requests to obtain documents that may be relevant to a case. Even if the statutes or rules do not provide for it, a simple request for disclosure may suffice. It is the advocate's responsibility to consider all of these avenues to obtain information relevant to the case.

If the disclosure is insufficient, the advocate should consider bringing a pre-hearing motion before the tribunal. Again, if the client is genuinely prejudiced, then a motion is necessary and appropriate and the proper remedy is a deferral of the decision or an adjournment of the hearing pending proper disclosure.

C. Oral or Written Hearing

Generally, the tribunal's constituent statute will simply state that a party is "entitled to a hearing." Procedural codes like the SPPA contain general provisions to the effect that a party is entitled to present evidence and make submissions.[30] However, the right to a hearing or to present evidence does not necessarily include the right to an oral hearing. The statutes, procedural code, or rules governing a tribunal may also permit hearings to be held electronically or in writing. The factors governing the determination of which form of hearing is required may or may not be listed or may be expressed in general terms only. For example, the SPPA provides that a tribunal "shall not hold a written hearing if a party satisfies the tribunal that there is a good reason for not doing so."[31] In that case, whether or not an oral hearing is required (if requested) is determined by the common law. Whether or not an oral hearing is required at common law depends on the application of the five *Baker* factors.

The advocate must always consider whether to request an oral hearing—that is, whether an oral hearing is necessary or desirable in the circumstances of the particular case. The case law suggests that the decision turns on whether there is an issue of credibility.[32] From an advocacy perspective, the considerations also include the relative strengths and weaknesses of the various witnesses, whether the public interest that may be generated by an oral hearing would be helpful to the client's cause, and the expense and time required for an oral hearing.

Finally, a tribunal may impose conditions when adding a party, restricting the party's evidence and argument to the party's specific interest. Faced with a request from a person

30 See, for example, s. 10.1 of the SPPA, *supra* note 1.

31 Section 5.1(2) of the SPPA, *supra* note 1. See also s. 5.2(2), which states that a "tribunal shall not hold an electronic hearing if a party satisfies the tribunal that holding an electronic hearing rather than an oral hearing is likely to cause the party significant prejudice."

32 *Khan v. University of Ottawa*, [1977] O.J. No. 2650, 34 O.R. (3d) 535 (C.A.).

to be added as a party, the advocate for another party should consider whether to seek such an order.

D. Agreed Statement of Facts

Many tribunals expect parties to cooperate in preparing an agreed statement of facts as well as an agreed book of documents. This expedites the hearing process, reflecting administrative law values of efficiency and expeditiousness. This exercise also forces the advocate to think about the issues that are truly contentious and deserve to be argued, and those that are not. It is good discipline, and helps in case planning, to turn one's mind to an agreed statement of facts. It will help to build a reputation as a good counsel and save the client time and money. However, the advocate cannot agree to any facts unless he or she has conducted a complete factual and legal examination of the case. Even if an agreed statement of facts is not achieved, the effort will not be wasted. The draft agreed statement will serve as the advocate's own chronology of the events. Often, much is revealed about a case by a review of a chronology—for example, whether there is truly a cause-and-effect relationship between certain events.

E. Witnesses

With regard to witnesses, there are two important issues to be considered in advance of the hearing: which witnesses to call and how to secure their attendance. The decision whether to call a witness will relate to the determination of what must be proved at the hearing. Is this witness essential? The good advocate must ruthlessly consider whether the witness has undesirable information or qualities. If so, the rule is, do not call the witness. Seek an agreed statement of facts so that a weak witness does not have to be called, or find an alternative source for the evidence.

Particularly before more sophisticated administrative tribunals, the advocate must consider whether expert evidence is required. If an expert is required, one must locate the best expert possible, retain and instruct him or her properly and ethically, and tender his or her evidence in accordance with tribunal rules and practice. Most tribunals require expert reports to be circulated well in advance of a scheduled hearing.

Generally, tribunals have the ability to summons witnesses to appear before them. Although procedures differ, often counsel is expected to obtain the executed summons from the hearing officer in advance of the hearing and serve the summons.

F. Other Considerations

Once the advocate has attended to all of the procedural and substantive issues that are anticipated to arise in the case, is there anything else to do before the case is argued before the tribunal? A good advocate will observe a tribunal in action prior to his or her first appearance before it. At an attendance to observe a proceeding, the advocate learns basic things like whether counsel slips are required, whether it is the practice to rise when the tribunal enters the hearing room, whether the tribunal makes preliminary remarks, whether opening statements from counsel are expected, and even where to sit. Lack of familiarity with a tribunal's practices betrays an advocate as a novice in the forum, and can impair the confidence of both the client and the tribunal in the advocate's abilities.

That is not to say that the advocate should adhere to the tribunal's practices when it is not in the client's interest to do so. For example, if the hearing is open to the public and the matter is a contentious one that has attracted media attention, it may be in the client's interest to make an opening statement in order to set out the client's position at the earliest possible opportunity, even if it is not the tribunal's practice to entertain one. In that case, counsel should acknowledge that it is not the tribunal's practice, but ask for permission to do so. That forestalls the inevitable response that it is not the tribunal's practice and signals to the tribunal that counsel has considered the tribunal's practice and is asking the tribunal to make an exception.

IV. ADVOCACY AT THE TRIBUNAL HEARING

The advocate must now present the case. He or she must build a persuasive case on the basis of relevant and admissible evidence. The advocate will have developed a theory of the case clearly tied to the statute under consideration, will have ensured that the remedy sought is within the statutory decision-maker's mandate, and will be prepared to argue general principles of administrative law in the course of the hearing.

A. Preliminary Motions at the Hearing

There are some types of serious preliminary motions that are generally argued at the commencement of a hearing. These include challenges to the jurisdiction of the tribunal, as well as challenges based on bias or tribunal independence. There are two aspects of bias: impartiality and independence. Impartiality refers to the state of mind of the decision-maker. Independence refers to the relationship of the decision-maker to others. Both impartiality and independence may operate at an individual or an institutional level.[33] Objecting to a member of a tribunal on the grounds of bias is a difficult judgment call even for an experienced advocate. The test is whether there is a reasonable apprehension of bias. What is "reasonable" varies greatly depending on the nature of the tribunal. For example, behaviour that would disqualify a member of an adjudicative tribunal may be perfectly acceptable in a member of a tribunal whose decisions are policy-based or whose functions approach the legislative end of the spectrum.[34] What is clear is that an objection on the grounds of bias must be made when it comes to the party's attention, failing which it will be deemed to have been waived.[35] It is important to inform the hearing officer of these motions in advance so that the tribunal is prepared to deal with such challenges.

A common mistake is to overuse preliminary motions at the hearing itself. A good advocate thinks carefully about the usefulness and the timing of a contemplated motion. For example, tribunals generally prefer to deal with motions for the production of documents

33 *Canadian Pacific Ltd. v. Matsqui Indian Band*, [1995] S.C.J. No. 1, 122 D.L.R. (4th) 12.

34 *Newfoundland Telephone Co. v. Newfoundland (Board of Commissioners of Public Utilities)*, [1992] S.C.J. No. 21, 89 D.L.R. (4th) 289.

35 *Canada (Human Rights Commission) v. Taylor*, [1990] S.C.J. No. 129, 75 D.L.R. (4th) 577.

before the hearing, to avoid adjournments. Even if a tribunal does not have rules governing pre-hearing disclosure of documents, a good advocate will contact counsel for the opposite party prior to the hearing, offer to share the documents on which he or she intends to rely, and ask for the same courtesy from opposing counsel. If there is a real issue and there is no opportunity for a pre-hearing motion or case conference, then, at a minimum, counsel should advise the hearing officer well in advance of the hearing that a disclosure motion will be brought that may necessitate an adjournment.

B. Opening Statements

There are similarities and differences between an opening statement before an administrative tribunal and an opening statement at a trial. As in a trial, the purpose of an opening statement is not to make legal argument. Rather, its chief purpose is to set out the theory of the case, to identify the issue from the perspective of the client, and to offer a simple solution. The opening statement is also an opportunity to "seize the moral high ground" of the case. A secondary purpose is to provide a road map for the tribunal as to how the case will unfold—that is, to identify the chief witnesses and the purposes for which they will be called. This aspect of the opening statement is generally briefer and less detailed than at trial, unless the tribunal has very court-like procedures or is dealing with a number of complex issues. It is important that the opening statement be flexible enough to take into account the inevitable vagaries of the evidence. It is crucial that the advocate not promise anything in an opening statement that cannot be delivered. Even if the tribunal does not remind the advocate of the promise, opposing counsel will. Many tribunals make opening statements of their own or have a checklist of questions they are expected to ask, or otherwise start the proceeding. Some may even question witnesses themselves.

C. Evidence

As a general rule, tribunals are not bound by the strict rules of evidence. This is not a licence to be lazy, however, as will be discussed in this section. Rather, it is a particular challenge faced by administrative advocates.

What does it mean to say that tribunals are not bound by the strict rules of evidence? A good example is s. 15 of the SPPA, which states:

> 15(1) Subject to subsection (2) and (3), a tribunal may admit evidence at a hearing, whether or not given or proven under oath or affirmation or admissible as evidence in a court,
>
> (a) any oral testimony; and
>
> (b) any document or thing,
>
> relevant to the subject matter of the proceeding and may act on such evidence, but the tribunal may exclude anything unduly repetitious.
>
> (2) Nothing is admissible in evidence at a hearing,
>
> (a) that would be inadmissible in a court by reason of any privilege under the law of evidence; or
>
> (b) that is inadmissible by the statute under which the proceeding arises or any other statute.

For each piece of evidence the advocate proposes to introduce, he or she should ask the following questions: What facts will be established with this evidence? How are the facts relevant to the issues in the hearing?

Is there any exclusionary rule that would prohibit calling the evidence (for example, privilege)? General privileges in the law of evidence continue to apply in administrative proceedings.[36]

Is there a better source? Although hearsay evidence is admissible, the common-law concern about hearsay is based on fairness. The more direct the evidence, the more likely it is to be accepted to establish the point that the advocate seeks to make.

Are there any rules that govern the admissibility of the evidence? For example, are there notice requirements? Tribunal rules often require that expert reports be produced in advance.

If another party objects to the admissibility of the evidence, is there an answer to those objections? In particular, what response is there to arguments about weight?

Some of these issues are discussed below in more detail.

D. Relevance

Tribunals do not have the jurisdiction to hear evidence that is not relevant to the proceedings. The type of evidence that may be considered by the tribunal relates directly to natural justice concerns. The tribunal may not take into account entirely irrelevant facts, or decide on the basis of facts for which there is no evidence. Relevant evidence means evidence having any tendency to make the existence of any fact that is of consequence to the determination of the matter more probable or less probable than it would be without the evidence.[37]

On the importance of presenting relevant evidence to support each component of a decision, see *Trinity Western University v. British Columbia College of Teachers.*[38] Trinity Western, a Christian university, was seeking accreditation to sponsor a teacher-training degree. The university's community standards document prohibited "biblically condemned" practices. From this, the college inferred that the outlook of graduates would have a detrimental effect on the learning environment in schools where they would subsequently teach. The College of Teachers denied the university the ability to sponsor a teaching-training program. The Supreme Court held that the College of Teachers erred in considering the beliefs of the institution, but not the actual impact of their beliefs on the teaching environment. The Court held:

> For the BCCT to have properly denied accreditation to TWU, *it should have based its concerns on specific evidence.* It could have asked for reports on student teachers, or opinions of school principals and superintendents. It could have examined discipline files involving TWU graduates and other teachers affiliated with a Christian school of that nature. Any concerns should go to risk, not general perceptions.[39]

---

36 *Pritchard v. Ontario (Human Rights Commission)*, [2004] 1 S.C.R. 809; SPPA s. 15(2).

37 *Canada (Attorney General) v. Gentles Inquest (Coroner of)* (1998), 116 O.A.C. 70 (Div. Ct.).

38 [2001] 1 S.C.R. 772.

39 *Ibid.* at para. 38 (emphasis added).

E. Weight

In addition to deciding whether evidence is relevant, a decision-maker must also decide how much weight to give to the tendered evidence. For example, an unsigned, undated letter regarding a fact in question may be relevant, but it would likely be afforded very little weight because its statements cannot be verified. The more reliable the evidence is, the more weight it should be accorded. The rules of evidence were developed by courts to prevent unfairness. Before an administrative tribunal, the advocate should be prepared to argue issues as to weight from first principles (natural justice, procedural fairness, quality of administrative decision-making, relevance given purpose of statute, and what is at stake for the individual).

F. Admissibility

The advocate should look to the tribunal's statutory provisions and to procedural codes like the SPPA to assist with admissibility issues. First, the statute may contain specific provisions on how evidence is to be dealt with. Second, the statute may describe the mandate of the tribunal and the scheme it administers, in terms that suggest what considerations and priorities should weigh heavily on the tribunal in making decisions—for example, whether the tribunal should favour protection of the public or some other value. If there is some question about the admissibility of evidence, reference to the policy and statutory mandate of the tribunal may assist in resolving it.

G. Standard of Proof

The standard of proof is the civil standard of the balance of probabilities. However, in administrative proceedings with a significant effect on the individual, the quality of evidence required to meet the standard of proof is "clear, cogent and convincing" evidence.[40] Again, the advocate must recognize the differences among administrative tribunals in assessing the nature of evidence required. In order to meet this exacting standard, the advocate should make efforts to call the best evidence available.

However, it is not an invariable rule that the more serious the subject matter of the proceeding, the less acceptable is hearsay evidence. For example, hearsay evidence is specifically permitted in child welfare proceedings, in light of the need to have all available information before the decision-maker, and in social welfare cases, in light of the need for expedition and informality. The lesson is: know the tribunal.

H. Judicial Notice

Expert tribunals may take notice of generally recognized facts within their specialized knowledge. For example, discipline panels in medical cases may make certain findings of fact based on their own knowledge of human anatomy.[41] Section 16 of the SPPA provides

40 See *Stetler v. Agriculture Food and Rural Affairs Appeal Tribunal*, [2005] O.J. No. 2817 (C.A.).

41 *Re Reddall and College of Nurses of Ontario* (1983), 149 D.L.R. (3d) 60 at 65 (Ont. C.A.); *Ringrose v. College of Physicians & Surgeons (No. 2)* (1978), 83 D.L.R. (3d) 680 at 695-96 (Alta. C.A.).

that a tribunal may take notice of facts that may be judicially noticed, and take notice of any generally recognized scientific or technical facts, information, or opinions within its scientific or specialized knowledge.

I. Examination-in-Chief

Perhaps surprisingly, examination-in-chief is a significantly more important skill than cross-examination. In case preparation, the advocate should focus on putting on the case well. More cases are won on direct examination than on cross-examination, because the advocate can (more or less) control direct examination. The most important thing to remember about examination-in-chief is that counsel is trying to assist the witness to tell the story in his or her own words. Counsel's job is to make it seem that the evidence comes out effortlessly and persuasively. It is the advocate's work in structuring the questions that helps the witness tell the story.

As discussed above, the strict civil and criminal rules of evidence do not apply. However, in practice, that may not make much of a difference, because the rules of evidence formally set out what is often a commonsense approach to developing evidence and also govern the expectations of most tribunals about the calling of evidence. For example, while in theory there may be more latitude to lead witnesses in an administrative tribunal, it is bad practice and bad advocacy to lead too much.

As also discussed above, the case should have a persuasive theme consistent with the purpose of the statute; one that is designed to take into account the normative policy choices reflected in the regulatory context. The evidence of each witness should advance the theme. What questions will do so? What facts should be highlighted?

Examinations-in-chief should be structured with headlines (for example, "I am now going to ask you about your health after the operation." "Turning to questions about your income before the accident …"). Such structuring helps both the witness and the tribunal understand where counsel is going—that is, flagging transitions in the evidence.

The usual rules of direct examination apply to administrative hearings. Any general advocacy textbook will summarize them. The most important rules of advocacy on direct examination include the following:

- Use open-ended questions: Who? What? Where? When? Why? How? Can you describe it? What happened next?
- Elicit short bits of information through targeted questions; avoid the "tell us about your complaint" type questions.
- Be prepared to introduce and use documents in the course of the examination-in-chief.
- Practise introducing exhibits and taking the witness through the documents in advance.

J. Cross-Examination

Cross-examination is one area that may differ substantially in administrative proceedings from other types of trials. Counsel should be aware that statutory procedural codes like the SPPA expressly limit cross-examination rights. Refusal to permit cross-examination altogether does not always amount to a denial of fairness at common law.

The primary purpose of cross-examination is to test the credibility of the witness. If the proceeding does not involve matters of credibility, then cross-examination may not be necessary or appropriate. Similarly, it may not be appropriate to permit cross-examination in a hearing that is intended to be informal and expeditious.[42]

In most proceedings, there will not have been any type of "discovery," so cross-examination in tribunal hearings is often much more fun (with greater opportunity for surprises, good and bad) than civil trials. That being said, in cross-examining a witness, the traditional techniques of advocacy apply:

- Control the witness.
- Ask short questions, one fact per question.
- Avoid open-ended questions (never ask why, how, etc., on cross).
- Impeachment on the basis of a prior inconsistent statement is an effective cross-examination tool. Make sure that the fact is material, that it helps the case, and that there is a genuine contradiction before attempting impeachment.
- Have a reason behind every area of questioning. Know where the question leads and think about how to get there with minimal damage. This is not discovery. Bad answers count against the client's case.

K. Tribunal Precedents

It is important for the purpose of argument to understand the composition of the tribunal. Mature tribunals like the Ontario Labour Relations Board or the Ontario Municipal Board have well-established jurisprudence. It is a bold step for an advocate to ask such a tribunal to depart from established precedent. However, occasionally a precedent requires re-examination. In that case, the best approach is to acknowledge the existence of and the policy reasons for the tribunal's line of authority and to argue that a modification of the jurisprudence is necessary to give continuing effect to the policies identified by the tribunal.

L. Closing Argument

Put bluntly, the purpose of a closing argument is to persuade the tribunal that the client should win. In the closing argument, the advocate should make submissions on the facts and law in the context of the regulatory scheme to establish the client's case and cast doubt on any other interpretation. Closing argument is the opportunity to summarize the evidence in a persuasive manner; argue about the evidence, challenging the other side's case directly; persuade the tribunal to make findings of fact that favour the client's case; argue about the application of the law to the facts of the case; and persuade the tribunal that the client's case is just and in accordance with the facts and the law.

Where there are factual disputes, the advocate should be prepared to argue issues such as:

- conclusion/inferences;
- circumstantial evidence;
- analogies;

42 *MacInnis v. Canada (Attorney General)*, [1996] F.C.J. No. 1117, 139 D.L.R. (4th) 72 (C.A.).

- credibility and motive;
- weight of evidence;
- application of the law/justice;
- role in statutory scheme, including public policy;
- which witnesses can be trusted, who should be believed, and why;
- reasonableness of witness testimony, especially in light of other evidence in case;
- importance of documents; and
- which expert is to be preferred, and why.

Some tribunals prefer to have only written submissions, and may restrict oral argument. Others will generally receive only oral arguments. Written submissions can be effective if it is the practice of the tribunal to reserve its decisions. Know the tribunal. If the case involves complex legal issues it may also be helpful to the tribunal to have written submissions. However, if the case is one in which the tribunal is being asked to depart from or to expand upon a line of authority, it may be preferable to have oral argument or at least a combination of oral and written argument to facilitate a full explanation of the issue and an opportunity for questions from the tribunal. If the opportunity for written submissions is offered to one party, it should be offered to all parties.[43]

Sometimes it may be advisable to request an opportunity to divide up the submissions. For example, it is more effective to make submissions on penalty only after there have been submissions on and a finding of misconduct.[44]

V. CONCLUSION

It is worth repeating that the cardinal rule of advocacy before administrative tribunals is: know the tribunal. Advocacy is concerned with how certain disputes reach tribunals (or courts on appeals or applications for judicial review) and how administrative law is advanced in those settings. The different contexts in which administrative tribunals operate is the key to understanding many administrative law concepts. For most of the concepts discussed in this text, there is no more important context than advocacy. Without clients who are willing (and able) to challenge administrative decision-making, and lawyers arguing for new approaches to existing doctrines, or tribunal members and judges articulating their understanding of administrative law, the rest of this book would not be possible.

43 *Communications, Energy and Paperworkers Union, Powell River Local 76 v. British Columbia (Power Engineers and Boiler and Pressure Vessel Safety Appeal Board)*, [2001] B.C.J. No. 2764, 209 D.L.R. (4th) 208 (C.A.).

44 *Brock-Berry v. Registered Nurses' Association*, [1995] B.C.J. No. 1876, 127 D.L.R. (4th) 674 (C.A.); *College of Physicians and Surgeons v. Petrie*, [1989] O.J. No. 187, 68 O.R. (2d) 100 (Div. Ct.).

SUGGESTED ADDITIONAL READINGS

SECONDARY SOURCES

Adair, Geoffrey D.E. *On Trial: Advocacy Skills, Law and Practice*, 2d ed. (Markham, ON: LexisNexis Butterworths, 2004).

Mauet, Thomas A. *Trials: Strategy, Skills, and the New Powers of Persuasion* (New York: Aspen Publishers, 2005).

Mauet, Thomas A., Donald G. Casswell & Gordon P. Macdonald. *Fundamentals of Trial Techniques*, 2d Canadian ed. (New York: Aspen Publishers, 1995).

Salhany, Roger E. *Cross-Examination: The Art of the Advocate*, 3d ed. (Markham, ON: LexisNexis Butterworths, 2006).

Index